The Palgrave Handbook of Global Migration in International Business

Audra I. Mockaitis
Editor

The Palgrave Handbook of Global Migration in International Business

palgrave
macmillan

Editor
Audra I. Mockaitis
Maynooth University
Maynooth, Ireland

ISBN 978-3-031-38885-9   ISBN 978-3-031-38886-6 (eBook)
https://doi.org/10.1007/978-3-031-38886-6

© The Editor(s) (if applicable) and The Author(s), under exclusive licence to Springer Nature Switzerland AG 2023

This work is subject to copyright. All rights are solely and exclusively licensed by the Publisher, whether the whole or part of the material is concerned, specifically the rights of translation, reprinting, reuse of illustrations, recitation, broadcasting, reproduction on microfilms or in any other physical way, and transmission or information storage and retrieval, electronic adaptation, computer software, or by similar or dissimilar methodology now known or hereafter developed.

The use of general descriptive names, registered names, trademarks, service marks, etc. in this publication does not imply, even in the absence of a specific statement, that such names are exempt from the relevant protective laws and regulations and therefore free for general use.

The publisher, the authors, and the editors are safe to assume that the advice and information in this book are believed to be true and accurate at the date of publication. Neither the publisher nor the authors or the editors give a warranty, expressed or implied, with respect to the material contained herein or for any errors or omissions that may have been made. The publisher remains neutral with regard to jurisdictional claims in published maps and institutional affiliations.

This Palgrave Macmillan imprint is published by the registered company Springer Nature Switzerland AG.
The registered company address is: Gewerbestrasse 11, 6330 Cham, Switzerland

Paper in this product is recyclable.

This book is dedicated to Sofija, my Third Culture Kid, who has traveled the globe and navigated different cultures, languages, and countries like a pro. May your world have no borders.

Foreword

As the editor of this Handbook affirms, migration represents a classic "grand challenge" to the global community because it is an empirical phenomenon with widespread ramifications that presents severe policy issues and has profound social, political, and economic consequences. The phrase "the kaleidoscope of global migration" is apposite not only (as the editor says) because of the shifting new images presented by a dynamic situation but also because it allows different viewpoints on the focal phenomenon. It is possible to take a bird's eye view of migration using social, political, or economic lenses of analysis. Migration can also be observed from the viewpoint of the boardroom by managers of multinational enterprises. The view from the individual migrant is a further important perspective. Admirably, this Handbook takes on board all of these perspectives. Organized under five themes, it encompasses many of the complexities surrounding (mainly) international migration.

The first section examines the theme of migration landscapes in international business including the socio-economic landscape, the impact of the COVID-19 pandemic, and the complex causality behind waves of migration. "Navigating the terrain of language and culture" is a rich treatment of the subject matter, including identity and diaspora issues. The multinational enterprise as a major player takes center stage in leveraging and managing the integration of migrants at the organizational level. The positive benefits and costs of such integration strategies are investigated and evaluated. Migration as an international business resource is the focus of theme 4 where knowledge sharing emerges as a key driver of impact. Finally, theme 5 takes an individual perspective including refugee entrepreneurship and repatriation.

Overall, this Handbook represents a major step forward in the international business approach to migration. The editor and authors are to be commended for their efforts in taking on a global grand challenge and subjecting it to analytical scrutiny. They would be the first to agree that far more research is needed in the furtherance of our understanding of the kaleidoscopic global phenomenon of migration, but their collective endeavours in pushing back the research frontier are to be applauded. We can but hope that their work will be emulated by successive researchers in search of improvements in global wellbeing.

University of Leeds Peter J. Buckley,
Leeds, UK
April 2023

Acknowledgments

This book would not have been possible without the successful collaboration between numerous individuals. I would like to foremost thank the authors, many of whom are migrants themselves, and have contributed their insights into a complex topic that will collectively help to shape this field and steer it in new directions going forward. Their knowledge, research, and dedication to the process have ensured the success of this handbook.

I am grateful to Liz Barlow of Palgrave Macmillan for guiding me throughout all steps of the process from conception to publication and to Paul Smith Jesudas for his help with the production of the book. I appreciate the helpful comments and input from colleagues in reviewing and providing constructive feedback along the way. Thank you to Petra Aigner, Shamika Almeida, Almina Bešić, Christina Butler, Janet Carruthers, Masud Chand, Richa Chugh, Marian Crowley-Henry, Francesco Di Lorenzo, Di Fan, Ariane Froidevaux, Jeannie Lee, Anh Nguyen, Johanna Niskavaara, Javad Nooshabadi, Edward O'Connor, Larissa Rabiosi, Xavier Salamin, Pallavi Shukla, Adele Smith-Auchmuty, Betina Szkudlarek, Heidi Wechtler, and Peter Zettinig.

I am grateful to my family, who provided me with a truly bicultural upbringing as a first-generation American and taught me to navigate my dual cultures seamlessly. The weekends devoted to attending Lithuanian school and immersion in the ethnic diaspora community throughout my childhood shaped my path in ways I could not have imagined. As a global migrant and scholar, I have a great appreciation for the issues that migrants encounter, having personally endured acculturation challenges in the many countries in which I have lived. The importance of migrant networks cannot be overemphasized, and I am grateful to various communities and professional and social support networks that have often helped me to return to my cultural roots and have fed my personal and research interests in migration issues. These are the diaspora communities in the United States and Australia, colleagues, and friends worldwide, as well as the community of migrants who tirelessly worked with me in establishing an ethnic school in Melbourne and gave me many insights into first-, second-, and third-generation migrants. These personal experiences were in large part the reason that this book came to be.

Audra I. Mockaitis

Contents

1 The Kaleidoscope of Global Migration: International Business Perspectives in a Turbulent World 1
Audra I. Mockaitis

Part I Migration Landscapes in International Business 23

2 Vulnerable Migrants, the COVID-19 Pandemic, and International Business: A Vicious Cycle 25
Eun Su Lee, Heidi Wechtler, Chiara Berardi, and Chris Brewster

3 The COVID-19 Pandemic: Immigration Policy Changes and Challenges 47
Masud Chand

4 Social Contagion and Migration: Sources and Implications of Migrant Ambivalence 67
Helena Barnard and Graham Nash

Part II Navigating the Terrain of Language and Culture 91

5 Migrants, Language, and Internationalization of Small- and Medium-Sized Enterprises: A Literature Review 93
Johanna Niskavaara and Rebecca Piekkari

6   Dissecting Generations of Migrant Identities within a
    Diaspora   119
    Audra I. Mockaitis and Lena Zander

7   Dual Perspectives: Immigrants' Comparisons of Host and
    Home Countries' Management of the COVID-19 Pandemic
    Emphasize the Salience of Cultural Differences   143
    Ariane Froidevaux and David J. G. Dwertmann

8   Can Intentions to Emigrate be Explained through Individual
    Values? An Exploratory Study in Lithuania   165
    Vilmantė Kumpikaitė-Valiūnienė, Audra I. Mockaitis,
    Jurga Duobienė, Ineta Žičkutė, and Vilmantė Liubinienė

9   From Working Hard to Being Hard Working: The
    Maintenance and Mobilization of Cultural Capital among
    Finnish Migrants in Florida   183
    Johanna Raitis, Riikka Harikkala-Laihinen, Niina Nummela,
    and Eriikka Paavilainen-Mäntymäki

10 [Adult] Third Culture Kids: Why Do Early Life International
    Experiences Matter?   205
    Mireka Caselius and Vesa Suutari

Part III   Leveraging and Managing Migration in the International
           Firm   225

11 Exploring the Missing Links between International Business
    and Domestic Migration: The Case of China   227
    Mingqiong Mike Zhang, Jiuhua Cherrie Zhu, Peter J. Dowling,
    and Di Fan

12 The Value of Migrants for International Joint Ventures   251
    Julia Mittermayr, Vera Kunczer, and Jonas Puck

13 Online Organizational Inclusion of Migrants in MNCs:
    Overcoming Cultural and Linguistic Barriers Virtually   279
    Charlotte Jonasson and Jakob Lauring

14	**A Balancing Act in Times of Crisis: Inclusion at Work and Career Advancement of Migrants in Austria** *Petra Aigner, Almina Bešić, and Christian Wenzler*	303
15	**Migrant Inclusion and Wider Workforce Well-being: Understanding the MNE Challenges and Solutions through the Diversity Climates Lens** *Christina L. Butler, Anna Paolillo, and Vittorio Edoardo Scuderi*	325

Part IV	**Migrants as an International Business Resource**	353
16	**Skilled Migrants: Stimulating Knowledge Creation and Flows in Firms** *Pallavi Shukla and John Cantwell*	355
17	**How Migration Enhanced a Mexican MNC's Socially Embedded Capability** *Anabella Davila*	385
18	**Female Diasporans and Diaspora Networks: A Neglected Resource for Business?** *Maria Elo, Ilia Gugenishvili, and Maria Ivanova-Gongne*	407
19	**Non-Ethnic Inventor Sourcing of Immigrant Knowledge: The Role of Social Communities** *Larissa Rabbiosi, Francesco Di Lorenzo, Anupama Phene, and Paul Almeida*	433

Part V	**The Migrant's Journey**	463
20	**Unfolding the Dynamics of Refugees' Entrepreneurial Journey in the Aftermath of Forced Displacement** *Solomon Akele Abebe and Ziad El-Awad*	465
21	**Supporting Skilled Migrants' International Career Success Across the Micro, Meso, and Macro Levels** *Marian Crowley-Henry, Shamika Almeida, Santina Bertone, and Asanka Gunasekara*	501

22 Career Capital Development of Highly Skilled Self-Initiated
    Expatriates   523
    Rodrigo Mello and Vesa Suutari

23 Expatriates' Quality of Life During the Pandemic: Two Sides
    of the Same Coin   547
    Anh Nguyen and Maike Andresen

24 "Bringing It All Back Home": Capital Utilization of Irish
    Repatriates in the Irish SME Animation Industry   573
    Adele Smith-Auchmuty and Edward O'Connor

Index   597

Notes on Contributors

Solomon Akele Abebe is a final year PhD candidate at the Sten K. Johnson Centre for Entrepreneurship, Lund University School of Economics & Management, Sweden.

Petra Aigner is an associate professor at the Institute of Sociology, Department of Empirical Social Research, at Johannes Kepler University (JKU), Linz (Austria). Her research interests relate to migration studies, specifically integration processes, labor market integration, ethnic entrepreneurship, diversity management, and qualitative methods. She graduated from Trinity College Dublin with a PhD in 2005. She was a researcher at numerous universities and research institutes (Germany, Ireland, UK, Austria), for example, Marie Curie Fellow at EFMS (European Forum for Migration Studies), University of Bamberg, Germany; University of Leeds (UK; 2008–2009). She was a Fulbright guest professor at University of Minnesota, Campus Twin Cities, USA (2022–2023). She has published monographs and several edited volumes under Springer and Palgrave, for instance, with Springer: 'Migrationssoziologie' (2017), as well as journal articles (e.g. *Journal of International Management, SWS Rundschau*).

Paul Almeida is Dean, William R. Berkley Chair, and Professor of Strategy and International Business at the McDonough School of Business at Georgetown University. He received his Ph.D. from the Wharton School of the University of Pennsylvania. Professor Almeida's research studies innovation, knowledge management, alliances and informal collaborations across firms and countries. He is particularly interested in understanding how knowledge builds across people and organizations and how this affects performance. His articles have appeared in leading journals such as *Strategic*

Management Journal, Management Science, Organization Science, Journal of International Business Studies, and *Research Policy* as well as in scholarly books. He has served on the editorial boards of several leading journals and as Area Editor for the *Journal of International Business Studies*. Professor Almeida was also previously Chair of the Technology and Innovation Management Division of the Academy of Management. paul.almeida@georgetown.edu

Shamika Almeida is an associate professor and associate dean (Equity, Diversity and Inclusion) in the Faculty of Business and Law at the University of Wollongong, Australia. Her articles have appeared in *Gender, Work, and Organization, International Migration* and *Asia Pacific Journal of Human Resources*, among others. Her research explores skilled migrant employment and careers, gender-inclusive practices supporting career progression, life journeys of transgender women, the wellbeing of healthcare professionals and holistic organizational and leadership practices that are founded on a care-based perspective. Prior to academia, Professor Almeida worked in different corporate roles in the fast-moving consumer goods, banking, apparel, travel, and recruitment consulting industries. Email: shamika@uow.edu.au

Maike Andresen is a Full Professor of Human Resource Management and Organizational Behavior at the University of Bamberg, Germany. She has served as a visiting professor, for example, at Copenhagen Business School, Denmark, and Deakin University, Australia. She is a faculty member of the joint European Human Resource Management program together with seven European universities and initiator and coordinator of the Horizon 2020 project GLOMO. Maike has authored numerous peer-reviewed articles in leading academic journals and edited volumes, and published and edited 25 books. She currently serves on several editorial boards of academic journals, including *the Human Resource Management Journal* and *The International Journal of Human Resource Management*. Her primary fields of expertise in terms of research are (global) careers, international mobility, and work flexibility.

Helena Barnard is the director of doctoral programs at the University of Pretoria's Gordon Institute of Business Science (GIBS), South Africa, having received her PhD in Management from Rutgers University. Her research interests are in how knowledge (and with it, technology, organizational practices, and innovation) moves between more and less developed countries, particularly in Africa. Her research on migration extends that work by looking at how people as the carriers of knowledge move between borders. Her work has been published inter alia in *Journal of Management, Research Policy, Journal of International Business Studies* and *Journal of World Business*.

Chiara Berardi is currently a PhD student in Economics at the University of Newcastle, Australia. Her research focuses on health economics and policy, healthcare system, mental health, and digital health technologies. Chiara completed Master's in Health Economics and Management at the University of Bologna, Italy. She was a member of the Economic Advisory Team on the Healthcare Insurance System Reform Proposal at the Chilean Ministry of Health.

Santina Bertone is deputy dean (Research) in the School of Business and Law at Central Queensland University, Melbourne (Australia). She is Professor of Management, specializing in diversity management and industrial relations. Professor Bertone has over 130 publications and has attracted more than $2 million in research funding. Her research interests span policy and administration, education management, and migration studies. Her articles have appeared in academic outlets including *Australian Journal of Public Administration, Ethnic and Racial Studies* and the *International Journal of Intercultural Relations*. Email: s.bertone@cqu.edu.au

Almina Bešić is an assistant professor at Johannes Kepler University Linz as well as an independent consultant and researcher for the European Migration Network and lecturer at the University of Graz. She obtained her doctoral degree in Economics and Social Sciences from the University of Graz, where she studied the human resource strategies of multinational companies in South-Eastern Europe, focusing on employment of highly skilled migrants. Almina's research and teaching interests include integration of migrants and refugees at work, European migration policy, gender and diversity, and international HRM. Her work has been published in academic journals such as *Journal of International Management, European Management Review, Comparative Migration Studies, Equality*, and *Diversity and Inclusion*. Almina has gained research and work experience in Austria, Bosnia and Herzegovina, Belgium, and the United Kingdom.

Chris Brewster is Professor of International Human Resource Management at Henley Business School, University of Reading, UK. In the course of a career in industry, he obtained his doctorate from the LSE and then became an academic, focusing on international and comparative human resource management. He has written or edited nearly 40 books and published more than 150 book chapters and over 250 articles in refereed journals. Chris was awarded an honorary doctorate by the University of Vaasa, Finland.

Christina L. Butler is Associate Professor of International Management and Organizational Behavior at Kingston University London, where she leads the Future of Work and Organizations Research Group. Her research focuses on global work and careers and the implications for well-being with a particular interest in global virtual teams and in the careers of migrant graduates. Her work has been published in leading international journals including *Journal of World Business*, *Journal of Vocational Behavior*, and *Organizational Behavior and Human Decision Processes*. She regularly presents her work at international conferences including *Academy of Management* and *European International Business Academy*.

John Cantwell is Distinguished Professor of International Business in Rutgers University (New Jersey, USA) since 2002. He was previously Professor of International Economics at the University of Reading in the United Kingdom. His work focuses on international technological knowledge networks. Professor Cantwell's total citation count on Google Scholar is over 20,000. His published research spans the fields of International Business and Management, Economics, Economic History, Economic Geography, Philosophy, and Innovation Studies.

Mireka Caselius is a Ph.D. candidate in The School of Management, Human Resource Management research group at the University of Vaasa, Finland. Her research interests are in the area of expatriation, and especially the experiences of accompanying expatriates' offspring (third culture kids/TCKs). Her dissertation examines the adjustment of TCKs, as well as the long-term impacts of an early international experience on adult third culture kids' (ATCKs) career capital and career interests and choices. She has recently published such research and has personal experience of living abroad as she comes from an expatriate family herself.

Masud Chand is Professor of International Business at the W. Frank Barton School of Business at Wichita State University. His research interests include the role of immigration and diasporas in driving cross-border trade and investment and the aging of populations and its effects on the global business environment. His work has been published in numerous journals including the *Academy of Management Perspectives*, *International Business Review*, *Journal of Business Ethics*, the *Asia Pacific Journal of Management*, and the *Journal of International Business Policy*.

Marian Crowley-Henry is Associate Professor in Human Resource Management and Organizational Behaviour at Maynooth University School of Business (Ireland). Marian teaches and researches in the fields of careers, skilled migration, diversity, and inclusion. She has published her research in international peer-reviewed journals, including *Human Relations* and *Journal of Business*. She currently serves on the editorial boards of the *International Journal of Human Resource Management* and the *Journal of Global Mobility* and is co-editor-in-chief of the open access, international, peer-reviewed (double blind), ABS-ranked *Irish Journal of Management*. She is member and mentor on MotherNet (EU Horizon 2020 Co-Ordination and Support project) and of the EU Horizon 2020 COST action on Connecting Theory and Practical Issues of Migration and Religious Diversity. Marian is also the academic program co-director of the BBS Business and Global Cultures undergraduate program. Email: marian.crowleyhenry@mu.ie

Anabella Davila (Ph.D. The Pennsylvania State University) is a Professor Emerita of Management at EGADE Business School, Tecnologico de Monterrey, Mexico. Her research interests include labor culture, human resource management, human development, and sustainability. In addition, her work examines the social logic that governs Latin American organizations. She is a founding member of the Emerging Multinationals Research Network, a certified evaluator of the Mexico Business Excellence Award, and a member of the Mexican Researchers System (Tier-II).

Francesco Di Lorenzo is Associate Professor in Strategy and Entrepreneurship at Copenhagen Business School in the department of Strategy and Innovation. He holds an MPhil and PhD in Management Science from ESADE Business School, a BA and an MSc in Business and Economics from Bocconi University. Before starting the academic career, Dr. Di Lorenzo worked as consultant for McKinsey & Co. and Accenture Strategy, focusing primarily on M&As operations in financial services. Dr. Di Lorenzo's main research interests are in the areas of strategic management and economics and management of innovation. More specifically, they include venture financing, inter-organizational knowledge flows, strategic human capital, impact investing. His research is empirically developed primarily in the pharmaceutical and semiconductor industries and got published in leading strategy and entrepreneurship journals as, among others, *Academy of Management Journal, Research Policy, Strategic Entrepreneurship Journal, Journal of Business Ethics*. Francesco is an active economic and strategy consultant and former entrepreneur. fdl.si@cbs.dk

Peter J. Dowling (PhD, Flinders University) is an Emeritus Professor of International Management & Strategy at La Trobe University, Australia. Professor Dowling is a Life Fellow of the Australian Human Resources

Institute. He has published over 100 articles in top journals and served as an editor of a number of prominent journals.

Jurga Duobienė is Associate Professor in Human Resource Management and a member of the Digitalization Research Group in the School of Economics and Business, at Kaunas University of Technology, Lithuania. Her research interests are in the fields of organizational development, business ethics and entrepreneurship in the frame of digitalization. Her research interests center on business ethics, digital transformation, human-technology interaction and international migration. See https://en.ktu.edu/scientist/jurga.duobiene/

David J. G. Dwertmann is Associate Professor of Management at Rutgers University, School of Business-Camden. He received his B.Sc. and M.Sc. from the University of Mannheim, Germany, and his Ph.D. in strategy and management from the University of St. Gallen, Switzerland. David is interested in the social and cognitive processes that result in feelings of otherness and how to overcome them. He published work on otherness in the form of people with versus without disabilities, immigrants versus non-immigrants, different levels of status and hierarchy, and more in several premier management journals. David is particularly interested in how social norms, organizational climate, and leadership influence these processes.

Ziad El-Awad is a Senior Lecturer in entrepreneurship and a researcher at the Sten K. Johnson Centre for Entrepreneurship, Lund University School of Economics & Management, Sweden; School of Business, Innovation and Sustainability, Halmstad University, Halmstad, Sweden.

Maria Elo Associate Professor, University of Southern Denmark, Professor, Belt and Road Institute of International Business at Shanghai University, senior research fellow, University of Turku and adjunct professor, Åbo Akademi University works on international business, entrepreneurship, and migration with topics such as internationalization, resources of skilled migrants and returnees, migrant and diaspora entrepreneurship, transnational and family businesses, diaspora networks, diaspora investment and remittances. She has published books and articles, for example, in *Journal of World Business*, *Journal of International Business Policy*, *Industrial Marketing Management*, *Regional Studies*, *Journal of International Entrepreneurship*, and *International Journal of Entrepreneurship and Small Business*.

Di Fan (Ph.D. Monash University, CPA) is a Professor of Management in the School of Management, RMIT University, Melbourne, Australia. He is an associate editor of *International Journal of Human Resource Management*. His current research interest includes, international business strategies, and international human resource management. His publications appear in journals, such as *Academy of Management Learning & Education, Entrepreneurship Theory and Practice, Human Resource Management* (US), *Human Resource Management Journal, Human Resource Management Review, Journal of Management Studies, Journal of World Business, International Journal of Human Resource Management, Long Range Planning, Public Administration Review, Organization Studies*, and *Regional Studies*, and among others.

Ariane Froidevaux is Assistant Professor of Management at the University of Texas at Arlington. Her research focuses on career transitions, retirement and aging at work, and identity negotiation. It appears in outlets such as *Journal of Applied Psychology, Journal of Organizational Behavior, Journal of Vocational Behavior*, and *Organizational Psychology Review*. She serves on the editorial boards of the *Journal of Vocational Behavior*, and of *Work, Aging and Retirement*. She received her Ph.D. from the University of Lausanne and was awarded two postdoctoral fellowships from the Swiss National Science Foundation to conduct her research at the University of Florida.

Ilia Gugenishvili (Ph.D., Åbo Akademi University) is an Assistant Professor in the department of International Marketing at the Åbo Akademi University, Turku, Finland. His research interests include sustainability, equality, consumer behavior, culture, and social psychology. Ilia has publications in the *Journal of Consumer Behavior, International Journal of E-Services and Mobile Applications*, and *Voluntary Sector Review*, among others. His name also appears in conference proceedings at the Association of Marketing Theory and Practice and the International Telecommunications Society.

Asanka Gunasekara is Lecturer in Management at Swinburne Business School, Melbourne (Australia). Dr. Gunasekara's main research interests are in the areas of social and organizational inclusion of migrants. In particular, she is interested in skilled migrants' acculturation, wellbeing, and career success. Email: agunasekara@swin.edu.au

Riikka Harikkala-Laihinen is a postdoctoral researcher in international business at Turku School of Economics at the University of Turku. Her main research foci are emotions in organizations and change management. She is particularly interested in exploring the role emotions have in individuals' life course, as well as increasing positivity surrounding difficult reorganization projects, such as cross-border mergers and acquisitions. riikka.m.harikkala@utu.fi

Maria Ivanova-Gongne works as an associate professor in International Marketing at Åbo Akademi University. Her research interests include migrant entrepreneurship and business-to-business marketing management, particularly the aspects of cross-cultural interaction and communication, as well as managerial sensemaking in international business. Another special interest lies in understanding sustainability in business from a cross-cultural and individual level perspective. Her works have appeared amongst all in such journals as *Industrial Marketing Management, Critical Perspectives on International Business, European Management Journal, Journal of Business and Industrial Marketing, Journal of Small Business & Entrepreneurship*, and *Scandinavian Journal of Management*.

Charlotte Jonasson is an associate professor at Department of Psychology and Behavioural Sciences, Aarhus University. Her research focuses on international management and virtual teams. She is currently conducting research on organizational failure and digitalization. Charlotte Jonasson's work has been published in *Organization Studies, British Journal of management*, and *Human Resource Management Journal*.

Vilmantė Kumpikaitė-Valiūnienė is Professor of Human Resource Management in the School of Economics and Business, a member of the Digitalization Research Group and a leader of the International Migration Research cluster at Kaunas University of Technology, Lithuania. She is also a member of the International Economics and Knowledge Research Group at the University of Granada in Spain. She is the author and co-author of more than 150 scientific publications and textbooks and has delivered 12 keynote presentations about migration and expatriation at different conferences. Her research interests center on self-initiated expatriation and international migration, cultural values, virtual work, well-being and modern educational methods. See https://en.ktu.edu/scientist/vilmante.kumpikaite/

Vera Kunczer is an assistant professor at the Institute for International Business at WU Vienna. She obtained her PhD in 2020 and was a visiting researcher at the University of Groningen. Her research focuses on international strategy in response to political and social developments. Her dissertation on foreign investment strategies and political dynamics was awarded the AIB Best Doctoral Dissertation Proposal Award 2020 and the IM Best Dissertation Award at the AOM Annual Meeting 2021. She was a finalist for the Gunnar Hedlund Award 2021 and received awards for her contributions at multiple conferences. Her work has been published in the *Journal of International Business Policy*.

Jakob Lauring is a professor at Department of management, Aarhus University. Jakob Lauring's research interests are focused on international management with specific interest in global virtual teams. Jakob Lauring has published more than 100 international articles in outlets such as *Journal of Worlds Business, British Journal of management, Human Resource Management Journal, and International Business Review.*

Eun Su Lee (PhD) is Lecturer in Management at the Newcastle Business School, the University of Newcastle, Australia. Her research interests are in the fields of international human resource management and global mobility, focusing on migrants' integration journeys in foreign countries and the role of multiple stakeholders, such as governmental organizations, businesses, and support organizations in facilitating such integrative efforts. Her recent research has appeared in top-tier international journals, including *Academy of Management Perspectives***,** *Human Resource Management Journal***, and** *International Journal of Management Reviews***.**

Vilmantė Liubinienė is a professor at the Faculty of Social Sciences, Arts and Humanities and a member of the Digital Culture Communication and Media Research Group at Kaunas University of Technology, Lithuania. Her research interests center on digital culture and intercultural communication, system of universal values and migration culture. See https://en.ktu.edu/scientist/vilmante.liubiniene/

Rodrigo Mello is a postdoctoral researcher at the University of Vaasa in Finland. During his doctoral program, he held one of the 15 highly competitive Ph.D. positions funded by Marie Skłodowska-Curie Action "Global mobility of employees" (Horizon, 2020). Leveraging such prestige international networking, Rodrigo published in high-ranking journals, such as the Human Resource Management Review and Gender, Work & Organization. Adding to his curriculum practical experiences in well-known multinational corporations such as Anheuser-Busch InBev and Lanxess and his international background of working and living in four countries, Rodrigo's research reflects his passion for understanding the influence of global mobility on the career of global workers.

Julia Mittermayr is a doctoral student at the Institute of International Business at WU Vienna and focuses her research on the effects of migration on multinational companies. In 2019, Julia was recognized for her research on hybrid and agile working models with the Austrian Honorary Award for academic achievements. In addition to her academic pursuits, she has been working as a consultant at McKinsey & Company, where she focuses on organizational design and key drivers for corporate performance. Through her research and practical experience, Julia aims to deepen our understanding of how migration impacts performance and internationalization efforts of multinational companies.

Audra I. Mockaitis is Professor (Chair) of International Business at Maynooth University School of Business, Ireland. She has been interested in migration and diaspora communities for most of her life. A bilingual first-generation American of Lithuanian descent, she spent her childhood navigating two very different cultures in the Lithuanian community in Chicago. Later, the experience of living as a foreigner in her parents' homeland and observing it as very different from the diaspora culture in which she grew up sparked her interest in studying cross-cultural issues in international business. She has lived and worked in ten countries and has been active in maintaining her heritage language and culture in the diaspora. In Melbourne, Australia, she founded an accredited Lithuanian ethnic school, attended by first-, second-, and third-generation children in the diaspora community. Audra has held tenured positions in Australia (Monash) and New Zealand (Victoria University of Wellington). Her research interests generally center on cross-cultural management, cultural values, migration, and identity. Her work has been published in various international business journals and has received multiple awards. This is Mockaitis' second book on migration. See www.mockaitis.com.

Graham Nash, himself a migrant, has always been intrigued as to what drives individuals to migrate, and the impact that such decisions have on the broader population. Graham has over 18 years' experience across diverse industries in leadership, project management and strategic implementation (process and system). He has a strong quantitative orientation, and holds a master of science degree in computational and applied mathematics from South Africa's University of the Witwatersrand (WITS) and an MBA from the University of Pretoria's Gordon Institute of Business Science (GIBS). He is currently based in Australia.

Anh Nguyen is a Ph.D. candidate of the Chair of Human Resource Management and Organisational Behaviour at the University of Bamberg, Germany, and an Early Stage Researcher in the Horizon 2020 project GLOMO. She has published peer-reviewed articles in academic journals such as Academy of Management Proceedings and Frontiers in Psychology, as well as edited volumes. Her research interests include internationally relocated employees, job embeddedness, work–life crossover effects, and emotions.

Johanna Niskavaara is doctoral researcher in International Business at Aalto University, School of Business in Finland. Her research interests center around the multifaceted role of language in international business. In her dissertation, she studies how language and cultural diversity can be leveraged in the internationalization of small- and medium-sized enterprises. Her research interests are inspired by professional experience from working in internationalizing SMEs as well as by personal experiences of international mobility.

Niina Nummela holds Professorship in International Business at the Turku School of Economics, University of Turku, Finland. She is also an adjunct professor at the Lappeenranta University of Technology and the University of Lapland. In 2022, she was invited to join EIBA Fellows, a group of distinguished scholars in the field of International Business. Her research focuses on cosmopolitan individuals, international entrepreneurship, and cross-border mergers and acquisitions. niina.nummela@utu.fi

Edward O'Connor is Assistant Professor of Management at Maynooth University, lecturing in the field of Human Resource. He gained his PhD at the Maynooth University, School of Business centring on an in-depth exploration of career motivations, actions, and experiences of skilled migrants from EU10 countries currently living and working in Ireland. His research interest is in the areas of Careers, Skilled Migration, Expatriation, and HRM. He has published in international peer-reviewed journals including the *Journal of Global Mobility*, *Human Relations*, *Journal of Business Ethics*, and the *European Management Review*. He regularly shares his research at national and international conferences. Edward is a John & Pat Hume scholar and an IRC Scholarship winner. Prior to joining academia, he worked in management, mainly in the SME sector.

Eriikka Paavilainen-Mäntymäki is Associate Professor of International Business at the Turku School of Economics, University of Turku, Finland, and an adjunct professor at the University of Vaasa, Finland. Her research interests focus on international entrepreneurship, qualitative research methods, the role of time and process in business research, and the internationalization process of the firm. eriikka.paavilainen-mantymaki@utu.fi

Anna Paolillo is Senior Lecturer in Organizational Psychology at Kingston University London. Her research interests and expertise concern the relationships between facet-specific climates and individual and organizational outcomes, in particular, the role of diversity, inclusion, and safety climates on organizational citizenship behaviors and safety performance. She has extensive research and consultancy experience in collaboration with international industries in the metal and mechanical, infrastructure, and educational sectors, with impact such as a significant decrease of injuries and accidents through the analysis and improvement of inclusion and well-being at work.

Anupama Phene is Professor of International Business and Phillip Grub Distinguished Scholar at the School of Business at George Washington University. Before joining GW, she was Associate Professor of Strategy at the University of Utah. She received her Ph.D. in international management from the University of Texas and her MBA from the Indian Institute of Management, Ahmedabad. Prior to beginning her doctoral studies, she worked for American Express Bank in the treasury department. Her research focuses on strategies to create innovation and enable knowledge transfer. She has authored publications in the *Administrative Science Quarterly, Journal of International Business Studies, Organization Science, Strategic Management Journal, Management International Review, Journal of Management Studies,* and the *Journal of Management.* She is Associate Editor at *Global Strategy Journal,* Consulting Editor at the *Journal of International Business Studies* and is on the editorial board of *Organization Science* and the *Strategic Management Journal.* anuphene@gwu.edu

Rebecca Piekkari is Marcus Wallenberg Professor of International Business at Aalto University, School of Business in Finland. Her current research focuses on managing multilingual organizations, qualitative cross-border language research, and applications of the translation approach to international business theory and practice. Her work has been published in a number of leading IB and management journals such as *Critical Perspectives on International Business, Global Strategy Journal, Journal of International Business Studies, International Business Review, Management International Review* as well as *Academy of Management Review, Journal of Management Studies* and *Organization Studies.* Together with Catherine Welch, she has edited two volumes on qualitative research published by Edward Elgar: *Handbook of Qualitative Research Methods for International Business* (2004) and *Rethinking the Case Study in International Business and Management Research* (2011). In 2021, she received, together with Catherine Welch and two co-authors, the *Journal of International Business Decade Award* for the article 'Theorising from case studies: Toward a pluralist future for international business research'.

Jonas Puck is a Full Professor at WU Vienna and the founding Head of WU's Institute for International Business. His current research interests lie in the overlaps of global strategy, finance, and political science. Jonas serves on the Editorial Boards of various journals, such as the *Journal of International*

Business Studies, *Journal of World Business*, *International Business Review*, and *European Management Journal*. He has published more than 50 papers in international journals and is an editor or author of 11 books and numerous book chapters.

Larissa Rabbiosi (PhD, Politecnico di Milano) is Professor (MSO) in International Business at Copenhagen Business School, Denmark. Her research concerns the relationship between the organization of firms and their strategic processes with a particular focus on knowledge transfer, innovation, and international expansion. Currently she is working on a variety of research projects including the study of the relationship between immigrants and firm innovative performance, multinational corporations' engagement in dialogue on issues of misconduct, and the effects of post-acquisition integration management on inventors' patenting activity. Her articles have appeared in leading academic journals such as *Journal of International Business Studies, Journal of World Business, Journal of Business Ethics*, and *Research Policy* among others. lr.si@cbs.dk

Johanna Raitis is an international business scholar. Currently she holds a postdoctoral position at Turku Institute for Advanced Studies (TIAS) and is a member of the Executive Committee of Cultural Memory and Social Change at the Turku University, Finland. Her research focuses on collective identity, values, social sustainability, socio-cultural integration and organizational fairness. johanna.raitis@utu.fi

Vittorio Edoardo Scuderi is a PhD Student in the Department of Management at Kingston University London. He has a master's degree in psychology from the University of Catania. His research areas focus on diversity, diversity practices, diversity climate, climate for inclusion, psychosocial safety climate, well-being, and workaholism.

Pallavi Shukla is Assistant Professor at Rutgers University (New Jersey, USA) since 2017. She received her Ph.D. in Management from Rutgers University and B.E. in Electronics & Communication Engineering from Birla Institute of Technology, Mesra, India. She has worked in the industry for over a decade for Tata Consultancy Services, Bear Stearns, and JP Morgan in Mumbai, India, and New York City, USA. Her current research interests lie at the intersection of global strategy, migration, and institutions literature streams. She has published in the *Journal of International Business Studies, Journal of World Business*, and *Rutgers Business Review*.

Adele Smith-Auchmuty lectures in International Business and Corporate Entrepreneurship at Maynooth University, Maynooth. Before joining Maynooth University, she was the Registrar at Galway Business School and an Associate Lecturer at the National University of Ireland, Galway. She earned her PhD from the Cairnes School of Business and Economics at the National University of Ireland, Galway. Her research explores born global companies with a particular focus on networks in evolving industries such as the animation industry. In her recent research, she analyzes the domestic horizontal network membership of accelerated international firms. She has published her research in the *International Marketing Review* and *European Journal of International Management* and presented at both National and International conferences. Beyond academia, she is the founder and Managing Director of a successful retail business for the past 16 years.

Vesa Suutari is a professor at the Department of Management at the University of Vaasa, Finland. Suutari has published various journal articles and book chapters on topics such as European management cultures, Expatriation, self-initiated Expatriation, global leadership, and global careers. Suutari is one of the permanent organizers of the EIASM Workshop on Expatriation and the EURAM Track on Expatriation. He has acted as one of the editors for books on topics such as Work-life Interface in International Career Context (Springer, 2015) and Management of Global Careers (Palgrave, 2018). Suutari has studied international HRM topics such as expatriation and global careers for 25 years. He is one of the permanent organizers of the EIASM Workshop on Expatriation and the EURAM track on Global Mobility, as well as an associate editor of the *International Journal of HRM*. He has also co-edited books on topics such as the *Work-life Interface in the International Career Context* (Springer, 2015), the *Management of Global Careers* (Palgrave, 2018), and *Self-Initiated Expatriates* (2021).

Heidi Wechtler holds a PhD in International Management from Macquarie University, Sydney (Australia), and is Senior Lecturer in Management at the University of Newcastle (Australia). She has carried out research related to various fields including expatriation, diversity management, employee selection, and turnover. Her work has appeared in outlets such as *Journal of Applied Psychology, Leadership Quarterly, Journal of World Business, International Business Review, Management International Review, Management Organization Review, Journal of Business Research, International Journal of Human Resource Management*, and *Contemporary Accounting Research*.

Christian Wenzler is currently completing his dissertation on "diversity management and work inclusion of migrants in Upper Austria" in the Department of Sociology at the Johannes Kepler University (JKU), Linz (Austria).

Lena Zander (Ph.D.) is Professor of International Business at Uppsala University in Sweden. She has earlier held positions at Victoria University of Wellington and the Stockholm School of Economics and as a visiting scholar at Chinese University of Hong Kong, Stanford University and the Wharton School. She currently carries out research on migrants and integration in Swedish organizations and on global virtual team leadership in multicultural settings. She has published in journals like *Journal of International Business Studies*, *Journal of World Business*, *International Business Review*, and *Organizational Dynamics*. Her work has received multiple best-dissertation, -paper, and -reviewer awards at AIB, ANZAM, and AOM. Lena Zander recently edited the *Research Handbook of Global Leadership: Making a Difference*, published by Edward Elgar.

Mingqiong Mike Zhang (PhD, Monash University) is an associate professor in the Department of Management, Monash University, Australia. Dr. Zhang's research is in the areas of human resource management and international business. His publications have appeared in journals such as *Academy of Management Learning & Education*, *Journal of Business Ethics*, *International Journal of Human Resource Management*, and *Human Resource Management*, among others.

Jiuhua Cherrie Zhu (PhD, University of Tasmania) is Professor of Human Resource Management and Chinese Studies in the Department of Management, Monash University. Australia. Professor Zhu's research areas cover cross-cultural management, human resource management, and Chinese studies. Her publications have appeared in many top-tier journals in the areas of HRM, international business, international management, and China-related studies.

Ineta Žičkutė is an associate professor at the School of Economics and Business, a member of the Digitalization Research Group and the International Migration Research Cluster at Kaunas University of Technology in Lithuania. In addition, she is a member of the Analysis of Migration, International Economics and Knowledge Research Group at the University of Granada in Spain. Her research interests center on international migration, application of artificial intelligence to business needs and behavioral economics. See https://en.ktu.edu/scientist/ineta.zickute/

List of Figures

Fig. 1.1	A kaleidoscope of global migration themes in IB	7
Fig. 4.1	Generalized model—State transition probabilities. Source: Dodds and Watts (2005)	72
Fig. 4.2	SCSM state transition probabilities	78
Fig. 4.3	General crisis: Crime	80
Fig. 4.4	Isolated crisis—Global job opportunities	82
Fig. 4.5	General combined with isolated crises	83
Fig. 4.6	Stifler and spreader with equivalent effects ($p_2 = p_1$)	84
Fig. 4.7	Stifler effect greater than that of spreader ($p_2 > p_1$)	84
Fig. 5.1	The four streams of literature included in the review	95
Fig. 6.1	Cultural values of migrants and home country nationals	131
Fig. 6.2	Cultural values of migrants by emigration wave	133
Fig. 7.1	Data structure	150
Fig. 11.1	Number of rural-urban migrants from 1982 to 2021. Source: Liang (2001); National Bureau of Statistics of China (2008–2021); Zhang (2016)	229
Fig. 11.2	FDI inflows into China from 1979 to 2021. Source: UNCTAD (2022). Investment statistics and trends. https://unctad.org/topic/investment/investment-statistics-and-trends	230
Fig. 11.3	Merchandise export from 1985 to 2021. Source: The World Bank (2022). https://data.worldbank.org.cn/topic/21	231
Fig. 11.4	Urbanization rate in China from 1978 to 2021. Source: The World bank. https://data.worldbank.org/indicator/SP.URB.TOTL.IN.ZS	234
Fig. 12.1	Plots visualizing the main effect of migrants on IJV performance (Plot 1), the moderating effect of female migrants (Plot 2) and the moderating effect of older migrants (Plot 3)	266

Fig. 16.1	Skilled migrants as international business resources: When, Why, and How	370
Fig. 18.1	Emigration from Finland. Source: Statistics Finland, compiled by the authors	415
Fig. 20.1	Data structure for the phases of RE	480
Fig. 20.2	Data structure for the enabling factors	480
Fig. 20.3	A dynamic process model of refugee entrepreneurship	488
Fig. 21.1	Intelligent career theory through a multi-level lens—supporting skilled migration and skilled migrants' career success. *Knowledge and understanding of intelligent career theory through micro, meso, and macro levels highlights positive policies and practices that support skilled migration and skilled migrants' careers across levels and stakeholders*	510
Fig. 23.1	Model illustration of 4-class LCA with covariates and distal outcomes	551
Fig. 23.2	Illustration of latent classes based on the experienced quality of life. *Note:* Scale ranging from 1 ("highly negative") to 7 ("highly positive") and a midpoint of 4 indicating no perceived impact ("neither negative nor positive")	560
Fig. 23.3	Illustration of differences in work outcomes between classes	561
Fig. 24.1	Bourdieu's Forms of Capital. Created by authors from Bourdieu (1986)	576

List of Tables

Table 2.1	Future research agenda in IB in light of migration trends post-pandemic	27
Table 3.1	Immigration changes during pandemic and steps taken post-pandemic	54
Table 3.2	Immigration and healthcare challenges during the pandemic	58
Table 4.1	Primary motive per demographic group	76
Table 4.2	Summary of results	85
Table 6.1	Effect of group differences in individual values	134
Table 8.1	Regression analysis results for Intention to Emigrate regressed on personal values	175
Table 8.2	Regression analysis results for Intention to Emigrate regressed on higher-order dimensions	176
Table 12.1	Results of regression analysis. $^*p < 0.05$; $^{***}p < 0.001$. Standard errors in parentheses	265
Table 13.1	Inclusiveness dimensions as identified in the existing literature	285
Table 14.1	Overview of interviews with experts	309
Table 14.2	Overview of interviews with migrants	310
Table 16.1	List of articles reviewed categorized by international business domains	359
Table 17.1	Country profile indicators of poverty, social inequality, and peace (in contrast to violence)	392
Table 18.1	Analysis of the interviews	419
Table 19.1	Correlation matrix and summary statistics	445
Table 19.2	Negative binomial regression for ethnic community knowledge sourced by non-Indian inventors	450
Table 20.1	Participant's characteristics	473
Table 20.2	Data sources	477

Table 21.1	Policy recommendations across levels, supporting skilled migration and skilled migrants' career success	517
Table 22.1	Sample characteristics (survey)	531
Table 22.2	Sample characteristics (interviews)	532
Table 22.3	Self-initiated expatriates' development abroad across three aspects of career capital	533
Table 22.4	Self-initiated expatriates' development abroad across subdimensions of knowing-why career capital	533
Table 22.5	Self-initiated expatriates' development abroad across subdimensions of knowing-how career capital	535
Table 22.6	Self-initiated expatriates' development abroad in terms of knowing-whom career capital	537
Table 23.1	Latent class analysis results	559
Table 23.2	Summary of the relationship between classes and covariates (predictors)	562
Table 24.1	SIE profile	583

1

The Kaleidoscope of Global Migration: International Business Perspectives in a Turbulent World

Audra I. Mockaitis

Introduction

In 2020, there were over 281 million international migrants worldwide, defined as individuals residing outside of their birth country (McAuliffe & Triandafyllidou, 2021). Migrants cross international borders temporarily or permanently and comprise migrant workers, refugees or humanitarian migrants, family migrants and international students (Batalova, 2022). The choice (or lack thereof) to migrate stems from various combinations of push factors, such as major events or shocks, such as conflict, war (such as in Syria and Ukraine), natural disasters, political, economic or societal crises (such as in Venezuela), deteriorating employment conditions and even a culture that encourages emigration (Kumpikaitė-Valiūnienė, Liubinienė, Žičkutė, Duobienė, Mockaitis & Mihi-Ramirez, 2021). Pull factors include the pursuit of better opportunities, such as employment or educational opportunities, a higher standard of living, incentives offered by host countries, the desire to join family members abroad, seeking certain freedoms (Castles, 2013), such as self-expression or congruence of values. In 2022, over 100 million individuals were forced migrants, an increase of almost 11 million on the previous year (UNHCR, 2022), and 40 million since 2015 (IOM, 2016). Most recently, Russia's war on Ukraine has left more than 14 million

A. I. Mockaitis (✉)
Maynooth University, Maynooth, Ireland
e-mail: audra.mockaitis@mu.ie

Ukrainians displaced (UNHCR, 2022). Importantly, most of these displaced persons are women and children; although, female migrants are increasingly more educated, they have higher unemployment rates than male migrants and native-born women (OECD, 2020).

These figures and the rise in migration in recent years appear daunting, and the impact on societies, institutions, organizations, and individuals is great, posing manifold challenges in managing population change, developing inclusive policy, migrant integration, workers' rights, personal adjustment, and well-being, to name a few. "Big questions" in international business research differ from "grand challenges," in that questions are posed and answered by researchers, whereas grand challenges are major societal issues that stem from the international business environment and cannot be easily addressed or answered via a research framework (Buckley, 2020). Migration, as a grand challenge (Buckley et al., 2017), has become an ever more apparent and difficult issue faced by societies in recent times; yet, studies on migration have only recently become more prominent in the international business (IB) field. Where do we begin to ask the necessary questions, and how do we integrate research on migration as IB scholars? Like a kaleidoscope, the parts of which shift and form new images when turned, the migration landscape is ever changing, leading IB scholars to ask questions (that lead to new issues) about the role of migration in IB and vice versa, and the facets of migration that affect societies, institutions, and people at various levels of analysis. The publication of recent special issues with a focus on migration in the *Journal of International Business Policy* (Barnard, Deeds, Mudambi & Vaaler, 2019) and *Journal of World Business* (Hajro, Caprar, Zikic & Stahl, 2021), and recent calls in the *Journal of International Business Studies* (Fitzsimmons, Minbaeva, Phene & Narula, 2021), and *Organization Science* (Choudhury, Hernandez, Khanna, Kulchina, Shaver, Wang & Zellmer-Bruhn, 2021) have drawn attention to the need for scholars to consider the significance of migration in the IB field.

Global Migration in International Business

International business (IB) is about the movement of firms, capital, goods and services, resources, and people across borders. People are arguably the most important resource of firms, and the unprecedented increase in the movement of people has had a marked impact on and is a reflection of globalization. Migration is often driven by inequalities and perceptions of (un)fairness, such as lower economic development, few job opportunities, wage and income inequality, inequalities in healthcare and education, discrimination, and corruption. Migrants often pursue better opportunities, attracted by career prospects or better quality of life; migrants fleeing war or environmental catastrophe seek the right to cross borders, refuge, and safety *en masse*. International business scholars should question the role that MNEs can play in mitigating the various push factors and reducing human displacement. MNEs have been encouraged to step up during the migration crisis (Reade, McKenna & Oetzel, 2019) and can play a major role in reducing these inequalities within and between countries.

This movement of people has potentially already changed the landscape of IB—its societal and organizational contexts. In advanced economies, such as Australia, for example, the percentage of foreign-born population has increased from 23.2% in 2000 to 29.9% in 2019 (OECD, 2021). The COVID-19 pandemic has had numerous implications for how firms have responded to pandemic restrictions in relation to migrant worker recruitment and retention and managing talent, implications for migrant work in different types of industries, in supply chains, or societal-level responses, such as to immigration policy. It has affected workers worldwide in various ways, but barriers to mobility, levels of support and inclusion, and well-being issues remain at the fore for migrants. Post-pandemic, the USA remains the largest recipient of permanent immigrants, and while migration in the EU has slowed somewhat, across the OECD, migrants comprise 10.6% of the total population (OECD, 2022). Multinational enterprises (MNEs), however, experienced a decline in intra-firm transfers of 52% in 2020 and 24% in 2021 (OECD, 2022).

For firms, navigating the landscape of migration to reap benefits from migrants is crucial. At the very least, the existence of MNEs depends on the mobility of people; MNEs source, develop, deploy, and utilize global talent. The development of global talent pools in MNEs by focusing on the strategic mobility of key talent (Collings, 2014) facilitates development of global mindsets and social capital, and the transfer of knowledge. Although traditionally global mobility in MNEs has been linked to the management of international assignments (Collings, 2014), this talent pool includes, but is not limited to, skilled expatriates, or corporate migrants (Barnard et al., 2019), as well as culturally and ethnically diverse workforces comprised of first- and second-generation migrants, highly skilled refugees that help organizations enhance their legitimacy in host countries (Reade et al., 2019), and returnee immigrants encouraged by changing home country conditions (Scullion & Collings, 2010). Migrants can assist MNEs to locate talent in their own countries of origin, as MNEs can tap into migrants' networks and experience to assist in international expansion (Morgan, Sui & Malhotra, 2020). Migrants bring unique skills, knowledge, experiences, networks, and identities to the international firm. They belong to diaspora networks that can assist in forming international alliances, entrepreneurial ties, and transferring knowledge; they can assist SMEs and MNEs in attaining their internationalization goals. Highly skilled migrants are a crucial source of global talent and global know-how. In these ways, migrants are a valuable international business resource as carriers of knowledge, social capital and ties. But migrants face numerous challenges related to living and working in a new environment: overcoming host country (and firm) barriers, maneuvring between countries, networks, cultures, and identities, forging (new) careers, seeking recognition of their skills and abilities within international firms, well-being, and repatriation challenges. A key question herein is: How can MNEs turn the benefit that they derive from migrants into gains for migrant communities?

Although the focus of much IB research is still on the sharing of knowledge between and among firms, more recently attention is shifting to a focus on people and, in particular, the transfer of knowledge via migrants and diasporas (Levin & Barnard, 2013), defined as communities of migrants and their descendants who maintain ties to their country of origin (Usher, 2005) and seek to preserve their heritage culture. Termed the "immigrant information effect" (Gould, 1994), the tacit knowledge that immigrants hold about their country of origin can be an invaluable resource to internationalizing firms. Diaspora communities that are large and have strong ties in the host country can not only serve as conduits of knowledge but may also influence internationalization location choice (Hernandez, 2014). Kunczer, Linder, and Puck (2019) demonstrated that this knowledge effect can help firms learn about a host country's environment and make informed decisions about FDI. In a similar vein, Levin and Barnard (2013) found that interpersonal ties with migrants, who are not necessarily employed within the firm, can also be a source of valuable business knowledge.

Migrant diaspora communities are often sources of innovation and international ventures (Riddle, Hrivnak & Nielsen, 2010; Elo, 2015). According to Kerr and Kerr (2019), first- or second-generation immigrants account for approximately 40% of Fortune 500 companies; immigrant-founded firms also engage more in international business activities. Diaspora communities dispersed worldwide provide members with access to networks, knowledge, and financial resources, aiding in the growth of international and transnational entrepreneurial firms. Often, first-generation immigrants engage with both their home and host countries, leading to international business opportunities but also idiosyncratic challenges (Zapata-Barrero & Rezaei, 2021). These challenges are difficult to study within existing theoretical IB perspectives due to business owners' varying degrees of embeddedness in both their countries of residence and origin (Morgan et al., 2020). Kunczer et al. (2019) have suggested that the IB institutional perspective should incorporate migration perspectives, by factoring in the endpoints of migrants' home and host countries. However, with regard to diaspora research, Elo (2015) cautions that the dichotomy between home and host is too black and white. Diaspora communities bridge the differences or distances that IB research so often deems as obstacles or barriers. Migrants can thus assist in decreasing liabilities of foreignness (Hajro et al., 2022).

At the micro and contextual levels, there is still much to learn about migrants' career development and career outcomes (Crowley-Henry et al., 2018; Guo & Al Ariss, 2015). Tales of migrants facing unfair treatment (Berry & Bell, 2012; Crowley-Henry & Al Ariss, 2016), a reduction in status (Al Ariss & Syed, 2011) and struggles in the host labor market (Pearson et al., 2011) while pursuing instrumental careers (O'Connor & Crowley Henry, 2020) are found in the extant literature. Many studies present a one-dimensional, homogeneous portrayal of migrant careers (Hajro et al., 2021). This is despite the many differences between the host country context and experiences of each migrant, such as the connection between voluntarily underemployed and subjective career success found in a study of Eastern European skilled migrants in Ireland (O'Connor & Crowley-Henry, 2020). Recent events in our world have introduced new and far-reaching challenges for international firms in managing their international workforces and international mobility while dealing with restrictions on international travel (and domestic movement). At the individual level, these issues are compounded for migrants having to cope with multiple work and nonwork demands. Because of the COVID-19 restrictions and isolation, these issues also differ in degree from those faced by domestic workers. Post-pandemic, the ongoing consequences on the well-being of migrants, especially, are unknown, and international firms must consider policies and practices to alleviate and remedy them. We need to consider how MNEs can close the chasm between migrants and home-country employees that has been so magnified by the COVID-19 pandemic.

The Focus of this Handbook

The focus of this handbook is the dynamic nature of global migration and its implications for international business. As a starting point, the aim is to raise and address some key questions from various perspectives. Societies, international organizations, and firms still face much work ahead in addressing, managing, and alleviating the challenges posed by influxes of refugees and voluntary migrants, and organizations, especially in developing appropriate policies and practices in ensuring the development, inclusiveness, and well-being of unskilled, under-skilled, and skilled migrants employed within them. There are numerous positive examples regarding the ways in which organizations can benefit from migration more generally, and the resources that migrants bring with them to organizations. Stories of positive migrant experiences, engagement with diaspora communities, sharing of knowledge and unique skills, and migrant career journeys abound. Many of these are highlighted in the chapters that follow. Many of the authors in this handbook have first-hand experience with migration, having lived and worked as migrant scholars. Readers who have migrated to another country or have some international experience may find that the descriptions, stories and findings throughout many of the chapters resonate with their own experiences.

The topics in this book point to a myriad of themes that have not been thoroughly addressed in the IB literature. The word "kaleidoscope" in the title of this introduction embodies the idea that the international business landscape is ever-changing. Among the drivers of this change is the rapid increase in global migration and mobility. Migration is often a response to events or circumstances within the home and host country environments. Recent events (the pandemic, Brexit, war) have dramatically impacted people's ability to physically relocate and firms' abilities to react to changes in timely and effective ways. This turbulence alters the global landscape of migration further, like a kaleidoscope in which the pieces shift to form new patterns. Thus, analyzing any of these issues or challenges necessitates a consideration of the dynamic and interconnected landscapes of global mobility and IB. The kaleidoscope of the migration-IB link has many moving parts in shifting patterns (global to micro-level). Here, we try to put the parts together through key themes across these levels.

The chapters in the handbook consider migration from the perspective of migrants and migrant communities as key contributors to international business and international firms that rely on the movement of people within them. They focus on the intersection between international business and migration issues, at the organizational (MNEs, SMEs) and/or the individual levels of analysis. The authors collectively contribute to furthering our understanding about the role of migration in IB. In keeping with the kaleidoscope metaphor, Fig. 1.1 depicts the various interconnected themes of the works by prevalence of keyword to illustrate their scope.

Fig. 1.1 A kaleidoscope of global migration themes in IB

Structure of the Book

The chapters in this book are grouped into five key themes. Each theme shifts the kaleidoscope to another broad focus, and within each theme the topics of the chapters cover a tapestry of questions, issues, and challenges within different contexts. As we navigate the "terrain" of global migration, we start with regional, country, and societal-level issues, and move throughout the book to migration issues affecting international firms and finally, to various issues and perspectives of migrants themselves.

Theme I: Migration Landscapes in International Business focuses on the socio-economic landscape of migration. Harjo et al. (2022) outline that the migration landscape has changed dramatically in recent decades, as larger numbers of highly skilled workers from developing and developed countries have settled in urban areas of advanced (mainly Anglo) economies. A shift from lower-skilled to more highly skilled migrants corresponds to an increase in the maintenance of social and economic ties by migrants with their home countries, including international business linkages. However, this change was especially evident during the COVID-19 pandemic, when migration was halted abruptly, and many countries experienced shortages of lower-skilled labor (e.g., in the garment industry in Southeast Asia). More than half of all countries had travel bans in place a year after the pandemic began on March 20, 2020 (McAuliffe & Triandafyllidou, 2021). The challenges and international business consequences of the pandemic for countries, industries, and migrants were severe. People were stranded outside their home countries. Vulnerable migrants faced additional health risks, poverty, and stigmatization (McAuliffe & Triandafyllidou, 2021). This changing migration context is the focus of the chapters in the first section. These recent studies address migration challenges from new perspectives, searching for new explanations underlying migration, as well as analyzing the impact of the COVID-19 pandemic on immigration and on migrants through the international business lens.

A common theme in this section is the extent to which migrants face various obstacles. Migrants have greater difficulties in overcoming various types of liabilities of foreignness, as outlined by Eun Su Lee, Heidi Wechtler, Chiara Berardi, and Chris Brewster in Chap. 2, "Vulnerable Migrants, the COVID-19 Pandemic, and International Business: A Vicious Cycle." The authors present a conceptual work outlining the reasons that vulnerable migrants have become entrapped in a downward spiral during the pandemic due to factors outside of their control. These factors have to do with lack of agency because of issues stemming from their vulnerable position in host societies, placing them in precarious employment that often does not match their skills with lower pay and higher risk, exacerbated further by a lack of resources and support. The authors discuss how these experiences can influence future IB practices and shape international organizations going forward. They urge IB scholars to give more heed to the importance of migrants as key stakeholders in IB, and to broaden the focus of research on migration to enable a shift from a predominant focus on elite skilled migrants to more inclusive conceptualizations of migrants and a (re)consideration of IB theories in turn.

In Chap. 3, "The COVID-19 Pandemic: Immigration Policy Changes and Challenges," Masud Chand analyzes the decline in immigration to select countries during the COVID-19 pandemic, due to restrictions, and the challenges that the aftermath of this decline will potentially pose for societies and organizations. The halting of immigration particularly highlighted shortages of healthcare workers. Chand outlines the changes in immigration policies that resulted from the pandemic in the United States, Canada, and Australia. These countries depend on immigrant workers in the health and sciences sectors. In the US, immigrants work in more than a quarter of jobs in the sciences, and a similar percentage of doctors are foreign trained (OECD, 2020); it is projected that the toll of the pandemic on health workers will lead to a severe shortage in the next decade. Likewise, in Canada, immigrants account for at least a quarter of healthcare workers. In Australia, a country that grows more due to immigration than natural births, the pandemic resulted in a talent shortage. These statistics raise questions about the future internationalization of the health sector, and the innovativeness and competitiveness of advanced nations going forward.

Helena Barnard and Graham Nash discuss migration waves from South Africa, and the reasons that the country has experienced higher than average emigration since the 1950s, in Chap. 4, "Social Contagion and Migration: Sources and Implications of Migrant Ambivalence." The evidence from their study points to different drivers of migration and migration events that influence individuals' decisions to emigrate inside a network, which they term "social contagion." The authors discuss the ambiguities that potential migrants from middle-income countries face when deciding to migrate and when they are faced with little certainty about the decision to migrate or the decision to stay. Migrants from middle-income countries are particularly sensitive to changes in their home country's institutional environment, yet the advantages of migrating are ambiguous. Barnard and Nash based their study in South Africa, where social and economic instability may provide an impetus for emigrating, but which also has a marked disparity between highly- and lower-skilled workers. They explain the decision to emigrate through social contagion, as a combination of perceptions about factors affecting the decision to emigrate that spreads among people. However, they also argue that social contagion processes may lead to distorted perceptions about destination countries that have implications for the adjustment of migrants.

Theme II: Navigating the Terrain of Language and Culture places a lens over the topics of language and culture. A focus on migrants and migration issues allows us to view these domains in new ways and question some extant paradigms. The chapters in this section explore language and culture via diaspora communities, the link between culture and identity formation and identity change, and the leveraging of culture by migrants and migrant groups to their advantage as "others" (e.g., liabilities of foreignness are viewed as advantages, as opposed to obstacles, challenging the traditional view). Language (in)competence places constraints on a firm's international activities. Migrant employees with language skills can help firms (especially SMEs) to select, enter, and thrive in new markets. In Chap. 5, "Migrants, Language, and Internationalization of Small- and Medium-sized Enterprises: A Literature Review," Johanna Niskavaara and Rebecca Piekkari discuss this missing element in the literature on language management. They argue that the link between language and internationalization is still overlooked in IB and demonstrate the role that migrants can play in the internationalization process, in a comprehensive review of the literature over a 65-year period. Their review encompasses and synthesizes the fields of IB, international entrepreneurship, industrial marketing, and economics and incorporates macro, meso, and micro perspectives. Migrants are a valuable resource for internationalization; their language skills and cultural knowledge can be used to overcome distance barriers and connect firms to other firms and markets. The focus in the migration literature has traditionally been on migrants' integration into host countries; the authors encourage researchers to move toward considerations of language issues in migrants' workplace integration and careers, particularly how firms can best utilize this resource.

In Chap. 6, "Dissecting Generations of Migrant Identities Within a Diaspora," Audra I. Mockaitis and Lena Zander present the results of a study that compares the cultural values of migrants comprising a single ethnic diaspora, more recent economic migrants, and home country nationals. They compare the cultural values of these groups across generations, migration waves, birth countries, and migrant ethnic generations. Although the cultural values of migrants become more distant over generations from those of Lithuanian nationals, in general, the authors find that migrant values are more similar than expected and differ from the values of nonemigrants in the home country, a finding that lends support to the stability of values. The differences between migrants and nonemigrants have implications for the ways in which culture is treated (e.g., using country of birth as a proxy for culture). The authors suggest that the timing of emigration may be less important than the act of migrating.

In Chap. 7, "Dual Perspectives: Immigrants' Comparisons of Host and Home Countries' Management of the COVID-19 Pandemic Emphasize the Salience of Cultural Differences," Ariane Froidevaux and David Dwertmann examine perceptions about and reactions to restrictions during the pandemic by immigrants from different cultures who reside in the USA. The authors show that the pandemic has accentuated cultural differences when migrants compare the handling of the pandemic in the USA to that in their home countries. In particular, the differences perceived by immigrant workers, the authors argue, can be a source of cognitive dissonance that may further have repercussions on their acculturation and decision to stay.

Vilmantė Kumpikaitė-Valiūnienė, Audra I. Mockaitis, Jurga Duobienė, Ineta Žičkutė, and Vilmantė Liubinienė (Chap. 8, "Can Intentions to Emigrate Be Explained Through Individual Values? An Exploratory Study in

Lithuania") apply Schwartz's individual values in examining the relationship between individual values and intentions to emigrate. Individualism was positively and collectivism negatively associated with emigration intention, openness to change and self-enhancement were also positively associated, while the conservation dimension negatively. With a few exceptions, the value dimensions were associated with emigration intentions in predicted ways and coincided with the bipolarity of dimensions. The results provide some insights into the characteristics that encourage migration in a country that has a long and turbulent history of migration.

Johanna Raitis, Riika Harikkala-Laihinen, Eriikka Paavilainen-Mäntymäki, and Niina Nummela, in Chap. 9, "From Working Hard to Being Hard Working: The Maintenance and Mobilization of Cultural Capital Among Finnish Migrants in Florida," focus on migrants' identity formation through combining national- and individual-level elements of culture. Based on interviews of Finnish migrant entrepreneurs in the USA, they find that migrants create hybrid and bicultural identities through de-emphasizing cultural differences. Instead of a challenge to be overcome, the authors argue that culture can enhance immigrants' entrepreneurial skills, by providing a source to tap into when integrating into a new host country. They found that positively valued elements of their native culture helped migrants to adapt to the host culture. The authors argue that liability of foreignness can be used as an advantage, as opposed to the traditional view of liability as an obstacle in international business.

In the next chapter, Chap. 10, "[Adult] Third Culture Kids: Why Do Early Life International Experiences Matter?" Mireka Caselius and Vesa Suutari argue that adult third culture kids (ATCK) are often overlooked in the migration and expatriation literatures, as they are "hidden" migrants. Although third culture migrants have grown up among various cultures, they face numerous challenges, as other migrants, in navigating cultural and language landscapes. The authors outline the challenges that third culture kids face as adults, in comparison to non-migrants, such as ambiguities around identities, rootlessness, detachment from their home culture and difficulties adjusting in new cultures and even as repatriates. On the other hand, the international experience of ATCKs is a valuable resource that can equip them for expatriate careers.

Five chapters are included under **Theme III: Leveraging and Managing Migration in the International Firm.** These consider migration from an organizational perspective and offer suggestions about how MNEs and SMEs can support migrants in the workplace through the development of inclusive policies and practices. In Chap. 11, "Exploring the Missing Links Between

International Business and Domestic Migration: The Case of China," Mike Zhang, Cherrie Zhu, Peter Dowling, and Di Fan look closely at practices that are implemented by MNEs in China in response to locally accepted discriminatory practices toward migrant workers, based on the *hukou* system of regulating domestic migration through the granting of different social and economic rights to rural and urban workers. Not all MNEs implement worker protection in China to the same degree; the authors argue that labor-intensive MNEs that seek location advantages via cheaper labor are more likely to adopt *hukou*-based HRM in contrast to capital- or technology-intensive MNEs. The authors highlight the need for IB research to consider domestic migration, especially in emerging economies, as international HRM policies and practices in MNEs reflect the institutional environment of home and host countries. Zhang et al. argue that MNEs should act as drivers of change via responsible HRM practices with a focus on migrant well-being in China, and they outline a series of practical recommendations for doing so.

Chapter 12, "The Value of Migrants for International Joint Ventures" discusses the benefits that migrants bring to international joint ventures (IJVs). Julia Mittermayr, Vera Kunczer, and Jonas Puck show that migrants can help IJVs enhance performance when they employ immigrants from the partner country. As migrants are knowledgeable about the partner country, they can reduce distance barriers by improving social ties, minimizing the negative impact of ingroup-outgroup distinctions by increasing the accuracy of perceptions about cultural and social norms, and help to improve relationships between IJV partners. The positive effects are also moderated by the share of female immigrants in the firms. The authors argue that females have a higher inclination toward developing and maintaining social connections, and this translates into better sharing of tacit knowledge. This study links migration and IB via IJV performance and moves beyond the focus on expatriates and inpatriates on temporary assignments, to permanent migrants, who bridge cultures in the longer term.

Charlotte Jonasson and Jacob Lauring in Chap. 13, "Online Organizational Inclusion of Migrants in MNCs: Overcoming Cultural and Linguistic Barriers Virtually," focus on what organizations can do to support migrants and international workers, who are relatively disadvantaged in organizations, as they face hurdles in skills-building, networking, and career advancement due in part to less favorable attitudes toward them. These vulnerabilities can be more pronounced when migrants also work remotely and don't have as much face-to-face interaction in their organizations. The authors provide suggestions for enhancing inclusiveness in organizations in the online space and present a typology of inclusiveness and its application in virtual settings with a focus on migrants in MNEs. In Chap. 14, "A Balancing Act in Times of Crisis: Inclusion at Work and Careers of Migrants in Austria," Petra Aigner and Almina Bešić also consider inclusiveness and support for migrants. They outline various barriers that migrants face in the labor market, at the country, organizational and personal levels. These barriers affect inclusion at work and career progression. Data in this study are gathered from interviews with HR managers, support organizations, and migrants in Austria.

Christina Butler, Anna Paolillo, and Vittorio Edoardo Scuderi present a comprehensive review of the importance of diversity climates and climates for inclusion to migrant well-being that in turn translate to well-being in MNEs, in Chap. 15, "Migrant Inclusion and Wider Workforce Well-being: Understanding the MNE Challenges and Solutions through the Diversity Climates Lens." The authors raise a series of challenges for MNEs in achieving the goals of positive diversity and inclusion climates that support migrants. For example, as migration continues to increase, the complexities of managing diversity in MNEs will amplify, and MNEs will face new tasks in integrating more vulnerable groups of migrants, such as refugees. MNEs in labor-intensive industries, in industries that traditionally employ migrant workers or that are located in emerging and developing countries, have shown little progress in improving migrant well-being, but they can and should work with external stakeholders to change their own and local practices, a point also noted by Zhang, Zhu, Dowling, and Fan in Chap. 11. MNEs must also consider the superdiversity of migrants, based on intersectionality characteristics and be wary of potential discrimination based on less apparent characteristics of migrants. The authors provide several solutions for MNEs to address these challenges. A key idea in the chapters under this theme is that organizations can make or break migrants' fragile structures of support, inclusiveness, and career progression. Often the resourcefulness and networks of migrants can be tapped into for this support, but organizations can and should do more.

The next set of chapters under **Theme IV: Migrants as an International Business Resource** consider the various benefits that migrants bring to international firms. Migration research has been traditionally overlooked in the IB literature, where a predominance is placed on global mobility; it is argued that these are two sides of the same coin, and that migrants (not only traditionally understood expatriates) are an important resource for international firms. The chapters within this theme address issues pertaining to the derived benefits from migrants for organizations: capital, social capital within the workplace and beyond (e.g., diaspora networks), expansion of global talent pools, innovativeness, access to markets, skills and internationalization, and the ways in which organizations can develop their human capital through various types of support and leverage the career capital of their international employees. There are four chapters under this theme.

Skilled migrants are a potential source of knowledge for firms, as they not only have unique knowledge about their countries of origin, but likely also have established ties with former colleagues, and actors in various communities in those countries. In Chap. 16, "Skilled Migrants: Stimulating Knowledge Creation and Flows in Firms," Pallavi Shukla and John Cantwell outline the ways in which skilled migrants can benefit international firms by assisting firms in navigating the complex cultural and language nuances that create barriers for non-migrant employees. Migrants can help their firms to identify new opportunities and to locate resources and capabilities in them. They can bring new knowledge through the migration process, and also bridge and integrate knowledge originating from their country of origin, acting as conduits of knowledge. The authors present a framework that encompasses the *when*, *why*, and *how* of migrants as sources of knowledge creation and flows in detail from the perspectives of both large and small international firms. They provide suggestions for firms to foster knowledge sharing by migrants, such as by developing more inclusive practices.

Anabella del Rosario Dávila Martínez extends this concept to Mexico (Chap. 17, "How Migration Enhanced Mexican MNEs' Social Capabilities"). Mexico has long been a recipient of refugees from the Latin American region. The chapter describes the activities of MNEs that have hired and trained refugees and the ways in which organizations can engage in community development through responsible migration governance. Dávila Martínez presents the case of one Mexican MNE in particular, in the beverages industry, that has hired refugees as part of its diversity and inclusion policy and through partnerships with international refugee organizations. The author traces the development of the firm's social embeddedness and CSR in gaining social legitimacy and highlights best practice examples about positively affecting migrant communities and their development.

Migrants, even in established diaspora communities, face disadvantages, such as being "other" in their host countries. But diasporans, by staying connected to their home countries, can be a source of various types of resources. Home countries can utilize the skills of diaspora members, by finding new avenues for marketing and exporting products and services, for example. Maria Elo, Ilia Gugenishvili, and Maria Ivanova-Gongne (Chap. 18 "Female Diasporans and Diaspora Networks: A Neglected Resource for Business?") examine this in the context of female diasporans, the extent of their engagement with home country actors and introduce the concept of reverse engagement from the perspective of migrant women from Finland. The authors present a taxonomy of female migrant resources, comprised of professional, social, cultural, and transnational resources. However, based on interviews with female migrants who possess sets of these resources, the authors conclude that, at least insofar as their sample of Finnish female migrants is concerned, there remains a disconnect with homeland institutions, who have not recognized this untapped pool of talent.

Adding further to this idea are Larissa Rabbiosi, Francesco Di Lorenzo, Anupama Phene, and Paul Almeida, who study the influence that innovativeness by immigrant inventors in the USA has on other communities of the host country. The authors examine the flows of knowledge sharing from Indian inventors to others in a knowledge-intensive industry in Chap. 19, "Non-ethnic Inventor Sourcing of Immigrant Knowledge: The Role of Social Communities." They find spillover effects of knowledge, especially where concentrations of immigrant inventors are larger in organizational, technological, and geographic communities; knowledge flows across the boundaries of ethnic communities, as well as within them. This has implications for the diffusion of innovation via migrant communities.

As we navigate through the landscapes, contexts, communities, organizations, and the challenges and opportunities therein, we turn our attention to our final **Theme V: The Migrant's Journey**. Here the focus naturally shifts to migrants, their issues, and first-hand accounts in different contexts. Five chapters comprise this final section. In Chap. 20, "Unfolding the Dynamics of Refugees' Entrepreneurial Journey in the Aftermath of Forced Displacement," Solomon Akele Abebe and Ziad El-Awad highlight the paradox of refugee entrepreneurship. Refugees are among the most vulnerable migrant groups, facing extreme disruption and crisis in their lives, due to the need to flee adverse circumstances, such as war; they face difficulties integrating into their host countries. Yet, many overcome these adversarial circumstances to thrive in their host countries, as Abebe and El-Awad demonstrate in a study of Syrian refugee entrepreneurs in Sweden. The authors unfold the experiences of refugee entrepreneurs over time at different phases of their journey; they discuss the loss of homeland resources and the creation and employment of new resources and networks in a dynamic process model of refugee entrepreneurship.

In Chap. 21, "Supporting Skilled Migrants' International Career Success Across the Micro, Meso and Macro Levels," Marian Crowley-Henry, Shamika Almeida, Santina Bertone, and Asanka Gunasekara highlight several career success stories of skilled migrants from multiple perspectives. These stories, based on the experiences of migrants from three Anglo countries, offer insights into the attainment of positive psychological outcomes. The authors discuss country-level policies and forms of organizational support that assist migrants in establishing or joining networks, and the personal characteristics that migrants use to take advantage of opportunities. Best practices for career success in organizations employing skilled migrants are proposed.

In Chap. 22, "Career Capital Development of Highly Skilled Self-initiated Expatriates," Rodrigo Mello and Vesa Suutari examine the career factors that differentiate self-initiated expatriates from traditional assignees from a career capital perspective. Although generally, the respondents in their study reported a high degree of accumulated career capital, the authors do note that self-initiated expatriates face some vulnerabilities compared to assigned expatriates due to the lower degree of organizational support available to them, especially as regards the development of social networks. Furthering the topics of well-being and career resources, in Chap. 23, "Expatriates' Quality of Life during the Pandemic: Two Sides of the Same Coin," Anh Nguyen and Maike Andresen conducted a study of 707 mainly self-initiated expatriates residing in France, Germany, and the UK and found that expatriates' experiences during the pandemic were related to the extent of available career resources, and that this in turn influenced their intention to stay or repatriate. The pandemic negatively influenced many expatriates' career resources; psychological and physiological stress contributed to resource losses.

Repatriation is the topic of the final chapter, bringing us full cycle in the migrant's journey. In Chap. 24, "Bringing It All Back Home: Capital Utilization of Irish Repatriates in the Irish SME Animation Industry," Adele Smith-Auchmuty and Edward O'Connor study Irish self-initiated repatriates, the push and pull factors associated with their repatriation, and the ways that these repatriates have acquired and used various resources, such as networks, collaborative social ties, market knowledge, economic and cultural capital. How these resources have been utilized in the careers of these skilled workers in a small but global industry with unique characteristics is unveiled through their career narratives.

Concluding Thoughts

As, in the next decade, it is predicted that the rate of migration will increase to at least 350 million people (Boutenko, Harnoss & Lang, 2022), the importance of migration in international business cannot be overstated. The contributors to this handbook have taken us on a journey through various contexts to address complex issues from multiple perspectives. There are still many questions that remain unanswered, yet a few of more highly contentious issues are briefly outlined that deserve attention going forward.

A first question regards the influence that the fourth industrial revolution will have on migration and IB. Remote working is expected to continue to increase post-pandemic. However, the pandemic had a large negative impact on lower wage jobs, and this may disproportionately affect lower-skilled migrants in favor of skilled migrants in the future. Already as high as 45% of skilled migrants in the EU end up in jobs that do not reflect their level of expertise (Baldassari, Hajro & Žilinskaitė, 2022). An increase in demand for skilled work in the science and health sectors, and a decrease in demand in food-based industries, office support, customer service, and sales are predicted to occur in the largest economies by 2030 (Lund et al., 2021). A related issue is the use of artificial intelligence (AI) in immigration; potentially it can increase the digital divide between countries by posing entry barriers to migrants from developing countries (McAuliffe, 2023). The use of AI could amplify inequalities between developed and developing countries (Carbonero et al., 2018). High-income countries with access to advanced technologies may sooner adapt to the new era through upskilling their workforce. Increasing use of AI could lead to a reduction by international firms in outsourcing or offshoring. Artificial Intelligence (AI) has the potential to transform the way international firms operate, leading to increased efficiency and productivity. However, the other side of the coin is that the increased use of AI could have significant implications for migrant workers, who may be working in low-skilled or repetitive tasks that are at a higher risk of being automated. Routine-based jobs with high automation potential are concentrated in developing countries and are conducted by unskilled or lower-skilled labor, often informal and migrant workers. These employees are less likely to receive or undertake training (ILO, 2021). As a result, migrant workers could be displaced from their jobs, leading to economic and social challenges for both the workers and the firms that rely on them. Whether the advent of new technologies will displace unskilled migrants and the extent that this will affect international businesses are of interest.

Modern slavery in global supply chains in MNEs remains a contentious and under-researched issue. The pandemic has increased the risk of modern slavery through a disruption of supply chains and the exploitation of vulnerable workers in essential industries and has made it more difficult to identify and support victims of modern slavery, especially workers in hidden industries or workers who were isolated during the pandemic. Industries such as agriculture, where workers might only be on site for relatively short periods of time, make it difficult to trace where workers come from (Crane et al., 2017).

Industries, such as electronics, hospitality, clothing, shoes, chocolate, coffee and tea, document copious instances of forced labor, unfair treatment of workers, and debt bondage. MNEs are not innocent observers; modern slavery thrives in MNE supply chains (Stringer & Michailova, 2018). Stringer and Michailova (2018) suggest that the complex IB environment, firms' low-cost strategies and seeking location advantages in developing countries, the outsourcing of low-value activities, and placing tight price and delivery requirements on (possibly hundreds of) intermediaries, create favorable conditions for poor treatment of workers. Within these chains of networks are labor intermediaries or brokers, typically offering up migrant workers from developing economies. Thus, MNE supply chains have a powerful influence on the distribution of wealth, international trade, and migration flows, as well as migrant workers (LeBaron, 2021). LeBaron (2021) argues that a shift in focus from product to labor supply chains, enabling an identification (and mapping) of the ways that migrant workers seek and obtain jobs and the intermediaries along the way from worker to worksite, could signal when workers become vulnerable and potentially curtail forced labor and other harmful practices. More research is needed in this area not just to map modern slavery in MNEs but to measure the positive and negative influence that MNEs have on (illegal) migration and vulnerable migrants. We need to question the dual role that MNEs play in affecting migration and their responsibility in alleviating the negative consequences and spillovers to various facets of societies.

References

Al Ariss, A., & Syed, J. (2011). Capital mobilization of skilled migrants: A relational perspective. *British Journal of Management, 22*, 286–304.

Baldassari, P., Hajro, A., & Žilinskaitė, M. (2022). *Fixing the global skills gap: Here's why firms need to get migrant management right*. World Economic Forum. https://www.weforum.org/agenda/2022/11/global-race-for-labour-why-companies-must-get-migrant-management-right/

Barnard, H., Deeds, D., Mudambi, R., & Vaaler, P. M. (2019). Migrants, migration policies, and international business research: Current trends and new directions. *Journal of International Business Policy, 2*, 275–288. https://doi.org/10.1057/s42214-019-00045-6

Batalova, J. (2022). Top statistics on global migration and migrants. *Migration Information Source*. Accessed September 28, 2022, from https://www.migrationpolicy.org/print/17530.

Berry, D. P., & Bell, M. P. (2012). 'Expatriates': Gender, race and class distinctions in international management. *Gender, Work and Organisation, 19*(1), 10–28.

Boutenko, V., Harnoss, J., & Lang, N. (2022). 5 key predictions for the future of talent migration. World Economic Forum. Source. Accessed April 1, 2023, from https://www.weforum.org/agenda/2022/11/5-key-predictions-for-the-future-of-talent-migration/.

Buckley, P. J. (2020). International business research and the world investment report: "Big questions" and grand challenges. *AIB Insights, 20*(4). https://doi.org/10.46697/001c.17987

Buckley, P. J., Doh, J. P., & Benischke, M. H. (2017). Toward a renaissance in international business research? Big questions, grand challenges, and the future of IB scholarship. *Journal of International Business Studies, 48*, 1045–1064.

Carbonero, F. Ernst, E., & Weber, E. (2018). Robots worldwide: The impact of automation on employment and trade. ILO Research Department Working Paper o. 36. ILO: Geneva.

Castles, S. (2013). The forces driving global migration. *Journal of Intercultural Studies, 34*, 122–140.

Choudhury, P., Hernandez, E., Khanna, T., Kulchina, E., Shaver, M., Wang, D., & Zellmer-Bruhn, M. (2021). Migration and organizations. Special issue of *Organization Science*. https://pubsonline.informs.org/pb-assets/Migration%20and%20Organizations-%20Call%20for%20Papers-1616425909783.pdf

Collings, D. G. (2014). Integrating global mobility and global talent management: Exploring the challenges and strategic opportunities. *Journal of World Business, 49*, 253–261.

Crane, A., LeBaron, G., Allain, J., & Behbahani, L. (2017). Governance gaps in eradicating forced labor: From global to domestic supply chains. *Regulation & Governance, 13*(1), 86–106. https://doi.org/10.1111/rego.12162

Crowley-Henry, M., & Al Ariss, A. (2016). Talent management of skilled migrants: Propositions and an agenda for future research. *The International Journal of Human Resource Management, 29*, 2054–2079.

Crowley-Henry, M., O'Connor, E., & Al Ariss, A. (2018). Portrayal of skilled migrants' careers in business and management studies: A review of the literature and future research agenda. *European Management Review, 15*, 375–394.

Elo, M. (2015). Diaspora networks in international business: A review on an emerging stream of research. In J. Larimo, N. Nummela, & T. Mainela (Eds.), *Handbook on international alliance and network research* (pp. 13–41). Edward Elgar.

Fitzsimmons, S., Minbaeva, D., Phene, A., & Narula, R. (2021). Global mobility of people: Challenges and opportunities for international business. *Special issue of Journal of International Business Studies*. http://resource-cms.springernature.com/springer-cms/rest/v1/content/18478310/data/v1

Gould, D. M. (1994). Immigrant links to the home country: Empirical implications for U.S. bilateral trade flows. *The Review of Economics and Statistics, 76*(2), 302–316.

Guo, C., & Al Ariss, A. (2015). Human resource management of international migrants: Current theories and future research. *The International Journal of Human Resource Management, 26*, 1287–1297.

Hajro, A., Brewster, C., Haak-Saheem, W., & Morley, M. J. (2022). Global migration: Implications for international business scholarship. *Journal of International Business Studies, 54*, 1134. https://doi.org/10.1057/s41267-022-00565-z

Hajro, A., Caprar, D. V., Zikic, J., & Stahl, G. K. (2021). Global migrants: Understanding the implications for international business and management. *Journal of World Business, 56*, 1–11.

Hernandez, E. (2014). Finding a home away from home: Effects of immigrants on firms' foreign location choice and performance. *Administrative Science Quarterly, 59*, 73–108.

ILO. (2021). *Changing demand for skills in digital economies and societies: Literature review and case studies from low- and middle-income countries*. ILO Publishing.

IOM. (2016). *2015 global migration trends, factsheet April 2016*. International Organization for Migration (IOM) Global Migration Data Analysis Centre GMDAC.

Kerr, S. P., & Kerr, W. R. (2019). Immigrant entrepreneurship in America: Evidence from the survey of business owners 2007 & 2012. *National Bureau of Economic Research* working paper 24494. https://doi.org/10.3386/w24494.

Kumpikaitė-Valiūnienė, V., Liubinienė, V., Žičkutė, I., Duobienė, J., Mockaitis, A. I., & Mihi-Ramirez, A. (2021). *Migration culture: A comparative perspective*. Springer.

Kunczer, V., Linder, T., & Puck, J. (2019). Benefitting from immigration: The value of immigrants' country knowledge for firm internationalization. *Journal of International Business Policy, 2*, 156–375.

LeBaron, G. (2021). The role of supply chains in the global business of forced labour. *Journal of Supply Chain Management, 57*(2), 29–42. https://doi.org/10.1111/jscm.12258

Levin, D. Z., & Barnard, H. (2013). Connections to distant knowledge: Interpersonal ties between more- and less-developed countries. *Journal of International Business Studies, 44*, 676–698.

Lund, S., Madgavkas, A., Manyika, J., Smit, S., Ellingrud, K., & Robinson, O. (2021). The future of work after COVID-19. McKinsey Global Institute report. https://www.mckinsey.com/featured-insights/future-of-work/the-future-of-work-after-covid-19#/.

McAuliffe, M. (2023). AI in migration is fueling global inequality: How can we bridge the gap? World Economic Forum. Source. Accessed April 2, 2023, from https://www.weforum.org/agenda/2023/01/ai-in-migration-is-fuelling-global-inequality-how-can-we-bridge-gap/.

McAuliffe, M., & A. Triandafyllidou (Eds.) (2021). World migration report 2022. International Organization for Migration (IOM), Geneva.

Morgan, H. M., Sui, S., & Malhotra, S. (2020). No place like home: The effect of exporting to country of origin on the financial performance of immigrant-owned SMEs. *Journal of International Business Studies, 52*, 504–524.

O'Connor, E., & Crowley-Henry, M. (2020). From home to host: The instrumental kaleidoscopic careers of skilled migrants. *Human Relations, 73*, 262–287.

OECD. (2020, November). How to strengthen the integration of migrant women? Migration Policy Debate No. 25. Accessed September 27, 2022, from https://www.oecd.org/migration/mig/migration-policy-debates-25.pdf.

OECD. (2021). *International migration database*. Accessed January 26, 2023, from https://data.oecd.org.

OECD. (2022). *International migration outlook*. Accessed January 26, 2023, from https://doi.org/10.1787/30fe16d2-en.

Pearson, J., Hammond, M., Heffernan, E., & Turner, T. (2011). Careers and talents not to be wasted. Skilled immigrants' journeys through psychological states en route to satisfying employment. *Journal of Management Development, 31*, 102–115.

Reade, C., McKenna, M., & Oetzel, J. (2019). Unmanaged migration and the role of MNEs in reducing push factors and promoting peace: A strategic HRM perspective. *Journal of International Business Policy, 2*, 377–396.

Riddle, L., Hrivnak, G. A., & Nielsen, T. M. (2010). Transnational diaspora entrepreneurship in emerging markets: Bridging institutional divides. *Journal of International Management, 16*, 398–411.

Scullion, H., & Collings, D. G. (2010). *Global Talent Management* (Vol. 45, p. 105). Routledge.

Stringer, C., & Michailova, S. (2018). Why modern slavery thrives in multinational corporations' global value chains. *Multinational Business Review, 26*(3), 194–206.

UNHCR. (2022). *UNHCR: The UN Refugee Agency*. https://www.unrefugees.org/, Accessed September 27, 2022.

Usher, E. (2005). The evolving role of diasporas. *Refugee Survey Quarterly, 24*(4), 47–49.

Zapata-Barrero, R., & Rezaei, S. (Eds.). (2021). *Diaspora governance and transnational entrepreneurship: The rise of an emerging global social pattern in migration studies*. Routledge.

Part I

Migration Landscapes in International Business

2

Vulnerable Migrants, the COVID-19 Pandemic, and International Business: A Vicious Cycle

Eun Su Lee, Heidi Wechtler, Chiara Berardi, and Chris Brewster

Introduction

Although migration has been much studied in other academic disciplines, the scholarly focus on migrants in international business (IB) as potentially part of the labor force or even as agents of change in organizations is comparatively recent (Hajro et al., 2023). Ironically, almost as IB scholarly interest in migration grew, the COVID-19 pandemic put an end to the previous steady year-on-year increase in migrant numbers and pushed migrants to the margins of the host economies. OECD numbers showed a sharp drop of 30% in migrant numbers in 2020, compared to 2019 (OECD, 2021). 'Temporary migrants' (expatriates) across the globe also decreased, showing falls of 58% in working holidaymakers, 53% in intra-company transfers, and a 9% decline in seasonal agricultural workers (OECD, 2021). There was even a reduction of 31% in the number of new asylum applications lodged in OECD countries in 2020 (OECD, 2021). The pandemic not only drove the migration rates down

E. S. Lee (✉) • H. Wechtler • C. Berardi
University of Newcastle, Callaghan, NSW, Australia
e-mail: jeannie.lee@newcastle.edu.au; heidi.wechtler@newcastle.edu.au; chiara.berardi@uon.edu.au

C. Brewster
University of Reading, Reading, UK
e-mail: c.brewster@henley.ac.uk

overall, but migrants experienced harsher reactions as many indigenous citizens became fearful of foreigners potentially spreading the virus (OECD, 2021).

Arguably, in many countries, migrants were particularly at risk during the pandemic, both in their health and their economic situations (Ngan & Sanip, 2021). Most countries adopted nationalistic approaches to managing the pandemic (Mukumbang, 2021) that resulted in negative implications for migrants. For example, migrants were often systematically excluded or disadvantaged in vaccination and testing policies. In Australia, for example, migrants had to wait in longer queues in public sites, as they were prevented from being vaccinated in private health practices. In many countries, little effort was taken to include migrants in the loop of up-to-date information. Often, updates around policies, vaccination, and the virus were translated into only a few languages, and even the translated versions were inaccurate or less detailed. The information disseminated was usually generic and did not take diversity of socio-cultural beliefs and norms into consideration. Overall, the pandemic left migrants vulnerable in their new country, often without proper support to enable them to survive or to make informed choices.

Combining conflict theory with the capability approach, De Haas (2021) defines mobility as a capability (or a freedom) to make a choice on where to live. Most migrants lack resources, liberty, or capability to move within their new society and 'are vulnerable to exploitation and extortion by state agents, employers or smugglers' (De Haas, 2021, p. 29). We argue that during the major disruption of international mobility that resulted from the pandemic, many (perhaps most) migrants were vulnerable and precarious, open to being exploited by the nationalistic approaches taken by state agents, politicians, businesses, and/or host communities. Migrants were often disadvantaged in getting vaccinated, tested, or informed of situations, and were also excluded from financial support and subsidies. Further, businesses and communities often formed biased conceptions of migrants spreading the virus. During the pandemic, many migrants experienced financial hardship, were more exposed to the risks of the virus, and suffered physical and psychological isolation. Migrants are found at all levels of society, of course, and although we will mention high-status migrants, this chapter is focused mostly on those who have suffered most from the turbulence created by the COVID-19 pandemic, the 'vulnerable' migrants and refugees at the bottom of the pyramid. We examine the mechanisms through which these more precarious migrants were trapped in a vicious cycle of nationalistic approaches to the pandemic.

Table 2.1 Future research agenda in IB in light of migration trends post-pandemic

Areas of improvement in IB theorization	Example research topics
Re-conceptualization of migrant workers	• Migrant workers as scapegoats in case of (socio-cultural, economic, or health) national disruptions • Implications around brain drain and brain waste, as well as under- and un-employment of migrants • Impact of nationalist policies for organizations • Understanding value of migrant workers in some industries, such as care work, agriculture, and manufacturing • Reinstating value of migrant workers
Re-conceptualizing the definition of "work"	• Re-conceptualizing value of work, talent, and skillsets • Moving beyond binary conceptualization of work: Skilled vs. unskilled, blue- and white collar, and essential vs. non-essential work • Re-evaluation of some work done by migrants in terms of their contribution to the national and global economy
Migrant workplace integration	• Importance of migrants' well-being and their working conditions • Migrants' integration conceptualized beyond economic value • Reinstating contribution of migrants in national economy as well as in creation of socio-cultural diversity • Cross-industry collaboration to assist in migrant workplace integration (e.g., businesses, non-profit organizations, educational institutes and community organizations) • Cross-cultural training and inclusive practices
Occupational health and safety in IB	• Highlighting importance of well-being, work-life balance, and working conditions • Impact of occupational health and safety rules, policies and programs on workers' performance and workplace integration • Context- and country-specific occupational health and safety policies and practices developed for MNEs • Role of employers in ensuring physical and psychological health of workers, especially in absence of national support • "New normal" practices and perceptions toward the importance of health and well-being
Expansion of HRM to be more inclusive	• Encompassing HRM practices and polices across multiple functions, such as recruitment, training, performance management, occupational health and safety, and socio-cultural diversity and inclusion • HRM with reference to other functions of the business, such as organizational strategy and responses to global, national, and regional disruptions • Multi-level theorization across global, national, regional, organizational, team and individual levels • Multi-stakeholder theorization, including internal and external stakeholders • Cross-case comparisons between different national, organizational, and individual contexts

Unpleasant and disadvantageous experiences in the workplace and in hosting communities are likely to reshape the perspectives of migrant workers, and thus impact future IB practices. We highlight the negative impacts suffered by migrant workers and the implications for IB. In particular, there are continued labor shortages and staffing issues, experienced by both multinational enterprises and local employers that rely on a pool of migrant workers. A 'new normal' set of criteria is being established to attract migrants, who are now better able to emphasize requirements for organizational support, such as workplace safety, (mental) health, well-being policies, and even flexible work arrangements. These dimensions, especially in regard to low-status migrants, have been neglected in management practice (Haak-Saheem et al., 2022). The extent of organizational support provided by host countries and communities needs more attention. We conclude the chapter by noting that, by understanding migrants' difficulties in integrating into the labor market, health inequities, barriers to healthcare access, and the combination of these factors together, IB scholars can better reflect on the changing trends in the labor market and workplaces, as well as migrants' perceptions of organizational practices and communities. These 'new normal' factors may shape business practice in IB and international human resources management, and at the same time, help scholars advance theoretical understanding through perspectives that intersect multiple levels of analysis (Syed, 2008), in different contexts (Beer et al., 2015).

Migrants during the Disruption of International Mobility

The pandemic disrupted many people's lives, but it particularly exacerbated the socio-cultural and economic vulnerability of migrants. International mobility was restricted with stricter regulations and, in some cases, border closures (Piccoli et al., 2021). Some people were stranded in foreign countries without work or proper living support, many of them isolated from their family members (Alcaraz et al., 2022), while others were forcibly repatriated without proper support and operational systems and protocols (ILO, 2021). In Malaysia, for example, more than 50% of the workers in several garment companies that closed down were migrants, leaving many unemployed (ILO, 2021). Countries like the United Arab Emirates, where residence is tied to employment had to amend their regulations to cope with unemployed migrants not allowed to go home (Haak-Saheem et al., 2022). The visa sponsorship system known as the Kafala program is in place in the Gulf Cooperation Council (GCC) countries of Bahrain, Kuwait, Oman, Qatar, Saudi Arabia, and the United Arab Emirates (UAE), as well as in Jordan and Lebanon, and requires businesses' approval for migrants' entry to and exit from the host country, which makes migrant workers completely dependent on their employers. This system often includes practices like passport confiscation, prohibition on joining unions and bargaining collectively, lack of minimum wage provision, and absence of guarantees to leave the workplace in case of abusive behaviors, that put migrants in a position of vulnerability and create favorable conditions for human rights violation and contemporary forms of slavery (ILO, 2017).

Migrants also had limited access to appropriate care, such as medical support with interpretation services, and thus, in some cases, suffered a combination of psychosocial and physical health issues (Chan & Kuan, 2020; Liem et al., 2020). A survey of approximately 30,000 participants with migrant and refugee backgrounds showed that about half felt greater levels of depression, anxiety, and loneliness during the pandemic, far more than pre-pandemic (WHO, 2020). Migrants related this increase to worries about their future and financial security, and concerns about their family and friends overseas (WHO, 2020). In short, migrants were disproportionally affected by the pandemic in terms of health outcomes, social and political exclusion, and economic and labor market trends. The key issues were as follows.

First, low-status migrants were more exposed to the risks of the COVID-19 virus because of their living conditions, which often involved overcrowded housing, insecure accommodation, asylum centers or refugee camps, as well as higher dependence on public transportation (WHO, 2020), making, for instance, physical distancing an issue (Lancet, 2020). Their poverty, and governmental immigration policies, meant that low-status migrants cluster in smaller, more crowded, and less favorable environments (e.g., dormitories, co-renting), which were ideal conditions for the virus to spread. For instance, in Singapore, more than 90% of cases, as of January 2021, were registered among migrants living in dormitories (Zheng et al., 2021). Evidence from Sweden suggests that the COVID-19 mortality rate among migrants from the low- and middle-income countries, such as those in the Middle East and North Africa, was three times higher for men and two times higher for women when compared to the local population (Hayward et al., 2021).

Second, treatment of the virus, and consequent healthcare issues, had to be managed in a situation where many low-status migrants had limited access to healthcare systems due to the pre-existing individual (e.g., language, education, immigration status) and systemic (e.g., underinsurance or uninsurance, limited or no entitlements to public health and healthcare) barriers. In terms of individual barriers, some were reluctant to be vaccinated either for sociocultural reasons, religious beliefs, or fear of stigmatization. Undocumented migrants, with no entitlements to healthcare, in particular, were hesitant about being vaccinated as they feared punitive action and deportation (Teerawattananon et al., 2021). In regard to systemic barriers, migrants were often systematically excluded or disadvantaged in preventative measures, such as vaccination and testing policies. Many migrants are healthcare workers and they were prioritized in most countries, but these aside, migrants, generally younger and healthier than indigenous populations (Lassetter & Callister, 2009), are rarely included in the 'prioritized groups' in the host countries, despite being at higher risk of contracting the virus due to riskier living and work conditions (Baggio et al., 2021).

Many countries used multiple languages in their vaccination campaigns and targeted a wide range of social and ethnic groups residing in their countries. Yet, the lack of details in these translated campaigns and gaps in the diversity of languages covered were consistently criticized as major hurdles in vaccinating migrants, and in creating the associated 'vaccine hesitancy' (Berardi et al., 2022; Crawshaw et al., 2021; Mukumbang, 2021). In addition, there was increased reliance on digital tools, such as telemedicine, mobile phone applications, and online websites, during the height of the pandemic, and these were less accessible, or not accessible at all, to many low-status migrants, limiting their access to online health, education, job seeking, and economic relief application forms. This exacerbated digital divide was amplified by limited digital literacy, lack of technological devices, and limited access to stable internet connections (Bastick & Mallet-Garcia, 2022). This combination of individual and systemic factors contributed to worsening the COVID-19 outcomes and health disparities for migrants.

Third, many migrants experienced economic challenges during the pandemic due to the nature of their jobs and employment conditions. Migrants had higher chance of having their employment suspended and/or terminated during the pandemic, having their working hours and rates of pay reduced, or being forced to 'take leave' (Jones et al., 2021; Hu, 2020). For example, in countries like Australia, Canada, Singapore, and the United Kingdom, migrants have traditionally been employed in services, manufacturing, construction, retail, hospitality, and healthcare, all of which were disproportionately impacted by the pandemic. Many such jobs cannot be performed remotely and have higher risks of exposure to the virus in the workplace. Thus, the employment positions in these sectors are seen to increase COVID-19-related risk factors and adverse outcomes among migrant populations. Migrants lost jobs in hospitality, tourism, agriculture, and food processing, contributing to a larger gap in (un)employment rates in comparison to the local population (Hu, 2020). Some migrants even faced higher risk of exploitation, such as longer hours and hazardous working conditions. This risk increased for those migrant workers that face language barriers or have their visa sponsorship tied to their employment status, as is the case in many Middle Eastern countries. There, individuals became unemployed, and therefore by definition unlawful, residents: They were unable to earn a living but also unable to return to their home countries due to border restrictions (Al-Ali, 2020; Alahmad et al., 2020). At the same time, others who contributed to essential social and economic activities did not have their visa renewed and were forced to return to their country of origin (Donà, 2021).

Fourth, inequalities in the labor market were increased by the pandemic which tended to reinforce intersectional differences amongst the migrant group and between the migrant groups and the indigenous population. Multiple intersectional disadvantages between gender, class, race, education, sexual orientation, religion, and language factors, contributed to discrimination against migrants in the labor market. For example, traditional gender roles are even more prevalent amongst migrant communities. Some women had to withdraw from paid labor to fulfill unpaid caregiving roles, childcare, and homeschooling, in their own family (Arora & Majumder, 2021; Yueping et al., 2021). Homeschooling is particularly difficult for migrant families where parents have limited national language competencies and are not familiar with the local education system. Even when women remained in their jobs, they were often in high-risk and demanding occupations, such as domestic roles, hospitality, and care services, worsening their work-life balance and increasing the risk of infection for themselves and their family members (Donà, 202; Swan, 2020). Working conditions often reflected and contributed disproportionately to migrants based on their socio-economic classes, races, and religious backgrounds. While some could reorganize their work remotely from home, undocumented, less educated, low-income migrants were found to be less likely to refuse essential work or employment in the informal sectors, despite not having social protection such as decent wages, sick pay, and lay-off payments (Maestripieri, 2021; Arora & Majumder, 2021; Swan, 2020). In the United Kingdom, during the height of the pandemic, women of color were disproportionally affected by food insecurity, due to their precarious job conditions (Swan, 2020). Despite facing higher financial hardship, there was discrimination against access to relief packages by the government, employers, and landlords, based on religious backgrounds (Noor et al., 2021). Furthermore, many LGBTQI+ people were perceived to be

COVID-19 spreaders and faced discrimination when searching for employment (Camminga, 2021; Cowper-Smith et al., 2022; Tschalaer, 2022).

Overall, exacerbating living, health status, and economic circumstances combined with low institutional and organizational support entrapped many migrants in a downward spiral during the pandemic. We argue, however, that these devastating conditions based on systemic and demographic discrimination are not new. The pandemic revealed and exacerbated the inequalities that have long existed and have worsened due to the overall nationalistic responses.

Nationalistic Approaches to the Pandemic: A Vicious Cycle

In their new countries, migrants always have to deal with a multiplicity of challenges (learning the local language, school system, expanding social networks, accessing appropriate healthcare and community support) in order to integrate into the local system, workplaces, and communities. These preexistent systemic inequalities for migrants in accessing the job market worsened during the pandemic. We examine these and the way they created a vicious cycle for migrants.

Migrants, and vulnerable migrants in particular, encounter a multiplicity of barriers to access employment in their new countries compared to domestic applicants. This is said to reflect migrants' liability-of-foreignness (e.g., Fang et al., 2013; Harvey et al., 2005), encompassing poorer language skills, a lack of local work experience, being perceived as less legitimate, having fewer resources: In sum, the social cost of being an outsider (e.g., Gurău et al., 2020). Migrants also face discrimination and injustice based on their ethnicity and while all migrants deal with discrimination of some form or extent, literature on ethnic hierarchies suggests that discrimination and racism do not affect all migrant groups the same way (e.g., Ahmad, 2022). We speculate that the race, ethnicity, and country of origin of vulnerable migrants, as a manifestation of ethnic hierarchies in society (e.g., Bobo & Zubrinsky, 1996), also contribute to the difficulty of accessing a job aligned with their qualifications and home-country experiences. The pandemic added another layer of Sinophobia, xenophobia, and general anti-migrant sentiment (Esses & Hamilton, 2021). As with previous infectious disease outbreaks, such as smallpox, SARS, and MERS, the transmission of the coronavirus increased the stigma of being a migrant and increased socio-cultural abuse toward migrants and ethnic minorities (Bhandari et al., 2021; Liu et al., 2020), reinforcing existing marginalization mechanisms and barriers to appropriate support (Nyblade et al., 2019). The processes of stigmatization and scapegoating have hardened labor market conditions for migrants who, at the same time, have been largely excluded from healthcare support and vaccination policies and, for example, subsidies for local (un)employment.

Because of language barriers, limitations around educational recognition, or discrimination, migrants can be forced to accept the first available jobs for survival reasons, rather than wait for one that fits their desired career prospects (Lee et al., 2020). As a consequence, vulnerable migrants tend to be more often unemployed and underemployed than their native-born counterparts (Guo et al., 2020; Lazarova et al., 2023; Nardon et al., 2022; Szkudlarek et al., 2021). Migrants also tend to hold precarious jobs and/or jobs with lower pay or status, so that migrants are often in frontline work (e.g., farm or care work) or excluded from safer working conditions (such as working from home) or from public benefits. The lack of fair job opportunities leads to jobs that require further and longer commuting using public transportations, that are more often in contact with people (e.g., frontline workers) and, in turn, put migrants at higher risk of exposure to the COVID-19 virus.

The pandemic widened the existing inequity between migrants and the local population (Berardi et al., 2022), disproportionately affecting the health and economic activities of vulnerable socio-economic groups (Büyüm et al., 2020). For vulnerable migrants, gender and mother tongue are barriers to career and financial advancement (e.g., Fitzsimmons et al., 2020). These typical disadvantages were exacerbated by media exposure and the general fear widespread during the pandemic that created additional stigma associated with migrants (Ittefaq et al., 2022) and, on the other side, increased migrants' distrust of institutions and health campaigns (Tjaden et al. 2022). The market disruption and unprecedented low level of economic activity due to the pandemic marginalized, isolated, and pushed vulnerable migrants even closer to the edge.

Security policies during the pandemic closed borders and imposed other health control regulations that grounded migrants, so that they were often unable to travel for emergencies or to reunite their family (IOM, 2020). This 'forced immobility' (Lazarova et al., 2023, p. 7), exacerbated by nationalist ideology from which a large number of the COVID-19 policies emanated (Givens & Mistur, 2021), is likely to have accentuated vulnerable migrants' physical and mental health issues during the pandemic, and thus impacted their ability to participate in economic activities even after the global health disruption.

Overall, the lack of support to migrants had repercussions on individuals' economic, social, health, and eventually career trajectories, created both by the nationalistic responses to the pandemic but also unraveled by a vicious cycle of health inequity where migrants have continued to face higher risks to their health and safety while being largely excluded or disadvantaged in the pandemic response (Berardi et al., 2022).

Migrants, Post-Pandemic and Implications for International Business

Migrants are increasingly becoming part of the everyday lives and local economies of many countries across the globe, particularly the developed economies (Hajro et al., 2023). Even though the pandemic, and the consequent travel restrictions, paused the international mobility trends, there is no reason to believe that the number of migrants will decrease in the longer term (Lazarova et al., 2023), and it has been argued that the world will be even more globalized post-pandemic (Contractor, 2022). The difference in the experience of the pandemic between migrants and the native-born populations has been striking, yet this might be an opportunity to rethink the role and space given to migrants and raise the relevance of migration in IB in the post-pandemic context (Barnard et al., 2019). There are important implications for IB scholarship and practice (see Table 2.1).

First, post-pandemic, IB scholars and practitioners need to re-consider the conceptualization of migrant workers and their roles in migrant integration. Migrants' workforce integration is the most important factor to their resettlement (Portes & Rumbaut, 2005). Yet, most Western countries continue to record discrimination and substantial barriers to migrants' integration into job markets and paths to sustainable career trajectories (e.g., Ahmad, 2022), including the widespread under-employment of migrants and associated economic loss of skills. The barriers, and hardships, faced by vulnerable migrants during the pandemic, exacerbated by nationalistic approaches to healthcare, vaccination, and economic recovery, could discourage migrants from investing in their job search effort as well as job commitment, and fulfilling their human capital more generally. This may become a key problem, given that migrants fill important gaps in local economies. For example, in Australia, in 2021, 20% of recent migrants worked in the healthcare and social assistance industry (Mackey et al., 2022). In Europe, migrants are overrepresented in occupations such as cleaning, construction, manufacturing, and transport (European Commission, 2021b). In the United States of America, migrants make up 22% of food supply chain workers and 69% of California agricultural workers (MPI, 2020). These figures may well increase as international borders open again. In Australia, Belgium, Denmark, Finland, and the United Kingdom, migrants' employment rates have started to increase, while rates remained constant or declined for locals (OECD, 2022).

Moreover, in the United States of America, as an example, more than 5 million essential workers are undocumented migrants (FWD, 2020). The pandemic helped us re-conceptualize work and especially those considered 'essential' (Bollard, 2020). Little of this 'essential' work is paid well or glamorous in its titles or duties performed, and these jobs have been ignored in the literature about 'talent management'. Yet, in the crunch situation created by the pandemic, it was nurses, carers, truck drivers, food workers, cleaners, and emergency services that were critical to the response to the crisis and the sustainability of the healthcare system and economy worldwide (Lazarova et al., 2023). These positions were often filled disproportionately by diverse employee groups, compared to those in higher organizational echelons. IB scholars have already pointed to the potential impact of reconceptualization of this 'essential' work, often filled by migrant employees at the fringes of local economy and society, and how practitioners implement different strategies to integrate these workers at the margins to continue to contribute to the ever more important roles in healthcare, hospitality, agriculture and more (Lazarova et al., 2023). Similarly, the question arises as to whether the crucial nature of certain work that the pandemic exposed will bring about more perceived value and sustainable diversity gains in these positions (Lazarova et al., 2023), a re-evaluation that would significantly improve the economic contributions of migrant workers. The signs are not good.

Second, scholars and practitioners alike need to restate the fact that migrants are key stakeholders in IB. Yet, evidence of the healthy migrant hypothesis shows that migrants' health decreases after arriving in their host country (e.g., Lassetter & Callister, 2009). This is due to the adjustment to local and relatively less healthy lifestyles, to the very limited access to healthcare among vulnerable migrants (e.g., Shakya et al., 2018), to the often less safe nature of the jobs held by vulnerable migrants, or to the strong control over migrants' rights (e.g., the American Zero Tolerance policy) discouraging access to healthcare. While vulnerable migrants are often depicted as a burden for receiving countries, they bring important economic opportunities that are often undervalued (Peri, 2016). While the pandemic did not create the health disparities between vulnerable migrants and domestic counterparts, the health crisis and associated policies, placing migrants' health far from national priorities, have exacerbated the problem.

All this leaves hanging the question of how host societies and employers can reinstate the value of migrant skillsets, integrate migrants better into work that meets their skillsets, and improve the treatment of migrants once they are employees in order to contribute to the development of 'world society' (Meyer, 2010), where multiple stakeholders including individuals, for-profit organizations, third sector organizations, and government actors adhere to discernible standards of care for migrants (Barnard et al., 2019).

Third, hiring migrants remains a complex and challenging task. Although IB scholars have devoted attention to cross-cultural training, they have primarily focused on the preparation of assigned expatriates, the most privileged members of the global workforce (e.g., Littrell et al., 2006; and see McNulty & Brewster, 2020). Indeed, refugees are not associated with talent in the academic discourse, where talent and its associated learnings are almost the exclusive domain of expatriates (e.g., Fan et al., 2022; Vaiman et al., 2015). This narrow view limits the understanding of how to support those who need it the most. 'Migrants' is a broad and heterogenous group that includes highly qualified migrants and refugees, voluntary and involuntary migrants as well as many other categories (Cerdin et al., 2014; Lee et al., 2020). We need to be inclusive in our approach. Migrants, especially those without recognized qualifications, rarely benefit from organizational training opportunities in order to facilitate smoother cross-cultural adjustment and workplace integration (Lee & Wechtler, 2022). This is detrimental to practitioners, who need up-to-date knowledge. It is becoming vital for IB scholars to invest in such issues. Our scholarship and practices also need to adjust to the reality of our societies, rethinking the increase of migrants and refugees through the lens of workplace equity, diversity, and inclusiveness (Lazarova et al., 2023). The literature around migrants and refugees is largely dominated by antidiscrimination rhetoric, focusing on the exclusion of minorities, rather than a more grounded discourse around inclusive practice and policies (e.g., Ponzoni et al., 2017). Despite stakeholders' good intentions, efforts to support diversity may unintentionally contain exclusionary practices, misinterpreting equal treatment as equity and inclusion. It seems urgent to go beyond the traditional layers of diversity (gender, age, sexuality, and religion) and appraise more carefully the complexity of migrants' needs to get fairer opportunities and eventually be fully included in the workplace.

Fourth, occupational health and safety (OHS) is rarely discussed in the IB literature (for exception, see De Cieri & Lazarova, 2021). This is despite the long-term concerns raised by many global health experts about the likelihood of pandemics and a substantial body of research conducted around previous health crises (Dovlo, 2005). Government bodies and for-profit organizations were not prepared for such a health crisis (Phan & Wood, 2020), and the global pandemic negatively influence the operations of many multinational enterprises (MNEs). Managing OHS has always been on the priority list for MNEs operating in multiple geographic locations with a diversity of employee groups (De Cieri & Lazarova, 2021), but research to date has focused mostly on mental health concerns such as depression, and physical or physiological outcomes, such as workplace injuries and infectious diseases (De Cieri & Lazarova, 2021). While the businesses' general duty of care for its workers are well recognized in practice and research, what is new was the extraordinary scale of the pandemic, and its impact on the health of many employees, as well as the urgency of the need for responses (Lazarova et al., 2023). Many employees also suffered the chronic health symptoms known as 'long COVID,' symptoms often accompanied by mental health problems (Gaspar et al., 2021).

Furthermore, the COVID-19 pandemic made such issues even more challenging with the 'new normal' perspectives of migrants having gone through difficult times without proper governmental or organizational support in the host countries. More migrant workers are expected to pay attention to OHS policies, procedures, and response plans in their employing organizations, and focus on organizational support and benefits such as health insurance. These 'new normal' and changed perspectives will point toward the need to reshape IB and international human resource management practices in order to attract and retain migrant talents. Unpleasant and disadvantageous experience in the workplace and in hosting communities during the pandemic is likely to influence the perspectives of migrant workers, and thus impact future IB practices. In particular, there exists in most developed countries a continued labor shortage and staffing issues, experienced by MNEs and local organizations that have relied on a pool of migrant workers. This is a serious challenge to the more or less explicit 'anti-immigrant' rhetoric of many political movements around the world. It is also a challenge for businesses. A 'new normal' set of criteria need to be established to attract migrants, who now place importance on traditionally less focused components of organizational support, such as healthcare insurance. The extent of organizational support provided by the host countries and communities to migrants' inclusivity is considered critical. There is a strong need for and relevance of theoretical research and policy actions to attract and retain the migrant workforce.

Fifth, theories in IB scholarship should play a role in gaining understanding of the post-pandemic scenarios in terms of migrant integration into the workforce. Both traditional human resource management, and a multi-sectoral interplay of different human resource functions, health management, OHS policies and procedures, inclusivity policies, and equity concerns, at different levels of analysis, will become crucial in future theorizations of IB in general and international human resource management in particular. Human resource management professionals in MNEs and local businesses that hire individuals with diverse cultural and ethnic backgrounds will need ever more encompassing systems and processes that not only look after the traditional employee issues, such as recruitment, selection, training, and performance management, but also embed newly arising issues, such OHS policies and procedures, into their system of human resource management operations. To this end, theories that cut across multiple levels of analysis will be ever more valued to understand issues (Hajro et al., 2019) around, for example, migrant workers and health insurance at individual, organizational, and policy levels. Theoretical perspectives, such as a relational perspective (e.g., Al Ariss & Syed, 2011; Syed, 2008; Lee et al., 2020) and the (multi-)stakeholder perspective (e.g., Beer et al., 2015; Lee & Szkudlarek, 2021), will be useful in capturing the diversity of concerns associated with recruitment, training, retaining, and integration of migrant workers. A relational perspective has long been applied to management of migrant workers, as there are multi-level issues that are inter-related (e.g., Al Ariss & Syed, 2011; Syed, 2008). For example, these multi-level, inter-related concerns around hiring and sustaining migrant workers include institutional policies around diversity and inclusion quotas, visa conditions (including private health insurance and access to public healthcare system) and policies, organizational practices including workplace safety policies, and entitlements to paid sick leave, as well as diversity and inclusion policies, and individual factors, such as drivers for work-life balance, access to private and public health insurance, and access to translation services during visits to healthcare support providers.

Traditional frameworks that include both external and internal factors in international human resource management and IB will also revitalize momentum in migrant discussion in the field. Examples of these frameworks include the Harvard model (Beer et al., 1984; Beer et al., 2015), Michigan model (Fombrun 1984), and the European model (Brewster, 1995; Gooderham & Nordhaug, 2011). The Harvard model, for example, includes the diversity of stakeholders in its theorization along with situational—what we would now call contextual—factors (Beer et al., 1984). When applied to the case of migrant workers, it is apparent that different stakeholders, such as support organizations, governmental bodies, qualification accreditation institutions, and local communities, as well as situational factors, including nationalistic approaches to healthcare, availability of translation services for healthcare and anti-migration ambiance, can altogether impact organizational practices, and thus, individual employment outcomes and negatively influence their experiences in the workplace. Similarly, the Michigan model (Fombrun 1984) can be extended to address the concerns regarding the recruitment of migrant workers by considering external factors, such as socio-cultural ambiance, political agendas, and macro-economic measures. Likewise, the European model can add significant value to understanding how to manage migrant workers as well by analyzing international and national contexts around health equity and perspectives toward migrants along with corporate-level factors, such as the existing HRM strategy and practices (Brewster, 2004, 2007). These three are selected only for illustrative purposes, as they are three of the most well-known frameworks in international human resource management. However, there can be more application of and extension of other frameworks to intersect across multiple levels by including diversity of external and internal stakeholders.

In particular, we emphasize the need to include situational and contextual factors beyond organizational boundaries to IB and international human resource management studies. Cross-country comparison can inform future research and practice to understand and identify what worked and what did not work when responding to the pandemic. Despite the fact that migrants in general experienced worsened health conditions, a comparative study across 11 OECD countries found that only in Ireland were positive tests for the COVID-19 virus for migrants equal to those for nationals (OECD, 2022). Similarly, an Italian study reported no difference in the probability of being tested and prevalence of infection between migrants and the native population (Rossi et al. 2020), although other research suggests an increased risk of death of non-Italians (Fabiani et al., 2021). Despite the higher probability of the COVID-19-related mortality among minorities in the Netherlands, the difference between the migrants and the native-born was smaller than those of other countries, such as Denmark, Sweden, Norway, the United Kingdom, and the United States of America (European Commission, 2021). While some countries might have performed better in protecting migrants from the virus, evidence across studies is mixed and results are limited to specific observational time periods, making them difficult to identify unequivocal and consistent factors or health policies that might have contributed to better outcomes in some countries compared to others. Further research would not only help countries revise their action plans for future health disruptions but would also help businesses' response plans in supporting and retaining migrant talents.

All in all, issues at the intersection of migration and IB were exacerbated by the COVID-19 pandemic, where the interplay of complex dynamics in IB including (re)conceptualization of work, migrant workforce integration, re-valuation of migrant talent, and the importance of occupational health and safety, points to a number of IB questions to (re-)emerge.

Conclusion

Migrants are key stakeholders of IB dynamism, constituting important bridges across personal, organizational, and national needs. As many migrants resume international travel, in-depth understanding of migrant workers' lived experiences during the pandemic is ever more critical. The restrictive border controls, reinforced with migrants' language, socio-cultural, legal, educational, economic, and religious barriers to appropriate support and care during the pandemic, all placed in a growing anti-immigration ambiance in hosting communities, contribute to compromised migrants' health and their experience overseas. This will no doubt contribute to the changed perceptions that migrant workers will have when moving across international borders. The COVID-19 pandemic is only an illustration of the health inequity faced by migrants and there are multiple intersections between vulnerability and grand societal challenges, in which social inequity is rooted.

References

Ahmad, A. (2022). Does the size of foreign population in a city affect the level of labour-market discrimination against job applicants of migrant origin? *Canadian Review of Sociology/Revue Canadienne de sociologie, 59*(S1), 134–150.

Al Ariss, A., & Syed, J. (2011). Capital mobilization of skilled migrants: A relational perspective. *British Journal of Management, 22*(2), 286–304.

Alahmad, B., Kurdi, H., Colonna, K., Gasana, J., Agnew, J., & Fox, M. A. (2020). COVID-19 stressors on migrant workers in Kuwait: Cumulative risk considerations. *BMJ Global Health, 5*(7), e002995. https://doi.org/10.1136/bmjgh-2020-002995

Al-Ali, N. (2020). Covid-19 and feminism in the global south: Challenges, initiatives and dilemmas. *European Journal of Women's Studies, 27*(4), 333–347.

Alcaraz, N., Lorenzetti, L., Thomas, S., & Dhungel, R. (2022). Breaking isolation: Social work in solidarity with migrant workers through and beyond COVID-19. *Social Work, 67*(1), 48–57.

Arora, S., & Majumder, M. (2021). Where is my home?: Gendered precarity and the experience of COVID-19 among women migrant workers from Delhi and National Capital Region, India. *Gender, Work and Organization, 28*, 307–320.

Baggio, S., Jacquerioz, F., Salamun, J., Spechbach, H., & Jackson, Y. (2021). Equity in access to COVID-19 testing for undocumented migrants and homeless persons during the initial phase of the pandemic. *Journal of Migration and Health., 4,* 100051. https://doi.org/10.1016/j.jmh.2021.100051

Barnard, B. H., Deeds, D., Mudambi, R., & Vaaler, P. M. (2019). Migrants, migration policies, and international business research: Current trends and new directions. *Journal of International Business Policy, 2*(4), 275–288.

Bastick, Z., & Mallet-Garcia, M. (2022). Double lockdown: The effects of digital exclusion on undocumented immigrants during the COVID-19 pandemic. *New Media & Society, 24*(2), 365–383.

Beer, M., Boselie, P., & Brewster, C. (2015). Back to the future: Implications for the field of HRM of the multistakeholder perspective proposed 30 years ago. *Human Resource Management, 54*(3), 427–438.

Beer, M., Spector, B., Lawrence, P., Mills, D. Q., & Walton, R. (1984). *Human resource management: A general manager's perspective.* Free Press.

Berardi, C., Lee, E. S., Wechtler, H., & Paolucci, F. (2022). A vicious cycle of health (in) equity: Migrant inclusion in light of COVID-19. *Health Policy and Technology, 11*(2), 100606.

Bhandari, D., Kotera, Y., Ozaki, A., Abeysinghe, S., Kosaka, M., & Tanimoto, T. (2021). COVID-19: Challenges faced by Nepalese migrants living in Japan. *BMC Public Health, 21*(1), 1–14.

Bobo, L., & Zubrinsky, C. L. (1996). Attitudes on residential integration: Perceived status differences, mere in-group preference, or racial prejudice? *Social Forces, 74*(3), 883–909.

Bollard, A. (2020). Globalisation in the time of coronavirus: Or one hundred years of solitude for New Zealand? *Policy Quarterly.* https://doi.org/10.26686/pq.v16i3.6549

Brewster, C. (1995). Toward a 'European' model of human resource management. *Journal of International Business Studies, 26*(1), 1–21.

Brewster, C. (2004). European perspectives on human resource management. *Human Resource Management Review, 14*(4), 365–382.

Brewster, C. (2007). Comparative HRM: European views and perspectives. *International Journal of Human Resource Management, 18*(5), 769–787.

Büyüm, A. M., Kenney, C., Koris, A., Mkumba, L., & Raveendran, Y. (2020). Decolonising global health: If not now, when? *BMJ Global Health, 5*(8), e003394.

Camminga, B. (2021). LGBTQI+ and nowhere to go: The makings of a refugee population without refuge. *African Security, 14*(4), 370–390.

Cerdin, J.-L., Abdeljalil-Diné, M., & Brewster, C. (2014). Qualified immigrants' success: Exploring the motivation to migrate and to adjust. *Journal of International Business Studies, 45*(2), 151–168.

Chan, L. G., & Kuan, B. (2020). Mental health and holistic care of migrant workers in Singapore during the COVID-19 pandemic. *Journal of Global Health, 10*(2), 020332.

Contractor, F. J. (2022). The world economy will need even more globalization in the post-pandemic 2021 decade. *Journal of International Business Studies, 53*(1), 156–171.

Cowper-Smith, Y., Su, Y., & Valiquette, T. (2022). Masks are for sissies: The story of LGBTQI+ asylum seekers in Brazil during COVID-19. *Journal of Gender Studies, 31*(6), 755–769.

Crawshaw, A. F., Deal, A., Rustage, K., Forster, A. S., Campos-Matos, I., Vandrevala, T., et al. (2021). What must be done to tackle vaccine hesitancy and barriers to COVID-19 vaccination in migrants? *Journal of Travel Medicine, 28*(4), taab048.

De Cieri, H., & Lazarova, M. (2021). "Your health and safety is of utmost importance to us": A review of research on the occupational health and safety of international employees. *Human Resource Management Review, 31*(4), 100790.

De Haas, H. (2021). A theory of migration: The aspirations-capabilities framework. *Comparative Migration Studies, 9*(1), 1–35.

Donà, G. (2021). Race, immigration and health: The hostile environment and public health responses to Covid-19. *Ethnic and Racial Studies, 44*(5), 906–918.

Dovlo, D. (2005). Wastage in the health workforce: Some perspectives from African countries. *Human Resources for Health, 3*(1), 1–9.

Esses, V. M., & Hamilton, L. K. (2021). Xenophobia and anti-immigrant attitudes in the time of COVID-19. *Group Processes & Intergroup Relations, 24*(2), 253–259.

European Commission. (2021). *Netherlands: Migrants less affected by COVID-19 than in other countries.* https://ec.europa.eu/migrant-integration/news/netherlands-migrants-less-affected-covid-19-other-countries_en.

European Commission. (2021b) *Statistics on migration to Europe.* European Commission. https://ec.europa.eu/info/strategy/priorities-2019-2024/promoting-our-european-way-life/statistics-migration-europe_en.

Fabiani, M., Mateo-Urdiales, A., Andrianou, X., Bella, A., Del Manso, M., Bellino, S., ... & COVID-19 Working Group. (2021). Epidemiological characteristics of COVID-19 cases in non-Italian nationals notified to the Italian surveillance system. *European Journal of Public Health, 31*(1), 37–44.

Fan, D., Wu, S., Su, Y., & Li, Y. (2022). Managing expatriates to achieve mutual benefits: An integrative model and analysis. *Journal of International Management, 28*(2), 100882.

Fang, T., Samnani, A. K., Novicevic, M. M., & Bing, M. N. (2013). Liability-of-foreignness effects on job success of immigrant job seekers. *Journal of World Business, 48*(1), 98–109.

Fitzsimmons, S. R., Baggs, J., & Brannen, M. Y. (2020). Intersectional arithmetic: How gender, race and mother tongue combine to impact immigrants' work outcomes. *Journal of World Business, 55*(1), 101013.

Fombrun, C. J. (1984). Structures of organizational governance. *Human Relations, 37*(3), 207–223.

FWD. (2020). *Immigrant essential workers are crucial to America's COVID-19 recovery*. FWD.us. https://www.fwd.us/wp-content/uploads/2020/12/FWD-essential-worker-report-FINAL-WEB.pdf

Gaspar, T., Paiva, T., & Matos, M. G. (2021). Impact of Covid-19 in global health and psychosocial risks at work. *Journal of Occupational and Environmental Medicine, 63*(7), 581–587.

Givens, J. W., & Mistur, E. (2021). The sincerest form of flattery: Nationalist emulation during the COVID-19 pandemic. *Journal of Chinese Political Science, 26*(1), 213–234.

Gooderham, P., & Nordhaug, O. (2011). One European model of HRM? Cranet empirical contributions. *Human Resource Management Review, 21*(1), 27–36.

Guo, G. C., Al Ariss, A., & Brewster, C. (2020). Understanding the global refugee crisis: Managerial consequences and policy implications. *Academy of Management Perspectives, 34*(4), 531–545.

Gurău, C., Dana, L. P., & Light, I. (2020). Overcoming the liability of foreignness: A typology and model of immigrant entrepreneurs. *European Management Review, 17*(3), 701–717.

Haak-Saheem, W., Holland, P., Brewster, C., & Liang, X. (2022). The family-oriented view on well-being amongst low-status expatriates in an international workplace. *Employee Relations, 44*(5), 1064–1076.

Hajro, A., Brewster, C., Haak-Saheem, W., & Morley, M. (2023). Global migration: Implications for international business scholarship. *Journal of International Business Studies.* https://doi.org/10.1057/s41267-022-00565-z

Hajro, A., Stahl, G., Clegg, C., & Lazarova, M. (2019). Integrating skilled migrants: A multi-level framework of the individual, organizational, and societal influences on migrants' acculturation outcomes. *Human Resource Management Journal, 29*(3), 328–352.

Harvey, M., Novicevic, M., Buckley, M., & Fung, H. (2005). Reducing inpatriate liability of foreignness by addressing stigmatization and stereotype threats. *Journal of World Business, 40*, 267–280.

Hayward, S. E., Deal, A., Cheng, C., Crawshaw, A., Orcutt, M., Vandrevala, T. F., et al. (2021). Clinical outcomes and risk factors for COVID-19 among migrant populations in high-income countries: A systematic review. *Journal of migration and health, 3*, 100041.

Hu, Y. (2020). Intersecting ethnic and native–migrant inequalities in the economic impact of the COVID-19 pandemic in the UK. *Research in Social Stratification and Mobility, 68*, 100528.

ILO. (2017). *Employer-migrant worker relationships in the Middle East: Exploring scope for internal labour market mobility and fair migration*. International Labour Organization, Regional Office for Arab States.

ILO. (2021, November 22). *COVID-19 has made life even more precarious for migrant workers*. International Labour Organization (ILO). https://www.ilo.org/global/about-the-ilo/newsroom/news/WCMS_829452/lang%2D%2Den/index.

htm#:~:text=ILO%2FSERC%20GENEVA%20(ILO%20News,International%20Labour%20Organization%20(ILO).

IOM. (2020). *World report migration*. International Organization for Migration (IOM). https://worldmigrationreport.iom.int/wmr-2020-interactive/

Ittefaq, M., Abwao, M., Baines, A., Belmas, G., Kamboh, S. A., & Figueroa, E. J. (2022). A pandemic of hate: Social representations of COVID-19 in the media. *Analyses of Social Issues and Public Policy, 22*(1), 225–252.

Jones, K., Mudaliar, S., & Piper, N. (2021). *Locked down and in limbo: The global impact of COVID-19 on migrant worker rights and recruitment*. International Labour Office.

Lancet, T. (2020). COVID-19 will not leave behind refugees and migrants. *Lancet (London, England), 395*(10230), 1090.

Lassetter, J. H., & Callister, L. C. (2009). The impact of migration on the health of voluntary migrants in western societies: A review of the literature. *Journal of Transcultural Nursing, 20*(1), 93–104.

Lazarova, M., Caligiuri, P., Collings, D. G., & De Cieri, H. (2023). Global work in a rapidly changing world: Implications for MNEs and individuals. *Journal of World Business, 58*(1), 101365.

Lee, E. S., Nguyen, D. C., & Szkudlarek, B. (2020). Global migration and cross-cultural management: Understanding the past, moving toward the future. In B. Szkudlarek, L. Romani, D. Caprar, & J. Osland (Eds.), *The SAGE handbook of contemporary cross-cultural management* (pp. 409–423). Sage Publications.

Lee, E. S., & Szkudlarek, B. (2021). Refugee employment support: The HRM–CSR nexus and stakeholder co-dependency. *Human Resource Management Journal, 31*(4), 936–955.

Lee, E. S., Szkudlarek, B., Nguyen, D. C., & Nardon, L. (2020). Unveiling the canvas ceiling: A multidisciplinary literature review of refugee employment and workforce integration. *International Journal of Management Reviews, 22*(2), 193–216.

Lee, E. S., & Wechtler, H. (2022). Cross-cultural training in context: Understanding refugee experience through the capability approach. *Academy of International Business Proceedings, Miami, the United States*.

Liem, A., Wang, C., Wariyanti, Y., Latkin, C. A., & Hall, B. J. (2020). The neglected health of international migrant workers in the COVID-19 epidemic. *The Lancet Psychiatry, 7*(4), e20.

Littrell, L. N., Salas, E., Hess, K. P., Paley, M., & Riedel, S. (2006). Expatriate preparation: A critical analysis of 25 years of cross-cultural training research. *Human Resource Development Review, 5*(3), 355–388.

Liu, Y., Finch, B. K., Brenneke, S. G., Thomas, K., & Le, P. D. (2020). Perceived discrimination and mental distress amid the COVID-19 pandemic: Evidence from the understanding America study. *American Journal of Preventive Medicine, 59*(4), 481–492.

Mackey, W., Coates, B., & Sherrell, H. (2022). *Migrants in the Australian workforce a guidebook for policy makers*. Grattan Institute.

Maestripieri, L. (2021). The Covid-19 pandemics: Why intersectionality matters. *Frontiers in Sociology, 6*, 642662.

McNulty, Y., & Brewster, C. (2020). From 'elites' to 'everyone': Re-framing international mobility scholarship to be all-encompassing. *International Studies of Management & Organization, 50*(4), 334–356.

Meyer, J. W. (2010). World society, institutional theories, and the actor. *Annual Review of Sociology, 36*, 1–20.

MPI. (2020). *The essential role of immigrants in the U.S. Food Supply Chain.* Migration Policy Institute. https://www.migrationpolicy.org/content/essential-role-immigrants-us-food-supply-chain

Mukumbang, F. C. (2021). Pervasive systemic drivers underpin COVID-19 vulnerabilities in migrants. *International Journal for Equity in Health, 20*(1), 1–7.

Nardon, L., Hari, A., Zhang, H., Hoselton, L. P., & Kuzhabekova, A. (2022). Skilled immigrant women's career trajectories during the COVID-19 pandemic in Canada. *Equality, Diversity and Inclusion, 41*(1), 112–128.

Ngan, O. M. Y., & Sanip, S. (2021). The vulnerability of migrant Workers in Global COVID-19 pandemic: Highlights from Malaysia and Hong Kong. *Asia-Pacific Journal of Public Health., 33*, 983. https://doi.org/10.1177/10105395211031367

Noor, Z., Wasif, R., Siddiqui, S., & Khan, S. (2021). Racialized minorities, trust, and crisis: Muslim-American nonprofits, their leadership and government relations during COVID-19. *Nonprofit Management and Leadership, 32*(3), 341–364.

Nyblade, L., Stockton, M. A., Giger, K., Bond, V., Ekstrand, M. L., Mc Lean, R., et al. (2019). Stigma in health facilities: Why it matters and how we can change it. *BMC Medicine, 17*(1), 1–15.

OECD. (2021). *International migration outlook 2021.* Organisation for Economic Co-operation and Development (OECD).

OECD. (2022). *What has been the impact of the COVID-19 pandemic on immigrants? An update on recent evidence.* Organisation for Economic Co-operation and Development (OECD). https://read.oecd-ilibrary.org/view/?ref=1155_1155529-kmivt4sbol&title=What-has-been-the-impact-of-the-COVID-19-pandemic-on-immigrants-An-update-on-recent-evidence

Peri, G. (2016). Immigrants, productivity, and labor markets. *Journal of Economic Perspectives, 30*(4), 3–30.

Phan, P. H., & Wood, G. (2020). Doomsday scenarios (or the black swan excuse for unpreparedness). *Academy of Management Perspectives, 34*(4), 425–433.

Piccoli, L., Dzankic, J., & Ruedin, D. (2021). Citizenship, migration and mobility in a pandemic (CMMP): A global dataset of COVID-19 restrictions on human movement. *PLoS One, 16*(3), e0248066. https://doi.org/10.1371/journal.pone.0248066

Ponzoni, E., Ghorashi, H., & van der Raad, S. (2017). Caught between norm and difference: Narratives on refugees' inclusion in organizations. *Equality, Diversity and Inclusion, 36*(3), 222–237.

Portes, A., & Rumbaut, R. G. (2005). Introduction: The second generation and the children of immigrants longitudinal study. *Ethnic and Racial Studies, 28*(6), 983–999.

Rossi, P. G., Costantini, M., Formoso, G., Bedeschi, M., Perilli, C., Venturi, I., et al. (2020). Prevalence of SARS-CoV-2 (Covid-19) in Italians and in immigrants in an area of northern Italy (Reggio Emilia). *Epidemiologia e Prevenzione, 44*(4), 304–307.

Shakya, P., Tanaka, M., Shibanuma, A., & Jimba, M. (2018). Nepalese migrants in Japan: What is holding them back in getting access to healthcare? *PLoS One, 13*(9), e0203645.

Swan, E. (2020). COVID-19 foodwork, race, gender, class and food justice: An intersectional feminist analysis. *Gender in Management, 35*(7/8), 693–703.

Syed, J. (2008). Employment prospects for skilled migrants: A relational perspective. *Human Resource Management Review, 18*(1), 28–45.

Szkudlarek, B., Nardon, L., Osland, J. S., Adler, N. J., & Lee, E. S. (2021). When context matters: What happens to international theory when researchers study refugees. *Academy of Management Perspectives, 35*(3), 461–484.

Teerawattananon, Y., Teo, Y. Y., Lim, J. F. Y., Hsu, L. Y., & Dabak, S. (2021). Vaccinating undocumented migrants against COVID-19. *British Medical Journal., 373*, n1608. https://doi.org/10.1136/bmj.n1608

Tjaden, J., Haarmann, E., & Savaskan, N. (2022). Experimental evidence on improving COVID-19 vaccine outreach among migrant communities on social media. *Scientific Reports, 12*(1), 1–10.

Tschalaer, M. (2022). Queer motherhood in the context of legal precarity: Experiences of lesbian mothers seeking asylum in Germany. *Ethnic and Racial Studies, 46*, 233. https://doi.org/10.1080/01419870.2022.2085055

Vaiman, V., Haslberger, A., & Vance, C. M. (2015). Recognizing the important role of self-initiated expatriates in effective global talent management. *Human Resource Management Review, 25*(3), 280–286.

WHO. (2020). *ApartTogether survey: Preliminary overview of refugees and migrants self-reported impact of Covid-19*. World Health Organization. https://apps.who.int/iris/handle/10665/337931.

Yueping, S., Hantao, W., Xiao-yuan, D., & Zhili, W. (2021). To return or stay? The gendered impact of the COVID-19 pandemic on migrant workers in China. *Feminist Economics, 27*(1–2), 236–253.

Zheng, K., Ortner, P., Lim, Y. W., & Zhi, T. J. (2021). Ventilation in worker dormitories and its impact on the spread of respiratory droplets. *Sustainable Cities and Society, 75*, 103327.

3

The COVID-19 Pandemic: Immigration Policy Changes and Challenges

Masud Chand

Introduction

The World Health Organization (WHO) declared COVID-19 a pandemic on March 10, 2020, and countries around the world started implementing restrictions on travel immediately. In total, 208 countries and territories implemented over 122,823 movement restrictions (International Organization for Migration, 2022). These restrictions included border closures, quarantines, entry restrictions, and bans for most international travelers, bringing the movement of people across international borders to a virtual standstill. Together with significantly slower immigration processing in host countries, the restrictions greatly reduced the flow of travelers and immigrants. Compared to pre-pandemic projections, it is estimated that the total number of international migrants dropped by nearly 2 million between 2019 and 2020 (Migration Data Portal, 2022). Permanent migration to Organization of Economic Cooperation and Development (OECD) countries fell by over 30% in 2020—the lowest migration numbers since 2003, with family-based migration showing the sharpest decline (International Migration Outlook, 2021).

M. Chand (✉)
Wichita State University, Wichita, KS, USA
e-mail: Masud.Chand@wichita.edu

The rising travel restrictions led to a hardening of national borders making the international business environment significantly more challenging for organizations and individuals alike. As immigration levels decreased, the global flow of talent across borders was disrupted leading to skill shortages in critical areas. This had important consequences in the "war for talent" (Beechler & Woodward, 2009; Chambers et al., 1998). Skilled immigrants often create connections between their countries of origin (COO) and countries of residence (COR) using their transnational social networks. These networks can act as conduits for trade, investment, and knowledge flows (Chand & Tung, 2019). Skilled immigrants also bring considerable economic benefits to receiving countries and are an important source of innovation (Blanding, 2018; Scheve & Slaughter, 2018; Norlander & Varma, 2019). International trade increasingly takes place within value chain activities (Mudambi, 2008), and this is where skilled immigrants often add value through their transnational social networks, trust facilitation, and tacit knowledge. The rising barriers to immigration made these connections more difficult and hampered global business activities.

The dramatic decline in travel and immigration flows during and in the immediate aftermath of the pandemic could lead to several challenges for both organizations and host countries. This is especially true in the case of attracting skilled immigrants who bring in much-needed skills and specialized knowledge. As immigration and travel slowed down, skill shortages were often exacerbated, and businesses and organizations had a difficult time in filling all their job openings. From the point of view of immigrants, the response to the pandemic in terms of border closures and longer immigration backlogs meant that both career and geographic mobility was hampered. There were additional issues in terms of family members being stranded and unable to travel to join family, and layoffs which often caused unique hardships to immigrants.

This is especially significant given that over the last few decades, we have seen a systematic rise in the cross-border mobility and migration of both skilled and unskilled workers, through expatriation by multinational corporations (MNCs), as well as through migration (Fitzsimmons et al., 2021). The United Nations Department of Economic and Social Affairs (2021) estimated that there were about 280 million immigrants worldwide in 2020, about 3.6% of the world's population. This is up from about 173 million in 2000 and 221 million in 2010. To put these numbers into perspective, if all immigrants were a hypothetical country ('Diasporia'), it would be the fifth largest in the world (Barnard et al., 2019). Migrants are also vital agents of change in their organizations and societies, and skilled migrants can often provide positive economic outcomes for their host countries (Hajro et al., 2021).

In this chapter, we examine how the pandemic led to changes in immigration policies and practices across several major immigrant countries, how these changes affected immigration and immigrants in these countries, and the extent to which these changes are still in place. In doing this, we will look specifically at three of the largest and most popular immigrant destinations—the United States (US), Canada, and Australia. The US with about 50 million immigrants—around 15% of its population—is the world's largest immigrant country. Canada and Australia also figure in the top ten, with the proportion of their immigrant populations even higher at 21% and 30%, respectively (World Population Review, 2022). These countries also rank in the top 15 on the 2022 Global Talent Competitiveness Index (The Global Talent Competitiveness Index, 2022). Collectively, the three countries attract about two-thirds of all skilled immigrants worldwide, as well as sharing a common cultural and institutional heritage that make comparisons across their policies easier (Chand & Tung, 2019). Immigrants in the US make up more than a quarter of all STEM (science, technology, engineering, and mathematics) jobs (Van Dam, 2018). About 35% of awardees of Canada Research Chairs (a Canadian government initiative to promote research excellence at Canadian universities) are foreign-born, almost twice the proportion of immigrants in the general population (Conference Board of Canada, 2010). Immigration to Australia is expected to increase average GDP growth by 1% between 2020 and 2050 (The Treasury and Department of Home Affairs, Government of Australia, 2018; Chand & Tung, 2019).

We start by looking at the immigration policy changes in response to the pandemic in these three countries. We compare their responses in terms of how this affected their immigration numbers, how quickly they recovered, and the steps that they took in the immediate aftermath of the pandemic. Next, we look at the healthcare sector to see how it has coped during the pandemic. We use the healthcare sector because of its critical nature during the pandemic as well as the high number of immigrants that work in it in all three countries. We compare the responses for these countries, point out the major challenges in the healthcare sector, and discuss programs and policies developed to deal with these. We conclude by synthesizing some policy recommendations for recovering from skilled worker shortages brought on by the pandemic, discuss some implications for healthcare managers, and point out some possible directions for future research.

Immigration during the Pandemic

The United States: The US has the largest immigrant population in the world in terms of absolute numbers, comprising about 15% of its total population, 17% of its civilian workforce, and about a sixth of all immigrants worldwide. Including children born to immigrants, about 85 million, or 26% of the population, live in immigrant families (Esterline & Batalova, 2022).

At the beginning of the pandemic, the US closed land borders with Canada and Mexico for most travel, while air travel was severely restricted (Passel & Cohn, 2022). Most US consulates closed due to the pandemic and only started gradually reopening in July 2020. Even after the gradual reopening, visa processing remained extremely slow especially in places with high covid cases or low vaccination rates. By July 2021, there was a backlog of over half a million immigrant visa interviews (up from about 61,000 pre-pandemic), and most consulates had very long waits for temporary visa interviews (Gelatt & Chishti, 2022). US Citizenship and Immigration Services, which processes applications for immigrants residing in the US, suspended many services during the pandemic. In addition, most other countries that were sources of immigrants or transit points closed borders, bringing legal immigration to almost a halt (Passel & Cohn, 2022).

As a result, the US saw a dramatic drop in the numbers of green cards (legal permanent residence) granted from about 240,000 in the January–March quarter of 2020 to about 79,000 in the April–June quarter of 2020 (Krogstad & Gonzalez-Barrera, 2022). Overall, the number of green cards issued declined 48% between FY 2019 and FY 2020, while temporary visas declined by 54% (Gelatt & Chishti, 2022). However, legal immigrant numbers recovered rapidly over the course of 2021 and regained their pre-pandemic levels by 2022. About 282,000 people received green cards in July–September 2021. That number was higher than in any quarter since April–June 2017, and slightly higher than the quarterly average for the period from October 2015 to March 2020 (Krogstad & Gonzalez-Barrera, 2022).

It should be noted that the number of temporary legal migrants, such as tourists, business visitors, and international students, while recovering somewhat, stayed significantly below their pre-pandemic levels. Arrivals of temporary migrants, which averaged 19.6 million per quarter from fiscal 2016 through March 2020, fell to about 600,000 during April–June 2020, only 3% of the pre-pandemic average. While tourist numbers have since risen considerably, data from July to September 2021 revealed that quarterly tourism reached less than a fourth of the average pre-pandemic level (Krogstad &

Gonzalez-Barrera, 2022). Student numbers were also greatly decreased, with 69% fewer students granted first-time students permits in 2020 compared to 2019. Temporary workers under the H-2A visa program, especially in the agricultural sector, were however relatively unaffected. These workers helped with seasonal crop harvests and were classified as critical to public health and safety (Migration Data Portal, 2022).

Between 2020 and 2021, partly because of the pandemic, the US population grew by just 0.1%, the lowest growth in over 120 years. Urban areas were particularly hard hit by the pandemic and actually shrank in population (Frey, 2022).

Canada: Immigration to Canada dropped significantly in 2020 due to the travel restrictions put in place due to the covid pandemic. Between 2019 and 2020, the number of immigrants coming in dropped almost by half—from 342,000 to 185,000. Given that Canada's population growth is largely dependent on immigration, in 2021 Canada recorded its lowest annual growth since 1916 (CIC News, 2022). The effects of the pandemic were felt in all types of migration. Between 2018 and 2021, permanent residence (PR) applications fell nearly 43% and asylum claims by almost 45%. Temporary visitor visas were down by over 80% (Griffith, 2022).

In response to the pandemic, the Canadian government announced a plan to support economic recovery leveraging immigration as a key component. The plan called for increasing the number of annual immigrants to 400,000 by 2021, 411,000 by 2022, and 421,000 by 2023 to help ensure that gaps in the workforce were plugged and Canadian industries remained competitive globally. In 2021, immigration increased about 25% over the 2020 level, though still somewhat below the pre-pandemic levels (CIC News, 2022). In 2022, the plan was revised upwards with a goal of attracting over 1.3 million immigrants in the next three-year period of 2022–2025, about 1% of the total population annually. Both the government and the Business Council of Canada have held immigration as key to Canada's recovery from the pandemic (Osman, 2022). Canada welcomed over 430,000 new immigrants in 2022, which was in line with its revised immigration targets (Government of Canada, 2023).

Since the pandemic, the Canadian government has modernized the immigration application process to help immigration numbers recover faster. It has prioritized urgent worker needs as well facilitating international students' entry and stay. Short- and long-term measures taken by the Canadian government to expedite immigration processes include the following (Griffith, 2022):

- Addressing the immediate need for temporary workers in essential sectors by providing exceptions to travel restrictions;
- A special pathway for international student graduates from Canadian institutions, healthcare workers, and other essential workers to become permanent residents;
- Greater flexibility for international students to continue their studies remotely;
- Increase in the number of permanent resident admissions, largely from temporary residents already in Canada;
- Temporary shutdown of the citizenship program, restarting with remote citizenship assessment and ceremonies;
- Major reduction in visitor visas, reflecting travel and related restrictions.

However, prioritizing certain applicants during the pandemic when processing was slower also meant that the overall backlog increased. As of April 2022, about a half million applications each for citizenship and permanent residence and about 850,000 for temporary residence were pending. Applications for permanent residence between 2018 and 2021 declined 43%; however, the number of permanent residents admitted to Canada actually increased from 321,000 to 404,000, reflecting faster processing times for those selected. This was partly done by enabling more temporary residents to become permanent residents in certain categories under the temporary residents to become permanent residents (TR2PR) program, which almost tripled to 279,000 in 2021. Other programs that were expanded during this time were the international mobility program (IMP—mainly intra-company transfers and post-graduate employment), international students, and the temporary foreign work program (TFWP—which includes caregivers, agriculture workers, and skilled workers). The number of agriculture workers rose by 14% and skilled workers by 59%. Study permit applications increased over 60%, reflecting the fact that studying in Canada has increasingly become a popular route for immigration (Griffith, 2022). Canada was the only G-7 country whose population increased from before the pandemic partly due to its openness to global talent and immigration (CIC News, 2022).

In implementing these programs, the Canadian government's priorities were to ensure fulfilling the needs of industry by allowing in temporary workers in specific sectors that needed more labor (e.g., agriculture, healthcare) and supporting educational institutions by allowing in more international students and letting them qualify for post-graduate employment. Reducing the backlog for citizenship applications for permanent residents was a lower priority and this was reflected in longer wait times (Griffith, 2022).

Australia: Australia closed its borders for nearly two years and greatly restricted travel and immigration during the pandemic. The fall in the numbers of immigrants was dramatic: in 2020, 3300 new immigrants moved to Australia, compared to 244,000 in the previous year (Mercer, 2021). There was also a simultaneous exodus of holiday workers and foreign students. Together these led to serious worker shortages after the pandemic as the economy rebounded and left many businesses struggling to find workers, with unemployment at a 50-year low of 3.4% (Jose & Jackson, 2022). For the first time in recent history, there were more jobs in the Australian market than job seekers (Menon & Holmes, 2022).

Between 2013 and 2019, Australia's annual immigration target was 190,000. This was cut by 15% to 160,000 just before the pandemic. In September of 2022, in a bid to attract more workers and skilled immigrants, the annual immigration target was set at 195,000 starting in 2023. Australia has been over the years competing with other industrialized countries to attract more high-skilled workers in a bid to help industry's need for workers and partly to counteract its aging population (Jose & Jackson, 2022). This was especially true in industries where the pandemic forced employers to cut jobs or push staff to work remotely. Over 600,000 temporary visa holders left Australia since the pandemic, creating worker shortages in the health, construction, and hospitality industries (Menon & Holmes, 2022). Immigration numbers started recovering in 2021 and net immigration in the 2022 fiscal year was about 170,000 (Australian Bureau of Statistics, 2022).

Traditionally, more people immigrate to than emigrate from Australia each year. Between 2006 and 2020, most of Australia's population growth was based on net migration rather than natural growth (births—deaths). However, in 2020–2021, arrivals to Australia declined over 70% due to the impact of the pandemic. International students were particularly hard hit (Australian Bureau of Statistics, 2021). The pandemic greatly hampered Australia's efforts to attract global talent. In the 2020–2021 fiscal year, overseas migration led to a net population loss of 89,000, the lowest growth on record since World War I (Jose & Jackson, 2022).

A major challenge for Australia since the pandemic has been the large increase in visa processing times, which has left nearly a million potential workers waiting for work visas while businesses deal with acute labor shortages. About 370,000 of the visas are in key temporary categories of visitors: students and skilled workers. Two major issues that are behind this increase in processing times are (a) resource shortages at Australian immigration offices and (b) a substantial backlog of applications that were not processed for nearly two years during the pandemic (Menon & Holmes, 2022). In a bid to reduce

Table 3.1 Immigration changes during pandemic and steps taken post-pandemic

	US	Canada	Australia
Immigrant visa decline 2019–2020	48%	46%	99%
Pre-pandemic-level immigration reached	2022	2022	Plans to reach pre-pandemic number by June 2023
Measures taken post-pandemic regarding immigration	Visa processing reopened at pre-pandemic levels	Increased annual immigration intake target, prioritized urgent workers and international students, lower priority for citizenship applications	Increased annual immigration intake target, extra resources to clear visa backlogs

processing times, the Australia government has devoted extra resources and increased funding by $25 million for extra staff to help clear visa processing backlogs (Turnbull, 2022).

Governments in both Australia and Canada expect that their efforts to increase immigration numbers, prioritize immigrants with critical skills, and reduce processing times for certain visas will hasten their recovery from the effects of the pandemic and help in attracting skilled immigrants in the global war for talent.

We summarize changes in immigration numbers during the pandemic and policies enacted in its aftermath in Table 3.1.

COVID-19, the Healthcare Sector, and Immigration

Immigrants are heavily represented in key economic sectors across industrialized countries. About seven in ten of all migrants in the US work in critical infrastructure sectors, while 13% of all key workers in the European Union (EU) are immigrants (Fasani & Mazza, 2020; Migration Data Portal, 2022). Immigrants comprise a critical and growing share of healthcare workers across industrialized countries. Over the past two decades, the shares of foreign-trained or foreign-born doctors and nurses have continued to rise. Across OECD countries, nearly one in four doctors are foreign-born and nearly one in five foreign-trained. Among nurses, nearly one in six are foreign-born and more than 7% foreign-trained (OECD, 2019). This exemplifies the international nature of the healthcare sector and its importance in the global war for talent.

A shortage of healthcare workers has been present globally for many years, and the demand for skilled health personnel was further exacerbated by the current pandemic. The International Council of Nurses warns of a global shortage of six million nurses, with another four million expected to retire in the next decade. According to the WHO, up to 180,000 health workers died in the first year of the pandemic (Jacks et al., 2022). In addition, stress and burnout levels were high affecting nearly half of US, Canadian, and Australian healthcare workers (Berg, 2021; Wright, 2022; Cabarkapa et al., 2020).

In the US, nearly 25% of doctors were foreign-trained (OECD, 2020). The American Medical Association (AMA) projects that by 2034, the US will face a shortage of between 37,800 and 124,000 doctors. Although bipartisan legislation to use 15,000 unused physician visas and 25,000 unused nurse visas has been proposed, it is as yet pending and has not been passed into law, pointing to the continuing gravity of the situation (Robeznieks, 2022).

The pandemic highlighted a critical shortage of healthcare professionals in the US. In 2018, there were 13 open healthcare job openings for every available unemployed healthcare worker (Liebert, 2021). Immigrants played an important role in alleviating shortages in healthcare: 29% of physicians, 38% of home health aides, 22% of nursing assistants, and 23% of pharmacists in 2018 were immigrants (Gelatt, 2020; Mathema, 2019).

However, it is estimated that as of 2020, there were over 260,000 immigrant physicians, nurses, and healthcare technicians in the US who were not using their training in their jobs (they might be working in different fields because of lack of credential recognition). With appropriate immigrant integration programs, they could be employed in health-related fields and thus alleviate some of the healthcare worker shortages. Such programs could include numerous levels such as assistance with credential recognition, local certification, apprenticeship/internship opportunities, mentoring, language training, and cultural sensitivity. There are, however, currently no formal integration programs for healthcare workers that arrive in the US (Liebert, 2021). Host country acculturation policies are important since they affect how immigrants interact with their host countries and the extent to which they feel at 'home' within them (Chand, 2014).

In spring of 2020, in response to the pandemic, the governors of six states—Colorado, Massachusetts, Michigan, New Jersey, New York, and Nevada—used their executive authority to temporarily suspend or adjust licensing requirements to increase the number of healthcare workers, particularly targeting internationally trained professionals (Batalova et al., 2021). However, these programs also illustrated the challenges in licensing foreign-trained professionals. For example, a New Jersey program launched in spring 2020 to recruit foreign physicians with licenses valid in other countries resulted in 1100 applications, but of these, less than 45 physicians had gained a license to practice in the state by fall 2020. A particularly limiting constraint for immigrants in the New Jersey program was a requirement that physicians have at least five years of practical experience and have practiced for at least one out of the last five years. Another constraint seen in Colorado was the requirement to carry malpractice insurance which is very expensive for temporary licensees (Batalova et al., 2021).

In Canada, more than 1.6 million people work in the healthcare sector. Almost half a million are over the age of 55, meaning that many will be retiring in the next decade, pointing to continuing and growing shortages in the sector. Immigrants account for one out of every four healthcare sector workers including 23% of registered nurses, 35% of nurse aides, 37% of pharmacists, 36% of physicians, 39% of dentists, and 54% of dental technologists and related occupations (Government of Canada, 2022). The shortage of healthcare workers, especially doctors and nurses, has led the Canadian government to start doing targeted draws for skilled immigrants beginning in 2023. This will allow the federal government to select applicants for faster processing with the most in-demand skills for underserved regions of the country, with a key focus on doctors and nurses. However, this will be done in conjunction only with provinces that make it easier for healthcare workers to validate their foreign credentials and start practicing when they arrive (Gordon, 2022). In addition, the Immigration Ministry announced a program in June 2022 to allocate about $1.5 million to help new migrants to Canada work in the healthcare sector faster. The funds are intended to promote collaboration and information sharing and help healthcare professionals get their credentials recognized faster (Thevenot, 2022).

Canadian provinces are also designing their own programs to alleviate some of these shortages in critical healthcare sectors. Ontario allowed international medical graduates (IMG) who passed their exams or graduated from medical school in the past two years to apply for a supervised 30-day medical license (called the Supervised Short Duration Certificate) to help fight the pandemic. In British Columbia, IMG who have at least two years of postgraduate training and who have completed Licentiate of the Medical Council of Canada qualifying exams can work as associate physicians supervised by fully certified doctors (OECD, 2020).

Among OECD countries, Australia is the most reliant on foreign-born healthcare workers. More than half of Australia's doctors and more than one-third of its nurses are born overseas. Their role is especially important in filling vacancies in regional remote hospitals and senior care settings (Jacks et al., 2022). The Australian Health Department modeling projects that an extra 14,000 nurses will be needed to deliver on the federal government's commitment for aged care homes to have a registered nurse on-site for 16 hours a day by October 2023. About 2500 more would be needed for 24/7 registered nurse coverage (Daniel, 2022).

State governments in Australia have also been active in attempting to recruit and retain foreign-trained health workers. In 2021, the Victorian government announced that they would hire up to 1000 overseas health professionals as part of a $255 million package to support frontline healthcare staff in Victoria. The package also included other benefits, such as relocation support, grants toward accommodation, and childcare in certain specialty fields (Waine, 2022). In 2022, it started a program offering up to $13,000 in relocation bonuses. Western Australia has a $2 million recruitment campaign for foreign healthcare workers and New South Wales actively advertises overseas and uses recruitment agents to attract healthcare workers (Jacks et al., 2022). At the federal level, about 4700 additional new immigrants in the healthcare sector will be allowed in from 2023 (Ryan, 2022).

There have also been calls to reform the system of recognizing foreign medical degrees and allowing foreign-trained doctors living in Australia to practice medicine. The Australian government is working on increasing the speed of credential recognition of foreign workers in the country as well as to reduce visa backlogs for those looking to immigrate (Martin, 2022).

We summarize the proportion of foreign healthcare professionals in the three countries, the immigration-related challenges faced by their healthcare sectors, and specific policies and programs adopted in the aftermath of the pandemic to deal with these challenges in Table 3.2.

Table 3.2 Immigration and healthcare challenges during the pandemic

	US	Canada	Australia
Foreign-trained/born doctors and nurses	29% (doctors) 22% (nurses and aides)	36% 23%	50% 33%
Major challenges	Over 250,000 foreign healthcare workers working in other fields, lack of credential recognition, no formal integration program, expensive malpractice insurance	Shortage of healthcare workers, aging population and healthcare workforce, lack of foreign credential recognition	Very reliant on foreign-born healthcare workers, acute need in rural areas, 14,000 more nurses needed for aged care homes, lack of foreign credential recognition
Specific programs to deal with medical professional shortage	State-level temporary suspension of licensing requirement (six states), bipartisan legislation to use unused visas for doctors and nurses (proposed)	Targeted immigration draws for healthcare professionals, faster provincial validation of foreign credentials, federal funding to accelerate information sharing and credential recognition, programs for supervised practice for foreign-trained physicians	State government efforts to recruit more foreign healthcare professionals, relocation bonuses, extra federal quota for healthcare immigrants, speeding up of foreign credential recognition (proposed)

Conclusion

The travel restrictions imposed during the pandemic had the effect of significantly lowering migration flows across borders. This in turn led to shortages of skilled workers in key sectors in immigrant-receiving countries as well as demographic changes. For example, a decline in immigration caused both Australia and Germany to lose population in 2021 and contributed to the slowest population growth of US in over a century. Organizations across industrialized countries had trouble recruiting enough skilled workers in the aftermath of the pandemic as economic activity rebounded and businesses stepped up operations. Critical areas that are especially dependent on skilled immigrants were affected more than others with the healthcare sector being a prime example.

In our look across the three countries—the US, Canada, and Australia, we see that permanent immigration levels declined markedly during the pandemic but are now close to their pre-pandemic levels. All three countries to a certain extent prioritized immigrants with needed critical skills during the pandemic even as overall immigration numbers dropped. This could have led to a sharper drop among family-based immigrants compared to skill-based immigrants. However, all three continue to see shortages in critical sectors, with healthcare being one of them. We see efforts at both the federal and state/provincial levels in Australia and Canada to help increase the recruitment and retention of foreign healthcare workers. These include dedicated immigration quotas for healthcare workers, recruitment and relocation bonuses, accelerated foreign credential recognition programs, and targeted drawing of immigrants already in the application process. In the US, while there were no specific federal programs to promote the integration of foreign medical professionals into the healthcare workforce, there were some state-level programs implemented on an emergency basis to help with critical shortages during the pandemic. However, their success was limited. Immigration integration programs are an area that could greatly benefit from public-private partnerships and include important stakeholders such as federal, state/provincial, and local governments, diaspora organizations, community colleges and universities, and healthcare organizations. It is important that governments at different levels work with industry and labor groups on a continuing basis to strategically design policies to attract skilled immigrants in sectors with the highest need.

In looking at the overall immigration responses, we can draw some preliminary lessons. Australia and Canada are both devoting additional resources to increase immigration processing in key identified areas (including healthcare). This could be one of the ways in which skill shortages can be overcome using immigration policy. Both countries, especially Canada, have put increasing skilled immigration at the forefront of their economic recovery. The targeted drawing of immigrants based on the skills needs of the host country along with accelerated processing could help with economic recovery from the pandemic and give countries an advantage in the global battle for talent. In the US, political gridlock continues to impede legislative action to deal with skilled immigration potentially hampering the long-term ability to attract needed talent.

Given the overall aging of the population in these three countries, it is important for governments to use skilled immigration as a strategic tool to help maintain or grow the workforce in key areas. This is especially important since skilled immigrants are an important source of innovation and entrepreneurship. In the healthcare sector, there is an additional need for talent as the aging population requires more care while simultaneously healthcare professionals themselves are aging and large numbers approaching retirement age. Targeted immigration quotas, shorter wait times through accelerated processing, ease of credential recognition without compromising quality, integration programs for healthcare workers, and federal/provincial/state cooperation for areas with specific needs should all be part of a comprehensive solution to growing healthcare worker needs. These programs could also help countries get an advantage in the global war for talent as economies worldwide recover from the pandemic and try to attract more skilled immigrants.

For healthcare managers, it is important to work with federal and state/provincial regulators to ensure that foreign credentials and experiences are recognized where appropriate. This should help reduce barriers to entry for foreign-trained workers and help boost the aging healthcare workforce. Healthcare managers should also be engaged in designing programs that help in the integration of foreign healthcare workers. Another possible avenue for healthcare managers to explore is the temporary licensing of foreign healthcare professionals, possibly under supervision of local doctors, as they gain the required experience and credentials. The previously mentioned Ontario and British Columbia programs could serve as useful models for this. These steps would help ensure that healthcare talent is nurtured, and artificial shortages not caused by unnecessary regulatory barriers. The shortage of talent worldwide means that managers should constantly be engaged with public policy officials to communicate the skills that are needed and update these skill needs periodically. They should also be working with federal and state/provincial regulators to design integration programs for skilled immigrants to facilitate their working in professional fields that they trained for. In addition, it is important to ensure that new immigrants get the support that they need in the workplace to navigate a new cultural and institutional environment.

An important area of future research is to study the effect of the slowdown in immigration on major emigrant countries. The World Bank estimated that remittances to low- and middle-income countries fell almost 14% between 2019 and 2021 because of the pandemic, pointing to the effect on millions of migrant families and their countries of origin (United Nations Department on Economic and Social Affairs, 2021). Another research direction is looking at how immigrants in different countries coped with the effects of the pandemic in their professional and personal lives (e.g., loss of mobility for self and family, family separation, job loss, stress, burnout) and how this affects their careers going forward. Case studies might be particularly suited to this. A further avenue for research is comparing immigration policy changes in response to the pandemic across more countries and how this affected their economic recovery and ongoing immigration. Future researchers should also look at how the shortage of skilled healthcare workers contributed to healthcare outcomes in the three countries. As the global economy emerges from the effects of the pandemic, and as countries step up their efforts to attract and retain skilled immigrants, it is important for policymakers and managers alike to understand the pandemic's continuing effects on the workforce and move proactively to better attract and retain talent that is needed to ensure continued global competitiveness.

References

Australian Bureau of Statistics. (2021). *Overseas migration*. ABS. https://www.abs.gov.au/statistics/people/population/overseas-migration/latest-release.

Australian Bureau of Statistics. (2022). Overseas Migration. Retrieved March 2, 2023, from https://www.abs.gov.au/statistics/people/population/overseas-migration/latest-release#:~:text=Net%20overseas%20migration,-Net%20overseas%20migration&text=In%20the%20year%20ending%2030,of%20171%2C000%20to%20Australia's%20population.

Barnard, H., Deeds, D., Mudambi, R., & Vaaler, P. M. (2019, November 8). Migrants, migration policies, and international business research: Current trends and new directions *Journal of International Business Policy, 2*(4), 275–288. https://link.springer.com/article/10.1057/s42214-019-00045-6.

Batalova, J., Fix, M., & Fernández-Peña, J. (2021, April). *The integration of immigrant health professionals*. Migration Policy Institute. Retrieved November 5, 2022, from https://www.migrationpolicy.org/sites/default/files/publications/mpi-immigrant-health-workers-beyond-pandemic_final.pdf

Beechler, S., & Woodward, I. (2009). The global "war for talent". *Journal of International Management, 15*, 273–285.

Berg, S. (2021). Half of health workers report burnout amid COVID-19. *AMA*. Retrieved March 1, 2023, from https://www.ama-assn.org/practice-management/physician-health/half-health-workers-report-burnout-amid-covid-19

Blanding, M. (2018, June 25). In America, immigrants really do get the job done. HBS Working Knowledge. Retrieved March 1, 2023, from https://hbswk.hbs.edu/item/in-america-immigrants-really-do-get-the-job-done

Cabarkapa, S., King, J., & Ng, C. H. (2020). The psychiatric impact of COVID-19 on healthcare workers. *Australian Journal of General Practice, 49*(12), 791. https://doi.org/10.31128/AJGP-07-20-5531

Chambers, E. G., Foulon, M., Hanfield-Jones, H., Hankin, S. M., & Michaels, E. G. (1998). The war for talent. *McKinsey Quarterly, 3*(3), 44–57.

Chand, M. (2014). Diaspora identity, acculturation policy and FDI: The Indian diaspora in Canada and the United States. *Asian Business and Management, 13*(4), 283–308.

Chand, M., & Tung, R. L. (2019). Skilled immigration to fill talent gaps: A comparison of the immigration policies of the United States, Canada, and Australia. *Journal of International Business Policy, 2*(4), 333–355. https://doi.org/10.1057/s42214-019-00039-4

CIC News. (2022, March 21). *How businesses can support newcomers to Canada.* Retrieved November 14, 2022, from https://www.cicnews.com/2021/06/why-canada-is-prioritizing-immigration-during-the-pandemic-0618502.html.

Conference Board of Canada. (2010). https://www.conferenceboard.ca/press/newsrelease/10-10-15/Immigrants_Make_Significant_Contributions_To_Innovation.aspx.

Daniel, D. (2022, April 26). *Overseas nurse recruitment drive needed to 'plug gaps' in aged care.* The Age. Retrieved November 12, 2022, from https://www.theage.com.au/politics/federal/overseas-nurse-recruitment-drive-needed-to-plug-gaps-in-aged-care-20220426-p5ag64.html.

Esterline, C., & Batalova, J. (2022, August 29). *Frequently requested statistics on immigrants and immigration in the United States.* migrationpolicy.org. Retrieved November 10, 2022, from https://www.migrationpolicy.org/article/frequently-requested-statistics-immigrants-and-immigration-united-states#:~:text=How%20many%20U.S.%20residents%20are,of%20approximately%20950%2C000%20from%202020.

Fasani, F., & Mazza, J. (2020). Immigrant key workers: Their contribution to Europe's COVID-19 response. SSRN Electronic Journal. https://doi.org/https://doi.org/10.2139/ssrn.3584941

Fitzsimmons, S., Minbaeva, D., Phene, A., & Narula, R. (2021). Global mobility of people: Challenges and opportunities for international business. *Special Issue of Journal of International Business Studies.* http://resource-cms.springernature.com/springer-cms/rest/v1/content/18478310/data/v1

Frey, W. H. (2022, April 14). New census data shows a huge spike in movement out of big metro areas during the pandemic. Brookings. Retrieved November 12, 2022, from https://www.brookings.edu/blog/the-avenue/2022/04/14/new-census-data-shows-a-huge-spike-in-movement-out-of-big-metro-areas-during-the-pandemic/

Gelatt, J. 2020. *Immigrant Workers: Vital to the U.S. COVID-19 Response, Disproportionately Vulnerable.* Migration Policy Institute Retrieved November 12, 2022 from https://www.migrationpolicy.org/research/immigrant-workers-us-covid-19-response#:~:text=March%202020-,Immigrant%20Workers%3A%20Vital%20to%20the,COVID%2D19%20Response%2C%20Disproportionately%20Vulnerable&text=Six%20million%20immigrant%20workers%20are,during%20the%20COVID%2D19%20pandemic.

Gelatt, J., & Chishti, M. (2022). *COVID-19's effects on U.S. immigration and immigrant communities, two years on.* Migration Policy Institute. Retrieved November 12, 2022, from https://www.migrationpolicy.org/sites/default/files/publications/mpi-covid-us-immigration-lookback_final.pdf.

Gordon, J. (2022, November 3). *Canada to start targeting draws for skilled immigrants next year.* Reuters. Retrieved November 15, 2022, from https://www.reuters.com/world/americas/canada-start-targeting-draws-skilled-immigrants-next-year-2022-11-03/

Government of Canada. (2022, June 7). *Immigration matters in healthcare.* Canada.ca. Retrieved November 15, 2022, from https://www.canada.ca/en/immigration-refugees-citizenship/campaigns/immigration-matters/growing-canada-future/health.html.

Government of Canada. (2023). *Canada welcomes historic number of newcomers in 2022.* Retrieved March 2, 2023, from https://www.canada.ca/en/immigration-refugees-citizenship/news/2022/12/canada-welcomes-historic-number-of-newcomers-in-2022.html.

Griffith, A. (2022, April 26). *How the government used the pandemic to sharply increase immigration.* Policy Options Retrieved November 7, 2022, from https://policyoptions.irpp.org/magazines/april-2022/immigration-increase-pandemic/

Hajro, A., Caprar, D. V., Zikic, J., & Stahl, G. K. (2021). Global migrants: Understanding the implications for international business and management. *Journal of World Business, 56*(2), 101192. https://doi.org/10.1016/j.jwb.2021.101192

International Migration Outlook. (2021). OECD library. Key facts and figures (infographic) | International Migration Outlook 2021 | OECD iLibrary (oecd-ilibrary.org)

International Organization for Migration (IOM). (2022, February 28). Global mobility restriction overview. COVID-19 Travel Restrictions Output — 28 February 2022 | Flow Monitoring (iom.int)

Jacks, T., Hall, B., & Dansie, M. (2022, May 6). *The global race to lure healthcare workers down under.* The Sydney Morning Herald. Retrieved November 13, 2022, from https://www.smh.com.au/healthcare/the-global-race-to-lure-healthcare-workers-down-under-20220505-p5aiza.html

Jose, R., & Jackson, L. (2022, September 2). *Australia raises migration target amid labour squeeze, global talent race.* Reuters. Retrieved November 12, 2022 from Australia raises migration target amid labour squeeze, global talent race | Reuters.

Krogstad, J. M., & Gonzalez-Barrera, A. (2022, January 11). *Key facts about U.S. immigration policies and Biden's proposed changes.* Pew Research Center. Retrieved

November 1, 2022, from https://www.pewresearch.org/fact-tank/2022/01/11/key-facts-about-u-s-immigration-policies-and-bidens-proposed-changes/

Liebert, S. (2021). U.S. immigrant integration policy in light of the covid -19 pandemic. *Public Administration Review, 81*(6), 1197–1203. https://doi.org/10.1111/puar.13331

Martin, S. (2022, July 23). International doctors unable to work in Australia due to 'broken system', experts say. The Guardian. Retrieved November 12, 2022, from https://www.theguardian.com/australia-news/2022/jul/24/international-doctors-unable-to-work-in-australia-due-to-broken-system-experts-say

Mathema, S. (2019, July 29). *Immigrant doctors can help lower physician shortages in rural America.* Center for American Progress. Retrieved November 13, 2022, from https://www.americanprogress.org/article/immigrant-doctors-can-help-lower-physician-shortages-rural-america/#:~:text=Jul%2029%2C%202019-,Immigrant%20Doctors%20Can%20Help%20Lower%20Physician%20Shortages%20in%20Rural%20America,and%20improving%20health%20care%20access.

Menon, P., & Holmes, S. (2022, August 31). *Australia needs workers but a million are stuck at the Door.* Reuters. Retrieved November 11, 2022, from https://www.reuters.com/business/australia-needs-workers-million-are-stuck-door-2022-08-31/

Mercer, P. (2021, June 21). *Covid-19 slashes immigration into Australia.* VOA. Retrieved November 9, 2022, from https://www.voanews.com/a/covid-19-pandemic_covid-19-slashes-immigration-australia/6207270.html

Migration Data Portal. (2022, March 18). *Migration data relevant for the COVID-19 pandemic.* Migration Data Portal. Retrieved November 1, 2022, from https://www.migrationdataportal.org/themes/migration-data-relevant-covid-19-pandemic

Mudambi, R. (2008). Location, control, and innovation in knowledge-intensive industries. *Journal of Economic Geography, 8*(5), 699–725.

Norlander, P., & Varma, A. (2019). H-1B and L-1 visa sponsored guest workers in the USA: An analysis of the strategic impact of Indian and other firms. *Thunderbird International Business Review, 65*(4), 565–579.

OECD. (2019, August 9). *Recent trends in international mobility of doctors and nurses.* OECD iLibrary. Retrieved November 15, 2022, from https://www.oecd-ilibrary.org/social-issues-migration-health/recent-trends-in-international-migration-of-doctors-nurses-and-medical-students_5ee49d97-en

OECD. (2020). *Contribution of migrant doctors and nurses to tackling COVID-19 crisis in OECD countries. OECD Policy Responses to Coronavirus (COVID-19).* OCED. https://doi.org/10.1787/2f7bace2-en

Osman, L. (2022, February 15). *Canada sets ambitious immigration targets for post-pandemic recovery.* The Globe and Mail. Retrieved November 11, 2022, from https://www.theglobeandmail.com/canada/article-canada-sets-ambitious-immigration-targets-for-post-pandemic-recovery-2/

Passel, J. S., & Cohn, D. V. (2022, April 4). *Legal immigration to the U.S. partially rebounds as national and global borders reopen.* Pew Research Center. Retrieved

November 5, 2022, from https://www.pewresearch.org/fact-tank/2022/04/04/legal-immigration-to-the-u-s-partially-rebounds-as-national-and-global-borders-reopen/#:~:text=During%20the%202020%20pandemic%20low,141%2C000%20for%20fiscal%202016%20onward.

Robeznieks, A. (2022, October 11). *Easing IMGs path to practice: What congress should do*. American Medical Association. Retrieved November 11, 2022, from https://www.ama-assn.org/education/international-medical-education/easing-imgs-path-practice-what-congress-should-do

Ryan, M. (2022, October 17). 'Fortress Australia' seeks to become immigration nation again. Nikkei Asia. Retrieved November 12, 2022, from https://asia.nikkei.com/Spotlight/Asia-Insight/Fortress-Australia-seeks-to-become-immigration-nation-again

Scheve, K., & Slaughter, M. (2018). How to save globalization. *Foreign Affairs, 97*(6), 98–108.

The Global Talent Competitiveness Index. (2022). INSEAD. Retrieved November 12, 2022, from https://www.insead.edu/sites/default/files/assets/dept/fr/gtci/GTCI-2022-report.pdf

The Treasury and Department of Home Affairs. (2018). *Shaping a nation - cdn.tspace.gov.au*. Shaping A Nation Population growth and immigration over time. https://cdn.tspace.gov.au/uploads/sites/107/2018/04/Shaping-a-Nation-2018.docx

Thevenot, S. (2022, June 6). *Canada to support internationally educated health professionals*. Retrieved November 10, 2022, from https://www.cicnews.com/2022/06/canada-to-support-internationally-educated-health-professionals-0626062.html

Turnbull, T. (2022, September 2). *Australia: Permanent migration Cap raised for first time in decade*. Retrieved November 11, 2022, from https://www.bbc.com/news/world-australia-62762158

United Nations Department on Economic and Social Affairs. (2021). *Growth of international migration slowed by 27%, or 2 million migrants, due to covid-19, says UN*. Growth of international migration slowed by 27%, or 2 million migrants, due to COVID-19. Retrieved November 5, 2022, from https://www.un.org/en/desa/growth-international-migration-slowed-27-or-2-million-migrants-due-covid-19-says-un#:~:text=Growth%20of%20international%20migration%20slowed,19%2C%20says%20UN%20%7C%20United%20Nations.

Van Dam, A. (2018, June 20). Analysis | how the U.S. cornered the market for skilled immigrants. The Washington Post. Retrieved November 11, 2022, from https://www.washingtonpost.com/news/wonk/wp/2018/06/20/how-the-u-s-cornered-the-market-for-skilled-immigrants/%3futm_term%3d.ffd28b4dc217%26noredirect%3don

Waine, M. (2022, September 19). *Solutions to address Australia's healthcare skills shortage*. GHE Australia. Retrieved November 10, 2022, from https://globalhealtheducation.com/au/categories/nursing/solutions-for-healthcare-skills-shortage-australia

World Population Review. (2022). *Immigration by Country 2022*. Retrieved November 11, 2022, from https://worldpopulationreview.com/country-rankings/immigration-by-country

Wright, T. (2022). *'We are absolutely destroyed': Health workers facing burnout, even as COVID levels ease*. Global News. Retrieved March 2, 2023, from https://globalnews.ca/news/8889103/covid-burnout-destroyed-health-workers/

4

Social Contagion and Migration: Sources and Implications of Migrant Ambivalence

Helena Barnard and Graham Nash

Introduction

Only a very small proportion of the world's people move away from the countries where they were born. Since 1950, the proportion has been between 2.7 and 3.3% of the global population (De Haas et al., 2019). An even smaller proportion is of interest to business, because although the word 'migrant' includes any individual who has crossed an international border, firms are mainly interested in skilled people who voluntarily and legally cross borders (rather than, e.g. refugees). Although it is clear why a persecuted person would want to leave for a safer location, skilled people also choose to leave their country of birth and home language, abandoning fairly secure employment options, family and friends to start again elsewhere. International business research has generally assumed that skilled migrants make a rational decision to migrate, and that managing them does not require the kind of care increasingly recognized as needed to manage refugees (e.g. Guo et al., 2020). We interrogate that assumption.

We situate our work against the backdrop of a continued global war for talent (Becker et al., 2020; Beechler & Woodward, 2009), but also the ongoing discrimination against foreign-born and educated employees (Esses, 2021; Oreopoulos, 2011). We suggest that social contagion processes can often

H. Barnard (✉) • G. Nash
University of Pretoria, Pretoria, South Africa
e-mail: barnardh@gibs.co.za

explain the decision to emigrate. Social contagion is a long-standing concept but has been little used in international business research, even though it was introduced to the field already in 1999 (Koka et al., 1999). The concept is increasingly used in management research generally (Anglin et al., 2018; Kensbock et al., 2022), and fear of migrants (in response to the European refugee crisis) has already been theorized through a social contagion lens (Guenichi et al., 2022). We make a contribution to international business research by showing that for potential migrants with the option of either leaving or staying, a contagion process seems to be at work. This has important implications for their needs and expectations in the new workplace.

Recognizing that most skilled migration originates in middle-income countries (Lucas, 2005), we suggest that the "middleness" of home countries affects the migration decision. Such middleness manifests in aspects like regulatory institutions that are present but not transparent, an education system with some but insufficient quality institutions, some but not complete political and economic freedoms, and other institutional imperfections (Marquis & Raynard, 2015). The fact that home country conditions provide neither a clear reason to remain nor a clear reason to leave combine with the challenges integral to migration (Bauloz et al., 2019) to make the decision about whether or not to emigrate non-obvious.

Our study is set in South Africa, a middle-income country with substantial inequality, a relatively small group of (typically well-paid) skilled people and a large group of people who suffer from hunger with the resultant social instability (Van der Berg et al., 2022). This duality provides clear motives for both staying and leaving. A model building approach was adopted to simulate the dynamics between social contagion and the determinants that drive migration. The nature of the determinants of migration was established by using a questionnaire about why people had left South Africa. Using this dataset in parallel to census data, parameters were developed for a model of social contagion in emigration.

Thus, we were able to identify the primary drivers of migration and their relative influence within the population. Drivers to emigrate include considerations that express pessimism about the country like concerns about crime and politics, but people also migrate because of "pull" factors, positive considerations like the search for further education, travel or job opportunities. These drivers were then used as inputs into a range of simulations, considering both general and isolated events. The simulations revealed that events related to the primary drivers of migration increase the likelihood of migration. However, those effect are fleeting and increased rates will subside in time. Positive messages also disseminate via social contagion and are found capable of negating the influence of the determinants of migration. Thus, our evidence suggests that potential migrants in middle-income countries are highly sensitive to changes in the socio-economic conditions of their home country.

Migrants are potentially a valuable resource for firms, especially multinational enterprises (MNEs). They are rarely "knowledge stars" (Hamilton & Davison, 2018) who can command premium salaries, but they are skilled. They do not receive the extensive financial and social support that expatriates do (Wang et al., 2022) but they bring with them valuable home country knowledge (Kunczer et al., 2019). Yet, there may be unexpected challenges in managing them. Although the literature on acculturation (Berry, 2001) suggests that commitment to and engagement with the new country is important, when the migration decision resulted from social contagion processes, this implies that migrants were not certain that they wanted to emigrate—and may not be certain whether they want to stay. Understanding how this ambivalence plays out in the workplace has important implications for business and requires future work.

Literature Review

Social Contagion in Social Science Research

Contagion processes occur as much in the social as in biological sphere (Dodds & Watts, 2005); in other words, behavior and/or emotion can traverse populations just as diseases are able to propagate. A characteristics of social contagion is that outcomes do not result from rational, evaluative choices, but instead that we are "infected" with positive or negative attitudes and behaviors like aggression, savings behavior and other outcomes in the same way as we are infected by biological contagions (Marsden, 1998). Simply put, social contagion occurs when behavior inside a network is imitated and thus spreads from one person to another.

After initial application to general individual states like emotions (Kimura et al., 2008) and obesity (Cohen-Cole & Fletcher, 2008), such network effects have also been documented in management research. Evidence of contagion has been found both when the impact is positive like that of optimism on new ventures (Anglin et al., 2018) or learning within networks (Peters et al., 2017), as well as for negative outcomes like performance-reducing "dark-side" relationship effects (Zhang et al., 2021) or the "epidemic" of mental disorders in business (Kensbock et al., 2022).

Contagion models have had very little application in international business research. The close conceptual links between social contagion and social networks have been recognized in studies on various dimensions of learning (Huang et al., 2011; Pérez-Nordtvedt et al., 2010), and the adoption of voluntary cross-national policies has also been ascribed to social contagion processes (Olabisi, 2019). In the context of migration, social contagion has also been used to explain the diffusion of policy related to migration (Brücker & Schröder, 2011). All of those applications deal with contagion at an institutional level, with the spread of the fear of migrants (in response to the European refugee crisis) as one of the few studies dealing with the topic at the level of the individual (Guenichi et al., 2022).

We argue that social contagion can also explain the very decision to emigrate. The non-rational nature of social contagion is arguably particularly useful to explain migration, because it is long known that migration itself is not an entirely rational decision: "it is not so much the actual factors at origin and destination as the perception of these factors that result in migration" (Lee, 1966: 51). In this regard, the conditions in middle-income countries are especially relevant.

The Challenges and Opportunities of Migration from Middle-Income Countries

Most skilled migrants come from middle-income countries (Lucas, 2005): Conditions in high-income countries are typically munificent enough for few people to consider emigration, whereas few people from low-income countries have the skills that allow them to legally emigrate. Marquis and Raynard (2015) differentiate between emerging (typically middle income) and developing (low income) markets, and show numerous dimensions according to which the institutions of middle-income countries are present, but imperfectly so. Whether in terms of infrastructure, capital markets, human development, political freedoms or others, people living in middle-income countries enjoy some benefits of institutions, although inconsistently.

Moreover, the position of middle-income countries in the middle of the global economic hierarchy does not mean that they are "average" across dimensions, but instead reflects the variability found inside them (Müller et al., 2018). This means that an important driver of migration, perceptions (Lee, 1966), is especially consequential. Looking at residents' associations in India, the widely varying standards of living of residents are clear, ranging from people who struggle to access basic services to those with skills who, reflecting the scarcity of skills in middle-income countries, experience a substantially higher quality of living conditions (Kamath & Vijayabaskar, 2009). Potential migrants from middle-income countries tend to be people with skills, and they must, therefore, decide how best to use their skills: Do they wish to continue living and working in a (familiar) country in which they have access to a level of institutional development, albeit uneven and unpredictable, or should they migrate in search of a better future?

This decision plays out against the backdrop of a persistent global labor shortage, both for employees who are highly skilled and for people with more general skills (Hajro et al., 2022). Given the global shortage of labor, it makes sense that firms would be keen to gain access to a global pool of labor. However, it is also known that migrants—called "self-initiated expatriates" if the move is not intended as permanent (Doherty, 2013)—can expect extensive employer discrimination for the fact that they are foreign-born and/or that their experience has been gained elsewhere (Esses, 2021; Oreopoulos, 2011).

This discrimination compares starkly with the experiences of traditional expatriates who typically receive support for themselves and their families (Cooke et al., 2019; Fan et al., 2022; Mendenhall et al., 1987). The study of expatriation started when senior executives were increasingly placed abroad, and indeed, the careers of senior executives remain the emphasis of that body of scholarship (Sanders & De Cieri, 2021). Much as it was strategically important to support them, the fact that living and working across borders is not easy is evidenced by the fact that expatriates require (and indeed are motivated by) costly financial and developmental support, and leave expatriate assignments if they do not receive such support (Maley et al., 2020; Suutari et al., 2018; Wang et al., 2022). Migrants are unlikely to receive such support and more likely to face discrimination. Moreover, their home country conditions are typically sub-optimal but seldom unbearable. In short, it is far from clear that a skilled person from a middle-income country will indeed benefit from migration.

A Model of Social Contagion

The Dodds and Watts (2005) generalized model of social contagion consists of a population of N individuals, each of which is assumed to occupy one of three states: Susceptible (S), Infected (I), or Recovered (R). As the names suggest, individuals falling into the 'susceptible' classification are vulnerable to being infected after exposure to an 'infected' individual, with vulnerability to the common cold being a useful analogy. Individuals who are 'removed' are analogous to people who had recovered from measles; they are no longer vulnerable to infection. Individuals maintain a memory of doses received from their last T contacts and the sum of individual i's last T doses (i's dose count) is denoted at the tth step by:

$$D_{t,i} = \sum_{t'=t-T+1}^{t} d_{t',i} \qquad (4.1)$$

In the event that a susceptible individual's dose count exceeds a specified threshold d^*, the individual will move into an infected state. Infected individuals whose dose count drops below the threshold may recover with probability r at each time step. Once in the recovered state, individuals may become susceptible again with probability ρ. The dynamics described are illustrated in Fig. 4.1.

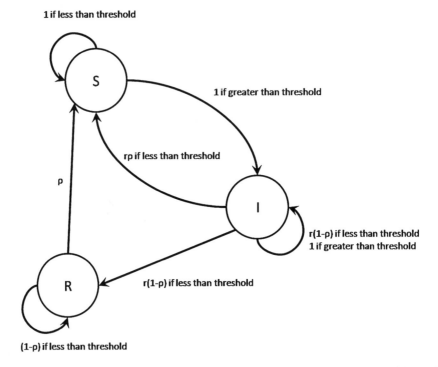

Fig. 4.1 Generalized model—State transition probabilities. Source: Dodds and Watts (2005)

This model can be developed further as per the rumor transmission model presented by Kawachi (2008). In this model, the states occupied are that of Susceptible (X), Spreader (Y) or Stifler (Z). A 'susceptible' individual is one who is not aware of the rumor while a 'spreader' knows about the rumor and spreads it actively. Lastly, 'stiflers' know about the rumor but do not spread it.

In the Dodds and Watts (2005) model, at each (discrete) time step t, each individual i comes into contact with another individual chosen uniformly at random from the population. The probability that individual i comes into contact with an infected individual is the current fraction of individuals infected in the population at time t, denoted Φ_t. If the contact is infected, an event occurring with probability p results in i receiving a 'dose' d drawn from a fixed-size distribution f, otherwise i receives a dose of zero.

Within the generalized model, the probability that a susceptible individual who comes into contact with K infected individuals in T time steps will become infected is the infection probability, denoted by P_{inf}. The quantity P_k is the expected fraction of a population that will be infected by k exposures (Dodds & Watts, 2005).

$$P_{inf}(K) = \sum_{k=1}^{K} \binom{K}{k} p^k (1-p)^{K-k} P_k \qquad (4.2)$$

where $K = 1, \ldots, T$ and

$$P_k = \int_0^\infty d\,d^* g(d^*) \int_0^\infty d\,d^* f^{k*}(d) \qquad (4.3)$$

The infection probability $P_{inf}(K)$ provides the 'dose-response' curve averaged over all members of the population and dose sizes distribution, where we note that K contacts with infected individuals will result in k actual exposures with probability $\binom{K}{k} p^k (1?p)^{K?k} P_k$ (Dodds & Watts, 2005).

Research Design

Migration in the South African Setting

Our study is set in South Africa, a middle-income country with substantial inequality. This inequality affects the labor market with "the paradox of a typical emerging market mismatch of demand and supply with a shortage of higher-level skills and a surplus of lower-level skills" (Wöcke & Barnard, 2021: 256). It means that skilled South Africans are in demand and able to command high salaries, but it also introduces substantial societal instability that has and continues to affect numerous dimensions of the South African economy (Luiz & Barnard, 2022).

Emigration from South African has tended to occur in "waves" (Louw & Mersham, 2001; Rule, 1994), providing prima facie evidence of a contagion process. Moreover, waves of migration have coincided with particularly disruptive periods in the history of the country, for example, starting with the election of the National Party on its Apartheid mandate in 1948. The fact that social negatives play an important role in triggering migration is also consistent with a contagion-type explanation.

Motives for Migration

To develop parameters for the model, we decided to use the structure of the population (derived from Census SA data) and to superimpose on that structure the motives people have for emigrating. The Census data provided evidence of the composition of the South African population in terms of race, gender, age and education level. We did not consider the full (and quite young) South African population, but only people who could make an independent decision to emigrate, 20 years and older.

To develop an understanding of why South Africans leave, we relied on a survey that was sent out by an organization concerned with gaining value from the South African diaspora, "Homecoming Revolution", and supported by the Development Bank of South Africa. Respondents were asked to select from the following list of motives, the primary reason why they left South Africa: global job opportunities, politics, crime, travel, exile, education, money, family and affirmative action. The survey was not representative; no reliable evidence exists of the size or composition of the number of South Africans living abroad (Barnard & Pendock, 2013). However, a large number of responses (6939) was received. Of those, 4399 responses were complete in terms of race, gender, age and education level, and thus usable.

Using the Apartheid-era racial designations, the bulk (87.5%) of respondents were white, reflecting the historical distribution of skills and thus ability to migrate. Black South Africans represented 4% of the respondents, Indian/Asian South Africans 3% and "Coloureds" (i.e. mixed-race South Africans) 5%. The level of skills of migrants was also high: 84.4% of respondents had completed tertiary education, with 15% of respondents having a masters or doctoral degree. Although some responses had been received from people who were younger than 20 years of age (often living with migrant parents), those responses were not considered, and the mean age at departure was 31 years old. The gender split was 48.5% female and 51.5% male.

This information allowed us to identify the relative weighting of the motives for each group. For ease of reference, Table 4.1 provides the single-most important motive for migration for each demographic grouping. The pattern observed suggests that younger white people go abroad in search of experiences: travel and work experience. Once they get to child-rearing age, concerns about crime is the dominant motive. For older people, family reunification is key. White women become preoccupied with both crime and with family reunification at a younger age than white men. Whereas crime is the primary reason why white South Africans emigrate, work opportunities abroad is the dominant reason for the migration decision of South Africans of color. The search for education also emerges as a far more important motive for South Africans of color than for white South Africans.

Social Contagion Simulation Model

Understanding the composition of the South African population as well as motives for migration for the different racial groups allowed us to develop the Social Contagion Simulation Model (SCSM). Using the widely used mathematical programming language, MATLAB, we adopted a phased approach in developing the model. To begin with, the generalized model was developed first and then evolved to incorporate elements of the rumor transition model.

The inputs to SCSM are comprised of a given population and an initial epidemic distribution, which are incorporated to establish an initial condition. As in the generalized model, SCSM considers a population of N individuals but differs in that it assumes that each individual may occupy one of four states as we incorporate the 'stifler' state of the rumor transition model. Unlike the rumor transition model, however, the recovered state of the generalized model is retained, hence the states considered are Spreader, Stifler, Susceptible and Recovered.

Within the context of migration, a spreader will expose a rumor encouraging emigration, either through general discussion regarding the determinants of migration or based on a particular determinant in alignment with the model's parameters, for example, an experience of 'crime'. The concept of the 'stifler' status is developed to be that of an individual who exposes individuals to

Table 4.1 Primary motive per demographic group

Race	Education	Gender	20–24 year	25–29 year	30–34 year	35–39 year	40–44 year	45–49 year	50–54 year	55–59 year	60–64 year	65–69 year	70–74 year	75+
White	High school	Male	Travel	Money	Crime	Crime	Crime*	Crime*	Crime*	Crime*	Crime*	Crime*		
		Female	Travel	Crime	Crime	Crime	Crime	Crime	Crime	Crime* Family*	Crime* Family*	Crime* Family*	Family*	
	Tertiary	Male	Jobs globally	Jobs globally	Jobs globally Crime	Crime	Crime	Crime	Crime	Crime*	Crime*	Family*	Education	Crime*
		Female	Travel Politics*	Travel	Crime	Crime	Crime	Crime Family	Crime	Crime*	Crime*	Politics*	Family*	
African/ black	High school	Male	Jobs globally*	Jobs globally*	Jobs globally*									
		Female	Education			Education								
	Tertiary	Male	Jobs globally*	Jobs globally	Jobs globally	Jobs globally* Education*	Jobs globally*	Money	Jobs globally*					
Colored	High school	Male	Jobs globally* Politics*	Jobs globally*	Jobs globally* Crime*	Jobs globally*	Jobs globally* Crime*	Family*						
		Female	Jobs globally*	Jobs globally* Travel*	Jobs globally*	Jobs globally*	Education*							
	Tertiary	Male	Jobs globally*	Travel*	Travel*	Jobs globally*	Crime*	Jobs globally*	Jobs globally*	Travel*				
		Female	Travel*	Travel*	Jobs globally*	Jobs globally*								
Indian/ Asian	High school	Male	Travel*	Jobs globally*	Jobs globally* Education	Jobs globally*	Politics*							
		Female	Jobs globally*	Jobs globally* Crime*	Education*	Jobs globally*								
	Tertiary	Male	Education*	Jobs globally	Jobs globally*	Jobs globally*	Jobs globally* Crime*	Jobs globally* Politics*	Jobs globally* Money*	Jobs globally Family*				
		Female	Jobs globally*	Jobs globally*	Jobs globally*	Jobs globally*								

* Indicates fewer than 30 observations

4 Social Contagion and Migration: Sources and Implications...

a rumor discouraging emigration through general discussion. Susceptible individuals may interact and be influenced by both spreaders and stiflers, while recovered individuals do not. Recovered individuals do, however, become susceptible over a period of time. Based on the demographic group to which an individual belongs, an individual may have an affinity to particularly themed rumors, for example, black South Africans may be particularly open to registering prospects for job opportunities or further education abroad. Individuals maintain a memory of both spreader and stifler doses received from their last T contacts and the sum of individual i's last T doses (i's dose count) is denoted at the tth step by:

$$D_{t,i} = \sum_{t'=t-T+1}^{t} b_{t,i} \times d_{t',i} \quad (4.4)$$

where,

$$b_{t,i} = \frac{1}{1+\alpha \times \log^{\beta}(1+t)}$$

Memory is managed slightly differently to that of the generalized model as an individual's memory fades with time, as opposed to remaining constant. When an individual receives a 'dose' (an event that causes a memory), there is a peak. Over time, there is a gradual decline.

In the event that a susceptible individual's dose count either exceeds a positive threshold $+d^*$ or drops below a negative threshold $-d^*$, the individual will move into the infected state of the spreader or stifler, respectively. Infected individuals whose dose count drops below the positive threshold $+d^*$ or rises above the negative threshold $-d^*$ may recover with probability r at each time step. Once in the recovered state, individuals may become susceptible again with probability ρ. Hence the simulation parameters of the generalized model are retained. However, it should be noted that the intensity of the dose is governed not only by dose size but in addition the individual's affinity toward determinant of migration as facilitated by the memory structure. Figure 4.2 illustrates the integrated dynamics of the SCSM.

At each (discrete) time step t, each individual i come into contact with another individual chosen uniformly at random from the population. This event occurs with probability Φ_{1t} and Φ_{2t}, the fraction of spreader and stifler individuals, respectively. Subsequently, with probability p_1 and p_2, the

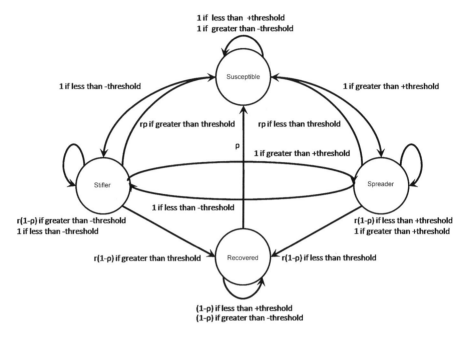

Fig. 4.2 SCSM state transition probabilities

susceptible individual will receive a dose d_+ or d_-, drawn from a distribution after exposure to a spreader or stifler.

In the SCSM, should p not be successful, the individual i may receive an 'anti-dose' depending on probability γ. Hence individual i may oppose a rumor and be influenced in the other direction, otherwise receiving a dose of zero. It should be noted that we now facilitate that a susceptible individual may oppose a spreader's rumor and receive a stifler dose, and vice versa. This interaction can be eliminated by setting the gamma to zero.

Results

In the next section, we discuss the results of the simulation. We first provide the baseline scenario, then the model in the case of both generalized and thematic crises, and then the case of successes.

Baseline Scenario

To ensure the integrity of the SCSM model, the model was first run with the simplest case of Dodds and Watts' (2005) generalized model of social and biological contagion. The model illustrated the presence of epidemic threshold dynamics where initial outbreaks either die out or else infect a finite fraction of the population, depending on whether or not p (the probability of exposure given contact with an infective) exceeds a specific critical value p_c.

The long history of migration from South Africa informed the values assigned in the model. The initial condition of each simulation was that the entire population was infected. The probability of exposure given contact with an infective, p, was set at 0.6. The value of r (the probability of moving from an infected to recovered state) was set at 0.5 and at 0.7 for ρ (the probability of moving from an immune to a susceptible state).

To develop the baseline model, ten iterations of the simulations were run with a population of 1000 individuals over 1600 time steps (days). A normal distribution with a mean of 4 and standard deviation of 0.25 was used to assign doses, whereas a normal distribution with a mean of 1.5 and standard deviation of 0.1 was used to assign thresholds. Thresholds were allocated to individuals at the onset of the simulation and remained unchanged for the duration of the simulation, while dose sizes varied. Thus, individuals were generally allocated thresholds of between 1.4 and 1.6 and received doses of 3.75–4.25. However, extremes were possible; an individual with a threshold of only 1.2 could receive a dose of 4.7. With no further exposure, based on the forgetting curve, the individual will only have the opportunity to recover after two days.

In addition to a general rumor advocating migration, themed rumors were also able to occur. Four such themed rumors were used, crime, foreign job opportunities, travel and 'money', earning in a hard currency. Both the rumors selected and the affinities toward determinants of migration were chosen in alignment with the findings from the Homecoming Revolution survey. The following heuristics are assumed with respect to themed rumors:

* Because individuals differ in terms of the key drivers of migration (e.g. crime versus foreign job opportunities), they will respond differently and in accordance with that affinity. Should an individual be exposed to a general rumor, it is assumed that the individual will be inclined to perpetuate the rumor in terms of their own natural affinity toward a determinant of migration. Thus, it is assumed that while general discussion may fuel an individual's decision to migrate, they will in general perpetuate the rumor in terms of the determinant toward which they are most sensitive.
* An individual will perpetuate rumors in terms of the determinant of migration to which they are inclined with a probability of 0.5 versus an alternate determinant to which they are exposed. Thus, should an individual who is naturally inclined to discuss crime as a reason for leaving be successfully

exposed to a rumor regarding foreign job opportunities, they may in future discuss that rumor with probability 0.5.

The baseline model behaved predictably and across ten iterations, stabilized after approximately 550 days. The initial epidemic in which the entire population was infected reached a state of equilibrium over time where 24% of the population was actively advocating for migration (spreader), 72% of the population might have considered it but were not actively engaged in thinking about (susceptible) it, while 4% of the population did not take note of the discussions about migration (recovered).

Generalized Crises

In order to determine how the dynamics of the baseline model react to a general crisis where a significant percentage of the population was exposed to a particular determinant of migration, the following scenario was constructed. A general crisis was introduced to the baseline model over 10 days (days 833 to 843). The crisis resulted in each individual being exposed to a determinant of migration, receiving a dose with a probability of 0.5. The scenario was run for ten iterations for each determinant of migration, respectively. A single iteration of a general crisis occurring because of crime is illustrated in Fig. 4.3.

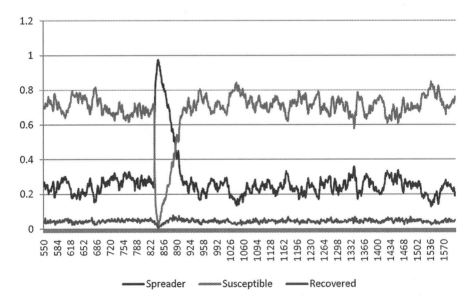

Fig. 4.3 General crisis: Crime

The sudden peak in the percentage of the population represented by the spreader state disrupted the state of equilibrium between time steps 833 and 843. The percentage of individuals within the recovered state remained at the level of the baseline model, but the percentage of spreaders increased by approximately 3%, subsequently reducing the percentage of susceptible individuals by the same value.

Four determinants of a general crisis were used: crime, global job opportunities, money and travel. The results held irrespective of the determinant causing the general crisis. For each case of general crisis, the equilibrium to which the model returned reflected a slightly higher proportion of spreaders and equally reduced susceptible individuals than that of the baseline model. With the increase in the number of infected individuals, the average number of successful exposures per day for the general determinant was higher than that of the baseline model.

Isolated Crises

The dynamics of the baseline model were also tested against isolated individual crises, where individuals were randomly exposed to a particular determinant of migration, introduced to the baseline model from day 833. The crisis resulted in an individual being exposed to a determinant of migration with probability 0.33 and probability 0.03 of actually receiving a dose. Each scenario was run for ten iterations for each determinant of migration, respectively. A single iteration of a general crisis occurring as a result of global job opportunities is illustrated in Fig. 4.4.

Once individuals started becoming exposed to random isolated crises (day 833); the gap between the percentage of spreader and susceptible individuals reduced. The percentage infected individuals increased, with the percentage of susceptible individuals decreasing. This trend persisted for the remainder of the simulation so that the percentage of spreaders in the population increased by approximately 7%. Again, four determinants of migration (crime, global job opportunities, money and travel) were used, and again the increase occurred irrespective of the determinant from which the isolated crises occurred.

Combined General and Isolated Crises

In reality, both general and isolated crises occur, thus a scenario was constructed incorporating both. A general crisis of crime coupled with isolated

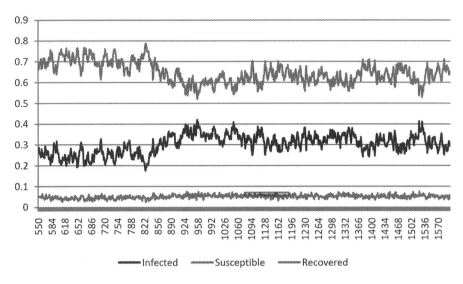

Fig. 4.4 Isolated crisis—Global job opportunities

cases of global job opportunities were introduced to the baseline model in the same manner that they were in previous scenarios. The scenario was run for ten iterations. As the system began to recover from the general crises, it reverted to a new equilibrium comprised of a substantially greater percentage of the population represented by the spreader state. Rather than 24% of the population being active spreaders as in the baseline model, the proportion increased to 34%, suggesting that general and isolated crises jointly contribute to a combined scenario. This is visually demonstrated in Fig. 4.5.

Stifling Messages about Migration

Given evidence that positives can also spread through processes of social contagion (Anglin et al., 2018; Peters et al., 2017), the effect of forces discouraging migration were analyzed by introducing a stifler state to the combined general and isolate crises scenario. The scenario was once again run for ten iterations with a general crisis pertaining to crime and isolated instances of global job opportunities affecting individuals within the population.

The stifler state was perpetuated using two mechanisms. Firstly, the parameter value γ was set to 0.05, thereby enabling individuals to disagree with an individual with whom they interact. Hence, a susceptible individual may

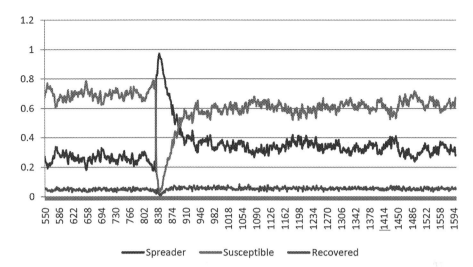

Fig. 4.5 General combined with isolated crises

interact with a spreader, receive a stifler dose, and vice versa. Secondly, individuals were deemed to have the same probability of being exposed to the stifler state as they were to isolated crises; thus, individuals were exposed with probability 0.33 and received a dose with probability 0.03. The threshold and doses with respect to the stifler state were of the same magnitude as the infected state, but with negative as opposed to positive values. Two versions of this scenario were analyzed.

First, the spreader's probability of infection p_1 was set as equal to that of the stifler's probability of infection p_2. Thus, it was assumed that an individual would be as likely to believe and spread rumors encouraging migration as they would be to those discouraging migration (Barsade, 2002). The stifler state was able to gain momentum over time despite the general and isolated crises unfolding. While the spreader state was not eliminated, it was drastically reduced. This scenario is shown in Fig. 4.6.

Second, it could be that the stifler's probability of infection p_2 is greater than that of the spreaders probability of infection p_1. We set it at $p_2 = p_1 + 0.05$. This case describes the situation where individuals are potentially more patriotic and are more likely to believe and spread messages discouraging rather than encouraging migration. Figure 4.7 shows the results of a simulation with such a strong stifler effect.

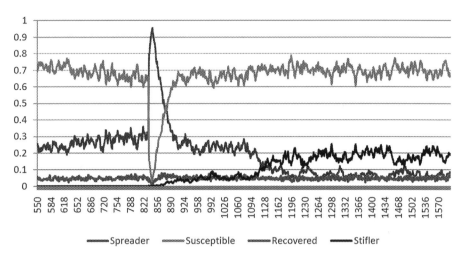

Fig. 4.6 Stifler and spreader with equivalent effects ($p_2 = p_1$)

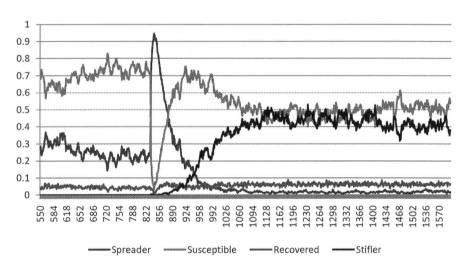

Fig. 4.7 Stifler effect greater than that of spreader ($p_2 > p_1$)

In both versions of the success versus crisis scenario, $p_2 = p_1$ and as expected as $p_2 > p_1$, the stifler discouraging migration more than counteracts the spreader state, and the number of successful exposures attributed to general discussion drops to below that of the baseline. Table 4.2 summarizes the results of the simulations.

Table 4.2 Summary of results

	Baseline	General crisis[a]	Isolated crises[a]	Combined general & isolated crises[b]	Stifling equal to promoting	Stifling greater than promoting
Infected	24.35%	27.17%	31.43%	34.10%	19.4%	12.5%
Susceptible	71.27%	68.50%	63.40%	60.80%	67.9%	55.8%
Recovered	4.38%	4.33%	5.17%	5.10%	4.6%	5.5%
Stifler	0%	0%	0%	0%	8%	26%

[a] The effect is shown for global job opportunities, but is very similar whether the driver relates to crime, travel or money
[b] Values reflect crime as general crisis and global job opportunities as isolated crises. Values for different permutations vary somewhat, but are within a similar range to that of this combination

Discussion

Our evidence suggests that the decision to emigrate could indeed be described in terms of contagion. There are sharp increases in people considering leaving South Africa when crises occur, with the rate slowing thereafter. 'Spreaders' of a message that migration is appropriate also increased and remain at high levels as the rate of especially specific events related to the primary drivers of migration increased in frequency and intensity. This included both push factors like crime and pull factors like opportunities for travel or global work opportunities. Although the latter would be a typical motive for a skilled person to migrate, it is also telling that even the lure of global work opportunities faded to the extent that positive discussion within the country became a greater feature of interactions. However, persistent isolated 'successes' were required to perpetuate and sustain discussion focusing on reasons not to leave the country, and subsequently lower levels of migration.

There are three main implications of our research. The first is theoretical: We show the benefit of applying social contagion as a theoretical base for understanding an important international business concept, migration. A core characteristic of both contagion and migration is that they do not reflect rational processes, but deal with complex layers of perceptions and beliefs. Research on management and business has a strong preference for theoretical models that offer rational explanations (Marsden, 1998), but as our work shows, some processes are not even boundedly rational (Simon, 2000), but non-rational. This is not a purely theoretical nuance, because of the profound practical implications of managing a process to which people may not even believe they are subjected. This is particularly the case when considering how to manage migrants in a workplace, leading to our second implication.

It has long been known that people who decide to emigrate have a largely perception-based and non-rational expectation that their new country will be 'better' than their country of birth (Lee, 1966). The ethnographic work of Jagtenberg among Afrikaans-speaking white South Africans in Australia captures some implications of these dynamics: Although Afrikaans migrants reported being forced to leave by negatives like job discrimination by the black-dominated government in South Africa, none of her respondents had actually experienced those negatives (Jagtenberg, 2017). And once in Australia, they reported disappointment at their lack of access to job opportunities (Jagtenberg, 2019). It is known that migrants face discrimination in the workplace (Esses, 2021), but South African migrants in Australia have long been acknowledged as particularly successful (Louw & Mersham, 2001). Jagtenberg (2019: 38) reports her findings:

> Australians are thought to specifically dislike Afrikaans immigrants due to their relatively high qualifications. Perceivably, this makes Australians feel threatened and insecure, scared that these foreigners will bypass them or take their jobs.

In a sense, it is immaterial whether these experiences are 'real' or perceived—unless migrants opt to become entrepreneurs, these disengaged and potentially divisive views need to be understood and managed in the workplace. Thus, such views represent a challenge to managers. Moreover, although migrants do not receive the support that expatriates do, they face similar adjustment challenges. This likely means that the challenge of creating functional workgroups will be discovered by (and become the responsibility of) the individual manager. How migrants experience the workplace or whether and why they see the workplace as place worth investing in are important areas for future research.

The final implication of our work is at the country level. We found the rumor transmission model useful to show how narratives that circulate in a country are amplified and eventually acted on. But these narratives have a basis in fact. Migrants do take on the tough task of resettling, at their own expense, away from family and friends, in a new country because they are dissatisfied with what is happening in the country of their birth. For countries struggling with waves of migration, the challenge is to change those narratives. This does not happen through a few isolated successes, but requires of leaders to change the underlying conditions in the country.

There are a number of limitations to the work. In addition to limitations to computing power, questions can be asked about the values assigned in the model. Specifically, the absence of a sampling frame, the under-presentation of South Africans of color (black, Asian/Indian and "Coloured") in the survey conducted, as well as the fact that the questionnaire was sent out by an organization with a name ("Homecoming Revolution") that suggests a specific stance toward migration all mean that we cannot rule out the possibility of inappropriate weightings. Moreover, although our work clearly indicates that many migrants decided to migrate on the basis of a collective perception rather than informed, rational criteria, we did not examine how they respond to workplaces in their adopted country. Although we believe that the basis for the migration decision is likely to result in some ambivalence, more work is needed to understand if and how this takes place, and plays out in the workplace. We thus join Hajro et al. (2019) in calling for more research on how skilled migrants adjust and acculturate in their adopted country.

References

Anglin, A. H., McKenny, A. F., & Short, J. C. (2018). The impact of collective optimism on new venture creation and growth: A social contagion perspective. *Entrepreneurship Theory and Practice, 42*(3), 390–425.

Barnard, H., & Pendock, C. (2013). To share or not to share: The role of affect in knowledge sharing by individuals in a diaspora. *Journal of International Management, 19*(1), 47–65.

Barsade, S. G. (2002). The ripple effect: Emotional contagion and its influence on group behavior. *Administrative Science Quarterly, 47*(4), 644–675.

Bauloz, C., Vathi, Z., & Acosta, D. (2019). Migration, inclusion and social cohesion: Challenges, recent developments and opportunities. *World Migration Report, 2020,* 186–206.

Becker, B., Driffield, N., Lancheros, S., & Love, J. H. (2020). FDI in hot labour markets: The implications of the war for talent. *Journal of International Business Policy, 3*(2), 107–133.

Beechler, S., & Woodward, I. C. (2009). The global "war for talent". *Journal of International Management, 15*(3), 273–285.

Berry, J. W. (2001). A psychology of immigration. *Journal of Social Issues, 57*(3), 615–631.

Brücker, H., & Schröder, P. J. (2011). Migration regulation contagion. *European Union Politics, 12*(3), 315–335.

Cohen-Cole, E., & Fletcher, J. M. (2008). Is obesity contagious? Social networks vs. environmental factors in the obesity epidemic. *Journal of Health Economics, 27*(5), 1382–1387.

Cooke, F. L., Wood, G., Wang, M., & Veen, A. (2019). How far has international HRM travelled? A systematic review of literature on multinational corporations (2000–2014). *Human Resource Management Review, 29*(1), 59–75.

De Haas, H., Czaika, M., Flahaux, M. L., Mahendra, E., Natter, K., Vezzoli, S., & Villares-Varela, M. (2019). International migration: Trends, determinants, and policy effects. *Population and Development Review, 45*(4), 885–922.

Dodds, P. S., & Watts, D. J. (2005). A generalized model of social and biological contagion. *Journal of Theoretical Biology, 232*(4), 587–604.

Doherty, N. (2013). Understanding the self-initiated expatriate: A review and directions for future research. *International Journal of Management Reviews, 15*(4), 447–469.

Esses, V. M. (2021). Prejudice and discrimination toward immigrants. *Annual Review of Psychology, 72*, 503–531.

Fan, D., Wu, S., Su, Y., & Li, Y. (2022). Managing expatriates to achieve mutual benefits: An integrative model and analysis. *Journal of International Management, 28*(2), 100882.

Guenichi, H., Chouaibi, N., & Khalfaoui, H. (2022). Contagion effect of migration fear in pre and European refugee's crisis period: Evidence from multivariate GARCH and wavelet empirical analysis. *Comparative Migration Studies, 10*(1), 1–20.

Guo, G. C., Al Ariss, A., & Brewster, C. (2020). Understanding the global refugee crisis: Managerial consequences and policy implications. *Academy of Management Perspectives, 34*(4), 531–545.

Hajro, A., Stahl, G. K., Clegg, C. C., & Lazarova, M. B. (2019). Acculturation, coping, and integration success of international skilled migrants: An integrative review and multilevel framework. *Human Resource Management Journal, 29*(3), 328–352.

Hajro, A., Žilinskaitė, M., & Baldassari, P. (2022). Addressing the elephant in the room: Global migration and its implications for business school teaching. *Academy of Management Learning and Education, 21*(1), 1–19.

Hamilton, R. H., & Davison, H. K. (2018). The search for skills: Knowledge stars and innovation in the hiring process. *Business Horizons, 61*(3), 409–419.

Huang, H. C., Shih, H. Y., & Wu, Y. C. (2011). Contagion effects of national innovative capacity: Comparing structural equivalence and cohesion models. *Technological Forecasting and Social Change, 78*(2), 244–255.

Jagtenberg, H. (2017). Afrikaner emigres in Australia: Perception vs. reality in human decision-making. *Australasian Review of African Studies, 38*(1), 86–104.

Jagtenberg, H. (2019). Invited in but kept out: Experiences of skilled Afrikaans-speaking south African immigrants in Australia. In *Strangers, Aliens, Foreigners* (pp. 33–46). Brill.

Kamath, L., & Vijayabaskar, M. (2009). Limits and possibilities of middle class associations as urban collective actors. *Economic and Political Weekly, 44*(26), 368–376.

Kawachi, K. S. (2008). A rumor tansmission model with various contact interactions. *Journal of Theoretical Biology, 253*, 55–60.

Kensbock, J. M., Alkærsig, L., & Lomberg, C. (2022). The epidemic of mental disorders in business—How depression, anxiety, and stress spread across organizations through employee mobility. *Administrative Science Quarterly, 67*(1), 1–48.

Kimura, M., Daibo, I., & Yogo, M. (2008). The study of emotional contagion from the perspective of interpersonal relationships. *Social Behavior and Personality: An International Journal, 36*(1), 27–42.

Koka, B. R., Prescott, J. E., & Madhavan, R. (1999). Contagion influence on trade and investment policy: A network perspective. *Journal of International Business Studies, 30*, 127–147.

Kunczer, V., Lindner, T., & Puck, J. (2019). Benefitting from immigration: The value of immigrants' country knowledge for firm internationalization. *Journal of International Business Policy, 2*(4), 356–375.

Lee, E. S. (1966). A theory of migration. *Demography, 3-1*, 47–57.

Louw, E., & Mersham, G. (2001). Packing for Perth: The growth of a southern African diaspora. *Asian and Pacific Migration Journal, 10*(2), 303–333.

Lucas, R. E. (2005). *International migration and economic development: Lessons from low-income countries*. Edward Elgar Publishing.

Luiz, J. M., & Barnard, H. (2022). Home country (in) stability and the locational portfolio construction of emerging market multinational enterprises. *Journal of Business Research, 151*, 17–32.

Maley, J. F., Moeller, M., & Ting, A. F. (2020). Sustainable expatriate compensation in an uncertain environment. *Journal of International Management, 26*(3), 100776.

Marquis, C., & Raynard, M. (2015). Institutional strategies in emerging markets. *Academy of Management Annals, 9*(1), 291–335.

Marsden, P. (1998). The selectionist paradigm: More implications for sociology. *Sociological Research Online, 3*(4), 26–36.

Mendenhall, M. E., Dunbar, E., & Oddou, G. R. (1987). Expatriate selection, training and career-pathing: A review and critique. *Human Resource Management, 26*(3), 331–345.

Müller, M., Cowan, R., & Barnard, H. (2018). On the value of foreign PhDs in the developing world: Training versus selection effects in the case of South Africa. *Research Policy, 47*(5), 886–900.

Olabisi, M. (2019). Bridging the enforcement gap in international trade: Participation in the New York convention on arbitration. *Journal of International Business Policy, 2*, 86–109.

Oreopoulos, P. (2011). Why do skilled immigrants struggle in the labor market? A field experiment with thirteen thousand resumes. *American Economic Journal: Economic Policy, 3*(4), 148–171.

Pérez-Nordtvedt, L., Babakus, E., & Kedia, B. L. (2010). Learning from international business affiliates: Developing resource-based learning capacity through networks and knowledge acquisition. *Journal of International Management, 16*(3), 262–274.

Peters, L. D., Pressey, A. D., & Johnston, W. J. (2017). Contagion and learning in business networks. *Industrial Marketing Management, 61*, 43–54.

Rule, S. P. (1994). A second-phase diaspora: South African migration to Australia. *Geoforum, 25*(1), 33–39.

Sanders, K., & De Cieri, H. (2021). Similarities and differences in international and comparative human resource management: A review of 60 years of research. *Human Resource Management, 60*(1), 55–88.

Simon, H. A. (2000). Bounded rationality in social science: Today and tomorrow. *Mind & Society, 1*(1), 25–39.

Suutari, V., Brewster, C., & Dickmann, M. (2018). Contrasting assigned expatriates and self-initiated expatriates: A review of extant research and a future research agenda. *The Management of Global Careers*, 63–89.

Van der Berg, S., Patel, L., & Bridgman, G. (2022). Food insecurity in South Africa: Evidence from NIDS-CRAM wave 5. *Development Southern Africa, 39*, 1–16.

Wang, C. H., Varma, A., Hung, L. S., & Wu, P. Y. (2022). A meta-analysis of the antecedents of employee willingness to expatriate. *Asia Pacific Journal of Human Resources*. https://doi.org/10.1111/1744-7941.12359

Wöcke, A., & Barnard, H. (2021). Turnover in South Africa: The effect of history. In *Global talent retention: Understanding employee turnover around the world*. Emerald Publishing Limited.

Zhang, Y., Leischnig, A., Heirati, N., & Henneberg, S. C. (2021). Dark-side-effect contagion in business relationships. *Journal of Business Research, 130*, 260–270.

Part II

Navigating the Terrain of Language and Culture

5

Migrants, Language, and Internationalization of Small- and Medium-Sized Enterprises: A Literature Review

Johanna Niskavaara and Rebecca Piekkari

Introduction

Many societies today rely on small and medium-sized enterprises (SMEs) to ensure future growth and well-being (Coviello & Munro, 1995). However, it is often reported that SMEs struggle to grow due to scarce resources and a lack of relevant knowledge (European Commission, 2020; OECD, 1996; Steinhäuser et al., 2020). Language proficiency in a firm can play a significant role in acquisition of knowledge about foreign markets and in the formation of new business relationships (Hurmerinta et al., 2015). Thus, language skills—or the lack thereof—may dramatically affect the availability of choices when SMEs seek international growth opportunities (Welch et al., 2001).

International Business (IB) scholars have tended to overlook the link between language and internationalization process (Welch & Welch, 2019). Moreover, migrants have received very limited attention in this context. The term 'migrant' refers to a person who has left his/her home country or country of origin, and now lives in a new host country. While migrants have been studied as entrepreneurs (Drori et al., 2009; Solano, 2015) and as skilled talent in international organizations (Crowley-Henry & Al Ariss, 2018), their

---

J. Niskavaara (✉) • R. Piekkari
Department of Management Studies, School of Business, Aalto University, Espoo, Finland
e-mail: johanna.niskavaara@aalto.fi; rebecca.piekkari@aalto.fi

© The Author(s), under exclusive license to Springer Nature Switzerland AG 2023
A. I. Mockaitis (ed.), *The Palgrave Handbook of Global Migration in International Business*,
https://doi.org/10.1007/978-3-031-38886-6_5

language skills have mainly been treated with respect to inclusion or exclusion in the host country (e.g. Shirmohammadi et al., 2019; Wei et al., 2019). Consequently, the focus has been on the proficiency of migrants in the host country language rather than on the role of their native language in firm internationalization. Overall, while the two themes of firm internationalization and migration have been studied separately (Hernandez, 2014), only few studies connect them (for exceptions, see e.g. Hatzigeorgiou & Lodefalk, 2016, 2021; Pennerstorfer, 2016; Sui et al., 2015).

Thus, in this chapter, we bring together migrants, language, and SME internationalization in undertaking an interdisciplinary literature review and pose the following research question: How has previous research addressed migrants, language, and SME internationalization simultaneously? The literature review, covering the period from 1968 to 2019, encompasses 59 publications in 4 disciplinary fields: IB, international entrepreneurship (IE), industrial marketing and purchasing (IMP), and economics. Each stream is relevant for a reason. IB literature offers a broad view of firm internationalization at the organizational level of analysis, whereas IE literature focuses more on decision-makers and language skills as antecedents of internationalization. IMP literature emphasizes inter-firm relationships, networks, and interaction, which are all language-dependent (Piekkari et al., 2014). Finally, research in economics, where some IB research is rooted, sheds light on the relationship between migrant populations and international trade.

Based on our review of publications scattered across four disciplinary fields, we found that the language skills and cultural knowledge of migrants are important resources for internationalizing companies. Migrants may serve as change agents and language bridges, triggering or confirming "the attractiveness of a selected market" (Welch et al., 2001, p. 194). Their proficiency in the languages of their home countries may contribute to how SMEs recognize international opportunities and access local business networks (Light et al., 2002; Sui et al., 2015). This in turn reduces the liability of outsidership experienced by internationalizing firms (Johanson & Vahlne, 2009). As many societies today are destinations for increasing migration, incoming talents could assist SMEs in achieving their internationalization ambitions.

The rest of the chapter is structured as follows. We start with an overview of our review methodology and then provide a historical account of how language has been addressed in the literature over time. The literature review consists of two main parts: (i) language in SME internationalization as it is used to recognize international opportunities and build inter-firm relationships, and (ii) the language skills of migrants in SME internationalization. In the latter section, we briefly take the perspective of migrant populations and then focus on individual migrants. In the concluding section, we discuss the findings and limitations of the review and offer suggestions for future research.

Review Methodology

This chapter is based on a review of 59 publications that have appeared between 1968 and 2019 in English. The publications were largely identified manually because language as a search term is seldom used in the title or among the key words of a publication. We initially relied on search terms such as 'language,' 'linguistic,' 'communicat(e/ion),' and/or 'interact(ion).' Furthermore, we combined 'migrant' and 'native' with 'international(ization)' and 'language' as search words. We also used 'SME' and 'export' as search words because SMEs commonly rely on exporting as a mode of operation. Since language often appeared together with concepts such as 'psychic distance,' 'international orientation/outlook,' 'international experience,' 'export antecedent,' and 'culture,' we added these search terms.

Figure 5.1 depicts the interdisciplinary nature of our literature review, which focuses on the intersection of the four streams of research. We soon realized that very few papers addressed simultaneously all three

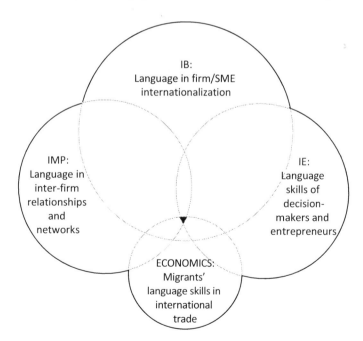

Fig. 5.1 The four streams of literature included in the review

topics—migrants, language, and firm internationalization (for exceptions, see Sui et al., 2015). The initial stage of the review resulted in more than 200 articles, books, and reports, but only a few of them were included in the final scope. As Fig. 5.1 shows, most of the publications were about language and internationalization but not about migration. We also came across a number of publications that focused on migrants as either domestic or cross-border entrepreneurs (e.g. Bolzani & Boari, 2018; Elo et al., 2021; Solano, 2015), but not on language (although it was often mentioned briefly). A limited number of publications addressed migrants and their language skills but not in the context of firm internationalization (Shirmohammadi et al., 2019; Wei et al., 2019).

Given the focus of our review, we considered 'language' a critical criterion for determining the scope of our sample. We, therefore, excluded work that addressed migrants and firm internationalization but not language. We also removed papers that only briefly mentioned language (e.g. Ojala, 2009; Sousa et al., 2008). This was characteristic of studies that approached language as a barrier. Furthermore, those publications that addressed migrants as an internal management issue in large multinational enterprises (MNEs) without a particular focus on firm internationalization were excluded. Although our focus is on SME internationalization, most authors did not explicitly distinguish between 'SME' and 'firm' and often referred to the firms as 'exporters.' Hence, papers dealing with both 'firm internationalization' and 'SME internationalization' were included, and we used these terms interchangeably (see e.g., Welch & Luostarinen, 1988).

After deciding on the scope of our review, we used 'snowballing,' that is, we looked up potential references mentioned in publications that had already been reviewed. Finally, we consulted two experts on internationalization process research and diaspora studies, respectively, to make sure our sample included the relevant studies. Thus, the final sample consists of 59 publications. Appendix lists all the publications included in our review.

Historical Overview

The story of language in firm internationalization began with occasional references in the 1950s, 1960s, and 1970s. In the early days of export research, scholars attempted to describe and explain patterns of international expansion and language was recognized as a factor. Beckerman (1956, p. 38) looked at both exports and imports and explained that if the actual transportation costs are the same for two suppliers, an Italian entrepreneur would be likely to choose a Swiss supplier over a Turkish one because "Switzerland will be 'nearer' to him in a psychic evaluation (fewer language difficulties, and so on)."

The notion of "psychic evaluation" was later developed into the concept of *psychic distance*, which was popularized by Johanson and Vahlne (1977). Psychic distance is defined as the "factors preventing or disturbing the flows of information between firm and market" (Johanson & Wiedersheim-Paul, 1975, p. 308). These factors include differences in language, culture, political systems, level of education, and level of industrial developments (Johanson & Vahlne, 1977; Johanson & Wiedersheim-Paul, 1975). According to Johanson and Vahlne (1977), companies first search for opportunities in countries with a lower psychic distance and gradually move to markets with a greater distance. Psychic distance is largely correlated with geographical distance, and in practice many firms began their international expansion from neighboring markets (Johanson & Wiedersheim-Paul, 1975). The concept has had a significant impact on subsequent IB research.

During the 1980s and early 1990s, scholars attached great importance to language in firm internationalization, particularly in the context of inter-firm relationships (Håkansson, 1982; Swift, 1991; Turnbull & Welham, 1985). However, toward the end of the 1990s and in the new millennium, the literature on inter-firm networks has paid limited attention to language while still highlighting the importance of interaction (e.g. Coviello & Munro, 1997; Naudé & Sutton-Brady, 2019). Since the late 1990s, language has been increasingly studied as an internal management issue in multinational enterprises (MNEs) (e.g. Marschan et al., 1997); this approach still dominates so-called language sensitive IB research (Tenzer et al., 2017).

The undisputed role of English as a lingua franca, that is, a language shared by non-native speakers, has contributed to the dominant understanding that language can be ignored in firm internationalization. Those who maintain that language is important underline its role as a resource for acquiring knowledge and discovering business opportunities internationally (Foreman-Peck & Zhou, 2015; Hurmerinta et al., 2015; Johnstone et al., 2018). It is, however, more common to look at language as a barrier. According to Kahiya (2018), who reviewed literature on export barriers from 1980 to 2016, a total of 40 papers mentioned language as a barrier; language ranked 11th on the list of the most common export barriers. However, while references to 'language' are common, they have been made only in passing. In fact, according to a recent review by Piekkari et al. (2022), IB researchers often regard language as a mechanical skill that is relatively easy to acquire; once it is acquired, the language barrier is expected to disappear (see also Welch et al., 2001). Language proficiency, however, is much more than grammar and vocabulary;

it also comprises the socio-cultural norms of language use (Vandermeeren, 2005). Thus, there is considerable potential to further develop our understanding of the role of language in firm internationalization.

In this chapter, we adopt the view of language as a resource for firm internationalization. Interestingly, our review shows that the importance of foreign language skills is often highlighted in studies conducted in English-speaking countries (e.g. Bilkey & Tesar, 1977; Clarke, 2000; Marcella & Davies, 2004; Stanley et al., 1990), whereas studies of non-English contexts rarely mention language at all (for exceptions, see Asasongtham & Wichadee, 2014; Lavric & Bäck, 2009; Rižnar & Rybnicek, 2017). Given the role of English as a lingua franca of international business, this was a surprising finding. Indeed, extant research from the resource perspective tends to focus on individuals with foreign language skills. Such skills are quite obviously something individuals possess *in addition to* their native language. What has received much less attention so far is how someone's native language can contribute as a resource to firm internationalization.

Literature Review

The following literature review makes two important assumptions: Firstly, SMEs are willing to employ migrants in their internationalization process, and secondly, migrants as entrepreneurs or employees of SMEs are willing to use their native language skills and knowledge of their country of origin to advance this process. These assumptions apply to some SMEs and migrants, but not all. We also assume that most migrants have spent their formative years in their country of origin and, therefore, speak the native language, know the native culture, and understand the local laws and customs as well as how the markets work.

Language in SME Internationalization

The first theme of our review is the role of language in firm internationalization especially from an SME perspective. We begin with a short introduction of what internationalization is in this context. Internationalization can be defined as "the process of adapting firms' operations (strategy, structure, resources, etc.) to international environments" (Calof & Beamish, 1995, p. 116). However, firms do not merely adapt passively to markets or react to them, but actively seek to transform them (Vahlne & Johanson, 2013). The actions a firm is able to take and the choices available to it depend on the resources and capabilities it possesses (Steinhäuser et al., 2020).

Many SMEs regard internationalization as a prerequisite for business success (Knowles et al., 2006), and exporting is often the first step in their internationalization process (Arteaga-Ortiz & Fernández-Ortiz, 2010; Cavusgil, 1980; Morgan & Katsikeas, 1997). Exporting is seen as a low-risk strategy to begin internationalization; it is a less resource-intensive and more flexible way to target international markets than other modes of internationalization that require higher levels of commitment (Bianchi & Wickramasekera, 2016). While the small size of SMEs may hinder internationalization (Haddoud et al., 2021), smallness may also be a source of flexibility that allows SMEs to adapt quickly to changes in the business environment (Steinhäuser et al., 2020).

Internationalization is typically described as a challenge for SMEs because they tend to lack resources compared with large MNCs (Steinhäuser et al., 2020). A critical factor in firm internationalization "is the possession of appropriate knowledge: this includes knowledge about foreign markets, about techniques of foreign operation, about ways of doing business, about key people in buyer organisations, and so on" (Welch & Luostarinen, 1988, p. 52). Firms also need to consider new language and cultural requirements (Rižnar & Rybnicek, 2017). In the following sections, we focus on the role of language when SMEs search for international opportunities and establish inter-firm relationships because these are the key steps in the internationalization process.

Language in the Recognition of International Opportunities

International opportunity recognition can be defined as "the potential [a] decision-maker sees for exchanging goods and services in selected markets" (Hurmerinta et al., 2015, p. 1084). Many scholars have referred to psychic distance in explaining the patterns used by firms in searching for opportunities. However, Welch et al. (2001) sought to unbundle language from psychic distance in order to explore the impact of language on firm internationalization in more detail. They found that language affects firm internationalization from its inception, either implicitly or explicitly. Furthermore, they suggest that companies tend to follow language paths in their internationalization and search for opportunities where they can use their home country language as long as possible (Welch et al., 2001). While, for example, companies from English- and Spanish-speaking countries can export to a variety of countries without the need to cross language borders, companies from countries such as

Finland or Japan face the language border immediately due to the limited number of speakers of their languages in the world.

The IE publications included in our review suggest that the personal experiences and characteristics of decision-makers "determine which export opportunities are perceived and how they are considered" (Morgan, 1997, p. 76). 'Decision-maker' refers to anyone in an SME with the authority to make decisions about where, when, and how to internationalize, for example, SME owners (Sui et al., 2015), export managers (Williams & Chaston, 2004), and managerial staff (Schlegelmilch & Crook, 1988). The articles reviewed associate the foreign language proficiency of decision-makers with the concept of international orientation or outlook (Bilkey, 1978; Dichtl et al., 1990). Hence the language skills of decision-makers can serve as an antecedent to exports (Fernández-Ortiz & Lombardo, 2009; Leonidou & Katsikeas, 2010; Suárez-Ortega & Álamo-Vera, 2005). A company may seem perfectly 'fit' to begin exporting, but without decision-makers with an international orientation the company is not likely to become an exporter (Dichtl et al., 1990). Compared with monolinguals, decision-makers with proficiency in foreign languages tend to be more likely to engage in exporting (Bilkey & Tesar, 1977; Burton & Schlegelmilch, 1987; Leonidou et al., 1998; Morgan, 1997). In addition, the number of languages spoken affects which markets they target and how many (Kubíčková & Peprný, 2011; Serra et al., 2012). Furthermore, successful exporting firms tend to be managed by executives with adequate foreign language proficiency (Clarke, 1999).

Hurmerinta et al. (2015) found that the ability of decision-makers to speak English as a foreign language "facilitated the recognition of international opportunities but did not direct interest towards any particular market" (2015, p. 1089). In contrast, their ability to speak other languages directed the search for opportunities to markets where those languages were spoken. Hurmerinta et al. (2015, p. 1089) described this effect as the "linguistic knowledge corridor." When the corridor effect is very strong (especially if decision-makers are fluent in only one foreign language), it may turn into "a linguistic blind" (Hurmerinta et al., 2015, p. 1090). Hence there is a risk that decision-makers will miss out on opportunities in markets where they lack language proficiency.

While foreign language skills can indeed encourage decision-makers to search for opportunities in certain markets, Hurmerinta et al. (2015) also found that language skills alone do not provide sufficient competences to do so. They argue that "fluency in a language may create false expectations for the decision-maker's understanding of the market and culture" (Hurmerinta et al., 2015, p. 1090). To successfully exploit international opportunities, linguistic knowledge must be accompanied by cultural knowledge which can be acquired through international experience (Hurmerinta et al., 2015). As Knowles et al. (2006, p. 638) point out, "it is the integrity of and relationship between these three decision-maker characteristics—language skills, intercultural competence, and business experience—that appear to hold the key to success for SMEs in international markets."

In the next section, we turn to the literature on inter-firm relationships and networks.

Language in Inter-Firm Relationships and Networks

An important sub-theme in our review deals with how SMEs establish inter-firm relationships and networks from a language perspective. We begin this section with a short overview of the concept of *networks* and its role in firm internationalization. In networks, "firms are linked to each other in various, complex and, to a considerable extent, invisible patterns" (Johanson & Vahlne, 2009, p. 1411). These relationships can also cross borders and create connections between different country markets (Vahlne & Johanson, 2013). Goods and services are exchanged between the members of a network, but networks also represent an important source of resources and knowledge for them (Johanson & Vahlne, 2009; Musteen et al., 2010; Schweizer, 2013; L. S. Welch & Luostarinen, 1988). Although networks are the basis of effective communication, they tend to be time-consuming and demanding to establish particularly when physical or cultural distance is involved (Welch & Luostarinen, 1988).

Given the importance of networks, Johanson and Vahlne (2009) argue that foreign-market entry should be studied as a process of building network positions where internationalization is the outcome. Improvement in a network position means access to more knowledge, leading to the discovery and/or creation of new business opportunities (Johanson & Vahlne, 2009). An insider position in relevant networks is paramount; otherwise a company may suffer from liability of outsidership (Johanson & Vahlne, 2009; Vahlne & Johanson, 2013). Liability of outsidership impedes learning, the building of trust, and the development of committed relationships as well as recognition and exploitation of opportunities (Johanson & Vahlne, 2009). To become an insider, however, it is necessary to first identify the relevant networks and the key members within them, and then build relationships with them (Valentino et al., 2018). Those already in a network must also be willing and motivated to connect with newcomers (Yamin & Kurt, 2018).

Although scholars often talk about inter-firm relationships, relationships are ultimately formed between people—not between firms. The importance of individuals in industrial relationships is underlined in IMP research (e.g. Håkansson, 1982; Turnbull & Welham, 1985). Hence individual characteristics such as experience, educational level, attitudes, and competences—including language skills—are influential in establishing international relationships (Turnbull & Welham, 1985). In addition to influencing *where* to look for international opportunities, language ability also affects *how* to internationalize (i.e., the choice of operation mode) and the quality of relationships.

Which mode of operation? Language differences are commonly seen as barriers to internationalization. Such barriers are situated between the target market and the internationalizing firm and are, therefore, external to the firm (Alrashidi, 2019; Leonidou, 2004). Intermediaries such as agents, distributors, or trading companies are frequently used to overcome language barriers (e.g., Håkansson, 1982). In such situations, the exporter outsources language matters (Welch et al., 2001) and relies on second-hand information about the foreign market instead of retrieving it directly (Williams & Chaston, 2004). Although trading companies play an important role in assisting firms of all sizes to internationalize, their services are particularly important for SMEs (Piekkari et al., 2014). In domestic indirect exports, the intermediary is based in the home country of the exporter who, in fact, may not have any direct contact with customers overseas. It is more common, however, for exporting companies to use foreign indirect export, in which the intermediary is located in the foreign market. In this form of exporting, there is great variation in how exporters and intermediaries 'share the work'; some companies are closely involved alongside the intermediary while others hand over more responsibility (Piekkari et al., 2014). Although intermediaries provide a bridge between the exporting company and foreign markets, psychic distance may play a role in the exporter-intermediary relationship as well (Safari & Chetty, 2019). Furthermore, according to Crick's (1999) study of UK companies looking for intermediaries, the ability of an intermediary to speak English was regarded almost as important as the ability to sell products in the target market. On the other hand, when exporting directly, that is, without any intermediaries, a company takes on the full responsibility for business relationships, including communication and, thus, language.

Whose language skills? Language skills assist in knowledge exchange and in building personal relationships with international customers (Håkansson, 1982; Turnbull & Welham, 1985). Although the language skills of decision-makers play a key role, successful exporters often employ foreign language specialists as well, particularly in marketing-related roles (Enderwick &

Akoorie, 1994). Furthermore, language skills are also important in, for example, credit control and quality assurance (Marcella & Davies, 2004). The ELAN study (2006) mentions companies that had targeted foreign markets based on use of the existing language skills of their employees and then hired additional staff with language skills that matched specific markets. In addition to the language skills of decision-makers and employees, Hurmerinta et al. (2015) report that even the language skills of family members are significant in recognizing and exploiting opportunities, especially in the case of SMEs.

Which language? Our review also provides insights into which language is valuable in inter-firm relationships. Many studies underline that the seller should speak the buyer's language (Conway & Swift, 2000; Knowles et al., 2006; Leonidou, 2004; Mughan, 1990; Nemkova et al., 2012; Swift, 1991; Turnbull & Welham, 1985; Vandermeeren, 1999). According to Mughan (1990, p. 22), "language skills can be the difference between failure and success in foreign markets." The above studies suggest that fluency in the customer's language provides the exporter with a deeper understanding of the target market, of its culture and of the customer's needs. Furthermore, the customer is also better able to recognize the abilities of exporters. Use of the customer's language can be seen as a sign of interest and respect which will promote development of a positive attitude toward the exporter and lead eventually to a relationship of mutual trust.

Lavric and Bäck (2009) offer an extensive analysis of language choice based on a study among Austrian exporters. They follow a three-level model that distinguishes between linguistic adaptation, non-adaptation, and standardization. Adaptation refers to speaking the customer's language, whereas non-adaptation means speaking one's own language; in other words, the customer is required to speak the exporter's language. Standardization, in turn, refers to use of a lingua franca. It is more common for exporters to adapt their language use to that of the customer's than the other way around (Piekkari et al., 2014).

The extent to which an exporting company can adapt language use depends on the language skills in the firm. From a broader perspective, the availability of language skills is subject to factors such as the educational system of a country, geographical location, historical ties, and business relationships with other countries (Johnstone et al., 2018; Lavric & Bäck, 2009). Fidrmuc and Fidrmuc (2016, p. 33) found that "[c]ountries whose residents can communicate easily are likely to trade more with each other, but residents of countries that trade a lot have also an incentive to learn each other's language." The reviewed publications suggest that members from smaller linguistic groups have stronger incentives to learn the language of larger groups than the other way around. This is due to the opportunities offered by majority languages (Foreman-Peck & Zhou, 2015).

Aaby and Slater (1989, p. 20) argue that "English is an important international language and may in export situations be the basis for the majority of international communications." Hurmerinta et al. (2015, p. 1089) agree by reporting that many of their Finnish interviewees saw English as a "safeguarding mechanism" with which the company could survive in a variety of markets even if they did not possess skills in the local languages of the target markets. In a study of exporting Australian companies, Stanley, Ingram, and Chittick (1990, p. 59) confirmed that a company can indeed get by in many markets without knowing the local language, "[b]ut getting by is not what business is about"; it is about having a competitive edge which can be derived from knowledge of local language and culture (Stanley et al., 1990).

While many rely on English as a lingua franca in cross-border business, it is not automatically the solution. First of all, Liu et al. (2015) remark that the proficiency and willingness to speak English should not be taken for granted. In fact, Fidrmuc and Fidrmuc (2016) show that even in Europe, English language proficiency is not as common as often assumed. Moreover, as Brannen et al. (2014) argue, it is only an illusion that a lingua franca makes communication unproblematic; in fact, it may become more complicated. While people speak English as a foreign language, they still draw on the language systems, interpretive frames, and socio-cultural norms of their mother tongues (Brannen et al., 2014; Jentjens, 2021; Vandermeeren, 2005). This may lead to misunderstandings since sharing a language does not necessarily mean that the interpretations and meanings attached are shared (Brannen et al., 2014; Jentjens, 2021).

Lavric and Bäck (2009) provide examples of how a mix of languages can serve different purposes in an exporter-customer relationship; while small-talk may be conducted in the customer's language, in the actual business negotiations both parties may use a lingua franca. Visser (1995) also notes that companies need to prioritize; it is unrealistic to expect proficiency in the languages of all potential customers. Finding employees with specific foreign language skills can be difficult, and language training is expensive, time-consuming, and slow in producing results (Visser, 1995). Hence it has been suggested by some studies (Asasongtham & Wichadee, 2014; ELAN, 2006; Foreman-Peck & Zhou, 2015; Marcella & Davies, 2004; Rižnar & Rybnicek, 2017; Sui et al., 2015; Welch et al., 2001) that the native language skills of migrants could offer important resources to SMEs. This is the next topic of our review.

The Language Skills of Migrants in SME Internationalization

Language skills and knowledge of international markets are often mentioned as key factors that make migrants an important resource for organizations (Al Ariss & Crowley-Henry, 2013). Migrants are also said to counter the effects of cultural differences (Tadesse & White, 2017). Yet, as indicated by Hernandez (2014), the themes of firm internationalization and migration have rarely been studied together. In this section, we add language to the equation and first review literature on migrant populations in firm internationalization and then turn to individual migrants.

Migrant Populations

Economists explain international trade flows by, for example, applying gravity models which commonly use language as a variable. There are indications that a shared language promotes trade between two countries (e.g. Hutchinson, 2002; Light et al., 2002; Melitz, 2008; Melitz & Toubal, 2014), excluding cases where the two countries experience or have a history of political tensions (Hernandez, 2014). Although there is still limited evidence on the participation of migrants in trade (Sui et al., 2015), there is some indication that the number of migrants from a certain country is positively related to trade toward their country of origin (e.g. Lücke & Stöhr, 2018; Pennerstorfer, 2016). Hernandez (2014), on the other hand, found that migrant populations also promote internationalization of companies from their country of origin toward the country of residence; they offer both a readily available customer base and a valuable source of market information. Some firms even follow migrant populations and co-locate their operations abroad (Hernandez, 2014). The importance of migrants for bilateral trade grows if the local host population has a limited proficiency in the migrants' native language (Light et al., 2002; Lücke & Stöhr, 2018). A shared national identity, language, and code of ethics form the basis of the bond between migrants and their country of origin; these factors enhance communication and ultimately promote trust (Cai et al., 2021; Hernandez, 2014; Jentjens, 2021; Melitz & Toubal, 2014).

Individual Migrants

Simmonds and Smith (1968) suggest that migrants may act as change agents who encourage non-exporting companies to start exporting and put the international experience and knowledge of migrants to use. Referring to Simmonds and Smith (1968), Welch et al. (2001, p. 194) theorize that migrants can serve as language bridges and influence a company at two levels: "as key decision maker, a migrant may select markets on the basis of former country familiarity" or as an employee, a migrant may reinforce the attractiveness of a selected market.

The study by Sui et al. (2015) is exceptional as it is the only one that falls directly into the focus of our review (see Fig. 5.1). They studied how the native languages of migrant SME owners affect the internationalization process. In line with the study of Hurmerinta et al. (2015), they found that the native language skills of migrants shape the firm's internationalization strategy; migrant entrepreneurs preferred to target markets with which they had "a linguistic match" and tended to avoid markets with "a linguistic mismatch" (Sui et al., 2015, p. 811). Sui et al. (2015) argue that their findings support the liability-of-outsidership hypothesis (Johanson & Vahlne, 2009). Migrant SME owners preferred to focus on markets where their language abilities provided easier access to network insidership as the lack of access, that is, outsidership, would hamper internationalization. Moghaddam et al. (2018, p. 52) argue that "[i]t would be very difficult, if not impossible, for a nonimmigrant entrepreneur to gain a high level of dual social embeddedness in two countries without spending a considerable amount of time in both countries learning their culture, language, and social norms." This view is supported by Light et al. (2002), who found that the right language and cultural skills allowed migrants to find export opportunities in their country of origin that non-migrants in the country of residence simply could not see.

Similar effects were also found in a study on migrants as employees. Jentjens (2021) (2021) studied the employability of German women who had migrated to France for family reasons, for example, had a French spouse. Her findings indicate that the women's fluency in German and cultural understanding and knowledge of their home country were highly beneficial in their international jobs, where these women needed to build networks between the French employing organization and stakeholders in Germany, and sometimes also deal with conflicts and misunderstandings. This highlights the importance of culture-sensitive communication skills that go beyond mere grammar and vocabulary (Jentjens, 2021), a view that is shared by Liu et al. (2015), who studied the role of migrants in international inter-firm knowledge transfer.

To sum up, Pennerstorfer (2016) details five advantages that migrants offer to firm internationalization compared with non-migrants: (i) migrants know more about business opportunities in their countries of origin; (ii) they are more likely to be connected with business networks in their countries of origin and are, therefore, better able to find customers and partners; (iii) they have more knowledge about preferences in their home country market; (iv) they face lower communication barriers due to language skills, and finally, (v) they are more likely to have both formal and informal knowledge about their home country, for example, legal systems, institutions, local business practices, and knowledge on whom to trust. Taken together, the positive impact that migrants have on international operations toward their country of origin is referred to as the "*immigrant effect*" (Chung, 2004, p. 706).

Discussion and Conclusion

In this chapter, we conducted a review of 59 publications in the fields of IB, IE, IMP, and Economics from 1968 to 2019. Despite the scant attention devoted to migrants, language, and firm internationalization to date, research across these fields seems to agree that migrants offer important resources for internationalizing SMEs.

The findings of our review showed that the way researchers have addressed language has varied over time. References to language first appeared in connection with the concept of psychic distance and patterns of international expansion (Beckerman, 1956; Johanson & Vahlne, 1977). During the 1980s and 1990s, when internationalization research turned its attention to the role of individuals in inter-firm relationships, language gained more traction (Håkansson, 1982; Swift, 1991; Turnbull & Welham, 1985). In the late 1990s, scholars developed an interest in language as a management challenge for MNEs, and since then it has been increasingly treated as an intra-firm issue (Brannen et al., 2014). Interestingly, recent work has called for renewed attention to language in developing business relationships to advance exports (Alteren & Tudoran, 2019).

Our review provides several avenues for future research. Extant research on language and internationalization tends to look at individuals' *foreign* language skills—or the lack thereof—leaving the perspective of migrants' *native* language skills underexplored. Future research could consider both perspectives and dig deeper into the social aspects of language in firm internationalization. While IB research commonly views language as a mechanical skill (Piekkari et al., 2022; Welch et al., 2001), our review reminds us that language skills should be complemented with cultural knowledge in order to advance internationalization (e.g., Hurmerinta et al., 2015; Knowles et al., 2006). This cultural knowledge includes communicative competence (Hymes, 1972), which means that, in addition to having knowledge of the vocabulary and grammar of the language in question, interlocutors must also follow the same socio-cultural norms of language use. This requires active and conscious learning of the socio-cultural norms of language use, such as the correct use of terms of address, in a foreign language, whereas the norms of a native language are learnt without much effort (Vandermeeren, 2005). In building and maintaining relationships, migrants using their native language to interact with customers have a clear advantage over non-native speakers and are better equipped to navigate various kinds of communicative contexts.

We acknowledge that our review treated migrants as a homogeneous group. However, this group is much more heterogeneous than what meets the eye. Future research could explore in more detail whether and under what circumstances migrants contribute to the internationalization of SMEs. The difference between first-generation migrants and their offspring may also be worth considering. Many migrants end up being self-employed and not all of them aspire to internationalize their businesses. However, based on our review, it would seem that the benefits for internationalizing firms of migrants' language skills are very similar regardless of whether the migrants are entrepreneurs or employees (e.g., Pennerstorfer, 2016), but this calls for further research.

In undertaking the review, we assumed that SMEs are willing to employ migrants in their internationalization process and that migrants are equally willing to use their native language skills and knowledge of their country of origin to advance this process. However, this may not always be the case (Kane & Levina, 2017). We invite future research to investigate the language-related roles of migrants among various stakeholders such as customers, suppliers, and co-workers. Companies may hire migrants proactively to initiate internationalization toward the migrant's country of origin, or reactively to maintain operations in the countries where the migrants are from (Hatzigeorgiou & Lodefalk, 2021). However, language-based advantages on the labor market are not static but dynamic; the competitive advantage of migrants that stems from their native language may start to fade as their skills in the host country language improve (Jentjens, 2021). Yet, we also suspect that some migrants may 'get stuck' in their language-related roles if they are unable to use or demonstrate their other competences. Future research could investigate turning points in their careers.

According to our review, much of the previous research conceptualizes internationalization as an outward process. However, as Welch and Luostarinen (1993) have pointed out, this view neglects inward internationalization, such as imports. Outward and inward internationalization are linked in such a way that the effectiveness of one influences the success of the other. Future research could theorize migrants as links between these two aspects of internationalization (Welch & Luostarinen, 1993). Migrants are an integral part of both processes; they represent a form of inward internationalization through which a company acquires resources from abroad. But they also affect the outward internationalization of SMEs by recognizing business opportunities that connect the exporting SME with foreign customers and by building business networks in their countries of origin. Migrants possess the requisite cultural and linguistic sensitivity (e.g. Jentjens, 2021; Pennerstorfer, 2016) that allows them to take on boundary-spanning roles.

Finally, our review suggests that extant research places the language barrier outside the internationalizing SME, in-between the firm and its customers or intermediaries abroad. However, migrants also present a new internal situation for SMEs that may have originally been entirely monolingual. Management of language diversity and inclusion have already been studied in the context of MNEs (e.g., Lauring & Klitmøller, 2017; Tenzer et al., 2014). We believe the increasing migration will make language and cultural diversity a critical management challenge for SMEs as well. How they deal with this challenge is for future research to uncover.

Acknowledgments We would like to thank Catherine Welch and Maria Elo for their valuable suggestions on an earlier version of this chapter. We are grateful to the anonymous reviewer for the feedback received during the review process. We would also like to thank Audra Mockaitis for her encouraging editorial guidance.

Appendix

Aaby and Slater (1989)
Al Ariss and Crowley-Henry (2013)
Alrashidi (2019)
Asasongtham and Wichadee (2014)
Bilkey and Tesar (1977)
Bilkey (1978)

Brannen et al. (2014)
Burton and Schlegelmilch (1987)
Cai et al. (2021)
Chung (2004)
Clarke (1999)
Conway and Swift (2000)
Crick (1999)
Dichtl et al. (1990)
ELAN (2006)
Enderwick and Akoorie (1994)
Fernández-Ortiz and Lombardo (2009)
Fidrmuc and Fidrmuc (2016)
Foreman-Peck and Zhou (2015)
Håkansson (1982)
Hernandez (2014)
Hutchinson (2002)
Jentjens (2021)
Johnstone et al. (2018)
Knowles et al. (2006)
Kubíčková and Peprný (2011)
Lavric and Bäck (2009)
Leonidou and Katsikeas (2010)
Leonidou et al. (1998)
Leonidou (2004)
Light et al. (2002)
Liu et al. (2015)
Lücke and Stöhr (2018)
Marcella and Davies (2004)
Melitz and Toubal (2014)
Melitz (2008)
Moghaddam et al. (2018)
Mughan (1990)
Nemkova et al. (20120
Pennerstorfer (2016)
Piekkari et al. (2014)
Safari and Chetty (2019)
Schlegelmilch and Crook (1988)
Serra et al. (2012)
Simmonds and Smith (1968)
Stanley et al. (1990)

Suárez-Ortega and Álamo-Vera (2005)
Sui et al. (2015)
Swift (1991)
Tadesse and White (2017)
Turnbull and Welham (1985)
Vandermeeren (1999)
Vandermeeren (2005)
Visser (1995)
Williams and Chaston (2004)
Hurmerinta et al. (2015)
Morgan (1997)
Rižnar and Rybnicek (2017)
Welch et al. (2001)

References

Aaby, N. E., & Slater, S. F. (1989). Management influences on export performance: A review of the empirical literature 1978-88. *International Marketing Review, 6*(4). https://doi.org/10.1108/EUM0000000001516

Al Ariss, A., & Crowley-Henry, M. (2013). Self-initiated expatriation and migration in the management literature: Present theorizations and future research directions. *Career Development International, 18*(1), 78–96. https://doi.org/10.1108/13620431311305962

Alrashidi, Y. A. (2019). Exporting barriers perceived by manufacturing SMEs: Evidence from emerging and advanced markets. *European Journal of Business and Management, 11*(12). https://doi.org/10.7176/EJBM

Alteren, G., & Tudoran, A. A. (2019). Open-mindedness and adaptive business style: Competences that contribute to building relationships in dissimilar export markets. *International Marketing Review, 36*(3), 365–390. https://doi.org/10.1108/IMR-08-2017-0142

Arteaga-Ortiz, J., & Fernández-Ortiz, R. (2010). Why don't we use the same export barrier measurement scale? An empirical analysis in small and medium-sized enterprises. *Journal of Small Business Management, 48*(3), 395–420. https://doi.org/10.1111/j.1540-627X.2010.00300.x

Asasongtham, J., & Wichadee, S. (2014). The roles of foreign language in export operations of Thai SMEs. *International Journal of Entrepreneurship, 18*, 41–58.

Beckerman, W. (1956). Distance and the pattern of intra-European trade. *The Review of Economics and Statistics, 38*(1), 31.

Bianchi, C., & Wickramasekera, R. (2016). Antecedents of SME export intensity in a Latin American market. *Journal of Business Research, 69*(10), 4368–4376. https://doi.org/10.1016/j.jbusres.2016.02.041

Bilkey, W. J. (1978). An attempted integration of the literature on the export behavior of firms. *Journal of International Business Studies, 9*(1), 33–46.

Bilkey, W. J., & Tesar, G. (1977). The export behavior of smaller-sized Wisconsin manufacturing firms. *Journal of International Business Studies, 8*(1), 93–98. https://doi.org/10.1057/palgrave.jibs.8490783

Bolzani, D., & Boari, C. (2018). Evaluations of export feasibility by immigrant and non-immigrant entrepreneurs in new technology-based firms. *Journal of International Entrepreneurship, 16*(2), 176–209. https://doi.org/10.1007/s10843-017-0217-0

Brannen, M. Y., Piekkari, R., & Tietze, S. (2014). The multifaceted role of language in international business: Unpacking the forms, functions and features of a critical challenge to MNC theory and performance. *Journal of International Business Studies, 45*(5), 495–507. https://doi.org/10.1057/jibs.2014.24

Burton, F. N., & Schlegelmilch, B. B. (1987). Profile analyses of non-exporters versus exporters grouped by export involvement. *Management International Review, 27*(1), 38–49.

Cai, H., Meng, Y., & Chakraborty, S. (2021). Migrants and exports: Decomposing the link. *Journal of World Business, 56*(2), 1090–9516. https://doi.org/10.1016/j.jwb.2020.101166

Calof, J. L., & Beamish, P. W. (1995). Adapting to foreign markets: Explaining internationalization. *International Business Review, 4*(2), 115–131. https://doi.org/10.1016/0969-5931(95)00001-G

Cavusgil, S. T. (1980). On the internationalisation process of firms. *European Research, 8*(6), 273–281. https://doi.org/10.1136/bmj.301.6765.1397-b

Chung, H. F. L. (2004). An empirical investigation of immigrant effects: The experience of firms operating in the emerging markets. *International Business Review, 13*(6), 705–728. https://doi.org/10.1016/j.ibusrev.2004.09.001

Clarke, W. M. (1999). An assessment of foreign language training for English-speaking exporters. *Journal of European Industrial Training, 23*(1), 9–15. https://doi.org/10.1108/03090599910253474

Clarke, W. M. (2000). The use of foreign languages by Irish exporters. *European Journal of Marketing, 34*(1/2), 80–90. https://doi.org/10.1108/03090560010306214

Conway, T., & Swift, J. S. (2000). International relationship marketing: The importance of psychic distance. *European Journal of Marketing, 34*(11), 309–0566.

Coviello, N. E., & Munro, H. J. (1995). Growing the entrepreneurial firm. *European Journal of Marketing, 29*(7), 49–61. https://doi.org/10.1108/03090569510095008

Coviello, N., & Munro, H. (1997). Network relationships and the internationalisation process of small software firms. *International Business Review, 6*(4), 361–386. https://doi.org/10.1016/S0969-5931(97)00010-3

Crick, D. (1999). An investigation into SMEs' use of languages in their export operations. *International Journal of Entrepreneurial Behaviour & Research, 5*(1), 19–31. https://doi.org/10.1108/13552559910259810

Crowley-Henry, M., & Al Ariss, A. (2018). Talent management of skilled migrants: Propositions and an agenda for future research. *International Journal of Human Resource Management, 29*(13), 2054–2079. https://doi.org/10.1080/09585192.2016.1262889

Dichtl, E., Koeglmayr, H.-G., & Mueller, S. (1990). International orientation as a precondition for export success. *Journal of International Business Studies, 21*(1), 23–40. https://doi.org/10.1057/palgrave.jibs.8490325

Drori, I., Honig, B., & Wright, M. (2009). Transnational entrepreneurship: An emergent field of study. *Entrepreneurship: Theory and Practice, 33*(5), 1001–1022. https://doi.org/10.1111/j.1540-6520.2009.00332.x

ELAN. (2006). *ELAN: Effects on the European economy of shortages of foreign language skills in enterprises* (Issue December).

Elo, M., Täube, F. A., & Servais, P. (2021). Who is doing "transnational diaspora entrepreneurship"? Understanding formal identity and status. *Journal of World Business, 57*(1), 101240. https://doi.org/10.1016/j.jwb.2021.101240

Enderwick, P., & Akoorie, M. E. M. (1994). Pilot study research note: The employment of foreign language specialists and export success - the case of New Zealand. *International Marketing Review, 11*(4), 4–18. https://doi.org/10.1108/02651339410069218

European Commission. (2020). *Unleashing the full potential of European SMEs* (Issue March).

Fernández-Ortiz, R., & Lombardo, G. F. (2009). Influence of the capacities of top management on the internationalization of SMEs. *Entrepreneurship and Regional Development, 21*(2), 131–154. https://doi.org/10.1080/08985620802176104

Fidrmuc, J., & Fidrmuc, J. (2016). Foreign languages and trade: Evidence from a natural experiment. *Empirical Economics, 50*(1), 31–49. https://doi.org/10.1007/s00181-015-0999-7

Foreman-Peck, J., & Zhou, P. (2015). Firm-level evidence for the language investment effect on SME exporters. *Scottish Journal of Political Economy, 62*(4), 351–377. https://doi.org/10.1111/sjpe.12072

Haddoud, M. Y., Onjewu, A. K. E., Nowiński, W., & Jones, P. (2021). The determinants of SMEs' export entry: A systematic review of the literature. In. *Journal of Business Research, 125*, 262–278. https://doi.org/10.1016/j.jbusres.2020.12.017

Håkansson, H. (Ed.). (1982). *International marketing and purchasing of industrial goods: An interaction approach.* John Wiley & Sons, Ltd.

Hatzigeorgiou, A., & Lodefalk, M. (2016). Migrants' influence on firm-level exports. *Journal of Industry, Competition and Trade, 16*(4), 477–497. https://doi.org/10.1007/s10842-015-0215-7

Hatzigeorgiou, A., & Lodefalk, M. (2021). A literature review of the nexus between migration and internationalization. *Journal of International Trade and Economic Development, 30*(3), 319–340. https://doi.org/10.1080/09638199.2021.1878257

Hernandez, E. (2014). Finding a home away from home: Effects of immigrants on firms' foreign location choice and performance. *Administrative Science Quarterly, 59*(1), 73–108. https://doi.org/10.1177/0001839214523428

Hurmerinta, L., Nummela, N., & Paavilainen-Mäntymäki, E. (2015). Opening and closing doors: The role of language in international opportunity recognition and exploitation. *International Business Review, 24*(6), 1082–1094. https://doi.org/10.1016/j.ibusrev.2015.04.010

Hutchinson, W. K. (2002). Does ease of communication increase trade? Commonality of language and bilateral trade. *Scottish Journal of Political Economy, 49*(5), 544–556. https://doi.org/10.1111/1467-9485.00247

Hymes, D. H. (1972). On communicative competence. In J. B. Pride & J. Holmes (Eds.), *Sociolinguistics. Selected readings* (pp. 269–293). Penguin.

Jentjens, S. (2021). Je ne parle pas français—So what? The impact of language on skilled German migrant women's employment in France. *International Journal of Cross Cultural Management, 21*(1), 71–93. https://doi.org/10.1177/1470595821999073

Johanson, J., & Vahlne, J.-E. (1977). The internationalization process of the firm-a model of knowledge development and increasing foreign market commitments. *Journal of International Business Studies, 8*(1), 23–32. https://doi.org/10.1057/palgrave.jibs.8490676

Johanson, J., & Vahlne, J. E. (2009). The Uppsala internationalization process model revisited: From liability of foreignness to liability of outsidership. *Journal of International Business Studies, 40*(9), 1411–1431. https://doi.org/10.1057/jibs.2009.24

Johanson, J., & Wiedersheim-Paul, F. (1975). The internationalization of the firm — Four SWEDISH cases. *Journal of Management Studies, 12*(3), 305–323. https://doi.org/10.1111/j.1467-6486.1975.tb00514.x

Johnstone, L., Monteiro, M. P., Ferreira, I., Westerlund, J., Aalto, R., & Marttinen, J. (2018). Language ability and entrepreneurship education: Necessary skills for Europe's start-ups? *Journal of International Entrepreneurship, 16*(3), 369–397. https://doi.org/10.1007/s10843-018-0230-y

Kahiya, E. T. (2018). Five decades of research on export barriers: Review and future directions. *International Business Review, 27*(6), 1172–1188. https://doi.org/10.1016/j.ibusrev.2018.04.008

Kane, A. A., & Levina, N. (2017). 'Am I still one of them?': Bicultural immigrant managers navigating social identity threats when spanning global boundaries. *Journal of Management Studies, 54*(4), 540–577. https://doi.org/10.1111/joms.12259

Knowles, D., Mughan, T., & Lloyd-Reason, L. (2006). Foreign language use among decision-makers of successfully internationalised SMEs. Questioning the language-training paradigm. *Journal of Small Business and Enterprise Development, 13*(4), 620–641. https://doi.org/10.1108/14626000610705787

Kubíčková, L., & Peprný, A. (2011). The internationalization of small and medium-sized enterprises in the viticulture. *Agricultural Economics (Czech Republic), 57*(7), 331–339. https://doi.org/10.17221/31/2011-AGRICECON

Lauring, J., & Klitmøller, A. (2017). Inclusive language use in multicultural business organizations: The effect on creativity and performance. *International Journal of Business Communication, 54*(3), 306–324. https://doi.org/10.1177/2329488415572779

Lavric, E., & Bäck, B. (2009). English, French, Spanish, Italian, Portuguese? Code choice and Austrian export. *International Journal of Multilingualism, 6*(1), 37–67. https://doi.org/10.1080/14790710802573039

Leonidou, L. C. (2004). An analysis of the barriers hindering small business export development. *Journal of Small Business Management, 42*(3), 279–302. https://doi.org/10.1111/j.1540-627X.2004.00112.x

Leonidou, L. C., & Katsikeas, C. S. (2010). Integrative assessment of exporting research articles in business journals during the period 1960-2007. *Journal of Business Research, 63*(8), 879–887. https://doi.org/10.1016/j.jbusres.2010.01.005

Leonidou, L. C., Katsikeas, C. S., & Piercy, N. F. (1998). Identifying managerial influences on exporting: Past research and future directions. *Journal of International Marketing, 6*(2), 74–102. https://www.jstor.org/stable/25048728

Light, I., Zhou, M., & Kim, R. (2002). Transnationalism and American exports in an English-speaking world. *International Migration Review, 36*(3), 702–725. https://doi.org/10.1111/j.1747-7379.2002.tb00101.x

Liu, X., Gao, L., Lu, J., & Wei, Y. (2015). The role of highly skilled migrants in the process of inter-firm knowledge transfer across borders. *Journal of World Business, 50*(1), 56–68. https://doi.org/10.1016/j.jwb.2014.01.006

Lücke, M., & Stöhr, T. (2018). Heterogeneous immigrants, exports and foreign direct investment: The role of language skills. *The World Economy, 41*(6), 1529–1548. https://doi.org/10.1111/twec.12598

Marcella, R., & Davies, S. (2004). The use of customer language in international marketing communication in the Scottish food and drink industry. *European Journal of Marketing, 38*(11/12), 1382–1395. https://doi.org/10.1108/03090560410560155

Marschan, R., Welch, D., & Welch, L. (1997). Language: The forgotten factor in multinational management. *European Management Journal, 15*(5), 591–598. https://doi.org/10.1016/S0263-2373(97)00038-8

Melitz, J. (2008). Language and foreign trade. *European Economic Review, 52*(4), 667–699. https://doi.org/10.1016/j.euroecorev.2007.05.002

Melitz, J., & Toubal, F. (2014). Native language, spoken language, translation and trade. *Journal of International Economics, 93*(2), 351–363. https://doi.org/10.1016/j.jinteco.2014.04.004

Moghaddam, K., Rustambekov, E., Weber, T., & Azarpanah, S. (2018). Transnational entrepreneurship, social networks, and institutional distance: Toward a theoretical framework. *New England Journal of Entrepreneurship, 21*(1), 45–64. https://doi.org/10.1108/NEJE-03-2018-0005

Morgan, R. E. (1997). Decision making for export strategy. *Journal of Small Business and Enterprise Development, 4*(2), 73–85. https://doi.org/10.1108/eb020982

Morgan, R. E., & Katsikeas, C. S. (1997). Obstacles to export initiation and expansion. *International Journal of Management Science, 25*(6), 677–690. https://doi.org/10.1016/S0305-0483(97)00035-2

Mughan, T. (1990). 1992 - is "languages for export" enough? *European Business Review, 90*(3), 22–25. https://doi.org/10.1108/EUM0000000001860

Musteen, M., Francis, J., & Datta, D. K. (2010). The influence of international networks on internationalization speed and performance: A study of Czech SMEs. *Journal of World Business, 45*(3), 197–205. https://doi.org/10.1016/j.jwb.2009.12.003

Naudé, P., & Sutton-Brady, C. (2019). Relationships and networks as examined in industrial marketing management. *Industrial Marketing Management, 79*, 27–35. https://doi.org/10.1016/j.indmarman.2019.03.006

Nemkova, E., Souchon, A. L., & Hughes, P. (2012). Export decision-making orientation: An exploratory study. *International Marketing Review, 29*(4), 349–378.

OECD. (1996). *Small businesses, job creation and growth: Facts, obstacles and best practices*. OECD.

Ojala, A. (2009). Internationalization of knowledge-intensive SMEs: The role of network relationships in the entry to a psychically distant market. *International Business Review, 18*(1), 50–59. https://doi.org/10.1016/j.ibusrev.2008.10.002

Pennerstorfer, D. (2016). Export, migration and costs of trade: Evidence from central European firms. *Regional Studies, 50*(5), 848–863. https://doi.org/10.1080/00343404.2014.947565

Piekkari, R., Gaibrois, C., & Johansson, M. (2022). A review of language-sensitive research in international business: A multi-paradigmatic Reading. *Journal of Comparative International Management, 25*(2), 144–174.

Piekkari, R., Welch, D. E., & Welch, L. S. (2014). *Language in international business: The multilingual reality of global business expansion*. Edward Elgar Publishing Ltd..

Rižnar, I., & Rybnicek, R. (2017). Language management strategies in Austrian and Slovenian SMEs. *Managing Global Transitions, 15*(4), 365–378. https://doi.org/10.26493/1854-6935.15.365-378

Safari, A., & Chetty, S. (2019). Multilevel psychic distance and its impact on SME internationalization. *International Business Review, 28*(4), 754–765. https://doi.org/10.1016/j.ibusrev.2019.03.001

Schlegelmilch, B. B., & Crook, J. N. N. (1988). Firm-level determinants of export intensity. *Managerial and Decision Economics, 9*(4), 291–300. https://doi.org/10.1002/mde.4090090408

Schweizer, R. (2013). SMEs and networks: Overcoming the liability of outsidership. *Journal of International Entrepreneurship, 11*(1), 80–103. https://doi.org/10.1007/s10843-012-0097-2

Serra, F., Pointon, J., & Abdou, H. (2012). Factors influencing the propensity to export: A study of UK and Portuguese textile firms. *International Business Review, 21*(2), 210–224. https://doi.org/10.1016/j.ibusrev.2011.02.006

Shirmohammadi, M., Beigi, M., & Stewart, J. (2019). Understanding skilled migrants' employment in the host country: A multidisciplinary review and a conceptual model. *International Journal of Human Resource Management, 30*(1), 96–121. https://doi.org/10.1080/09585192.2018.1511615

Simmonds, K., & Smith, H. (1968). The first export order: A marketing innovation. *European Journal of Marketing, 2*(2), 93–100. https://doi.org/10.1108/EUM0000000005244

Solano, G. (2015). Transnational vs. domestic immigrant entrepreneurs: A comparative literature analysis of the use of personal skills and social networks. *American Journal of Entrepreneurship, 8*(2), 1–20.

Sousa, C. M. P., Martínez-López, F. J., & Coelho, F. (2008). The determinants of export performance: A review of the research in the literature between 1998 and 2005. *International Journal of Management Reviews, 10*(4), 343–374. https://doi.org/10.1111/j.1468-2370.2008.00232.x

Stanley, J., Ingram, D., & Chittick, G. (1990). The relationship between International Trade & Linguistic Competence (report to the Australian advisory council on languages and multicultural education).

Steinhäuser, V. P. S., Paula, F., & de Macedo-Soares, T. D. L. (2020). Internationalization of SMEs : A systematic review of 20 years of research. *Journal of International Entrepreneurship, 19*, 164. https://doi.org/10.1007/s10843-020-00271-7

Suárez-Ortega, S. M., & Álamo-Vera, F. R. (2005). SMES' internationalization: Firms and managerial factors. *International Journal of Entrepreneurial Behaviour and Research, 11*(4), 258–279. https://doi.org/10.1108/13552550510603298

Sui, S., Morgan, H. M., & Baum, M. (2015). Internationalization of immigrant-owned SMEs: The role of language. *Journal of World Business, 50*(4), 804–814. https://doi.org/10.1016/j.jwb.2015.04.002

Swift, J. S. (1991). Foreign language ability and international marketing. *European Journal of Marketing, 25*(12), 36–49. https://doi.org/10.1108/eum0000000000634

Tadesse, B., & White, R. (2017). Immigrants, cultural differences, and trade costs. *International Migration, 55*(1), 51–74. https://doi.org/10.1111/imig.12291

Tenzer, H., Pudelko, M., & Harzing, A. W. (2014). The impact of language barriers on trust formation in multinational teams. *Journal of International Business Studies, 45*(5), 508–535. https://doi.org/10.1057/jibs.2013.64

Tenzer, H., Terjesen, S., & Harzing, A. W. (2017). Language in international business: A review and agenda for future research. *Management International Review, 57*(6), 815–854. https://doi.org/10.1007/s11575-017-0319-x

Turnbull, & Welham, G. F. (1985). The characteristics of European export marketing staff. *European Journal of Marketing, 19*(2), 31–41. https://doi.org/10.1108/EUM0000000004752

Vahlne, J.-E., & Johanson, J. (2013). The Uppsala model on evolution of the multinational business enterprise-from internalization to coordination of networks. *International Marketing Review, 30*(3), 189–210. https://doi.org/10.1108/02651331311321963

Valentino, A., Caroli, M., & Mayrhofer, U. (2018). Establishment modes and network relationships of foreign subsidiaries. *International Business Review, 27*, 1250–1258. https://doi.org/10.1016/j.ibusrev.2018.05.006

Vandermeeren, S. (1999). English as a lingua franca in written corporate communication: Findings from a European survey. In F. Bargiela-Chiappini & C. Nickerson (Eds.), *Writing business: Genres, media and discourses* (pp. 273–291). Pearson.

Vandermeeren, S. (2005). Foreign language needs of business firms. In M. H. Long (Ed.), *Second language needs analysis* (pp. 159–181). Cambridge University Press. https://doi.org/10.1017/cbo9780511667299

Visser, C. (1995). Theory and practice: A defence of small business language strategies. *European Business Journal*, 49–55.

Wei, X., Jiao, Y., & Growe, G. (2019). Language skills and migrant entrepreneurship: Evidence from China. *Small Business Economics, 53*(4), 981–999. https://doi.org/10.1007/s11187-018-0105-6

Welch, L. S., & Luostarinen, R. (1988). Internationalization: Evolution of a concept. *Journal of General Management, 14*(2), 34–55. https://doi.org/10.1177/030630708801400203

Welch, L. S., & Luostarinen, R. K. (1993). Inward-outward connections in internationalization. *Journal of International Marketing, 1*(1), 44–56. https://doi.org/10.1177/1069031x9300100104

Welch, D. E., & Welch, L. S. (2019). Coping with multilingualism: Internationalization and the evolution of language strategy. *Global Strategy Journal, 9*(4), 618–639. https://doi.org/10.1002/gsj.1191

Welch, D. E., Welch, L. S., & Marschan-Piekkari, R. (2001). The persistent impact of language on global operations. *Prometheus, 19*(3), 193–209. https://doi.org/10.1080/08109020110072180

Williams, J. E. M. M., & Chaston, I. (2004). Links between the linguistic ability and international experience of export managers and their export marketing intelligence behaviour. *International Small Business Journal, 22*(5), 463–486. https://doi.org/10.1177/0266242604046296

Yamin, M., & Kurt, Y. (2018). Revisiting the Uppsala internationalization model: Social network theory and overcoming the liability of outsidership. *International Marketing Review, 35*(1), 2–17. https://doi.org/10.1108/IMR-11-2014-0345

6

Dissecting Generations of Migrant Identities within a Diaspora

Audra I. Mockaitis and Lena Zander

Introduction

"Our cultural identities reflect the common historical experiences and shared cultural codes which provide us, as 'one people,' with stable, unchanging and continuous frames of reference and meaning, beneath the shifting divisions and vicissitudes of our actual history" (Hall, 1990: 223). In explaining the culture of a diasporic people, Hall emphasizes the oneness or sameness in a shared experience and shared history. In the context of ethnic diasporas, especially those that have formed through shared trauma (displacement and forced migration from their homelands), sense of identity, belongingness and loyalty in ethnic diaspora communities is especially strong and a shared identity is passed to subsequent ethnic generations through family and community socialization. However, the quote above also emphasizes the strength of these ties as unchanging and stable. Cultural identity in the collective sense is a set of traits that members of the group or community share; these traits include values and attitudes (Adler, 1977). Cultural identity reflects one's belonging

---

A. I. Mockaitis (✉)
Maynooth University, Maynooth, Ireland
e-mail: audra.mockaitis@mu.ie

L. Zander
Uppsala University, Uppsala, Sweden
e-mail: lena.zander@fek.uu.se

to and identification with this group, whose values and worldviews are shared, stable and identifiable over time.

In this chapter, we aim to dissect the cultural values composition of a worldwide group of ethnic Lithuanian migrants. Some of these migrants belong to a worldwide diaspora, while others are more recent migrants from Lithuania. Although these migrants all technically belong to a single culture, migration in itself brings about the need to reconsider, restructure or even rebuild the cultural identity for migrants (Liu, 2015). Migrants' identities can change, to become even stronger representations of their homeland cultures, or become hybridized, depending on numerous contextual and personal factors. Some migrants enter a space "in between" cultures (Bhabha, 1990) forming a hybrid identity; some learn to effectively move between two cultures while keeping each separate. A question emerges about where one's cultural home is once the decision to migrate is made. In addition, how stable are diasporic communities in terms of their cultural values, and where do recent economic migrants fit in to long-established diasporas?

When we speak of national cultures in empirical terms, we render a group of individuals a single country score that we compare to other such scores across societies. Yet, we know that individuals within a culture, even when they identify with that culture, are not uniform. Values are the primary drivers of cultures and are standards by which people form their judgments, opinions, attitudes and behaviors (Rokeach, 1973). Individuals carry their own sets of values, and we tend to compare these sets of values across national culture groups. Past studies (Mockaitis, 2002a, 2002b) have identified Lithuanian national culture as high on uncertainty avoidance, masculinity and medium high on power distance and individualism (Hofstede, 2001). These findings of national values have been applied to comparisons of workplace attitudes across countries, such as leadership (Mockaitis, 2005), cooperation and communication (Moustafa et al., 2009, 2011) and ethical preferences (Ralston et al., 2009).

However, national-level measures of cultural values are rather poor representations of individuals (Steel & Taras, 2010). Recent studies have argued that values at the individual level are better predictors of individuals' attitudes and behaviors with respect to workplace factors across cultures (e.g., Ralston et al., 2014) as they allow for within-society or within-group analyses across countries or cultures (Lenartowicz & Roth, 2001; Fischer et al., 2011) and capture within and across group variability. In this study, we are interested in the personal values of migrant members of a worldwide diaspora. As the subgroups of migrants span multiple generations and periods of migration, a comparison of individual-level values (Sivadas, Bruvold & Nelson, 2008; Yoo et al., 2011) will allow us to answer the following questions: How different are migrant groups that share an ethnicity? Are individuals who decide to emigrate from their home country different from nonemigrants? How similar or different in their cultural values composition are migrants representing different generations, and different emigration waves?

In answering these questions, we compare values within and across age cohorts, emigration waves and ethnic generation. We will explore the cultural values of migrants, who share a common ethnic heritage to examine the stability of their values over generations. It is expected that these within-culture findings will help to form a more accurate picture of current and evolving migrant ethnic identity than societal-level cultural values. Implications of the findings for international business are discussed.

Background

Diaspora Culture

Diaspora is defined as the worldwide dispersal of people with the same national origin (Dufoix, 2008) of an "expatriate minority community" (Safran, 1991), who maintain strong emotional and material links to their homeland (Shuval, 2002). A characteristic that distinguishes diaspora is the attachment that its members have to their previous homeland and culture (Kearney, 1995; Shuval, 2002). Diasporas have a collective identity that is defined by the relationship they have with their homeland (Clifford, 1994). And this sense of attachment to one's homeland through the diaspora community can be transmitted to several generations of (already) non-immigrant diaspora members, even though there may not be an intention (or possibility of) repatriating to the original homeland. In this sense, it is held that adjustment and acculturation to the host environment do not lead to loss of the group's original ethnic identity. Interestingly, although we often equate diasporas with assimilated communities in host cultures, Safran (1991) maintains that diaspora members believe that they will never be fully accepted by their host country, and this contributes to the reason that diaspora communities so strongly maintain their cultures. The collective memory of their homeland helps to kindle the hope of returning to it, and keeps the diasporic community active in maintaining solidarity, ties and the maintenance of the homeland (Safran, 1991). That does not mean that diasporic communities are always strong. They may be characterized as more or less diasporic, as the relationship between them and their home and host countries changes (Clifford, 1994).

Clifford (1994) argues that we need not equate diaspora populations with immigrant groups. The differences between diasporas and immigrant groups lies in the different relationships each has with their homeland. Diasporas are marked by *traumatic* emigration, a collective memory of displacement and loss. Immigrants may also experience feelings of loss or nostalgia, but this is related more to the natural process of acculturation to their new host country. Diasporas experience a paradoxical duality of simultaneous cultural accommodation and resistance to host country cultures and norms. Diasporas maintain a connection to their homeland that is strong enough to resist "normalizing processes of forgetting, assimilating, and distancing" (Clifford, 1994: 310). Diaspora has both positive and negative aspects of their collective consciousness. The negative aspects are formed by memories of trauma, threat, exclusion, discrimination and marginalization. Often these facets are emphasized within the community and the trauma and wounds are "reopened" for decades. The positive aspects relate to a (re)identification with their homeland, the collective sharing in being 'other,' the need to maneuver between the past and the present, suffering (survival) and opportunity, all of which dynamically shape the diaspora culture.

The Lithuanian diaspora has been evolving and transforming over the past century due to various political and economic events adversely affecting the country. Although Lithuania has a vast history of migration, over the last century, relatively more Lithuanians have emigrated than from other European nations (Kumpikaitė-Valiūnienė et al., 2021). The late nineteenth century saw large numbers of Lithuanians move to the USA due to various economic and political factors and establish the first communities, mostly around the coal mining areas of Pennsylvania (Cadzow, 2020). This period was followed by the period between 1918 and 1940, during which economic migrants settled in Canada and South America, with fewer numbers in the USA. The Second World War brought mass exodus, deportations and exile. It was during this period that highly educated members of the intellectual elite fled for fear of deportation, to refugee camps, before finding new homes in the Americas, Australia and Europe. During the Soviet era, there was little movement beyond the Iron Curtain, except within the 15 Soviet republics (Kumpikaitė-Valiūnienė et al., 2021). Emigration was allowed only in exceptional circumstances. After the restoration of Lithuanian independence in 1990, migration increased and has continued to this day. Kumpikaitė-Valiūnienė et al. (2021) have identified several key events during this period that have seen increases in emigration, marked by distinct waves: the post-independence period (1990–2003), EU accession in 2004 and visa-free movement, the economic crisis in 2009, and joining the Eurozone followed by Brexit (2015 to the present).

A key difference between the post-war migrants and post-Soviet and EU-era migrants is that migration was a free choice for the latter. The displaced post-war migrant generation established cultural communities, ethnic schools and organizations to maintain their cultural identities, while balancing and nurturing a simultaneous identification with both the heritage and host country cultures. For the post-war diaspora, homeland attachment is expressed through what Shuval (2002) describes as a selective presentation and recovery of traditions that creates a longing for a time and place far-reaching in history and culture. Belonging to the diaspora community and speaking the language were matters of course for preserving the culture from which people were forcefully uprooted. For more recent economic migrants, diaspora belongingness is more of a pragmatic or instrumental choice that is not seeped in loss and longing. These emigrants of the post-independence period have left mainly in search of better opportunities (Kumpikaitė-Valiūnienė et al., 2021).

Migrant Identities

The different migrant groups are also national subcultures (Smith & Schwartz, 1997), born in different countries but sharing a common national or cultural heritage, some also identifying with the diaspora communities that have evolved over the generations in different countries. We might expect that given the length of time that migrant groups have spent away from their original homeland, they will have experienced different degrees of acculturation to their host countries and have assimilated to varying degrees. Though more generally, as argued by Schiefer (2013), immigrants are less likely, compared to host country nationals, to be influenced by the cultural values of their destination country, as they carry the values of their country of origin, we might expect to see differences according to when people migrated, their birth country and ethnic generation (i.e., whether they identify as first-, second-, third-generation members of the heritage culture).

People also hold different beliefs and exhibit different behaviors in different life stages (Baltes & Baltes, 1990; Mockaitis et al., 2022). Slightly differently from life stages theory, which purports that each major period in one's life represents new developmental challenges and outcomes that continue throughout the life span (Baltes, 1987), generation subculture theory holds that age groups differ in their beliefs and values, and that the values define generation subcultures or cohorts, as values acquired in people's youth remain stable over time. In his socialization hypothesis, Inglehart (1997, 2018) proposed that individuals acquire values that reflect the socioeconomic conditions of their formative years. As different generations are socialized under different historical, social and economic conditions, we would expect that their belief systems would reflect these differences. Inglehart (1997, 2018) proposed that people give priority to their most pressing needs, especially during early adulthood; generations that grew up under times of economic and social stress would reflect survival values (such as materialism, conformity, respect for authority), while generations during times of social and economic prosperity would reflect postmodern values, such as egalitarianism, individualism, tolerance and trust. Where political or economic change is great so too might be the generation effect; this may mean that different generations grow up in essentially different worlds (Mishler & Rose, 2007).

What could be starker than the drastic political and economic change in what was to become the Soviet Union? Lithuania was annexed into the Soviet Union in 1940 and endured Soviet occupation from 1944 to 1990. The first decade (1944–1953) witnessed the reign of terror under Stalin, followed by the Khrushchev-era "thaw" (1953–1964), followed by 20 years (1984–1984) of stagnation under Brezhnev, Gorbachev's *glasnost* and *perestroika* (1985–1990), and Lithuanian independence post-1990. During Soviet times, individuals were taught from birth to live the attitudes, values and beliefs of the authoritarian regime (Mishler & Rose, 2007). Yet older generations were coming of age during the reign of terror. Younger generations would have had a different socialization experience during the *glasnost* period and beyond. In a society with such a turbulent history, we might expect value differences between these younger and older generations. Post-war migrants fled the country as young children with their parents. They will have acquired their values through primary socialization in a different environment than their parents did. Yet also, they will have transmitted their own values to their offspring.

Migrant identities and acculturation. Migrants naturally belong to multiple groups that shape their identities. These identities vary depending on the social context that individuals are in (Naujoks, 2010). Migrant identities have been discussed in terms of being finite (e.g., individuals must divide their identity among groups, where membership to one group reduces identification with another), hybrid or hyphenated (e.g., Lithuanian-American) in which identities are borrowed from the different groups with which one identifies. The strength of these identities and loyalty to different home (or homeland) and host cultures depends on the strength of the groups, but also on the degree of the individuals' and their ethnic group's identity and acculturation, and the individuals' socialization into the group.

Acculturation occurs "when groups of individuals having different cultures come into continuous first-hand contact, with subsequent changes in the original cultural patterns of either or both groups" (Redfield et al., 1936: 149). Berry (1992) suggests that this contact results in changes to one's personal and ethnic identity that verge toward attitudes, preferences and behaviors typical of the host country, depending on the extent of acculturative stress that individuals (and their groups) experience. According to Berry (2005), acculturation and the acculturation strategies that people adopt occur to varying degree depending on an individual's or group's attitudes toward the host culture (including their values) and their attitudes toward their home culture (i.e., the extent to which they maintain their home culture). Individuals and groups can opt to relinquish their cultural identities and adopt that of the new culture (assimilation), maintain some parts of their cultural identity while integrating into the host culture (integration), withdraw from the host culture while maintaining their own culture (separation), or relinquish their own and the host culture (marginalization). Thus, within migrant groups and diasporas, we may see different extents of culture change within individuals, as well as changes to their identity as their identification with their home and host cultures shifts.

The extent to which immigrants have contact with the host culture, as well as the attitudes of the host country toward migrants, determine the extent of the group's acculturation. Chand (2014) has argued that host country policies determine migrants' degree of integration, citing the assimilation policies of the USA compared with a policy of multiculturalism in Canada. In his study of Indian immigrants to both countries, Chand (2014) found that the host country policies influenced migrants' attitudes toward the host country. Indian immigrants in Canada were more likely to feel at home due to its policy of multiculturalism and were more likely to invest in Canada, compared to those in the USA (with an assimilation policy), who felt a greater affinity to their home country and directed more of their investments toward India.

Acculturation also depends on the migrant group. Migrants who voluntarily relocate with a greater emphasis on "pull" factors may assimilate more to the host culture than temporary sojourners (e.g., diplomats, expatriates), refugees or forced migrants, who are pushed out of their home countries and often have little choice of the society in which they settle (Berry, 2006). Long-established diasporas may be well-settled while maintaining a strong sense of identity.

Measuring migrants' values. Cultural values determine how individuals think about their identities (Ting-Toomey, 2005). Several studies to date have been conducted on Lithuanian values at the level of society, with most relying on variants of the Schwartz (2006) instruments of values. The European Social Survey (ESS) included a series of questions from the Portrait Value Questionnaire by Schwartz et al. (2001) at the individual level that were aggregated to country level. One of the questions asked about the importance placed on personal enjoyment. Lithuania ranked 19th out of 23 countries. Another ranked Lithuania 22nd on happiness. With respect to the Schwartz (2006) value dimensions, a study by Ralston et al. (2011) in 50 countries identified Lithuanian values as low on affective autonomy, high on embeddedness, low on mastery and medium low on harmony; its egalitarianism score is similar to that of China, India and Vietnam (35th of 50).

In the World Values Surveys (WVS) by Inglehart et al. (2014), Lithuania scores higher on secular values (22nd of 71 countries), and low on emancipative values (43rd). Mockaitis (2002a, 2002b) measured Lithuania at the country level on Hofstede's dimensions and found a medium high individualism and power distance and high masculinity and uncertainty avoidance. Mockaitis provides a full societal-level cultural portrait of Lithuania in Kumpikaitė-Valiūnienė et al. (2021).

In a large study comparing generations of migrants with nonemigrants from EU and non-EU origins across 24 countries on attitudes toward others (enmity) and Schwartz's personal values, Schiefer (2013) revealed that Lithuania was second only to Ukraine on mastery. Lithuanians were the most hierarchical, and second to Israel on embeddedness. Attitudes of nonemigrant Lithuanians toward others were more like those of non-EU immigrants than of EU-immigrants. These findings may suggest that those emigrating from the country have values that are different from nonemigrants.

As we are comparing individuals in different countries of one national heritage, we explore individual-level group differences in values. Individual values are considered as "part of the self-concept and identity of the person" and "are influenced by individual experience during individual development in a sociocultural context" (Trommsdorff et al., 2004: 160). Individual values are more malleable; they are influenced by people's interactions with others and with one's environment (Trommsdorff et al., 2004). Hofstede's study does not directly replicate to the individual level, and his dimensions cannot be applied in individual-level comparisons (Hofstede, 1980, 2001). A few scholars have conducted studies at the individual-level in Lithuania by applying Schwartz's (2006) values (Ralston et al., 2014; Kumpikaitė-Valiūnienė et al., 2022). Schwartz (2006) argued that values dimensions at the individual and societal levels should appropriately reflect the characteristics of those levels. Fischer et al. (2010) found that values show structural similarity across individual and societal levels. Egri et al. (2012) have applied Schwartz's individual values in comparing respondents across countries, life-stages and gender to compare value orientations within and across societies. Ralston et al. (2014) concluded that individual-level values are far better predictors of people's workplace behaviors than values at the societal level. Individual-level values can be attributed to societal culture, they influence decision-making, behaviors and attitudes (Ralston et al., 2014) and are in turn influenced by demographic characteristics. Thus, individual-level values can be studied with respect to cohort differences among migrants.

We apply the individual-level value dimensions framework developed by Yoo et al. (2011) in assessing whether there are differences in values between migrant groups. Yoo et al. (2011) developed a measure of cultural orientations at the individual level, the Individual Cultural Values Scale (CVSCALE) to enable researchers to avoid linking Hofstede's metric to individual attitudes and behaviors, which has been shown to be unstable at the individual level (e.g., Hoppe, 1990). A focus on individual values will allow us to distinguish among groups of migrants with exposure to different environments, life events and socialization conditions. Specifically, we seek answers as to whether there are significant value differences between migrant groups, whether migrants differ from nonemigrants, and how values differ between more recent migrants and second- and third-generation migrant groups.

Method

Sample and Data Collection Procedure

Data for this study were collected from diaspora members of Lithuanian heritage worldwide. Participants were contacted via community organizations, chambers of commerce, and publications in Lithuanian language media (including newspapers, magazines, newsletters and social media). Participants chose whether to respond to the questionnaire in English or Lithuanian. Translation and backtranslation procedures followed recommendations by Brislin (1970). Items were initially translated from English by an English/Lithuanian bilingual native Lithuanian speaker. The Lithuanian version was reviewed by a second English/Lithuanian bilingual native Lithuanian speaker to check for clarity and any awkward or confusing wording. Items were then backtranslated by a third English/Lithuanian bilingual native Lithuanian speaker. The original English version was compared to the backtranslated version, inconsistencies were discussed among the team of translators, and a final Lithuanian version was adopted based on consensus.

In all, 1538 responses were received; incomplete questionnaires were removed, leaving 1110 usable questionnaires. Nonresponse bias was checked by conducting T-tests to compare respondents of completed surveys to those who began the survey but did not finish. Groups were compared on gender, citizenship, and place of birth (Lithuania, other). No significant differences between groups were found on any of the variables apart from marital status, where the mean was slightly higher for the responding group. Given that this mean difference was only marginally significant ($T = -2.016$, $p = 0.05$), we may be reasonably confident that nonresponse bias was not an issue in our data.

The final sample was skewed on gender, with 75.5% female ($N = 838$). The mean age was 39.22 years (SD 13.59, min 18, max 84). Most of the respondents were married (73.2%) and Lithuanian-born (74.1%). The remaining respondents represented 16 birth countries, with the most born in the United States ($N = 165$), followed by Canada ($N = 30$) and Australia ($N = 28$). These individuals represented first- (11.9%), second- (4.1%) and third- (9.7%) generation born migrants of Lithuanian descent.[1] Most non-Lithuanian-born respondents indicated that they live in their birth country, and 65.1% of all respondents indicated that they live outside of their birth country. Most of the respondents (45%) emigrated in the last 18 years (post-2004). The post-Soviet era (1991–2003) saw 15.9% of our sample emigrate. A small percentage (1.8%) migrated during the Soviet era (1960–1990),[2] and 2.5% during the post-war period (1942–1958). Finally, respondents were highly educated, with 38.2% having a university degree, and 39.8% a master's degree or higher.[3]

Measures

We compared the values of migrant groups by emigration wave, native-born status and age cohorts. There are generally four major emigration waves represented by the respondents in this study: (1) 2004 to current (EU era), (2) 1991–2003 (post-Soviet era), (3) 1960–1990 (Soviet era), and (4) 1942–1958 (post-war era). Age groups were represented by birth cohorts in decades (up to 1949, 1950–1959, 1960–1969, 1970–1979, 1980–1989 and 1990–2000). Lithuanian-born migrants (LBMs) ($N = 657$) include only those born in

Lithuania who emigrated in emigration wave 3 or later, that is, it does not include post-war displaced person emigrants. This is because it is fair to assume that these individuals, despite being born in Lithuania, emigrated at a young age with their own parents. Foreign-born Lithuanians (FBLs) (N = 288) include post-war emigrants. There were also 165 nonemigrant nationals. In calculating differences in mean scores between groups of migrants, we controlled for gender (0 = female, 1 = male) and level of education (1 = unfinished secondary school, 6 = graduate degree).

Individual-level values were measured using the CVSCALE by Yoo et al. (2011), a scale developed to measure values at the individual level with similar labels to Hofstede's (1980) societal-level cultural dimensions. Items for the scale were drawn from individual-level studies such as Bochner and Hesketh (1994), Triandis et al. (1993) and others. A pool of 230 original items was reduced to 26 items on 5 dimensions and validated in cross-cultural samples (see Yoo et al., 2011). In our sample, the dimensions were tested across two groups of Lithuanian-born nationals (LBN) and foreign-born Lithuanian (FBL) respondents. Cronbach alphas[4] for the five individual-level values dimensions were as follows: Power distance α_{LBN} = 0.62, α_{FBL} = 0.70; Collectivism α_{LBN} = 0.79, α_{FBL} = 0.76; Uncertainty avoidance α_{LBN} = 0.82, α_{FBL} = 0.83; Masculinity α_{LBN} = 0.71, α_{FBL} = 0.78; Long-term orientation α_{LBN} = 0.78, α_{FBL} = 0.82. We examined the dimensionality of the CVSCALE and whether its components are invariant across the two groups of interest. A description of the procedure follows.

Factor Structure of the Individual-Level Values

Given that migrants are likely to have different value sets from home country nationals that are influenced by different environmental and situational factors (Kumpikaitė-Valiūnienė et al., 2021), we first assess whether the components of the CVSCALE model are invariant across groups, that is, whether the five-factor cultural dimensions model is equivalent for our sample of LBNs and FBLs. We measure whether the items comprising the cultural dimensions operate equivalently across the two groups; we also test the dimensionality of the individual-level cultural value model for equivalence. We test for measurement invariance of both the item scores and the underlying latent structure across the two groups. In our preliminary single-group analysis, we deleted one problematic item and proposed a model with 25 items as the baseline model for each group, and 2 error covariances specified. If the model fits the data well for both groups, it will become the hypothesized model used for testing for equivalence across the two groups, or it will be modified accordingly. The model fits for LBNs ($X^2_{(262)}$ = 604.439; CFI = 0.935; RMSEA = 0.040) and for FBLs ($X^2_{(262)}$ = 421.401; CFI = 0.928; RMSEA = 0.046) were both excellent.

We next estimated the same parameters in the baseline model for each group separately within the framework of a multigroup model, or the configural model. We are interested in the extent to which the configural model fits the multigroup data (whether the same configuration holds across the groups) (Byrne, 2016). We find that configural invariance is achieved, with excellent model fit measures ($X^2_{(528)}$ = 1441.0; CFI = 0.924; RMSEA = 0.031). We thus proceed with the 25-item model in our group comparisons.

Analysis and Results

Comparing Values of Migrants and Nonemigrants

We ran a series of UNIANOVAs with the GLM procedure in SPSS on each cultural value dimension to plot marginal means for each migrant group and to assess any group differences. We plotted the results in Fig. 6.1, with age cohorts represented by decade of birth on the X-axis and cultural dimensions scores on the Y-axis. Significant differences were found on a few of the cultural dimensions between migrant groups. For example, both nonemigrants (mean difference 0.518, $p < 0.05$) and Lithuanian-born migrants (LBMs) (mean difference 0.450, $p < 0.001$) scored significantly higher on masculinity than FBLs. LBMs scored higher on power distance than FBLs (mean difference 0.302, $p < 0.001$). No significant differences were found between migrant groups on collectivism, uncertainty avoidance, long-term orientation.

We can see, generally, a similar pattern in value scores between the migrant groups across the age cohorts. For instance, a downward trend is observed on power distance from older to younger generations. A similar pattern occurs in masculinity and uncertainty avoidance, whereas collectivism slightly increases in the younger generations. There are some differences between age groups, however. In power distance, the age effect is strongest between the older (1950s) (mean difference 0.611, $p < 0.001$), 1960s (mean difference 0.615, $p < 0.001$), 1970s (mean difference 0.349, $p < 0.001$) and youngest (1990s) cohorts. Collectivism drops significantly between the 1960s and 1970s cohorts (mean difference 0.26, $p < 0.05$). The greatest differences on masculinity, driven by higher masculinity for both Lithuanian-born groups, is

6 Dissecting Generations of Migrant Identities within a Diaspora 131

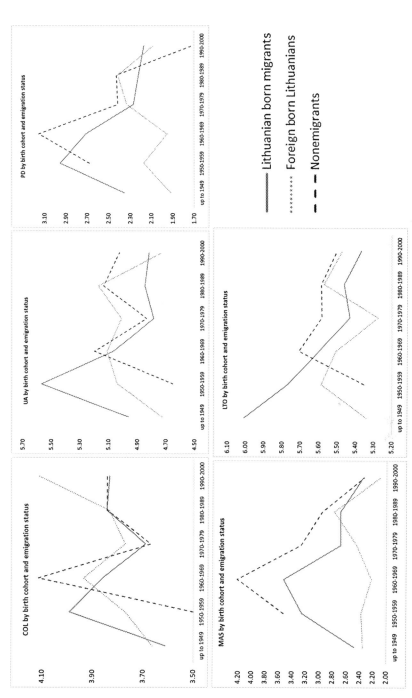

Fig. 6.1 Cultural values of migrants and home country nationals

between the 1960s cohort and all others, except those born in the 1950s, for example, pre-1950 (mean difference 1.34, $p < 0.01$), 1970s (mean difference 0.521, $p < 0.01$), 1980s (mean difference 0.517, $p < 0.01$), and 1990s (mean difference 1.058, $p < 0.001$). No significant differences were found between age cohorts on uncertainty avoidance and long-term orientation, which both remain above average across all age cohorts.

Comparing Values by Emigration Waves

We also compared LBMs to FBLs with regards to when emigration took place. Foreign-born first-generation respondents indicated the year in which their parents immigrated to their birth country. We controlled for education, age and gender. In Fig. 6.2, we can see some trends in values over migration waves. Collectivism levels were slightly higher during the post-war and Soviet eras than the post-Soviet and EU eras, though not significantly so. There were also no differences between migrant groups. Similarly, in uncertainty avoidance values, there were no significant differences between groups, with relatively stable levels in different migrant groups and migration waves. Long-term orientation scores were likewise relatively high across migrant groups and waves with no significant differences.

With regard to power distance, there is a significant difference between migrants in the post-war era and both the post-Soviet (mean difference 0.721, $p = 0.01$) and EU eras (mean difference 0.487, $p < 0.05$). Overall, power distance has increased across emigration waves, but especially for LBMs, who exhibited a higher power distance in the Soviet-era migration waves and beyond. Differences in masculinity are driven by LBMs. The graph depicts a spike in masculinity in Soviet-era migrants, and a slight decrease no significant differences between mean scores in later waves. There are significant differences in overall scores between the post-war era and the post-Soviet era (mean difference 0.795, $p < 0.05$) and the EU era (mean difference 1.314, $p < 0.001$).

Comparing Values by Migrant Ethnic Generations

We also compared values across ethnic generations, that is, first-, second- and third-generation foreign-born respondents of Lithuanian descent, and Lithuanian-born respondents. Lithuanian-born respondents scored significantly higher on power distance than first (mean difference 0.318, $p = 0.001$)

6 Dissecting Generations of Migrant Identities within a Diaspora

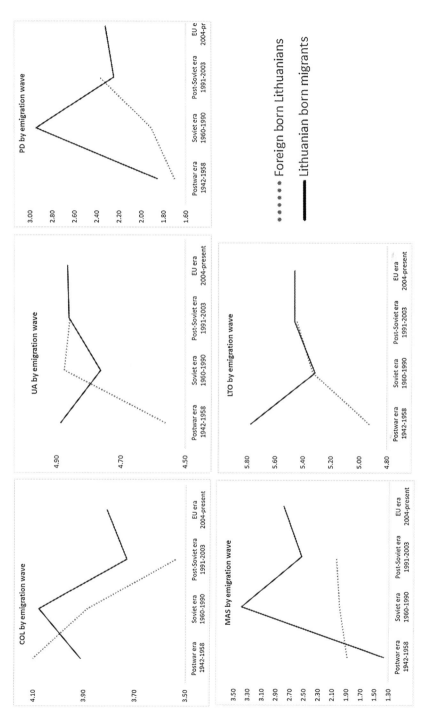

Fig. 6.2 Cultural values of migrants by emigration wave

Table 6.1 Effect of group differences in individual values

Variables	COL	UA	PD	MAS	LTO
	F	F	F	F	F
Migrant group	0.39	0.09	6.60***	8.32***	1.49
Generation cohort	1.33	1.31	7.82***	10.11***	0.73
Emigration wave	0.58	0.78	2.14	2.67*	0.94
Ethnic generation	0.76	1.32	6.22***	12.12***	0.47

* $p < 0.05$, ** $p < 0.01$, *** $p < 0.001$

and third-generation (mean difference 0.245, $p = 0.01$) respondents, while second-generation (born to one Lithuanian-born parent) respondents did not significantly differ from Lithuanian born but scored higher than first ($p < 0.01$) and third-generation ($p < 0.05$) respondents. Lithuanian-born respondents scored significantly higher on masculinity than first- (mean difference 0.704, $p < 0.001$) and third- (mean difference 0.518, $p < 0.001$) generation respondents, and there was a significant difference between higher-scoring second (mean difference 0.532, $p < 0.05$) and first-generation respondents, and no differences between second-generation and Lithuanian-born respondents. There were no significant differences between ethnic generation groups on uncertainty avoidance, collectivism and long-term orientation. Table 6.1 presents the effect sizes of group differences in individual values.

Discussion

In this preliminary study of migrant diaspora values, we set out to examine differences in groups of migrants that share a cultural heritage. We applied the individual-level value framework developed by Yoo et al. (2011), and we compared individual-level values across generation cohorts, emigration waves and ethnic generations. Some of our findings are consistent with prior research on generation effects. But they also lend evidence both to the stability of values over time, as well as to differences between migrants and nonmigrants.

Trommsdorff et al. (2004) studied the transmission of values through three generations within families to address the question of cultural stability and change; individualism values increased with subsequent generations. Egri and Ralston (2004) likewise found that personal values changed over generations in a comparison of US and Chinese values. Younger generations of Chinese exhibited more modern values, consistent with Chinese political and economic reforms. Our findings point to a decrease in power distance and masculinity values across generation cohorts, with younger generations exhibiting more egalitarian values. A change in these values was also consistent with political shifts in Lithuanian society as it moved from the Soviet to post-Soviet and EU eras. Specifically, individuals who migrated during the Soviet era exhibited higher levels of power distance and masculinity, reflecting the cultural context of the times. Higher levels of power distance among respondents born during the post-Soviet era abroad may suggest that these values were transmitted to them by their parents, who were of the Soviet political generation. Also, the observation that these values are held by individuals who emigrated from their home country between 20 and 60 years ago, reflects the enduring nature of personal values. Our comparison of ethnic generation cohorts revealed that LBMs exhibited higher levels of power distance and masculinity than second- and third-generation respondents, suggesting that subsequent generations born abroad are less like native Lithuanians.

Do individuals, who share a cultural heritage, share more similarities than differences in individual-level cultural values? Our preliminary findings based on one framework of individual-level cultural values might so suggest. We observed the greatest differences on the two value orientations discussed above. Yet, in explaining cultural value differences, it appears to matter less *when* migration occurred and more *that* it has occurred, lending support to what Kumpikaitė-Valiūnienė et al. (2021) suggest as a phenomenon of migration culture in Lithuania.

Limitations and Future Research Directions

In our view, these findings expose the complexity of diaspora identity. The migrant groups in our study do not share the collective memory that defines diaspora. How do the similarities and differences identified in migrants' cultural values inform their identification with their heritage culture, diaspora identity, and host country cultures? Ward (2008) has suggested that more work still needs to be done generally on examining the processes by which groups and individuals integrate into a new culture. What elements of cultural identity are retained or merged or changed and how does this change take place over time? How do individuals manage identity conflict? How strong is cultural and ethnic identity within diaspora communities? How are these identities maintained and how do they change over medium-term and long-term group acculturation processes (Ward, 2008)? Importantly, given that diaspora communities are long-established across ethnic generations, how do newcomers to these communities integrate into them, and what are the characteristics that determine whether an individual joins a diaspora community or chooses to integrate into the mainstream host country culture?

Berry's (1980) theory of acculturation asserts that an individual's degree of acculturation depends on the cultural distance between home and host countries. That is, individuals, whose values are very different from those of the host country will find it more difficult (or be less willing) to adopt its values and norms. However, other explanations, such as questions about how immigrants are treated by host countries and organizations, whether host country institutions promote assimilation or not (marginalization), the extent that migrants rely on members from their ethnic communities, personal characteristics of the migrants (such as their economic background, employment status, linguistic abilities), must be considered in the study of migrant identities and are future steps in providing a more detailed picture of diaspora values.

A limitation in this study is that we have not examined how individual values can shape people's personal experiences and identities depending on the above factors. In addition, first-, second-, and third-generation migrants are more likely to be assimilated, speak the language of their country of birth and perhaps do not speak Lithuanian as well if at all, whereas new immigrants have a different experience altogether. They may not speak the language of the host country, may rely on compatriots, and may have different levels of acculturation depending on whether they are skilled migrants, their language abilities, and other distinguishing characteristics that would place them into different groups that shape their experiences and identities. In this study, we also did not account for host country. Comparing individuals in narrower groups, such as destination countries of regions could reveal interesting and rich findings.

With the large exodus of migrants in the modern era due to the opening of societies (in the 1990s) and the removal of barriers for migration (2000s), we may revisit the concept of diaspora to assess whether and how we may speak of collective identity. Although collective identities are ever changing, and individuals' experiences within diasporas are determined by various demographic characteristics, diasporas as traditionally defined, perhaps have more in common than the masses of economic migrants of late. In the case of countries such as Ukraine, we see a new diaspora being formed of refugees again fleeing Russian invasion; the extent to which the shared memory and collective identity of this diaspora will differ from that of the old post-war diaspora is of interest.

Finally, for international business research, when we speak of national culture, we may question whether and how much the concept bears relevance in this new era of the migrant. We have shown that behind a national average score, we see distinctions that are not considered, among subgroups with different migration histories and circumstances, whose values formed during vastly different epochs of terror, scarcity and prosperity, who fled or voluntarily migrated to countries all around the world, and whose values, for reasons unknown, differ more from the values of home country nonemigrants than from one another. Can we be comfortable as scholars in amalgamating these differences to a single score that we call 'culture'? We urge IB scholars to delve beyond the numbers to reveal the links between the many layers of identity within the many layers of culture. Future studies of migration in international business could consider the 'dissection' of these complexities in developing new frameworks of culture and identity.

Notes

1. First generation was defined as individuals born outside of Lithuania to both Lithuanian-born parents. Second generation are individuals whose either one parent was Lithuanian-born. Third-generation individuals were born to both foreign-born parents of Lithuanian descent.
2. This percentage is unsurprisingly low, given the almost zero migration policy during this era. Movement of people was limited to within the Soviet bloc.
3. Rates of tertiary education completion are traditionally higher in Lithuania than the OECD average (OECD, 2019).
4. The Cronbach's alphas were calculated after establishing the final factor structure.

References

Adler, P. S. (1977). Beyond cultural identity: Reflections on cultural and multicultural man. In R. Brislin (Ed.), *Culture learning: Concepts, application and research* (pp. 24–41). University of Hawaii Press.

Baltes, P. B. (1987). Theoretical propositions of lifespan developmental psychology: On the dynamics between growth and decline. *Developmental Psychology, 23*, 611–626.

Baltes, P. B., & Baltes, M. M. (1990). In P. B. Baltes & M. M. Baltes (Eds.), *Successful aging: Perspectives from the behavioral sciences*. Cambridge University Press.

Berry, J. W. (1980). Acculturation as varieties of adaptation. In A. M. Padilla (Ed.), *Acculturation: Theory, models and some new findings*. Westview.

Berry, J. W. (1992). Acculturation and adaptation in a new society. *International Migration, 30*(1), 69–85.

Berry, J. W. (2005). Acculturation: Living successfully in two cultures. *International Journal of Intercultural Relations, 29*, 697–712.

Berry, J. W. (2006). Context of acculturation. In D. L. Sam & J. W. Berry (Eds.), *The Cambridge handbook of acculturation psychology* (pp. 27–42). Cambridge University Press.

Bhabha, H. K. (1990). The third space. Interview with Homi Bhabha. In J. Rutherford (Ed.), *Identity: Community, culture, difference*. Lawrence and Wishart.

Bochner, S., & Hesketh, B. (1994). Power distance, individualism/collectivism, and job-related attitudes in a culturally diverse work group. *Journal of Cross-Cultural Psychology, 25*(2), 253–257.

Brislin, R. W. (1970). Back-translation for cross-cultural research. *Journal of Cross-Cultural Psychology, 1*(3), 185–216.

Byrne, B. M. (2016). *Structural equation modeling with AMOS*. Routledge.

Cadzow, J. (2020). *Lithuanian Americans and their communities of Cleveland. Cleveland Ethnic Heritage Studies*. Cleveland State University.

Chand, M. (2014). Diaspora identity, acculturation policy and FDI: The Indian diaspora in Canada and the United States. *Asian Business & Management, 13*(4), 283–308.

Clifford, J. (1994). Diasporas. *Cultural Anthropology, 9*(3), 302–338.

Dufoix, S. (2008). *Diasporas*. University of California Press.

Egri, C. P., Khilji, S. E., Ralston, D. A., Palmer, I., Girson, I., Milton, L., Richards, M., Ramburuth, P., & Mockaitis, A. I. (2012). Do Anglo countries still form a values cluster? Evidence of the complexity of value change. *Journal of World Business, 47*, 267–276.

Egri, C., & Ralston, D. A. (2004). Generation cohorts and personal values: A comparison of China and the United States. *Organization Science, 15*(2), 210–220.

Fischer, R., Milfont, T. L., & Gouveia, V. V. (2011). Does social context affect value structures? Testing the within-country stability of value structures with a functional theory of values. *Journal of Cross-Cultural Psychology, 42*, 253–270.

Fischer, R., Vauclair, C. M., Fontaine, J. R. J., & Schwartz, S. H. (2010). Are individual-level and country-level value structures different? Testing Hofstede's legacy with the Schwartz value survey. *Journal of Cross-Cultural Psychology, 41*, 135–151.

Hall, S. (1990). Cultural identity and diaspora. In J. Rutherford (Ed.), *Identity: Community, culture, difference*. Lawrence & Wishart.

Hofstede, G. (1980). Culture's Consequences. In *International differences in work-related values*. Sage.

Hofstede, G. (2001). *Culture's consequences: Comparing values, behaviors, institutions and organizations across nations*. Sage.

Hoppe, M. H. (1990). *A comprehensive study of country elites: International differences in work-related values and learning and their implications for management*. Unpublished PhD diss., University of North Carolina at Chapel Hill.

Inglehart, R. (1997). *Modernization and Postmodernization: Cultural, economic, and political change in 43 societies*. Princeton University Press.

Inglehart, R. (2018). *Cultural evolution: People's motivations are changing, and reshaping the world*. Cambridge University Press.

Inglehart, R., Haerpfer, C., Moreno, A., Welzel, C., Kizilova, K., Diez-Medrano, J., Lagos, M., Norris, P., Ponarin, E., & Puranen, B., et al. (eds.) (2014). World values survey: Round three - country-pooled Datafile version: www.worldvaluessurvey.org/ WVSDocumentationWV3.jsp. Madrid: JD Systems Institute.

Kearney, M. (1995). The local and the global: The anthropology of globalization and transnationalism. *Annual Review of Anthropology, 24*, 547–565.

Kumpikaitė-Valiūnienė, V., Duobienė, J., & Pinnington, A.H. (2022). Values in different career paths: Emigrants, returnees and immobile locals. Academy of Management Best Paper Proceedings.

Kumpikaitė-Valiūnienė, V., Liubinienė, V., Žičkutė, I., Duobienė, J., Mockaitis, A. I., & Mihi-Ramirez, A. (2021). *Migration culture: A comparative perspective*. Springer.

Lenartowicz, T., & Roth, K. (2001). Does subculture within a country matter? A cross-cultural study of motivational domains and business performance in Brazil. *Journal of International Business Studies, 32*(2), 305–326.

Liu, S. (2015). *Identity, hybridity and cultural home: Chinese migrants and diaspora in multicultural societies*. Rowman & Littlefield.

Mishler, W., & Rose, R. (2007). Generation, age, and time: The dynamics of political learning during Russia's transformation. *American Journal of Political Science, 51*(4), 822–834.

Mockaitis, A. I. (2002a). *The influence of national cultural values on management attitudes: A comparative study across three countries*. Unpublished PhD dissertation. Vilnius University.

Mockaitis, A. I. (2002b). The national cultural dimensions of Lithuania. *Ekonomika, 59*(1), 67–77.

Mockaitis, A. I. (2005). A cross-cultural study of leadership attitudes in three Baltic Sea region countries. *International Journal of Leadership Studies, 1*(1), 44–63.

Mockaitis, A. I., Butler, C. L., & Ojo, A. (2022). COVID-19 pandemic disruptions to working lives: A multilevel examination of impacts across career stages. *Journal of Vocational Behavior, 138*, 103768. https://doi.org/10.1016/j.jvb.2022.103768. Advance online publication.

Moustafa, K. L., et al. (2009). Culture and communication: Cultural variations and media effectiveness. *Administration and Society, 41*(7), 850–877.

Moustafa, K. L., et al. (2011). Examining media effectiveness across cultures and national borders: A review and multilevel framework. *International Journal of Cross Cultural Management, 11*(1), 83–103.

Naujoks, D. (2010). Diasporic identity. Reflections on transnational belonging. *Diaspora Studies, 3*(1), 1–21.

OECD. (2019). *Country note: Education at a glance*. Accessed February 2, 2022, from https://www.oecd.org/education/education-at-a-glance/EAG2019_CN_LTU.pdf.

Ralston, D. A., Egri, C. P., Mockaitis, A. I., et al. (2011). A twenty-first century assessment of values across the global workforce. *Journal of Business Ethics, 104*, 1–31.

Ralston, D. A., et al. (2009). Ethical preferences for influencing superiors: A 41-society study. *Journal of International Business Studies, 40*(6), 1022–1045.

Ralston, D. A., et al. (2014). Societal-level versus individual-level predictions of ethical behavior: A 48-society study of collectivism and individualism. *Journal of Business Ethics, 122*, 283–306.

Redfield, R., Linton, E., & Herskovits, M. J. (1936). Memorandum for the study of acculturation. *American Anthropologist, 38*(1), 149–152.

Rokeach, M. (1973). *The nature of human values*. Free Press.

Safran, W. (1991). Diasporas in modern societies: Myths of homeland and return. *Diaspora, 1*(1), 83–99.

Schiefer, D. (2013). Cultural values and group-related attitudes: A comparison of individuals with and without migration background across 24 countries. *Journal of Cross-Cultural Psychology, 44*(2), 245–262.

Schwartz, S. H. (2006). A theory of cultural value orientations: Explication and applications. *Comparative Sociology, 5*(2–3), 137–182.

Schwartz, S. H., Melech, G., Lehmann, A., Burgess, S., & Harris, M. (2001). Extending the cross-cultural validity of the theory of basic human values with a different method of measurement. *Journal of Cross-Cultural Psychology, 32*, 519–542.

Shuval, J. T. (2002). Diaspora migration: Definitional ambiguities and a theoretical paradigm. *International Migration, 38*(5), 41–56.

Sivadas, E., Bruvold, N. T., & Nelson, M. R. (2008). A reduced version of the horizontal and vertical individualism and collectivism scale: A four-country assessment. *Journal of Business Research, 61*(3), 201–210.

Smith, P., & Schwartz, S. (1997). Values. In C. Kagitcibasi & M. H. Segall (Eds.), *Handbook of cross-cultural psychology*. Allyn and Bacon.

Steel, P., & Taras, V. (2010). Culture as a consequence: A multi-level multivariate meta-analysis of the effects of individual and country characteristics on work-related cultural values. *Journal of International Management, 16*, 211–233.

Ting-Toomey, S. (2005). Identity negotiation theory: Crossing cultural boundaries. In W. B. Gudykunst (Ed.), *Theorizing about intercultural communication*. Sage.

Triandis, H. C., Betancourt, H., Iwao, S., Leung, K., Salazar, J. M., Setiadi, B., Sinha, J. B. P., Touzard, H., & Zaleski, Z. (1993). An etic-emic analysis of individualism and collectivism. *Journal of Cross-Cultural Psychology, 24*(3), 366–383.

Trommsdorff, G., Mayer, B., & Albert, I. (2004). Dimensions of culture in intra-cultural comparisons: Individualism/collectivism and family-related values in three generations. In H. Vinken, J. Soeters, & P. Ester (Eds.), *Comparing cultures: Dimensions of culture in a comparative perspective* (pp. 157–184). Brill.

Ward, C. (2008). Thinking outside the Berry boxes: New perspectives on identity, acculturation and intercultural relations. *International Journal of Intercultural Relations, 32*(2), 105–114.

Yoo, B., Donthu, N., & Lenartowicz, T. (2011). Measuring Hofstede's five dimensions of cultural values at the individual level: Development and validation of CVSCALE. *Journal of International Consumer Marketing, 23*(3/4), 193–210.

7

Dual Perspectives: Immigrants' Comparisons of Host and Home Countries' Management of the COVID-19 Pandemic Emphasize the Salience of Cultural Differences

Ariane Froidevaux and David J. G. Dwertmann

International migration has been on the rise. Between 2000 and 2015, the number of immigrants worldwide has increased from 173 million to 244 million (United Nations, 2015). The U.S. is the country with the largest population of migrants (United Nations, 2019) and has historically been an immigrant country. The importance of migrants for society and business is apparent in many ways. For example, immigrants founded about 25% of all U.S. companies (Pekkala Kerr & Kerr, 2020) and about 40% of Fortune 500 companies were founded by first- or second-generation immigrants (Partnership for a New American Economy, 2011). Immigrants also represent

---

Both authors have contributed equally to this work. Correspondence concerning this chapter should be addressed to Ariane Froidevaux, University of Texas at Arlington, USA. Contact: ariane.froidevaux@uta.edu

A. Froidevaux (✉)
University of Texas at Arlington College of Business, Arlington, TX, USA
e-mail: ariane.froidevaux@uta.edu

D. J. G. Dwertmann
Rutgers University School of Business-Camden, Camden, NJ, USA
e-mail: david.dwertmann@rutgers.edu

a critical source of talent for U.S. organizations (Harrison et al., 2019). In 2019, 17.4% (28.4 million) of the U.S. labor force was comprised of foreign-born individuals (BLS, 2020).

The COVID-19 pandemic emerged in the U.S. in early 2020 and has changed society and business practices in many ways. The U.S. closed its borders and restricted travel from many parts of the world from March 2020 onward. In November 2021, borders were finally opened for travel from the European Union but shortly after, restrictions were added for South African countries to slow the spread of the emerging Omicron variant. As of spring 2023, health restrictions continue to limit international travel, with individuals who are not citizens or permanent residents of the U.S. needing to show proof of their full vaccination status to be allowed to enter the country. Such travel restrictions may partly explain that, according to the U.S. Census Bureau, net international migration added only 247,000 to the nation's population between 2020 and 2021, compared to the 477,000 added between 2019 and 2020, and to the 1,049,000 between 2015 and 2016 before the election of President Trump followed by the adoption of more restrictive immigration laws (Schachter et al., 2021). With the resurgence of the COVID-19 pandemic in China as of spring 2023, uncertainty remains. Still, lessons for management scholarship can be already learned from the first surge of the pandemic in 2020. At that time, countries took very different routes in terms of pandemic management (Claeson & Hanson, 2020). Even within the U.S., states varied greatly in how they approached COVID-19, with Republican-governed states imposing relatively fewer or no restrictions compared to states governed by Democrats. In parallel, organizations implemented different measures with many moving toward increasing remote work arrangements (Hickman & Saad, 2020; Kniffin et al., 2021).

The sensemaking perspective (Weick, 1995) has been recently identified as a key theoretical approach to study immigrants' experiences, providing "a research lens to examine how immigrants make sense of their new environment" (Farashah & Blomquist, 2021, p. 2050) by learning a new culture while discounting their past foreign experiences. Prior research has applied a sensemaking framework to understand the shock of migrating to another country and adapting to differences (Fernando & Patriotta, 2020). The COVID-19 pandemic provided a unique context to explore how such an additional shock or incisive event (Vaziri et al., 2020) may prompt novel sensemaking in immigrants as they compare pandemic management strategies between both their host and home countries. While adjustments to a COVID-19 world have been noticeable for everyone, immigrants are particularly likely to notice differences in how the pandemic is managed. This is because they have another frame of reference—their home country (the same could apply to multiculturals; Hong et al., 2000; Martin & Shao, 2016; Vora et al., 2019). Being exposed to the way in which the U.S. managed the COVID-19 pandemic and to the way in which their respective home countries handled it, likely makes cultural differences more salient as such management is presumably in line with cultural norms. This heightened salience could influence feelings of otherness and alienation and ultimately influence immigration outcomes. Hence, the pandemic provided a unique context to further explore immigrants' engagement in sensemaking (Farashah & Blomquist, 2021), enabling us to highlight the retrospective nature of sensemaking in interpreting their present situation in the U.S. based on their past experiences in their home country. Put differently, the pandemic context provided a unique opportunity for immigrants to compare their host and home countries' culture via respective pandemic management strategies, adding a frame of reference for immigrants to interpret their immigration experience in their host country. Accordingly, in this chapter we specifically focus on the initial surge of the COVID-19 pandemic in 2020 and its impact on immigrants' sensemaking experiences.

Considering the importance of migrants for their host countries and organizations worldwide, it is not surprising that scholars have identified migration as a significant challenge for societies, to which research in management should contribute (George et al., 2016). The pandemic context provides a unique opportunity that allows us to analyze the role of cultural differences for immigrant employees' experiences and, thus, help address the significant neglect of the topic of migration in management research (Bell et al., 2010; Dwertmann & Kunze, 2021; Jonsen et al., 2011). Among the limited findings, cultural differences have been associated with greater conflict and difficulties to collaborate between immigrants and host country nationals at work (Castaneda et al., 2013). With this manuscript, we further contribute to expanding management research on migrants with a qualitative study, an approach that has been underutilized in migration studies (Doz, 2011). We offer an analysis of qualitative interview data from 25 immigrants who legally entered the U.S. to explore if and to what extent different reactions to the COVID-19 pandemic emphasized cultural differences between host (i.e., U.S.) and respective home countries. By doing so, we address calls for "future research [to] consider how employees' and organizations' responses to COVID-19" might have been affected by their "sociocultural differences (e.g., in collectivism)" and values (Kniffin et al., 2021, p. 71).

Research Questions

During the first surge of the pandemic in 2020, countries took very different approaches to managing COVID-19. On the one end of the spectrum, countries like China, Italy, Austria, and Spain took restrictive measures that included curfews, lockdowns, strict mask mandates, and strict vaccine mandates. On the other end of the spectrum, countries like Sweden embarked on a herd immunity approach and imposed almost no restrictions (Bjorklund & Ewing, 2020). Even within countries, individual states and different regions used different approaches and citizens accepted and followed them to varying degrees. Such differences were arguably driven by political and health considerations on the one hand, and culture and accepted norms on the other hand.

According to Hofstede (Hofstede, 2011, p. 3) "culture is the collective programming of the mind that distinguishes the members of one group or category of people from others." It influences the way people interpret the world and what behaviors they expect and accept. We argue that immigrants in our sample are likely to make specific sense of their comparison between the approach the U.S. took, and the way in which Americans reacted to this approach, to the way that their home countries handled the pandemic and citizens reacted. This should result in an assessment of the quality of the approaches and the varying approaches and reactions likely made cultural differences (Hofstede, 2011) between the U.S. and the respective home countries more salient (Guan et al., 2020). Because of this, we investigate the question *to what extent did different approaches to managing COVID-19 highlight cultural differences between the U.S. and home countries?* Furthermore, we refine our understanding by asking (a) *Which cultural differences were particularly salient?* and (b) *How did immigrants evaluate the response of the U.S. relative to the response of their home country?*

Methods

A qualitative research method was the most appropriate to assess participants' unique perceptions of cultural differences between the U.S. and their respective home countries in the context of the pandemic. Using qualitative data allowed us to generate rich insights into the sensemaking process of immigrants. To align with our sensemaking perspective, we relied on an interpretivist paradigm to report participants' experiences and meanings of their own reality, each of these realities being considered as socially constructed and equally valid (Ponterotto, 2005).

Procedure and Participants

We recruited participants via networking sites for foreigners such as Facebook groups. To be included in the study, participants had to be over 18 years old, currently reside but not being born in the U.S., and be fluent in English. Note that some of our participants had gained U.S. citizenship. Immigrant participants were living in multiple regions of the U.S. (i.e., Northeast, Southwest, Midwest, and South) at the time of data collection and came originally from Africa, Asia, Europe, and South America. All participants provided informed consent in line with the Institutional Review Board at Rutgers University. No compensation was offered for participation in this research.

After sharing their demographics and immigration history via Qualtrics, participants took part in an audio-recorded, semi-structured interview via Zoom, Cisco WebEx, or Skype. The interviews lasted about 60 minutes each. Our data collection was originally not built with specific COVID-19 research questions in mind, but focused on immigrants' experiences more generally. Yet, since we started data collection in early April 2020, we added a question to control for potential biases in responses due to this unique situation: "Given the current COVID-19 pandemic, do you think this situation affects the answers you gave in this interview?" with the prompt: "If so, why?" After the eighth interview, we noticed interesting response patterns to the COVID-19 question; that is, that the pandemic affected participants' sensemaking of their immigration experience in that immigrants often provided examples of how their home country was dealing with the pandemic. They emphasized how different that strategy was from that of the U.S., both in a positive and a negative sense. They also commented on the fact that office closures, general concerns, and so on led them to speak less to coworkers and more to loved ones. Hence, in August 2020, we modified the prompt from "If so, why?" to "What about your workplace experience as an immigrant, your relationships with your family and friends in your home country, people here, and with other immigrants, your travel to your home country, your overall immigration plans?" Furthermore, to follow up on interesting response patterns in our interviews to the COVID-19 answers, we sent out an email to all participants in December 2020 asking for additional written answers to several open-ended questions focusing on the impact of COVID-19 on their immigrant experience. Examples of these questions are "Has the COVID-19 pandemic highlighted specific cultural differences between your home country and the United States? If yes, which ones?" "If you compare the ways your home country and the United States have dealt with the COVID-19 pandemic, respectively, what are your conclusions?"

Data used in the present chapter solely represent answers to the COVID-19 interview question and to the follow-up written COVID-19 questions. A total of 25 participants answered both, and hence, constitute the final sample for the present study. They were between 23 and 74 years old [M = 40.5, SD = 12.1)], 64% female, and only 8% did not have a college degree. Approximately 12% held master's and 20% doctoral degrees. Thus, our sample is above average in terms of educational level compared to the population. On average, participants had been in the U.S. for 12.7 years (SD = 11.4; range = 2–47 years), and before the pandemic, 12% visited their home country two to five times a year, 40% once a year, 32% once every few years, and 16% never.

Data Analysis

We used thematic analysis to identify patterns (i.e., themes) within our data for the current study. Themes capture "something important about the data in relation to the research question, and represents some level of patterned response or meaning within the data set" (Braun & Clarke, 2006, p. 82). The research team consisted of two coders, a primary coder who conducted the data analysis, and a secondary coder who served as an auditor, providing feedback and modifications to the initial coding.

Braun and Clarke's (2006) clearly defined steps for thematic analysis allowed us to cross-examine the answers to COVID-19 questions in both interviews and written follow-up responses with a bottom-up approach. First, after having read and re-read the interview transcripts to allow coders to get familiarized with the data, initial codes were generated. That is, any interesting aspect that may represent the basis for repeated patterns (i.e., themes) was recorded. Concretely, data was broken down into passages providing initial codes with sufficient context. This led to a first list of codes.

Second, we searched for themes by "re-focus[ing] the analysis at the broader level of themes, rather than codes[, by] sorting the different codes into potential themes" (Braun & Clarke, 2006, p. 89). It was during this step that an initial reflection about the relationships between codes, themes, and overarching themes was conducted. Specifically, the first list of codes was refined into a second list. The first list of themes was created by extracting from the codes based on the former highlights.

Third, the first list of themes was refined into a pre-final list by deleting, adding, integrating, or splitting themes. Themes were named by identifying their specific interest and by making sure they were not overly broad. Given our focus on culture, we relied on Hofstede's (2011) and Meyer's (2015) theories for these themes and when presenting the results. To be specific, such themes (e.g., U.S. is more individualistic) were of second order, that is, we used a similar language to that of the management literature the study intends to contribute to (Rogers et al., 2017). This step led to a satisfactory pre-final data structure that was discussed by the two coders to ensure agreement.

Results

Our model, which is depicted in Fig. 7.1, shows that COVID-19 and its management resulted in different quality assessments for the U.S. and the respective home countries. In addition, it highlights that identification of COVID-19 pandemic management strategies made cultural differences between the U.S. and the respective home countries more salient. This was particularly the case for uncertainty avoidance, power distance, and individualism versus collectivism (Hofstede, 2011), as well as the decision-making, leadership, and disagreement dimensions of Meyer's (2015) cultural map.

Differences in Pandemic Management between Countries

Immigrants are often connected to their home country through families, friends, and/or local media they still follow. Because of this, they were aware of the situation in their home countries and strategies selected by the respective governments to manage the COVID-19 pandemic. This enabled them to draw comparisons between both countries' approaches to managing the pandemic. Our data indicates that participants indeed engaged in these types of comparisons but that they did not come to uniform conclusions. Hence, the pandemic context led them to make comparisons and to engage in sense making that resulted in three main types of evaluations regarding the U.S. pandemic management.

Favorable Assessment of U.S. Participants relied on various reasons to explain why they believed the U.S. managed the pandemic better than their home country. Typically, they perceived lockdowns and other restrictions at home as unreasonably rigid as demonstrated by Participant (P) 13 (40-year-old female, working in administration, originally from South Africa):

> They [in South Africa] had a very regimented lockdown, like sometimes worse than here. You couldn't walk your dog, you couldn't go for a run, you were like in your house and if you went out the house, you could only go for groceries. They weren't allowed to buy cigarettes or alcohol at all.

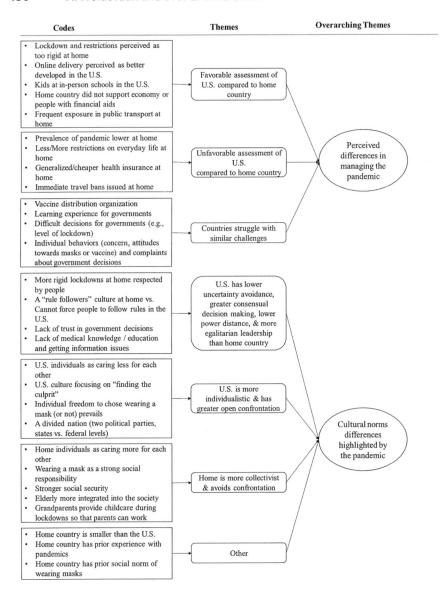

Fig. 7.1 Data structure

Similarly, P14 (45-year-old female, working in science, originally from France) described that in her country of origin "*you can only leave the house for one hour and a half … you know it was hard to see for us because at least we weren't as restricted.*" The notion of the U.S. doing better was further clear in P9's (32-year-old female, working in education, originally from Switzerland) experience, when she shared that "*half-lockdown is stronger in Switzerland where all the restaurants, museums, and fitness centers are closed and for that reason I'm happy to be in the U.S. right now."* For P15 (31-year-old male, working in arts and media, originally from Peru), restrictions were even more extreme:

> *The quarantine was worse than here [in the U.S.]. There was military in the streets every single night from 9 pm–5 am from Monday to Saturday. Sunday, they let the people go out. It was extreme, but sadly, not all people in Peru are well educated or well raised, so they don't really understand the weight of the quarantine. So, it was done to prevent all these people from going out on the streets.*

Further, one participant commented on a lack of resources in their home country: P18 (32-year-old male, working in computer and mathematics, originally from Kenya):

> *Kenya is a poorer country and lacked the financial feasibility to provide stimulus to the unemployed or anyone affected by the pandemic and so the country was probably forced to let people work since they had no way to help anyone who suffered in anyway.*

Unfavorable Assessment of U.S. Participants indicated several reasons why they believed the U.S. managed the pandemic worse than their home country. These mostly relied on lower infection rates in their home countries. P25 (35-year-old male, working in education, originally from Taiwan) states: *"Taiwan has 0 cases of COVID. Zero. They haven't had a case of COVID in 300 days, like 250 days. They're having parades and baseball games and everybody's living a totally normal life."* The results were explained by "good" decisions, such as immediate travel bans and greater reliance on—and application of—health safety measures. For instance, P8 (38-year-old male, working in education, originally from Germany): *"Germany and Europe more generally had a few lockdowns and they worked."*

Countries Struggle with Similar Challenges. Interestingly, several participants did not make better or worse judgments; rather, they highlighted common struggles without perfect responses in terms of pandemic management. P19 (49-year-old female, working in arts, originally from Germany): *"[My conclusion is] that we all don't know how to properly deal with it and just do our best and learn as we go."* Such challenges included vaccine distribution, the difficulty of governmental decision-making (e.g., lockdown modalities), dealing with complaints about these decisions, and individuals' behaviors (e.g., degree of personal concern about the pandemic, attitudes toward safety guidelines and vaccines). P7 (36-year-old female, working in education, originally from France) explains: "*Different complaints, but still ... that governments were not ready, and that people are too individualistic to care about others ... In each country there are anti-maskers and anti-vaccine people.*"

Furthermore, these comparisons appeared in the assessment of individuals' reactions to the imposed measures. They made cultural differences between the U.S. and the respective home country more salient as we outline now.

Cultural Differences Highlighted by the COVID-19 Pandemic

Immigrant workers' perceptions of cultural differences between the U.S. and their home countries were fairly representative of some of Hofstede's (2011) national culture dimensions, as well as Meyer's (2015) cultural map dimensions. Specifically, first, the U.S. has lower degrees of uncertainty avoidance (i.e., feeling "comfortable in unstructured situations"; Hofstede, 2011, p. 10); that is, in Meyer's (2015) terms, participants' perceptions of pandemic management emphasized that their home countries practiced a more "top-down" approach when making decisions about the best pandemic management strategy; that is, such decisions were made by the government or president, as unique individuals, with greater power, rather than in concertation or consensus with the population.

Second, such management revealed U.S.'s lower power distance ("the extent to which the less powerful members of organizations and institutions [like the family] accept and expect that power is distributed unequally"; Hofstede, 2011, p. 9), or in Meyer's (2015) terms, U.S.'s leadership being more egalitarian than hierarchical (i.e., with a lower distance between people of lower and higher statuses and a flat organization).

Third and finally, our participants' perceptions emphasized U.S. higher degree of individualism ("is the degree to which people in a society are integrated into groups. On the individualist side we find cultures in which the ties between individuals are loose: everyone is expected to look after him/herself and his/her immediate family"; Hofstede, 2011, p. 11); or, as put by Meyer (2015), in situations of disagreement, open confrontation (versus avoiding confrontation) is appropriate as it is perceived as less likely to negatively affect the group or relationships among people.

Lower Uncertainty avoidance, Consensual decision-making, Lower Power Distance, and Egalitarian leadership in the U.S. Overall, participants talked about U.S. decisions of lockdowns and restrictions being less respected. For instance, P22 (23-year-old female, working in education, originally from China) emphasizes the more consensual decision-making process in the U.S. compared to China, her home country: "*Why it is not very realistic to practice lockdown in the U.S. is because of this cultural thing, you can't really force people to do anything.*" Similarly, P25 (35-year-old male, working in education, originally from Taiwan) explains:

> *My relatives from home ask me: Why don't stores and restaurants shut down?"* He *[President Trump] says the economy is more important than the elderly. He is encouraging people to fight the lockdown restrictions. "Doesn't he care if his citizens die?" He is blaming it on China and individual States. "Is there contact tracing?" No, the Americans will not accept it. "Why don't people wear masks?" It is not required in many States. Also, a lot of people think it is a hoax and that their individual rights are more important.*

Relatedly, some participants emphasized the greater top-down approach when making decisions about pandemic management in their home countries, evoking a culture of *rule followers* at home. For instance, P11 (55-year-old female, working in legal occupation, originally from Germany) stated that "*Germans are rule followers, Americans struggle with this concept,*" and P14 (45-year-old female, working in science, originally from France) explaining that "*from the beginning lockdown was stricter in France and people took it seriously.*"

Similarly, other participants highlighted the inability of the U.S. government to reach agreement on the pandemic among citizens, resulting in a lack of unified decision-making regarding pandemic management. Notably, "*there's a lot of information shared based on fear, nothing can be verified*" (P16, 40-year-old female, working in management, originally from Cuba). Hence, as a top-down decision-making strategy would not be appropriate in the U.S. context compared to their home countries, our immigrant workers emphasized that individuals in the U.S. were critical of experts, and more open to opinions from "anyone". Relatedly, several participants mentioned perceptions of a more prevalent lack of medical knowledge in the U.S. (often associated with the challenge to get reliable information). Hence, participants shared perceptions of a divided nation (e.g., different views based on political party, and states versus federal levels) where information was politicized: "*Culturally I find the American people very divided and that they politicize the advice of Health officials which is unlike my culture*" (P13, 40-year-old female, working in administration, originally from South Africa).

Of note, a few participants reported an opposite sensemaking process, representing "negative cases" important to highlight in qualitative research.

Notably, two participants' home countries ranked lower than the U.S. in terms of uncertainty avoidance and power distance. For P13 (40-year-old female, working in administration, originally from South Africa), "*coming from Africa, we don't want to stop living, … we still go out to restaurants and bars and whatever's open. Some people [in the U.S.] are just really scared, so they just don't want to go anywhere.*" Similarly, for P6 (46-year-old female, working in legal occupation, originally from Russia), "*people in the USA trust the government more than in Russia … The Russians do not like to follow rules too much.*"

Higher Individualism and Open Confrontation in U.S. Overall, individual reactions to U.S. pandemic management were perceived by immigrant workers as more openly confrontational, at the risk of harming the collective interest. This is in line with a more individualistic U.S. society compared to that of their home countries. Participants strongly evoked the extent to which individuals cared for each other in their home countries, and in contrast, perceived a lower likelihood of U.S. nationals to be willing to wear a mask. As stated by P8 (38-year-old male, working in education, originally from Germany):

I was struck by the individual freedom notion in the U.S. I always felt like the U.S. were less communal than Europe, but this was particularly clear during this pandemic. The idea that people would refuse to wear a mask because it restricts their individual rights is mindboggling. It doesn't feel like people realize that we are all in this together.

Further, examples of home countries' more collectivist culture were shared, including better integration of elderly in society (e.g., P25, 35-year-old male, working in education, originally from Taiwan): "*nursing homes are not a part of the culture at all—[it is] very unfilial to neglect your duty to care for the elderly*"); stronger social security systems (e.g., P8, 38-year-old male, working in education, originally from Germany): "*So many people here [in the U.S.] are poor and struggle to make ends meet. I am German and we have a much stronger social safety net. No one has to starve on the street*"; and strong social norms toward protecting others (e.g., P1, 30-year-old male, working in education, originally from South Korea): "*In South Korea every citizen wears a mask. It is considered rude for a person not to wear a mask*". As P25 (35-year-old male, working in education, originally from Taiwan) explains: "*People in Asia may not agree with one another about everything, but they do generally trust one another to do the right thing for society, and they also expect their institutions to do the right thing for the people.*"

Discussion

A focus on immigrants is important because this group of workers contributes significantly to society and the business sphere in general (Dwertmann & Kunze, 2021; Harrison et al., 2019). While the U.S. hosts the largest population of immigrants worldwide, with migration numbers being on the rise over the past decades (United Nations, 2019), a shortage of migrants was noticed in the labor market due to the pandemic (Rose, 2021; Schachter et al., 2021). Considering this, it is important to understand how the COVID-19 pandemic, an unprecedented event, affected migrants' experience in the U.S. to better understand the possible long-term consequences for organizations. In this chapter, we uncovered the extent to which different COVID-19 pandemic management strategies led migrants to perceive cultural differences between the U.S. and their respective home countries. Furthermore, we explored how migrants assessed the quality of the response to COVID-19 by the U.S., relative to their home countries.

Implications

Our findings suggest that immigrants' sensemaking of the way in which the U.S. has managed the COVID-19 pandemic is not homogenous. Instead, some participants had favorable views of the ways in which the U.S. has managed the pandemic in comparison to their respective home countries, while others had an unfavorable view. A third group simply acknowledged that handling the pandemic is hard for all countries. This suggests a high and diverse level of sensemaking, calling into question generalized analyses of migrants, and instead signaling heterogeneity within this group (Crowley-Henry et al., 2018; Farashah & Blomquist, 2021; Jonczyk Sédès et al., 2022). While our sample and methodology were not designed to conduct moderator analyses, participants' home country could affect these judgments. Notably, African (e.g., Kenya, South Africa) participants tended to be more positive about the U.S., whereas participants from Asia (e.g., Chinese, Korean, Taiwanese) were more critical of the measures taken (or not taken) by the U.S. government, with those from Europe appearing to be the most diverse in their assessments. As one participant from Kenya mentioned a lack of financial resources as one reason why Kenya did worse than the U.S., it would be interesting to investigate such patterns in larger-scale quantitative investigations among immigrants from developing countries.

We also believe that such varying sensemaking outcomes could reflect, at least in part, an expression of cultural values. Indeed, the role of national culture was highlighted by our analyses. Answering our research question, participants' responses suggested that different approaches to managing the COVID-19 pandemic have emphasized cultural differences between the U.S. and the respective home countries in several ways.

First, U.S. culture is characterized by low levels of power distance and greater egalitarian leadership, where less powerful individuals are less likely to accept unequally distributed power and feel entitled to a certain amount of power (Hofstede, 2021; Meyer, 2015). In U.S. culture, freedom of speech is protected with the First Amendment, allowing for greater tolerance of ideas or opinions from anyone. This could be one reason why "*there's a lot of information shared based on fear, nothing can be verified*" (P16, Cuba) and "*American people [are] very divided and that they politicize the advice of Health officials*" (P17, South Africa). Further, in our study, immigrants' sensemaking of the COVID-19 pandemic management may be explained by U.S. culture being characterized by low levels of uncertainty avoidance. Indeed, in U.S. culture, individuals are comfortable with uncertainty and are thus low on willingness to avoid uncertainty. This may lead to observations such that "*it is not very realistic to practice lockdown in the U.S.*" (P22, China), something that is very different from "*rule followers*" in other countries, something that Americans "*struggle with*" (P11, Germany). It may also explain why "*lockdown was stricter in France and people took it seriously*" (P14, France). Indeed, this finding and interpretation are in line with research by Huynh (2020), who found that countries scoring higher on uncertainty avoidance had lower proportions of people gathering in public spaces (e.g., retail and recreation, grocery and pharmacy, parks, transit stations, workplaces) during the first surge of the pandemic (i.e., March 2020). Further, we did not find a clear pattern of, for example, only participants from Asian countries noticing these differences in lower uncertainty avoidance and power distance in the U.S., instead, as indicated by the quotes, participants from various regions (e.g., Europe, Asia, Africa) showed a similar pattern of responses. In comparison, consistency in responses relative to individualism are less surprising since the U.S. represents an extreme case (i.e., the country that ranks highest in individualism in the world; Hofstede, 2021).

Second, the U.S. is the most individualistic country in the world, where, according to Hofstede (2021), "the expectation is that people look after themselves and their immediate families only and should not rely (too much) on authorities for support." Multiple participants commented in various ways on the individualistic culture in the U.S. that is observable in COVID-19 measures and reactions to them. Participants mentioned "*the individual freedom*" and that people in the U.S. "*do not realize that we are all in this together*" (P8, Germany), that people in the U.S. are "*very divided*" (P13, South Africa), and do not trust their government (P25, Taiwan). This leads to individuals unwilling to wear masks to protect others (P1, South Korea). Such statements about COVID-19 can be explained by U.S. individualism (Hofstede, 2001, 2011) and open confrontation when disagreements occur (Meyer, 2015), as wearing a mask is associated with an individual decision (in U.S.) versus a collective responsibility (e.g., in the respective home country) that further allows to avoid confrontation. Interestingly, the notion of individualism was mentioned broadly by participants from various regions of the world, and it seemed clear that the pandemic emphasized this perception. This was the most apparent from this quote by P8 (Germany), who said, "*I always felt like the U.S. were less communal than Europe, but this was particularly clear during this pandemic.*"

In particular, Asian participants from more collectivistic cultures (Oyserman et al., 2002) that generally avoid confrontation in case of disagreements and had implemented the usage of masks to protect others when sick well before the pandemic, seemed to prefer stricter measures that would restrain individual rights from a U.S. perspective. Follow-up studies could provide more clarity on these observations (see also, Guan et al., 2020; Kniffin et al., 2021), in particular as following the initial surge of the pandemic, the Chinese population did become more openly confrontational when they disagreed with their country's pandemic management and top-down decision-making. Hence, an interesting future research question is the extent to which the COVID-19 pandemic management may not only have emphasized immigrant workers' perceptions of cultural differences between their two countries, but also made countries' citizens more aware of their own country's culture—in comparison to other cultures' pandemic management as shared in the news. In extension, it is also possible that not only the awareness and salience of cultural dimensions may have increased, but that such increase may lead to a cultural shift toward greater uniformity around the world (e.g., decreasing the top-down decision-making culture in China toward greater consensual decision-making following 2023).

Overall, our finding of increased perceptions of cultural differences between the U.S. and the participants' home countries as a means of making sense of COVID-19 pandemic management is important for organizations and management research because such perceptions may affect immigrants' acculturation to the U.S. (Berry, 2005), and in turn, their turnover intentions—which are already higher among cultural minority employees (Hofhuis et al., 2014).

Indeed, as highlighted by the sensemaking perspective on immigrants (Farashah & Blomquist, 2021), interpreting events and expecting certain courses of action based on how such events used to unfold in one's home country is likely to be unsuccessful in a new cultural context. Accordingly, our results stress the need for future management research to explore the role of such increased salience of cultural differences on workplace outcomes in the long term. Notably, future studies could explore the sensemaking process immigrants engage in to not only determine which career directions to pursue next, but also to address immigrants' potential anxiety or cognitive dissonance resulting from perceptions that the U.S. managed the pandemic worse than the home country. Finally, future work may explicitly examine the consequences of increased salience of cultural differences following the pandemic on work-related identity construction, as it represents a key characteristic of the sensemaking perspective (Farashah & Blomquist, 2021). Generally, we believe that these questions are valuable following larger societal events and shocks and not just the COVID-19 pandemic. Examples could include racial violence and police brutality, mass shootings, elections, and others.

Practical Implications

Our results are also relevant for organizations since they suggest that organizations may need to help immigrant workers make sense of their environment (Weick, 1995) and reconcile the cultural differences highlighted by how the U.S. and their home country dealt with the pandemic following this first surge. To do so, organizations are, for example, encouraged to facilitate positive group climates (Dwertmann et al., 2016), that is, the extent to which cultural differences are valued (Luijters et al., 2008). Concretely, this can include offering their immigrant employees diversity training, intercultural workshops, and supportive organizational policies (Bezrukova et al., 2016; Hayes et al., 2020). These may enable a better understanding between immigrants and Americans of both the U.S. culture and the immigration backgrounds for various countries of origin. This is important as positive intercultural group climate has been shown to increase the likelihood that immigrants embrace acculturation strategies that include an adoption of the host country culture (Valenzuela et al., 2020) and should, thus, be more likely to remain in the country and with their organization. Based on our results, organizations may offer specific trainings to their international employees, in which the Hofstede and Meyer models and their application to the U.S. as a country could be shared. Parallels with the measures taken to manage the pandemic could be drawn to foster immigrants' understanding of the reasons behind the differences they may have noted between their home country and the U.S. pandemic management strategies during the surge of the pandemic. Such a measure should strengthen immigrants' bond to the U.S. and facilitate the development of a positive immigrant identity (Dwertmann & Kunze, 2021), increasing their likelihood of staying in the country, hence continuing to contribute to the U.S. economy.

Limitations and Future Research Directions

First, our data collection in, and focus on, the U.S. context (Johns, 2006, 2017) and its specific cultural profile limit the generalizability of our findings to other countries. It would, for example, be interesting to examine if European immigrants in Asia would comment on the relatively higher collectivism of their host countries. This may have led such participants to be more skeptical of restrictive measures relative to host-country nationals. Indeed, in line with this logic, before the protests in China against the zero-COVID-19 policy in winter 2022, many European immigrants had already left the country (Bickenbach & Liu, 2022), in part because of imposed restrictions. We recommend future research to investigate such possibilities.

Second, our findings are based on U.S. management of the first surge of the pandemic, mostly in 2020, before the rise of the Omicron variant. Yet, the COVID-19 pandemic is still evolving, and countries continue to impose and lift restrictions. Also, the political climate in the U.S. has continued to evolve after the election of President Biden. These changes are not accounted for in our data, but they could have influenced our results. In fact, several participants expressed hope that the outcomes of the 2020 election would affect the way in which the U.S. managed the pandemic and others highlighted the hostility toward minority groups during the Trump presidency (Konrad, 2018). Thus, follow-up studies would be interesting to investigate whether changes in the political landscape have influenced the experience of U.S.-based immigrants.

Finally, based on our initial qualitative findings, a quantitative perspective may also be interesting for future studies. It would allow including a greater number of participants and the empirical test of the role of specific immigration variables such as country or cultural region of origin, the numbers of years residing in the U.S., frequency of visits to the home country before the pandemic, and participants' levels of knowledge about pandemic-related policies in both the U.S. and their home countries in determining the reactions of immigrants to pandemic measures.

Conclusion

Migrants are critical for economies worldwide. As for everyone else, the COVID-19 pandemic represented a shock that changed many of their lives. As our results show, the influence of the first surge of the pandemic on immigrants' sensemaking of their host- and home-countries was a salient event for many immigrants, as they had to account for multiple frames of reference, comparing how governments in both countries reacted. By adopting a sensemaking perspective on immigrants and showing how the differences in pandemic management approaches increased perceived cultural differences between countries, we hope that this chapter will open novel academic conversations among diversity scholars to conduct future research on immigrant workers and explore whether the salience of these cultural differences may have long-lasting influences on immigrants' career decisions and work outcomes, not just following the pandemic but also other major societal events.

References

Bell, M. P., Kwesiga, E. N., & Berry, D. P. (2010). The new "invisible men and women" in diversity research. *Journal of Managerial Psychology, 25*(2), 177–188. https://doi.org/10.1108/02683941011019375

Berry, J. W. (2005). Acculturation: Living successfully in two cultures. *International Journal of Intercultural Relations, 29*, 697–712. https://doi.org/10.1016/j.ijintrel.2005.07.013

Bezrukova, K., Spell, C. S., Perry, J. L., & Jehn, K. A. (2016). A meta-analytical integration of over 40 years of research on diversity training evaluation. *Psychological Bulletin, 142*(11), 1227–1274. https://doi.org/10.1037/bul0000067

Bickenbach, F., & Liu, W. H. (2022). Goodbye China: What do fewer foreigners mean for multinationals and the Chinese economy? *Intereconomics, 57*(5), 306–312. https://doi.org/10.1007/s10272-022-1075-0

Bjorklund, K., & Ewing, A. (2020, October 14). The Swedish COVID-19 response is a disaster. It shouldn't be a model for the rest of the world. *Time.* https://time.com/5899432/sweden-coronavirus-disaster/

BLS. (2020). *Foreign-born workers: Labor force characteristics—2019.* U.S. Department of Labor.

Braun, V., & Clarke, V. (2006). Using thematic analysis in psychology. *Qualitative Research in Psychology, 3*(2), 77–101. https://doi.org/10.1191/1478088706qp063oa

Castaneda, M. E., Bateh, J., & Heyliger, W. (2013). Areas of cross-cultural difference in the workplace. *Journal of International Education Research, 9*(2), 165–170. https://doi.org/10.19030/jier.v9i2.7721

Claeson, M., & Hanson, S. (2020). COVID-19 and the Swedish enigma. *The Lancet, 6736*(20), 2020–2021. https://doi.org/10.1016/s0140-6736(20)32750-1

Crowley-Henry, M., O'Connor, E., & Al Ariss, A. (2018). Portrayal of skilled migrants' careers in business and management studies: A review of the literature and future research agenda. *European Management Review, 15*(3), 375–394. https://doi.org/10.1111/emre.12072

Doz, Y. (2011). Qualitative research for international business. *Journal of International Business Studies, 42*(5), 582–590. https://doi.org/10.1057/jibs.2011.18

Dwertmann, D. J. G., & Kunze, F. (2021). More than meets the eye: The role of immigration background for social identity effects. *Journal of Management, 47*(8), 2074–2104. https://doi.org/10.1177/0149206320929080

Dwertmann, D. J. G., Nishii, L. H., & van Knippenberg, D. (2016). Disentangling the fairness & discrimination and synergy perspectives on diversity climate: Moving the field forward. *Journal of Management, 42*(5), 1136–1168. https://doi.org/10.1177/0149206316630380

Farashah, A. D., & Blomquist, T. (2021). Work experiences of qualified immigrants: A review of theoretical progress. *Equality, Diversity and Inclusion*. https://doi.org/10.1108/EDI-01-2019-0046

Fernando, D., & Patriotta, G. (2020). "Us versus them": Sensemaking and identity processes in skilled migrants' experiences of occupational downgrading. *Journal of World Business, 55*(4), 101109. https://doi.org/10.1016/j.jwb.2020.101109

George, G., Howard-Grenville, J., Joshi, A., & Tihanyi, L. (2016). Understanding and tackling societal grand challenges through management research. *Academy of Management Journal, 59*(6), 1880–1895. https://doi.org/10.5465/amj.2016.4007

Guan, Y., Deng, H., & Zhou, X. (2020). Understanding the impact of the COVID-19 pandemic on career development: Insights from cultural psychology. *Journal of Vocational Behavior, 119*(May), 1–5. https://doi.org/10.1016/j.jvb.2020.103438

Harrison, D. A., Harrison, T., & Shaffer, M. A. (2019). Strangers in strained lands: Learning from workplace experiences of immigrant employees. *Journal of Management, 45*(2), 600–619. https://doi.org/10.1177/0149206318790648

Hayes, T. L., Kaylor, L. E., & Oltman, K. A. (2020). Coffee and controversy: How applied psychology can revitalize sexual harassment and racial discrimination training. *Industrial and Organizational Psychology, 13*(2), 117–136. https://doi.org/10.1017/iop.2019.84

Hickman, A., & Saad, L. (2020). *Reviewing remote work in the U.S. under COVID-19*. Gallup. https://news.gallup.com/poll/311375/reviewing-remote-work-covid.aspx

Hofhuis, J., Van der Zee, K. I., & Otten, S. (2014). Comparing antecedents of voluntary job turnover among majority and minority employees. *Equality, Diversity and Inclusion: An International Journal, 33*(8), 735–749. https://doi.org/10.1108/EDI-09-2013-0071

Hofstede, G. (2001). *Culture's consequences: Comparing values, behaviors, institutions, and organizations across nations*. Sage.

Hofstede, G. (2011). Dimensionalizing cultures: The Hofstede model in context. *Online Readings in Psychology and Culture, 2*(1), 1–26. https://doi.org/10.9707/2307-0919.1014

Hofstede, G. (2021). *Country comparison.* https://www.hofstede-insights.com/country-comparison/the-usa/.

Hong, Y. Y., Morris, M. W., Chiu, C. Y., & Benet-Martínez, V. (2000). Multiculrtrial minds: A dynamic constructivist approach to culture and cognition. *American Psychologist, 55*(7), 709–720. https://doi.org/10.1037/0003-066X.55.7.709

Huynh, T. L. D. (2020). Does culture matter social distancing under the COVID-19 pandemic? *Safety Science, 130*(April), 104872. https://doi.org/10.1016/j.ssci.2020.104872

Johns, G. (2006). The essential impact of context on organizational behavior. *Academy of Management Review, 31*(2), 386–408. https://doi.org/10.5465/amr.2006.20208687

Johns, G. (2017). Incorporating context in organizational research: Reflections on the 2016 AMR decade award. *Academy of Management Review, 42*(4), 577–595. https://doi.org/10.5465/amr.2017.0044

Jonczyk Sédès, C., Miedtank, T., & Oliver, D. (2022). Suddenly I felt like a migrant: Identity and mobility threats facing European self-initiated expatriates in the UK under Brexit. *Academy of Management Discoveries.* https://doi.org/10.5465/amd.2020.0162

Jonsen, K., Maznevski, M. L., & Schneider, S. C. (2011). Diversity and its not so diverse literature: An international perspective. *International Journal of Cross Cultural Management, 11*(1), 35–62. https://doi.org/10.1177/1470595811398798

Kniffin, K. M., Narayanan, J., Anseel, F., Antonakis, J., Ashford, S. P., Bakker, A. B., Bamberger, P., Bapuji, H., Bhave, D. P., Choi, V. K., Creary, S. J., Demerouti, E., Flynn, F. J., Gelfand, M. J., Greer, L. L., Johns, G., Kesebir, S., Klein, P. G., Lee, S. Y., et al. (2021). COVID-19 and the workplace: Implications, issues, and insights for future research and action. *American Psychologist, 76*(1), 63–77. https://doi.org/10.1037/amp0000716

Konrad, A. M. (2018). Denial of racism and the trump presidency. *Equality, Diversity and Inclusion, 37*(1), 14–30. https://doi.org/10.1108/EDI-07-2017-0155

Luijters, K., Van der Zee, K. I., & Otten, S. (2008). Cultural diversity in organizations: Enhancing identification by valuing differences. *International Journal of Intercultural Relations, 32*(2), 154–163. https://doi.org/10.1016/j.ijintrel.2007.09.003

Martin, L., & Shao, B. (2016). Early immersive culture mixing: The key to understanding cognitive and identity differences among multiculturals. *Journal of Cross-Cultural Psychology, 47*(10), 1409–1429. https://doi.org/10.1177/0022022116639391

Meyer, E. (2015). *The culture map: Decoding how people think, lead, and get things done across cultures.* PublicAffairs.

Oyserman, D., Coon, H. M., & Kemmelmeier, M. (2002). Rethinking individualism and collectivism: Evaluation of theoretical assumptions and meta-analyses. *Psychological Bulletin, 128*(1), 3–72. https://doi.org/10.1037/0033-2909.128.1.3

Partnership for a New American Economy. (2011). *The "New American" Fortune 500* (Issue 4).

Pekkala Kerr, S., & Kerr, W. (2020). Immigrant entrepreneurship in America: Evidence from the survey of business owners 2007 & 2012. *Research Policy, 49*(3), 103918. https://doi.org/10.1016/j.respol.2019.103918

Ponterotto, J. G. (2005). Qualitative research in counseling psychology: A primer on research paradigms and philosophy of science. *Journal of Counseling Psychology, 52*(2), 126–136. https://doi.org/10.1037/0022-0167.52.2.126

Rogers, K. M., Corley, K. G., & Ashforth, B. E. (2017). Seeing more than Orange: Organizational respect and positive identity transformation in a prison context. *Administrative Science Quarterly, 62*(2), 219–269. https://doi.org/10.1177/0001839216678842

Rose, J. (2021). *Fewer immigrant workers are coming to fill key jobs. That has slowed the U.S. Economy*. NPR.Org. https://www.npr.org/2021/12/22/1063104262/immigrant-workers-us-economy-key-jobs.

Schachter, J., Borsella, P., & Knapp, A. (2021). *New population estimates show COVID-19 pandemic significantly disrupted migration across Borders*. U.S. Census Bureau. https://www.census.gov/library/stories/2021/12/net-international-migration-at-lowest-levels-in-decades.html.

United Nations. (2015). *International Migration Report 2015*. www.un.org/en/development/desa/population/migration/publications/migrationreport/docs/MigrationReport2015_Highlights.pdf

United Nations. (2019). *International migration 2019*.

Valenzuela, M. A., Flinchbaugh, C., & Rogers, S. E. (2020). Can organizations help adjust?: The effect of perceived organizational climate on immigrants' acculturation and consequent effect on perceived fit. *Journal of International Management, 26*(3), 100775. https://doi.org/10.1016/j.intman.2020.100775

Vaziri, H., Casper, W. J., Wayne, J. H., & Matthews, R. A. (2020). Changes to the work-family interface during the COVID-19 pandemic: Examining predictors and implications using latent transition analysis. *Journal of Applied Psychology, 105*(10), 1073–1087. https://doi.org/10.1037/apl0000819

Vora, D., Martin, L., Fitzsimmons, S. R., Pekerti, A. A., Lakshman, C., & Raheem, S. (2019). Multiculturalism within individuals: A review, critique, and agenda for future research. *Journal of International Business Studies, 50*(4), 499–524. https://doi.org/10.1057/s41267-018-0191-3

Weick, K. E. (1995). *Sensemaking in organizations*. Sage.

8

Can Intentions to Emigrate be Explained through Individual Values? An Exploratory Study in Lithuania

Vilmantė Kumpikaitė-Valiūnienė, Audra I. Mockaitis, Jurga Duobienė, Ineta Žičkutė, and Vilmantė Liubinienė

Introduction

Global changes and developments increased the international demand for skilled and specialized labor (Fernando & Cohen, 2016). The flexibility of the labor market in the European Union and the Schengen area has led to increased internal migration in these regions (e.g., 1.9 million people who previously resided in one EU member state migrated to another EU member state in 2017 [Eurostat, 2020]). Millions of people work abroad every year resulting from migration, expatriation, or short overseas assignments. Therefore, finding a skilled, specialized foreigner in an organization is no longer exceptional (Dang et al., 2020).

When people migrate, they move between societies that can have different value systems (Fischer & Schwartz, 2011). Therefore, the value differences

---

V. Kumpikaitė-Valiūnienė (✉) • J. Duobienė • I. Žičkutė • V. Liubinienė
Kaunas University of Technology, Kaunas, Lithuania
e-mail: vilmante.kumpikaite@ktu.lt; jurga.duobiene@ktu.lt; ineta.zickute@ktu.lt; vilmante.liubiniene@ktu.lt

A. I. Mockaitis
Maynooth University, Maynooth, Ireland
e-mail: audra.mockaitis@mu.ie

between locals and migrants could pose different challenges at work and in the daily life of migrants. However, Bhugra (2004) points out that it does not matter what migration reasons are and when individuals migrate abroad for economic, political, or educational purposes; their cultural and ethnic identity is likely to change. Previous studies have focused on the values of migrants and value change. Several authors (e.g., Alba & Nee, 2009; Bardi et al., 2014; Leong, 2013; Lönnqvist et al., 2011, 2013; Rudnev, 2014; Tartakovsky, 2009) have investigated value changes and provided insights on how the values of immigrants change in the process of immigration, and what value system immigrants hold after some years of life in the new country. Others (e.g., Bobowik et al., 2011; Kumpikaitė-Valiūnienė et al., 2020; Tartakovsky et al., 2017) have compared migrants with the non-migrant population in the destination country or their country of origin. Kumpikaitė-Valiūnienė et al. (2020) highlighted that values differ significantly between people who have migration experience and intention to migrate in relation to citizens who do not have such experience or intention to move.

Studies have long highlighted challenges that international employees face within organizations due to their different cultural backgrounds and values (Perlstein & Ciuk, 2019; Kim et al., 2018), and the challenges that organizations face in managing multinational teams of employees (Mockaitis et al., 2018; Zander et al., 2012), as well as local firms (Makkonen, 2016). Some knowledge about the types of values that are tied to decisions to emigrate can help to understand if and how values might change during the migration or acculturation process in a new host country, and also provide a baseline for assessing these differences. In this chapter, we examine the relationship between individual-level cultural values and individuals' intentions to emigrate. We apply the Schwartz Value Survey (Schwartz, 1992, 2006a, 2012) in Lithuania, which is known as one of the most emigrating countries in the European Union (Kumpikaitė-Valiūnienė, 2019a). In fact, its rates of emigration were so high that between 1990 and 2018, every sixth citizen left the country (Migration in numbers, 2020).

The structure of this chapter consists of a theoretical background that describes push and pull factors that motivate migration values in the context of migration. We next present the research method followed by the empirical research results, and finally, we discuss the findings and future research directions.

Theoretical Background

Push and Pull Factors in the Decision to Emigrate

Although our focus is on cultural factors affecting the migration decision, much attention is given in the literature to a range of individual, social, and economic factors, with a focus on the institutional environments of countries as drivers of migration. The conventional push-pull models in migration research represent these socioeconomic factors that motivate people to migrate (Van Hear et al., 2018; Ojeda-Gonzalez et al., 2018). *Push factors* are factors that stimulate people to leave their country of origin, and *pull factors* are those factors that attract individuals to a destination country or region (Lee, 1966). In studies on Lithuania, Kumpikaitė and Žičkutė (2012) and Kumpikaitė-Valiūnienė et al. (2017) identified the pull factors that are most important for Lithuanian emigrants. Among the most important were factors related to employment opportunities and financial stability, followed by factors that ease transition into a host society, such as the existence of a large ethnic community in the host country, and having relatives in the host country.

Push-pull factors have the opposite mirror image in both countries; for example, the low wage is a factor pushing from the country of origin and a higher wage in the destination country is a pull factor. Piore (1971) has argued that pull factors in host countries and primarily in developed countries are more important than push factors in the country of origin. Poire claimed that migrants flow from poorer to richer countries because of the labor market pulling a labor-intensive workforce. Push-pull theories have been criticized for their overly simplistic approach to migration, as they might only skim the surface in explaining the decision to migrate (and do not explain the process) (de Haas, 2021). But in this study, we are interested more in explaining the reasons for migration rather than the process per se. We also understand that lists of push-pull factors are insufficient in themselves in explaining migration intentions. But understanding the context is important; that is, we should understand the institutional context of our sample country, as well as the wider migration context, as Lithuania has long been a country of migrants.

The Lithuanian Migration Context

Lithuania is a former Soviet republic that gained its independence in 1990 and joined the European Union in 2004. It is held to be one of the most emigrating countries in the EU; its population decreased by almost 890,000 during its independence and almost 700,000 due to emigration in 1990–2018, resulting in a population of less than 2.8 million (Migration in numbers, 2020). Only since 2019 has Lithuania begun experiencing positive net migration.

Previous studies (see Kumpikaitė-Valiūnienė, 2019a; Kumpikaitė-Valiūnienė & Žičkutė, 2017) revealed that the main push factors on Lithuanian emigrants were economic, such as (1) low wages, (2) personal life conditions, (3) income inequality, and (4) price levels of products. However, non-economic push factors, such as wishing for a change in life and family reasons also were important factors for migration. Kumpikaitė-Valiūnienė and Žičkutė (2017) highlighted following five main pull factors fostering migration of Lithuanians: (1) higher income in the host country, (2) relatives living in the host country, (3) the possibility of self-development, (4) better job opportunities, and (5) self-realization.

Different destination countries and migration reasons have been attracting Lithuanians since 1990. Before Lithuanian accession to the EU, the United States was the most attractive destination for Lithuanians, as it was before World War II (Kumpikaitė-Valiūnienė & Žičkutė, 2017). Germany and the UK were also preferred for their levels of economic development and language (during the Soviet regime, Lithuanians primarily studied Russian as their first language and English or German as their second). When Lithuania joined the European Union in 2004, the United Kingdom became the top destination country until 2017, when most settled migrants remained, but and the uncertainty of Brexit put off potential new migrants (Kumpikaitė-Valiūnienė, 2019b). While the USA lost its popularity after 2004, the popularity of the Scandinavian countries grew. During 2010–2019, the largest numbers of Lithuanians emigrated to the UK, Ireland, Norway, Germany, Russia, the USA, Spain, Denmark, Sweden, and the Netherlands (Migration in numbers, 2020). Kumpikaitė-Valiūnienė (2019a) analyzed the various pull factors in the main destination countries for Lithuanians (UK, Norway, Germany, and Ireland) and highlighted that economic factors were of highest importance (higher income, better job opportunities) for most emigrants, as well as opportunities for personal development. Family reasons were also high on the list, while in the UK, language was also a key determinant. Although the order of importance of these factors differed slightly among countries, economic pull factors were a priority.

Values in the Context of Migration

Values affect perception and attitudes and guide people's behavior (Boer & Fischer, 2013; Schwartz, 2006a; Schwartz & Butenko, 2014; Schwartz et al., 2012). Migrants do not abandon their beliefs overnight or leave all their values behind. They leave the country with their ethnic and cultural identities based on a certain system of values, which is usually formed during the pre-adult years. However, migration scholars have been interested in the adaptation and acculturation of migrants, such as whether or not they adopt the culture of the host country in favor of those of their country of origin. Welzel and Inglehart (2010) argue that people's values do change in response to changing living conditions. But little is known about the process of value change in migrants, especially as pertains to their personal values and over time. That is, we know relatively little about whether (or how) values may change as a result of permanent migration compared to short-term migration, and whether change in values is more prominent in migrants who have little to no contact with their country of origin, compared to migrants who do. Moreover, the reasons for migrating differ among individuals. Can different reasons for migrating lead to different degrees of change in individuals' values?

Individual-level values can be traced to the Rokeach Values Survey (RVS), the seminar work of Rokeach (1973). Although societal-level values have been used to compare national cultures (e.g., Hofstede, 1984; House et al., 2004; Lnglehart, 1997), and individuals do have values or characteristics that can be reflective of their societal cultures, prior research has shown that individuals' decisions are influenced by individual-level values (Tsui et al., 2007; Ralston et al., 2014), and to compare individuals (and behaviors of individuals), we should consider characteristics of individuals (not societies). Comparisons across groups of individuals, especially if they are from a single source country or culture, should be conducted at the individual level of analysis, and include personal values. Ultimately, as argued by Ralston et al. (2014: 287), "individuals are individuals."

As the RVS was developed in the USA, it was limited in its application in cross-cultural research. In response, Schwartz and Bilsky (1987) adapted the instrument to cross-cultural research. The Schwartz Values Survey (SVS), developed based on samples in 73 countries (Schwartz, 2006b), has been used to measure values at the societal and individual levels. At the individual level, there are ten primary value sub-dimensions: (1) *self-direction* (involving independent thought and action), (2) *stimulation* (the need for variety), (3) *hedonism* (the drive for pleasure and self-gratification), (4) *achievement* (which involves the self-attainment of personal success), (5) *power* (the attainment of a dominant position in the social system), (6) *security* (safety, harmony and stability), (7) *conformity* (behaving according to social expectations or norms), (8) *tradition* (respect and commitment to cultural or religious customs and ideas), (9) *benevolence* (concern for the welfare of one's closest affiliate), and (10) *universalism* (concern for the welfare of all people). These sub-dimensions have been grouped into two higher-order sets of value dimensions: individualism and collectivism. Individualism includes power, achievement, hedonism, self-direction and stimulation. Collectivism includes the values of benevolence, tradition and conformity. An additional set of four higher-order values represent sets of opposing dimensions in the Schwartz circumplex model. Openness to change versus conservation (e.g., stimulation and self-direction versus conformity, security and tradition), self-enhancement versus self-transcendence (e.g., power, achievement and hedonism versus benevolence and universalism).

The SVS has been tested for internal consistency across national samples at both the societal and individual levels. Ralston et al. (2011) conducted a test across 50 countries and concluded that the SVS is a better predictor of individual-level values than at the level of societies, especially the higher-order individual-level value dimensions, using more varied samples than the original SVS samples, that is, of working adults. However, they found that only 8 of the 50 countries in their sample demonstrated acceptable scale reliabilities for all 10 of the SVS values. A few of the sub-dimensions, such as hedonism, security and self-direction, were problematic across a larger percentage of countries. However, the higher-order dimensions of individualism and collectivism were highly reliable across all societies, as were openness to change, conservation, self-transcendence and self-enhancement. Ralston et al. (2011) have proposed that researchers can use the higher-order value dimensions meaningfully in cross-cultural research, as these demonstrated more acceptable reliability scores within country samples than the internal reliabilities of the individual-level sub-dimensions.

The SVS values have been found in a number of studies to influence individuals' decision-making. For example, Ralston et al. (2014) found that values are predictors of ethical decision-making across societies. Other study by Piurko et al. (2011) explored the SVS values in relation to left-right political orientations in 20 countries. A study by Brosch and Sander (2014) provided insights into the role of universal core values and emotions in decision-making.

The SVS values may influence individuals' decision to migrate as well, by affecting priorities and goals. For example, individuals who place a high value on security and stability may be less likely to emigrate, as they would be concerned about leaving behind the familiar and taking on the risks and uncertainties of a new environment. Individuals who value conformity and tradition might likewise be less likely to emigrate, as moving to a new culture might go against the grain, would introduce the unfamiliar and involve adapting to new customs. On the other hand, individuals who are self-directed and value achievement might be up for a challenge and might pursue new avenues for achieving their personal ambitions if they are dissatisfied in the home country. Individuals who seek novelty and excitement (stimulation) or self-expression may be more likely to emigrate to pursue new opportunities and experiences that align with their values.

Regarding the higher-order value dimensions of the SVS, we might expect that individuals higher on the individualism dimension would be more inclined to emigrate than individuals higher on collectivism. Individualism includes the sub-dimensions that would stimulate emigration, which necessitates a high degree of individual initiative and reliance on oneself. The group orientation of collectivism, focus on tradition and upholding established norms, would work in the opposite direction. We thus propose that:

Hypothesis 1a: The value dimension of individualism will be positively associated with intention to emigrate.
Hypothesis 1b: The value dimension of collectivism will be negatively associated with intention to emigrate.

We would expect that the opposing higher-order dimensions would also influence intentions to emigrate in opposing ways. Openness to change is comprised of the sub-dimensions of stimulation and self-direction that would also help individuals take on or overcome the challenge of emigrating, while conservation would restrict individuals through the adherence to rules and norms within the values of conformity, security and tradition (e.g., maintaining the status quo). We propose that:

Hypothesis 2a: The value dimension of openness to change will be positively associated with intention to emigrate.
Hypothesis 2b: The value dimension of conservation will be negatively associated with intention to emigrate.

We would also expect the final two dimensions to affect intention to emigrate in different ways. Individuals higher on self-enhancement would be more likely to emigrate than individuals who place more value on self-transcendence. Individuals who value and pursue self-enhancement might seek out better opportunities wherever they present themselves. Self-transcendent individuals need a sense of belonging, have concern for others. Being surrounded by (and not leaving behind) people they know, and value would be important. We propose that:

Hypothesis 3a: The value dimension of self-enhancement will be positively associated with intention to emigrate.
Hypothesis 3b: The value dimension of self-transcendence will be negatively associated with intention to emigrate.

Limited research has compared emigrants to nonemigrants on individual-level values and found differences between them. Tartakovsky et al. (2017) found that migrants place greater value on *power* and *security* and less emphasis on *universalism, benevolence* and *self-direction* than non-migrants. Kumpikaitė-Valiūnienė et al. (2020) found that *universalism* is more important and *security* and *achievement*—less. These studies also suggest that the decision to migrate might lie in certain types of values differences that act as drivers of migration. In this study, we explore the link between individual-level values and emigration intention, by testing the Schwartz value sub-dimensions and higher-order dimensions as predictors of the intention to migrate. Our study considers the values of home country respondents.

Method

Data Collection and Sample

A questionnaire was administered online to working-age respondents residing in Lithuania. A market research firm was employed to collect the data. A total of 1250 completed questionnaires were received. The questionnaire consisted of three parts, asking for demographic information, their intentions to emigrate from Lithuania and a series of questions pertaining to their personal values. The language of the questionnaire was Lithuanian. The sample consisted of 59% females and 40.8% males. The median age of respondents was 36 years. More than half of the respondents (56%) were university educated.

Measures

The dependent variable, *Intention to emigrate*, was measured as a single Likert-scale item asking respondents whether they intend to emigrate for settlement or work in another country over the next ten years, on a scale from 1 = not at all to 7 = absolutely.

Individual values. For the measurement of values, the 56-item Schwartz Value Survey (SVS) was used (Schwartz, 1992). A previously published translation into Lithuanian by Liubinienė (1999) was used. The original 8-point Likert scale (where '-1' means 'opposed to my values', '0' means 'not important' with the following growing importance up to '7' with the meaning of 'supreme important') by Schwartz was used for coding. Following Schwartz (1992), the 56 values were grouped into 10 sub-dimensions and aggregated to higher-order dimensions. Cronbach's alphas for each of the sub-dimensions are as follows: Conformity (4 items), α = 0.74; Tradition (5 items), α = 0.77; Benevolence (7 items), α = 0.89; Universalism (8 items), α = 0.89; Self-direction (6 items), α = 0.86; Stimulation (3 items), α = 0.78; Hedonism (2 items) α = 0.81; Achievement (5 items) α = 0.81; Power (5 items) α = 0.77; and Security (7 items) α = 0.81. The four items measuring Spirituality were not included in this study.

The value sub-dimensions were also classified into individual-level higher-order value dimensions. Collectivism (α = 0.83) includes the values of benevolence, tradition and conformity. Individualism (α = 0.87) includes power, achievement, hedonism, stimulation and self-direction. The other four higher-order dimensions are bi-polar in the Schwartz model, as follows: openness to change, α = 0.80 (including stimulation and self-direction) versus conservation, α = 0.81 (including conformity, tradition and security), and self-enhancement, α = 0.79 (power, achievement and hedonism) versus self-transcendence, α = 0.88 (universalism and benevolence).

Control variables. We included the following demographic variables as controls in the study. Gender was a binary variable (0 = male, 1 = female). Age was measured by the number of years at the time of data collection. Education was scored on a 5-point scale, where 1 = primary education and 5 = university degree. For the correlation analysis, to account for differences in respondents' use of the SVS and correct for scale use, we include the variable *MRAT*, as recommended in Schwartz (1992). The MRAT is computed as each individual's score on all value items, divided by the total number of items. This variable is included as a covariate to enable partialling out of the relationships of the ten values to the MRAT.

Analysis and Results

To test our hypotheses, we conducted OLS regressions, regressing the dependent variable on each of the value sub-dimensions, as well as the higher-order individual-level value dimensions. The results are depicted in Tables 8.1 and 8.2. Table 8.1 depicts the results of the value sub-dimensions predictors. Table 8.2 depicts the higher-order dimension results. Due to multicollinearity among the dimensions and sub-dimensions, separate regressions were conducted for each, depicted in separate models. Multicollinearity was not an issue in the final results, as VIF values were all below 4.3 for the value sub-dimensions, and below 6.60 for the higher-order dimensions.

We first regressed intention to emigrate on the ten value sub-dimensions. Model 1 (Table 8.1) includes the base model with control variables. Each of the value sub-dimensions is included as a predictor in subsequent models. We can see that all of the sub-dimensions were significantly related to intention to emigrate with the exception of benevolence. Significant positive associations are found between intention to emigrate and power ($B = 0.13$, $p < 0.05$), achievement ($B = 0.21$, $p < 0.01$), hedonism ($B = 0.29$, $p < 0.001$), stimulation ($B = 0.53$, $p < 0.001$) and self-direction ($B = 0.30$, $p < 0.01$). Significant negative relationships were found between the dependent variable and conformity ($B = -28$, $p < 0.001$), universalism ($B = -0.20$, $p < 0.05$), tradition ($B = -0.37$, $p < 0.001$) and security ($B = -0.32$, $p < 0.001$). These results suggest that the individuals who place more importance on those values that are associated with security, tradition and conformity (e.g., maintaining the status quo), have fewer intentions to uproot and emigrate. Individuals who place more emphasis on the self and who value power, achievement, self-direction and stimulation are more inclined to pursue their personal ambitions and are more likely to express their intention to emigrate. These values act in combination to influence emigration intentions via the higher-order value dimensions.

Our first set of hypotheses (hypothesis 1a and hypothesis 1b) predicted that the dimensions of individualism and collectivism would be associated with intentions to emigrate in opposing ways. Table 8.2 depicts the results for each of the higher-order dimensions in separate models. The results for the individualism and collectivism dimensions are depicted in models 6 ad 7. The association between individualism and intention to emigrate was positive and significant ($B = 0.95$, $p < 0.001$). The association between collectivism and intention to emigrate was negative and significant ($B = -0.77, p < 0.001$). Our first hypotheses (1a and 1b) are supported.

Table 8.1 Regression analysis results for Intention to Emigrate regressed on personal values

	1	2	3	4	5	6	7	8	9	10	11
Constant	4.73***	4.77***	4.78***	4.66***	4.69***	4.79***	4.96***	4.72***	4.69***	4.45***	4.94***
	(0.46)	(0.46)	(0.46)	(0.45)	(0.44)	(0.45)	(0.46)	(0.46)	(0.46)	(0.45)	(0.46)
Age	-0.01	-.1	-0.01	-0.01	-0.01	-0.01	-0.01	-0.01	-0.01	-0.01	-0.01
	(0.01)	(0.01)	(0.01)	(0.01)	(0.01)	(0.01)	(0.01)	(0.01)	(0.01)	(0.01)	(0.01)
Gender	0.00	0.01	-0.00	0.06	0.00	0.01	0.02	0.01	-0.01	-0.06	0.03
	(0.11)	(0.11)	(0.11)	(0.11)	(0.11)	(0.11)	(0.11)	(0.11)	(0.11)	(0.11)	(0.11)
Education	-0.06	-0.06	-0.08	-0.08	-0.09	-0.09	-0.09	-0.07	-0.06	-0.10	-0.06
	(0.06)	(0.06)	(0.06)	(0.06)	(0.06)	(0.06)	(0.06)	(0.06)	(0.06)	(0.06)	(0.06)
MRAT	-0.14*	-0.26**	-0.34***	-0.41***	-0.65***	0.13	-0.45***	0.07	-0.28*	0.24**	0.17
	(0.06)	(0.08)	(0.09)	(0.07)	(0.08)	(0.10)	(0.11)	(0.12)	(0.12)	(0.08)	(0.10)
Power		0.13*									
		(0.06)									
Achievement			0.21**								
			(0.08)								
Hedonism				0.29***							
				(0.04)							
Stimulation					0.53***						
					(0.06)						
Conformity						-0.28***					
						(0.07)					
Self-direction							0.30**				
							(0.09)				
Universalism								-0.20*			
								(0.10)			
Benevolence									0.13		
									(0.10)		
Tradition										-0.37***	
										(0.05)	
Security											-0.32***
											(0.08)
F-ratio	2.39*	2.80*	3.47***	11.02***	16.75***	4.80***	3.95**	2.77*	2.27*	12.83***	4.86***
Max VIF	1.06	2.02	2.62	1.56	2.18	2.72	3.93	4.11	4.29	1.90	2.99

Notes: * $p<0.05$, ** $p<0.01$, *** $p<0.001$. $N = 1250$. Coefficients are unstandardized. Standard errors in parentheses

Table 8.2 Regression analysis results for Intention to Emigrate regressed on higher-order dimensions

	1	2	3	4	5	6	7
Constant	4.73***	4.77***	4.80***	4.76***	4.73***	4.66***	4.86***
	(0.46)	(0.44)	(0.46)	(0.44)	(0.46)	(0.45)	(0.44)
Age	−0.01	−0.01	−0.01	−0.01	−0.01	−0.01	−0.01
	(0.01)	(0.01)	(0.01)	(0.01)	(0.01)	(0.01)	(0.01)
Gender	0.00	0.06	0.00	−0.01	0.01	−0.02	0.05
	(0.11)	(0.11)	(0.11)	(0.11)	(0.11)	(0.11)	(0.11)
Education	−0.05	−0.12*	−0.07	−0.11	−0.07	−0.12*	−0.11
	(0.06)	(0.06)	(0.06)	(0.06)	(0.06)	(0.06)	(0.06)
MRAT	−0.14*	−0.90***	−0.38***	0.74***	−0.07	0.66***	−1.05***
	(0.06)	(10)	(0.10)	(0.12)	(0.15)	(0.13)	(0.06)
Openness to change		0.77***					
		(0.08)					
Self-enhancement			0.26**				
			(0.09)				
Conservation				−0.89***			
				(0.10)			
Self-transcendence					−0.06		
					(0.13)		
Collectivism						−0.77***	
						(0.11)	
Individualism							0.95***
							(0.11)
F-ratio	2.39*	19.38***	3.71**	16.89***	1.97	11.40***	17.51***
Max VIF	1.06	3.18	2.98	4.39	6.51	5.25	4.47

Notes: * $p<0.05$, ** $p<0.01$, *** $p<0.001$. N = 1250. Coefficients are unstandardized. Standard errors in parentheses

Hypotheses 2a predicted a positive relationship between openness to change and intention to emigrate, while hypothesis 2b predicted a negative relationship between the conservation dimension and intention to emigrate. The results in models 2 and 4 support the hypotheses. The coefficient for openness to change was positive and significant ($B = 0.77$, $p < 0.001$), while the coefficient for conservation was significant and negative ($B = -0.89$, $p < 0.001$). These results are consistent with the bi-polar alignment of the dimensions.

Hypothesis 3a predicted a positive relationship between intention to emigrate and self-enhancement, while hypothesis 3b—a negative relationship between self-transcendence and intention to emigrate. The results for our hypotheses tests are in models 3 and 5. The coefficient for self-enhancement was significant and positive ($B = 0.26$, $p < 0.01$) in support of hypothesis 3a. The coefficient for self-transcendence, however, was nonsignificant. Hypothesis 3b is not supported.

Discussion and Future Research Direction

This study is cross-sectional, exploratory study and its main findings represent a first step in exploring intentions to emigrate through individual values. We focused on Lithuania and found that willingness to migrate was positively related to certain values. Five of our hypotheses were supported. We found Lithuanians who score higher on the values of power, achievement, hedonism, stimulation and self-direction showed a higher willingness to emigrate. This makes sense, as uprooting one's life and taking the decision to move to another country requires a high degree of personal sacrifice, and acceptance of unknowns. In line with this, of the higher-order dimensions, openness to change was positively related to intentions to emigrate, alongside self-enhancement and individualism. Although we did not test pull-factors, previous studies by Kumpikaitė-Valiūnienė (2019a) had highlighted that opportunities for personal growth and career advancement were important considerations in choosing a host country for migrants; the importance placed on individualism and self-enhancement (e.g., power, achievement, hedonism, self-direction, stimulation) appears to align with these preferences. On the other hand, individuals who value tradition, security and conformity, and are more particularistic, are less likely to migrate, preferring instead the status quo. Conservation and collectivism were the higher-order dimensions associated with lower intentions to emigrate.

Our study is a first step in identifying migrants' values. A limitation is that we only considered values, but we note that other factors will also influence migration intentions, such as personal circumstances of migrants, financial circumstances, employment (unemployment), and various push factors from Lithuania that can compound individuals' personal circumstances. Leong (2014) argues that congruence in values is an important factor in immigrant acculturation in the host country. Time spent in the destination country is also a key variable in the acculturation process, as it is suggested that migrant values can undergo change. Lönnqvist et al. (2011, 2013) found that migrant values do change, affected by different migrant experiences in their host countries. However, this change depends on numerous additional factors, such as the degree to which people interact with host country nationals, the extent to which they live in enclaves of other migrants and the extent to which they rely on their native language versus the host country language, the commitment to their home country, various support networks, migrant demographic characteristics, and a range of additional factors. We focused on individuals still resident in their home country. A comparison of values between potential migrants and immigrants could be of interest in future studies, as would a longitudinal study to capture migrants' value change over time.

Additionally, looking from the perspective of international companies, individual values of international employees could be explored and compared with the values of host nationals. For example, a study by Rudnev (2014) highlighted that the values of migrants are more similar to values that are common in the host country than to values commonly held in their country of origin. We also did not explore demographic differences in relation to values in this study, although we found that intentions to migrate were not significantly related to demographic respondent profiles. However, Sawyerr et al. (2005) revealed that values of individuals depend on age and Alonso-Almeida and Llach (2019) explored the divergences between millennials in high-income countries in relation to the attractiveness of organizations according to their profile of work values. Thus, future studies that compare further the values of different migrant groups could be of benefit for international firms and provide insights for international human resource management.

Acknowledgments This research was funded by a grant (No. S-MIP-17-118) from the Research Council of Lithuania.

References

Alba, R., & Nee, V. (2009). *Remaking the American mainstream: Assimilation and contemporary immigration.* MA, Harvard University Press.

Alonso-Almeida, M. D. M., & Llach, J. (2019). Socially responsible companies: Are they the best workplace for millennials? A cross-national analysis. *Corporate Social Responsibility and Environmental Management, 26*(1), 238–247. https://doi.org/10.1002/csr.1675

Bardi, A., Buchanan, K. E., Goodwin, R., Slabu, L., & Robinson, M. (2014). Value stability and change during self-chosen life transitions: Self-selection versus socialization effects. *Journal of Personality and Social Psychology, 106*(1), 131–147. https://doi.org/10.1037/a0034818

Bhugra, D. (2004). Migration, distress and cultural identity. *British Medical Bulletin, 69*(1), 129–141. https://doi.org/10.1093/bmb/ldh007

Bobowik, M., Basabe, N., Paez, D., Jimenez, A., & Bilbao, M. A. (2011). Personal values and well-being among Europeans, Spanish natives and immigrants to Spain: Does the culture matter? *Journal of Happiness Studies, 12*, 401–419. https://doi.org/10.1007/s10902-010-9202-1

Boer, D., & Fischer, R. (2013). How and when do personal values guide our attitudes and sociality? Explaining cross-cultural variability in attitude–value linkages. *Psychological Bulletin, 139*(5), 1113–1147. https://doi.org/10.1037/a0031347

Brosch, T., & Sander, D. (2014). Appraising value: The role of universal core values and emotions in decision-making. *Cortex: A Journal Devoted to the Study of the Nervous System and Behavior, 59*, 203–205. https://doi.org/10.1016/j.cortex.2014.03.012

Dang, V. T., Vu, T. T., & Nguyen, P. T. (2020). Workplace learning and foreign workers' commitment to host cultural organization: The effects of cross-cultural adjustment and supervisor trust. *Employee Relations: The International Journal, 43*(1), 297–317. https://doi.org/10.1108/ER-02-2020-0039

de Haas, H. (2021). A theory of migration: The aspirations-capabilities framework. Comparative. *Migration Studies, 9*(8), 8. https://doi.org/10.1186/s40878-020-00210-4

Eurostat. (2020). *Emigration by age group, sex and country of next usual residence*. Retrieved December 20, 2022, from https://appsso.eurostat.ec.europa.eu/nui/show.do?dataset=migr_emi3nxt&lang=en

Fernando, W. D. A., & Cohen, L. (2016). Exploring career advantages of highly skilled migrants: A study of Indian academics in the UK. *International Journal of Human Resource Management, 27*(12), 1277–1298. https://doi.org/10.1080/09585192.2015.1072101

Fischer, R., & Schwartz, S. (2011). Whence differences in value priorities? Individual, cultural, or artifactual sources. *Journal of Cross-Cultural Psychology, 42*(7), 1127–1144. https://doi.org/10.1177/0022022110381429

Hofstede, G. (1984). *Culture's consequences: International differences in work-related values* (Vol. 5).

House, R. J., Hanges, P. J., Javidan, M., Dorfman, P. W., & Gupta, V. (Eds.). (2004). *Culture, leadership and organizations : The GLOBE study of 62 societies*. Sage Publications.

Kim, S., Mori, I., & Rahim, A. R. A. (2018). Cultural values matter: Attractiveness of Japanese companies in Malaysia. *International Journal of Cross Cultural Management, 18*(1), 87–103. https://doi.org/10.1177/1470595818759570

Kumpikaitė, V., & Žičkutė, I. (2012). Darnus vystymasis emigracijos kontekste: Lietuvos atvejis. *Vadybos mokslas ir studijos-kaimo verslų ir jų infrastruktūros plėtrai, 3*, 89–97.

Kumpikaitė-Valiūnienė, V. (2019a). Four Lithuanian emigration waves: Comparison analysis of the main host countries. In *Diaspora networks in international business* (pp. 159–181). Springer. https://doi.org/10.1007/978-3-319-91095-6_9

Kumpikaitė-Valiūnienė, V. (2019b). Endangered Lithuania. *Migration Letters, 16*(4), 637–646. https://doi.org/10.33182/ml.v16i4.619

Kumpikaitė-Valiūnienė, V., Duobienė, J., Liubinienė, V., Žičkutė, I., & Pinnington, A. (2020). The contribution of universal values in migration decisions. Who stays and who leaves? In EURAM 2020 Conference, 4–6 December, Dublin, Ireland (online).

Kumpikaitė-Valiūnienė, V., & Žičkutė, I. (2017). Emigration after socialist regime in Lithuania: Why the west is still the best? *Baltic Journal of Management, 12*(1), 86–110. https://doi.org/10.1108/BJM-02-2016-0053

Lee, E. (1966). A theory of migration. *Demography, 3*(1), 47–57. https://doi.org/10.2307/2060063

Leong, C. H. (2013). The socio-psychological profile of prospective emigrants: Singaporeans leaving Singapore. In E. Tartakovsky (Ed.), *Immigration: Policies, challenges, and impact* (pp. 29–50). Nova Science.

Liubinienė, V. (1999). *National Identity in Lithuania: Processes during the period of changes*. Praha: Research Support Scheme. Retrieved December 10, 2020, from http://rss.archives.ceu.hu/archive/00001032/01/33.pdf

Lnglehart, R. (1997). *Modernization and postmodernization: Cultural, economic and political change in 43 societies*. Princeton University Press.

Lönnqvist, J. E., Jasinskaja-Lahti, I., & Verkasalo, M. (2011). Personal values before and after migration: A longitudinal case study on value change in Ingrian–Finnish migrants. *Social Psychological and Personality Science, 2*(6), 584–591. https://doi.org/10.1177/1948550611402362

Lönnqvist, J.-E., Jasinskaja-Lahti, I., & Verkasalo, M. (2013). Rebound effect in personal values: Ingrian Finnish migrants' values two years after migration. *Journal of Cross-Cultural Psychology, 44*(7), 1122–1126. https://doi.org/10.1177/0022022113480040

Makkonen, P. (2016). Career self-management behaviour of Western self-initiated expatriates in local organizations in China. *The International Journal of Human Resource Management, 27*(11), 1135–1157. https://doi.org/10.1080/09585192.2015.1061580

Migration in numbers. (2020). Retrieved December 10, 2020, from https://123.emn.lt/en/

Mockaitis, A. I., Zander, L., & De Cieri, H. (2018). The benefits of global teams for international organizations: HR implications. *International Journal of Human Resource Management, 29*(14), 2137–2158. https://doi.org/10.1080/09585192.2018.1428722

Ojeda-Gonzalez, S., Mihi-Ramirez, A., Arteaga-Ortíz, J., & Cuenca-Garcia, E. (2018). Spain trade in view of some migratory and economic considerations. *Engineering Economics, 29*(1), 53–61. https://doi.org/10.5755/j01.ee.29.1.19387

Perlstein, M., & Ciuk, S. (2019). HRM roles in cross culture training provision: Insights from Israeli companies. *Personnel Review, 48*(1), 273–287. https://doi.org/10.1108/PR-10-2016-0279

Piore, M. J. (1971). *The dual labor market: Theory and implications* (pp. 93–97). Routledge.

Piurko, Y., Schwartz, S. H., & Davidov, E. (2011). Basic personal values and the meaning of left-right political orientations in 20 countries. *Political Psychology, 32*(4), 537–561. https://doi.org/10.1111/j.1467-9221.2011.00828.x

Ralston, D. A., Egri, C. P., Furrer, O., Kuo, M. H., Li, Y., Wangenheim, F., Dabic, M., Naoumova, I., Shimizu, K., Carranza, M., Fu, P. P., Potocan, V. V., Pekerti, A., Lenartoqicz, T., Srinivasan, N., Casado, T., Rossi, A. M., Szabo, E., Butt, A., Palmer, I., Ramburuth, P., Brock, D. M., Terpstra-Tong, J., Grison, I., Reynaud, E., Richards, M., Hallinger, P., Castro, F. B., Ruiz-Gutierrez, J., Milton, L., Ansari, M., Starkus, A., Mockaitis, A., Dalgic, T., Leon-Darner, F., Thanh, H., Moon, Y., Molteni, M., Fang, Y., Pla-Barner, J., Alas, R., Maignan, I., Jesuino, J. C., Lee, C., Nicholson, J. D., Chia, H., Danis, W., Dharmasiri, A. S., & Wber, M. (2014). Societal-level versus individual-level predictions of ethical behavior: A 48-society study of collectivism and individualism. *Journal of Business Ethics, 122*, 283–306.

Ralston, D. A., Egri, C. P., Reynaud, E., Srinivasan, N., Furrer, O., Brock, D., et al. (2011). A twenty-first century assessment of values across the global workforce. *Journal of Business Ethics, 104*(1), 1–31. https://www.jstor.org/stable/41476064

Rokeach, M. (1973). *The nature of human values*. Free press.

Rudnev, M. (2014). Value adaptation among intra-European migrants: Role of country of birth and country of residence. *Journal of Cross-Cultural Psychology, 45*(10), 1626–1642. https://doi.org/10.1177/0022022114548482

Sawyerr, O. O., Strauss, J., & Yan, J. (2005). Individual value structure and diversity attitudes: The moderating effects of age, gender, race, and religiosity. *Journal of Managerial Psychology, 20*(6), 498–521. https://doi.org/10.1108/02683940510615442

Schwartz, S. H. (1992). Universals in the content and structure of values: Theory and empirical tests in 20 countries. In M. Zanna (Ed.), *Advances in experimental social psychology* (Vol. 25, pp. 1–65). Academic Press.

Schwartz, S. H. (2006a). Les valeurs de base de la personne: Théorie, mesures et applications [Basic human values: Theory, measurement, and applications]. *Revue Française de Sociologie, 47*, 249–288. https://doi.org/10.3917/rfs.474.0929

Schwartz, S. H. (2006b). A theory of cultural value orientations: Explication and applications. *Comparative Sociology, 5*, 137–182.

Schwartz, S. H. (2012). An overview of the Schwartz theory of basic values. *Online Readings in Psychology and Culture, 2*(1). https://doi.org/10.9707/2307-0919.1116

Schwartz, S. H., & Butenko, T. (2014). Values and behavior: Validating the refined value theory in Russia. *European Journal of Social Psychology, 44*(7), 799–813. https://doi.org/10.1002/ejsp.2053

Schwartz, S. H., Cieciuch, J., Vecchione, M., Davidov, E., Fischer, R., Beierlein, C., Ramos, A., Verkasalo, M., Lönnqvist, J.-E., Demirutku, K., Dirilen-Gumus, O., & Konty, M. (2012). Refining the theory of basic individual values. *Journal of Personality and Social Psychology, 103*(4), 663–688. https://doi.org/10.1037/a0029393

Tartakovsky, E. (2009). Cultural identities of adolescent immigrants: A three-year longitudinal study including the pre-migration period. *Journal of Youth and Adolescence, 38*(5), 654–671. https://doi.org/10.1007/s10964-008-9370-z

Tartakovsky, E., Walsh, S. D., Patrakov, E., & Nikulina, M. (2017). Between two worlds? Value preferences of immigrants compared to local-born populations in the receiving country and in the country of origin. *Journal of Cross-Cultural Psychology, 48*(6), 835–853. https://doi.org/10.1177/0022022117709534

Tsui, A. S., Nifadkar, S. S., & Ou, A. Y. (2007). Cross-national, cross-cultural organizational behavior research: Advances, gaps, and recommendations. *Journal of Management, 33*(3), 426–478. https://doi.org/10.1177/0149206307300818

Van Hear, N., Bakewell, O., & Long, K. (2018). Push-pull plus: Reconsidering the drivers of migration. *Journal of Ethnic and Migration Studies, 44*(6), 927–944. https://doi.org/10.1080/1369183X.2017.1384135

Welzel, C., & Inglehart, R. (2010). Agency, values, and well-being: A human development model. *Social Indicators Research, 97*(1), 43–63. https://doi.org/10.1007/s11205-009-9557-z

Zander, L., Mockaitis, A. I., & Butler, C. L. (2012). Leading global teams. *Journal of World Business, 47*, 592–603. https://doi.org/10.1016/j.jwb.2012.01.012

9

From Working Hard to Being Hard Working: The Maintenance and Mobilization of Cultural Capital among Finnish Migrants in Florida

Johanna Raitis, Riikka Harikkala-Laihinen, Niina Nummela, and Eriikka Paavilainen-Mäntymäki

Introduction

In today's global world, it has become increasingly common, possible, and even necessary for individuals to relocate to different countries for work or other reasons for short periods of time, temporarily, or for good. Despite the reason or motivation for relocation (e.g., expatriate, sojourner, or migrant entrepreneur) or the length of the stay, moving to a new country is likely to cause stress and require an individual to change. Consequently, socio-cultural adaptation—or the ability of individuals to adapt to and function in a foreign culture—is becoming an increasingly important skill (Bierwiaczonek & Waldzus, 2016; Huff et al., 2021). Considering the phenomenon's importance to individuals' well-being and to organizations and societies, as the notion of well-integrated migrants may be critical in terms of competitive resources and economic assets (Dana et al., 2019), understanding the factors that drive successful cultural adaptation is of the utmost significance. However, the increasing complexity of the global environment and connectivity of

---

J. Raitis (✉) • R. Harikkala-Laihinen • N. Nummela • E. Paavilainen-Mäntymäki
University of Turku, Turku, Finland
e-mail: johanna.raitis@utu.fi; riikka.m.harikkala@utu.fi; niina.nummela@utu.fi; eriikka.paavilainen-mantymaki@utu.fi

people require researchers to take more systematic approaches and dynamic perspectives. Traditionally, research on socio-cultural adaptation and related processes of acculturation has largely focused on the importance of the "receiving" culture, ignoring the wider range of individual, situational, and cultural-level influences and complexities (Ward et al., 2004; Weinreich, 2009). Consequently, an important but empirically less studied question continues to circle around the topic of individual–host country interactivity.

In the field of international business, culture, and cultural differences in particular, is and has long been at the center of various streams of research, but it has mainly been seen as the root and cause of challenges and obstacles at both the organizational and individual levels. Such a limited and negative view of culture inevitably hinders our understanding of the processes and conditions needed to help organizations and individuals adapt to and leverage the benefits of cultural differences (Shenkar, 2001, 2012; Stahl & Tung, 2015). Thus, there has been a call for a more "positive treatment of culture" and its distinguishing features (Cameron, 2017; Stahl & Tung, 2015; Srivastava et al., 2020) and for a more intense focus on the interfaces rather than on the voids between the transacting entities (Shenkar, 2001). From the viewpoint of migrating individuals, recent research has suggested that certain geographical or cultural areas might be more appealing to certain groups of people (cf. Nummela et al., 2021), emphasizing the need to respond to the call to incorporate individual-level attributes and desires into the model (Berry, 2005; Potosky, 2016; Ward & Geeraert, 2016).

At a more fundamental level, mobility has permanent consequences on who we are and what we do (Weinreich, 2009; Özkazanç-Pan, 2019). However, to understand how the new forms of belonging and identities emerge from the interplay between cultures, further research is required. Thus, in the field of international migration and diasporas, the focus has started to shift from the deficit-and-problem view to the agency-and-opportunity view (Elo & Minto-Coy, 2019; see also Annique Un et al., 2022). In other words, the state of multiple belonging, formerly seen as a negative feature of diaspora, is now viewed as an advantage, offering, for example, opportunities for networking and facilitating recognition in individuals' entrepreneurial activities (Elo & Minto-Coy, 2019; see also Calhoun, 2003). Extant literature has already shown linkages between mobility and entrepreneurial efforts (e.g., Frederiksen et al., 2016; Nummela et al., 2021) and highlighted the relatively high entrepreneurial activity in migrant communities (Zubair & Brzozowski, 2018). Although these ideas were first found in the entrepreneurship literature, they could also be relevant and applicable to individuals seeking, recognizing, and engaging in any type of work in a new host country. Moreover, although it is suggested that entrepreneurship is affected by both actors and contexts (Welter, 2011), prior studies have neglected to explain how opportunities and activities may emerge from the interplay between the individual, the host population, and the socio-cultural environment (Ozasir Kacar & Essers, 2019).

To address the gaps identified above, we aim to dig deeper into the interactivity between contexts and individuals by asking *how migrants can draw from and utilize their cultural capital in their new host environment in the domain of work*. Regarding the term "cultural capital," we refer to the Bourdeausian "rucksack approach" from migration studies that defines culture-specific competencies (fitting or not fitting) as those that migrants bring with them to the new country of residence (Bourdieu, 1986; Cutler et al., 2005; Erel, 2010). Thus, we follow the idea that context—both home and host—is an important driver of cultural adaptation (Berry, 1997; Bierwiaczonek & Waldzus, 2016; Ward & Geeraert, 2016), but equally important are the "matching" features of the home and host cultures that individuals can mobilize in the domain of work. We seek to unveil the dynamics between the different levels (individual and contextual) by drawing from the identity literature that puts forth that individual identities are constructed in interactions with others (e.g., Ashforth & Mael, 1996; Hall, 1991).

To address the research question, we conducted an empirical study of the Finnish diaspora in Florida, United States. A central feature of overseas ethnic communities, diasporas, is their retained affinity for both their native lands and their members. While adapting to their local environments, diasporas often retain elements of the culture, language, religion, food, family structures, and other cultural features of their homelands. Florida has a unique history as a melting pot of different cultures, hosting many immigrant communities with a "settler nationality" (see Bell, 2009), and the Finnish community was one of the earliest diasporas in the region, established more than 100 years ago. The data analyzed in this study consist of 12 face-to-face interviews with Finnish-origin, first- and second-generation residents in Florida, secondary data, and participant observations collected in the spring of 2022. The study results are expected to enrich our understanding of the conditions and drivers of interactivity by illustrating what specific contents of cultural capital are utilized and how. Despite the focus on the Finnish–Florida context, the results could have a wider impact on the ongoing discussions surrounding international migration, socio-cultural adaptation, and the "positivity" of culture in international business.

Theoretical Framework

The extant literature on cross-cultural adaptation has introduced various individual- and context-level factors that explain and drive successful (or unsuccessful) migration to a new environment. A commonly applied theoretical lens is a cultural fit pertaining to both psychological and socio-cultural adjustment (Peltokorpi & Froese, 2014; Ward et al., 2004, 2020). These studies have emphasized the interaction between migrating individuals' personalities, or personal attributes, and the cultural norms in the host country that together determine the adjustment process and its outcome. In other words, cultural fit does not require all personality traits to resemble the host culture's norms to be adaptive; some characteristics may function as psychological resources and drivers of psychological well-being, while others relate to more tangible intercultural skills and competencies (Caligiuri, 2000; Ward et al., 2004). In this study, we focus on the latter domain to understand the dynamics between the contextual and individual levels.

In the literature, there is ample evidence that the societal environment of the host country (i.e., the country of relocation) can be a powerful predictor of cultural adaptation (e.g., Ward & Geeraert, 2016; Wilson, 2013). Sociocultural adaptation is influenced by the amount of contact with host nationals and the length of stay in a new culture (Stahl & Caligiuri, 2005; Ward & Kennedy, 1993), but the specificity of the context(s) also plays a role. Studies have suggested that host country policies, whether they are based on assimilation or multiculturalism (Kunst & Sam, 2013; Ait Ouarasse & Van De Vijver, 2004) and the level of economic development, may facilitate or hinder adaptation (Greenman, 2011). A recent study by Huff et al. (2021) introduced the concept of "historical heterogeneity," which accentuates the host country's traditions and history as a variable explaining adaptation. The researchers argued that successful cultural adaptation may be more dependent on a society's long-standing traditions of diversity than on its current situation and outlook (Huff et al., 2021; Richardson, 2022). Prior studies have drawn from the idea that cultural norms, especially those related to the acceptance of foreigners, typically take generations to develop (Leung & Morris, 2015; Schwartz, 2011). Indeed, past migrant generations' positive experiences may generate more positive expectations, motivation, and confidence among newcomers, facilitating their engagement with and adjustment to the host country. Thus, perceiving the host culture as more welcoming could encourage newcomers to engage more deeply, seek out interactions with locals, and adjust their behaviors (Berry, 1997).

A widely applied construct incorporating both home and host cultures in predicting adaptation is "cultural distance" (e.g., Demes & Geeraert, 2014; Stahl & Caligiuri, 2005), suggesting that cultures with similarities pair up better than those with differences. However, the construct has been criticized for its simplicity and "illusions," such as its assumption of cultural stability over time and the linearity in the amount of distance and number of challenges (Beugelsdijk et al., 2018; Shenkar, 2001, 2012; Stoessel et al., 2014). The asymmetrical effect of cultural distance was further confirmed by Selmer et al. (2007) in their empirical study of both German and American managers. They discovered that despite the equal cultural distance, it was easier for German managers to adapt to the United States than it was for U.S. managers to adapt to Germany. Thus, although it is important to understand both cultures that are in contact, if we are to understand the individuals in contact (Berry, 2005), we also need to look into various other factors, such as by exploring the situational, motivational, or temporal aspects, to fully understand interactivity. For example, in the case of Chinese immigrants entering and integrating into an engineering culture in Canada, migrants devalued the emotional and relational values endorsed in their home country's culture and instead started to endorse masculine, competitive, and individualistic values, which they perceived to be essential in their new work environment (Shan, 2012).

Berry's model of acculturation is grounded in the idea that individuals' cultural orientation toward the home and host cultures impacts their acculturation strategies in a new environment (Berry, 1997, 2005; see also Ward & Geeraert, 2016). According to the model, migrants choose to either maintain or discard their own home/heritage cultures and to adopt or reject the new host/settlement culture. Although this model offers a usable framework for understanding the variety of individual approaches, it has been criticized for its bipolar conceptualization, mainly focusing on the settlement culture rather than the heritage culture (Shenkar, 2012). In a recent study, Valenzuela and Rogers (2021) suggested that the selection of the chosen acculturation strategy may depend on a perceived match between immigrants' abilities and traits and the demands of the host culture. They further highlighted that the process of how immigrants draw upon certain personal attributes to meet the demands of the host culture has been inadequately explored. Weinreich (2009) suggested replacing acculturation with the "enculturation" strategy, highlighting the incorporation of any available cultural elements, mainstream or otherwise, that a person considers relevant and thus significant to the construction of their overall identity. Moreover, while acculturation typically indicates migrants' movements on a single continuum toward the adoption of the mainstream "receiving" culture, enculturation equally emphasizes the relevance of the heritage culture in the identity formation process (Weinreich, 2009). Thus, rather than switching their cultural framework (Ivanova-Gongne et al., 2021), they could incorporate, leverage, or even take advantage of it.

The identity literature has put forth the idea that individual identities are constructed and negotiated in interactions with others (e.g., Ashforth & Mael, 1996). In the case of migrants, however, social negotiations and construction entail more diverse identity dimensions and audiences. In their study, Killian and Johnson (2006) suggested that migrants have at least three distinct identities: immigrant, ethnic, and national/host country. The influence of and interplay between these identities differ depending on the context or situation. Thus, migrants may selectively use different repertoires or traits of their cultures and showcase only a distinct part of themselves. An individual can carry a portfolio of identities and activate them at different times, depending on, for example, the restrictions imposed by social settings and identity audiences (Nagel, 1997). However, this also means that although people can choose how they wish to identify themselves, they cannot always control others' attempts to classify them (Nagel, 1997). For example, Morris et al. (2011) discovered that a sudden increase in the number of migrants in a host country may be perceived as a threat to cultural identity by locals, leading to unwelcoming attitudes that potentially undermine the migrants' cultural adaptation.

Indeed, perceptions and pre-classifications by the constituents of the host country may differ greatly in different domains and situations. These perceptions may also date back in history. In his study of the hybrid identity construction of first- and second-generation Caribbeans in Canada, Plaza (2006) discovered that depending on the domain and groups of the host population, the immigrants either needed to deal with racial stereotyping dating back to the time of colonialism, or they could be more open and proud about their roots and own cultural ideologies. Similarly, Killian and Johnson (2006) found that belonging to a certain ethnic group gave African women immigrants a low-status image in France, marking them permanently by their place of birth or the milieu in which they grew up. To counteract these negative images, they employed various strategies of refusing certain labels of identity, such as through the management of appearance, "Not-Me" narratives, the redefinition of labels, and the use of educational resources (Killian & Johnson, 2006).

Thus, the experiences of demarcation based on ethnic background may be shaped not only by present relationships, rules, and practices but also by past experiences, indicating that there might be considerable fluidity, and also stability, across generations (cf. Plaza, 2006). Usually, however, classifications or stereotypes are built on "typical" values and oversimplified images that others perceive to reflect a specific group (Helkama, 2015; Schwartz, 2011). Migrant individuals can refuse a given classification or image (Hunt, 2003) or then welcome and leverage it, depending on the nature and type of classification. Fewer studies have focused on the latter, specifically how individuals may maintain and utilize the given classifications in the socio-cultural adaptation process.

Methods

The data for this chapter stem from a Finnish community located in South Florida. The community centers around Lake Worth and Lantana but has contributed to the construction and development of large areas in the Palm Beach County area since its establishment approximately 100 years ago. At the time of data collection, this included two "club houses" (Finland House and American Finnish Club), several street names sourced from Finnish surnames (e.g., Alho drive), a residential area named by its Finnish builder (Nurmi Isles), a Finnish bakery (Polar Bakery, Lantana), and statues donated by and dedicated to Finns in a public park (Bryant Park, Lake Worth). We describe this settlement as a transnational community stemming from the notion that the "nation" in transnationality usually refers to the territorial, social, and cultural aspects of the nations concerned (Kearney, 1995). What is particular to this community is the dual existence of both Finnish and American elements.

The members of the community identify as "amerikansuomalainen," American Finns, who actively leverage their Finnish heritage to adapt to the surrounding American culture. The community is residentially scattered but closely tied together through informal networks and ethnic organizations. According to U.S. census data, foreign-born Finns have been present in Florida since at least 1850, growing steadily in number and reaching over 400,000 in 1910. In the 1960s, the foreign-born Finnish population still accounted for over 150,000 people. From there, the number of foreign-born Finns in Florida began to decline, amounting to approximately 30,000 in 2000. According to the interviewees, the area still houses at least 10,000 Finns. However, nowadays, the majority are "snowbirds" who fly in for the winter season and spend summers in Finland or in the northern states. This has made the community vulnerable, and locals expect that the COVID-19 pandemic has mortally wounded the area in terms of the vibrancy of the winter season.

One of the authors lived in this community in Florida for four months in the spring of 2022. During her stay, she conducted qualitative, semi-structured life-course interviews with 42 members of the community. These interviews enabled the obtaining of detailed information on the life stories of the participants, paying special attention to experiences of identity formation, community, and work. The interview guide was inspired by Atkinson's (1998; see also Shan, 2012) life story interview protocol, utilizing questions such as "please tell me about yourself," "where are you from," "what kind of identity is closest to your heart," "how active are you in the surrounding community," "what has been the role of the community in settling into the area," "please describe your work history," "what does work mean for you," "how are Finns perceived in working life in Florida," and "do you consider yourself entrepreneurial." The purpose of using life-course interviews was to explore the stories of the people within a society, enabling the retelling of lives across time and the interaction between individual lives and the community (cf. Atkinson, 1998). The interviews were conducted in Finnish and translated by the research team.

Of the 42 interviews, all of which informed our understanding of the community, 14 (including four interviews with two participants) were selected for this chapter to reflect on how individuals draw strengths from different cultures. These interviewees were either entrepreneurs (13) or individuals with entrepreneurial attitudes toward work (4). At the same time, these interviewees represented the clearest reflection of both of the two cultures, Finnish and American, whereas others reported that they were primarily Finnish, perceived themselves as American, or perceived themselves as cosmopolitans, with no clear sense of drawing from any cultural heritage. Appendix 1 lists the participants who were interviewed in this study.

In addition to the interviews, the prolonged visit to Florida allowed the researcher to participate in gatherings and events hosted by the Finnish community, such as morning coffee chats at the Finnish bakery, lunch at Kerhotalo (American Finnish Club), meetings of the heritage society at Suomi Talo (Finland House), and the Finnish summer festival. This prolonged and "idle" stay (cf. Coates, 2017) opened access to the casual interactions with and between people, which provided a more profound understanding of the history and the bicultural makeup of Florida Finns that ultimately informed the data analysis. Secondary data, which were used to understand the historical role and relevance of the early Finnish migrants in the region, consisted of history books written by various authors from that area, pictures, and other historical objects.

Findings

The data in our study suggest that coming from a culture that is seen to possess certain values and characteristics helped the migrants start and run their businesses and engage in other types of work in their host environment. The stereotype given to Finns in the region—labeling them as hard-working, diligent, and trustworthy workers and business partners—inculcated the migrants with a positive image that helped them to boost their self-image in the domain of work. We discovered that the roots of the given stereotype had already been established at the time of the first Finnish settlers arriving in the area in the 1920s. The same stereotype has pervaded until today, and it has been adopted by current migrants in the region. The following explains the premises of the cultural match between the Finnish migrants and the work context (and population) in Florida and shows how the historically built image of the Finns and the activities by and in the diaspora have helped and informed the migrants in adapting to the host society, interactively leveraging both their home and host countries' cultures.

Matching the Host Country Context and Migrants' Cultural Capital

The work environment in the United States is characterized by special features, the most central of which is the value of hard work. The story of the American dream postulates that by working hard, anyone can achieve the "American dream," which highlights opportunity, economic success, and security (Adams, 2017; Geary, 2019; Waldron et al., 2004). It is also a central component of the nation's story, as immigration has played an essential role in the country's economy and cultural make-up for centuries, being a major source of population and economic growth (Barrett, 1992; Porter, 2010). Many will associate the phrase "American dream" with "the land of opportunity for immigrants," although attitudes toward migrants have cycled between favorable and hostile since the 1790s (Geary, 2019).

The value of hard work was familiar and equally important to the Finnish migrant interviewees, who perceived work as an intrinsic part of themselves and their lives. Although the value of hard work is and has been central to Finnish people throughout their history (Helkama, 2015; Taramaa, 2009), the American emphasis and pace was yet at another level. Consequently, the encouraging work environment and interactions with locals further bolstered their diligence and attitude toward work:

> It's the way of life (work), which is very strong here ... Even my neighbor always says, "You work hard, you work hard, and you work hard." Yes, I work very hard. Work always comes first for Americans. Well, for all of us Finns, it has always been very important as well, and we have worked a lot. But Finnish visitors who come here say that they never work as much in Finland as we do here. (MK).

Although the interviewees stated that working hard was the only way to survive in the host country, they also enjoyed it immensely. They considered themselves to be in a fitting and supporting environment that pushed them to work even harder. Furthermore, they considered themselves to be living the American dream and thus had been integrated into society through their work:

> Well, you have to work here. You will always have to work, but we have always enjoyed working like crazy! So, now we're living the American dream. (ER).

However, the tendency and attitude toward the "purpose" and "fruits" of hard work were perceived to be different in their home and host countries:

> In Finland, there is a lot of envy. People envy you when you become successful. Here, they say, "Well done, great, and we encourage you." Here, they are proud to have friends who are successful. You boast about it. (JK)

This difference in the interpretation and accepted outcomes may be explained by the origin of the values, where the Finnish value of hard work is the legacy of Lutheranism and the Protestant work ethic and the work itself is valued and cherished (Helkama & Portman, 2019). In the United States, hard work is linked to "dream" and "economic freedom" (Geary, 2019). Thus, although the values are similar, their interpretations vary between the home and host countries.

Manifesting and Maintaining the "Hard Working" Stereotype over Time

The image of Finnish migrants as hard-working people was already established in the 1920s, when the first Finnish settlers came to the region and started building the community and its surroundings. At that time, the local community was in a strong phase of growth and development, and a lot of construction work was available. There were many skillful carpenters and craftsmen among the Finnish migrants, and they participated in the development and construction work. Over time, their reputation as skillful, reliable, and hardworking craftsmen grew. Their construction work still exists today and is visible in various parts of the region, such as the grand houses on Palm Beach Island, reminding the residents of their accomplishments. In the 1940s, a Finnish migrant, Victor Nurmi, bought undeveloped small islands formerly known as Las Olas near Fort Lauderdale, developing them into a prestigious upper-middle-class residential area now known as the Nurmi Isles. The residential Alho drive in Lantana, named and completely built by Finns, has also housed many Finns over the decades. The interviewees seemed to be very familiar with and often referred to the buildings and places built by the early Finns:

> In the old days … everything here is built by Finnish migrants. There were big areas in Lake Worth, Lantana, where they were working. So, Finnish people have always been diligent and hardworking, very professional craftsmen and builders. And we are very well known for that. We always discuss how Finnishness is also visible outside, in the exteriors. (MK).

Thus, the past images of the early settlers continue to influence the current residents' perceptions of themselves. Present-day migrants' awareness of the past and of the Finns' central role in the region makes them proud of their roots in the area. Furthermore, the image that was created in the past is being actively maintained by the Finnish community. For example, they actively engage in cultural remembering (Goncharova, 2016) and celebrate the historical past. Thus, rather than defying the historical stereotype or their background, they enforce it in a type of "us-too" rather than "not-me" narrative. An interviewee referred to it as a *positive stamp* demarcating both the previous and current generations.

The images from the past are also fortified and maintained by the Finnish community, especially the active clubs and associations (Suomi Talo and Kerhotalo, meeting places for the Finnish community and locals interested in their events, such as plays and dances) maintaining Finnish culture, heritage, and traditions. Interestingly, the observer-researcher noted that the "Finnishness" innate to the Florida community dates back decades, but the Finnish culture embraced by the community seemed somewhat outdated. For example, reflections on dances every Wednesday and Saturday seemed foreign to the participating researcher. The community organizes activities and gathers people together, but it also disseminates information from the community's history. The role of the Finnish people in the community, and especially the image of Finnish workers as diligent and hardworking, is shared and perpetuated through various stories and books written about the early years (e.g., Hiironniemi, 2021). In addition, in club houses, there are many pictures, ornaments, and objects reminding people of the past. The concrete settings of the various community venues, namely the club houses and churches built by the Finns, also reinforce these stories.

The maintenance of collective cultural capital is also notable in a more performative way. The community's club houses, administration, and activities are organized and run by community members on a voluntary basis. Depending on the volunteer's role, whether it is cleaning, financial management, preparing coffee and refreshments for the events, organizing flea markets, or impersonating Santa Claus at the Christmas party, the work can be very time-consuming. A general perception among the interviewees was, however, that it was not a problem because the work itself is thought to be very rewarding, giving them *a lot of joy*. In addition, this work connected to and showcased the migrants' similarity in terms of their perceptions of work in the host culture but in another domain:

> What does working mean to you? (Interviewer)
> Well, it's in a way my way of life. That's also why I am (working voluntarily) here at (the club house), without pay. (AA).

The quote demonstrates that the migrants have maintained a very strong Finnish cultural practice: joint voluntary work for the common good, referred to in Finnish as *talkoot*. This means that as the community engages its members in voluntary work, it also makes them participants—enablers, creators, and communicators—in the heritage work. On the one hand, voluntary work promotes desirable attitudes toward the work. On the other hand, it brings people together and engages them in cultural remembering and preservation that also support the maintenance and durability of cultural capital and the perceptions of themselves over time.

Utilization of Cultural and Social Capital in the Domain of Work

According to the interview data, the host environment offered many possibilities and encouraged the migrants to enter and engage in different types of work. Whether they had businesses of their own or were employed by others, the "Finnishness" was perceived to be a clear advantage in the eyes of the employers, partners, or collaborators:

9 From Working Hard to Being Hard Working: The Maintenance...

> Being a Finn gives you a lot of benefits. It has definitely helped me because people respect it. I have been working (cleaning houses) in a very good neighborhood here, and the word has gone around. They really respect the fact that I am a Finn. I have been told that many times ... (MK).

Although they identified with the ideals of the American way of working, the interviewees also noted some controversies in local business conduct, which were in stark contrast to their cultural ideals and conduct. This was especially the case regarding the value of honesty, which is central to Finnish national identity (Helkama & Portman, 2019). This juxtaposition and value conflict was particularly evident in interactions with other foreign-origin businesses that were infamous for being unreliable and untrustworthy. Reportedly, doing business with some "other migrants" always included risks, which the Finnish migrants also had experiences of:

> You can't trust anybody here. Just today, I drove to see a car that was supposed to be in good condition, but it was crap. So, before you have the names on the paper and money in our pocket, you can't trust anyone. It's that simple. (JT).

The interviewee continued and dispositioned himself partly from the prevailing business culture:

> Business-wise, I am more American, but if you look at the basic stuff about life, honesty, and so forth, then yeah, I'm Finnish. (JT).

This negative attitude toward some migrants prevailing in the business environment did not deter Finns. Even if the Finns identified strongly with the American dream, they maintained their national values of integrity and honesty, which helped them distinguish themselves from the notorious "other migrants." The interviewees highlighted that the Americans' trust in the Finnish people made it easier for them to do business, impacting their economic performance. Thus, when positioning themselves in the host context, they purposefully emphasized the group-specific cultural traits that were appreciated by others and distinguished them from the other locally based migrant groups. In other words, they deliberately emphasized their origins to create a positive and desired image. The Finnish origin did not go un-noticed in interactions with others. On the contrary, migrants even used it to influence the perceptions of others. When asked if their response to the question "Where are you from?" is Finland, an interviewee explained:

> Yes, absolutely, always. It is also that Finns are considered trustworthy and honest. And it creates the image that I can be trusted, too. Especially in business, honesty is the top priority. (JT).

This positive and distinguishing feature made the Finnish migrants enforce and cultivate this part of their national identity, making them feel even "more Finnish" in a context where such features are not generally prevailing:

> It (being Finnish) is somehow refined here. It has become stronger than it was in Finland. In Finland, certain things are normal and regular, nothing special, but here, we become even more Finnish in certain aspects. (AA).

In addition to utilizing the positive image of being a Finn, the interviewees also highlighted the important role of the Finnish diaspora in their work endeavors. This was evident, especially among the newcomers, who were establishing themselves and their businesses in the region. They could, for example, get help and advice from other community members for many practical matters, such as bookkeeping and facilitating and hastening their adaptation. This guidance was particularly important in situations where the migrant worker was not very fluent in the native language. Reportedly, getting advice in their mother tongue eased their anxiety in adapting to a new business or work environment whose customs and terminology were unfamiliar to them.

Furthermore, their first customers or employers often came from within the community or through the community members' connections. Thus, in a sense, the community operated as a link between migrants and work/business opportunities by providing opportunities to interact with and access other community members' networks. In establishing these new relationships, trust, rather than prior experience, was often the decisive factor. One interviewee explained this when asked about the relevance of the Finnish community in their settlement into the region:

> I would say it has been huge. I am an entrepreneur, and I am almost fully employed by a company that has been established by Finns ... So it (the Finnish community) has definitely made things easier. We don't engage very much with Finnish people in our leisure time, but in business, we do. Let's put it this way: Finns prefer to buy from other Finns because they are reliable. (MA).

Sometimes, the demands or ideas from the community members even guided the entrepreneurs to recognize business opportunities and enter certain business fields:

We have had all kinds of businesses. It doesn't matter what it is. But initially, they (community members) came to us with lots of ideas, like why don't you start mowing lawns? And that's how we started our lawn-mowing business. (ER)

Conclusions

This chapter addressed the question of *how migrants can draw from and utilize their cultural capital in their new host country in the domain of work*. We looked into the interfaces between the contextual and individual levels and sought to explore factors driving interactivity and facilitating migrants' adaptation. While there seems to be more research on migrants rejecting or devaluing their distinctive home culture characteristics, we presented an opposite type of case, where the migrants successfully utilized and even emphasized their cultural capital facilitating their adaptation. Our empirical findings indicate that contextual-level cultural match, a historically built group image, and activities of and in the migrant community may facilitate and guide migrant workers in their adaptation processes and in constructing a bicultural identity (Brannen & Thomas, 2010), leveraging both their home and host cultures. Such an approach does not require the migrants to change or reject their heritage culture but rather to strategically select and enforce some aspects of it that are most fitting, usable, or positively distinguishing in their host environment. However, the successful selection of these traits requires matching individual-level attributes with socially desirable features, where the experience of past generations, comparisons to other migrant groups, and feedback from external audiences are pivotal.

The difference between acculturation and enculturation processes is that the former is inclined toward the settlement culture, while the latter emphasizes settlement and heritage cultures equally in individuals' adaptation and identity formation processes (cf. Berry, 1997; Weinreich, 2009). The findings of this study also highlighted the relevance of both cultures, but rather than seeing the process on a continuum, moving toward either end, we should look for the crossings of the lines as opposed to specific positions on them. In other words, we suggest that adaptation does not necessarily require giving up the culture of origin (see Ryder et al., 2000). We believe that our study enriches the understanding of migrant identity construction by illustrating how migrants can build partly overlapping yet unique bicultural identities by identifying with both cultures (Brannen & Thomas, 2010). We show how individuals may build linkages over time and across the home and host cultures. The process is situational and dynamic, leading to the creation of a new, negotiated identity (see also Freedman & Tarr, 2000). According to Malkki (2008), the homeland is one of the most powerful unifying symbols for mobile individuals, but it can be constructed in different ways in different settings. In our case, migrant identity was negotiated and founded in the domain of work. Our empirical study illustrates one case of a slightly differently reconstructed homeland, where some features were positively enforced (honesty) and others dismissed (language) based on the perceived contextual and situational relevance.

As a response to the call for more research on contextualized settings and their impact on international migration (Elo & Minto-Coy, 2019), this study offers a historically and geographically specific explanation of the Finnish migrants' settlement in Florida. Moreover, the study shifted the lens away from the historical victim perspective of diasporas to a more modern stance (Brubaker, 2005) by illustrating how the Finnish community in Florida has thrived by maintaining and utilizing its cultural capital. In doing so, the community has persisted over time, showing a long-standing and stable status in society (Dana et al., 2019). Thus, it matters not only where one goes but also who went there first. The experiences of earlier migrants may create strong and enduring impressions in the host environment and among its population, and in the migrants' perceptions of themselves. Thus, in addition to the host society's heritage and historical stances (Huff et al., 2021), we emphasized the early settlers' role in present-day migrants' lives and status in society.

Finally, we believe that our findings could advance the "positivity" of cultural discussions in the field of international business. We have shown how foreign cultures can also be evaluated and matched by their compatible features. In this study, this was found to occur through values that transcended countries, companies, professions, types of employment, and even generations. It was geographically confirmed and bounded in past and current experiences and utilized for economic benefit. These findings could be relevant and applied to migrant entrepreneurship studies that seek to understand how to capitalize on distinctiveness and conformance in the international business arena (Abd Hamid et al., 2019), how cultural capital can be formed and utilized differently (e.g., Andrejuk, 2017).

References

Abd Hamid, H., O'Kane, C., & Everett, A. M. (2019). Conforming to the host country versus being distinct to our home countries: Ethnic migrant entrepreneurs' identity work in cross-cultural setting. *International Journal of Entrepreneurial Behavior & Research, 25*(5), 919–935.

Adams, J. T. (2017). *The epic of America*. Routledge.

Ait Ouarasse, O., & Van de Vijver, F. J. (2004). Structure and function of the perceived acculturation context of young Moroccans in The Netherlands. *International Journal of Psychology, 39*(3), 190–204.

Andrejuk, K. (2017). Self-employed migrants from EU member states in Poland: Differentiated professional trajectories and explanations of entrepreneurial success. *Journal of Ethnic and Migration Studies, 43*(4), 560–577.

Annique Un, C., Ou, C., & Lafayette, S. U. (2022). From the liability to the advantage of refugeeness. *Journal of International Business Policy.*, Palgrave Macmillan, 5(4), 530–561.

Ashforth, B. E., & Mael, F. A. (1996). Organizational identity and strategy as a context for the individual. *Advances in Strategic Management, 13*, 19–64.

Atkinson, R. (1998). *The life story interview*. Sage.

Barrett, J. R. (1992). Americanization from the bottom up: Immigration and the remaking of the working class in the United States, 1880–1930. *The Journal of American History, 79*(3), 996–1020.

Bell, A. (2009). Dilemmas of settler belonging: Roots, routes and redemption in New Zealand national identity claims. *The Sociological Review, 57*(1), 145–162.

Berry, J. W. (1997). Immigration, acculturation, and adaptation. *Applied Psychology, 46*(1), 5–34.

Berry, J. W. (2005). Acculturation. In *Culture and human development* (pp. 263–273). Psychology Press.

Beugelsdijk, S., Ambos, B., & Nell, P. C. (2018). Conceptualizing and measuring distance in international business research: Recurring questions and best practice guidelines. *Journal of International Business Studies, 49*, 1113–1137. https://doi.org/10.1057/s41267-018-0182-4

Bierwiaczonek, K., & Waldzus, S. (2016). Socio-cultural factors as antecedents of cross-cultural adaptation in expatriates, international students, and migrants: A review. *Journal of Cross-Cultural Psychology, 47*(6), 767–817.

Bourdieu, P. (1986). The forms of capital. In J. G. Richardson (Ed.), *Handbook of theory and research for the sociology of education* (pp. 241–259). Greenwood.

Brannen, M. Y., & Thomas, D. C. (2010). Bicultural individuals in organizations: Implications and opportunity. *International Journal of Cross Cultural Management, 10*(1), 5–16.

Brubaker, R. (2005). The 'diaspora'diaspora. *Ethnic and Racial Studies, 28*(1), 1–19.

Calhoun, C. (2003). "Belonging" in the cosmopolitan imaginary. *Ethnicities, 3*(4), 531–553.

Caligiuri, P. M. (2000). The big five personality characteristics as predictors of expatriate's desire to terminate the assignment and supervisor-rated performance. *Personnel Psychology, 53*(1), 67–88.

Cameron, K. (2017). Cross-cultural research and positive organizational scholarship. *Cross Cultural & Strategic Management, 24*(1), 13–32.

Coates, J. (2017). Idleness as method: Hairdressers and Chinese urban mobility in Tokyo. In A. Elliot, R. Norum, & N. B. Salazar (Eds.), *Methodologies of mobility: Ethnography and experiment* (pp. 109–128). Berghahn.

Cutler, D., Glaeser, E., & Vigdor, J. (2005). Ghettos and the transmission of ethnic capital. In G. Loury, T. Modood, & S. Teles (Eds.), *Ethnicity, social mobility, and public policy: Comparing the US and the UK* (pp. 204–221). Cambridge University Press.

Dana, L. P., Virtanen, M., & Barner-Rasmussen, W. (2019). Shaking the minority box: Conceptualizing the impact of context and social capital on the entrepreneurial activity of minorities. In *Diaspora networks in international business: Perspectives for understanding and managing diaspora business and resources* (pp. 205–228). Springer.

Demes, K. A., & Geeraert, N. (2014). Measures matter: Scales for adaptation, cultural distance, and acculturation orientation revisited. *Journal of Cross-Cultural Psychology, 45*(1), 91–109.

Elo, M., & Minto-Coy, I. (2019). The concept of diaspora from the perspective of international business and economy: An introduction to the book. In *Diaspora networks in international business: Perspectives for understanding and managing diaspora business and resources* (pp. 1–14). Springer.

Erel, U. (2010). Migrating cultural capital: Bourdieu in migration studies. *Sociology, 44*(4), 642–660.

Frederiksen, L., Wennberg, K., & Balachandran, C. (2016). Mobility and entrepreneurship: Evaluating the scope of knowledge–based theories of entrepreneurship. *Entrepreneurship Theory and Practice, 40*(2), 359–380.

Freedman, J., & Tarr, C. (2000). *Women, immigration and identities in France*. Berg.

Geary, D. (2019). Behold, America: The entangled history of "America first" and "the American dream.". *Journal of American History, 106*(2), 502–503.

Goncharova, G. N. (2016). Getting inside the migrants' world(s): Biographical interview as a tool for (re)searching transcultural memory. *Crossings: Journal of Migration & Culture, 7*(1), 43–61.

Greenman, E. (2011). Assimilation choices among immigrant families: Does school context matter? *International Migration Review, 45*(1), 29–67.

Hall, S. (1991). Old and new identities, old and new ethnicities. In *Culture, globalization and the world system* (pp. 41–68). Macmillan.

Helkama, K. (2015). (The values of the Finnish people: What is really important to us?). Suomalaisen kirjallisuuden seura.

Helkama, K., & Portman, A. (2019). Protestant roots of honesty and other Finnish values. On the Legacy of Lutheranism in Finland, 81.

Hiironniemi, S. (2021). (The travelers to the USA). Siirtolaisuusinstituutti.

Huff, S. T., Hanek, K. J., Lee, F., & Brannen, M. Y. (2021). Cultural adaptation and societal context: The role of historical heterogeneity in cultural adaptation of newcomers. *International Journal of Intercultural Relations, 85*, 141–155.

Hunt, M. O. (2003). Identities and inequalities. In *Advances in identity theory and research* (pp. 71–84). Springer.

Ivanova-Gongne, M., Lång, S., Brännback, M., & Carsrud, A. (2021). Sensemaking by minority entrepreneurs: Role identities and linguistic embeddedness. *Journal of Small Business & Entrepreneurship, 27*, 1–24.

Kearney, M. (1995). The local and the global: The anthropology of globalization and transnationalism. *Annual Review of Anthropology, 24*, 547–565.

Killian, C., & Johnson, C. (2006). "I'm not an immigrant!" resistance, redefinition, and the role of resources in identity work. *Social Psychology Quarterly, 69*(1), 60–80. https://doi.org/10.1177/019027250606900105

Kunst, J. R., & Sam, D. L. (2013). Relationship between perceived acculturation expectations and Muslim minority youth's acculturation and adaptation. *International Journal of Intercultural Relations, 37*(4), 477–490.

Leung, K., & Morris, M. W. (2015). Values, schemas, and norms in the culture–behavior nexus: A situated dynamics framework. *Journal of International Business Studies, 46*, 1028–1050.

Malkki, L. (2008). National geographic: The rooting of peoples and the territorialization of national identity among scholars and refugees. In *The cultural geography reader* (pp. 287–294). Routledge.

Morris, M. W., Mok, A., & Mor, S. (2011). Cultural identity threat: The role of cultural identifications in moderating closure responses to foreign cultural inflow. *Journal of Social Issues, 67*(4), 760–773.

Nagel, J. (1997). *American Indian ethnic renewal: Red power and the resurgence of identity and culture*. Oxford University Press on Demand.

Nummela, N., Paavilainen-Mäntymäki, E., Harikkala-Laihinen, R., & Raitis, J. (2021). Cosmopolitans as migrant entrepreneurs. In *Global migration, entrepreneurship and society* (Vol. 13, pp. 55–70). Emerald Publishing Limited.

Ozasir Kacar, S., & Essers, C. (2019). The interplay between identity construction and opportunity structures: Narratives of Turkish migrant women entrepreneurs in The Netherlands. *International Small Business Journal, 37*(7), 713–731. https://doi.org/10.1177/0266242619856809

Özkazanç-Pan, B. (2019). *Transnational migration and the new subjects of work: Transmigrants, hybrids and cosmopolitans*. Policy Press.

Peltokorpi, V., & Froese, F. (2014). Expatriate personality and cultural fit: The moderating role of host country context on job satisfaction. *International Business Review, 23*(1), 293–302.

Plaza, D. (2006). The construction of a segmented hybrid identity among one-and-a-half-generation and second-generation indo-Caribbean and African Caribbean Canadians. *Identity, 6*(3), 207–229.

Porter, G. (2010). Work ethic and ethical work: Distortions in the American dream. *Journal of Business Ethics, 96*(4), 535–550. http://www.jstor.org/stable/29789736

Potosky, D. (2016). A framework and typology of adjustment responses to extracultural disorientation experienced during intercultural assignments. *Human Resource Management Review, 26*(3), 227–241.

Richardson, C. (2022). It's all in the past: How do colonial legacies between host and home countries affect the expatriate experience? *Journal of Global Mobility: The Home of Expatriate Management Research, 10*(1), 36–54.

Ryder, A. G., Alden, L. E., & Paulhus, D. L. (2000). Is acculturation unidimensional or bidimensional? A head-to-head comparison in the prediction of personality, self-identity, and adjustment. *Journal of Personality and Social Psychology, 79*(1), 49.

Schwartz, S. H. (2011). Values: Cultural and individual. In F. J. R. van de Vijver, A. Chasiotis, & S. M. Breugelmans (Eds.), *Fundamental questions in cross-cultural psychology* (pp. 463–493). Cambridge University Press. https://doi.org/10.1017/CBO9780511974090.019

Selmer, J., Chiu, R. K., & Shenkar, O. (2007). Cultural distance asymmetry in expatriate adjustment. *Cross Cultural Management: An International Journal, 14*(2), 150–160.

Shan, H. (2012). Learning to "fit in:" The emotional work of Chinese immigrants in Canadian engineering workplaces. *Journal of Workplace Learning, 24*(5), 351–364.

Shenkar, O. (2001). Cultural distance revisited: Towards a more rigorous conceptualization and measurement of cultural differences. *Journal of International Business Studies, 32*, 519–535.

Shenkar, O. (2012). Beyond cultural distance: Switching to a friction lens in the study of cultural differences. *Journal of International Business Studies, 43*, 12–17.

Srivastava, S., Singh, S., & Dhir, S. (2020). Culture and international business research: A review and research agenda. *International Business Review, 29*(4), 101709.

Stahl, G. K., & Caligiuri, P. (2005). The effectiveness of expatriate coping strategies: The moderating role of cultural distance, position level, and time on the international assignment. *Journal of Applied Psychology, 90*(4), 603.

Stahl, G. K., & Tung, R. L. (2015). Towards a more balanced treatment of culture in international business studies: The need for positive cross-cultural scholarship. *Journal of International Business Studies, 46*, 391–414.

Stoessel, K., Titzmann, P. F., & Silbereisen, R. K. (2014). Being "them" and "us" at the same time? Subgroups of cultural identification change among adolescent diaspora immigrants. *Journal of Cross-Cultural Psychology, 45*(7), 1089–1109.

Taramaa, R. (2009). Sisu as a central marker of Finnish-American culture: Stubbornness beyond reason. *American Studies in Scandinavia, 41*(1), 36–60.

Valenzuela, M. A., & Rogers, S. E. (2021). Strategizing personality traits: An acculturation approach to person–environment fit and expatriate adjustment. *The International Journal of Human Resource Management, 32*(7), 1591–1619.

Waldron, T., Roberts, B., & Reamer, A. (2004). *Working hard, falling short: America's working families and the pursuit of economic security*. Annie E. Casey Foundation.

Ward, C., Bochner, S., & Furnham, A. (2020). *The psychology of culture shock*. Routledge.

Ward, C., & Geeraert, N. (2016). Advancing acculturation theory and research: The acculturation process in its ecological context. *Current Opinion in Psychology, 8*, 98–104.

Ward, C., & Kennedy, A. (1993). Psychological and socio-cultural adjustment during cross-cultural transitions: A comparison of secondary students overseas and at home. *International Journal of Psychology, 28*(2), 129–147.

Ward, C., Leong, C.-H., & Low, M. (2004). Personality and sojourner adjustment: An exploration of the big five and the cultural fit proposition. *Journal of Cross-Cultural Psychology, 35*(2), 137–151. https://doi.org/10.1177/0022022103260719

Weinreich, P. (2009). "Enculturation," not "acculturation:" Conceptualising and assessing identity processes in migrant communities. *International Journal of Intercultural Relations, 33*(2), 124–139.

Welter, F. (2011). Contextualizing entrepreneurship—Conceptual challenges and ways forward. *Entrepreneurship Theory and Practice, 35*(1), 165–184.

Wilson, J. K. (2013). *Exploring the past, present, and future of cultural competency research: The revision and expansion of the sociocultural adaptation construct*.

Zubair, M., & Brzozowski, J. (2018). Entrepreneurs from recent migrant communities and their business sustainability. *Sociologica, 12*(2), 57–72.

10

[Adult] Third Culture Kids: Why Do Early Life International Experiences Matter?

Mireka Caselius and Vesa Suutari

Introduction

Owing to the increasing globalization of business life and societies, increasing numbers of individuals are moving across borders during their lives. Due to the importance of the topic for both companies as well as for individuals and their families, expatriation has become probably the most widely studied area within international human resource management. Some expatriates are sent abroad for a few years by their employers as assigned expatriates (AEs) for reasons such as control, coordination, knowledge transfer, or personal development (Suutari, 2003). Others head abroad on their own initiative and seek work abroad as self-initiated expatriates (SIEs) (Brewster et al., 2021; Doherty et al., 2011). A common factor affecting all kinds of expatriates is that many of them have families who follow them abroad (Shaffer et al., 2012). It is therefore important to note that moving and living abroad is at least as challenging for partners and children as it is for the expatriates themselves (Shaffer et al., 2001; Richardson, 2006; Kanstrén & Suutari, 2021). In the light of such evidence on the centrality of family concerns to successful expatriation, expatriate children are seen to be an increasingly important part of the entire expatriate discussion (Lazarova et al., 2015) though their personal participation in such studies is still often missing (see e.g., Shah et al., 2022). While the

M. Caselius (✉) • V. Suutari
School of Management, University of Vaasa, Vaasa, Finland
e-mail: mireka.caselius@gmail.com; vesa.suutari@uwasa.fi

© The Author(s), under exclusive license to Springer Nature Switzerland AG 2023
A. I. Mockaitis (ed.), *The Palgrave Handbook of Global Migration in International Business*,
https://doi.org/10.1007/978-3-031-38886-6_10

experiences of partners during the expatriation process are becoming increasingly understood, it has been stressed that more research is needed on the experiences of the children, and the impacts such experiences have on them during their time abroad and also in the long term (Weeks et al., 2010; Lazarova et al., 2015; Adams, 2016; Caselius & Mäkelä, 2022).

The experiences of such children have also been discussed in the cross-cultural management literature, where globally mobile children are often referred to as *third culture kids (TCKs)* and later when they come of age, as *adult third culture kids (ATCKs)*. The term was coined by Ruth Useem, who was active in studying American expatriate families living in India already since the late 1950s. We adopt a definition by Pollock et al. (2017, p. 404) who define a TCK as "a person who spends a significant part of his or her first eighteen years of life accompanying parent(s) into a country that is different from at least one parent's passport country(ies) due to a parent's choice of work or advanced training". However, there is no standardized definition of a TCK (Dillon & Ali, 2019) which would help clarify the use of the term. Also, what constitutes a 'significant time abroad' during the developmental years has not yet been defined and varies significantly since scholars have used time periods from less than a year up to six years (Tan et al., 2021), or in some cases the time spent abroad has not even been presented.

In the literature on TCKs, the 'third culture' is often described as an expatriate culture which is neither like the home or host country but has blended elements from the person's home or passport culture (the 'first culture') and the host culture where the family has moved to (the 'second culture') (Pollock et al., 2017). TCKs have been known to build relationships with various cultures, despite not having full ownership of any of them (Useem, 2001). The term 'TCK' has been commonly applied to study children who are raised by parents from different sectors such as corporate expatriates (Selmer, 2003; Lam & Selmer, 2004), missionaries (Bikos et al., 2009; Davis et al., 2010), foreign service and military personnel (Pollock et al., 2017).

Given this background, the present chapter looks to review the existing research on TCKs and, based on the findings, to develop a future research agenda that can help to further increase our understanding of TCKs. When carrying out the review, we searched Google Scholar, and the Web of Science, EBSCO and SCOPUS databases. In our search, we used the terms 'third culture kid', 'TCK', 'expatriate children', 'adult third culture kid', 'ATCK', 'third culture individual', and 'global nomad'. We searched for empirical studies in which the selected terms were used without imposing any specific time limits with regard to the length of the experience abroad as a TCK as that had been seen to vary across studies. Finally, we included full English text articles from peer-reviewed academic journals and books. As an outcome, our review covers research carried out within different disciplines, in particular research in international business, education, and psychology. On the basis of our review findings, we have organized our review into two different sections. First, we discuss the findings on TCKs and their experiences during their stay abroad by following the expatriation cycle from the pre-departure stage to repatriation. Second, we review the findings on the longer-term impacts of such experiences, and divide such impacts into the challenges and benefits associated with a TCK background, as both were reported in studies among ATCKs. In the last section, we discuss the key findings from the review and identify future research avenues, as well as discussing the implications of our findings for expatriates, their expatriate families, and companies.

The TCK Journey: Facing Early International Exposure During Childhood

There has been a gradually increasing amount of research on TCKs, especially when seen in comparison with expatriates. Such research has been carried out across different stages of the TCK journey, from their pre-departure expectations and preparations, further on to their adjustment abroad, and finally to repatriation. These stages form an appropriate base on which to structure our review.

Starting from the *pre-departure views or expectations of children*, it can be noted that such views have not attracted as much attention as have experiences abroad, despite that stage being a very important part of the cycle (see e.g., De Sivatte et al., 2019). While the evidence is limited, it has been suggested that it would be important to involve children in the family-level decision-making process concerning the move abroad, because the decision affects the lives of all of the family members (Chew & Zhu, 2002). It has also been raised that the decision-making process is quite different among AEs and SIEs as AEs need to follow an organizational logic (e.g., timing, length, host country, type of job), while SIEs can decide these issues on their own and thus may be in a better position to take into account the family needs (Mäkelä & Suutari, 2013). An issue that has received considerable research interest in the pre-departure stage is the difficulty of leaving friends behind (Banerjee et al., 2020; De Sivatte et al., 2019; Weeks et al., 2010), as this strongly impacts on TCKs' willingness to move abroad. The age of the TCK impacts such feelings, since younger children deal better with these relocations due to having less significant friendships before the move when compared to adolescents (De Sivatte et al., 2019). They have also been used to following the decisions of the parents, but gradually start to have more independent personal views and expectations when they become older. Therefore, the pre-departure views or expectations of children are important as they are connected with the later adjustment abroad (Pollock et al., 2017).

De Sivatte et al. (2019) found in their interviews that previous international experience and language fluency were pre-departure viewpoints that supported TCKs' later adjustment abroad, since subsequent relocations routinized the globally mobile lifestyle and having inadequate host country language skills was seen to pose difficulties. In turn, Weeks et al. (2010) did not find any evidence that language fluency before a move would be a significant issue for the adjustment of TCKs, although in their study the participants already spoke the school language before their relocation. However, school language proficiency may be significant for non-native speakers who need to learn the destination school language, as well as being able to cope in everyday situations with the local language.

The importance of training and support for TCKs has also been widely discussed in literature. Existing research indicates that it would be wise for organizations to provide in-depth pre-departure training for TCKs (Weeks et al., 2010), so as to facilitate their language abilities and cross-cultural adjustment. For example, Rosenbusch and Cseh (2012) stress the importance of such cross-cultural training, and their case study highlights the importance of building programs where the whole expatriate family may receive training before departure, during an assignment, and also in the repatriation phase (see also Okpara & Kabongo, 2011). Interestingly, Selmer (2001) reported that families would have preferred post-arrival cross-cultural training in the host country, since their motivation to learn is seen to be stronger abroad than in the pre-departure period. The reason for this might be the intense nature of the period before relocation, as all of the practical arrangements for the move have to be addressed. Therefore, there might not be enough time to concentrate on deep cross-cultural learning. Although the importance of training and support has already been addressed for some time in the literature, proper pre-departure training of TCKs is still almost non-existent (Banerjee et al., 2020), even within multinational corporations (MNCs) that have expatriate programs. Among those who leave to go abroad on their own initiative and search for a job abroad, both expatriates and their families are likely to be beyond the scope of corporate practices like family training and support (Mäkelä & Suutari, 2013). Thus, families must deal with most of the challenges they encounter on their own. Consequently, it is not surprising that parents have reported stress and emotional pain arising from relocating their children abroad (McLachlan, 2005).

TCKs' *adjustment abroad* (see e.g., Alston & Nieuwoudt, 1992; Weeks et al., 2010; De Sivatte et al., 2019; Banerjee et al., 2020) has already received more research attention than the topics of pre-departure experiences and expectations. It has now been increasingly recognized that moving abroad poses a significant change for TCKs (Weeks et al., 2010; Banerjee et al., 2020). Recently, De Sivatte et al. (2019) have reported findings on the factors impacting the adjustment of TCKs. They build their work on the model by Weeks et al. (2010) who have studied the adjustment of students. Their model consists of three key factors affecting teenagers' adjustment: individual factors (open-mindedness, freedom, and academic success), environmental factors (cultural differences and living conditions), and interpersonal relationships (friends, family, and repatriation training). De Sivatte et al. (2019) expanded such work by recognizing additional factors such as social and academic self-efficacy, the type of international school, academic system differences, and the different academic requirement levels that were found to affect the adjustment of TCKs.

The social adjustment of children is affected by the nature of their relationships. Expatriate parents have reported that their children's friendships become more casual when they lose their original friendships (McLachlan, 2005), and that they tend to approach new relationships cautiously (Walters & Auton-Cuff, 2009). When TCKs are in international schools, there are always new people arriving and leaving owing to the limited lengths of stay in the host country. Thus, expatriate children regularly face the fear of losing their friends, which also concerned their parents (McLachlan, 2005) as their children may already have at least to some extent lost connections with their friends in the home country owing to expatriation (Banerjee et al., 2020).

There is also a separate track of research on TCKs that focuses on their education abroad. While such studies could be connected with the adjustment perspective outlined above, they are introduced here as a separate area of interest as it appears as a separate discussion also in the literature and research on TCKs. In such discussions, the main focus has been on the specifics of the education in international schools across countries. Children of assigned expatriates are often found to study in private institutions where the tuition fees are paid by the expatriate's employer (Wilkins, 2013), and in a few cases by the parents themselves. However, the same might not be applicable to TCKs of SIEs since SIEs typically sign local contracts and do not have such benefits for their children that are common among assigned expatriates (Suutari et al., 2018). Other examples of schools that TCKs attend are

European Schools (schools for children of EU staff), or local schools in the host country (Caselius & Mäkelä, 2022). While research exists on the experiences of TCKs in these international schools (McLachlan, 2005; Tanu, 2016), much less research can be found relating to those who have studied in local schools.

These different types of schools offer quite different study environments for students to become integrated into. The major reason for using an international school for TCKs' education during their time abroad is language (Hayden & Thompson, 2008). English is the dominant language in the international schools around the world, and in some countries, the local children are not even allowed to attend these schools (Hayden & Thompson, 2008). While there are also international schools that operate in languages other than English, it is still typical for non-native English-speaker expatriate parents to value their children learning to speak English almost as well as their own mother tongue (Hayden & Thompson, 2008). By studying in English, it may also be easier to continue their studies in another country if a family constantly relocates.

Small nuances can have a significant effect on TCKs' adjustment to an education institution. For example, Japanese expatriate children in the USA felt good about their American school because the homework was relatively easy for them compared to that assigned in their Japanese schools (Miyamoto & Kuhlman, 2001), and such an experience also eased their initial adjustment. From an opposite perspective, De Sivatte et al. (2019) reported that a harder academic requirement level of the host country negatively impacted the adjustment of TCKs. However, in spite of a harder academic level, students with high academic capabilities might still be able to raise their academic abilities in the host country rather quickly, although further research is needed to confirm this. After adjusting to local requirements, TCKs typically achieve above-average grades compared to their home country peers (Wilkins, 2013), and they are often motivated students and eager to start their higher education (Caselius & Mäkelä, 2022). One reason for this might be that their parents are typically well-educated professionals, have high expectations toward their children, and are also able to support them in their education and adjustment abroad.

TCKs' experiences of their *repatriation stage* have not yet been analyzed in great detail (Gambhir & Rhein, 2021; Smith & Kearney, 2016). However, there is some evidence on missionary kids' repatriation experiences (see e.g. Bikos et al., 2009; Davis et al., 2013), and some studies have been conducted on their repatriation experiences to college and university (Purnell & Hoban, 2014; Smith & Kearney, 2016; Ra et al., 2023); all demonstrating how difficult the process of repatriation adjustment can be. It has been found that TCKs often face a reverse culture shock on repatriation because they feel themselves as foreigners in their home country after living abroad (Fail et al., 2004; Gambhir & Rhein, 2021). Thus, TCKs are sometimes positioned as 'hidden immigrants' since they look alike but think differently. Particularly, while they often view life through the lens of a 'foreigner', people around them tend to consider them to share similar worldview due to them looking like they belong to the dominant cultural group (Pollock et al., 2017). As an outcome, TCKs may end up with the sense of not being understood in their home culture (Hervey, 2009), and such struggles have been found to correlate with a changed sense of identity for TCKs (Smith & Kearney, 2016; Kortegast & Yount, 2016).

After studying in a foreign language for several years, TCKs sometimes find it difficult to continue their studies in their home country education system in the TCK's mother tongue. For that reason, some children choose to attend an international school in their home country after repatriation (Kierner & Suutari, 2018). However, TCKs are often interested in both international study programs in their home country and also studies abroad, due to their international background (Caselius & Mäkelä, 2022).

Repatriation support and training for TCKs is underresearched, although it has been stressed that TCKs should receive proper preparation for their repatriation from their school and parents (Purnell & Hoban, 2014). Also, family-related studies have highlighted the importance of individual proactive strategies together with corporate-sponsored repatriation programs, in order to ensure realistic expectations, since inaccurate expectations are often seen as the biggest challenges in repatriation (Andreason & Kinneer, 2005).

Adult Third Culture Kids: Impacts of Early Life International Exposure on Later Life

While the main focus of TCK research has been on the experiences of TCKs abroad, there has also been an increasing amount of research on ATCKs (Adult Third Culture Kids) to complement the view on the impacts of early life international exposure on individuals in the longer term. We group these studies into two categories; those that have focused on the challenges faced by ATCKs, and those that have focused on the more positive sides of a TCK background.

Challenges Associated with a TCK Background

ATCKs are found to face a number of challenges due to their international background. First, their identity formation is often influenced by several different cultures that they face along their journey (Pollock et al., 2017; Mosanya & Kwiatkowska, 2023). From an identity perspective, individuals with an international background often have difficulties with their sense of belonging due to feelings of being disconnect from a place (Fail et al., 2004; Westropp et al., 2016; Jeon, 2022). Also, insecurity is associated with their identity (Cranston, 2017) as well as their grief for the loss of their personal identity (Gilbert, 2008), and their identity challenges have been seen to involve feelings of being rootless and restless (Pollock et al., 2017). Such feelings are typical among ATCKs who may still be exploring their personal identity, as they often do not feel as if they have full ownership of the different home/host cultures they have lived in. They also often have difficulties with answering seemingly simple questions such as "Where are you from" (Pollock et al., 2017, p. 185) since they might have lived abroad for a significant part of their life, while not fully owning the home culture identity (Hervey, 2009). This cultural homelessness has been found to be connected with a lower degree of self-esteem (Hoersting & Jenkins, 2011), and interestingly, recent findings also show that TCKs tie a stronger identity bond to their host culture compared to their home culture (De Waal & Born, 2021).

In turn, a sense of restlessness derives from the learned lifestyle of moving around, especially if one has experienced several such moves. Typically, ATCKs build their home in the current place of residence, even though they might stay there for just a limited period of time (Westropp et al., 2016) and are no longer satisfied with permanently living in a single location (Moore & Barker, 2012). Their significant life changes also increase the risks of mental health challenges (Thomas et al., 2021) such as depression, anxiety, and stress (Davis et al., 2010; Davis et al., 2013). Thus, the well-being of ATCKs has raised attention among researchers (Abe, 2018; Mosanya & Kwiatkowska, 2021). ATCKs may also feel grief from being separated from people living far away, and sometimes the losses of such relationships in the long term (Pollock et al., 2017). This factor might explain why ATCKs often gravitate toward other individuals with a TCK background, as they have also experienced similar kinds of losses, and understand the feelings of grief associated with their support network (Gilbert, 2008).

Benefits Associated with a TCK Background

While the time spent abroad often creates challenges for ATCKs, researchers have started to become increasingly interested about the longer-term benefits of such unique early international exposures to other cultures. From the perspective of skills such as social skills, ATCKs have been found to have a high degree of social sensitivity (Lyttle et al., 2011) and social intelligence, due to the experience of living in multicultural environments (Caselius & Mäkelä, 2022).

ATCKs have been shown to have strong cross-cultural skills (Bonebright, 2010; Tarique & Weisbord, 2013), and thus, to be culturally adaptable (Selmer & Lauring, 2014) and able to fit in and survive in new cultures more easily (Westropp et al., 2016). ATCKs are also seen to be typically more open-minded toward different cultures than their home country peers (Westropp et al., 2016; De Waal & Born, 2020; de Waal et al., 2020) due to their globally expanded worldview (Pollock et al., 2017). Furthermore, good language skills and cross-cultural skills also facilitate future studies abroad (Caselius & Mäkelä, 2022), and may open up new international study options.

TCKs typically have clear plans for their future (Wilkins, 2013), and when becoming an adult are attracted to different international roles, work tasks, and careers (Caselius & Mäkelä, 2022). They are typically suitable for expatriate work as well as other types of global work because they have special international capabilities (Westropp et al., 2016) which are not easy to be developed in any other way (Selmer & Lauring, 2014), and are therefore an interesting population for a variety of international jobs.

Conclusions and Future Research Directions

The aim of the present chapter was to review existing research on TCKs in order to analyze what we know about their early life international experience and their later life as ATCKs, and as an outcome, frame a research agenda for future studies.

The focus of extant research on TCKs has mainly been on their experiences abroad, while the pre-departure issues that impact their experiences abroad have received less attention (De Sivatte et al., 2019). Although the evidence is still very limited, anticipatory factors such as leaving home country friends, previous international experience, language fluency, and training and support have all been found to impact the adjustment of TCKs (De Sivatte et al.,

2019; Weeks et al., 2010; Pollock et al., 2017). With regard to pre-departure decision-making, people decide to expatriate for various reasons such as career development, employment, or financial reasons, but it is also evident that family-related motives and concerns are typically highly relevant to the process (Suutari et al., 2012). Family members have an active role in deciding whether to accept an assignment (Chew & Zhu, 2002), and determining what kind of assignments are considered. It has also been raised that the situation of SIEs differs from assigned expatriates as they have more autonomy to decide about matters surrounding their expatriation than those sent abroad by their employers (Mäkelä & Suutari, 2013). The evidence on SIE families is still limited and we therefore need further research on such decision-making processes of SIEs and their families before expatriation.

It is also widely understood that moving and living abroad presents a challenging time for family members (Shaffer et al., 2001; Richardson, 2006), especially if the children of the family are not willing to relocate. While expatriates' motives and expectations and increasingly also the pre-departure views of partners (Chew & Zhu, 2002; Richardson & Mallon, 2005) are now better understood, we do not have a similar level of understanding of the motives, expectations, or concerns of children before moving abroad, or the impacts they may have. Thus, further research is needed with samples from different contexts, in order to fully understand the role of these anticipatory factors in the experiences of TCKs abroad.

Family-related training and support practices have been discussed in the literature (e.g., Lazarova et al., 2015; Shah et al., 2022), but often the companies assigning expatriates appear to lack an understanding of the need for family training and support (Rosenbusch & Cseh, 2012; De Sivatte et al., 2019), and do not arrange such support for TCKs (Banerjee et al., 2020). More investigation is also needed on the specific training and support needs of TCKs, as well as on the impact of different training and support activities on their adjustment before, during, and after the assignment. While we still have gaps even in understanding the training and support needs of TCKs of assigned expatriates, further research is needed to build an understanding about which resources the TCKs of SIEs rely on and could benefit from, since organizational training and support is not generally available for them.

Within the research on expatriation, adjustment has historically received the most intensive attention. It is also widely agreed that family issues have a great impact on expatriate adjustment and, therefore, also on an expatriate's performance at work (e.g., Takeuchi, 2010; Cole, 2011). The existing research among TCKs highlights that the key concerns affecting the adjustment to a host-country scenario include the ability to make friends, social life in general, and children's academic success (Weeks et al., 2010; De Sivatte et al., 2019). In comparison to the extensive amount of research on the adjustment of expatriates, it may be concluded that research on TCKs is very limited, and more research is needed on their adjustment as well as the antecedents and outcomes of their adjustment. Furthermore, research on TCK adjustment among different types of families would add to the understanding of overall TCK adjustment (Banerjee et al., 2020).

One specific strand of the research on TCKs focuses on their educational experiences. The focus has mainly been on international schools as expatriate children are often sent to these schools owing to the language used for tuition (which is typically English: Hayden & Thompson, 2008), although there are exceptions depending on the host country (Haslberger & Brewster, 2008). The popularity of international schools among expatriate families is understandable, especially if the family relocates on more than one occasion to different countries with different national languages (Hayden & Thompson, 2008). Nevertheless, further studies that examine the experiences of TCKs from different kinds of schools and national education systems would be welcome.

While the overall research on repatriation has recently increased (Chiang et al., 2018; Mello et al., 2023), there is a clear lack of research on the repatriation experiences of TCKs. Therefore, further studies are needed on repatriation adjustment as well as its antecedents and outcomes (Smith & Kearney, 2016), encompassing the views of both children and their family members. Communication options have also improved significantly over recent years, and it is typical for adolescents to have their own smartphones and laptops, which makes their communication with friends at home easier. Accordingly, it would be interesting to see how social media platforms may support the repatriation of TCKs today. So, while the research suggests that repatriation training and support could ease the repatriation adjustment (Rosenbusch & Cseh, 2012; Smith & Kearney, 2016), we still need more evidence on what kind of repatriation practices would be most suitable for TCKs.

ATCKs present a population who have had to adjust to changes and challenges that non-expatriate children do not typically face in their lives (De Sivatte et al., 2019). This has been found to impact ATCKs in the long-term, although the evidence is still limited. It is typical that after their international periods in childhood, ATCKs face challenges with the development of their personal identity (Gilbert, 2008) due to emotional detachments from their home culture (De Waal & Born, 2021). In addition, rootlessness and restlessness are often a reality for these 'hidden immigrants'. A TCK background has also been connected to a variety of later-life challenges, and consequently their psychological perspectives have attracted attention (see e.g., Davis et al., 2013; Thomas et al., 2021). They may also become tired of constant relocations (De Sivatte et al., 2019), and face challenges in managing their networks. So, while we have increasingly come to understand the different difficulties and challenges associated with a TCK background, more research is needed to understand how long lasting these challenges are in ATCKs' lives. Moreover, there is lack of research on whether a TCK childhood might generate any long-term detrimental aspects for later studies or careers.

However, it is also important to highlight the need to further study the positive impacts of a TCK background on ATCKs. In a recent study, it was reported that ATCKs saw that the advantages of a globally mobile childhood outweigh the challenges related to their later career and life (Caselius & Mäkelä, 2022). This is important, as when many families consider whether to accept international assignments (Hartman, 2022), they estimate the possible negative effects that the time abroad may have on their children in the long term. As ATCKs have been exposed to international experiences at a highly receptive age, they often obtain valuable international strengths, skills, and knowledge that they are able to transfer to their later education, careers, and life (Caselius & Mäkelä, 2022). They have also been found to be eager to develop international careers (Westropp et al., 2016; Caselius & Mäkelä, 2022). Nevertheless, we still need more information on where these individuals live and work in the long run, and on how they might have benefited from their early international experiences. But given that such research is very limited, any actual links from TCK experiences to later work life are often missing from the discussion.

Lately, expatriation research has been increasingly interested in more long-term global career perspectives, as high numbers of expatriates (and their families) are found to have multiple expatriation experiences during their career (Dickmann et al., 2018b). Thus, instead of repatriating, the expatriates and their families may decide to stay in the host country over a longer term and thus become permanent immigrants, or decide to re-expatriate somewhere else immediately after the previous expatriation or after staying for a while back in their home country (Ho et al., 2016; Mello et al., 2023; Suutari, 2003). It has also been found that such decisions are even more common among SIEs than among assigned expatriates, and overall, SIEs tend to stay longer abroad than assigned expatriates (Selmer et al., 2022). All of these different life and career choices by parents of TCKs create different circumstances for the TCKs who may have been living abroad for the whole or at least an extensive part for their youth. Existing studies indicate that work-life balance issues are very challenging for such mobile global careerists and their families

(Mäkelä & Suutari, 2011; Mäkelä et al., 2022). However, the research on the experiences of TCKs in such circumstances is very limited. For example, there is currently little understanding about TCKs who migrate more permanently, and who may thus never return to their home countries. Furthermore, questions surrounding the educational decisions, career paths, and life choices of these individuals are currently unanswered, as are those relating to how their migration or longer-term mobile lifestyle through frequent re-expatriation across countries impacts them, their well-being, and their career success in the long run.

TCKs are claimed to be 'cultural hybrids' (Greenholtz & Kim, 2009) and, therefore, ideal future business expatriates (Bonebright, 2010; Tarique & Weisbord, 2013; Westropp et al., 2016). However, more knowledge would be useful on how cross-cultural learnings transfer into different work and life contexts. Also, we should develop a better understanding of what kinds of overall skills and knowledge TCKs develop abroad, how the extent of their learning depends on the context of the experience, and how they benefit from these skills in their future life. Therefore, future studies could use, for example, *career capital theory* to find out whether early international experience develops a similar career capital for ATCKs as it does for partners and expatriates (see e.g., Dickmann et al., 2018a; Kanstrén & Suutari, 2021). Theories previously used in expatriate research could also provide possibilities to study aspects of ATCKs' career expectations, decision-making, career identities, tracks, and commitment. As a further related point, more research is needed on whether a TCK background develops unique strengths compared to peers without such experience, or those with different types of international exposure such as experiences as an exchange student.

While there is a need for the research perspectives noted above, gathering data from family members can be difficult (Rosenbusch & Cseh, 2012), and especially when the data concerns internationally mobile children. Such methodological challenges for studying TCKs might partly explain the limited amount of research that has so far been conducted among them, and accordingly, researchers should consider new and alternative ways of collecting data (see e.g., Bikos et al., 2009) such as email interviews, blogs, and different social media platforms that might offer potential for collecting data from TCKs around the world. We also need to consider the methodological challenges involved in conducting studies among TCKs themselves, especially if we involve very young TCKs. Such research efforts would clearly require cross-disciplinary cooperation and the involvement of specialists in studying childhood experiences. It would be good to include both the views of TCKs as well as the views of their parents in studies, so as to offer a broader view of the TCK experience and the overall family experience related with parenthood during international relocations. But more generally, we also need more longitudinal studies among TCKs, in order to better understand the process they go though and to gather stronger evidence on the causal relationships between such experiences and different outcomes.

Practical Implications

The current review suggests practical implications for both organizations and families. First, according to the reviewed literature, organizations have overlooked support and training (Banerjee et al., 2020) in relation to the anticipatory, in-country, and repatriation phases of expatriation assignments. Proper training programs may have a significant impact on the realistic expectations surrounding the coming life abroad. Therefore, sending organizations could arrange groups on social media where TCK experiences could already be exchanged in the anticipatory phase, or where the platform can be used for distributing digital content (as suggested by Banerjee et al., 2020). Adolescents could be shown videos with TCKs discussing their life abroad (Weeks et al., 2010). In addition, as organizations may have families who have carried out assignments in the same location, they could even arrange training sessions with previous TCKs and new departing children together, in order to promote positive attitudes, answer specific questions, and explain matters of life abroad. Departing children could also benefit from having TCK 'mentors' who could support and advise them along the way. As SIEs typically do not receive training and support from their employer (Suutari et al., 2018), the parents have a highly important role in arranging proper training and preparation for their children, as well as in supporting them in their overseas adjustment.

As a second consideration, organizations could look into hiring ATCKs since they have special international strengths, skills, and knowledge. In light of their international capabilities, the reviewed literature highlights that ATCKs might be ideally placed to become future expatriates, and if they are individually suited for expatriate assignments, then they might be ideal for a variety of jobs that have an international perspective. By hiring ATCKs, organizations might gain an employee who would be suited for multinational teams or serving customers from various countries, due to their specially developed cross-cultural and social skills. However, it is also recognized that while ATCKs might present a restless population which organizations could use to their benefit, they could periodically ensure that their interests in changing locations or any other desired new aspects of their work are considered.

References

Abe, J. A. A. (2018). Personality, well-being, and cognitive-affective styles: A cross-sectional study of adult third culture kids. *Journal of Cross-Cultural Psychology, 49*(5), 811–830. https://doi.org/10.1177/0022022118761116

Adams, M. (2016). Young expatriate children forming friendships: A cultural-historical perspective. *International Research in Early Childhood Education, 7*(1), 85–105.

Alston, E. A., & Nieuwoudt, J. (1992). Adjustment problems experienced by children during cross-cultural orientation: A pilot study. *The Journal of Genetic Psychology, 153*(3), 321–329.

Andreason, A. W., & Kinneer, K. D. (2005). Repatriation adjustment problems and the successful reintegration of expatriates and their families. *Journal of Behavioral and Applied Management, 6*(2), 109–126. https://doi.org/10.21818/001c.14525

Banerjee, P., Gupta, R., Shaheen, M., David, R., Chenji, K., & Priyadarshini, C. (2020). Exploring adjustment mechanisms of adolescent expat kids from South Asia against sociopolitical stigma. *Journal of Global Mobility, 8*(3–4), 273–290. https://doi.org/10.1108/JGM-06-2020-0041

Bikos, L. H., Kocheleva, J., King, D., Chang, G. C., McKenzie, A., Roenicke, C., Campbell, V., & Eckard, K. (2009). A consensual qualitative investigation into the repatriation experiences of young adult, missionary kids. *Mental Health, Religion & Culture, 12*(7), 735–754. https://doi.org/10.1080/13674670903032637

Bonebright, D. A. (2010). Adult third culture kids: HRD challenges and opportunities. *Human Resource Development International, 13*(3), 351–359. https://doi.org/10.1080/13678861003746822

Brewster, C., Suutari, V., & Waxin, M. (2021). Two decades of research into SIEs and what do we know? A systematic review of the most influential literature and a proposed research agenda. *Journal of Global Mobility, 9*(3), 311–337. https://doi.org/10.1108/JGM-05-2021-0054

Caselius, M., & Mäkelä, L. (2022). Expatriate childhood as the first domino: Does early international exposure lead to a later international career? *Journal of Global Mobility: The Home of Expatriate Management Research, 10*(3), 332–350. https://doi.org/10.1108/JGM-11-2021-0093

Chew, I. K. H., & Zhu, W. (2002). Factors influencing Singapore managers' career aspiration in international assignments. *Career Development International, 7*(2), 96–108. https://doi.org/10.1108/13620430210421623

Chiang, F. F. T., Van Esch, E., Birtch, T. A., & Shaffer, M. (2018). Repatriation: What do we know and where do we go from here. *International Journal of Human Resource Management, 29*(1), 188–226. https://doi.org/10.1080/09585192.2017.1380065

Cole, N. D. (2011). Managing global talent: Solving the spousal adjustment problem. *International Journal of Human Resource Management, 22*(7), 1504–1530. https://doi.org/10.1080/09585192.2011.561963

Cranston, S. (2017). Self-help and the surfacing of identity: Producing the third culture kid. *Emotion, Space and Society, 24*, 27–33. https://doi.org/10.1016/j.emospa.2017.07.006

Davis, P., Headley, K., Bazemore, T., Cervo, J., Sickinger, P., Windham, M., & Rehfuss, M. C. (2010). Evaluating impact of transition seminars on missionary kids' depression, anxiety, stress, and well-being. *Journal of Psychology and Theology, 38*(3), 186–194.

Davis, P. S., Suarez, E. C., Crawford, N. A., & Rehfuss, M. C. (2013). Reentry program impact on missionary kid depression, anxiety, and stress: A three-year study. *Journal of Psychology and Theology, 41*(2), 128–140. https://doi.org/10.1177/009164711304100203

De Sivatte, I., Bullinger, B., Cañamero, M., & del Martel Gomez, M. P. (2019). Children of expatriates: Key factors affecting their adjustment. *Journal of Global Mobility, 7*(2), 213–236. https://doi.org/10.1108/JGM-11-2018-0058

De Waal, M. F., & Born, M. P. (2020). Growing up among cultures: Intercultural competences, personality, and leadership styles of third culture kids. *European Journal of International Management, 14*(2), 327–356. https://doi.org/10.1504/EJIM.2020.105548

De Waal, M. F., & Born, M. P. (2021). Where I'm from? Third culture kids about their cultural identity shifts and belonging. *International Journal of Intercultural Relations, 83*, 67–83. https://doi.org/10.1016/j.ijintrel.2021.04.004

De Waal, M. F., Born, M. P., Brinkmann, U., & Frasch, J. J. F. (2020). Third culture kids, their diversity beliefs and their intercultural competences. *International Journal of Intercultural Relations, 79*, 177–190. https://doi.org/10.1016/j.ijintrel.2020.09.002

Dickmann, M., Suutari, V., Brewster, C., Mäkelä, L., Tanskanen, J., & Tornikoski, C. (2018a). The career competencies of self-initiated and assigned expatriates: Assessing the development of career capital over time. *The International Journal of Human Resource Management, 29*(16), 2353–2371. https://doi.org/10.1080/09585192.2016.1172657

Dickmann, M., Suutari, V., & Wurtz, O. (2018b). The management of global careers: Exploring the rise of international work. In M. Dickmann, V. Suutari, & O. Wurtz (Eds.), *The Management of Global Careers*. Springer International Publishing. https://doi.org/10.1007/978-3-319-76529-7

Dillon, A., & Ali, T. (2019). Global nomads, cultural chameleons, strange ones or immigrants? An exploration of third culture kid terminology with reference to The United Arab Emirates. *Journal of Research in International Education, 18*(1), 77–89. https://doi.org/10.1177/1475240919835013

Doherty, N., Dickmann, M., & Mills, T. (2011). Exploring the motives of company-backed and self-initiated expatriates. *International Journal of Human Resource Management, 22*(3), 595–611. https://doi.org/10.1080/09585192.2011.543637

Fail, H., Thompson, J., & Walker, G. (2004). Belonging, identity and third culture kids life histories of former international school students. *Journal of Research in International Education, 3*(3), 319–338. https://doi.org/10.1177/1475240904047358

Gambhir, R., & Rhein, D. (2021). A qualitative analysis of the repatriation of Thai-Indian third culture kids in Thailand. *Asian Ethnicity, 22*(3), 464–480. https://doi.org/10.1080/14631369.2019.1661770

Gilbert, K. R. (2008). Loss and grief between and among cultures: The experience of third culture kids. *Illness, Crisis & Loss, 16*(2), 93–109. https://doi.org/10.2190/il.16.2.a

Greenholtz, J., & Kim, J. (2009). The cultural hybridity of Lena: A multi-method case study of a third culture kid. *International Journal of Intercultural Relations, 33*(5), 391–398. https://doi.org/10.1016/j.ijintrel.2009.05.004

Hartman, C. J. (2022). Adult third culture kids: Impacts on adult lives of living internationally and attending boarding school. *International Journal of Intercultural Relations, 86*, 122–133. https://doi.org/10.1016/j.ijintrel.2021.11.007

Haslberger, A., & Brewster, C. (2008). The expatriate family: An international perspective. *Journal of Managerial Psychology, 23*(3), 324–346. https://doi.org/10.1108/02683940810861400

Hayden, M., & Thompson, J. (2008). *International schools: Growth and influence.* United Nations Eductional, Scientific and Cultural Organization.

Hervey, E. G. (2009). Cultural transitions during childhood and adjustment to college. *Journal of Psychology and Christianity, 28*(1), 3–12. https://doi.org/10.1037/e649172007-001

Ho, N. T. T., Seet, P. S., & Jones, J. (2016). Understanding re-expatriation intentions among overseas returnees – An emerging economy perspective. *International Journal of Human Resource Management, 27*(17), 1938–1966. https://doi.org/10.1080/09585192.2015.1088884

Hoersting, R. C., & Jenkins, S. R. (2011). No place to call home: Cultural homelessness, self-esteem and cross-cultural identities. *International Journal of Intercultural Relations, 35*, 17–30. https://doi.org/10.1016/j.ijintrel.2010.11.005

Jeon, A. (2022). Growing up (un)bounded: Globalization, mobility and belonging among Korean third culture kids. *International Multilingual Research Journal, 16*(1), 65–77. https://doi.org/10.1080/19313152.2021.1951941

Kanstrén, K., & Suutari, V. (2021). Development of career capital during expatriation: Partners' perspectives. *Career Development International, 26*(6), 824–849. https://doi.org/10.1108/cdi-12-2020-0314

Kierner, A., & Suutari, V. (2018). Repatriation of international dual-career couples. *Thunderbird International Business Review, 60*(6), 885–895. https://doi.org/10.1002/tie.21947

Kortegast, C., & Yount, E. M. (2016). Identity, family, and faith: U.S. third culture kids transition to college. *Journal of Student Affairs Research and Practice, 53*(2), 230–242. https://doi.org/10.1080/19496591.2016.1121148

Lam, H., & Selmer, J. (2004). Are former "third-culture kids" the ideal business expatriates? *Career Development International, 9*(2), 109–122. https://doi.org/10.1108/13620430410526166

Lazarova, M., McNulty, Y., & Semeniuk, M. (2015). Expatriate family narratives on international mobility: Key characteristics of the successful moveable family. In V. Suutari & L. Mäkelä (Eds.), *Work and family Interface in the international career context* (pp. 29–51). Springer.

Lyttle, A. D., Barker, G. G., & Cornwell, T. L. (2011). Adept through adaptation: Third culture individuals' interpersonal sensitivity. *International Journal of Intercultural Relations, 35*(5), 686–694. https://doi.org/10.1016/j.ijintrel.2011.02.015

Mäkelä, L., & Suutari, V. (2011). Coping with work-family conflicts in the global career context. *Thunderbird International Business Review, 53*(3), 365–375. https://doi.org/10.1002/tie.20414

Mäkelä, L., & Suutari, V. (2013). The work-life interface of self-initiated expatriates: Conflicts and enrichment. In V. Vaiman & A. Haslberger (Eds.), *Talent Management of Self-Initiated Expatriates* (pp. 278–303). Palgrave Macmillan.

Mäkelä, L., Suutari, V., & Biswas, T. (2022). Expatriates' work-nonwork Interface – What do we know about it and what should we learn? In S. Toh & A. DeNisi (Eds.), *Expatriates and managing global mobility*. Routledge; SIOP Organizational Frontiers Series.

McLachlan, D. A. (2005). Global nomads in an international school. *Journal of Research in International Education, 6*(2), 233–249. https://doi.org/10.1177/1475240907078615

Mello, R., Suutari, V., & Dickmann, M. (2023). Taking stock of expatriates' career success after international assignments: A review and future research agenda. *Human Resource Management Review, 33*(1), 100913. https://doi.org/10.1016/j.hrmr.2022.100913

Miyamoto, Y., & Kuhlman, N. (2001). Ameliorating culture shock in Japanese expatriate children in the US. *International Journal of Intercultural Relations, 25*, 21–40.

Moore, A. M., & Barker, G. G. (2012). Confused or multicultural: Third culture individuals' cultural identity. *International Journal of Intercultural Relations, 36*(4), 553–562. https://doi.org/10.1016/j.ijintrel.2011.11.002

Mosanya, M., & Kwiatkowska, A. (2021). Complex but integrated: Exploring social and cultural identities of women third culture kids (TCK) and factors predicting life satisfaction. *International Journal of Intercultural Relations, 84*, 65–78. https://doi.org/10.1016/j.ijintrel.2021.07.001

Mosanya, M., & Kwiatkowska, A. (2023). New ecological paradigm and third culture kids: Multicultural identity configurations, global mindset and values as predictors of environmental worldviews. *International Journal of Psychology*, [Early View] 05 January 2023. https://doi.org/10.1002/ijop.12887

Okpara, J. O., & Kabongo, J. D. (2011). Cross-cultural training and expatriate adjustment: A study of western expatriates in Nigeria. *Journal of World Business*, 46, 22–30. https://doi.org/10.1016/j.jwb.2010.05.014

Pollock, D. C., Van Reken, R. E., & Pollock, M. V. (2017). Third Culture Kids: Growing up Among Worlds, 3rd ed. Boston: Nicholas Brealey Publishing.

Purnell, L., & Hoban, E. (2014). The lived experiences of third culture kids transitioning into university life in Australia. *International Journal of Intercultural Relations*, 41, 80–90. https://doi.org/10.1016/j.ijintrel.2014.05.002

Ra, Y. A., Ko, H., Cha, I., & Kim, H. (2023). A qualitative exploration on repatriate experiences of south korean third culture kids in college. *Current Psychology*. https://doi.org/10.1007/s12144-023-04654-6

Richardson, J. (2006). Self-directed expatriation: Family matters. *Personnel Review*, 35(4), 469–486. https://doi.org/10.1108/00483480610670616

Richardson, J., & Mallon, M. (2005). Career interrupted? The case of the self-directed expatriate. *Journal of World Business*, 40, 409–420. https://doi.org/10.1016/j.jwb.2005.08.008

Rosenbusch, K., & Cseh, M. (2012). The cross-cultural adjustment process of expatriate families in a multinational organization: A family system theory perspective. *Human Resource Development International*, 15(1), 61–77. https://doi.org/10.1080/13678868.2011.646895

Selmer, J. (2001). The preference for predeparture or postarrival cross-cultural training – An exploratory approach. *Journal of Managerial Psychology*, 16(1), 50–58. https://doi.org/10.1108/02683940110366560

Selmer, J. (2003). "Third-culture kids": Future business expatriates? *Personnel Review*, 33(4), 430–445. https://doi.org/10.1108/00483480410539506

Selmer, J., & Lauring, J. (2014). Self-initiated expatriates: An exploratory study of adjustment of adult third-culture kids vs. adult mono-culture kids. *Cross Cultural Management*, 21(4), 422–436. https://doi.org/10.1108/CCM-01-2013-0005

Selmer, J., Suutari, V., & Brewster, C. (2022). Self-initiated expatriates. In S. Toh & A. DeNisi (Eds.), *Expatriates and Managing Global Mobility*. Routledge; SIOP Organizational Frontiers Series.

Shaffer, M. A., Harrison, D. A., Gilley, K. M., & Luk, D. M. (2001). Struggling for balance amid turbulence on international assignments: Work-family conflict, support and commitment. *Journal of Management*, 27(1), 99–121. https://doi.org/10.1016/S0149-2063(00)00088-X

Shaffer, M. A., Kraimer, M. L., Chen, Y.-P., & Bolino, M. C. (2012). Choices, challenges, and career consequences of global work experiences. *Journal of Management*, 38(4), 1282–1327. https://doi.org/10.1177/0149206312441834

Shah, D., De Oliveira, R. T., Barker, M., Moeller, M., & Nguyen, T. (2022). Expatriate family adjustment: How organisational support on international assignments matters. *Journal of International Management*, 28, 100880. https://doi.org/10.1016/j.intman.2021.100880

Smith, V. J., & Kearney, K. S. (2016). A qualitative exploration of the repatriation experiences of US third culture kids in college. *Journal of College Student Development, 57*(8), 958–972. https://doi.org/10.1353/csd.2016.0093

Suutari, V. (2003). Global managers: Career orientation, career tracks, life-style implications and career commitment. *Journal of Managerial Psychology, 18*(3), 185–207. https://doi.org/10.1108/02683940310465225

Suutari, V., Tornikoski, C., & Mäkelä, L. (2012). Career decision making of global careerists. *The International Journal of Human Resource Management, 23*(16), 3455–3478. https://doi.org/10.1080/09585192.2011.639026

Suutari, V., Brewster, C., & Dickmann, M. (2018). Contrasting assigned expatriates and self-initiated expatriates: A review of extant research and a future research agenda. In M. Dickman, V. Suutari, & O. Wurtz (Eds.), *The management of global careers: Exploring the rise of international work* (pp. 63–89). Palgrave.

Takeuchi, R. (2010). A critical review of expatriate adjustment research through a multiple stakeholder view: Progress, emerging trends, and prospects. *Journal of Management, 36*(4), 1040–1064. https://doi.org/10.1177/0149206309349308

Tan, E. C., Wang, K. T., & Cottrell, A. B. (2021). A systematic review of third culture kids empirical research. *International Journal of Intercultural Relations, 82*, 81–98. https://doi.org/10.1016/j.ijintrel.2021.03.002

Tanu, D. (2016). Going to school in "Disneyland": Imagining an international school community in Indonesia. *Asian and Pacific Migration Journal, 25*(4), 429–450. https://doi.org/10.1177/0117196816672467

Tarique, I., & Weisbord, E. (2013). Antecedents of dynamic cross-cultural competence in adult third culture kids (ATCKs). *Journal of Global Mobility, 1*(2), 139–160. https://doi.org/10.1108/JGM-12-2012-0021

Thomas, J., Humeidan, M., Barrack, C., & Huffman, K. L. (2021). Mindfulness, stress reactivity, and depressive symptoms among "third culture kids" in The United Arab Emirates. *Journal of Cross-Cultural Psychology, 52*(2), 192–208. https://doi.org/10.1177/0022022120987620

Useem, R. H. (2001). *Third culture kids: focus of major study – TCK "mother" pens history of field*, from http://www.tckworld.com/useem/art1.html

Walters, K. A., & Auton-Cuff, F. P. (2009). A story to tell: The identity development of women growing up as third culture kids. *Mental Health, Religion and Culture, 12*(7), 755–772. https://doi.org/10.1080/13674670903029153

Weeks, K. P., Weeks, M., & Willis-Muller, K. (2010). The adjustment of expatriate teenagers. *Personnel Review, 39*(1), 24–43. https://doi.org/10.1108/00483481011007841

Westropp, S., Cathro, V., & Everett, A. M. (2016). Adult third culture kids' suitability as expatriates. *Review of International Business and Strategy, 26*(3), 334–348. https://doi.org/10.1108/RIBS-12-2015-0080

Wilkins, S. (2013). 'Home' or away? The higher education choices of expatriate children in The United Arab Emirates. *Journal of Research in International Education, 12*(1), 33–48. https://doi.org/10.1177/1475240913479519

Part III

Leveraging and Managing Migration in the International Firm

11

Exploring the Missing Links between International Business and Domestic Migration: The Case of China

Mingqiong Mike Zhang, Jiuhua Cherrie Zhu, Peter J. Dowling, and Di Fan

Introduction

Foreign direct investment (FDI) and population migration are two closely associated phenomena that often go hand in hand and augment each other, constituting two major pillars of globalization in recent decades. On the one hand, multinational enterprises (MNEs) produce expatriates, inpatriates, and flexipatriates across countries (Collings, 2014); on the other hand, MNEs rely on local labor markets and shape domestic migration in host countries. Therefore, scholars are increasingly realizing the importance of migration for international business (IB) since both international and domestic migrants are important forces for international operations. However, extant IB studies on migration mainly focus on international migration (Hajro et al., 2021), few studies have systematically explored the relationship between IB and

---

M. M. Zhang (✉) • J. C. Zhu
Department of Management, Monash University, Melbourne, VIC, Australia
e-mail: mike.zhang@monash.edu; cherrie.zhu@monash.edu

P. J. Dowling
Department of Management, La Trobe University, Melbourne, VIC, Australia
e-mail: p.dowling@latrobe.edu.au

D. Fan
School of Management, RMIT University, Melbourne, VIC, Australia
e-mail: david.fan@rmit.edu.au

domestic migration. We do not have enough knowledge about the implications of IB for domestic migration and vice versa, how FDI and MNEs have shaped and been shaped by domestic migration and migrant workers, and how to achieve the virtuous circle of IB and migration.

To close the gaps in the literature, based on an extensive literature review, this study takes the unprecedented domestic rural-urban migration in recent decades in China as an example to examine how foreign direct investment and domestic migration have influenced each other, and how MNEs have exerted influence on and responded to the rural-urban migration and local institutional changes such as the migration regime and labor market of China over the past decades. Given that academic discussions on international business and domestic migration have remained separate in the literature, the aim of this study is not to take stock of the existing studies but to surface the linkage between IB and domestic migration. Our study has several significant contributions to the literature. First, it is among the first to examine the relationship between IB and domestic migration and narrows the gaps in the literature. Second, it develops a future research agenda, and hence, provides a starting point for this newly emerged research area.

The Unprecedented Rural-Urban Migration and FDI Inflows in China

Since 1978 when China initiated economic reforms and reopened up to the outside world, it has experienced the largest domestic migration in human history and entered into the age of urbanization through rural-urban migration (Liang & White, 1996; Zhang et al., 2014). The number of rural-urban migrants was only 2 million in the mid-1980s (Liang, 2001), quickly climbed to 50 million by the late 1980s, and 100 million when China re-joined the World Trade Organization in 2001 (Zhang et al., 2014).[1] As can be seen from Fig. 11.1, since 2008, this number has been steady above 200 million and increased from 225.42 million in 2008 to 292.51 in 2021 (NBSC, 2022). Every year, millions of farmers flock into cities for work and return to the countryside in the busy farming season or when they are unemployed. Although some of them have migrated to cities or towns permanently, most

---

[1] China was one of the 23 founding members of the WTO's predecessor, the General Agreement on Tariffs and Trade (GATT). It withdrew from GATT in 1950 due to the change in government and reapplied for membership in GATT in 1986. Since then, negotiations on China's accession to GATT continued for 15 years, until an accession protocol was adopted by WTO members in 2001. Therefore, China claims that it re-joined the WTO as a founding member of GATT.

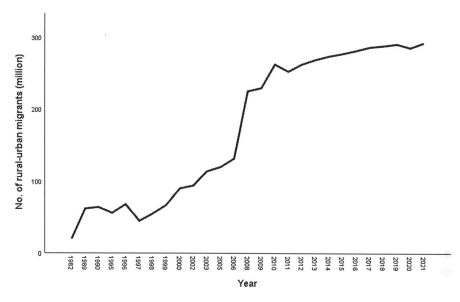

Fig. 11.1 Number of rural-urban migrants from 1982 to 2021. Source: Liang (2001); National Bureau of Statistics of China (2008–2021); Zhang (2016)

of them repeat such a life as migratory birds, forming the largest mobile workforce in the world and significantly shaping the Chinese economy and society (Zhang, 2016).

This unprecedented rural-urban migration in human history might never happen without the massive FDI inflows into China. It is the continuous FDI inflows and the rapid increase of MNEs in China that initiate this decades-long enormous rural-urban migration. This does not mean that all domestic migrants in China have only worked for foreign-funded firms. Although the township and village enterprises emerged in costal provinces of China also rely on migrants, most of their employees were local farmers transferred from local agricultural production (Zhang, 2021). Before the reform and opening up in 1978, China had adopted an urban-rural segregation strategy since the late 1950s (Solinger, 1999a), and the household-registration system (hukou hereafter) imposed strict limits on mobility of citizens. It was extremely difficult for people to change their permanent registration place of residence and find a job outside of their place of residence (Solinger, 1999b). There was few unofficial and voluntary migration that existed in the era of planned economy before 1978 (Zhang, 2016).

The re-entry of MNEs into mainland China in the early 1980s weakened the restrictions on domestic migration. Given that most urban dwellers who had a permanent job in state-owned or collectively owned enterprises were reluctant to quit their life-time jobs and switch to MNEs at that time, to ensure an adequate supply of labor for MNEs so as to encourage foreign investment, farmers were allowed to migrate outside of their place of residence for work, which translated surplus rural labor force into an army of rural-urban migrants (Zhang et al., 2017). Since then, FDI inflows into China and the domestic rural-urban migration have stepped into a mutually reinforcing positive spiral. On the one hand, more than 50% of inward FDI has flown into labor-intensive industries such as garments and footwear, creating a lot of jobs for rural-urban migrants (Davies, 2013; Tseng & Zebregs, 2002). On the other hand, tens of millions of mobile migrants constitute an ample supply of cheap labor, making China an attractive investment destination. As a result, China has become the largest FDI recipient among developing countries and the second largest foreign capital recipient in the world since the early 1990s (MOFCOM, 2019; OECD, 2000). As can be seen from Fig. 11.2, FDI inflows into China had increased from negligible US$ 0.08 million in 1979 to over US$ 180.96 billion in 2021 (UNCTAD, 2022). According to the 2019 Report on Foreign Investment in China (MOFCOM, 2019), by the end of 2018, about 960,000 foreign-invested enterprises had been established in China since 1978, and the total amount of foreign investment actually used was about US$ 2000 billion. In 2017, 25.81 million

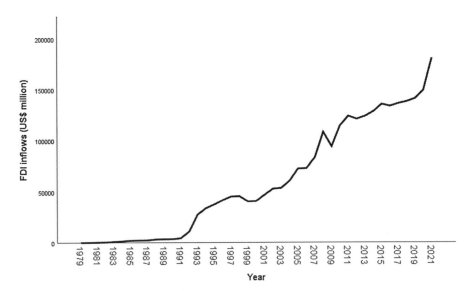

Fig. 11.2 FDI inflows into China from 1979 to 2021. Source: UNCTAD (2022). Investment statistics and trends. https://unctad.org/topic/investment/investment-statistics-and-trends

Chinese workers were employed directly by MNEs, accounting for 6.1% of urban employment (MOFCOM, 2019).

The continuous and massive FDI inflows and domestic rural-urban migration have significantly changed modern China, leading to China's decades of export-oriented rapid growth, and helping China become the "world factory" (Yang, 2012). While the massive FDI inflows inject adequate capital into the Chinese economy and expand China's access to the world, a steady stream of industrious and disciplined rural migrant workers has reduced the costs of labor and enhanced the competitiveness of foreign-funded enterprises. Statistics show that MNEs have contributed around 20% of China's tax revenue, around half of its foreign trade, and one in ten urban jobs in China (MOFCOM, 2019). As can be seen from Fig. 11.3, China's merchandise exports increased from US$ 27.35 billion in 1985 to US$ 3363.96 billion in 2021 (UNCTAD, 2022). China has been the largest trading country in goods since 2017 and the largest trading partner of more than 120 countries and regions in the world (MOFCOM, 2019).

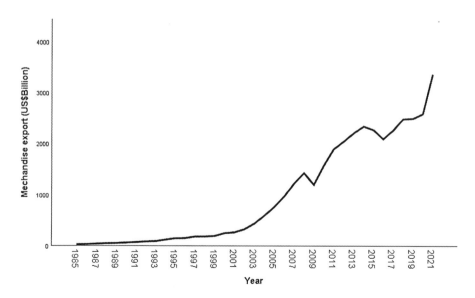

Fig. 11.3 Merchandise export from 1985 to 2021. Source: The World Bank (2022). https://data.worldbank.org.cn/topic/21

FDI Inflows and the Institutional Environment of Domestic Migration in China

Foreign direct investment has been an important driving force not only for local economic development, technological progress, and employment but also for institutional innovations (MOFCOM, 2019), as well as the change of institutional environment of domestic migration. Without considering the influence of foreign direct investment, it is impossible for us to fully understand the institutional changes in China in recent decades, including the institutional environment of domestic migration. However, few studies have systematically examined how foreign investment has shaped domestic migration in China. This study seeks to close this gap in the literature by exploring how FDI inflows have shaped domestic migration and rural-urban migrants in China.

Erode the Hukou System

One major impact of FDI inflows on domestic migration in China is that foreign direct investment has eroded the China's hukou system and initiated the massive rural-urban migration (Kerswell & Lin, 2017). Hukou is a household registration system introduced by the Chinese central government in 1958 (Fan, 2008). It is a residence permit associated with different social statuses and economic rights. Citizens have different social and economic rights based on their registered residency status (Cheng & Selden, 1994). Therefore, the hukou system is de facto a scheme of domestic migration, social control, and resource distribution based on residency status (Zhang et al., 2014). China is one of the few countries in the world that impose strict household registration control on citizens. The original hukou system before reform had some unique features (Chan & Zhang, 1999; Cheng & Selden, 1994; Zhang, 2016). First, based on their permanent residence and occupation, the hukou system classified Chinese citizens into rural-hukou holders and urban-hukou holders. Roughly, urban dwellers and all workers employed by state-owned enterprises, no matter where they live, were urban-hukou holders, while famers were rural-hukou holders (Chan & Zhang, 1999). Second, the hukou status of citizens was inherited at birth and passed down from generation to generation (Cheng & Selden, 1994). Third, urban-hukou and rural-hukou holders were treated differently and entitled to different social and economic rights, with the former enjoying more benefits in terms of social welfare, education, and employment (Chan & Zhang, 1999). Fourth, rural-urban hukou conversion was strictly regulated by government with quota control. Rural-hukou holders had few opportunities to become urban-hukou holders except for obtaining a college degree or joining the army and being promoted as a cadre before 1978 (Zhang, 2016). Fifth, citizens were not allowed to migrate outside of their registered permanent place of residence for work without official permission (Chan & Zhang, 1999). Therefore, in the planned economy, there was only officially organized planned internal migration, and there was no spontaneous domestic migration in China (Zhang, 2016).

The strict official control over voluntary rural-urban migration was gradually relaxed when more and more MNEs entered the Chinese market since the late 1980s (Kerswell & Lin, 2017). To ensure sufficient labor supply to attract foreign investment and foster employment, farmers were allowed to migrate for work outside their registered place of residence (Zhang, 2016). Since the government soon realized that the benefits of rural-urban migration for economy development far outweigh its disadvantages such as traffic pressure, both the central and local governments started to encourage rural-urban migration (Sun & Liu, 2019). Therefore, since the early 1990s, the massive rural-urban migration has become a hot topic every year in China, and citizens have gained an increased freedom to live and work outside their registered place of residence (Zhang, 2016). FDI has attracted a large number of rural migrant workers to work and live in urban areas and contributed a lot to the level of urbanization (Wu & Chen, 2016). Given that FDI inflows have overwhelmingly concentrated in the eastern region of China (MOFCOM, 2019; OECD, 2000), the coastal areas including the Pearl River Delta and Yangtze River Delta have been the major destinations of the domestic rural-urban migration (Zhang, 2016). In recent decades, more and more rural-hukou holders obtain their urban hukou in cities and towns through more channels such as higher education, buying an apartment in the host city, and the local points-based migration system (Zhang et al., 2014). In 2011, urban population in China exceeded the rural population for the first time. As can be seen from Fig. 11.4, the urbanization rate in China increased from 17.9% in 1978 to 64.72% in 2021 (The World Bank, 2022). In recent decades, people in China can freely decide where to live and work, although obtaining an urban hukou is still not easy in some mega-cities such as Beijing and Shanghai (Sun & Liu, 2019). Such an unprecedented institutional change may not occur without the contribution of continuous and massive foreign direct investment inflows into China.

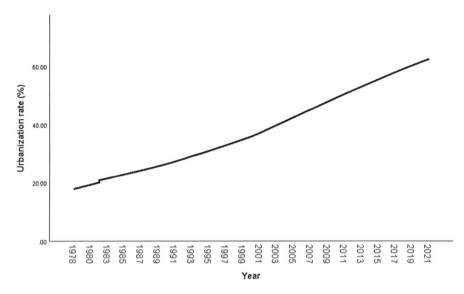

Fig. 11.4 Urbanization rate in China from 1978 to 2021. Source: The World bank. https://data.worldbank.org/indicator/SP.URB.TOTL.IN.ZS

Introduce Market Mechanisms into the Chinese Workplace

The second major impact of FDI inflows on the domestic migration and rural-urban migrants in China is that foreign direct investment has shaken up some established local institutional arrangements through introducing market mechanisms into the Chinese workplace. China is a former socialist country and has followed some unique managerial practices (Warner, 2008). For example, in the planned economy era before 1978, the Chinese workplace was dominated by the "iron-rice bowl" which is "a fusion of Soviet regulation with Buddhist values for harmony and obedience, resulting in centrally regulated job allocation, high job security, egalitarian pay systems and cradle-to-grave social welfare systems" (Chen & Wilson, 2003, p. 398). Under the "iron-rice bowl" system, employees were allocated to companies by government; wages were centrally administrated by government based on post, skill level, and region; senior managerial staff were appointed by government; workers enjoyed life-time employment and could not be dismissed unless they did not go to work for a few months, made a fatal mistake which resulted in serious losses, or violated laws and were sentenced by the court (Tsang, 1994); and companies offered employees cradle-to-grave social welfare including housing, medical care, and other social services such as nursery schools (Warner, 2008; Xia et al., 2020). Obviously, in the planned economy, state-owned enterprises were not efficient organizations in the economic sense, but mini societies where employees were viewed as the masters (Gong, 2015; Lee, 2007).[2]

The re-entry of MNEs into China has introduced labor market, employment contract, and various market-oriented managerial practices into China; shaken the iron-rice bowl system based on the socialist logic; and created a workplace fully dominated by the capitalist logic for rural-urban migrants. In the newly created workplace, jobs are obtained from informal or formal labor market; life-time employment rarely exists; egalitarian and stable salary is usually replaced by efficiency wage based on piece rates (Warner, 2003, 2014); and adequate social welfare is only a luxurious dream for rural-urban migrants. Under the capitalist logic, companies are dominated by investors and management, employees are no longer the masters of companies, but cheap labor for creating surplus value (Zhang, 2016). Since MNEs have been more productive than state-owned enterprises, they have become role models for domestic companies, and their managerial practices based on the capitalist logic have been widely adopted by local firms as benchmarks (Warner, 2003, 2014). As a result, the decades of massive rural-urban migration have created a mobile and low-wage army of workforce (Solinger, 1999b) that is incorporated into the global supply chain by foreign capital.

The Hukou-Based Human Resource Management (HRM) Discrimination

The capitalist logic reintroduced into China by MNEs, combined with China's weak labor protections for workers, has dumped rural-urban migrants on the market to fend for themselves, leading to prevalent hukou-based discrimination against rural-urban migrants (Solinger, 1999a; Zhang, 2016). The attitude of government toward rural-urban migration can be classified into four stages (Hu & Yang, 2019; Zhang, 2021). During the first stage in 1980s, the

---

[2] "Workers are the masters of the enterprise" is a socialist rhetoric in China during the era of planned economy before 1978. This "master" narrative emphasizes that the socialist revolution in China in 1949 had transformed the proletariat class into the leading class and risen workers from slaves in the old society to the owners of the nation. Therefore, the interests of workers are fully aligned with the interests of the nation and the state-owned enterprises. As the leading class, they need to exercise leadership during work for the interests of their enterprises and the nation. At the same time, the nation should look after workers by offering them life-time employment and cradle-to-grave welfare. The "master" narrative helped workers gain a sense of dignity and avoid being marginalized. In an age of reform since the late 1990s, this "master" narrative has become Chinese workers' collective memories of the past in the Mao era (Gong, 2015; Lee, 2007).

central government and city governments adopted a hands-off approach to rural-urban migration for work (Zhang, 2021). However, the enormous influx of migrant workers into cities also led to some social problems such as the increased crime rate, traffic congestion, and energy shortages. To maintain social stability and avoid "urban ills" such as slums and high unemployment rate, during the second stage from the late 1980s to the early 2000s, both the central government and local city governments issued many regulations to restrict the employment of rural migrants and protect the privilege of urban residents (Hu & Yang, 2019; Zhang et al., 2014). As a result, rural migrants had to apply for various certificates and permits in order to live and work in cities. Apart from the temporary residence permit, they had to apply for a permit to work away from their hometown, a one-child certificate, and a work permit for the destination city (Alexander & Chan, 2004; Wang et al., 2002). Prior to 2003, it was legal for city governments to detain rural migrants without certificates, fine them, and then deport them back to their permanent registration place of residence (Zhang, 2016). To reduce urban unemployment rate, city governments also issued regulations to reserve decent jobs for urban residents and limited rural migrants to the "three-D" (difficult, dangerous, and demeaning) jobs (Solinger, 1999a). Moreover, before the mid-2000s, city governments had no responsibility for non-local rural migrants and did not provide them any public services such as kindergarten services and legally compulsory education for children of rural migrants (Research Office of the State Council, 2006). Even if their children had graduated from high schools in cities, they were not allowed to take the college entrance examination in cities and had to return to their hometown where they registered their permanent residence to take the test (Solinger, 1999a; Zhang, 2016).

In brief, the regulations and restrictions on rural migrants provided a legal basis for discriminating against rural workers in the urban workplace (Solinger, 1999a). As a result, migrant workers in China had been treated as an inferior ethnic group and suffered structural discrimination before the mid-2000s. They had to congest in the secondary labor market characterized by low pay, poor working environment, and no job security. They had to undertake the "three-D" (dirty, dangerous, and difficult) jobs avoided by urbanites. They often worked long hours at a low wage, and their labor rights were often violated. Their health tended to be affected by noise, dust, and pollution associated with their poor working conditions, and they were frequent victims of work-related injury and illness (Research Office of the State Council, 2006; Zhang et al., 2014; Zhang et al., 2017).

The discriminatory government regulations and policies have received increasing criticism in China. Under the pressure of urban labor shortage which was supposedly induced by the prevalent hukou-based discrimination, during the third stage since 2003, the central government has abolished the discriminatory regulations, and required city governments to stop discriminating against rural migrants, to help migrant workers solve problems such as unpaid wages, and to provide migrants public services such as offering compulsory education for their children (Hu & Yang, 2019; Zhang, 2016). Since 2013, the attitude of the central government has entered into the fourth stage, emphasizing the need to integrate rural migrants into cities and towns. At the same time, city governments have also realized the benefits of migrant workers for tax revenue and local economy, and made an effort to lower the requirements for hukou transfer and encourage migrants to permanently move to cities (Hu & Yang, 2019; Sun & Liu, 2019).

However, although discriminatory regulations and formal rules can be changed overnight, direct and indirect discrimination against rural migrants in the form of informal rules, social stigma, and established managerial routines in workplaces usually take decades to change (Zhang et al., 2017). Although the Chinese government has advocated in the recent decade that rural migrant workers should be treated equally with urbanites in cities, the division between urbanites as core employees and rural migrants as peripheral workers in the workplace is still common, and rural workers still suffer from job and wage discrimination (Zhang et al., 2010; Zhang, 2016). Consequently, rural workers have less access to training, social insurance, welfare benefits, and promotion than urban-hukou holders. Job, wage, training, social insurance, welfare, and promotion hierarchies based on hukou status remain in firms, and rural migrants are usually at the bottom of each hierarchy (Wong et al., 2007; Zhang et al., 2017). Such hierarchies in employee management between urban workers and rural migrants can be conceptualized as hukou-based HRM discrimination, that is, the hukou-based managerial practices discriminating against rural migrants in terms of recruitment, wage, training, social insurance, and promotion (Zhang et al., 2010; Zhang, 2016; Zhang et al., 2017). It has constituted a unique institutional environment in the Chinese workplace before the mid-2000s (Zhang et al., 2014; Zhang, 2016).

Strategies of MNEs Toward Local Institutional Environment

The prevalent hukou-based HRM discrimination against rural migrants in the Chinese workplace for several decades has led to a natural question: how did MNEs respond to such a local distinctive management practice which had constituted an important part of the Chinese indigenous institutional environment (Zhang et al., 2017). As discussed earlier, China has received massive FDI since the early 1980s. More than half of the inward FDI has gone into labor-intensive manufacturing industries, employing millions of rural migrant workers (Davies, 2013; MOFCOM, 2019; OECD, 2000; Tseng & Zebregs, 2002). The prevailing discrimination against rural migrants represents an institutional tension or challenge for MNEs operating in China. MNE subsidiaries, when employing both urban and rural employees, have to decide how they respond to the discriminatory hukou-based HRM in the Chinese workplace (Zhang et al., 2017).

The strategic response of MNEs toward institutional environments of host countries is an important topic for international business since MNEs operate across multiple institutional environments, and choosing the right responsive strategy is vital for their survival and success (Mudambi & Navarra, 2002; Regnér & Edman, 2014). Institutional environment refers to a social web of rules, norms, values, patterned practices, and taken-for-granted assumptions that surround organizations (Kostova, 1996; Matten & Geppert, 2004; Scott, 2001). There are different understandings about how MNEs respond to the local institutional environment. The old institutionalism emphasizes institutional isomorphism and denies organization and management agency, arguing that organizations have to adapt to local environments for social legitimacy and acceptance (DiMaggio & Powell, 1983). By contrast, neo-institutionalism argues that organizations are not just passive recipients of institutional environments but have the desire, ability, and power to influence external institutional environments (Oliver, 1991; Scott, 2001). Therefore, the theory of institution co-evolution assumes that organizations and external institutional environments co-evolve (Cantwell et al., 2010). On the one hand, organizations are shaped by external environments and follow local formal and informal institutions through institutional adaptation; on the other hand, they actively mobilize resources to shape institutional environments for their interests and survival. Given that MNEs operate across multiple institutional environments and are exposed to multiple institutional powers such as home country institutions, host country factors, international regulations, and the practices of other MNEs, scholars tend to assume that MNEs often form an independent organizational field, behaving in new ways different from that of both home and host country firms. Therefore, MNEs tend to be change agents, actively engaging in institutional entrepreneurship in host countries (Bartlett & Ghoshal, 1989; Cantwell et al., 2010; Paul & Feliciano-Cestero, 2021; Zhang et al., 2017).

These perspectives on MNEs' strategic response to local institutional environments are somewhat normative and prescriptive. In fact, MNEs are not a homogeneous group (Sally, 1994). Foreign-owned enterprises come from different economies with different levels of development and different home country institutional environments. Some of them come from leading economies with strict anti-discrimination laws, while others come from emerging economies with less perfect legal environment. Some are labor-intensive while others are technology- or capital-intensive, and MNEs engage in foreign investment with different objectives (Paul & Feliciano-Cestero, 2021). Different MNEs may adopt different strategies toward hukou-based HRM discrimination (Zhang et al., 2017). For example, large MNEs of leading economies are less likely to take advantage of the hukou-based HRM discrimination since such managerial practices might damage their international reputation. By contrast, labor-intensive MNEs are more likely to adopt hukou-based HRM to cut labor costs and maintain competitiveness (Smith & Pun, 2006).

Empirical research findings also support such judgments. There have been no consistent strategies adopted by all types of MNEs (Zhang et al., 2017; Zhu, 2004). Cooke (2004) finds that even in one foreign-owned company, both hard and soft HR practices are adopted at the same time. On the one hand, HR practices in the MNE display strong paternalism in terms of employee welfare and care arrangements such as offering rural migrant workers night school education; on the other hand, there are also strong elements of managerial prerogatives and opportunistic behavior in its HR practices that take advantage of migrant workers. Based on the perception of rural migrant workers, Zhang et al. (2017) find that there is no statistically significant difference between the strategies of MNE subsidiaries and domestic firms toward hukou-based HRM discrimination. Although HR managers of foreign-funded firms report that they tend to adopt avoidance and defiance strategies toward hukou-based HRM, they are reluctant to play a leadership role in eliminating hukou-based discrimination. The findings of this study reveal that MNEs from different economies had different reputations among rural migrant workers in terms of their treatment of employees (Zhang et al., 2017), indicating a more nuanced understanding of the strategic responses of MNEs to host country institutional environment. In general, the findings of this study reveal that the governance quality of MNEs' home countries shapes MNEs' behavior and strategies toward hukou-based HRM discrimination.

Research on IB and Domestic Migration: Toward a Future Research Agenda

As discussed earlier, although migration has attracted attention in the international business field recently, existing studies have focused on international migration, there is a dearth of discussions on domestic migration in the IB literature. Given that FDI inflows and rural-urban migration are two important forces that are significantly shaping modern China, the lack of attention to the implications of domestic migration for international business and vice versa is an important omission. Since studies on IB and domestic migration have been largely paralleling to each other, there are many gaps in the literature which constitute future research opportunities. Specifically, in the case of China, the following are some potential topics worth exploring further.

Eliminate Hukou-based Discrimination Migrants in many countries are often vulnerable to discrimination and exploitation (ILO, 2001). As discussed earlier, rural migrant workers in China have suffered from hukou-based discrimination in urban areas. Although the Chinese government has abolished policies and regulations discriminating against rural migrants and made efforts to improve the situations of rural migrant workers since the mid-2000s, rural migrants in cities are still disadvantaged and vulnerable in terms of job security, social insurance, welfare benefits, employability, and opportunities of upward social mobility (Zhang et al., 2017). It is worth to explore how MNEs as change agents show leadership in eliminating various hukou-based discrimination through responsible HRM practices. In recent years, Scholars (e.g., Reiche et al., 2019, p. 360) are calling for integrating IB and HRM research in order to obtain "a more integrative understanding of various aspects of global work." Exploring how MNEs manage rural migrant workers in a responsible way can deepen our understanding of international business.

Improve Migrant Wellbeing Rural migrant workers in China tend to be trapped in the secondary labor market with low pay and inferior working environment, undertaking repetitive, dirty, or difficult work avoided by urban residents. Therefore, they are more likely to suffer from work-related injuries and mental health issues (Zhang, 2016). Research has revealed that ignoring employee well-being can be expensive since happy workers are healthy and more productive (Zelenski et al., 2008). How to improve the well-being of rural migrant workers is also important for MNEs operating in China as responsible investors. However, international business studies have been dominated by the efficiency-driven logic, and employee well-being has been largely overlooked by the mainstream literature.

Foster Social Integration of Migrants in Urban Communities Migrant integration refers to the process that migrants gain basic economic and social insurance, acculturate to living and working in host cities, and actively engage in positive interactions with local residents on the basis of equal treatment and mutual respect (Zheng et al., 2021). In the recent decade, migration from rural areas to cities has few policy and legal barriers, but it is still difficult for rural migrants to integrate into host cities. Differing from the older generation of rural migrants who are expected to be city sojourners and eventually return to the countryside (Solinger, 1999a), the new generations of rural migrants prefer city life and will not return to their hometown even if they are unemployed in cities (Hu & Yang, 2019; Sun & Liu, 2019). Since 2013, the central government and city governments have encouraged rural migrants to permanently move into cities to improve the level of urbanization. Nevertheless, there are still various social and economic barriers for rural migrants to settle down in cities, and social segregation is still common (Sun & Liu, 2019). However, scant literature exists on how MNEs operating in China can contribute to the integration of rural migrants into city life.

Leverage Skills, Knowledge, and Experiences of Migrants in MNEs MNEs in China recruit both rural migrant workers and urban migrants (MOFCOM, 2019). Migrants constitute valuable human assets of MNEs and significantly influence organizational performance. Given that migrants may have needs different from that of local employees, how to effectively motivate them with personalized HRM packages is an important topic for MNEs operating in China. However, domestic migrants are usually not viewed as migrants in their home country, and hence, their distinctive needs are often ignored. Integrating domestic migration in host countries into international business studies can help MNEs effectively manage domestic migrant employees.

Upskill and Reskill Rural Migrant Workers Most rural-urban migrants are not well educated and low-skilled workers. According to the 2021 Survey Report on Rural Migrant Workers (NBSC, 2022), 70.5% of rural migrants had received junior high school education or less, and only 13% of them had a junior college diploma. If they are not well trained, it is more likely that they are locked into the "three-D" low-paid jobs that keep them impoverished and difficult to really integrate into city life. Moreover, it is believed that we are now in the early stage of the Fourth Industrial Revolution (Raisch & Krakowski, 2021). With the development of digitalization and AI technology, it is possible that the low-skilled, "three D," and repetitive work will be performed by machines in the near future. Rural migrants, especially the new generations of migrant workers, need to be upskilled and reskilled so as to obtain employability in the process of industrial upgrading and digitalization. MNEs need to explore how to upskill and reskill their migrant workers for sustainable development.

Explore New Theoretical Perspectives on IB and Domestic Migration The relationship between IB and domestic migration should be much more complicated than the relationship between pull and push forces (Hare, 1999). Similarly, domestic migration is also much more than just a change of residence for migrants or a location advantage for MNEs (Mathews & Zander, 2007). Moreover, we are now living in a digital age, and the rapid development of technologies and digitalization is changing the way organizations operate and people work (Mourtzis et al., 2022). Such development may influence the way of organizational internationalization (Ipsmiller et al., 2022) and the pattern of international and domestic migration, leading to new ways of interaction between IB and domestic migration. Therefore, to integrate IB and domestic migration studies, new theoretical perspectives are necessary. In the special issue on global work in multinational enterprises, Reiche et al. (2019) propose a framework to examine global work in multinational enterprises from both IB and HRM perspectives. This framework integrates actors, structure, and processes to obtain a more integrative understanding of various aspects of global work. Such a framework integrating actors, structures, and processes of global work can also help integrate theoretical and empirical research in the fields of IB and domestic migration. IB scholars can explore more theoretical perspectives and methodological approaches to achieve the cross-fertilization between IB and domestical migration studies.

Discussion and Conclusion

This chapter seeks to examine the relationship between international business and domestic migration in China. The findings show that both the unprecedented FDI inflows and domestic rural-urban migration have been interdependent. At the same time, FDI and MNEs contribute to and are shaped by the host country institutional environment in China. Therefore, examining the relationship between IB and domestic migration is an important topic for IB studies.

China represents an ideal context to test international business theories and explore the relationship between international business and domestic migration. For example, decades-long massive rural-migration has created an army of cheap labor, constituting a unique location advantage for MNEs and helping China become an attractive investment destination for labor-intensive MNEs that seek to reduce operational costs and maximize output in countries with low labor and safety standards. As one of the largest FDI recipient in the world for decades, China is also an ideal setting to examine the role of MNEs in society. This study reveals how MNEs, as a whole, have significantly challenged the hukou system, the way companies operate, and the way employees are managed in China over the past decades. For China that has just opened its doors to the outside world, the foreignness of MNE behaviors tend to be viewed as the representatives of modernity and superiority. Therefore, MNEs operating in emerging economies such as China are generally in a position to act as a powerful change agent that challenges existing structures and established institutional arrangements by introducing new managerial practices (Collings et al., 2011). However, although MNEs are powerful change agents in host countries, the positive spillover effects of MNEs on host countries has been limited while "research has found evidence of negative economic, social, and environmental spillovers from MNE activity" (Oetzel & Doh, 2009, p. 110). This study also shows that MNEs in China, usually driven by the economic efficiency logic, have not contributed much to the elimination of hukou-based HRM discrimination and the improvement of rural-urban migrant well-being, although they have the ability and resources to do so. How to play a more positive role in improving employee well-being of host countries is still an important task for MNEs.

This study has significant theoretical and practical implications. Theoretically, it helps us understand the interaction between MNEs and institutional environments, as well as the behavior and roles of MNEs in host countries. There is a de-contextualization tendency in the HRM literature, assuming that management has full autonomy to choose their HRM policies and practices and focusing on examining the effects of HRM but downplaying the effects of institutional environments (Cook, 2018; Zhang et al., 2010). This study shows that HRM policies and practices of an MNE, deliberately or unintentionally, reflect institutional environments of both host and home countries and can be fully understood only when both home and host country institutional contexts are considered. This finding lends support to the notion of "socially embedded HRM" which emphasizes contextualization in HRM research (Morishima, 1995; Zhang et al., 2010; Zhang et al., 2017). Moreover, our study shows that international investment and domestic migration are not unrelated but influence each other, especially in developing countries. International business studies should not ignore domestic migration in host countries. Studies on both international business and domestic migration should go beyond disciplinary silos to enrich each other.

Practically, this study has implications for managing multinationals and fostering socially responsible MNEs. Given that different MNEs adopt different strategies toward the hukou-based HRM discrimination, indicating that HRM policies and practices of MNE subsidiaries are shaped by the institutional environments of both home and host countries. Therefore, governments of both home and host countries play an important role in shaping MNE behavior and creating socially responsible MNEs (Wu et al., 2008). However, when discussing the management of MNEs, scholars tend to ignore the governance quality of their home countries. Our study reveals that when encouraging MNEs to adopt ethical practices toward employees in host countries, it is important to consider the role of the home country institutional environment in shaping MNE behavior when operating abroad (Zhang et al., 2017).

This study also has implications for MNEs to manage local institutional factors to obtain legitimacy and reduce reputation risk. The hukou-based HRM discrimination against rural migrant workers represents a challenge that MNEs face in China and requires MNEs to manage it carefully. In recent decades, conducting business in a responsible and ethical manner has become a basic requirement for MNEs. There are many international regulations emphasizing the elimination of discrimination in employment such as the *ILO Declaration on Fundamental Principles and Rights at Work* (1998), *the United Nations Global Compact* (2000), and the *OECD Guidelines for Multinational Enterprises* (2011). Simultaneously, the rise of ethical consumer and investor movements has also pushed MNEs to behave responsibly in host countries (Devinney et al., 2010). MNE subsidiaries should exercise greater care to manage legitimacy when responding to the host country institutional environment.

References

Alexander, P., & Chan, A. (2004). Does China have an apartheid pass system? *Journal of Ethnic and Migration Studies, 30*(4), 609–629.

Bartlett, C. A., & Ghoshal, S. (1989). *Managing across Borders: The transitional solution*. Harvard Business School Press.

Cantwell, J., Dunning, J., & Lundan, S. M. (2010). An evolutionary approach to understanding business activity: The co-evolution of MNEs and the institutional environment. *Journal of International Business Studies, 41*(4), 567–586.

Chan, K. W., & Zhang, L. (1999). The hukou system and rural-urban migration in China: Processes and changes. *The China Quarterly, 160*, 818–855.

Chen, S. H., & Wilson, M. (2003). Standardization and localization of human resource management in Sino-foreign joint ventures. *Asia Pacific Journal of Management, 20*(3), 397–408.

Cheng, T., & Selden, M. (1994). The origins and social consequences of China's hukou system. *The China Quarterly, 139*, 644–668.

Collings, D. G. (2014). Integrating global mobility and global talent management: Exploring the challenges and strategic opportunities. *Journal of World Business, 49*, 253–261.

Collings, D., Lavelle, J., & Gunnigle, P. (2011). The role of MNEs. In M. Barry & A. Wilkinson (Eds.), *Research handbook of comparative employment relations* (pp. 402–420). Edward Elgar Publishing. https://doi.org/10.4337/9780857936318.00025

Cook, F. L. (2018). Concepts, contexts and mindsets: Putting human resource management research in perspectives. *Human Resource Management Journal, 28*(1), 1–13.

Cooke, F. L. (2004). Foreign firms in China: Modelling HRM in a toy manufacturing corporation. *Human Resource Management Journal, 14*(3), 31–52.

Davies, K. (2013). *China investment policy: An update. OECD working papers on international investment*. OECD Publishing.

Devinney, T. M., Auger, P., & Eckhardt, G. M. (2010). *The myth of the ethical consumer*. Cambridge University Press.

DiMaggio, P. J., & Powell, W. W. (1983). The iron cage revisited: Institutional isomorphism and collective rationality in organizational fields. *American Sociological Review, 48*(2), 147–160.

Fan, C. C. (2008). *China on the move: Migration, the state, and the household*. Routledge.

Gong, Q. (2015). Masters of the nation: Representation of the industrial worker in films of the cultural revolution period (1966–1976). *China Perspectives, 2*, 15–23.

Hajro, A., Caprar, D. V., Zikic, J., & Stahl, G. K. (2021). Global migrants: Understanding the implications for international business and management. *Journal of World Business, 56*, 1–11.

Hare, D. (1999). Push' versus 'pull' factors in migration outflows and returns: Determinants of migration status and spell duration among China's rural population. *The Journal of Development Studies, 35*(3), 45–72.

Hu, Y. W., & Yang, K. (2019). Forty years of research on migrant workers in China: Evolution, characteristics, and trends: A visualized study based on CiteSpace V. *Journal of South China University of Technology (Social Science Edition), 21*(4), 100–110. https://doi.org/10.19366/j.cnki.1009-055X.2019.04.011

ILO (2001). International migration, racism, discrimination and xenophobia (for distribution at the world conference against racism, racial discrimination, xenophobia and related intolerance). International Labour Office, International Organization for Migration, Office of the United Nations High Commissioner for Human Rights. Retrieved from http://www.unesco.org/most/migration/imrdx.pdf.

Ipsmiller, E., Dikova, D., & Brouthers, K. D. (2022). Digital internationalization of traditional firms: Virtual presence and entrepreneurial orientation. *Journal of International Management, 28*(4), 100940. https://doi.org/10.1016/j.intman.2022.100940

Kerswell, T., & Lin, J. (2017). Capitalism denied with Chinese characteristics. *Socialism and Democracy, 31*(2), 33–52.

Kostova, T. (1996). *Success of the transnational transfer of organizational practices within multinational companies*. Unpublished manuscript. University of Minnesota.

Lee, C. K. (2007). What was socialism to Chinese workers? Collective memories and labor politics in an age of reform. In C. K. Lee & G. B. Yang (Eds.), *Re-envisioning the Chinese revolution: The politics and poetics of collective memories in reform China* (pp. 141–165). Stanford University Press.

Liang, Z. (2001). The age of migration in China. *Population and Development Review, 27*(3), 499–524.

Liang, Z., & White, M. J. (1996). Internal migration in China, 1950–1988. *Demography, 33*(3), 375–384.

Mathews, J. A., & Zander, I. (2007). The international entrepreneurial dynamics of accelerated internationalisation. *Journal of International Business Studies, 38*(3), 387–403.

Matten, D., & Geppert, M. (2004). Work systems in heavy engineering: The role of national culture and national institutions in multinational corporations. *Journal of International Management, 10*(2), 177–198.

MOFCOM. (2019). *China's foreign investment report 2019*. The Ministry of Commerce of the People's Republic of China. Retrieved from http://images.mofcom.gov.cn/wzs/202008/20200819101923422.pdf

Morishima, M. (1995). Embedding HRM in a social context. *British Journal of Industrial Relations, 33*(4), 617–640.

Mourtzis, D., Angelopoulos, J., & Panopoulos, N. (2022). A literature review of the challenges and opportunities of the transition from industry 4.0 to society 5.0. *Energies, 15*(17), 6276. https://doi.org/10.3390/en15176276

Mudambi, R., & Navarra, P. (2002). Institutions and international business: A theoretical overview. *International Business Review, 11*(6), 635–646.

NBSC. (2022). *2008–2021 Survey reports on migrant workers*. National Bureau of Statistics of China. http://www.stats.gov.cn

OECD. (2000). *Main determinants and impacts of foreign direct investment on China's economy*. OECD working papers on international investment, 2000/04. OECD Publishing. https://doi.org/10.1787/321677880185

Oetzel, J., & Doh, J. P. (2009). MNEs and development: A review and reconceptualization. *Journal of World Business, 44*(2), 108–120.

Oliver, C. (1991). Strategic responses to institutional processes. *The Academy of Management Review, 16*(1), 145–179.

Paul, J., & Feliciano-Cestero, M. M. (2021). Five decades of research on foreign direct investment by MNEs: An overview and research agenda. *Journal of Business Research, 124*, 800–812.

Raisch, S., & Krakowski, S. (2021). Artificial intelligence and management: The automation–augmentation paradox. *Academy of Management Review, 46*(1), 192–210.

Regnér, P., & Edman, J. (2014). MNE institutional advantage: How subunits shape, transpose and evade host country institutions. *Journal of International Business Studies, 45*(3), 275–302.

Reiche, B. S., Lee, Y. T., & Allen, D. G. (2019). Actors, structure, and processes: A review and conceptualization of global work integrating IB and HRM research. *Journal of Management, 45*(2), 359–383.

Research Office of the State Council. (2006). *Survey reports on the problems of rural migrant workers in China*【《中国农民工问题调研报告》】. China Yanshi Press. (In Chinese).

Sally, R. (1994). Multinational enterprises, political economy and institutional theory: Domestic embeddedness in the context of internationalization. *Review of International Political Economy, 1*(1), 161–192.

Scott, W. R. (2001). *Institutions and organizations*. Sage.

Smith, C., & Pun, N. (2006). The dormitory labour regime in China as a site for control and resistance. *The International Journal of Human Resource Management, 17*(8), 1456–1470.

Solinger, D. J. (1999a). *Contesting citizenship in urban China: Peasant migrants, the state, and the logic of the market*. University of California Press.

Solinger, D. J. (1999b). Citizenship issues in China's internal migration: Comparisons with Germany and Japan. *Political Science Quarterly, 114*(3), 455–478.

Sun, Z.W., & Liu, L. P. (2019, August 2). *Forty years of research on migrant workers in China: From "Surplus labor force" to "New urban immigrants"*. Retrieved from https://www.aisixiang.com/data/117533.html

The World Bank. (2022). Urban population (% of total population) - China. https://data.worldbank.org/indicator/SP.URB.TOTL.IN.ZS?locations=CN

Tsang, E. W. K. (1994). Human resource management problems in Sino-foreign joint ventures. *International Journal of Manpower, 15*(9), 4–21.

Tseng, W., & Zebregs, H. (2002). *Foreign direct investment in China: Some lessons for other countries.* International Monetary Fund, Asia and Pacific Dept. Retrieved from https://www.imf.org/external/pubs/ft/pdp/2002/pdp03.pdf

UNCTAD (2022). *Investment statistics and trends.* https://unctad.org/topic/investment/investment-statistics-and-trends

Wang, F., Zuo, X., & Ruan, D. (2002). Rural migrants in Shanghai: Living under the shadow of socialism. *International Migration Review, 36*, 520–545.

Warner, M. (2003). China's HRM revisited: A step-wise path to convergence? *Asia Pacific Business Review, 9*(4), 15–31.

Warner, M. (2008). Reassessing human resource management 'with Chinese characteristics': An overview. *International Journal of Human Resource Management, 19*(5), 771–801.

Warner, M. (2014). *Understanding management in China: Past, present and future.* Routledge.

Wong, D. F. K., Li, C. Y., & Song, H. X. (2007). Rural migrant workers in urban China: Living a marginalised life. *International Journal of Social Welfare, 16*(1), 32–40.

Wu, Y., & Chen, C. L. (2016). The impact of foreign direct investment on urbanization in China. *Journal of the Asia Pacific Economy, 21*(3), 339–356.

Wu, C., Lawler, J. J., & Yi, X. (2008). Overt employment discrimination in MNC affiliates: Home-country cultural and institutional effects. *Journal of International Business Studies, 39*, 772–794.

Xia, J., Zhu, C. J., Fan, D., & Zhang, M. M. (2020). The 'iron Rice-bowl' regime revisited: Whither human resource Management in Chinese Universities? *Asia Pacific Journal of Human Resources, 58*, 289–310.

Yang, C. (2012). Restructuring the export-oriented industrialization in the Pearl River Delta, China: Institutional evolution and emerging tension. *Applied Geography, 32*, 143–157.

Zelenski, J. M., Murphy, S. A., & Jenkins, D. A. (2008). The happy-productive worker thesis revisited. *Journal of Happiness Studies, 9*(4), 521–537.

Zhang, M. M. (2016). *The institution of Hukou-based social exclusion in contemporary China and strategies of multinationals: An institutional analysis.* Nova Science Publishers.

Zhang, S. W. (2021). Social development and the management of migrant workers since reform and opening up in China. *Cultural Review.* Retrieved from http://www.21bcr.com/gaigekaifangyilaizhongguoshehuifazhanhenongmingongzhili/.

Zhang, M., Nyland, C., & Zhu, J. C. (2010). Hukou-based HRM in contemporary China: The case of Jiangsu and Shanghai. *Asia Pacific Business Review, 16*(3), 377–393.

Zhang, M., Zhu, C. J., & Nyland, C. (2014). The institution of Hukou-based social exclusion: A unique institution reshaping the characteristics of contemporary urban China. *International Journal of Urban and Regional Research, 38*(4), 1437–1457.

Zhang, M. M., Zhu, C. J., Dowling, P., & Fan, D. (2017). Subsidiary responses to the institutional characteristics of the host country: Strategies of multinational enterprises towards hukou-based discriminatory HRM practices in China. *Personnel Review, 46*(5), 870–890.

Zheng, R., Mei, L., Guo, Y., Zhen, S., & Fu, Z. (2021). How do city-specific factors affect migrant integration in China? A study based on a hierarchical linear model of migrants and cities. *PLoS One, 16*(1), e0244665. https://doi.org/10.1371/journal.pone.0244665

Zhu, Y. (2004). Workers, unions and the state: Migrant workers in China's labour-intensive foreign enterprises. *Development and Change, 35*(5), 1011–1035.

12

The Value of Migrants for International Joint Ventures

Julia Mittermayr, Vera Kunczer, and Jonas Puck

Introduction

International joint ventures (IJVs) are a popular choice for companies looking to expand into foreign markets, but they can be difficult to manage due to cultural differences between IJV partners. Cultural differences are cited as one of the main reasons for the high failure rate and potentially bad performance of international alliances (Beugelsdijk et al., 2018; Hennart & Zeng, 2002; Slangen, 2006). Cultural differences are rooted in the distinct norms and practices of each IJV partner, and they are generally greater across than within national cultures (Hofstede, 1980). These differences can lead to the formation of separate "in-group" (the local IJV partner) and "out-group" (the foreign IJV partner) identities within the venture, hindering team cohesion and motivation and ultimately lowering IJV success rates (Mohr et al., 2016b; Salk & Shenkar, 2001).

Knowing that cultural differences are problematic in IJVs, the role of national origin and other social identities in sense-making for IJV members merits a closer investigation than has been the case so far. While some researchers (e.g., Ren et al., 2009) point out that social networks within culturally diverse teams that link people from different cultures might play an

---

J. Mittermayr (✉) • V. Kunczer • J. Puck
Vienna University of Economics and Business, Vienna, Austria
e-mail: julia.mittermayr@s.wu.ac.at; vera.kunczer@wu.ac.at; Jonas.Puck@wu.ac.at

© The Author(s), under exclusive license to Springer Nature Switzerland AG 2023
A. I. Mockaitis (ed.), *The Palgrave Handbook of Global Migration in International Business*,
https://doi.org/10.1007/978-3-031-38886-6_12

interesting role in counteracting conflict, empirical confirmation of that effect remains scarce. Despite over 30 years of research on IJV performance (Harrigan, 1988; Dutta & Beamish, 2013; Mohr et al., 2016a), negligible attention has been paid to social and cognitive processes in this regard. The study by Salk and Shenkar (2001) is one of the few to have done so. We seek to advance these lines of research by elucidating the black box of social identity building in IJVs to better explain the performance of these alliances.

In doing so, the focus of the present study is on the role of migrants as a valuable source of knowledge about foreign cultures and thus as a potential driver of identity formation for IJVs. Migrants possess significant knowledge about their country of origin (COO) and its culture and can act as a bridge between their COO and firms in their new host country (Hernandez, 2014). Several researchers (e.g., Gould, 1994; Javorcik et al., 2011) have noted that the presence of individuals with a shared national origin on both sides of a border can alleviate many of the challenges for MNEs when conducting business in other countries. Migrants may play a key role in reducing perceived cultural differences as they can make their own culture appear less "alien" to others. It is argued that if the cultural differences are less pronounced, IJV members start focusing more on the similarities and form a stronger connection with the foreign partner. A stronger identification with the out-group (the foreign IJV partner) reduces conflict and enhances alliance performance (Salk & Shenkar, 2001).

At the same time, we investigate how this effect behaves depending on certain demographic characteristics of the migrants as drivers for social identity building. More specifically, we focus on two demographic characteristics: gender and age. According to the literature on the social identity theory (SIT) (e.g., Tajfel & Turner, 1985), characteristics such as gender and age are among the factors most likely to trigger social identification processes among members. Due to the salience of demographic characteristics, they are readily and frequently taken as a basis of individuals to assess how much they are socially attracted to a group and to what extent they can identitfy with its members. In summary, this chapter aims to answer the following research question: *What is the impact of migrants on International Joint Ventures, and what role do migrants' characteristics play?*

To answer this research question, we investigated migration patterns in Austria and IJVs formed between Austrian firms and at least one international partner. Austria's strategic location at the heart of Europe not only facilitates trade and transportation of goods and services between Eastern and Western Europe but also acts as a hub for the flow of people. With over 2.24 million people with a migration background residing in Austria, accounting for around 25% of the total population in 2021 (Statistik Austria, 2022), the country is a popular destination for migration and attracts individuals from diverse countries and cultures. Furthermore, Austria is characterized by an international economy with almost 60% of its GDP attributable to business activities abroad (Ministry of Foreign Affairs Austria, 2022). This combination of factors provides a unique opportunity to investigate the impact of migration on international business performance.

In doing so, our study contributes to the international business literature in four different ways. First, it enriches the IJV literature by linking it to migration literature and connecting the two streams. It goes beyond the insights that cultural differences can cause performance problems in IJVs (e.g., Beugelsdijk et al., 2018) and provides insights into how migrants as informants about foreign cultures can make a difference in performance outcomes for IJVs, cultural differences between the IJV partners notwithstanding. Second, this chapter contributes to the SIT. Existing research leaves a gap as to how migrants can affect social identity building within firms and especially firm alliances. This is an important omission, given that social identities are formed primarily on the basis of differences or similarities in demographic characteristics such as nationality and origin. Third, this chapter examines migrants as a broad group of people who left their COOs to settle in a new home country. Past research has primarily concentrated on expatriates who are not representative of the overall migrant population as they are typically staffed on temporary assignments with the intention to repatriate (Hajro et al., 2021). Fourth, the chapter sheds light on the characteristics of migrants that moderate the relationship between migrants and IJV performance, thereby extending research on migrants' characteristics in the realm of business activities (e.g., Gheasi et al., 2013; Kugler & Rapoport, 2011).

State of Research

IJV Performance

IJVs offer access to foreign markets and partner resources, but are also known for high conflict and dissolution rates. IJVs are defined as a temporary and mutually beneficial alliance established between a local parent and at least one foreign partner for the purpose of jointly undertaking specific projects. These collaborations offer access to foreign markets and to the complementary skills and resources of the other partner, allowing firms to produce and sell products and services more effectively and efficiently than they could do alone. Furthermore, the IJV partner can assist in better navigating the foreign business environment in the host country (Makino & Delios, 1996). However, despite their popularity, IJVs are known to have high dissolution rates due to a high degree of conflict between the IJV partners. Harrigan (1988) found that half of the alliances investigated dissolved prematurely. Similar results were found in studies by Kogut (1989) and Franko (1971). In a more recent study (Mohr et al., 2016a), around 20% of the IJVs analyzed were dissolved. Consequently, it is not surprising that the underlying drivers for IJV performance have been researched extensively (e.g., Mohr & Puck, 2005; Mohr et al., 2016b; Reus & Rottig, 2009).

Scholars agree that IJVs are particularly susceptible to *cultural* conflict between partner firms (e.g., Beugelsdijk et al., 2018; Hennart & Zeng, 2002). Culture, in this context, refers to the shared values, norms, and priorities that are prevalent among the members of a specific group or nation (Hofstede, 1980). These cultural elements determine how things are to be evaluated and which behaviors are desirable or to be omitted. Despite cultural conflicts being a frequently cited cause of IJV breakups, research on the impact of cultural differences between partners has yielded mixed results. On the one hand, cultural distance between partner firms can increase the likelihood of ambiguities in the relationship and misunderstandings about the alliance goals and objectives (e.g., Beugelsdijk et al., 2018; Hennart & Zeng, 2002; Reus & Rottig, 2009). Furthermore, cultural distance can make it more difficult for partners to value each others' working habits and business approaches (Reus & Rottig, 2009), which negatively impacts the perceived performance of the IJV (Yeheskel et al., 2001) and destabilizes the IJV overall (Meschi & Riccio, 2008). On the other hand, cultural differences may also serve as a source of admiration, resulting in more information exchange and collaboration (Ren et al., 2009). Berry et al. (2010) report that several researchers discovered a relationship between greater cultural distance and lower dissolution rates of foreign subsidiaries. For example, Park and Ungson (1997) found that IJVs that are characterized by a relatively higher level of cultural differences are less likely to dissolve compared to national joint ventures. Similarly, Vasilaki (2011) showed that cultural distance has a positive effect on the performance of acquired entities. A study by Tihanyi et al. (2005) discovered a positive impact of cultural differences for developed country investments, suggesting that diversity and heterogeneity can lead to increased benefits and opportunities for synergies. It can thus be concluded that the relationship between IJV performance and cultural differences is complex.

While the significance of understanding cultural differences in alliances and investments has been acknowledged in the field (e.g., Barkema & Vermeulen, 1997; Beugelsdijk et al., 2018; Dikova & Sahib, 2013; Hutzschenreuter et al., 2014), there is a lack of research on how and under which conditions cultural sensitivity is established. It is argued that "if there is greater cultural sensitivity in the culturally distant partners, the cultural difference may not be a strong obstacle (…) because partners appreciate their counterpart's culture and can behave with sensitivity and understanding" (Ren et al., 2009, p. 821). Migrants, with their valuable cultural knowledge, could serve as a vehicle to create conditions that foster cultural sensitivity within IJVs. But the role migrants play in this context has yet to be explored.

Migration in International Business

Migrants are valuable "agents of change" in organizations as well as in local communities, making migration a relevant field for international business researchers (Hajro et al., 2021). Due to the specific knowledge of migrants about their COOs, they can support the creation of a knowledge pool that can serve as a source for knowledge spillovers to local companies (Gould, 1994; Kunczer et al., 2019). This knowledge pool can provide firms with foreign-country knowledge that is rare, valuable, difficult to reproduce, and has the potential to allow firms to build a unique competitive advantage (Chung et al., 2012). Through the accumulation of foreign-country knowledge, a company's lack of familiarity with the foreign market environment can be reduced, ultimately supporting the operations of that firm in the foreign country (Hernandez, 2014).

The sharing of migrants' knowledge can happen directly, when migrants are employed by a company, or indirectly through interactions and relationships with people in the local community (Kunczer et al., 2019). Indirect knowledge spillovers can be explained by the relationships migrants build with people in the local community either in a professional context (e.g., conferences) or in everyday life (e.g., coincidental meetings) (Oettl & Agrawal, 2008). In fact, Singh (2005) found that social interactions and interpersonal ties are key in determining knowledge diffusion, while firm boundaries (i.e., being employed by the same firm) have little impact on the probability of knowledge flow between actors. Therefore, companies can also benefit from the knowledge of their employees acquired through relationships and interactions with people outside the company (Kunczer et al., 2019).

In the past decade, IB literature has begun to explore the role that migrants' characteristics play in the acquisition and transfer of knowledge, as well as its absorption and use by companies. A study by Gheasi et al. (2013) demonstrates that the higher the level of education of migrants from a certain country, the stronger the positive impact they have on foreign direct investment (FDI). Similarly, a study conducted by Federici and Giannetti (2010) presents strong evidence of network externalities which are mainly associated with the skilled diaspora. Javorcik et al. (2011) also find a positive relationship between US FDI abroad and the presence of migrants from the host country, with the link being stronger for migrants with tertiary education.

Some scholars endorse the migrants' occupational position rather than education as an indicator of migrants' job skill levels (e.g., Aleksynska & Peri, 2014; Cuadros et al., 2019). Higher occupations, such as managerial positions, are more influential compared to lower occupations in channeling relevant knowledge and in establishing an understanding for the differences in culture and applied business approaches. Apart from their formal knowledge or capabilities, these occupations are characterized by a higher decision-making power which is expected to explain the greater, positive influence of such occupations on internationalization activities (Cuadros et al., 2019).

The gender of migrants has long been neglected and we still know very little about the role of gender or gender relations in migration and international business research. Most research has inexplicitly assumed a male-dominated pool of migrants. The long prevailing invisibility of women in the migration literature can be attributed to a false stereotype of female migrants as unskilled dependents of their spouses (Guo & Al Ariss, 2015). Today, however, we know that migrant men and women face different hurdles as well as opportunties when they emigrate to a new country, and they differ in terms of their roles in new communities, the professions they pursue, and their access to resources and services (Piper, 2006). Unsurprisingly, research has started to pay increasing attention to gender difference and recognize the importance of gender-disaggregated studies (e.g., Guo & Al Ariss, 2015; Mintz & Krymkowski, 2010).

Hypotheses

According to the SIT, cultural differences between IJV partners can lead to the formation of different social identities and nationality-based subgroups (Salk & Shenkar, 2001). The SIT was first proposed by Tajfel and Turner (1979) and explains how individuals form social identities based on their membership in groups. Accordingly, we tend to demonstrate group behavior, such as solidarity, within the groups we identify with (i.e., in-groups), while we show discrimination against groups we do not identify with (i.e., out-groups) as part of a process to build a positive social identity and self-esteem. The following three psychological steps are central in this process:

First, social categorization describes the classification of individuals into categories based on characteristics such as organizational membership, religious affiliation, gender, age, and nationality (Hogg & Terry, 2000). IJVs which by their very nature involve parent firms from different countries tend to strongly use nationality as a differentiating factor in social identity building. In the sense of the SIT, the different nationalities of the companies can be understood as social categories (Salk & Shenkar, 2001).

Second, during the step of social identification, members of a group adopt the identity of the group they have categorized themselves as belonging to (Tajfel & Turner, 1979). The identification with a group is associated with establishing an emotional connection to that group, linking one's self-esteem to the group's social standing as well as creating a sense of identity. Salk & Shenkar (2001, p. 163) propose that the formation of social identities which are based on differences in nationality is likely within IJVs since "homogeneity of imported norms and practices might typically be greater within than across national cultures (…), and distinctiveness is theorized to be a vital basis for social identification".

The third step is social comparison, where group members evaluate their own group's prestige and social standing in relation to other groups. As Turner (1975) noted, social categorization serves to form an in-group by encouraging evaluative distinctions between in-group and out-group. More specifically, members tend to view their own group as superior to others in order to maintain self-esteem and a positive connection to the group. In an IJV context, an IJV partner is thus likely to classify the foreign partner as an out-group and categorize its own members into the in-group (Salk & Shenkar, 2001).

Salk and Shenkar (2001) point out that the formation of nationality-based subgroups (i.e., the in-group and the out-group) as part of the social identity building process can have negative consequences for the IJV, such as stereotyping and in-group favoritism. First, the perception of the foreign IJV partner as the out-group encourages generalization across individuals and groups. The in-group may deindividuate and depersonalize the members of the out-group (Ashforth & Mael, 1989). This stereotyping behavior lowers the awareness for individual characteristics while group characteristics become more prominent (Hogg, 2001). Consequently, members of the in-group tend to overlook the positive characteristics of individuals of the foreign partner firm and attribute negative qualities to them, which they might associate with the foreign partner firm (i.e., the out-group).

Second, another consequence is in-group favoritism and the resulting justification of creating and maintaining social distance to the out-group (Smith, 1983). Members of the in-group tend to emphasize the negative aspects of the foreign partner while accentuating the positive aspects of their own group, thereby reinforcing the distinction between the two groups and strengthening identification with their in-group. Furthermore, in-group and out-group formation is associated with lower levels of interaction and information exchange since members tend to favor information from within one group over information from another group (Harrison & Klein, 2007; Mohr et al., 2016b). Also, while the out-group is seen as deserving its failures and not its successes, the opposite holds for the in-group. These underlying perceptions inevitably lead to tensions between the groups. As Ashforth and Mael (1989, p. 32) note, "in-group and out-group relations may be marked by competition and hostility even in the absence of 'objective' sources of conflict". Overall, this behavior has been demonstrated to negatively impact collaboration, motivation, team cohesion, and, ultimately, performance (Killing, 1983; Salk & Shenkar, 2001). Conversely, if the out-group is perceived as less distant and is evaluated less negatively, the IJV partners will benefit from lower levels of conflict, increased trust, and cooperation. We can conclude that it is of importance to IJVs to reduce the perceived distinctiveness between in-group and out-group and encourage a more favorable perception of the out-group's characteristics.

The process of categorizing others in an out-group can, however, also provide advantages. For example, when there is little information about individuals, social categorization helps us ascribe characteristics of a particular social group to those individuals we believe belong to that group (i.e., stereotypes) (Allport, 1954). In general, the more information is available about individuals, the lower the need to categorize them into groups based on salient demographic categories (Ertrug et al., 2013). As a result, the formation of in-groups and out-groups is less likely, and potential group affiliations are less strong the more information is available about an individual or group of individuals.

One lever to get more information is increased contact between the groups. Following Allport's (1954) contact hypothesis, contact between different groups can lessen social categorization and intergroup discrimination. Contact makes it possible to discover similarities in values and beliefs. At the same time, it increases the opportunity to learn stereotype-inconsistent information about members of the out-group (Brewer & Miller, 1984). As individual characteristics become more apparent with increasing contact, there is less need to rely on ascribed group characteristics. Masson and Verkuyten (1993) reported findings consistent with this reasoning. They found that contact between people of different ethnicities is associated with less in-group and out-group formation, in-group favoritism, as well as less prejudiced attitudes toward ethnic minorities. As a result, more frequent contact between social groups makes social categorization and stereotyping less likely (Chatman & Flynn, 2001), while at the same time increasing liking and respect for out-group members (Brewer & Miller, 1984).

In the IJV and migration context, this means that the more social contact members of one IJV partner (in-group) have with migrants who have knowledge of the norms, values, and practices prevailing in their COOs, the more information the IJV can gain about the cultural aspects of the other IJV partner (out-group) who shares the same culture. The information gained through more contact with knowledgeable individuals can either be negative or positive for the IJV firm's perception of the other culture. Irrespective of this, the IJV firm has more knowledge about the foreign partner that it can use to evaluate the partner (Ertrug et al., 2013). This makes social categorization, stereotyping, and group formation less likely (Brewer & Miller, 1984; Ertrug et al., 2013) and makes it easier for an IJV partner to perceive the other IJV partner's positive attributes. A more positive perception of the out-group (i.e., the foreign IJV partner) strengthens relationship characteristics such as cooperation, commitment, and trust (Salk & Shenkar, 2001)—the three key ingredients for a functioning relationship between alliance partners (Demirbag & Mirza, 2000). A strong relationship is key to prevent and manage conflicts and is ultimately reflected in a relatively stronger performance of IJVs (Krishnan et al., 2006). Accordingly, we hypothesize:

Hypothesis 1: Migration from the migrants' COO to the location of an IJV partner firm in a new host country leads to increased performance of IJVs involving partner firms of home and host country.

An IJV partner's ability to get access to the migrants' valuable knowledge depends on the individuals' willingness to invest time and energy in sharing knowledge. Important factors influencing the willingness of individuals to engage in knowledge sharing are (1) the strength of social ties (Hansen, 1999), and (2) the type of knowledge to be shared (Reagans & McEvily, 2003).

First, an individual will be more inclined to share information with another person the stronger the interpersonal connection between the two (Hansen, 1999). "The more emotionally involved two individuals are with each other, the more time and effort they are willing to put forth on behalf of each other, including effort in the form of transferring knowledge" (Reagans & McEvily, 2003, p. 244). It has been argued that there are gender difference in the strength of social ties and, consequently, in the extent of knowledge sharing between individuals and groups. Women are more inclined to form strong social ties with other people as opposed to men (Baumeister & Sommer, 1997). While men tend to gravitate toward relationships in a broader social sphere with a larger number of people, women tend to focus more on dyadic, close relationships and seek intimate connections in which information is shared more openly (Cross & Madson, 1997). Additionally, people tend to have stronger social ties as they age. In the process of getting older, people tend to maintain emotionally significant relationships while abandoning less significant and potentially unpleasant ones (Carstensen et al., 2003). As opposed to younger individuals, elderly people put a greater emphasis on the quality of socio-emotional experiences and social interactions in the present (Fasbender et al., 2020). Hence, older people tend to have smaller networks consisting of disproportionately more meaningful and emotionally close social partners (Carstensen et al., 2003).

The influence of social tie strength on information sharing also depends on tacitness or "stickiness" of the knowledge being transferred as this affects the ease of transferring knowledge (Reagans & McEvily, 2003; Szulanski, 1996). Tacit knowledge is generally described as "any form of non-quantifiable knowledge, particularly the knowledge about social interactions, social practices, and most generally, how a group or an institution gets things done" (Linde, 2001, p. 160). Cultural knowledge which is relevant for one IJV partner to know about the other IJV partner in our scope of research represents to a large extent not explicit but tacit knowledge.

Tacit knowledge requires more effort to be transferred which is why women and older people—given their stronger social ties—might have an advantage in passing on tacit cultural knowledge. Tacit knowledge, as opposed to explicit knowledge, is difficult to codify and articulate and thus requires greater effort to be transferred (Reagans & McEvily, 2003). The transfer of tacit knowledge might be easier between strong social ties as the individuals are willing to spend more time and effort in transferring information to their close social partners as opposed to weak social ties (Hansen, 1999; Reagans & McEvily, 2003). Additionally, the specialized language and relationship-specific heuristics that tend to emerge in a strong and close relationships make it easier to communicate complex chunks of knowledge (Uzzi, 1996). A study by Balogun (2014) supports this reasoning by showing that the willingness to pass on tacit knowledge increases with age and that female study participants were generally more willing to pass on tacit knowledge than their male counterparts.

Summing up, due to their stronger social ties, we argue that female migrants and older migrants facilitate knowledge transfer which reduces in-group and out-group formation in IJVs. Accordingly, we expect that they positively moderate the effect migrants can have on the creation of a shared social identity within IJVs and increased IJV performance:

Hypothesis 2: The positive relationship between migration and IJV performance (H1) is positively moderated by an increasing share of female migrants.

Hypothesis 3: The positive relationship between migration and IJV performance (H1) is positively moderated by an increasing share of older migrants.

Empirical Setting and Data

The data on IJV performance is provided by the Austrian Central Bank. It focuses on Austrian firms with a voting capital share of at least EUR 100,000 and includes annual data on the international operations of these firms. Data on migration in Austria at the level of political districts is provided by Statistik Austria. This chapter analyzes the performance of IJVs, defined as subsidiaries in which the Austrian multinational holds between 5% and 95% of the shares (Dhanaraj & Beamish, 2004). Wholly owned subsidiaries (>95% share) and portfolio investments (<5% share) are excluded from the sample. Additionally, this chapter excludes data of indirect subsidiaries (i.e., subsidiaries of subsidiaries).

Austria constitutes an optimal research ground for this study for two reasons. First, it has an open and international economy that is heavily reliant on foreign business activities. According to the Ministry of Foreign Affairs Austria (2022), approximately six out of ten euros generated in Austria are attributable to business activities abroad. Second, Austria is home to a significant and rapidly growing population of migrants. As of 2021, around 2 million individuals residing in Austria have a migration background, accounting for nearly one quarter of the total population (Statistik Austria, 2022).

To account for the fact that migrants' knowledge is not only passed on directly by migrants to their respective firms but also indirectly through migrants' interactions with others who reside in the same geographic area and pass on this knowledge to firms (Hernandez, 2014), two measures were taken: first, we conduct our analysis on a political district level to account for regional differences of migration and knowledge flows. And second, the sample was limited to companies based in areas in which the knowledge provided by migrants adds an extra value to the firm. This would not be the case for global cities as companies would be surrounded by other international firms that disseminate knowledge. Consequently, we exclude firms located in Austria's capital city, Vienna, which we classify as a "global city" due to its interconnectedness to global markets, availability of advanced producer services, and cosmopolitan environment (Chakravarty et al., 2021).

Measurements

IJV Performance In this study, we examine the impact of migrants on the performance of international joint ventures (IJVs), which is operationalized as annual profits. According to Ainuddin et al. (2007), most IJVs are established with the main goal to generate profits, making annual profit a key indicator of IJV success. Annual profit data of IJVs is derived from the ADI dataset from the Austrian Central Bank and is expressed in EUR.

Migration Migration represents the main independent variable investigated. It is measured as the number of migrants who come from a subsidiary's host country (migrants' COO) and live in the political district where the parent company is situated. This measurement is consistent with previous studies that have used similar variables to capture migration flows, albeit at different levels of geographical granularity (e.g., Javorcik et al., 2011; Oettl & Agrawal, 2008). To rule out reverse causality, the migration variable is standardized and lagged by one year.

Migrants' Characteristics This study investigates the moderating effects of gender and age of migrants on the performance of IJVs. Age and gender data are available without the respective information on the migrants' COOs. Thus, we use proxy variables by multiplying the percentage of migrants in each political district belonging to a certain gender or age group by the number of migrants from the different COOs. To examine the moderating effect of older migrants on IJV performance, we consider migrants in the 40–64-year age range. This measurement aligns with prior research on the influence of age on group identification, social identification, and the formation of in-groups and out-groups (e.g., Barker, 2012).

Control Variables In this study, several control variables are considered at the country and firm level. At the country level, we control for geographic distance and cultural distance between the parent firm and the IJV. Cultural distance is measured as linguistic and religious distance. The larger the distance between countries, the more difficult communication, mutual understanding, and access to general market information might be (Dow, 2000; Hennart & Zeng, 2002). The data are sourced from Douglas Dow (Dow, n.d.). We also control for GDP per capita, GDP growth, and FDI inflows to control for the performance effects that the economic situation of a country can have on an IJV (García-Canal & Guillén, 2008). The GDP and FDI data are retrieved from the World Development Indicators provided by the World Bank. Additionally, we use the Political Constraints Index (POLCON) as a proxy for political stability, with the assumption that a higher number of political constraints indicates greater stability and reduces political hazards (Garrido et al., 2014). The stability of a political environment can influence the performance of companies due to potential adaptation costs that might arise in case of political changes in a country (Delios & Henisz, 2003). At the firm level, we control for the size of the IJV and the MNC in terms of number of employees and IJV equity ownership. The underlying assumptions are that larger firms can draw on more human resources which may influence a venture's performance (Barkema & Vermeulen, 1997) and that a higher share in the foreign subsidiary is associated with a higher willingness to allocate more resources to it (Luo, 2004) and a lower likelihood of a premature dissolution of the venture (Dhanaraj & Beamish, 2004). All firm-level variables are standardized.

Methodology

This study examines profits of foreign subsidiaries per parent company, host country, and year. We assume a linear relationship between the variables together with a hierarchical structure in the data. Thus, we use a linear mixed-effects model as an estimation technique. While the host country per se is not the focus of the present study, but migrants are, it is expected that the migrants' COO might impact the dependent variable (i.e., IJV performance). Consequently, we include the host country as a random intercept in our model. More specifically, we estimate the performance of an IJV, depending on migration from host country into the political district in Austria with the random intercept on the host country level.

Hierarchical (or multi-level) regression models are regarded as particularly fitting for IJV research settings of this kind (Hox et al., 2017; Kwon et al., 2016). Numerous researchers in IB assume a hierarchical structure as they combine different levels of analysis, integrating characteristics of a market or country with those of joint ventures (e.g., Hennart, 1988) or other firm-level characteristics (e.g., Rugman & Verbeke, 2008; Lederman, 2010). Methodologically, our analyses are carried out in accordance with the guidelines put forth by Lindner et al. (2021) to ensure our study conforms to rigorous standards and protocols when using multi-level analyses in the field of IB research.

Results

Table 12.1 depicts the results of the conducted regression analyses. Model 1 represents the control model as it relies exclusively on control variables. From among the 10 control variables included in the analyses, only one variable enters on a statistically significant level. The IJV size measured by the employee headcount has a positive effect on IJV performance. Model 2 extends the control model by the main effect of migration flows. In Models 3 and 4, we include the moderating effects of the share of female and older migrants, respectively. Model 5 represents the full model including all variables. The data lend support for Hypothesis 1 suggesting that higher levels of migration flows improve IJV performance. In Model 5, the migration inflow coefficient is positive and significant at the 0.05 level (β = 0.045; p = 0.041). The positive effect of migrants on IJV performance is further enhanced by an increase in the share of female migrants, thereby providing evidence for Hypothesis 2. The findings show a statistically significant positive moderating effect of female migrants in Model 5 (β = 0.140; p = 0.000). However, while the data reveal a significant moderating effect for older migrants (β = 0.029; p = 0.037) in Model 4, the full model (Model 5), including all variables, does not provide significant results (β = -0.019; p = 0.212). Consequently, the results provide evidence for Hypotheses 1 and 2, but not for Hypothesis 3.

The plots created in Fig. 12.1 depict the main effect and both moderating effects. All panels rely on data from Model 5. Plot 1 shows the main effect of migrants on IJV performance. The effect appears to be positive and is thus in line with Hypothesis 1. Plot 2 depicts the moderating effect of the share of female migrants. A strong positive effect of migration on IJV performance can be seen if the share of female migrants is high (upper bold line). This effect turns negative if the share of female migrants is low (lower thin line). Contrary

Table 12.1 Results of regression analysis. *p < 0.05; ***p < 0.001. Standard errors in parentheses

	(1)	(2)	(3)	(4)	(5)
Constant	0.009(0.039)	0.017	0.009	0.025	0.003
		(0.041)	(0.040)	(0.041)	(0.040)
Parent firm employees	0.004	0.002	0.007	0.003	0.007
	(0.013)	(0.013)	(0.013)	(0.013)	(0.013)
IJV employees	0.231***	0.235***	0.236***	0.234***	0.236***
	(0.013)	(0.013)	(0.013)	(0.013)	(0.013)
Ownership share	0.009	0.011	0.007	0.011	0.007
	(0.013)	(0.013)	(0.013)	(0.013)	(0.013)
Host country FDI inflows	0.013	0.012	0.008	0.012	0.010
	(0.021)	(0.021)	(0.021)	(0.021)	(0.021)
Host country GDP growth	0.010	0.010	0.011	0.008	0.010
	(0.015)	(0.015)	(0.015)	(0.015)	(0.015)
Host country GDP/capita	0.005	0.013	0.024	0.019	0.025
	(0.031)	(0.032)	(0.032)	(0.032)	(0.031)
Geographic distance	−0.036	−0.031	−0.031	−0.029	−0.030
	(0.024)	(0.025)	(0.025)	(0.025)	(0.025)
Religious distance	0.014	0.015	0.016	0.015	0.016
	(0.026)	(0.026)	(0.026)	(0.026)	(0.026)
Linguistic distance	−0.078	−0.040	−0.023	−0.030	−0.029
	(0.060)	(0.064)	(0.064)	(0.064)	(0.063)
Policy stability	−0.031	−0.033	−0.034	−0.034	−0.034
	(0.021)	(0.022)	(0.022)	(0.022)	(0.022)
Migrant inflows		0.076***	0.069***	0.095***	0.045*
		(0.017)	(0.017)	(0.021)	(0.022)
Share of female migrants			0.025		0.032*
			(0.013)		(0.014)
Migrant inflows* share of female migrants			0.129***		0.140***
			(0.017)		(0.018)
Share of older migrants				−0.010	−0.023
				(0.014)	(0.014)
Migrant inflows* share of older migrants				0.029*	−0.019
				(0.014)	(0.015)
Observations	4525	4525	4525	4525	4525
Log likelihood	−5855.522	−5849.070	−5826.146	−5853.147	−5830.945
Akaike Inf. Crit.	11,737.040	11,726.140	11,684.290	11,738.290	11,697.890
Bayesian Inf. Crit.	11,820.470	11,815.980	11,786.970	11,840.970	11,813.400

to Hypothesis 3, Plot 3 shows that the share of older migrants has no significant moderating effect on the relationship between migrants and IJV performance. The panel shows a slight (almost negligible) positive effect of migration on IJV performance when the share of older migrants is high (lower bold line).

To check for the overall robustness of the empirical results, we further performed the following analyses: we used three other dependent variables as an

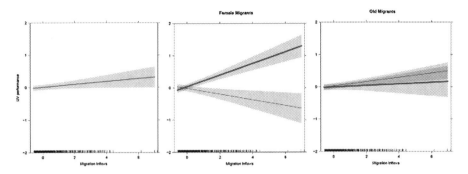

Fig. 12.1 Plots visualizing the main effect of migrants on IJV performance (Plot 1), the moderating effect of female migrants (Plot 2) and the moderating effect of older migrants (Plot 3)

alternative to annual profit to represent the performance of IJVs. The variables chosen are operating income, operating profit, and equity (or market value).[1] Furthermore, we repeated the analysis using a different random intercept (i.e., the OENACE level)[2] and we performed the analyses using ordinary least square (OLS) regressions as alternative econometric models. All robustness checks provide additional support for the results of this study.[3]

Discussion and Conclusion

This chapter extends our understanding of the impact migrants have on international business activities due to their valuable knowledge about their COOs. The findings of this study also shed light on the characteristics of migrants and their impact on the relationship between migration and IJV performance. Our empirical results are in line with previous migration research that finds that migrants are a valuable source of knowledge for MNCs and positively impact business activities abroad. Liu et al. (2015), for example, found that skilled migrants play a key role in the transfer of knowledge between firms of two countries. Migrants supported the identification of potential key contacts, the establishment of relationships, as well as the exchange of knowledge. Similarly, research by Enderwick et al. (2011) shows that firms—even those with low international experience—can still be successful in new host markets

---

[1] If the IJV is listed on a stock exchange market, equity equals market value. Otherwise, the variable represents the reported equity in the balance sheet.
[2] The OENACE represents a national classification of the economic sector the Austrian IJV partner is active in.
[3] Output tables of the robustness checks can be requested from the authors.

by leveraging the knowledge and experience provided by key contacts. Thus, the findings of the present study are consistent with previous migration research in that migrants have a positive influence on the success of foreign business and internationalization operations due to the valuable knowledge and experience that they bring with them, which can be used by firms in the migrants' new home country.

In addition, the reasoning of this study is also in conformity with research on alliance success. Scholars such as Mowery et al. (1996), Rosenkopf and Almeida (2003), and Singh (2005) conclude that the success of IJVs is dependent on the strength of the relationship between the alliance partners as well as the strength of the interpersonal ties between employees from both sides. Gomes-Casseres et al. (2006) found that knowledge exchange and collaboration between different partners are highest for firms that have a close relationship with each other, share similar interests, and pull in the same direction. The present study also suggests that increasing the empathy and understanding of the members of one IJV partner (in-group) toward members of the other IJV partner (out-group) will translate into elevated levels of success for the alliance overall.

We further find that the positive effect of migrants on IJV performance can be enhanced by the influence of female migrants. The higher the share of female migrants in a certain district in Austria, the more successful the IJVs formed between Austrian MNCs based in this district and a foreign partner based in the migrants' COO (Hypothesis 2). The rationale behind this effect can be explained as follows:

First, an individual will be more inclined to share information with another person the stronger the interpersonal connection between the two (Hansen, 1999). Studies have found that there are gender differences in the strength of social ties, with women typically having stronger connections than men (Cross & Madson, 1997). Second, cultural knowledge can be classified as tacit or "sticky" knowledge (Linde, 2001) which is more easily transferred between strong social ties. This is why women—given their stronger social ties—might have an advantage in passing on tacit cultural knowledge (Balogun, 2014). Overall, it appears that the strength of social ties and the type of the knowledge being shared are both important factors in determining the extent to which knowledge is shared among individuals. Women's generally stronger social ties and tendency to share tacit knowledge may contribute to their advantage in this regard.

The empirical results do not lend support for Hypothesis 3 stating that higher age of migrants positively moderates the relationship between migrants and IJV performance. We approach the question of why age might not be a significant moderator in this context from two perspectives: first, from the perspective of the *value of knowledge*, Foad (2009) found that age has a negative effect on FDI. He suggests that older migrants tend to have weaker ties to their COOs. Therefore, the knowledge these migrants provide to MNCs in their new home countries might be less valuable as it is less up to date. Second, from a *knowledge dissemination* perspective, empirical evidence suggests that older people, relative to their younger peers, have smaller social networks consisting of emotionally closer social partners (Carstensen et al., 2003). The consequence might be that the knowledge of older migrants is passed on to a smaller group of recipients and thus less accessible for IJVs. We conclude that the assumed benefits that older migrants can bring to IJVs may not be fully exploitable or accessible enough for firms to take advantage of.

Contributions This study contributes to IB literature in four different ways. First, we suggest a structured way of how theory can accommodate both migration and IJV success. On the one hand, researchers have devoted much effort to identifying the drivers of IJV performance (e.g., Demirbag & Mirza, 2000; Ren et al., 2009). On the other hand, scholars have expressed a great interest in the advantages migrants can bring to MNEs (e.g., Chung & Tung, 2013; Kugler & Rapoport, 2011). However, existing research has not yet connected the two streams. This study enriches the IJV literature by linking it to migration literature and connecting the two streams. It goes beyond the insights that cultural differences may cause performance problems in IJVs (e.g., Lane & Beamish, 1990) and provides insights into how migrants as informants about foreign cultures can make a difference in performance outcomes for IJVs, cultural differences between the IJV partners notwithstanding.

Second, this chapter contributes to the SIT. Existing research leaves a gap as to how migrants can affect social identity building within firms and especially firm alliances. This is an important omission given that social identities are formed primarily on the basis of differences or similarities in origin and nationality (Brewer & Brown, 1998). To our knowledge, this chapter is one of the first if not the first to take this fact into account and to discuss how social identity building in IJVs may be influenced by migrants. We argue that migrants create vital conditions for dissolving nationality-based boundaries and building a common IJV-based social identification.

Additionally, it shall be mentioned that we contribute to IB and migration literature by studying migrants as a broad group of people who left their COOs in order to settle in a new home country. In the past, the link between migration and IB has been primarily studied from the perspective of expatriates, a subcategory of migrants (e.g., Black, 1988; Olsen & Martins, 2009). Expatriates, however, are not representative of the broader migrant population as they are staffed on temporary assignments predominantly with the intention to repatriate (Hajro et al., 2021). This study complements the small number of IB studies by properly recognizing the diversity of migrants who have a longer-term impact on business activities in their new home countries.

Fourth, the chapter sheds light on the characteristics of migrants that moderate the relationship between migrants and IJV performance. It extends research on migrants' characteristics in the realm of business activities (e.g., Foad, 2009; Gheasi et al., 2013; Kugler & Rapoport, 2011) by demonstrating that gender of migrants is a central factor to consider as it may strengthen the positive effect of migration on IJV performance.

Practical Implications Our finding that migrants can have a positive impact on IJV performance (Hypothesis 1) has several implications for practitioners. First, policymakers may actively educate the local society about the benefits of migrants for the local economy to fight the general assumption that migration and the development of a country are negatively correlated—an assumption that still governs much of the political discussion today. This may counteract xenophobic sentiments as well as the call for protectionist measures against migrants. Second, to promote successful integration, migration policies should lower job barriers and support language and cultural understanding for migrants. This is essential as migrants often struggle with the devaluation of their foreign education and experiences, hindering their ability to integrate and find employment (Hajro et al., 2021). Without effective integration policies, governments will fail to reap the full benefits migrants bring to a country as migrants' skills and knowledge remain underutilized. Third, companies seeking to expand into foreign markets by partnering with foreign firms should actively try to leverage the knowledge of migrants from their foreign partner's country by locating in areas with high migrant populations or hiring migrants directly. Additionally, implementing "migrant-friendly" policies and processes can facilitate knowledge exchange with them and even attract migrant talent to the company. Our results also show that female migrants have a positive impact on the performance of international joint ventures (Hypothesis 2). Yet, their contributions are not always recognized or compensated fairly. To address this, policymakers should educate businesses and communities on the value of female migrants and MNEs should strive to provide equal pay and a supportive work environment for this minority group.

Limitations This empirical study has several limitations. First, we only have access to limited information on migrants, such as age, gender, political district of residence in Austria, as well as COO. However, we acknowledge that it would be interesting to consider additional variables that potentially affect the knowledge of migrants and its diffusion process, such as education, employment, and occupational position. It may be worthwhile examining how many of the migrants are employed by IJV partner companies. Another limitation is that this study examined IJV performance in a single home country, Austria. We encourage future studies to validate the findings for IJVs formed between other home-host country pairs and test whether different institutional or economical contexts affect the relationship between migration and IJV performance. Additionally, this study only used annual profit as a measure of IJV performance. However, the IJV partners may consider the venture a success even though it generates low financial returns in the short term (Geringer & Herbert, 1991). We concede that financial measures assess only one dimension of IJV performance. Future research could consider using other performance measures, including non-financial measures like achievement of goals and satisfaction with the venture.

References

Ainuddin, R. A., Beamish, P. W., Hulland, J. S., & Rouse, M. J. (2007). Resource attributes and firm performance in international joint ventures. *Journal of World Business, 42*(1), 47–60. https://doi.org/10.1016/j.jwb.2006.11.001

Aleksynska, M., & Peri, G. (2014). Isolating the network effect of immigrants on trade. *The World Economy, 37*(3), 434–455. https://doi.org/10.1111/twec.12079

Allport, G. (1954). *The nature of prejudice*. Addison-Wesley.

Ashforth, B. E., & Mael, F. (1989). Social identity theory and the organization. *Academy of Management Review, 14*(1), 20–39. https://doi.org/10.5465/amr.1989.4278999

Balogun, A. (2014). Demographic variables predicting employee willingness to share tacit knowledge in service occupations. *IFE Psychologia: An International Journal, 22*(2), 42–49. https://journals.co.za/content/ifepsyc/22/2/EJC163463

Barkema, H., & Vermeulen, F. (1997). What differences in the cultural backgrounds of partners are detrimental for international joint ventures. *Journal of International Business Studies, 28*(4), 845–864. https://doi.org/10.1057/palgrave.jibs.8490122

Barker, V. (2012). A generational comparison of social networking site use: The influence of age and social identity. *International Journal of Aging and Human Development, 74*(2), 163–187. https://doi.org/10.2190/ag.74.2.d

Baumeister, R., & Sommer, K. (1997). What do men want? Gender differences and two spheres of belongingness: Comment on cross and Madson (1997). *Psychological Bulletin, 122*(1), 38–44. https://doi.org/10.1037/0033-2909.122.1.38

Berry, H., Guillen, M., & Zhou, N. (2010). An institutional approach to cross-national distance. *Journal of International Business Studies, 41*(9), 1460–1480. https://doi.org/10.1057/jibs.2010.28

Beugelsdijk, S., Kostova, T., Kunst, V. E., Spadafora, E., & van Essen, M. (2018). Cultural distance and firm internationalization: A meta-analytical review and theoretical implications. *Journal of Management, 44*(1), 89–130. https://doi.org/10.1177/0149206317729027

Black, J. (1988). Work role transitions: A study of American expatriate managers in Japan. *Journal of International Business Studies, 19*(2), 277–294. https://doi.org/10.1057/palgrave.jibs.8490383

Brewer, M., & Brown, R. (1998). Intergroup relations. In D. Gilbert, S. Fiske, & G. Lindzey (Eds.), *The handbook of social psychology* (pp. 554–594). McGraw-Hill.

Brewer, M., & Miller, N. (1984). Beyond the contact hypothesis: Theoretical perspectives on desegregation. In N. Miller & M. Brewer (Eds.), *Groups in contact: The psychology of desegregation* (pp. 281–302). Academic Press.

Carstensen, L. L., Fung, H. H., & Charles, S. T. (2003). Socioemotional selectivity theory and the regulation of emotion in the second half of life. *Motivation and Emotion, 27*(2), 103–123. https://doi.org/10.1023/A:1024569803230

Chakravarty, D., Goerzen, A., Musteen, M., & Ahsan, M. (2021). Global cities: A multi-disciplinary review and research agenda. *Journal of World Business, 56*(3), 1–16. https://doi.org/10.1016/j.jwb.2020.101182

Chatman, J., & Flynn, F. (2001). The influence of demographic heterogeneity on the emergence and consequences of cooperative norms in work teams. *Academy of Management Journal, 44*(5), 956–974. https://doi.org/10.5465/3069440

Chung, H., & Tung, R. (2013). Immigrant social networks and foreign entry: Australia and New Zealand firms in the European Union and greater China. *International Business Review, 22*(1), 18–31. https://doi.org/10.1016/j.ibusrev.2012.01.005

Chung, H., Rose, E., & Huang, P.-H. (2012). Linking international adaptation strategy, immigrant effect, and performance: The case of home–host and cross-market scenario. *International Business Review, 21*(1), 40–58. https://doi.org/10.1016/j.ibusrev.2010.11.001

Cross, S., & Madson, L. (1997). Models of the self: Self-construals and gender. *Psychological Bulletin, 122*(1), 5–37. https://doi.org/10.1037/0033-2909.122.1.5

Cuadros, A., Martín-Montaner, J., & Paniagua, J. (2019). Migration and FDI: The role of job skills. *International Review of Economics and Finance, 59*, 318–332. https://doi.org/10.1016/j.iref.2018.09.007

Delios, A., & Henisz, W. (2003). Policy uncertainty and the sequence of entry by Japanese firms, 1980-1998. *Journal of International Business Studies, 34*(3), 227–241. https://doi.org/10.1057/palgrave.jibs.8400031

Demirbag, M., & Mirza, H. (2000). Factors affecting international joint venture success. An empirical analysis of foreign-local partner relationships and performance in joint ventures in Turkey. *International Business Review, 9*(1), 1–35. https://doi.org/10.1016/S0969-5931(99)00027-X

Dhanaraj, C., & Beamish, P. W. (2004). Effect of equity ownership on the survival of international joint ventures. *Strategic Management Journal, 25*(3), 295–305. https://doi.org/10.1002/smj.372

Dikova, D., & Sahib, P. R. (2013). Is cultural distance a bane or a boon for cross-border acquisition performance? *Journal of World Business, 48*(1), 77–86. https://doi.org/10.1016/j.jwb.2012.06.009

Dow, D. (2000). A note on psychological distance and export market selection. *Journal of International Marketing, 8*(1), 51–64. https://doi.org/10.1509/jimk.8.1.51.19563

Dow, D. (n.d.). *The research page for Douglas Dow*. Distance and diversity scales for International Business research. Retrieved January 2, 2023, from http://dow.net.au/

Dutta, D., & Beamish, P. (2013). Expatriate managers, product relatedness, and IJV performance: A resource and knowledge-based perspective. *Journal of International Management, 19*(2), 152–162. https://doi.org/10.1016/j.intman.2012.11.002

Enderwick, P., Tung, R., & Chung, H. (2011). Immigrant effects and international business. *Journal of Asia Business Studies, 5*(1), 6–22. https://doi.org/10.1108/15587891111100778

Ertrug, G., Cuypers, I., Noorderhaven, N., & Bensaou, B. (2013). Trust between international joint venture partners: Effects of home countries. *Journal of International Business Studies, 44*(3), 263–282. https://doi.org/10.1057/jibs.2013.6

Fasbender, U., Burmeister, A., & Wang, M. (2020). Motivated to be socially mindful: Explaining age differences in the effect of employees' contact quality with coworkers on their coworker support. *Personnel Psychology, 73*(3), 407–430. https://doi.org/10.1111/peps.12359

Federici, D., & Giannetti, M. (2010). Temporary migration and foreign direct investment. *Open Economies Review, 21*(1), 293–308. https://doi.org/10.1007/s11079-008-9092-6

Foad, H. (2009). FDI and immigration: A regional analysis. *The Annals of Regional Science, 49*(1), 237–259. https://doi.org/10.1007/s00168-011-0438-4

Franko, L. G. (1971). *Joint venture survival in multinational corporations*. Praeger Publishers.

García-Canal, E., & Guillén, M. (2008). Risk and the strategy of foreign location choice in regulated industries. *Strategic Management Journal, 29*(10), 1097–1115. https://doi.org/10.1002/smj.692

Garrido, E., Gomez, J., Maicas, J. P., & Orcos, R. (2014). The institution-based view of strategy: How to measure it? *BRQ Business Research Quarterly, 17*(2), 82–101. https://doi.org/10.1016/j.brq.2013.11.001

Geringer, M., & Herbert, L. (1991). Measuring performance of international joint ventures. *Journal of International Business Studies, 22*(2), 249–263. https://doi.org/10.1057/palgrave.jibs.8490302

Gheasi, M., Nijkamp, P., & Rietveld, P. (2013). Migration and foreign direct investment: Education matters. *The Annals of Regional Science, 51*(1), 73–87. https://doi.org/10.1007/s00168-012-0533-1

Gomes-Casseres, B., Hagedorn, J., & Jaffe, A. B. (2006). Do alliances promote knowledge flows? *Journal of Financial Economics, 80*(1), 5–33. https://doi.org/10.1016/j.jfineco.2004.08.011

Gould, D. (1994). Immigrant links to the home country: Empirical implications for U.S. bilateral trade flows. *The Review of Economics and Statistics, 76*(2), 302–316. https://doi.org/10.2307/2109884

Guo, C., & Al Ariss, A. (2015). Human resource management of international migrants: Current theories and future research. *The International Journal of Human Resource Management, 26*(10), 1287–1297. https://doi.org/10.1080/09585192.2015.1011844

Hajro, A., Caprar, D., Zikic, J., & Stahl, G. (2021). Global migrants: Understanding the implications for international business and management. *Journal of World Business, 56*(2), 101192. https://doi.org/10.1016/j.jwb.2021.101192

Hansen, M. (1999). The search-transfer problem: The role of weak ties in sharing knowledge across organization subunits. *Administrative Science Quarterly, 44*(1), 82–111. https://doi.org/10.2307/2667032

Harrigan, K. R. (1988). Strategic alliances and partner asymmetries. *Management International Review, 28*, 53–72. https://www0.gsb.columbia.edu/mygsb/faculty/research/pubfiles/2230/Strategic%20Alliances%20and%20Partner%20Asymmetries.pdf

Harrison, D. A., & Klein, K. J. (2007). What's the difference? Diversity constructs as separation, variety, or disparity in organizations. *Academy of Management Review, 32*(4), 1199–1228. https://doi.org/10.5465/amr.2007.26586096

Hennart, J. (1988). A transaction costs theory of equity joint ventures. *Strategic Management Journal, 9*(4), 361–374. https://doi.org/10.1002/smj.4250090406

Hennart, J.-F., & Zeng, M. (2002). Cross-cultural differences and joint venture longevity. *Journal of International Business Studies, 33*(4), 699–716. https://doi.org/10.1057/palgrave.jibs.8491040

Hernandez, E. (2014). Finding a home away from home: Effects of immigrants on firms' foreign location choice and performance. *Administrative Science Quarterly, 59*(1), 73–108. https://doi.org/10.1177/0001839214523428

Hofstede, G. (1980). *Culture's consequences. International differences in work-related values*. Sage.

Hogg, M. (2001). A social identity theory of leadership. *Personality and Social Psychology Review, 5*(3), 184–200. https://doi.org/10.1207/s15327957pspr0503_1

Hogg, M. A., & Terry, D. J. (2000). Social identity and self-categorization processes in organizational contexts. *Academy of Management Review, 25*(1), 121–140. https://doi.org/10.5465/amr.2000.2791606

Hox, J. J., Moerbeek, M., & Van de Schoot, R. (2017). *Multilevel analysis: Techniques and applications.* Routledge.

Hutzschenreuter, T., Kleindienst, I., & Lange, S. (2014). Added psychic distance stimuli and MNE performance. Performance effects of added cultural, governance, geographic, and economic distance in MNEs' international expansion. *Journal of International Management, 20*(1), 38–54. https://doi.org/10.1016/j.intman.2013.02.003

Javorcik, B., Özden, Ç., Spatareanu, M., & Neagu, C. (2011). Migrant networks and foreign direct investment. *Journal of Development Economics, 94*(2), 231–241. https://doi.org/10.1016/j.jdeveco.2010.01.012

Killing, J. P. (1983). *Strategies for joint venture success.* Croom Helm.

Kogut, B. (1989). The stability of joint ventures: Reciprocity and competitive rivalry. *Journal of Industrial Economics, 38*(2), 183–198. https://doi.org/10.2307/2098529

Krishnan, R., Martin, X., & Noorderhaven, N. (2006). When does trust matter to alliance performance? *Academy of Management Journal, 49*(5), 894–917. https://doi.org/10.5465/amj.2006.22798171

Kugler, M., & Rapoport, H. (2011). *Migration, FDI, and the margins of trade.* CID Working Paper Series. Harvard University. https://dash.harvard.edu/handle/1/37366246

Kunczer, V., Lindner, T., & Puck, J. (2019). Benefitting from immigration: The value of immigrants' country knowledge for firm internationalization. *Journal of International Business Policy, 2*(4), 356–375. https://doi.org/10.1057/s42214-019-00034-9

Kwon, S.-W., Haleblian, J., & Hagedoorn, J. (2016). In country we trust? National trust and the governance of international R&D alliances. *Journal of International Business Studies, 47*(7), 807–829. https://doi.org/10.1057/s41267-016-0006-3

Lane, H. W., & Beamish, P. W. (1990). Cross-cultural cooperative behaviour in joint ventures in LDCs. *Management International Review, 30,* 87–102. https://www.proquest.com/scholarly-journals/cross-cultural-cooperative-behavior-joint/docview/202689921/se-2

Lederman, D. (2010). An international multilevel analysis of product innovation. *Journal of International Business Studies, 41*(4), 606–619. https://doi.org/10.1057/jibs.2009.30

Linde, C. (2001). Narrative and social tacit knowledge. *Journal of Knowledge Management, 5*(2), 160–170. https://doi.org/10.1108/13673270110393202

Lindner, T., Puck, J., & Doh, J. (2021). Hierarchical modelling in international business research: Patterns, problems, and practical guidelines. *Journal of World Business, 56*(4), 101224. https://doi.org/10.1016/j.jwb.2021.101224

Liu, X., Gao, L., Lu, J., & Wei, Y. (2015). The role of highly skilled migrants in the process of inter-firm knowledge transfer across borders. *Journal of World Business, 50*(1), 56–68. https://doi.org/10.1016/j.jwb.2014.01.006

Luo, Y. (2004). Building a strong foothold in an emerging market: A link between resource commitment and environment conditions. *Journal of Management Studies, 41*(5), 749–773. https://doi.org/10.1111/j.1467-6486.2004.00452.x

Makino, S., & Delios, A. (1996). Local knowledge transfer and performance: Implications for alliance formation in Asia. *Journal of International Business Studies, 27*(5), 905–927. https://doi.org/10.1057/palgrave.jibs.8490156

Masson, C., & Verkuyten, M. (1993). Prejudice, ethnic identity, contact and ethnic group preferences among Dutch young adolescents. *Journal of Applied Social Psychology, 23*(2), 156–168. https://doi.org/10.1111/j.1559-1816.1993.tb01058.x

Meschi, P., & Riccio, E. (2008). Country risk, national cultural differences between partners and survival of international joint ventures in Brazil. *International Business Review, 17*(3), 250–266. https://doi.org/10.1016/j.ibusrev.2007.11.001

Ministry of Foreign Affairs Austria. (2022). Foreign trade. *European and Foreign Policy*. Retrieved April 2, 2022, from https://www.bmeia.gv.at/en/european-foreign-policy/foreign-policy/

Mintz, B., & Krymkowski, D. H. (2010). The ethnic, race, and gender gaps in workplace authority: Changes over time in the United States. *The Sociological Quarterly, 51*(1), 20–45. https://doi.org/10.1111/j.1533-8525.2009.01165.x

Mohr, A. T., & Puck, J. F. (2005). Managing functional diversity to improve the performance of international joint ventures. *Long Range Planning, 38*(2), 163–182. https://doi.org/10.1016/j.lrp.2005.02.004

Mohr, A., Wang, C., & Fastoso, F. (2016a). The contingent effect of state participation on the dissolution of international joint ventures: A resource dependence approach. *Journal of International Business Studies, 47*(4), 408–426. https://doi.org/10.1057/jibs.2016.14

Mohr, A., Wang, C., & Goerzen, A. (2016b). The impact of partner diversity within multiparty international joint ventures. *International Business Review, 25*(4), 883–894. https://doi.org/10.1016/j.ibusrev.2015.11.001

Mowery, D. C., Oxley, J. E., & Silverman, B. S. (1996). Strategic alliances and inter-firm knowledge transfer. *Strategic Management Journal, 17*(2), 77–91. https://doi.org/10.1002/smj.4250171108

Oettl, A., & Agrawal, A. (2008). International labor mobility and knowledge flow externalities. *Journal of International Business Studies, 39*(8), 1242–1260. https://doi.org/10.1057/palgrave.jibs.8400358

Olsen, J., & Martins, L. (2009). The effects of expatriate demographic characteristics on adjustment: A social identity approach. *Human Resource Management, 48*(2), 311–328. https://doi.org/10.1002/hrm.20281

Park, S., & Ungson, G. (1997). The effect of national culture, organizational complementarity, and economic motivation on joint venture dissolution. *Academy of Management Journal, 40*(2), 279–307. https://doi.org/10.2307/256884

Piper, N. (2006). Gendering the politics of migration. *International Migration Review, 40*(1), 133–164. https://doi.org/10.1111/j.1747-7379.2006.00006.x

Reagans, R., & McEvily, B. (2003). Network structure and knowledge transfer: The effects of cohesion and range. *Administrative Science Quarterly, 48*(2), 240–267. https://doi.org/10.2307/3556658

Ren, H., Gray, B., & Kim, K. (2009). Performance of international joint ventures: What factors really make a difference and how? *Journal of Management, 35*(3), 805–832. https://doi.org/10.1177/0149206308331165

Reus, T., & Rottig, D. (2009). Meta-analyses of international joint venture performance determinants. *Management International Review, 49*(5), 607–640. https://doi.org/10.1007/s11575-009-0009-4

Rosenkopf, L., & Almeida, P. (2003). Overcoming local search through alliances and mobility. *Management Science, 49*(6), 751–766. https://doi.org/10.1287/mnsc.49.6.751.16026

Rugman, A. M., & Verbeke, A. (2008). A new perspective on the regional and global strategies of multinational service firms. *Management International Review, 48*(4), 397–411. https://doi.org/10.1007/s11575-008-0023-y

Salk, J., & Shenkar, O. (2001). Social identities in an international joint venture: An exploratory case study. *Organization Science, 12*(2), 161–178. https://doi.org/10.1287/orsc.12.2.161.10111

Singh, J. (2005). Collaborative networks as determinants of knowledge diffusion patterns. *Management Science, 51*(5), 756–770. https://doi.org/10.1287/mnsc.1040.0349

Slangen, A. (2006). National cultural distance and initial foreign acquisition performance: The moderating effect of integration. *Journal of World Business, 41*(2), 161–170. https://doi.org/10.1016/j.jwb.2006.01.003

Smith, K. (1983). Social comparison processes and dynamic conservatism in intergroup relations. In L. Cummings & B. Staw (Eds.), *Research in organizational behavior* (pp. 199–233). JAI Press.

Statistik Austria. (2022, July 25). *More than a quarter of the total Austrian population has a migration background*. Statistik Austria Press Release. Retrieved January 2, 2023, from https://www.statistik.at/fileadmin/announcement/2022/07/20220725MigrationIntegration2022EN.pdf

Szulanski, G. (1996). Exploring internal stickiness: Impediments to the transfer of best practice within the firm. *Strategic Management Journal, 17*(2), 27–43. https://doi.org/10.1002/smj.4250171105

Tajfel, H., & Turner, J. (1979). The social psychology of intergroup relations. In S. Worchel & W. G. Austin (Eds.), *An integrative theory of intergroup conflict*. Brooks/Cole.

Tajfel, H., & Turner, J. (1985). The social identity theory of intergroup behaviour. In S. Worchel & W. Austin (Eds.), *Psychology of intergroup relations* (pp. 7–24). Nelson-Hall Publishers.

Tihanyi, L., Griffith, D. A., & Russell, C. J. (2005). The effect of cultural distance on entry mode choice, international diversification, and MNE performance: A meta-analysis. *Journal of International Business Studies, 36*(3), 270–283. https://doi.org/10.1057/palgrave.jibs.8400136

Turner, J. (1975). Social comparison and social identity: Some prospects for intergroup behaviour. *European Journal of Social Psychology, 5*(1), 1–34. https://doi.org/10.1002/ejsp.2420050102

Uzzi, B. (1996). The sources and consequences of embeddedness for the economic performance of organizations: The network effect. *American Sociological Review, 61*(4), 674–698. https://doi.org/10.2307/2096399

Vasilaki, A. (2011). Culture distance and cross-border acquisition performance: The moderating effect of transformational leadership. *European Journal of International Management, 5*(4), 394–412. https://doi.org/10.1504/ejim.2011.040912

Yeheskel, O., Zeira, Y., Shenkar, O., & Newburry, W. (2001). Parent company dissimilarity and equity international joint venture effectiveness. *Journal of International Management, 7*(2), 81–104. https://doi.org/10.1016/s1075-4253(01)00039-4

13

Online Organizational Inclusion of Migrants in MNCs: Overcoming Cultural and Linguistic Barriers Virtually

Charlotte Jonasson and Jakob Lauring

Introduction

The shortage of labor caused by the economic upsurge in recent years has increased MNCs' effort to recruit migrants and other foreign nationality minorities (cf. Charlton & Kostandini, 2021; Karan & Asgari, 2021). Traditionally, such international minorities have in many situations been met with a negative cultural bias from host country nationals (Sonesh & DeNisi, 2016; Varma et al., 2021; Zhang & Peltokorpi, 2016). Therefore, they are generally evaluated less favorably in relation to competence and leadership (Heilman & Welle, 2006), and they are disadvantaged in promotion decisions (Powell & Butterfield, 1997), as well as excluded from important networking opportunities (Dreher & Cox, 2000). Thus, it might be difficult for migrants working in MNCs to acquire job-relevant information and find out who to contact in regard to work-related matters, and the assistance from host country nationals is, therefore, highly important. Nevertheless, it is often expected that migrants by themselves find useful information through their personal social networks (Bayraktar, 2019). Such expectancies do not take into account that migrants may find it hard to obtain information from locals due to their cultural and linguistic dissimilarities (Wang & Kanungo, 2004) and due to

C. Jonasson • J. Lauring (✉)
Aarhus University, Aarhus, Denmark
e-mail: charlotte@psy.au.dk; jala@mgmt.au.dk

© The Author(s), under exclusive license to Springer Nature Switzerland AG 2023
A. I. Mockaitis (ed.), *The Palgrave Handbook of Global Migration in International Business*,
https://doi.org/10.1007/978-3-031-38886-6_13

their holding more peripheral positions in the local business unit of the MNC (Jonasson, et al., 2017).

In order to overcome cultural biases in international organizations, a number of practices have been designed to generally accommodate diversity and facilitate workplace inclusion (cf. Egorov et al., 2020; Leroy et al., 2022; Onyeador et al., 2021). This emphasis on inclusion in organizations has been seen as a response to a more diversified employee pool where access to global talent is essential for maintaining competitive advantages (Bouncken et al., 2016).

The core argument for managing inclusiveness in MNCs is that this will allow such organizations to utilize available staff resources in the best way despite inherent employee dissimilarities. If handled well, it has been maintained that MNCs can create an environment that is valuing the contributions of all their different employees (Boehm et al., 2014; van Knippenberg et al., 2013). In such an inclusive organizational setting, migrants are likely to engage more in debates and knowledge sharing from their unique perspectives (Hartgerink et al., 2014; van Knippenberg & van Ginkel, 2021; Selmer et al., 2014). As a consequence, this will give the organization a greater potential for creativity and, in turn, a better performance (Leroy et al., 2022).

A prominent, recent development in the business community, however, has not been taken into account in the international business literature on migrants (Anier et al., 2018; Turchick Hakak & Al Ariss, 2013; Verkuyten, 2005). Namely, the introduction of online or virtual work environments. Here, virtual work could be described as flexible work arrangements whereby employees predominantly collaborate in locations at a distance from their central offices or production facilities (Raghuram & Wiesenfeld, 2004). During this process, employees have little physical contact with colleagues but can communicate with them using technological appliances, the so-called information and communications technology (Asatiani & Penttinen, 2019; Gibson & Gibbs, 2006; Golden, 2007).

Although businesses have become increasingly virtual, scant research has focused on online inclusion. Among those studies that have combined virtuality and inclusiveness is the work by Taras et al. (2019) on the different types of diversity in global virtual teams. Their most prominent finding was that the negative effect of personal dissimilarities was stronger on satisfaction than on objective performance. Moreover, a number of multilevel studies focus on an inclusive linguistic environment. For example, Lauring and Jonasson (2018) demonstrated that when inclusiveness, in terms of openness to language diversity, was low, inspirational leadership could compensate for this deficiency. In another language diversity study, Klitmøller and Lauring (2016) showed that different types of virtuality led to different perceptions of linguistic inclusiveness. In addition to that Lauring et al. (2022) focus on the role of inclusive attitudes toward cultural diversity. Here they show that acceptance of culturally dissimilar team members assisted in overcoming distance-related problems such as low levels of trust and time zone adjustment. Finally, a conceptual article on the relation between inclusion and virtual work has recently be published by Lauring and Jonasson (2023).

Hence, although it is well known that virtual ways of working have great effect on the interaction in an organization (Cramton, 2001; Marlow et al., 2017; Zakaria, 2017), there has been relatively limited attention to how an online environment influences the inclusion of migrants in MNCs. This is unfortunate due to the general acknowledgment of the important role of inclusion across cultural and linguistic boundaries in today's international business environment (Davies et al., 2019). Therefore, we believe that the interest in inclusive management in international business should be extended to the online domain.

Accordingly, the aim of the current chapter is to address the challenge for MNCs of being inclusive while facilitating integration and involvement of employed migrants through virtual means. This can support MNCs in launching successful inclusionary online activities directed at foreign nationality workers while overcoming cultural and linguistic barriers in the organization. We focus on migrants working, at least partially, online in units of global companies such as MNCs defined by having subsidiaries or sales divisions in more than one country. These migrants comprise individuals that have chosen relocation to a foreign country to live and work for an international or multinational corporation.

Migrants Being Subject to Social Categorization Processes in a Global Labor Market

Migrants have in many contexts been considered a needed source of labor. However, a significant problem has been to integrate them in order to retain them in the job (Polek et al., 2010; Turchick Hakak & Al Ariss, 2013). This means that migrants are more likely to leave their jobs than their non-migrant counterparts. For example, Heponiemi et al. (2019) highlighted that foreign-born physicians had substantially higher turnover rates compared to native-born physicians in Finland (see also Kuusio et al., 2013). Studies have also found this to be the case in Australia (Halvorsen et al., 2015) and Ireland

(Brugha et al., 2016). Such difficulties with retaining migrants is problematic because already the hiring of skilled migrants in MNCs requires a greater investment and more training compared to local staff (McNulty & Tharenou, 2004).

In terms of integration challenges, it has been found that migrants face severe problems such as acculturation stress (Andresen et al., 2018; Finch & Vega, 2003) and negative responses from fellow local employees or customers (Dos Santos, 2020; Eneroth et al., 2017; Louis et al., 2013). In regard to unfavorable attitudes toward migrants, these can be rooted in dissimilarities with regard to linguistic skills and cultural values (Kalmijn & Kraaykamp, 2018). Such differences might lead to migrants experiencing difficulties with forming social bonds in the workplace (Hakak et al., 2010; Mansoor et al., 2019) and with achieving a good fit with the organization (Farh et al., 2010; MacKenzie & Forde, 2009). Moreover, Ford (2011) suggests that the local, majority workplace group will provide migrants who are more distinct from the local community in relation to culture and language with a less welcoming reception. This is because such individuals are often considered to pose a greater threat to the host nationals as compared to migrants from regions with greater similarity. An example of this is provided by Baltes and Rudolph (2010), who found that in Germany the acceptance of a negative stereotype significantly affected ratings for highly qualified Turkish candidates. Along the same lines, Storm et al. (2017) found that, due to pronounced differences in cultural values, Muslim immigrants in the United Kingdom were considered more problematic than other ethnic minority groups.

In terms of language differences, being unable to master the local language can have negative consequences such as a reduction of social status (Lauring et al., 2023). This may be due to a general perception among host country locals that an immigrant is less competent when he or she is unable to communicate freely in the local language (Neeley, 2013). In addition, linguistic inadequacies lower the possibility of being integrated because communication is central to making connections and facilitating understanding (Miller, 2000; Selmer et al., 2013). As an example, it has been found that if a person has a strong accent or struggles to find the words, others may avoid this individual in social situations, for example, in a company canteen or in a meeting break (Lauring & Klitmøller, 2015; Pot et al., 2020).

Migrants working in local units of MNCs thus face the risk of being subject to certain social categorization dynamics. We suggest that social categorization theory (Turner, 1978) can provide a framework to examine integration barriers in MNCs. In this regard, it is suggested that when a differentiating category, such as difference in nationality, culture, or language, becomes salient to the work group, differential treatment often follows (Giles et al., 1977; Giles & Johnson, 1981; Giles & St Clair, 1979). This distinctiveness brings greater attention to examine how locals categorize migrant's foreignness and whether this, dependent on the salience of such categories, increases the likelihood of being perceived as an outsider (Bonache et al., 2016). Indeed, studies have found that majority group members use these categorizations to assign in-group or out-group status to others, and that this perception subsequently guides their behavior (Gudykunst, 2004; Gudykunst & Kim, 1997; Tajfel, 1982). This could explain why migrants might face some difficulties being integrated in the local MNC unit. In such cases, the organization needs to have inclusionary activities in place if migrants are to be well integrated, and thus fully functioning members, in the workplace.

Organizational Inclusiveness

In this section of the chapter, we apply insights from inclusiveness research to develop an initial framework that can help us to understand culturally and linguistically dissimilarities of migrants.

At a general level, inclusion can be said to be the involvement of every group member but to the extent that individual dissimilarities are not muted in the process (Schutz, 1958). Inclusion, in other words, requires all individuals to feel they are able to contribute meaningfully to shared goals regardless of group affiliation and to do so without conforming to dominating norms and values (Ferdman, 2014). In this way, managing inclusiveness entails the establishment of participation and dialogue to encourage shared decision-making as well as an appreciation of both high- and low-status employees' contributions to the functioning of an organization (Nembhard & Edmondson, 2006a).

Shore et al. (2011) created a conceptual model of inclusion based on two themes, namely the need for feeling belongingness and the need for feeling uniqueness. Thereby, Shore et al. (2011) rely on thoughts from Mor Barak and Cherin (1998) who distinguish between dimensions of inclusiveness as having (1) group-oriented as well as (2) individual-oriented elements. It is argued that in order to fulfill the need for belongingness, people should have frequent and positive interactions and should feel accepted in a stable group. At the same time, however, individuals also have a fundamental need to see themselves as a unique, differentiated being (Chung et al., 2020). In this perspective, Shore et al. (2011) focus on socio-emotional needs and feelings in relation to the larger group and to the person's self-perception. Little attention, however, is paid to actual concrete experiences and the functional practicalities of being involved in task-relevant work.

In the current article, we, therefore, take inspiration from van Knippenberg et al. (2004) integrative model that combines socio-emotional and task-relevant consequences of integrating diverse group members in organizations. Examples of socio-emotional elements of inclusion are experiencing reciprocal recognition and affection in the group (e.g. Jansen et al., 2014) and being able to preserve authenticity and self-worth (e.g. Pless & Maak, 2004; Randel et al., 2018). Task-oriented activities as elements of inclusion comprise being included in a work group (e.g. Mor Barak et al., 1998; Pelled et al., 1999) and can entail participation in work tasks and related dialogue leading to shared decision-making (Mor Barak, 2000). Moreover, task-oriented inclusion has been argued to comprise appreciation and use of employees' dissimilar knowledge and expertise for problem solving (Roberson, 2006).

A combined perspective has also been tentatively proposed by Leroy et al. (2022). They describe inclusiveness in terms of "cultivating value-in-diversity beliefs" as an emotional perspective and "harvesting the benefits of diversity on work tasks" as a more instrumental orientation, thereby including a distinction between task-related and socio-emotional orientations of inclusiveness. In this regard, it can be argued that central elements of task-related inclusion should also be related to the group and the individual. Here, diversity scholars have argued for the importance of focusing on the person's task-related access to the group (O'Hara et al., 1994; Pelled et al., 1999). Furthermore, at the individual level of task-related inclusion, the experience of usefulness in relation to one's distinct knowledge and skills is mentioned to be an important element of inclusion (Gruenfeld et al., 2000).

Based on the above, we divide elements of inclusiveness, on the one hand, into those concerning *being an equal group member* and those relating to *being valued as an individual* (Mor Barak & Cherin, 1998; Shore et al., 2011). On the other hand, we include dimensions related to *socio-emotional orientations* (subjective feelings) and *task-related orientations* (functional actions) (Leroy et al., 2022; van Knippenberg et al., 2004). This provides us with a matrix comprising four cells, namely (1) *belongingness* (socio-emotional; equal group member), (2) *uniqueness* (socio-emotional; valued individual), (3) *accessibleness* (task-related; equal group member), and (4) *usefulness* (task-related; valued individual). Those elements are described in greater detail below in Table 13.1. The listed labels could be relevant in relation to collocated as well as online inclusion of migrants in local MNC units. However, achieving the different types of inclusiveness may function differently in virtual settings. We unfold this in the following section.

Table 13.1 Inclusiveness dimensions as identified in the existing literature

	Socio-emotional	Task related
Group-oriented	*Belongingness* Satisfied need of belonging in a group while being accepted as insider. Experience of reciprocal recognition and affection (Jansen et al., 2014; Pelled et al., 1999; Pless & Maak, 2004; Shore et al., 2011)	*Accessibleness* Access to the group's information and resources needed to conduct the work. Being involved in the group's central decision-making (e.g. Ferdman, 2014; Mor Barak, 2000; Pelled et al., 1999; Roberson, 2006)
Individual oriented	*Uniqueness* Satisfied need of individual uniqueness, preserving authenticity, integrity, and self-worth. Acknowledgment of the individual's voice (Nishii, 2013; Pless & Maak, 2004; Randel et al., 2018; Shore et al., 2011)	*Usefulness* Application of the individual's useful unique information, opinions, and expertise. The person contributing to work group functionality and having influence on decision-making (e.g. Ferdman, 2014; Mor-Barak et al., 1998; Nembhard & Edmondson, 2006b; Roberson, 2006)

Online Work in Today's Organizations

Wiesenfeld et al. (2001) early on described online work as comprising individuals conducting their job from home, while traveling, or in other cases being outside of traditional physical work spaces. More recent advances in technology have changed the structure of work dramatically, and online work is even considered the "new normal" (Field & Chan, 2018; Raišienė et al., 2021). Online work entails that employees can perform their job away from the office without necessarily having much physical contact with colleagues (Bartel et al., 2012; Raghuram & Wiesenfeld, 2004; Watson-Manheim, 2019). Such online, virtual work is considered to be widely applied in today's organizations being part of digital information societies (Hodson, 2018).

The use of information and communication technology for exchanging information, documents, and ideas between employees is central to virtual work. Such use can vary from standard applications like email or voice mail to online collaboration platforms and web solutions (Dwivedi et al., 2015; Hu et al., 2021). Smartphones and other mobile devices supplement computers in handling job-related information and collaboration (Li & Lin, 2019). Despite such widespread online work and the use of advanced technology, there remain important differences between work interaction by use of information and communication technology and face-to-face interaction.

Examples of this are that body language and voice tonality are less present in information and communication technology-driven dialogues (Cramton, 2001). Relatedly, this can entail that communication in the virtual workplace becomes more formal and more task-related and thus the spontaneous and informal interaction is reduced (Eisenberg & DiTomaso, 2021; Eisenberg & Krishnan, 2018; Montoya et al., 2009). Instead, formal communication, often in the context of scheduled meetings structured for purposes such as defining and assigning task contributions as well as assessing and reporting on progress, prevail (Eisenberg & Mattarelli, 2017; Gibbs et al., 2013). This, as well as the general physical distance, can lead to a feeling of social isolation and loneliness due to "out of sight out of mind" impressions (Adamovic, 2022; Heiden et al., 2021; Sarfraz et al., 2021). The loss of informal face-to-face interaction with other organizational members makes it difficult for employees to maintain a connection with the organization when working virtually (Belle et al., 2015; Liu et al., 2022). A consequence of such isolation, social fragmentation, and lack of embeddedness can be that the individual shows a greater tendency to resign should other opportunities arise.

Additionally, the tendency to more lean and task-related than informal communication creates a situation in which organization members are unable to develop accurate perceptions of others, thereby further lowering subsequent interactions (Johri, 2012). Wilson et al. (2008) argue that, in a virtual context, perceived social distance is created as a result of a weak interrelation between communication and group identification. If the communication level in a group is low, its members will not identify as strongly as a joint social unit, and, in turn, they will reduce the communication frequency even further. Accordingly, working virtually leads to challenges caused by physical distance and by the need to use technology-mediated communication that in turn creates social indifference and neutrality with regard to differences, for example, in relation to culture and language (Eisenberg & DiTomaso, 2021; Klitmøller & Lauring, 2016). This evolves because technology-mediated interaction provides reduced access to social cues, thus diminishing the interpersonal appeal (Montoya et al., 2009; Montoya & Horton, 2013). Thereby, the individual primarily working online often behaves in a way that separates the persons from the group and establishes independence from others (Kitayama et al., 2006). This could be in the form of low levels of prosocial initiative and high levels of social withdrawal (Caldwell et al., 2004). In consequence, individuals may to a greater extent objectify each other, often causing some degree of psychological detachment (Hinds & Mortensen, 2005; Kiesler & Cummings, 2002). This could be problematic for international minorities because of their already weak affiliation and low identification with other persons in the group (cf. Eisenberg & Mattarelli, 2017; O'Leary et al., 2014; Wilson et al., 2008).

This type of distance-generated social disengagement, however, does not only have negative consequences for inclusion in international organizations. Instead, it can actually reduce the focus on how international minorities are different from home country nationals (cf. Driskell et al., 2003). In line with this, a number of researchers argue that in the virtual environment, home country nationals will perceive migrants in a neutral rather than a negatively biased perspective which could otherwise be the case when dealing with foreign organization members (cf. Liberman & Trope, 2008; Wilson et al., 2013). Hence, it can be argued that the use of information technology in interaction tones down overt dissimilarities and behavioral differences and thus counters some important barriers for intergroup interaction (Han & Beyerlein, 2016; Lauring & Klitmøller, 2015). In line with this, Stahl et al. (2010) state that cultural differences matter less in online work due to the lean communication.

Online Inclusion of International Minorities

In this section of the chapter, we combine insights from inclusiveness research with those from the virtual work literature. Here the four-dimensional framework, we developed based on existing inclusiveness research, can be applied to provide a more nuanced understanding on how international minority group members are affected by the online environment. Below we discuss how the online environment influence inclusion of international minorities specified for each of the four inclusiveness dimensions: belongingness, uniqueness, accessibleness, and usefulness.

In relation to belongingness, the virtual environment may not improve the often-difficult situation of migrants in international organizations as the increased general neutrality will reduce feelings of belongingness. The physical distance and the need to interact by means of communication technology will lower the general urge to contact other people and the social disengagement will increase (O'Leary & Cummings, 2007). Therefore, it will often be particularly difficult to promote belongingness as part of the inclusion effort in relation to minority group members in organizations working virtually. Although the virtual environment may lead to a decline in belongingness for both host country national and international minorities employees, this could have most severe consequence for the foreigners, as they often already have low feelings of belongingness.

With regard to uniqueness, there are some opportunities in the online environment for allowing international minorities to develop a unique, positive self-image (Han & Beyerlein, 2016). This is because the social requirement for conformity and struggles for status positions are less prominent in online contexts (Bhappu et al., 2001; Stahl et al., 2010). In this way, the neutrality with regard to cultural and linguistic differences in the online environment could be an advantage for international minorities. Moreover, the overall low interaction frequency may not be too problematic because feeling positively unique is not necessarily dependent on close contact with others. This is because such contact could both confirm and disconfirm one's self-perception.

Concerning accessibleness, the online setting often provides structures, policies, and systems that are more transparent and objective and can more easily be installed virtually than in the case where the informal interaction between collocated colleagues is prominent (cf. Bourgault et al., 2008; Rice et al., 2007). Because informal interaction within a specific group is not as frequent and because more can be documented directly in the online setting, this could potentially be an advantage for inclusion of minority group members such as migrants. Nonetheless, the generally decreased interaction throughout the organization would hamper all communication processes and, in consequence, upset the networking for all organization members (Marlow et al., 2017). Therefore, while it is generally more difficult for international minorities to get access to the resources of the host country nationals the online environment can enable more objective systems. Hence, the virtual context may have a favorable or neutral influence on minority group members' experience of accessibleness that is normally challenged by cultural and linguistic differences.

Usefulness could also be affected by the online environment. In the virtual context, as communication and interaction are generally reduced (Charlier et al., 2016; Zakaria, 2017), it may be more difficult to express valuable viewpoints or to match certain skills to specific tasks. However, the increased intercultural neutrality could have some positive consequences for the experience of usefulness by diverse group members. In this regard, it has been argued that the usefulness of including dissimilar members in the work group is greater in virtual settings compared to physical workplaces. This is because the general social neutrality reduces conformity and group assimilation in virtual work groups, and because individuals are more free to express deviant viewpoints (Bhappu et al., 2001). As such, the general intercultural neutrality between organization members during online interactions may actually facilitate the sharing of differentiated and useful knowledge among organization members

(Mesmer-Magnus et al., 2011). Accordingly, the virtual setting could have a slightly positive effect on this.

Based on the above discussion of the four inclusiveness dimensions, it can be argued that the special nature of the virtual organization can affect different dimensions of inclusiveness differently. It can be concluded that for international minority group members in a virtual setting, feelings of belongingness will most likely be more difficult to develop in this context.

However, the experience of accessibleness may be somewhat easier to achieve. For both feelings of uniqueness and experiences of usefulness, there could be both advantages and disadvantages for international minority group members in virtual work situations. As with accessibleness, positive aspects of virtuality mainly originate from the increased neutrality with regard to being a foreign nationality organization member. To this extent, the virtuality could counter negative aspects of the cultural biases that international minority group members often experience.

Conclusion and Implications

Organizations in large parts of the world are increasingly dependent on the use of migrants to work along the host country staff and thereby add needed talent that cannot be easily acquired locally (Kubovcikova & van Bakel, 2022; Setti et al., 2020). Such employees can add expertise, foster knowledge transfers, and enhance international business strategy and opportunities (van der Laken et al., 2019). However, to an increasing extent, the single unit of the multinational corporation does not host all migrant workers physically (Au & Fukuda, 2002; Eisenberg & Mattarelli, 2017). This means that migrants have to be included and integrated to function in the work group primarily through online virtual means (Mattarelli & Gupta, 2009).

Accordingly, as virtual work becomes more common, it is necessary that sufficient theory is available to guide both researchers and practitioners regarding this theme's role in different domains of the international business conversation. In connection to online work, one issue, that we feel needs further theorizing, is inclusion of migrants in local MNC units. To address this deficiency and inform future international business research, we outlined a four-dimensional framework based on socio-emotional versus task orientation and group versus individual orientation. We find this is suitable to explore inclusiveness in general but also to gage into how inclusion of migrants becomes affected by the online environment that exists in most MNCs. This can be used to get a deeper understanding of how different aspects of inclusion may potentially be affected in various ways by the context.

Theoretical Implications

Foreignness in terms of culture and linguistics will often result in migrants being faced by negative biases and reduced contact with host country representatives. The online environment reduces contact and feelings of belongingness as well as creates indifference toward differences between group members. Such diminished contact is not specific to any particular national group. In addition to that, virtuality tends to promote a more neutral perception of other organization members regardless of cultural and linguistic differences. Online work can hold both positive and negative consequences for the integration of migrants, and we, therefore, suggest paying attention to the different types of inclusion and how they proceed under specific conditions of virtual work.

By discussing each of the different types of inclusion in relation to the online environment, we have provided a more detailed picture of pitfalls and opportunities in virtual inclusiveness of international minorities. From the knowledge provided by existing research, it becomes relatively clear that the different elements of inclusion are not affected equally by the online environment. While all types of inclusion to some extent are hampered by cultural and linguistic differences, certain aspects of inclusion are benefitted by the virtual context. This is predominantly due to the reduced focus on factors such as culture and language and thus a more neutral perception of migrants that are working virtually in local MNC units.

The present study mainly contributes to the ongoing scholarly debate in international business by integrating the international differences theme and inclusion literature (Davies et al., 2019) with existing knowledge on virtual work and online interaction (Eisenberg & DiTomaso, 2021; Wilson et al., 2008). So far, they have not been sufficiently connected, and the current practical development toward a more virtual work life leaves many important questions concerning the management of international minorities and inclusion unanswered.

Here, we have emphasized the complexity of the relation between international minorities and host country nationals and dimensions of inclusiveness in the online environment. The understanding of potentially contrasting or varying effects of virtuality on different dimensions of inclusiveness may be integral to moving the theoretical conversation on inclusion of migrants in online environments forward. Based on the discussion in this article, MNCs may be provided with a clearer idea regarding how to foster inclusive activities, given the online circumstances under which they are to an increasing extent functioning.

Practical Implications

Because the different types of inclusiveness are not affected in the same way by the virtual context, there is not one single managerial practice that could handle virtual inclusiveness in its entirety. Rather, there is a need to focus on the four different consequences influencing online inclusion of international minority group members and provide managerial interventions that are designed to tackle them separately and in combination. Below we suggest different approaches to deal with those issues. We will first describe managerial practices that could reduce the negative impact of cultural and linguistic differences in the virtual organization. This will lead us to ways of increasing interpersonal interaction. Finally, we will discuss how the nature of the online environment and its tendency to increase an intercultural neutrality can be applied constructively to create more objective structures in the organization.

Social categorization is an element of social interaction in international settings also when working virtually (Mortensen & Hinds, 2001). In order to deal with group-related biases, activities can be launched to avoid direct or subtle discrimination or to encourage online interaction across group boundaries. To avoid discrimination of foreign nationals, organization managers can review rules and practices applied in the virtual organization to make sure that they do not differentiate any minority groups (cf. Wilton et al., 2020). This could, for example, be related to language use in online meetings or to when the meetings are held during the day. If specific practices are found to disadvantage certain groups, measures could be taken to compensate for this. For example, tools such as auto-translation can help migrants with weak language skills. In relation to that, official rules that proscribe biased and discriminatory behavior can also be important in order to ensure that specific individuals can potentially be held accountable if policies are clearly disregarded, for example, in relation to derogatory expressions (Kalev et al., 2006). Such initiatives should not only allow greater access but also increase feelings of belongingness in the organization. To further reduce the feeling of discrimination among migrants and other international workers, inclusive communication about the value of such minority employees' special usefulness and contribution to the organization should be provided by managers and openly presented on corporate webpages. Such messages could, for example, include descriptions of the organization's online cultural diversity management profile (Onyeador et al., 2021).

Another way to counter discrimination in virtual work is to increase contact across cultural and linguistic barriers. This is because social categorization and negative biases tend to decrease as a result of contact with other dissimilar persons (Pettigrew, 1998). The frequent interaction needed for this to take place, however, can be difficult to achieve virtually, where general interaction is decreased. Moreover, in relation to minorities of, for example, different nationalities, their weaker host country language skills communicated through information-lean technological media could worsen the understanding across groups (Klitmøller & Lauring, 2013). Therefore, the virtual manager needs to pay special attention to potential declines in interaction and contact in the virtual organization. He or she could use video sessions where both international minority and host country national organization members are encouraged to present personal information so that they will know each other better and develop more social closeness. As such, organization managers have to offer opportunities for remote individuals to get to know each other and build stronger informal relationships to increase the quality of online interaction and the experience of one's skills and knowledge being useful (Liao, 2017). Another way to increase intergroup interaction, but in the task-related context, is to organize the work to cross between different types of host country and international minority group members to increase job task integration (Ahuja & Galvin, 2003). As such, formalization and routinization of the virtual organization has the potential for reducing discrimination and increasing intergroup interaction and thereby increasing experiences of having access to necessary information and resources as well as of being useful as a person. This could also lead the individual minority group member to develop more positive feelings about the organization and one's own place belonging to it.

In terms of supporting increased cultural neutrality of the virtual setting, which may positively affect several of the inclusiveness dimensions, formalizing work processes could be a way to avoid subtle discrimination and achieve objectivity and transparency. In this regard, it has been argued that virtual managers should adopt a clear and open management style and that necessary information must be communicated explicitly to all nationalities (Rice et al., 2007). This could be done by extensive use of email, blogs, audio/video conferencing. At the same time, organization members should be encouraged to state clearly what they are working on and convey to others if they encounter problems or opportunities (Olson & Olson, 2006). This is because spontaneity and informality are difficult to achieve in the virtual organization but also because a formalization of procedures provides less room for cultural biases. As a way of formalizing work, Maznevski and Chudoba (2000) argue that, because debate and communication do not occur naturally in this context, the virtual manager should ensure that interaction follows rhythmic patterns. This could be an advantage for international minorities that might otherwise not get a clear voice in the organizational debate. Meetings should also to a greater extent follow a formal and repeated routine and the virtual manager must explicitly solicit comments and contributions from everyone, even online polling of organization members for commentary (Olson & Olson, 2006). This not only ensures that needed information and opinions are included; it also makes it more likely that foreign nationalities feel respected and heard. By developing such clear and inclusive work routines, international minority group members could experience that their knowledge is better used and thus also feel a greater sense of belongingness, which, contrary to other inclusiveness dimensions, may be negatively affected by the virtual setting.

References

Adamovic, M. (2022). How does employee cultural background influence the effects of telework on job stress? The roles of power distance, individualism, and beliefs about telework. *International Journal of Information Management, 62*, 102437.

Ahuja, M., & Galvin, J. (2003). Socialization in virtual groups. *Journal of Management, 29*(2), 161–185.

Andresen, M., Goldmann, P., & Volodina, A. (2018). Do overwhelmed expatriates intend to leave? The effects of sensory processing sensitivity, stress, and social capital on expatriates' turnover intention. *European Management Review, 15*(3), 315–328.

Anier, N., Badea, C., Berthon, M., & Guimond, S. (2018). Perceived acculturation preferences of minority groups and intergroup discrimination: When cultural norms of integration matter. *Journal of Applied Social Psychology, 48*(9), 506–518.

Asatiani, A., & Penttinen, E. (2019). Constructing continuities in virtual work environments: A multiple case study of two firms with differing degrees of virtuality. *Information Systems Journal, 29*(2), 484–513.

Au, K. Y., & Fukuda, J. (2002). Boundary spanning behaviors of expatriates. *Journal of World Business, 37*, 285–296.

Baltes, B. B., & Rudolph, C. W. (2010). Examining the effect of negative Turkish stereotypes on evaluative workplace outcomes in Germany. *Journal of Managerial Psychology, 25*(2), 148–158.

Bartel, C. A., Wrzesniewski, A., & Wiesenfeld, B. M. (2012). Knowing where you stand: Physical isolation, perceived respect, and organizational identification among virtual employees. *Organization Science, 23*(3), 743–757.

Bayraktar, S. (2019). A diary study of expatriate adjustment: Collaborative mechanisms of social support. *International Journal of Cross Cultural Management, 19*(1), 47–70.

Belle, S. M., Burley, D. L., & Long, S. D. (2015). Where do I belong? High-intensity teleworkers' experience of organizational belonging. *Human Resource Development International, 18*(1), 76–96.

Bhappu, A. D., Zellmer-Bruhn, M., & Anand, V. (2001). The effects of demographic diversity and virtual work environments on knowledge processing in teams. In M. M. Beyerlein, D. A. Johnson, & S. T. Beyerlein (Eds.), *Virtual teams* (pp. 149–165). Wiley.

Boehm, S. A., Dwertmann, D. J. G., Kunze, F., Michaelis, B., Parks, K. M., & McDonald, D. P. (2014). Expanding insights on the diversity climate-performance link: The role of work group discrimination and group size. *Human Resource Management, 53*(3), 379–402.

Bonache, J., Langinier, H., & Zárraga-Oberty, C. (2016). Antecedents and effects of host country nationals negative stereotyping of corporate expatriates. A social identity analysis. *Human Resource Management Review, 26*(1), 59–68.

Bouncken, S., Brem, A., & Kraus, S. (2016). Multi-cultural teams as sources for creativity and innovation: The role of cultural diversity on team performance. *International Journal of Innovation Management, 20*(1), 1650012.

Bourgault, M., Drouin, N., & Hamel, E. (2008). Decision making within distributed project teams: An exploration of formalization and autonomy as determinants of success. *Project Management Journal, 39*(1), 97–110.

Brugha, R., McAleese, S., Dicker, P., Tyrrell, E., Thomas, S., Normand, C., & Humphries, N. (2016). Passing through–reasons why migrant doctors in Ireland plan to stay, return home or migrate onward to new destination countries. *Human Resources for Health, 14*(1), 45–54.

Caldwell, M. S., Rudolph, K. D., Troop-Gordon, W., & Do-Yeong, K. (2004). Reciprocal influences among relational self-views, social disengagement, and peer stress during early adolescence. *Child Development, 75*(4), 1140–1154.

Charlier, S. D., Stewart, G. L., Greco, L. M., & Reeves, C. J. (2016). Emergent leadership in virtual teams: A multilevel investigation of individual communication and team dispersion antecedents. *Leadership Quarterly, 27*(5), 745–764.

Charlton, D., & Kostandini, G. (2021). Can technology compensate for a labor shortage? Effects of 287(g) immigration policies on the U.S. dairy industry. *American Journal of Agricultural Economics, 103*(1), 70–89.

Chung, B. G., Ehrhart, K. H., Shore, L. M., Randel, A. E., Dean, M. A., & Kedharnath, U. (2020). Work group inclusion: Test of a scale and model. *Group and Organization Management, 45*(1), 75–102.

Cramton, C. D. (2001). The mutual knowledge problem and its consequences for dispersed collaboration. *Organization Science, 12*(3), 346–371.

Davies, S. E., Stoermer, S., & Froese, F. J. (2019). When the going gets tough: The influence of expatriate resilience and perceived organizational inclusion climate on work adjustment and turnover intentions. *The International Journal of Human Resource Management, 30*(8), 1393–1417. https://doi.org/10.1080/09585192.2018.1528558

Dos Santos, L. M. (2020). Stress, burnout, and turnover issues of black expatriate education professionals in South Korea: Social biases, discrimination, and workplace bullying. *International Journal of Environmental Research and Public Health, 17*(11), 3851–3866.

Dreher, G. F., & Cox, T. H. (2000). Labor market mobility and cash compensation: The moderating effects of race and gender. *Academy of Management Journal, 43*(5), 890–900.

Driskell, J. E., Radtke, P. H., & Salas, E. (2003). Virtual teams: Effects of technological mediation on team performance. *Group Dynamics: Theory, Research, and Practice, 7*(4), 297.

Dwivedi, Y. K., Wastell, D., Laumer, S., Henriksen, H. Z., Myers, M. D., Bunker, D., Elbanna, A., Ravishankar, M., & Srivastava, S. C. (2015). Research on information systems failures and successes: Status update and future directions. *Information Systems Frontiers, 17*(1), 143–157.

Egorov, G., Enikolopov, R., Makarin, A., & Petrova, M. (2020). Divided we stay home: Social distancing and ethnic diversity.

Eisenberg, J., & DiTomaso, N. (2021). Structural decisions about configuration, assignments, and geographical distribution in teams: Influences on team communications and trust. *Human Resource Management Review, 31*(2), 100739.

Eisenberg, J., & Krishnan, A. (2018). Addressing virtual work challenges: Learning from the field. *Organization Management Journal, 15*(2), 78–94.

Eisenberg, J., & Mattarelli, E. (2017). Building bridges in global virtual teams: The role of multicultural brokers in overcoming the negative effects of identity threats on knowledge sharing across subgroups. *Journal of International Management, 23*(4), 399–411.

Eneroth, M., Gustafsson Sendén, M., Schenck Gustafsson, K., Wall, M., & Fridner, A. (2017). Threats or violence from patients was associated with turnover intention among foreign-born GPs: A comparison of four workplace factors associated with attitudes of wanting to quit one's job as a GP. *Scandinavian Journal of Primary Health Care, 35*(2), 208–213.

Farh, C. I. C., Bartol, K. M., Shapiro, D. L., & Shin, J. (2010). Networking abroad: A process model of how expatriates form support ties to facilitate adjustment. *Academy of Management Review, 35*(3), 434–454.

Ferdman, B. M. (2014). The practice of inclusion in diverse organizations: Toward a systemic and inclusive framework. In B. M. Ferdman & B. R. Deane (Eds.), *Diversity at work: The practice of inclusion.* Jossey-Bass.

Field, J. C., & Chan, X. W. (2018). Contemporary knowledge workers and the boundaryless work–life interface: Implications for the human resource management of the knowledge workforce. *Frontiers in Psychology, 9*(1), 2414.

Finch, B. K., & Vega, W. A. (2003). Acculturation stress, social support, and self-rated health among Latinos in California. *Journal of Immigrant Health, 5*(3), 109–117.

Ford, R. (2011). Acceptable and unacceptable immigrants: How opposition to immigration in Britain is affected by migrants' region of origin. *Journal of Ethnic and Migration Studies, 37*(7), 1017–1037.

Gibbs, J. L., Rozaidi, N. A., & Eisenberg, J. (2013). Overcoming the "ideology of openness": Probing the affordances of social media for organizational knowledge sharing. *Journal of Computer-Mediated Communication, 19*(1), 102–120. https://doi.org/10.1111/jcc4.12034

Gibson, C. B., & Gibbs, J. L. (2006). Unpacking the concept of virtuality: The effects of geographic dispersion, electronic dependence, dynamic structure, and national diversity on team innovation. *Administrative Science Quarterly, 51*(3), 451–495.

Giles, H., Bourhis, R. Y., & Taylor, D. M. (1977). Towards a theory of language in ethnic group relations. In H. Giles (Ed.), *Language, ethnicity and intergroup relations* (pp. 307–348). Academic Press.

Giles, H., & Johnson, P. (1981). The role of language in ethnic group relations. In J. C. Turner & H. Giles (Eds.), *Intergroup behavior* (pp. 199–243). Blackwell.

Giles, H., & St Clair, R. (1979). *Language and social psychology*. Blackwell.

Golden, T. (2007). Co-workers who telework and the impact on those in the office: Understanding the implications of virtual work for co-worker satisfaction and turnover intentions. *Human Relations, 60*(11), 1641–1667.

Gruenfeld, D. H., Martorana, P. V., & Fan, E. T. (2000). What do groups learn from their worldliest members? Direct and indirect influence in dynamic teams. *Organizational Behavior and Human Decision Processes, 82*(1), 45–59.

Gudykunst, W. B. (2004). *Bridging differences: Effective intergroup communication*. Sage.

Gudykunst, W. B., & Kim, Y. Y. (1997). *Communicating with strangers: An approach to intercultural communication*. McGraw-Hill.

Hakak, L. T., Holzinger, I., & Zikic, J. (2010). Barriers and paths to success: Latin American MBAs' views of employment in Canada. *Journal of Managerial Psychology, 25*(2), 159–176.

Halvorsen, B., Treuren, G. J. M., & Kulik, C. T. (2015). Job embeddedness among migrants: Fit and links without sacrifice. *International Journal of Human Resource Management, 26*(10), 1298–1317.

Han, S. J., & Beyerlein, M. (2016). Framing the effects of multinational cultural diversity on virtual team processes. *Small Group Research, 47*(4), 351–383.

Hartgerink, J. M., Cramm, J. M., Bakker, T. J., van Eijsden, A. M., Mackenbach, J. P., & Nieboer, A. P. (2014). The importance of multidisciplinary teamwork and team climate for relational coordination among teams delivering care to older patients. *Journal of Advanced Nursing, 70*(4), 791–799.

Heiden, M., Widar, L., Wiitavaara, B., & Boman, E. (2021). Telework in academia: Associations with health and well-being among staff. *Higher Education, 81*(4), 707–722.

Heilman, M. E., & Welle, B. (2006). Disadvantaged by diversity? The effects of diversity goals on competence perceptions. *Journal of Applied Social Psychology, 36*(5), 1291–1319.

Heponiemi, T., Hietapakka, L., Kaihlanen, A., & Aalto, A.-M. (2019). The turnover intentions and intentions to leave the country of foreign-born physicians in Finland: A cross-sectional questionnaire study. *BMC Health Services Research, 19*(1), 1–10.

Hinds, P. J., & Mortensen, M. (2005). Understanding conflict in geographically distributed teams: The moderating effects of shared identity, shared context, and spontaneous communication. *Organization Science, 16*, 290–307.

Hodson, R. (2018). Digital revolution. *Nature, 563*(7733), 131–131.

Hu, X., Park, Y., Day, A., & Barber, L. K. (2021). Time to disentangle the information and communication technology (ICT) constructs: Developing a taxonomy around ICT use for occupational health research. *Occupational Health Science, 5*(1), 217–245.

Jansen, W. S., Otten, S., van der Zee, K. I., & Jans, L. (2014). Inclusion: Conceptualization and measurement. *European Journal of Social Psychology, 44*(4), 370–385.

Johri, A. (2012). From a distance: Impression formation and impression accuracy among geographically distributed coworkers. *Computers in Human Behavior, 28*(6), 1997–2006. https://www.sciencedirect.com/science/article/pii/S0747563212001999

Kalev, A., Dobbin, F., & Kelly, E. (2006). Best practices or best guesses? Assessing the efficacy of corporate affirmative action and diversity policies. *American Sociological Review, 71*(4), 589–617.

Kalmijn, M., & Kraaykamp, G. (2018). Determinants of cultural assimilation in the second generation. A longitudinal analysis of values about marriage and sexuality among Moroccan and Turkish migrants. *Journal of Ethnic and Migration Studies, 44*(5), 697–717.

Karan, E., & Asgari, S. (2021). Resilience of food, energy, and water systems to a sudden labor shortage. *Environment Systems and Decisions, 41*(1), 63–81.

Kiesler, S., & Cummings, J. N. (2002). What do we know about proximity and distance in work groups? A legacy of research. In P. Hinds & S. Kiesler (Eds.), *Distributed work* (Vol. 1, pp. 57–80). MIT Press.

Kitayama, S., Mesquita, B., & Karasawa, M. (2006). Cultural affordances and emotional experience: Socially engaging and disengaging emotions in Japan and the United States. *Journal of Personality and Social Psychology, 91*(5), 890–903.

Klitmøller, A., & Lauring, J. (2013). When global virtual teams share knowledge: Media richness, cultural distance and language commonality. *Journal of World Business, 48*(3), 398–406.

Klitmøller, A., & Lauring, J. (2016). When distance is good: A construal level perspective on perceptions of inclusive international language use. *International Business Review, 25*(1), 276–285.

Kubovcikova, A., & van Bakel, M. (2022). Social support abroad: How do self-initiated expatriates gain support through their social networks? *International Business Review, 31*(1), 101894.

Kuusio, H., Heponiemi, T., Vänskä, J., Aalto, A.-M., Ruskoaho, J., & Elovainio, M. (2013). Psychosocial stress factors and intention to leave job: Differences between foreign-born and Finnish-born general practitioners. *Scandinavian Journal of Public Health, 41*(4), 405–411.

Lauring, J., Drogendijk, R., & Kubovcikova, A. (2022). The role of context in overcoming distance-related problems in global virtual teams: An organizational discontinuity theory perspective. *International Journal of Human Resource Management, 33*(21), 4251–4283.

Lauring, J., & Jonasson, C. (2018). Can leadership compensate for deficient inclusiveness in global virtual teams? *Human Resource Management Journal, 28*(3), 392–409.

Lauring, J., & Jonasson, C. (2023). How is work group inclusiveness influenced by working virtually? *Human Resource Management Review, 33*(2), 100930.

Lauring, J., & Klitmøller, A. (2015). Corporate language-based communication avoidance in MNCs: A multi-sited ethnography approach. *Journal of World Business, 50*(1), 46–55.

Lauring, J., Vulchanov, I. O., & Stoermer, S. (2023). Linguistic capital and status: The interaction between language skills, personal reputation, and perceived collaboration performance. *European Management Review, 20*(1), 61–75.

Leroy, H. L., Buengeler, C., Veestraeten, M., Shemla, M., & Hoever, I. J. (2022). Fostering team creativity through team-derived inclusion: The role of leader harvesting the benefits of diversity and cultivating value-in-diversity beliefs. *Group and Organization Management, 47*(4), 798–839.

Li, L., & Lin, T. T. C. (2019). Smartphones at work: A qualitative exploration of psychological antecedents and impacts of work-related smartphone dependency. *International Journal of Qualitative Methods, 18*(1), 1609406918822240.

Liao, C. (2017). Leadership in virtual teams: A multilevel perspective. *Human Resource Management Review, 27*(4), 648–659. https://www.sciencedirect.com/science/article/pii/S1053482216301024

Liberman, N., & Trope, Y. (2008). The psychology of transcending the here and the now. *Science, 322*(21), 1201–1205.

Liu, Y., Xu, N., Yuan, Q., Liu, Z., & Tian, Z. (2022). The relationship between feedback quality, perceived organizational support, and sense of belongingness among conscientious teleworkers. *Frontiers in Psychology, 13*(1), 806443.

Louis, W. R., Esses, V. M., & Lalonde, R. N. (2013). National identification, perceived threat, and dehumanization as antecedents of negative attitudes toward immigrants in Australia and Canada. *Journal of Applied Social Psychology, 43*(1), 156–165.

MacKenzie, R., & Forde, C. (2009). The rhetoric of thegood worker versus the realities of employers' use and the experiences of migrant workers. *Work, Employment and Society, 23*(1), 142–159.

Mansoor, S., French, E., & Ali, M. (2019). Demographic diversity, processes and outcomes: An integrated multilevel framework. *Management Research Review, 43*(5), 521–543.

Marlow, S. L., Lacerenza, C. N., & Salas, E. (2017). Communication in virtual teams: A conceptual framework and research agenda. *Human Resource Management Review, 27*(4), 575–589.

Mattarelli, E., & Gupta, A. (2009). Offshore-onsite subgroup dynamics in globally distributed teams. *Information Technology and People, 22*(3), 242–269.

Maznevski, M. L., & Chudoba, K. M. (2000). Bridging space over time: Global virtual team dynamics and effectiveness. *Organization Science, 11*(5), 473–492.

McNulty, Y. M., & Tharenou, P. (2004). Expatriate return on investment: A definition and antecedents. *International Studies of Management and Organization, 34*(3), 68–95.

Mesmer-Magnus, J. R., DeChurch, L. A., Jimenez-Rodriguez, M., Wildman, J., & Shuffler, M. (2011). A meta-analytic investigation of virtuality and information sharing in teams. *Organizational Behavior and Human Decision Processes, 115*(2), 214–225.

Miller, J. M. (2000). Language use, identity, and social interaction: Migrant students in Australia. *Research on Language and Social Interaction, 33*(1), 69–100.

Montoya, M. M., Massey, A. P., Hung, Y. T. C., & Crisp, C. B. (2009). Can you hear me now? Communication in virtual product development teams. *Journal of Product Innovation Management, 26*(2), 139–155.

Montoya, R. M., & Horton, R. S. (2013). A meta-analytic investigation of the processes underlying the similarity-attraction effect. *Journal of Social and Personal Relationships, 30*(1), 64–94.

Mor-Barak, M. E., Cherin, D. A., & Berkman, S. (1998). Organizational and personal dimensions in diversity climate. *Journal of Applied Behavioral Science, 43*(1), 82–104.

Mor Barak, M. (2000). The inclusive workplace. *Social Work*, 1–12.

Mor Barak, M. E., & Cherin, D. (1998). A tool to expand organizational understanding of workforce diversity. *Administration in Social Work, 22*(1), 47–64.

Mor Barak, M. E., Cherin, D. A., & Berkman, S. (1998). Organizational and personal dimensions in diversity climate. *Journal of Applied Behavioral Science, 43*(1), 82–104.

Mortensen, M., & Hinds, P. J. (2001). Conflict and shared identity in geographically distributed teams. *International Journal of Conflict Management, 12*(3), 212–238.

Neeley, T. B. (2013). Language matters: Status loss and achieved status distinctions in global organizations. *Organization Science, 24*(2), 476–497.

Nembhard, I. M., & Edmondson, A. C. (2006a). Making it safe: The effects of leader inclusiveness and professional status on psychological safety and improvement efforts in health care teams. *Journal of Organizational Behavior, 27*(7), 941–966.

Nembhard, I. M., & Edmondson, A. C. (2006b). Making it safe: The effects of leader inclusiveness and professional status on psychological safety and improvement efforts in health care teams. *Journal of Organizational Behavior: The International Journal of Industrial, Occupational and Organizational Psychology and Behavior, 27*(7), 941–966.

Nishii, L. H. (2013). The benefits of climate for inclusion for gender-diverse groups. *Academy of Management Journal, 56*(6), 1754–1774.

O'Leary, M. B., & Cummings, J. N. (2007). The spatial, temporal, and configurational characteristics of geographic dispersion in teams. *MIS Quarterly, 31*(3), 433–452.

O'Hara, K. B., Beehr, T. A., & Colarelli, S. M. (1994). Organizational centrality: A third dimension of intraorganizational career movements. *Journal of Applied Behavioral Science, 30*(2), 198–216.

O'Leary, M. B., Wilson, J. M., & Metiu, A. (2014). Beyond being there. *MIS Quarterly, 38*(4), 1219–1244.

Olson, J. S., & Olson, G. M. (2006). Bridging distance: Empirical studies of distributed teams. In D. Galletta & P. Zhang (Eds.), *Human computer interaction in management information system* (pp. 23–28). M.E Sharp Publishers.

Onyeador, I. N., Hudson, S. T. J., & Lewis, N. A. (2021). Moving beyond implicit bias training: Policy insights for increasing organizational diversity. *Policy Insights From the Behavioral and Brain Sciences, 8*(1), 19–26.

Pelled, L. H., Ledford, G. E., & Mohrman, S. A. (1999). Demographic dissimilarity and workplace inclusion. *Journal of Management Studies, 36*(7), 1013–1031.

Pettigrew, T. F. (1998). Intergroup contact theory. *Annual Revue of Psychology, 49*, 65–85.

Pless, N., & Maak, T. (2004). Building an inclusive diversity culture: Principles, processes and practice. *Journal of Business Ethics, 54*(2), 129–147.

Polek, E., Wöhrle, J., & Pieter van Oudenhoven, J. (2010). The role of attachment styles, perceived discrimination, and cultural distance in adjustment of German and eastern European immigrants in The Netherlands. *Cross-Cultural Research, 44*(1), 60–88.

Pot, A., Keijzer, M., & De Bot, K. (2020). The language barrier in migrant aging. *International Journal of Bilingual Education and Bilingualism, 23*(9), 1139–1157.

Powell, G. N., & Butterfield, D. A. (1997). Effect of race on promotions to top management in a federal department. *Academy of Management Journal, 40*(1), 112–128.

Raghuram, S., & Wiesenfeld, B. (2004). Work-nonwork conflict and job stress among virtual workers. *Human Resource Management Review, 43*, 259–277.

Raišienė, A. G., Rapuano, V., Dőry, T., & Varkulevičiūtė, K. (2021). Does telework work? Gauging challenges of telecommuting to adapt to a "new normal". *Human Technology, 17*(2), 126–144.

Randel, A. E., Galvin, B. M., Shore, L. M., Ehrhart, K. H., Chung, B. G., Dean, M. A., & Kedharnath, U. (2018). Inclusive leadership: Realizing positive outcomes through belongingness and being valued for uniqueness. *Human Resource Management Review, 28*(2), 190–203.

Rice, D. J., Davidson, B. D., Dannenhoffer, J. F., & Gay, G. K. (2007). Improving the effectiveness of virtual teams by adapting team processes. *Computer Supported Cooperative Work, 16*(1), 567–594.

Roberson, Q. M. (2006). Disentangling the meanings of diversity and inclusion in organizations. *Group & Organization Management, 31*, 212–236.

Selmer, J., Jonasson, C., & Lauring, J. (2014). Knowledge processing and faculty engagement in multicultural university settings: A social learning perspective. *Journal of Further and Higher Education, 38*(2), 211–229.

Selmer, J., Lauring, J., & Jonasson, C. (2013). Academic staff involvement and openness to diversity in international educational organisations: Is there a moderating effect of shared language? *Higher Education Quarterly, 67*(2), 135–156.

Sarfraz, M., Ivascu, L., Khawaja, K. F., Vevera, A. V., & Dragan, F. (2021). ICT revolution from traditional office to virtual office: A study on teleworking during the COVID-19 pandemic. *Studies in Informatics and Control, 30*(4), 77–86.

Schutz, W. (1958). *FIRO: A three-dimensional theory of interpersonal behavior*. Rinehart.

Setti, I., Sommovigo, V., & Argentero, P. (2020). Enhancing expatriates' assignments success: The relationships between cultural intelligence, cross-cultural adaptation and performance. *Current Psychology, 41*, 1–21. https://doi.org/10.1007/s12144-020-00931-w

Shore, L. M., Randel, A., Chung, B., Dean, M. A., Ehrhart, K. H., & Singh, G. (2011). Inclusion and diversity in work groups: A review and model for future research. *Journal of Management, 37*(4), 1262–1289.

Sonesh, S. C., & DeNisi, A. S. (2016). The categorization of expatriates and the support offered by host country nationals. *Journal of Global Mobility, 4*(1), 18–43.

Stahl, G., Maznevski, M., Voigt, A., & Jonsen, K. (2010). Unraveling the effects of cultural diversity in teams: A meta-analysis of research on multicultural work groups. *Journal of International Business Studies, 41*(4), 690–709.

Storm, I., Sobolewska, M., & Ford, R. (2017). Is ethnic prejudice declining in Britain? Change in social distance attitudes among ethnic majority and minority Britons. *British Journal of Sociology, 68*(3), 410–434.

Tajfel, H. (1982). Social psychology of intergroup relations. *Annual Review of Psychology, 33*, 1–39.

Taras, V., Baack, D., Caprar, D., Dow, D., Froese, F., Jimenez, A., & Magnusson, P. (2019). Diverse effects of diversity: Disaggregating effects of diversity in global virtual teams. *Journal of International Management, 25*(1), 1–15.

Turchick Hakak, L., & Al Ariss, A. (2013). Vulnerable work and international migrants: A relational human resource management perspective. *International Journal of Human Resource Management, 24*(22), 4116–4131.

Turner, J. C. (1978). Social categorization and social discrimination in the minimal group paradigm. In H. Tajfel (Ed.), *Vol. differentiation between social groups: Studies in the social psychology of intergroup relations* (pp. 235–250). Academic Press.

van der Laken, P., van Engen, M., van Veldhoven, M., & Paauwe, J. (2019). Fostering expatriate success: A meta-analysis of the differential benefits of social support. *Human Resource Management Review, 29*(4), 100679.

van Knippenberg, D., De Dreu, C. K. W., & Homan, A. C. (2004). Work group diversity and group performance: An integrative model and research agenda. *Journal of Applied Psychology, 89*(6), 1008–1022.

van Knippenberg, D., & van Ginkel, W. (2021). A diversity mindsets perspective on inclusive leadership. *Group and Organization Management, 47*(4). https://doi.org/10.1177/1059601121997229

van Knippenberg, D., van Ginkel, W. P., & Homan, A. C. (2013). Diversity mindsets and the performance of diverse teams. *Organizational Behavior and Human Decision Processes, 212*, 183–193.

Varma, A., Yoon, Y., & Froese, F. J. (2021). Expatriate demographic characteristics and host country national support: An empirical investigation in central/South America. *Cross Cultural and Strategic Management, 28*(2), 407–423. https://doi.org/10.1108/CCSM-02-2020-0036

Verkuyten, M. (2005). Ethnic group identification and group evaluation among minority and majority groups: Testing the multiculturalism hypothesis. *Journal of Personality and Social Psychology, 88*(1), 121–138.

Watson-Manheim, M. B. (2019). Discontinuities, continuities, and hidden work in virtual collaboration. In K. Riemer, S. Schellhammer, & M. Meinert (Eds.), *Collaboration in the digital age* (pp. 121–132). Springer.

Wiesenfeld, B. M., Raghuram, S., & Garud, R. (2001). Organizational identification among virtual workers: The role of need for affiliation and perceived work-based social support. *Journal of Management, 27*(2), 213–229.

Wilson, J., Crisp, C. B., & Mortensen, M. (2013). Extending contrual-level theory to distributed groups: Understanding the effects of virtuality. *Organization Science, 24*(2), 629–644.

Wilson, J. M., O'Leary, M. B., Metiu, A., & Jett, Q. R. (2008). Perceived proximity in virtual work: Explaining the paradox of far-butclose. *Organization Studies, 29*(7), 979–1002.

Wilton, L. S., Bell, A. N., Vahradyan, M., & Kaiser, C. R. (2020). Show don't tell: Diversity dishonesty harms racial/ethnic minorities at work. *Personality and Social Psychology Bulletin, 46*(8), 1171–1185.

Zakaria, N. (2017). Emergent patterns of switching behaviors and intercultural communication styles of global virtual teams during distributed decision making. *Journal of International Management, 23*(4), 350–366.

Zhang, L. E., & Peltokorpi, V. (2016). Multifaceted effects of host country language proficiency in expatriate cross-cultural adjustments: A qualitative study in China. *International Journal of Human Resource Management, 27*(13), 1448–1469.

14

A Balancing Act in Times of Crisis: Inclusion at Work and Career Advancement of Migrants in Austria

Petra Aigner, Almina Bešić, and Christian Wenzler

Introduction

Recent events, foremost the Covid-19 pandemic have globally affected labor markets and employment of migrants and other vulnerable groups such as refugees. In connection with well-known challenges that migrants face when entering labor markets in receiving societies, these events lead to the following questions to be addressed in this chapter: *How do major crises such as the Covid-19 pandemic impact migrants' inclusion at work and their career progression? How can organizations support such inclusion?* We address these questions in the context of Austria, an EU member state, with a sizeable migrant population, and a complex web of employment-related integration support for these.

Migrants face multiple challenges when entering the receiving country's labor market and aiming to progress in their careers. These challenges are context dependent (Aigner & Bešić, 2023), and crisis might exacerbate them (Bešić & Aigner, 2023). At the macro level, migration and integration policies, as well as policies addressing the recognition of qualifications (Kirilova et al., 2016; Stadler et al., 2010), affect employment, career development, and the overall integration processes. At the organizational level, company policies can have an impact on migrants' inclusion at work and their career

P. Aigner (✉) • A. Bešić • C. Wenzler
Johannes Kepler University, Linz, Austria
e-mail: petra.aigner@jku.at; almina.besic@jku.at

perspectives (see Ortlieb et al., 2021; Barnard et al., 2019; Bendl et al., 2010, 2012). And at the individual level, migrants, despite frequently being highly qualified, are thus often discriminated against (see Weichselbaumer, 2017) and end up in low-wage professions, characterized by little chance of career development (Aigner, 2019; Harris & Todaro, 1970; Piore, 1979).

To better understand these challenges and their role in migrants' inclusion and career progression in light of the global pandemic and its impacts regarding the ethnically diverse workforce in the specific case of Austria, in this chapter, we position ourselves in the career-related literature (e.g. Zikic & Klehe, 2021; Crowley-Henry et al., 2018; Zikic, 2015; Bendl et al., 2012). Various studies have addressed challenges migrants face when entering receiving country labor markets (e.g. Syed, 2008; Shirmohammadi et al., 2019); however, less is known about their agency in dealing with such challenges, especially in a crisis setting. By addressing strategies migrants employ with regard to employment and career progression during a crisis, this chapter sheds light on the individuals and their adaptation to the changing environment. We contribute to career literature by showcasing various paths migrants take to progress in their careers in challenging circumstances, and we thus answer calls for a better understanding of migrant career trajectories in different contexts (see Crowley-Henry et al., 2018).

In terms of our methodological approach, we conducted 36 semi-structured interviews with HR managers, representatives of support organizations, and migrants between 2020 and 2022 in Austria. The qualitative data analysis followed a grounded theory approach (Glaser & Strauss, 1967).

We proceed in this chapter by first outlining the literature, and second, our methodology, before addressing the findings as well discussing these in light of the Covid-19 pandemic.

Migrant Inclusion at Work and Career Trajectories: Pluralist Challenges and Agency

The challenges migrants face when entering labor markets and aiming for career progression are well known and multifaceted. The vulnerability of migrants at the workplace and at the intersection of labor markets at macro, meso, and micro level is caused by problems related to overall national contexts, networks, employment relations, and individual acculturation (see Lee et al., 2020).

One challenge at the macro and meso level consists of positioning migrants in meaningful employment, which fits their skills and educational background. In practical settings, however, de-skilling and de-qualification processes often take place upon entering the receiving country's labor markets, when education and qualifications acquired in the country of origin are not recognized, and migrants are frequently positioned in low-skilled or at least lower-skilled employments than they are qualified for (Kirilova et al., 2016; Stadler et al., 2010; Currie, 2007). The dominant narrative deploys that premigration-acquired qualifications and abilities remain in theory celebrated assets, however, in practice turn into a barrier for career development. Thereby, target policies need to be addressed to reduce barriers to meaningful employment and employment discrimination, which, in turn, have negative effects on overall settlement processes (Udah et al., 2019).

At the organizational level, company policies can have an impact on migrants' inclusion at work (see Ortlieb et al., 2021; Barnard et al., 2019; Bendl et al., 2010, 2012). The praise of the promotion of equality and diversity, in turn, in practical settings changes to inequalities in accessing the workplace and social inclusion at the workplace (Omanović & Langley, 2023). Successful organizational integration is associated with language skills, the acquisition of social knowledge and skills, as well as networks with colleagues (Rajendran et al., 2020). The attitude of employers (Fossland, 2013; Schein, 1988; Van Maanen & Schein, 1979; Omanović & Langley, 2023), hard and soft barriers, can be counteracted by the provision of language-support programs, mentoring programs, and a positive work climate (Gabrielli & Impicciatore, 2022), which organizations in theory provide, but in practice often fail to implement. Additionally, as a result of crisis, companies face a lack of funding for labor market and company integration programs (see Ortlieb et al., 2021), which, moreover, limits the measurements that can be directed toward successful work integration and career progression of migrants. In addition, support organizations responsible for labor market integration measures and initiatives shifted their focus elsewhere (e.g. on furlough programs) during the Covid-19 pandemic, leaving limited focused support (see Bešić et al., 2021).

At the individual level, migrants, despite frequently being highly qualified, are often discriminated against (see Weichselbaumer, 2017) and are found in low-wage professions, characterized by little chance of career development (Aigner, 2019; Harris & Todaro, 1970; Piore, 1979). Mismatched employment often leads to settlement difficulties, precarious work contexts, accreditation problems, and identity-based discrimination (Sert, 2016). Lack of meaningful integration in the labor market, combined with a lack of German language knowledge, or an absence of networks and support measures

(Brücker et al., 2014; Esser, 2006) accelerate the social exclusion of migrants, thereby counteracting successful long-term settlement. Crises such as Covid-19 accelerated existing inequalities, and processes of social exclusions, counteracting settlement processes all the more (Barker, 2021; Bešić & Aigner, 2023). Additionally, the Covid-19 pandemic accelerated the digital divide and thereby obstructed job applications, participation in training, and successful employment throughout times of social distancing during Covid-19 (Bešić et al., 2021; Aigner & Bešić, 2023; Barker, 2021).

Fewer studies address migrant agency within job search and employment, which is, as we show further below, crucial in unfavorable times such as the Covid-19 crisis. Still, research has shown how migrants can proactively move toward better employment quality including, for example, career planning (see Zikic & Klehe, 2021; Bešić & Aigner, 2023).

Overall, studies suggest that career patterns of migrants (including skilled migrants) are affected across the aforementioned levels. Crowley-Henry et al. (2018) in their systematic literature review of skilled migrants' careers identify career patterns instead of career paths, which can vary due to the multifaceted factors that affect job entry and progression in receiving societies. As we show in our results further below, the repercussions of the Covid-19 pandemic have led to a rethinking of employment and career trajectories by migrants.

Austria's Culturally and Ethnically Diverse Labor Force

Austria has a long-standing history of immigration, shaping its sociodemographic profile and diversity of workforce. From the 1960s and 1970s onward, labor migration, specifically, the guest worker migration from Turkey and former Yugoslavian countries, shaped Austrian post-Second World War history of immigration (Aigner, 2017). Throughout the 1990s, refugee movements, such as those occurring as a result of the break-up of former Yugoslavia, further defined the immigration history and, in consequence, the ethnically diverse workforce of contemporary Austria. The 1994 Austrian membership of the European Union, on the one hand, and the EU enlargements of 2004, 2007, and 2013, [1] on the other hand, additionally shaped—as a result of the free movement of labor policies of the EU—the diversity of the Austrian

---

[1] EU enlargement 2004: Estonia; Latvia; Lithuania, Malta, Poland, Slovakia, Slovenia, Czech Republic, Hungary, Cyprus.
 EU enlargement 2007: Bulgaria, Rumania
 EU enlargement 2013: Croatia

workforce. Regarding the migrant population of EU member states in contemporary Austria, predominately citizens from Germany, Romania, Croatia, and Hungary reside (Statistic Austria, 2022). Regarding third-country nationals, citizens from Serbia, Turkey, Bosnia, and Herzegovina, as well as Afghanistan, Syria, and, lately, the Ukraine, reside in Austria, a considerable number of those having entered as refugees (ibid.).

Recently, two main refugee movements have increased Austria's workforce diversity. The first, predominately originating in Afghanistan and Syria, peaked in 2015 with approximately 88,000 refugees entering Austria (ibid.; BMI, 2023). However, subsequently, the overall number of asylum seeker numbers dropped between 2019 and 2021, but peaked again in 2022, with over 112,000 applications, predominately from Afghanistan, India, Syria, and Tunisia (ibid.; BMI, 2023). Additionally, since February 2022, approximately 95,000 displaced persons from Ukraine have entered Austria by early 2023 (ÖIF, 2023). Over 70% of Ukrainian refugees are women and minor children (ÖIF, 2023).

As a result, a culturally and ethnically diverse workforce shapes the Austrian labor market at present. In 2021, approximately a quarter of the Austrian population (25.4%) had a migrant background, and 22% of the Austrian labor force (in total 839,632 persons) had no Austrian citizenship (Statistics Austria, 2022; BMA, 2022). The number of migrants in employment rose alongside the overall immigration rate, specifically, EU labor migrants of "new" EU member states since 2004 increased from 2020 to 2021 by 8% (17,197 persons) (BMA, 2022). Among the migrant labor force, in 2021, the majority of migrants (16%) were employed in the sectors of *manufacturing and trade*, followed by *catering* (11%), as well as the *building industry* (11%) (ibid.). The sector of *health and social services*, in which 6% (50,717) of the total migrant labor force was employed, increased by 12% (5612 persons) within the sector from 2020 to 2021 (ibid.).

However, some sectors rely more heavily on migrant labor than others. For example, in the sector *agriculture, forestry, and fishing industry*, 53% of the employees have a migrant background, followed by the sector *catering and gastronomy* with a 51% share of migrant labor. In the sector of *catering* almost 50% of the migrant labor originated in the "new" EU member states,[2] 19% were third-country nationals from outside Europe, and 17% were European third-country nationals (ibid.). Additionally, the sector of the *building industry* with a 31% share of migrant workforce, followed by the sector of *transport and storage* with a 27% share of migrant workforce, rely strongly on migrant

---

[2] The "new" EU member states consist of EU member states joining the European Union after 2004.

workforce (BMA, 2022). In the *health and social service* sector, 17% of the labor force had a migrant background in 2021 (ibid.). In the *health care* sector, a quarter of the workforce came from "old" EU member states,[3] 36% from "new" EU member states, and a further quarter originated from European countries outside the EU (ibid.).

Overall, the data explains that migrants are employed in a mixture of sectors, but that increasingly important sectors for migrants are the sectors of *health care* and *catering*. In addition, employments in those sectors may range from temporary low-skilled work to (in fewer cases) highly skilled jobs with options for career progression (Ortlieb et al., 2021).

Generally, the employment and labor market inclusion of migrants remains a challenge for policy makers, organizations, and individuals. On the one hand, institutional barriers (e.g. barriers with regard to the recognition of qualifications), and, on the other hand, discrimination at the labor market entry points, as well as the individuals' lack of networks and credentials, coupled with the unfamiliarity with the labor market (Eggenhofer-Rehart et al., 2018; Verwiebe et al., 2019) contribute to challenges at the macro, meso, and micro levels.

Following the Covid-19 pandemic, the Austrian labor market faces shortages across specific sectors (e.g. in care and technology), which has led to a more vocal role of employers when it comes to enabling and including migrants in the labor market.

Methodology

To answer our research questions, *how major crises such as the Covid-19 pandemic impact migrants' inclusion at work and their career progression, and how organizations can support such inclusion*, we conducted a qualitative study, based on 36 semi-structured interviews, in 2 separate spheres, to highlight the career advancement and employment opportunities of migrants during Covid-19 from differing perspectives. In Upper Austria, 18[4] interviews with experts and officials and 18[5] interviews with migrants were carried out. Mainly theoretical and snowball sampling (Patton, 2015; Denscombe, 2010) were

---

[3] The "old" EU member states consist of EU member states joining the European Union before 2004.

[4] The first nine expert interviews (E1–E9), which were carried out in 2020 and 2021 were conducted as part of a study on the impact of Covid-19 on labor market integration and work inclusion by the first two authors. The second set of nine expert interviews (E10–E18) were conducted by the third author as part of a dissertation project on labor market integration, work inclusion, and diversity management.

[5] The 18 interviews with migrants were conducted as part of the dissertation project of the third author.

used to reach out to experts as well as migrants. We interviewed 18 experts, including 3 HR managers, 2 project managers, 9 handling officers at employment support organizations, 2 trainers, 1 coach, and 1 social worker (see Table 14.1 for an overview). Furthermore, we interviewed 18 migrants, with differing countries of origin. The interviewees originated in "old" and "new" EU member states (e.g. Slovakia, Romania, Germany), but also arrived from outside the EU (e.g. Mexico, Kazakhstan, Iran), covering the age range from 28 to 60 years. The sample consisted of 7 men and 11 women (see Table 14.2 for an overview).

The interviews were conducted between November 2020 and August 2022 and took between 20 and 70 minutes. During the operationalization of the field work, we used two interview guides for experts, and a third interview guide for migrants. Both semi-structured interview guidelines for experts included questions which were directed at measurements taken to combat de-skilling processes, at support tools utilized by companies and support organizations to support labor market integration of migrants and refugees as such, to employ migrants in meaningful positions, before, during, and after Covid-19. Additionally, the implementation of support measures for career advancement was investigated in light of Covid-19. Migrants, on the other hand, were interrogated about their experiences of employment, their work placement in meaningful positions, their experiences of training and possibilities of career advancement, and workplace inclusion in light of Covid-19.

Table 14.1 Overview of interviews with experts

Officials	Gender	Job Title	Organization	Interview Date
E1	M	Handling Officer	Private support org. 1	2020
E2	M	Project Manager	NGO1	2020
E3	M	Handling Officer	Private support org. 2	2020
E4	M	Handling Officer	NGO2	2020
E5	M	Handling Officer	NGO3	2020
E6	M	Trainer	NGO1	2020
E7	M	Social Worker	NGO1	2020
E8	M	Handling Officer	APES	2021
E9	F	Handling Officer	NGO4	2021
E10	M	Handling Officer	Support Organization	2021
E11	F	Coach	NGO	2021
E12	M	Handling Officer	Support Organization	2022
E13	M	Handling Officer	Support Organization	2022
E14	F	Project Manager	Support Organization	2022
E15	M	Trainer	NGO	2022
E16	F	HRM Management	Company	2022
E17	F	HRM Management	Company	2022
E18	M	HRM Management	Company	2022

Table 14.2 Overview of interviews with migrants

Interviewee	Gender	Age	Age at immigration	CoO	Education CoO	Additional Education Austria	Employment before migration	First employment after migration	Present employment
B1	M	31	24	Germany	Apprenticeship	Course	Butcher	Butcher	Quality management butcher
B2	F	52	31	Romania	University	Course	Sales pharmaceuticals	Research in timber products	Sales management
B3	M	31	28	Slovakia	University	No	Quality engineer	Industry consultant	Job seeking
B4	F	40	28	Moldavia	University	No	Translator; teacher	Sales personnel	Office work
B5	F	40	24	Romania	University	Course	Lobbyist	Department management transport	Pregnancy leave
B6	F	38	27	Slovakia	Nursing Diploma University	Nostrification of diploma	Nurse with diploma (DGKS)	Elderly care	Nurse with diploma DGKS
B7	M	40	36	Mexico	University	No	Research (waterpower)	Research	Research
B8	F	42	21	Slovakia	Nursing Diploma	Nostrification of diploma	Nurse with diploma (DGKS)	Elderly care	Nurse with diploma (DGKS)
B9	F	48	19	Romania	High School	No	Waitress and cleaner	Housekeeper	Low-skilled job production
B10	F	50	35	Kazakhstan	University	Repeat of the educational path from CoO	Management of hospital station; specialist doctor	Doctor	Specialist doctor

			CoO		Nostrification of diploma			
B11	F	45	35	Romania	Nursing Diploma		Nurse with diploma (DGKS)	Cleaner	Nurse with diploma (DGKS)
B12	M	28	24	Romania	Apprenticeship	No	Carpenter	Logistic and repair	Logistic and repair
B13	M	29	28	Libya	University	University	International trader	International trader	International trader
B14	F	53	33	Bosnia & Herzegovina	Nursing Diploma	Nostrification of diploma	Nurse with diploma (DGKS)	Low-skilled production	Nursing assistant
B15	F	29	23	Hungary	University	No	Student of midwifery	Cleaner	Midwife
B16	M	38	31	Iran	University	University	Quality manager, engineer composer	Music teacher	Store manager food trade
B17	F	44	28	Bulgaria	University	University	Student law	Law assistant	Consultant at IT company
B18	M	60	20	Iran	University	University		Newspaper sales	Self-employed physiotherapy

Note: CoO Country of Origin

The interviews were predominantly conducted online or by telephone (due to Covid-19 restrictions during the interview process) and were carried out to the point of theoretical saturation (Glaser & Strauss, 1967). The digital interviewing process can be understood as equivalent to face-to-face interviews. One advantage ascribed to digital interviewing processes is the removal of the interviewer effect, as a greater social distance is created between the interviewer and the interviewee, while at the same time the interviewees feel more comfortable in their own home environment and are therefore more likely to give detailed answers to questions (Thunberg & Arnell, 2022).

All interviews were digitally recorded, transcribed, and coded with MAXQDA. The qualitative data analysis followed an inductive grounded theory approach (Glaser & Strauss, 1967); therefore, it was "data driven". Applying this approach, during the initial coding process open codes evolved out of the data material, in a second coding process by axial and selective coding, the main themes evolved. Those focus on (1) challenges and opportunities regarding employment and career advancement through training; (2) sector-specific career development strategies of migrants; and (3) meaningful employment in times of crisis and social integration at work. Those will be presented in the following section in detail, in which we aim to highlight how major crisis, such as Covid-19, affect migrants' inclusion at work and career development, and what role HR management and support organizations play in the receiving country context, as well as the career advancement of migrants in light of the global pandemic with a specific focus on Austria.

Findings

Our findings show that crises such as Covid-19 impact in multiple ways the migrants' inclusion at work and their career advancement. Furthermore, the findings indicate the drastic impact on the abilities of support organizations and companies to implement training measurements and provide paths to career advancement. Our findings point to multiple impacts of crises, often specific sectors were differently impacted than others, mostly accelerating existing barriers, as a result of social distancing and a consequent switch to digital communication, while at the same time, a number of positive side effects evolved. For example, the crisis triggered new forms of coping strategies adopted by migrants, which contributed to a restructuring and turn taking, a replanning, of career advancement or employments. Specifically, the following themes evolved: (1) *Challenges and opportunities regarding employment and career advancement through training;* (2) *career development strategies of migrants—sector-specific challenges and opportunities*; and (3) *Meaningful employment in times of crisis and social integration at work.*

Challenges and Opportunities Regarding Employment and Career Advancement Through Training

During Covid-19, a major change occurred as suddenly the world went into lockdown mode and social distancing. Social distancing was followed by a unique switch to digitalization regarding work and employment-related measurements, from training to language courses, to job applications, and employment as such. This acceleration of digitalization became a challenge as well as an opportunity at the organizational level, the companies and the support organizations, but similarly affected migrants' employments and labor market integration (and beyond) equally. For support organizations, going digital resulted in managerial, technical, organizational, and financial challenges, both on an individual level and on an organizational level (e.g. Orru et al., 2021). The majority of experts from support organizations and company HR representatives pointed out that the digital divide was a challenge to overcome when reaching out to migrants, specifically, in regard to career advancement. A handling officer exemplified in this respect:

> *What was and still is a challenge, of course, is our support with application documents, because the clients, if they don't have a computer at home themselves, are then partly dependent on other people who help them to complete these application documents, and this is now an empowerment approach and to help the clients to become independent, [this situation/Covid-19] is really not ideal, because the clients cannot work on the applications themselves [.….].* (E5)

The majority of the interviewed migrants, on the other hand, and depending on their digital skills, were appreciative of the courses that were on offer and made use of the opportunity created by lockdowns and social distancing. However, career advancement courses and professional training courses were mainly provided by their employers, thereby only useable by and useful to already employed migrants, leaving specifically unemployed migrants and job seekers to their own devices (Aigner & Bešić, 2023). A 28-year-old migrant, who originally was a carpenter in Romania, and presently works in low-skilled employment in the logistics and repair sector reasoned:

> *Yes. Of course, that is also an advantage of the company where I work. Training courses, also for foreigners, for example, there are German training courses, in which*

you can register and learn German. And this is always an alternative, particularly now in Lockdown with online German training courses, where you can learn German and so on. I think that's also good from the company's point of view, that there's such possibility and that the company provides this possibility and it's all paid for by the company. You don't have to pay anything or anything like that. (B12)

As pointed out by most experts and migrants, trainings provided in specific sectors, for example, for the technical sector, were difficult to deliver due to social distancing and the need to do training on site. The pandemic, therefore, also impeded training possibilities in some sectors due to the sheer impossibility to attend personally and face to face on site. A German migrant indicated in this matter:

Well, I would say that further training in the technical area already exists, partly because of the increasing technology. Everything is becoming more and more extensive, the machines are becoming more extensive and so on, so the technical staff has to keep learning and learning and learning. Further and further training, but the normal production employee is probably less likely to undergo further training. In the office area, I can't define it so precisely, whether or not, but it also depends on whether you think it makes sense or not. And now, in the Corona case, it is much more difficult anyway, so I would say that at the moment probably no one continues his education. (B1)

Career Development Strategies of Migrants: Sector-Specific Challenges and Opportunities

Overall, the majority of experts, as well as migrants, noted that the migrants' strategic response to the challenges of lockdowns, possible unemployment and furlough work, as a result of Covid-19 appeared twofold. First, it seemed attractive to make use of additionally available time to engage in further career development by participating in online courses, if such possibilities arose. Alternatively, university education or courses subsidized by employers were another option to take. Consequently, opportunities as a result of the crisis arose for migrants: Using the extra time often created by the circumstances of the pandemic to advance their skills and acquire additional qualifications. This was summed up by a handling officer of career advancement programs, from a support organization, the following way:

It was always latently there, but Corona has reinforced that 100%, that awareness, so to speak, "Now I also have the time, now I can also think". I have also noticed in the counselling that in many cases the requests for a change of profession or a change of career have increased significantly. (E12)

A 29-year-old migrant from Libya, who worked in international trade, acquired a university degree in Libya and was at the time of interview in the process of further university education in Austria, exemplified the possibility of making use of the additional time to gather education:

Well, I started the master's program at the beginning of Covid-19. I had a little bit more time and that's when I had a little bit more time to study. And also, the company also welcomed it, because the studies were in a way related to my work. So, it was kind of an improvement to do that. So, it was both. It was my decision to take the time and the intention of the company was to support an employee's career development. The company, so HR, always looks at personal and career development programs for the team and when I came with the proposal, they helped me make that happen. (B13)

Second, as indicated by a large number of experts and migrants alike, it appeared a strategic response to overcome negative side effects of lockdowns and Covid-19 impacts, to switch careers specifically toward professions and sectors in demand, often essential sectors, such as health care (nursing). Such switch often occurred from sectors most adversely affected by Covid-19, and with most job losses or income cuts as a result of furlough work, such as occurring in the catering industry. The motivational factors to switch professions, as reported by the interviewees, included the interest in less precarious work situations, being in demand, and a raise in income. Shortages in specific labor segments were observed as opportunities for and by migrants, strategizing about taking different directions in their career professions, thereby professionally advancing and additionally being able to move to professions with higher incomes. In this respect, a handling officer of a support organization claimed that:

I've experienced it that way before, although now the urgency—or let's say—the clarity of how we [...] are dependent on care in hospitals or in nursing homes, so the awareness has risen, not only among legislators and employers, but also among migrants, migrant women, in the sense that "I'd have a job that's safe". Of course, you have to like that job, because it's not very pleasant, but I think that some awareness has already been created in the sense of "I'm going into an area where I'll have a secure job and a secure salary and where I have job prospects/perspectives". [...] This is a consideration that perhaps Corona has made people even more aware of. (E10)

Despite the recognition of such shortages by the macro-level organizations, for instance, by governments, the entry barriers for migrant workers were not lowered, when it came to specific qualifications needed, for those sectors in demand. According to most experts interviewed, while companies made an effort in recruiting, being aware of the situation of labor shortage, the legislative restrictions, nevertheless, remained in place. A handling officer from a support organization suggested:

> *I personally know 2 large companies, but basically it is the case that skilled personnel is really needed, especially in the medical field […] although there are very rigid frameworks and structures. Whereby the companies can't help it, they actually make an effort and try to somehow to find personnel. But we have other obstacles and framework conditions that are difficult. Because the care sector is regulated, formal recognition is required, and without that it is not possible. Companies and entrepreneurs are trying very hard, but it is very difficult at the moment—difficult.* (E11)

Contrary to sectors with labor shortages, other sectors, such as the catering sector, were affected the opposite way by Covid-19. People lost jobs or were sent into furlough work, and often appeared to have no other choice but to redirect and replan their careers, as was argued by a majority of experts and migrant interviewees. A handling officer reported:

> *The shortage of skilled workers has actually always been an issue, in this intensity and also due to Corona, I would see it much more intensified now, because the industry was affected by short-time work [furlough work] and therefore many people were forced to look for alternatives. So, an insane number of employees have now moved away from the catering industry.* (E12)

Many of the interviewed migrants highlighted the change Covid-19 drastically caused for possibilities of employment. An Iranian migrant exemplified, that due to labor shortages, the pandemic had opened up further employment opportunities for migrants, albeit solely regarding specific sectors, which were in demand of labor.

> *But it is not so simple. […] it is not easy because I have sent out more than 100 resumes and applications. It was not easy at all in the beginning. […] - 7 years ago—as a normal employee, as a shelf supervisor in the grocery store, but they didn't give me a chance. They said "You are a foreigner, you don't know German and we'll give this chance to an Austrian". They said that so honestly. That was already very, very different—8 years ago.*

> *Right now, it's great because all the stores need employees and they are giving opportunities to foreigners. At the moment everything is perfect, but 8 years ago everything was already full. I sent way too many applications, way too much with PES, again and again, but I couldn't get a chance.* (B16)

Meaningful Employment and Social Integration at Work in Times of Crisis

The positioning of migrants in meaningful employment corresponding to their skills has been hotly debated prior to Covid-19 (Kirilova et al., 2016; Stadler et al., 2010; Currie, 2007). Language skills and cultural and social knowledge amount to essential assets for social integration at work (Fossland, 2013; Schein, 1988; Van Maanen & Schein, 1979; Omanović & Langley, 2023). A majority of interviewed experts from Austrian support organizations and companies argued that language skills were generally and independent of the crisis, a precondition for the recognition of educational qualifications acquired abroad. A handling officer indicated:

> *And the typical entry-level jobs often, because it's so often also about language barriers or the qualifications from the home country, if there is a university degree or another school degree, which are perhaps not yet recognized in Austria, or there are no certificates, then there are indeed already opportunities to catch up on these degrees in Austria, but of course you first need the language skills for it and that is a very long process.* (E5)

Equally, the majority of interviewed migrants communicated similar points. An Iranian migrant with an engineering background from his country of origin also mentioned the importance of the ability to speak German to achieve successful labor market integration and meaningful job placements.

> *But I have been in Austria since 12/2012, you could say that. Since then, I have been in Austria. In the first year I couldn't work properly, because I was already working for a band and took part in concerts and so on, because I still had language problems. I could only speak English, but in Austria you really need German. you absolutely need German. And that's why I couldn't find a job [...].* (B16)

Often formal recognitions of university degrees obtained in the country of origin are considered essential for meaningful employment by Austrian companies (Titelbacher et al., 2021). In this project, a number of interviewed experts stated that reasons behind the rejection of home country qualifications by companies can be—besides the recognition of the education itself—attributed to payment schemes. For companies, to employ migrants in low-skilled sectors, despite high-skilled qualifications, has multiple advantages, as reasoned by a support officer:

> *[…] there are also many companies that hire people with qualifications they have brought with them, but do not want to pay them [migrant workers] accordingly, but rather in auxiliary activities. And they demand formal recognition where it is not necessary.* (E2)

Covid-19-specific impacts regarding meaningful employments were also reported by a majority of interviewed migrants. A viewpoint the interviewees repeatedly highlighted was related to a perceived *hierarchy of migrants* when it came to labor market integration and work inclusion, and, in consequence, meaningful employments. Covid-19 and subsequent shortages in specific sectors of the labor market appeared to be a game changer in those hierarchies, leading toward more equality in the workplace. An Iranian migrant observed:

> *Now it doesn't matter if you're a foreigner or not. But in the past, […] it was the case that Austrians were always in first place, then EU countries. Austrians, then EU countries. Or you can put it this way: Austrians, Austrian citizenship, the current EU and then the other countries. You can say it like this. You have always been on the 4th place, that's why you could never find anything. But now for the past 2 years everything has become great, everything has changed. It has become much better, yes. With the current company it doesn't matter. […] I think because of Corona, I think. […] Because for 2 years it has already become quite better.* (B16)

Finally, Covid-19 impacted on the overall work situation. Social distancing measures and the inability to work together with colleagues and meet them in person impacted the possibilities of the advancement of social inclusion at the workplace. A 40-year-old Romanian woman with a university degree reported, similar to a number of interviewees, on the inabilities to meet face to face during the pandemic:

> *The colleagues in my department work in various locations in Austria and the corporate headquarters are actually in […]. Of course we meet somewhere for meetings—less so now—but before the lockdown or pandemic, we always met somewhere, and that was mostly in […], because one of the colleagues was there and that was actually the middle ground between Western Austria and Eastern Austria.* (B5)

Thus, although the pandemic-related restrictions have largely been lifted in Austria since mid-2021, various long-term impacts on work inclusion remain. For instance, the current situation at the labor market, with increased prominence of labor and skills shortages across sectors, partly as a result of the long-term impact of Covid-19 on the overall labor market, is favorable for job entry of migrants. On the other hand, local and global challenges around the recognition of qualifications and language skills as well as potential underemployment remain, but new developments at the policy level might ease the challenges for some migrants (see also Anderson et al., 2021; Sommarribas & Nienaber, 2021). For instance, the enlargement of opportunities for remote and flexible work, as well as the lowered entry barriers for skilled third-country nationals with experience in occupations of labor shortages (even without a formal degree), might simplify and lower barriers to employment for some migrants. Others, however, might remain marginalized, including those migrants already situated in the receiving country, in the case of our project, in Austria, but with limited chances for labor market entry and career progression (e.g. asylum seekers).

Discussion and Conclusions

In this chapter, we analyzed how major crises, such as Covid-19, affect migrants' career development and inclusion at work. Thereby we highlighted the barriers, challenges, and opportunities that a crisis like Covid-19 conveys.

Going digital caused challenges at the individual level of migrants' possibilities to participate in digital training courses as a result of the digital divide (Bešić et al., 2021; Aigner & Bešić, 2023). However, new opportunities were also created, as migrants understood the phase of lockdowns and social distancing, brought about by the pandemic, as an opportunity, and utilized strategies to turn the negative side effects into advantages, thereby planning and re-planning their careers (Bešić & Aigner, 2023). One common deployed response to the crisis was to turn to alternative employments in sectors in demand, such as health care and nursing. Those were perceived as better paid and with more secure employment contracts, partially opening up new career advancement opportunities. Moreover, career re-planning took place as a strategic response to unemployment or furlough work in sectors with low labor demand during times of crisis (such the catering industry). Migrants also turned to opportunities created by added available time as a result of the pandemic to pursue further education and gain additional qualifications, thus planning their career more carefully (see also Zikic & Klehe, 2021).

The positioning of migrants in meaningful employment corresponding to their skills appears to be obstructed by barriers of the macro-level legislations and policies, as well as around companies and employers insisting on additional qualifications on top of abroad-acquired education, or by excessive waiting periods to formalize and acknowledge in CoO-acquired qualifications. This is an issue globally (Kirilova et al., 2016; Stadler et al., 2010; Currie, 2007) and has not changed during times of crisis, at least in the case of Austria (see also Dobusch & Kreissl, 2020). Additionally, it is, irrespective of the crisis, convenient for organizations to downgrade wages by employing migrants without recognition of skills and qualifications (Brunow & Jost, 2022). However, the Covid-19 pandemic might have also served as a game changer specifically in some sectors, where labor shortages occurred. Additionally, the hierarchichal structures of a - by the interviewees detected- *migrant employment hierarchy* were broken up.

Successful social integration at work continues to be associated with language skills, the acquisition of social knowledge and skills, and the attitude of employers (Fossland, 2013; Schein, 1988; Van Maanen & Schein, 1979; Omanović & Langley, 2023), which has been proven to be the case in the Austrian context also. The acquisition of language skills in the Austrian employment context remains a necessity for labor market integration, and even though language courses are provided, both by support organizations and employers, those were heavily impacted by the pandemic due to the challenges of going digital, in turn overall impeding labor market integration. Furthermore, a positive work climate and so-called welcome culture as a precondition for successful integration at work (Gabrielli & Impicciatore, 2022) continues to be a, in theory, celebrated asset, but in practical contexts, as outlined in our findings, only partially operationalized, whereby in times of social distancing, social integration in work was hindered by little possibilities of social interactions.

Hence, the pandemic caused disruptions to pathways toward successful work integration. The impact of Covid-19, a global crisis, subsequently, appears to have impacted—at least in the Austrian context—as a double-edged sword regarding labor market integration, work inclusion, and career advancement of migrants, creating opportunities, on the one hand, while accelerating challenges and drawbacks, on the other.

References

Aigner, P. (2017). *Migrationssoziologie*. Springer.
Aigner, P. (2019). *Multidimensionale Betrachtungsweisen zu Ethnic Entrepreneurship*. Peter Lang.

Aigner, P., & Bešić, A. (2023). Left to their own devices: Refugees' labour-market integration challenges in Austria during the Covid-19 pandemic. In M. L. Jakobson, R. King, L. Moroşanu, & R. Vetik (Eds.), *Anxieties of migration and integration in turbulent times* (IMISCOE research series) (pp. 77–95). Springer. https://doi.org/10.1007/978-3-031-23996-0_5

Anderson, B., Poeschel, F., & Ruhs, M. (2021). Rethinking labour migration: Covid-19, essential work, and systemic resilience. *Comparative Migration Studies, 9*(45), 1–19.

Barnard, H., Deeds, D., Mudambi, R., & Vaaler, P. M. (2019). Migrants, migration policies, and international business research: Current trends and new directions. *Journal of International Business Policy, 2*, 275–228.

Barker, M. (2021). Social integration in social isolation: Newcomers' integration during the Covid-19 pandemic. *New Horizons in Adult Education and Human Resource Development, 33*, 34–45.

Bendl, R., Hanappi-Egger, E., & Hofmann, R. (2012). Diversität und Diversitätsmanagement: Ein vielschichtiges Thema. In R. Bendl, E. Hanappi-Egger, & R. Hofmann (Eds.), *Diversität und Diversitätsmanagement* (pp. 11–21). Facultas.

Bendl, R., Hanappi-Egger, E., & Hofmann, R. (2010). Austrian perspectives on diversity management and equal treatment: Regulations, debates, practices and trends. In *International handbook on diversity Management at Work*. Edward Elgar Publishing.

Bešić, A., Diedrich, A., & Aigner, P. (2021). Organizing labor market integration support for refugees in Austria and Sweden during the Covid-19 pandemic. *Comparative Migration Studies, 9*(1), 1–18.

Bešić, A., & Aigner, P. (2023). Action, reaction and resignation: How refugee women and support Organisations respond to labour market integration challenges during the Covid-19 pandemic. *Journal of International Management*, 101031. https://doi.org/10.1016/j.intman.2023.101031

BMA. (2022). *Arbeitsmarktinfo AMIS*. Accessed December 28, 2022, from https://www.dnet.at/amis/Default.aspx. Bundesministerium für Arbeit und Wirtschaft.

BMI. (2023). *Statistics on Asylum applications*. Accessed August 19, 2023, from https://www.bmi.gv.at/301/Statistiken/. Bundesministerium für Inneres.

Brücker, H., Liebau, E., Romiti, A., & Vallizadeh, E. (2014). *Arbeitsmarktintegration von Migranten in Deutschland: Anerkannte Abschlüsse und Deutschkenntnisse lohnen sich. IAB-Kurzbericht*. Informationszentrum.

Brunow, S., & Jost, O. (2022). Wages of skilled migrant and native employees in Germany: New light on an old issue. *International Migration Review, 56*(2), 410–432. https://doi.org/10.1177/01979183211040505

Crowley-Henry, M., O'Connor, E., & Al Ariss, A. (2018). Portrayal of skilled migrants' careers in business and management studies: A review of the literature and future research agenda. *European Management Review, 15*, 375–394.

Currie, S. (2007). De-skilled and devalued: The labor market experience of polish migrants in the UK following EU enlargement. *International Journal of Comparative Labor Law and Industrial Relations, 1*(23), 83–116.

Denscombe, M. (2010). *The good research guide*. Open University Press.

Dobusch, L., & Kreissl, K. (2020). Privilege and burden of Im-/mobility governance: On the reinforcement of inequalities during a pandemic lockdown. *Gender, Work and Organization, 27*(5), 709–716.

Eggenhofer-Rehart, P. M., Latzke, M., Pernkopf, K., Zellhofer, D., Mayrhofer, W. and Steyrer, J. (2018). Refugees' career capital welcome? Afghan and Syrian refugee job seekers in Austria. *Journal of Vocational Behavior, 105*, 31–45.

Esser, H. (2006). *Sprache und Integration. Die sozialen Bedingungen und Folgen des Spracherwerbs von Migranten*. Campus.

Fossland, T. (2013). Negotiating future careers: A relational perspective on skilled migrants' labor market participation. *Journal of Management Development, 32*(2), 193–203.

Gabrielli, G., & Impicciatore, R. (2022). Breaking down the barriers: Educational paths, labor market outcomes and wellbeing of children of immigrants. *Journal of Ethnic and Migration Studies, 48*(10), 2305–2323.

Glaser, B. G., & Strauss, A. L. (1967). *The discovery of grounded theory. Strategies for qualitative research*. Chigaco.

Harris, J. R., & Todaro, M. P. (1970). Migration, unemployment and development: A two-sector analysis. *American Economic Review, 60*, 126–142.

Kirilova, S., Biffl, G., Pfeffer, T., Skrivanek, I., Egger, A., Kerler, M. & Doll, E., (2016). *Anerkennung von Qualifikationen*. Accessed January 26, 2022, from OEIF_Anerkennung_von_Qualifikationen_Forschungsbericht_web.pdf&usg=AOvVaw38-v-Xjjbnm-MtcbxIDcJl

ÖIF- Austrian Integration Fund. (2023). *UkrainerInnen in Österreich 2023: Stand April/Mai 2023*. https://www.integrationsfonds.at/statistiken/. Accessed April 2023.

Lee, E. S., Szkudlarek, B., Nguyen, D. C. and Nardon, L. (2020). Unveiling the canvas ceiling: A multidisciplinary literature review of refugee employment and workforce integration. *International Journal of Management Reviews, 22*(2), 193–216.

Omanović, V., & Langley, A. (2023). Assimilation, integration or inclusion? A dialectical perspective on the organizational socialization of migrants. *Journal of Management Inquiry, 32*(1), 76–97.

Ortlieb, R., Glauninger, E., & Weiss, R. (2021). Organizational inclusion and identity regulation: How inclusive organizations form 'good', 'glorious', and 'grateful' refugees. *Organization, 28*(2), 266–288.

Orru, K., Nero, K., Nævestad, T. -O., Schieffelers, A., Olson, A., Airola, M., Kazemekaityte, A., Lovasz, G., Scurci, G., Ludvigsen, J. and de los Rios Pérez, D. A. (2021). Resilience in care organisations: challenges in maintaining support for vulnerable people in Europe during the Covid-19 pandemic. *Disasters, 45*, 48-75.

Patton, M. (2015). *Qualitative Research and Evaluation Methods: Integrating Theory and Practice.* SAGE

Piore, M. J. (1979). *Birds of passage. Migrant labor in industrial societies.* Cambridge University Press.

Rajendran, D., Ng, E. S., Sears, G., & Ayub, N. (2020). Determinants of migrant career success: A study of recent skilled migrants in Australia. *International Migration, 58*, 30–51. https://doi.org/10.1111/imig.12586

Syed, J. (2008). Employment prospects for skilled migrants: A relational perspective. *Human Resource Management Review, 18*(1), 28–45.

Schein, E. H. (1988). Organizational socialization and the profession of management. *MIT Sloan Management Review, 30*(1), 53.

Shirmohammadi, M., Beigi, M., & Stewart, J. (2019). Understanding skilled migrants' employment in the host country: A multidisciplinary review and a conceptual model. *International Journal of Human Resource Management, 30*(1), 96–121.

Sert, D. (2016). From skill translation to devaluation: The de-qualification of migrants in Turkey. *New Perspectives on Turkey, 54*, 97–117.

Sommarribas, A., & Nienaber, B. (2021). Migration and mobility of third-country national labour workers to and inside Europe during the covid-19 pandemic – A legal analysis. *Comparative Migration Studies, 9*(22), 1–17.

Stadler B., Wiedenhofer & Galik, B. (2010). *Dequalifizierung von Migrantinnen und Migranten am österreichischen Arbeitsmarkt.* Accessed January 26, 2022, from http://pic.statistik.at/web_de/static/dequalifizierung_von_migrantinnen_und_migranten_am_oesterreichischen_arbei_064155.pdf

Statistik Austria. (2022). *Statcube.* Accessed December 20, 2022, from https://statcube.at/statistik.at/ext/statcube/jsf/login.xhtml

Thunberg, S., & Arnell, L. (2022). Pioneering the use of technologies in qualitative research – A research review of the use of digital interviews. *International Journal of Social Research Methodology, 25*(6), 757–768.

Titelbacher, G., Fink, M., & Vogtenhuber, S. (2021). *Dequalifizierung am Wiener Arbeitsmarkt.* IHS Wien.

Udah, H., Singh, P., Hiruy, K., & Mwanri, L. (2019). African immigrants to Australia: Barriers and challenges to labor market success. *Journal of Asian and African Studies, 54*(8), 1159–1174.

Van Maanen, J. E., & Schein, E. H. (1979). Toward a theory of organizational socialization. In B. M. Staw (Ed.), *Research in organizational behavior* (Vol. 1, pp. 209–264). JAI Press.

Verwiebe, R., B. Kittel, F. Dellinger, C. Liebhart, D. Schiestl, R. Haindorfer & Liedl, B. (2019). Finding your way into employment against all odds? Successful job search of refugees in Austria. *Journal of Ethnic and Migration Studies, 9*, 1401–1418.

Weichselbaumer, D. (2017). Discrimination against migrant job applicants in Austria. An experimental study. *German Economic Review, 18*(2), 237–265.

Zikic, J. (2015). Skilled migrants' career capital as a source of competitive advantage: Implications for strategic HRM. *The International Journal of Human Resource Management, 26*(10), 1360–1381.

Zikic, J., & Klehe, U.-C. (2021). Going against the grain: The role of skilled migrants' self-regulation in finding quality employment. *Journal of Organizational Behavior, 42*(8), 1023–1041.

15

Migrant Inclusion and Wider Workforce Well-being: Understanding the MNE Challenges and Solutions through the Diversity Climates Lens

Christina L. Butler, Anna Paolillo, and Vittorio Edoardo Scuderi

Introduction

Migration is a global phenomenon that is affecting more and more countries and is having an impact at individual, organizational, and societal levels. As the International Organization for Migration (IOM) has reported (2020), 272 million people live in a country other than their home country. While the overall proportion of the global population classed as migrant has remained steady at 3% for the past 60 years, the proportion of developed economies' populations so classed has risen to 12%, while the proportion of migrants in emerging economies has remained at 2% (Engler et al., 2020). The absolute increase in and diversification of international migratory movements and greater politicization of this phenomenon (e.g., Esipova et al., 2020) have led to this period being defined as the "Age of Migration" (Castles & Miller, 2009, p. 3).

Workforce well-being has risen up political agendas within developed economies separately from but alongside that of migration. In 2010, the Organisation for Economic Co-operation and Development (OECD) launched its "How's Life?" survey (OECD, 2020) in 37 countries, followed

---

C. L. Butler (✉) • A. Paolillo • V. E. Scuderi
Kingston University London, London, UK
e-mail: Christina.Butler@kingston.ac.uk; A.Paolillo@kingston.ac.uk; k2036224@kingston.ac.uk

by the Better Life Index in 2011 (OECD, 2020). Well-being was also subsumed into the UN's Sustainable Development Goal (SDG) #3 together with health when the SDG program was launched in 2016 (United Nations, 2015). Additionally, various countries have adopted their own measures (e.g., Canadian Index of Wellbeing (CIW, 2022) and frameworks (e.g., Italy's Equitable and Sustainable Wellbeing Framework (Blazey et al., 2022)) over the past couple of decades.

It is estimated that between 2011 and 2030 mental health will cost $16 trillion in lost economic output worldwide (Broom, 2020). While limited coverage of migrant well-being is offered by the various national and international measures and frameworks (Wong Espejo, 2021), the data that is available suggests significantly poorer outcomes for migrants including lower resilience, greater poverty, and lower quality working and housing conditions (Wong Espejo, 2021). Further, other studies suggest that migrant populations are at greater risk of mental illnesses (Hashemi et al., 2019; Liddell et al., 2016). Recently, the COVID-19 Mental Disorders Collaborators (2021) found the pandemic was responsible for generating an additional 53 million cases of major depressive disorder and 76 million additional cases of anxiety disorders worldwide which has compounded the situation. In line with earlier evidence, the pandemic turbulence experienced by migrants was found to be more severe than that experienced by non-migrants (Kothari, 2021). As promoted by various national and international bodies, well-being in the workplace is a recognized business priority (see, e.g., McCain & Sen, 2021) with migrants likely experiencing a greater need for support.

To grow the research agenda on migration to incorporate a well-being at work perspective within the community of international business scholars, in this chapter, we choose to adopt the International Organization on Migration's (IOM) (2019) broad definition of migration. In doing so, we shine a spotlight on the many and varied characteristics of the migrant population (e.g., gender, age, and marital status) which may differentially impact migrant well-being outcomes.[1] Worthy of special mention among these characteristics is that of refugee as defined, for example, by the UNHCR (2021) under the IOM's (2019) broad umbrella definition of migrants. The purpose of selecting the IOM's broad definition in this piece is to illustrate the potential for very varied and complex migrant well-being outcomes.

We introduce international business scholars to the diversity and inclusion literature to enhance the research richness of the former. First, we provide an

---

[1] Empirical studies stemming from this initial discussion will of course need to adopt the usual rigorous definitions for sampling as appropriate to the research question(s).

overview of the growing diversity of organizations. Second, we define and differentiate the concepts of diversity climate and climate for inclusion. Third, we analyze the interplay between such climates and well-being. We conclude with a discussion of multinational enterprise (MNE) challenges and potential solutions to support migrant inclusion and wider workforce well-being.

Diverse Organizations as a Growing Global Phenomenon

Over the past 60 years, scholars and organizations have paid increasing attention to workforce diversity in terms of gender, ethnicity, age, sexual orientation, nationality, and other demographic and social differences (Bellotti et al., 2022; Guillaume et al., 2013; Williams & O'Reilly, 1998). As the forces of globalization have deepened and broadened, and the absolute numbers of migrants have risen, such phenomena have led to much higher heterogeneity in working environments. Concomitantly, organizations have started recognizing the need to be better equipped to manage such a diversified talent pool to create a competitive advantage as well as to fulfill their humanistic mission (Mor Barak, 2017, 2019).

Companies are interested in hiring migrants not only to enter diverse markets and reach a diverse range of customers but also to obtain local resources and to share information across national borders (e.g., Hajro et al., 2017). According to the extant literature, there are additional benefits for culturally savvy organizations and teams, such as increased work performance, job satisfaction, and problem-solving skills, as well as improved organizational image and employee well-being, just to mention a few (Cox, 1994; Hofhuis et al., 2012; Pitts, 2009; Richard et al., 2013). Nevertheless, inadequate management and poor understanding of the complex dynamics pertaining to the level of homogeneity/heterogeneity in a workgroup can also lead to negative outcomes, including dissatisfaction, conflicts, and discrimination episodes (Jayne & Dipboye, 2004; Ogbonna & Harris, 2006), turning eventually to what has been called "a paradoxical dilemma" (Mor Barak, 2019, p. 939). Specifically, embracing diversity represents a risk for a company, in terms of intergroup conflicts, mistrust, and tensions which can result in negative social and economic consequences (Bassett-Jones, 2005). However, avoiding diversity can result in negative outcomes too, such as losing creativity, innovation, and potential economic competitive edge (Mor Barak, 2017).

As the IOM has reported (2020), 272 million people live in a country other than their home country; hence this phenomenon has become one of the main contributors to the cultural diversity of the world's workforce. Prompted by government legislation in certain countries/regions aimed at promoting diversity and inclusion and, sometimes, addressing colonial pasts and privilege (OHCHR, 2012), organizations become subject to social imperatives to reflect the cultural composition of society in their employment policies and practices (i.e., equal employment opportunities and affirmative action programs; D'Netto et al., 2014). Despite those efforts, recent studies in multinational companies have found that ethnocentric staffing practices are still in place and that they cause workers to show favoritism toward their own national ingroup and to create distance with others belonging to a different nationality (i.e., the outgroup; Lee et al., 2022). Examples of ethnocentric practices include showing loyalty, pride, and cohesiveness toward an individual's own group, namely, intragroup cohesiveness or ingroup positivity (e.g., House et al., 2004), as well as putting trust in ingroup members relative to outgroup members, namely, intergroup distance or outgroup negativity (Kramer, 2018).

When migrants leave their home country for the host country, a certain degree of acculturation is required to facilitate adjustment to the new environment (Volpone et al., 2018). Acculturation is defined as the internal psychological change involving the individual when he/she comes into contact with a new culture (Zea et al., 2003). People differ in the extent to which they can acculturate to new environments (Ang et al., 2007), with the most successful becoming truly bicultural and able to alternate between their two cultures (Benet-Martínez & Haritatos, 2005; Lafromboise et al., 1993). Further, field research seems to support the idea that the more minority statuses an individual holds, the better and the quicker they will acculturate to the new environment (Volpone et al., 2018). This faster process is due to the greater personal resources such minorities can rely upon when navigating cross-cultural situations. Their greater and more frequent experiences of social exchanges with others different from them enhance their ability to transfer that knowledge and experience across different situations and cultures (e.g., Barnett & Ceci, 2002; Hinds et al., 2001). Ultimately, such bi- and multicultural individuals can engage easily and quickly in code-switching, adapting their behavior to participate competently in their multiple cultures (Chen et al., 2008). In theory, a superdiverse migrant who has moved to a developed economy (e.g., older female Black migrant who is the mother to several teenage children; young male Brown refugee who speaks English and a variety of

Afghani languages) should be well-positioned to become a successful multicultural individual (Kothari et al., 2022).

At the same time, the process of acculturation can be strongly and negatively impacted by at least two key factors. First, migrants' own social resources can play a significant role. For example, Hashemi et al. (2019) found that the well-being of Middle Eastern migrants in Australia was positively influenced by their perceived social support which they defined as "the resources people perceive to be available or that are actually provided to them by non-professionals in the context of both formal support groups and informal helping relationships" (p. 47). Second, acculturation is also impacted by the interactions migrants have with other people. Individuals associate themselves with an identity group based on demographic characteristics and tend to negotiate these identities through their daily interactions (Stryker, 1980; Tajfel & Turner, 1986). Through those transactions, minorities get to learn the disadvantaged status they hold in society, because of the discrimination they are pervasively exposed to and the negative feelings associated with that (Utsey et al., 2002), and remain marginalized. When applying this to a context which includes migrant workers, this means, for example, that being from a different country in an otherwise nationally homogeneous team does not imply that migrants will inevitably perceive themselves as foreigners. This negative type of self-categorization will more likely occur if the rest of the team discusses cultural differences, comments on a team member's different accent (Gonzalez & Denisi, 2009), or performs other acts of exclusion.

As illustrated above, social interactions and daily work practices directly impact individuals in their daily working life. For this reason, it is important to move from a focus on the organizational rhetoric about how diversity is managed (including the official HR policies and programs) to an assessment of how all employees—those from the majority as well as minorities *including migrants*—in all locations experience and interpret the implementation of those practices, namely, the organization's diversity climate (Kossek & Zonia, 1993; Li et al., 2019). In the next section, we formally introduce the concept of diversity climate.

Diversity Climate

Several definitions of diversity climate can be found in the literature. Some highlight the aggregated employee perception of the formal structure and informal values concerning diversity as provided by the organization (Gonzalez & DeNisi, 2009). Others refer to employees' shared perception of practices and policies that are implicitly and explicitly focused on supporting diversity, making it priority for businesses to eradicate discrimination (Gelfand et al., 2005). Yet other definitions have put the emphasis on the perception of how company policies promote the integration of minorities in the organization (McKay et al., 2008). Drawing from these definitions, we argue that a diversity climate consists of the degree to which employees perceive that the organizational practices, policies, and procedures are able to create a work environment that values, promotes, and integrates all employees—especially minorities *including migrants*—while standing against all forms of discrimination.

Stemming from Cox's Interactional Model of Cultural Diversity (IMCD) developed in 1994, current research centered on diversity climate draws from Mor Barak's bi-dimensional model which includes Organizational and Personal dimensions (Mor Barak et al., 1998). The organizational dimension concerns the extent to which company policies and practices promote fairness in employees' selection, promotion, and treatment and establish official programs to support their inclusion within the company; the personal dimension refers to the value attributed by individual employees to diversity and the degree to which they feel comfortable to interact with co-workers belonging to a different social/cultural group.

Existing research findings around diversity climate have shown its significant positive impact at the individual level, thus promoting job satisfaction (Wolfson et al., 2011) and organizational commitment (McKay et al., 2007) while reducing the employee's intention to leave the company (Buttner & Lowe, 2017; Jolly & Self, 2020; Lee et al., 2020a). Although these findings are not focused on the migrant experience, research should be undertaken to confirm whether these results also hold for various categories of migrants. At the organizational/unit level, diversity climate appeared to foster unit sales performance (McKay et al., 2008, 2009) and firm unit performance (Gonzalez & Denisi, 2009; Moon & Christensen, 2020). As some researchers have investigated the effects of diversity climate at the personal level and others at the organizational level, more recent studies have started to refer to "diversity climates", which acts as an umbrella term encompassing constructs such as value diversity climate and fairness diversity climate (Leslie & Flynn, 2022). More specifically, diversity climates have been defined as work environments that enable the entire workforce to be treated fairly and socially integrated (Holmes et al., 2021). Again, the migrant experience needs to be specifically targeted in future research. It is crucial to emphasize that, alongside fostering a diversity climate within the workplace, it is also necessary to develop a climate for inclusion, which is closely related to the former but also needs to be clearly distinguished (Cox, 1994; Mor Barak, 2017; Nishii, 2013). In the next section, we introduce the concept of climate for inclusion and distinguish between the different types of diversity climates.

Promoting a Climate for Inclusion

Nishii (2013) and Roberson (2006) argued that diversity climate and climate for inclusion are separate constructs. Diversity climate focuses on the fair treatment of those belonging to a minority group (i.e., managing organizational demography). Inclusion climate concentrates on removing all obstacles to encourage the participation and contribution of all employees and the integration of their different competencies and opinions within the organization. Despite companies' efforts to try to integrate minorities and promote an environment supportive of diversity, minorities can still experience exclusion in the everyday working life, which is manifested as a lack of opportunities to participate fully and contribute to organizational life and core processes (Mor Barak, 2017). This means that focusing only on ensuring fairness through complying with equal opportunity-related laws (e.g., in recruitment and development, such as through training and mentoring programs, advocacy groups, and flexible working policies) ensures demographic representation at every organizational level but might not translate into actual opportunities to belong to and participate meaningfully in the organizational system, at the formal and informal level (Mor Barak, 2019). Specifically, the compliance approach does not value personal differences, nor it makes use of them in a beneficial way (Shen et al., 2009), since it does not guarantee that all employees—especially minorities *including migrants*—are enabled to actively participate in the business life and key organizational activities (Guillaume et al., 2014; Mor Barak, 2017; Roberson, 2006).

Organizations are now moving away from a focus on diversity climate aimed at resolving the issue of how to manage a diverse workforce. Instead, they are working to generate a positive climate for inclusion. Although still a work in progress for many organizations (McKinsey & Co., 2020), the aim of the latter climate type is that all employees perceive themselves to be involved in company decision-making processes, information and communication networks, and formal and informal activities, irrespective of the employees' social, demographic, and cultural background (Nishii, 2013; Shore et al., 2011). Such a climate does not only make employees feel valued and respected by offering equality and fairness of opportunities but also makes employees feel empowered (Guillaume et al., 2014), being considered valuable members of the team through the achievement of a balance between their need of belongingness and their need of uniqueness (Roberson, 2006). Therefore, a climate for inclusion is broader than a climate for diversity, as it involves the removal of the obstacles to the full contribution of all employees in organizations (Roberson, 2006); for that reason, it goes beyond the specific issue of how to deal with the organizational demography (Paolillo et al., 2020).

Experiencing a climate of inclusion at work likely leads employees to feel more comfortable when interacting with members of other groups; this results in higher likelihood to participate in organizational life and wider society, together with a greater acceptance of all individuals for who they are (Mor Barak, 2019). Additionally, this helps to develop a work environment where the full spectrum of talents is used (Shore et al., 2011; Nishii, 2013; Mor Barak, 2017), making the most of individual and cultural differences.

Obviously, diversity climate and inclusion climate are related concepts; however, inclusive organizations and diverse organizations do not seem to have the same attributes (Roberson, 2006); for example, inclusion attributes incorporate broader human resource initiatives, such as "collaborative work arrangements and conflict resolution processes, which are designed to involve all employees in organizational decision-making processes" (Roberson, 2006, p. 231). Diversity attributes, instead, cover the representation of different demographic groups in the organization, fair treatment, and top management commitment to diversity (Roberson, 2006; Konrad & Linnehan, 1995). This suggests that both types of climates illustrate two different—although related—approaches to benefit from the potential of a diverse workforce (Paolillo et al., 2016).

The Interplay between Diversity Climate and Climate for Inclusion on Migrants' Well-being

Work environment is an integral part of individuals' lives, given people spend most of their time at work; therefore, well-being in the workplace has become central to an individual's overall health and welfare (Haile, 2012; Wilks & Neto, 2013). Hence, the UN has not only highlighted the relevance of well-being as the third of the SDGs that need to be achieved by 2030 (United Nations, 2015) but also included as other core objectives Decent Work (SDG #8) and Reduced Inequality (SDG #10). Those goals, taken together and with the initiatives of the OECD and others noted above, emphasize the importance of inclusion and well-being of migrants in the workplace.

Despite well-being being a recognized priority, throughout the years, there have been different conceptualizations, often measuring it in the positive terms of job satisfaction and work engagement (namely, as pleasant or fulfilling feelings and/or states of mind related to work; Bakker & Demerouti, 2008) or, conversely, through negative definitions, such as burnout, intention to quit, or "the implementation of disinterested and neglectful behaviour" (Kowalski & Loretto, 2017; Platania et al., 2022, p. 8). Several disciplines have shown interest in exploring and defining well-being, including psychology, medicine, sociology, and anthropology, thus making it a multidimensional concept with multiple definitions. Nevertheless, a common thread across different perspectives aims at defining it as an individual's overall positive state, manifested on multiple levels—that is, physical, psychological, social, and occupational—and with spill-over effects of one dimension over the others and vice versa (Kowalski & Loretto, 2017). With regards to work-related well-being, the UK's Chartered Institute of Personnel and Development (CIPD) refers to a work environment which promotes an employee's state of contentment, allowing them to flourish and achieve their full potential for the organization and the individual's benefit (CIPD, 2007).

Studies have established that being in employment is better for physical and mental health than being unemployed (e.g., Marmot, 2010; Waddell & Burton, 2006). Nevertheless, the quality of work matters and poor work-related well-being is a key reason for workplace absence (CIPD/SimplyHealth, 2016) and a series of potential adverse effects (e.g., Goetzel et al., 2002). We noted above extant research that points to migrants experiencing poorer working conditions and worse outcomes than non-migrants (Wong Espejo, 2021).

Research has highlighted that well-being at work can be identified as one of the main outcomes of both diversity and inclusion climates (Findler et al., 2007; Hofhuis et al., 2012; Sliter et al., 2014; Ward et al., 2020). Specifically, creating an inclusive and diverse work environment can reduce the experience of discrimination and promote better mental health, lower stress levels, decreased turnover and absenteeism (Greenglass et al., 1996; Michie & Williams, 2003; Mor Barak & Levin, 2002; Sabharwal, 2014); additional positive outcomes would include greater job satisfaction and perceived job recognition, especially for minority employees (Clark et al., 1999; Hofhuis et al., 2012; McKay et al., 2007; Williams et al., 1997). As discrimination negatively affects the well-being of minorities *including migrants,* creating a working environment that promotes both diversity and inclusion has been shown to reduce the experience of discrimination, hence establishing a positive individual's state (Clark et al., 1999; McKay et al., 2007; Williams et al., 1997).

The extant literature on migrants and well-being is limited and mainly focused on mental health. Specifically, migrants are at higher risk of developing depression, anxiety, schizophrenia, post-traumatic stress disorder (PTSD), and other mental problems compared to the majority settled populations (Abbott, 2016; Liddell et al., 2016; Zimmerman et al., 2011). Yet, the results of existing studies on identification and acculturation and well-being are inconsistent. Some studies suggest successful identification with a new ethnic culture enhances migrants' self-esteem, decreasing anxiety and depression (Berry & Sabatier, 2011; Moztarzadeh & O'Rourke, 2015; Sheldon et al., 2015). Other scholars, in contrast, indicate that the same process of acculturation creates stress or depression (Abu-Rayya & Abu-Rayya, 2009; Amer & Hovey, 2007). It seems that these opposing results are probably due "to the existing differences between host countries, migrant populations, as well as immigration policies and attitudes" (Hashemi et al., 2019, p. 46), which would also lead to different experiences of discrimination and levels of acculturation (Hashemi et al., 2019).

Research on refugees and well-being at work is even more limited and at an infant stage. Nonetheless, we do know that, to a greater extent than other migrants, refugees are often subjected to additional challenges, such as discrimination due to their ethnic identity and social status. Additionally, refugees find it more difficult to obtain work (Jackson & Bauder, 2014); as such, they may strive to maintain employment even when they are not treated with respect (Newman et al., 2018). Nevertheless, existing studies on refugees illustrate a similar pattern as for other migrants, namely, refugees display higher levels of commitment and lower turnover intentions if working in an environment that values diversity and fosters inclusion. Moreover, these effects seem to be particularly pronounced for refugees coming from more collectivistic cultures (such as those in the Middle East and Central Asia; Newman et al., 2018); a reason for this lies in the fact that individuals from collectivistic cultures have strong in-group identities, seek mutual protection from one another (Hennekam & Tahssain-Gay, 2015; Herrera et al., 2011; Muchiri, 2011), and are aware of the importance of acting altruistically to others members of the group (Nadeem, 2013; Tlaiss & Kauser, 2011; Triandis, 2001). Individuals from collectivistic cultures are also likely to place greater value on building social ties with others and setting group goals (Randall, 1993); these actions make them more committed toward their employer (Meyer et al., 2012). In other words, the extent to which workers—especially cultural minorities *including migrants*—are accepted and included rather than rejected and excluded in their workplace is crucial for their attitudes and behaviors toward the organization (McKay et al., 2007; Hicks-Clarke & Iles, 2000; Hopkins et al., 2001), as well as for their personal well-being (Leary & Downs, 1995).

A diverse and inclusive climate, where employees feel supported, equitably treated, encouraged, and empowered to contribute to the effectiveness of the work group, makes employees perceive that their organization cares and looks after their well-being (McKay & Avery, 2015). The fulfillment of the psychological contract on the part of the employer will make the employees reciprocate such care and concern by engaging in behaviors that benefit the whole organization, including higher organizational commitment and lower turnover intentions (Buttner et al., 2010; Hopkins et al., 2001; Lo & Aryee, 2003; Tekleab et al., 2005).

MNE Challenges in Supporting Migrant Inclusion and Workforce Well-being

The extant literature on diversity climate and climate for inclusion reviewed above suggests that there is value in the workforce perceiving positive diversity and inclusion climates, especially for minorities, notwithstanding the gaps resulting from our limited knowledge around migrant experiences. Nevertheless, this body of research suggests that MNEs face a series of significant multilevel significant challenges to achieving migrant inclusion and wider workforce well-being through diversity climates, as these practices need to be implemented and managed against the background of population diversification, politicization of migration, and superdiversity of migrants.

The First Challenge: Diversification of the Workforce and Breadth of MNE Operations

The first challenge to migrant inclusion and wider workforce well-being is found at the national societal or macro level. MNEs operate across national boundaries. North America, Europe, and, to a lesser extent, other developed economies around the globe remain the top locations for MNE headquarters and their subsidiaries (Cheung, 2022). MNE management is inherently more complex than many other organizations, at least in part, owing to the cultural and institutional complexity (Sasikala & Sankaranarayanan, 2022) of the organization's operations. Specifically, diversity is increasing within those geographical areas mentioned above with migrants arriving from all four corners of the world. These regions are also the recipients of the majority of economic migrants (Edmond, 2020) and the majority of asylum seekers (UNHCR, 2021). Additionally, MNEs are venturing more and more into emerging markets, increasing the number of countries within which they operate, and making the diversity picture even more complex (Cheung, 2022).

Refugees remain largely, although not exclusively, in emerging economies. The top five countries for refugee resettlement are Turkey, Columbia, Uganda, Pakistan, and Germany (UNHCR, 2021). Refugee workforce integration is thus a grand challenge even for MNEs that consider it an important humanistic mission and not simply a route to filling low-cost labor shortages (Lee et al., 2020b; Vaara et al., 2021). Multilevel and multidimensional challenges vary across regions of MNE operation including, among others, limitations or restrictions on the rights to work (Meyer et al., 2020), a mismatch between refugees' skills and the receiving countries' labor needs, lack of formal recognition of qualifications, and employer biases, which together create a canvas ceiling (Szkudlarek et al., 2022). These challenges inevitably limit refugees' employment opportunities and, although further research is needed, possibly compromise individual well-being even for those refugees who find employment in an MNE with a positive diversity climate.

Solutions: A global strategic approach to integrating refugees is not feasible; localized customized and collaborative solutions (Szkudlarek et al., 2022) and diversity management practices (Georgiadou et al., 2019a) are needed. Such solutions require state, society, and multinational enterprises to collaborate on diversity and inclusion initiatives (Ghauri, 2022). As discussed by Szkudlarek et al. (2022), IKEA is a leading example, committed to supporting 2500 refugees globally by 2023 with a locally customized program of job training and language skills, after which refugees are free to apply for a job with IKEA or another organization. As part of locally customized—but still global—strategies, MNEs can help refugees become employees, diversify supply chains, or offer direct interventions to support refugees (Wainwright, 2017), among many other initiatives. Those firms that are already engaging in such collaborations can also raise awareness more generally both inside (Szkudlarek, 2019) and outside the organization. The Tent Partnership for Refugees (2022)—which now counts 180 organizations from around the supporters—is one such global example; however, a variety of initiatives are needed, given overall refugee numbers. It is no longer enough for MNEs to act alone to tackle this challenge. With a significant investment of time and energy, sensitively and strategically focused, diversity climates may take root and/or broaden to integrate refugees and create flourishing inclusive societies.

The Second Challenge: The Politicization of Migration and the Organizational Field

The second challenge to the inclusion of migrants and wider well-being that MNEs face is positioned at the meso or industry level. Some sectors like financial services, technology and communications, and construction are dominated by MNEs (Barklie, 2021). UNCTAD (2020) considers mining to be the most international industry in the world, contributing nearly 7% of world GDP. As discussed by Sasikala and Sankaranarayanan (2022), mining is dominated by corporations headquartered in the developed world, while most of the industry's operations are located in emerging markets and make a significant (negative) impact on the local environment, often stemming from colonial and patriarchal pasts (Mackenzie, 2019; Hoffman, 2001). Attempts to address the diversity and inclusion agenda in this industry start from a position of extreme privilege with little evidence of progress. For example, the percentage of women executives in the mining sector has largely remained static over time (MacDougall et al., 2020) and the median wage gap is still one of the largest of any industry (McKinsey & Co., 2021). If women executives are excluded from this industry, that is, the diversity climate is weak, there are unlikely to be real opportunities for others *especially migrants (of any background)* to be included, let alone feel included.

Depending on the organizational field, that is, the specific macro-level context for diversity and inclusion for a particular operation, global mining companies adopt one of four stances in that field: Pro-active, Accommodative, Defensive, Reactive (Sasikala & Sankaranarayanan, 2022). The operations that are more likely to adopt a pro-active approach are based in countries which also pro-actively support diversity and inclusion; these are the national and societal contexts where migrants are more likely to be welcomed. In other countries, instead, the approach is more muted or merely reactive. Other MNE-dominated industries—for example, construction, IT, and finance—may start from a less extreme position of privilege, but where disparities and exclusion are still predominant. The construction industry remains largely male-dominated (e.g., Gerber, 2022; Uribes, 2021) with echoes of a colonial past (Austin et al., 2016). Technology may be seen as a relatively new sector, and so less subject to such deeply rooted historical forces; nevertheless, it has a long-standing problem with respect to equal opportunities for women (e.g., PwC, 2017). The financial services sector has made some progress on gender and race, but significant challenges remain (e.g., Ellingrud et al., 2021); socio-economic class also continues to impact recruitment processes (Tobias Neely,

2018). Unless the organizational field (e.g., country-specific mining, technology, or finance sectors) promotes pro-activity, developing a positive diversity climate may not be possible, and even in pro-active organizational fields, fostering a positive climate for inclusion might be at the early stages of development (Sasikala & Sankaranarayanan, 2022). Therefore migrants, *even more than other minority employees*, are likely not to feel included (Gonzalez & Denisi, 2009) and their well-being compromised.

Solutions: Most MNEs find themselves in organizational fields that are not pro-active (Sasikala & Sankaranarayanan, 2022); nevertheless, their leaders will likely understand the value of diversity to organizational performance (Ely & Thomas, 2020; Gulati, 2022). To progress, they need to consider initiatives beyond the organization itself to contribute to the development of a pro-active organizational field. Sasikala and Sankaranarayanan (2022) recommend three actions. First, they advise firms to establish non-discrimination practices, such as merit-based decision-making, co-created with external stakeholders including government. Next, resources and resource development practices, such as targeted training for specific groups, are needed and are best initiated with industry bodies or other similar external organizations. Lastly, accountability practices are required. Diversity plans and grievance systems are two examples. Enforcement by industry bodies or equivalents must be secured through prior collaboration. Nevertheless, such solutions are not easy or quick to develop. MNEs with operations in organizational fields that are not pro-active are likely to be limited in these ways to establishing a diversity climate, rather than a climate for inclusion, in such regions, and thus to still face internal challenges to migrant inclusion and well-being.

The Third Challenge: Superdiversity of Migrants and Intersectionality

The third challenge to migrant inclusion and wider workforce well-being sits at the micro level or level of the individual employee. While the key characteristics of diversity have been well-established (Bellotti et al., 2022; Georgiadou et al., 2019b; Guillaume et al., 2013; Williams & O'Reilly, 1998), less attention has been paid to the intersectionality of these various characteristics (Kothari et al., 2022). Crenshaw's work on intersectionality (Crenshaw, 1989) highlighted the challenges of being both female and Black, both of which are—the often negatively perceived—minority valences of the gender and racio-ethnicity categories. Neither researchers nor practitioners have really grappled successfully with these double (or more) intersections; characteristics are often still considered separately (Kothari et al., 2022).

Applying an intersectionality lens to the challenge of migrant integration highlights the superdiversity of migrants relative to other minorities (Kothari et al., 2022; Vertovec, 2007). For example, a White woman in a predominantly White society faces potential discrimination on the basis of gender. A migrant Black woman living in a predominantly White area faces potential discrimination, not only based on gender and racio-ethnicity but also based on the basis of migrant status, which may be compounded by language, citizenship, and other differences (Kothari et al., 2022). Therefore, there are multiple potentially unrecognized obstacles for such migrant employees or potential employees (Aman et al., 2021; Elo et al., 2021). Even highly skilled migrants face bottlenecks in entering the workforce (Kothari et al., 2022) and developing successful careers (Jackson & Bauder, 2014; Newman et al., 2018). It seems that, where international migrant flows are concerned, we are only starting to appreciate the different and varied forms of capital being transferred (Stahl et al., 2016).

Solutions: Implementing diversity and inclusion in a way that accommodates migrants' superdiversity requires a remit to work directly with employee groups and charitable/governmental organizations (Kothari et al., 2022). Building a diversity climate and a climate for inclusion means supporting not only prospective migrant candidates, including *refugees,* but also existing privileged employees and minorities. The challenge of doing so should not be underestimated given that each group will have different needs.

The superdiversity richness of the migrant workforce needs to be carefully explored, and then creativity, sensitively and sustainably employed (Kothari et al., 2022). A strengths-based approach to recruitment, for example, may be beneficial in increasing the diversity of the workforce (Ott et al., 2022). SAP successfully employs such an approach with neurodivergent candidates (Austin & Pisano, 2017). Allowing migrants, including *refugees*, to showcase talents may, therefore, offer a more equitable recruitment playing field and a more inclusive management of the wider workforce. Likewise, considering carefully who holds global virtual team leader roles (Zander et al., 2012) will enable an inclusive approach to blending (Butler et al., 2012). Well-considered locally customized and well-supported initiatives, if grounded in evidence, will enable diversity climates to be created with time and determination and lead to wider workforce well-being.

Conclusion

In this chapter, we have highlighted the importance of diversity climates to migrant well-being as well as the wider well-being of MNCs (and other organizations which operate internationally). We highlighted three significant challenges, one each at the macro, meso, and micro levels, to the successful embedding of a climate for inclusion which enables both migrants and majority settled workforces to flourish: (1) diversification of migration and breadth of MNC operations, (2) politicization of migration and the organizational field, and (3) intersectionality and the superdiversity of migrants. We shared some possible solutions to the challenges already in practice by a limited number of organizations or proposed by scholars and other experts.

Diversity without inclusion is an illusion (Ott et al., 2022). Futureproofing MNEs, therefore, needs to include strengthened workforce management with the focus shifting from *human resources* to *human beings* (Korn Ferry, 2022) to enable inclusive well-being through climates of diversity. Although the challenges to achieving such climates are significant, especially as MNEs become more diverse by employing migrants and attempting to recruit refugees, MNEs are important agents of change (Kwok & Tadesse, 2006) to stimulate cultural shifts to effect social change (Raskovic, 2021) toward more inclusive and well workforces and societies.

References

Abbott, A. (2016). The mental-health crisis among migrants. *Nature, 538*, 158–160. https://doi.org/10.1038/538158a

Abu-Rayya, H. M., & Abu-Rayya, M. H. (2009). Acculturation, religious identity, and psychological well-being among Palestinians in Israel. *International Journal of Intercultural Relations, 33*(4), 325–331. https://doi.org/10.1016/j.ijintrel.2009.05.006

Aman, R., Ahokangas, P., Elo, M., & Zhang, X. (2021). Migrant women entrepreneurship and the entrepreneurial ecosystem. In D. G. Pickernell, M. Battisti, Z. Dann, & C. Ekinsmyth (Eds.), *Disadvantaged entrepreneurship and the entrepreneurial ecosystem* (pp. 87–119). Emerald Group Publishing.

Amer, M. M., & Hovey, J. D. (2007). Socio-demographic differences in acculturation and mental health for a sample of 2nd generation/early immigrant Arab Americans. *Journal of Immigrant and Minority Health, 9*(4), 335. https://doi.org/10.1007/s10903-007-9045-y

Ang, S., Van Dyne, L., Koh, C., Ng, K. Y., Templar, K. J., Tay, C., & Chandrasekar, N. A. (2007). Cultural intelligence: Its measurement and effects on cultural judgement and decision making, cultural adaptation and task performance. *Management and Organization Review, 3*(3), 335–371. https://doi.org/10.1111/j.1740-8784.2007.00082.x

Austin, G., Frankema, E., & Jerven, M. (2016). Patterns of manufacturing growth in sub-Saharan Africa: From colonization to the present. In K. O'Rourke & J. G. Williamson (Eds.), *The spread of modern manufacturing to the periphery, 1870 to the present* (pp. 345–373). Oxford University Press.

Austin, R. D., & Pisano, G. P. (2017). Neurodiversity as a competitive advantage. *Harvard Business Review, 95*(3), 96–103.

Bakker, A. B., & Demerouti, E. (2008). Towards a model of work engagement. *Career Development International, 13*, 209–223. https://doi.org/10.1108/13620430810870476

Barklie, G. (2021, January 28). Where are the global hotspots for MNC subsidiaries? *Insights*. Retrieved October 25, 2022, from https://www.investmentmonitor.ai/uncategorized/where-are-the-global-hotspots-for-mnc-subsidiaries

Barnett, S. M., & Ceci, S. J. (2002). When and where do we apply what we learn? A taxonomy for far transfer. *Psychological Bulletin, 128*(4), 612–637. https://doi.org/10.1037/0033-2909.128.4.612

Bassett-Jones, N. (2005). The paradox of diversity management: Creativity and innovation. *Creativity and Innovation Management, 14*(2), 169–175. https://doi.org/10.1111/j.1467-8691.00337.x

Bellotti, L., Zaniboni, S., Balducci, C., Menghini, L., Cadiz, D. M., & Toderi, S. (2022). Age diversity climate affecting individual-level work-related outcomes. *International Journal of Environmental Research and Public Health, 19*(5), 30–41. https://doi.org/10.3390/ijerph19053041

Benet-Martínez, V., & Haritatos, J. (2005). Bicultural identity integration (BII): Components and psychosocial antecedents. *Journal of Personality, 73*(4), 1015–1050. https://doi.org/10.1111/j.1467-6494.2005.00337.x

Berry, J. W., & Sabatier, C. (2011). Variations in the assessment of acculturation attitudes: Their relationships with psychological wellbeing. *International Journal of Intercultural Relations, 35*(5), 658–669. https://doi.org/10.1016/j.ijintrel.2011.02.002

Blazey, A., Lelong, M., & Giannini, F. (2022). The equitable and sustainable well-being framework in Italy: An action plan for its use in policy and budget decision making. *OECD Working Papers on Public Governance, 56*, 1–34. https://doi.org/10.1787/4f48c504-en

Broom, D. (2020, October 9). *5 things to know about mental health across the world*. World *Economic Forum*. Retrieved October 25, 2022, from https://www.weforum.org/agenda/2020/10/mental-health-day-covid19-coronavirus-global/

Butler, C. L., Zander, L., Mockaitis, A. I., & Sutton, C. (2012). The global leader as boundary spanner, bridge maker and blender. *Industrial Organizational Psychologist: Perspectives on Science and Practice, 5*(2), 246–243. https://doi.org/10.1111/j.17549434.2012.01439.x

Buttner, E. H., & Lowe, K. B. (2017). Addressing internal stakeholders' concerns: The interactive effect of perceived pay equity and diversity climate on turnover intentions. *Journal of Business Ethics, 143*, 621–633. https://doi.org/10.1007/s10551-015-2795-x

Buttner, E. H., Lowe, K. B., & Billings-Harris, L. (2010). Diversity climate impact on employee of color outcomes: Does justice matter? *Career Development International, 15*(3), 239–258. https://doi.org/10.1108/13620431011053721

Canadian Index of Wellbeing. (2022). *About the Canadian Index of Wellbeing.* Retrieved January 27, 2023, from https://uwaterloo.ca/canadian-index-wellbeing/about-canadian-index-wellbeing/history

Castles, S., & Miller, M. J. (2009). *The age of migration: International population movements in the modern world* (4th ed.). Palgrave Macmillan.

Chartered Institute of Personnel and Development. (2007). *Absence management survey.* Retrieved October 25, 2022, from https://www.cipd.co.uk/knowledge/fundamentals/relations/absence/absence-management-surveys#gref

Chen, S. X., Benet-Martinez, V., & Bond, M. (2008). Bicultural identity, bilingualism, and psychological adjustment in multicultural societies: Immigration-based and globalization-based acculturation. *Journal of Personality, 76*(4), 803–838. https://doi.org/10.1111/j.1467-6494.2008.00505.x

Cheung, B. (2022). What countries are most multinational corporations based in? *Investopedia.* Retrieved October 25, 2022, from https://www.investopedia.com/ask/answers/021715/why-are-most-multinational-corporations-either-us-europe-or-japan.asp

Chartered Institute of Personnel and Development/SimplyHealth. (2016). *Absence management survey.* Retrieved October 25, 2022, from https://www.cipd.co.uk/knowledge/fundamentals/relations/absence/absence-management-surveys#gref

Clark, R., Anderson, N. B., Clark, V. R., & Williams, D. R. (1999). Racism as a stressor for African Americans: A biopsychosocial model. *American Psychologist, 54*(10), 805–816.

COVID-19 Mental Disorders Collaborators. (2021). Global prevalence and burden of depressive and anxiety disorders in 204 countries and territories in 2020 due to the COVID-19 pandemic. *Lancet, 398*, 1700–1712. https://doi.org/10.1016/S0140-6736(21)02143-7

Cox, T. H. (1994). *Cultural diversity in organizations: Theory, research, & practice.* Berrett-Koehler.

Crenshaw, K. (1989). Demarginalizing the intersection of race and sex: A black feminist critique of antidiscrimination doctrine, feminist theory and antiracist politics. *University of Chicago Legal Forum, 1989*(1), 139–167.

D'Netto, B., Shen, J., Chelliah, J., & Monga, M. (2014). Human resource diversity management practices in the Australian manufacturing sector. *International Journal of Human Resource Management, 25*(9), 1243–1266. https://doi.org/10.1080/09585192.2013.826714

Edmond, C. (2020). Global migration by the numbers: Who migrates, where they go, and why. *World Economic Forum*. Retrieved October 25, 2022, from https://www.weforum.org/agenda/2020/01/iom-global-migration-report-international-migrants-2020/#:~:text=There%20are%20an%20estimated%20272,conflict%2C%20violence%20and%20climate%20change.

Ellingrud, K., Krivkovich, A., Nadeau, M-C., & Zucker, J. (2021, October 21). *Closing the gender and race gaps in north American financial services*. McKinsey & Company. Retrieved October 25, 2022, from https://www.mckinsey.com/industries/financial-services/our-insights/closing-the-gender-and-race-gaps-in-north-american-financial-services

Elo, M., Taube, F. A., & Servais, P. (2021). Who is doing "transnational diaspora entrepreneurship"? Understanding formal identify & status. *Journal of World Business, 57*(1), 101240. https://doi.org/10.1016/j.jwb.2021.101240

Ely, R. J., & Thomas, D. A. (2020). Getting serious about diversity: Enough already with the business case. *Harvard Business Review, 98*(6), 68–77.

Engler, P., MacDonald, M., Piazza, R., & Sher, G. (2020). Migration to advanced economies can raise growth. *IMFBlog*. Retrieved October 25, 2022, from https://www.imf.org/en/Blogs/Articles/2020/06/19/blog-weo-chapter4-migration-to-advanced-economies-can-raise-growth

Esipova, N., Ray, J., & Pugliese, A. (2020). World grows less accepting of migrants. *Gallup News*. Retrieved October 25, 2022, from https://news.gallup.com/poll/320678/world-grows-less-accepting-migrants.aspx

Findler, L., Wind, L., & Mor Barak, M. E. (2007). The challenge of workforce management in a global society: Modeling the relationship between diversity, inclusion, organizational culture, and employee well-being, job satisfaction and organizational commitment. *Administration in Social Work, 31*(3), 63–94. https://doi.org/10.1300/J147v31n03_05

Gelfand, M. J., Nishii, L. H., Raver, J., & Schneider, B. (2005). Discrimination in organizations: An organizational level systems perspective. In R. Dipboye & A. Colella (Eds.), *Discrimination at work: The psychological and organizational bases* (pp. 89–116). Taylor & Francis Group.

Georgiadou, A., Gonzalez-Perez, M. A., & Olivas-Lujan, M. R. (2019a). *Diversity with diversity management: Country-based perspectives*. Emerald Group Publishing Limited.

Georgiadou, A., Gonzalez-Perez, M. A., & Olivas-Lujan, M. R. (2019b). *Diversity with diversity management: Types of diversity in organizations*. Emerald Group Publishing Limited.

Gerber, P. (2022, March 7). Women in construction: Smashing down the concrete walls that keep them out. *Lens*. Monash University. Retrieved October 25, 2022, from https://lens.monash.edu/@politics-society/2022/03/07/1384504/women-in-construction-smashing-down-the-concrete-walls-that-keep-them-out

Ghauri, P. N. (2022). The role of multinational enterprises in achieving sustainable development goals. *AIB Insights, 22*(1), 1–5. https://doi.org/10.46697/001c.31077

Goetzel, R. Z., Ozminkowaksi, R. J., Sederer, L. I., & Mark, T. L. (2002). The business case for quality mental health services: Why employers should care about the mental health and wellbeing of their employees. *Journal of Occupational & Environmental Medicine, 44*(4), 320–330.

Gonzalez, J. A., & DeNisi, A. S. (2009). Cross-level effects of demography and diversity climate on organizational attachment and firm effectiveness. *Journal of Organizational Behavior, 30*(1), 21–40. https://doi.org/10.1002/job.498

Greenglass, E., Fiskenbaum, L., & Burke, R. J. (1996). Components of social support, buffering effects and burnout: Implications for psychological functioning. *Anxiety, Stress and Coping, 9*(3), 185–197. https://doi.org/10.1080/10615809608249401

Guillaume, Y. R. F., Dawson, J. F., Priola, V., Sacramento, C. A., Woods, S. A., Higson, H. E., Budhwar, P. S., & West, M. A. (2014). Managing diversity in organizations: An integrative model and agenda for future research. *European Journal of Work and Organizational Psychology, 23*(5), 783–802. https://doi.org/10.1080/1359432X.2013.805485

Guillaume, Y. R. F., Dawson, J. F., Woods, S. A., Sacramento, C. A., & West, M. A. (2013). Getting diversity at work to work: What we know and what we still don't know. *Journal of Occupational and Organizational Psychology, 86*(2), 123–141. https://doi.org/10.1111/joop.12009

Gulati, R. (2022). *Deep purpose: The heart and soul of high-performance companies.* Harper Business/HarperCollins Publishers.

Haile, G. A. (2012). Unhappy working with men? Workplace gender diversity and job-related well-being in Britain. *Labour Economics, 19*(3), 329–350. https://doi.org/10.1016/j.labeco.2012.02.002

Hajro, A., Gibson, C., & Pudelko, M. (2017). Knowledge exchange processes in multicultural teams: Linking organizational diversity climates to teams' effectiveness. *The Academy of Management Journal, 60*(1), 345–372. https://doi.org/10.5465/amj.2014.0442

Hashemi, N., Marzban, M., Sebar, B., & Harris, N. (2019). Acculturation and psychological well-being among middle eastern migrants in Australia: The mediating role of social support and perceived discrimination. *International Journal of Intercultural Relations, 72*, 45–60. https://doi.org/10.1016/j.ijintrel.2019.07.002

Hennekam, S., & Tahssain-Gay, L. (2015). Changing attitudes towards diversity: The Netherlands and Morocco compared. *Management Decision, 53*(9), 2135–2155. https://doi.org/10.1108/MD-04-2015-0119

Herrera, R., Duncan, P. A., Green, M., Ree, M., & Skaggs, S. L. (2011). The relationship between attitudes toward diversity management in the Southwest USA and the GLOBE study cultural preferences. *The International Journal of Human Resource Management, 22*(12), 2629–2646. https://doi.org/10.1080/09585192.2011.588037

Hicks-Clarke, D., & Iles, P. (2000). Climate for diversity and its effects on career and organizational attitudes and perceptions. *Personnel Review, 29*(3), 324–345. https://doi.org/10.1108/00483480010324689

Hinds, P. J., Patterson, M., & Pfeffer, J. (2001). Bothered by abstraction: The effect of expertise on knowledge transfer and subsequent novice performance. *Journal of Applied Psychology, 86*(6), 1232–1243. https://doi.org/10.1037/0021-9010.86.6.1232

Hofhuis, J., Van der Zee, K. I., & Otten, S. (2012). Social identity patterns in culturally diverse organizations: The role of diversity climate. *Journal of Applied Social Psychology, 42*(4), 964–989. https://doi.org/10.1111/j.1559-1816.2011.00848.x

Hoffman, J. (2001). Patriarchy and Anti-Statist Theory. In *Gender and Sovereignty*. London: Palgrave Macmillan. https://doi.org/10.1057/9780230288188_8

Holmes, O., Jiang, K., Avery, D. R., McKay, P. F., Oh, I., & Tillman, C. J. (2021). A meta-analysis integrating 25 years of diversity climate research. *Journal of Management, 47*(6), 1357–1382. https://doi.org/10.1177/0149206320934547

Hopkins, W. E., Hopkins, S. A., & Mallette, P. (2001). Diversity and managerial value commitment: A test of some proposed relationships. *Journal of Managerial Issues, 13*(3), 288–306.

House, R. J., Hanges, P. J., Javidan, M., Dorfman, P. W., & Gupta, V. (2004). *Culture, leadership, and organizations*. SAGE Publications.

International Organization for Migration. (2019). Glossary on Migration. *International Migration Law #34*. Retrieved October 25, 2022, from https://www.weforum.org/agenda/2020/01/iom-global-migration-report-international-migrants-2020/#:~:text=There%20are%20an%20estimated%20272,conflict%2C%20violence%20and%20climate%20change

International Organization for Migration (IOM). (2020). *UN world migration report 2020*. Retrieved September 06, 2022, from https://publications.iom.int/system/files/pdf/wmr_2020.pdf

Jackson, S., & Bauder, H. (2014). Neither temporary, nor permanent: The precarious employment experience of refugee claimants in Canada. *Journal of Refugee Studies, 27*(3), 360–381. https://doi.org/10.1093/jrs/fet048

Jayne, M. E. A., & Dipboye, R. L. (2004). Leveraging diversity to improve business performance: Research findings and recommendations for organizations. *Human Resource Management, 43*(4), 409–424. https://doi.org/10.1002/hrm.20033

Jolly, P. M., & Self, T. T. (2020). Psychological diversity climate, organizational embeddedness, and turnover intentions: A conservation of resources perspective. *Cornell Hospitality Quarterly, 61*(4), 416–431. https://doi.org/10.1177/1938965519899935

Konrad, A. M., & Linnehan, F. (1995). Formalized HRM structures: Coordinating equal employment opportunity or concealing organizational practices? *Academy of Management Journal, 38*, 787–820. https://doi.org/10.2307/256746

Korn Ferry. (2022). What is radically human transformation, and how can you get started? *Korn Ferry*. Retrieved October 25, 2022, from https://www.kornferry.

com/insights/this-week-in-leadership/what-is-radically-human-transformation-and-how-can-you-get-started

Kothari, T. (2021). Can the Biden Administration's immigration policy reignite America's innovation engine? *The Visible Magazine*. Retrieved October 25, 2022, from https://visiblemagazine.com/bidenadministrations-immigration-policy-reignite-americas-innovation-engine/

Kothari, T., Elo, M., & Wiese, N. (2022). Born as a citizen and reborn as an alien: Migrant superdiversity in global business. *AIB Insights, 22*(3), 1–6. https://doi.org/10.46697/001c.35243

Kossek, E. E., & Zonia, S. C. (1993). Assessing diversity climate: A field study of reactions to employer efforts to promote diversity. *Journal of Organizational Behavior, 14*(1), 61–81. https://doi.org/10.1002/job.4030140107

Kowalski, T. H. P., & Loretto, W. (2017). Well-being and HRM in the changing workplace. *The International Journal of Human Resource Management, 28*(16), 2229–2255. https://doi.org/10.1080/09585192.2017.1345205

Kramer, R. M. (2018). Ingroup–outgroup trust: Barriers, benefits, and bridges. In E. M. Uslaner (Ed.), *The Oxford handbook of social and political trust* (pp. 95–116). Oxford University Press.

Kwok, C. C. Y., & Tadesse, S. (2006). The MNC as an agent of change of host-country institutions: FDI and corruption. *Journal of International Business Studies, 37*(6), 767–785. https://doi.org/10.1057/palgrave.jibs.8400228

Lafromboise, T., Coleman, H. L. K., & Gerton, J. (1993). Psychological impact of biculturalism: Evidence and theory. *Psychological Bulletin, 114*(3), 395–412. https://doi.org/10.1037/0033-2909.114.3.395

Leary, M. R., & Downs, D. L. (1995). Interpersonal functions of the self-esteem motive: The self-esteem system as a sociometer. In M. R. Leary & D. L. Downs (Eds.), *Efficacy, agency, and self-esteem* (pp. 123–144). Plenum Press.

Lee, H. J., Yoshikawa, K., & Harzing, A. W. (2022). Cultures and institutions: Dispositional and contextual explanations for country-of-origin effects in MNC 'ethnocentric' staffing practices. *Organization Studies, 43*(4), 497–519. https://doi.org/10.1177/01708406211006247

Lee, J., Kim, S., & Kim, Y. (2020a). Diversity climate on turnover intentions: A sequential mediating effect of personal diversity value and affective commitment. *Personnel Review, 50*(5), 1397–1408. https://doi.org/10.1108/PR-11-2019-0636

Lee, E. S., Szkudlarek, B., Nguyen, D. C., & Nardon, L. (2020b). Unveiling the canvas ceiling: A multidisciplinary literature review of refugee employment and workforce integration. *International Journal of Management Reviews, 22*(2), 193–216. https://doi.org/10.1111/ijmr.12222

Leslie, L. M., & Flynn, E. (2022). Diversity ideologies, beliefs, and climates: A review, integration, and set of recommendations. *Journal of Management, 1-28*, 014920632210862. https://doi.org/10.1177/01492063221086238

Li, Y., Perera, S., Kulik, C. T., & Metz, I. (2019). Inclusion climate: A multilevel investigation of its antecedents and consequences. *Human Resource Management, 58*(4), 353–369. https://doi.org/10.1002/hrm.21956

Liddell, B. J., Nickerson, A., Sartor, L., Ivancic, L., & Bryant, R. A. (2016). The generational gap: Mental disorder prevalence and disability amongst first and second generation immigrants in Australia. *Journal of Psychiatric Research, 83*, 103–111. https://doi.org/10.1016/j.jpsychires.2016.08.011

Lo, S., & Aryee, S. (2003). Psychological contract breach in a Chinese context: An integrative approach. *Journal of Management Studies, 40*(4), 1005–1020. https://doi.org/10.1111/1467-6486.00368

McCain, K. & Sen, N. (2021, September 16). Is there a doctor in the boardroom? 6 health chiefs explain why employee wellbeing matters more than ever. *World Economic Forum*. Retrieved October 25, 2022, from https://www.weforum.org/agenda/2021/09/is-there-a-doctor-in-the-boardroom-here-s-how-6-organizations-are-prioritizing-employee-wellbeing/

MacDougall, A., Valley, J. M., & Jeffrey, J. (2020, October 5). *Diversity disclosure practices report – Mining industry*. Osler, Hoskin & Harcourt LLP. Retsrieved October 25, 2022, from https://www.osler.com/en/resources/governance/2020/report-2020-diversity-disclosure-practices-diversity-and-leadership-at-canadian-public-companies

Mackenzie, W., 2019. Why the Mining Industry Needs More Women. *Forbes*. May 24, 2019. Available at: https://www.forbes.com/sites/woodmackenzie/2019/05/24/why-the-mining-industry-needs-more-women/?sh=1229b7f0585c

Marmot, M. (2010). *Fair society, healthy lives: The marmot review. Strategic review of health inequalities in England post 2010*. The Marmot Review.

McKay, P. F., Avery, D. R., & Morris, M. A. (2009). A tale of two climates: Diversity climate from subordinates' and managers' perspectives and their role in store unit sales performance. *Personnel Psychology, 62*(4), 767–791. https://doi.org/10.1111/j.1744-6570.2009.01157.x

McKay, P. F., & Avery, D. R. (2015). Diversity climate in organizations: Current wisdom and domains of uncertainty. *Research in Personnel and Human Resources Management, 33*, 191–233. https://doi.org/10.1108/S0742-730120150000033008

McKay, P. F., Avery, D. R., & Morris, M. A. (2008). Mean racial-ethnic differences in employee sales performance: The moderating role of diversity climate. *Personnel Psychology, 61*(2), 349–374. https://doi.org/10.1111/j.1744-6570.2008.00116.x

McKay, P. F., Avery, D. R., Tonidandel, S., Morris, M. A., Hernandez, M., & Hebl, M. R. (2007). Racial differences in employee retention: Are diversity climate perceptions the key? *Personnel Psychology, 60*(1), 35–62. https://doi.org/10.1111/j.1744-6570.2007.00064.x

McKinsey & Co. (2020, June 23). Understanding organizational barriers to a more inclusive workplace. *McKinsey & Co*. Retrieved January 28, 2023, from https://

www.mckinsey.com/capabilities/people-and-organizational-performance/our-insights/understanding-organizational-barriers-to-a-more-inclusive-workplace

McKinsey & Co. (2021, September 13). Why women are leaving the mining industry and what mining companies can do about it. *McKinsey & Co*. Retrieved October 25, 2022, from https://www.mckinsey.com/industries/metals-and-mining/our-insights/why-women-are-leaving-the-mining-industry-and-what-mining-companies-can-do-about-it

Meyer, J. P., Stanley, D. J., Jackson, T. A., McInnis, K. J., Maltin, E. R., & Sheppard, L. (2012). Affective, normative, and continuance commitment levels across cultures: A meta-analysis. *Journal of Vocational Behavior, 80*(2), 225–245. https://doi.org/10.1016/j.jvb.2011.09.005

Meyer, K. E., Li, C., & Schotter, A. P. J. (2020). Managing the MNE subsidiary: Advancing a multi-level and dynamic research agenda. *Journal of International Business Studies, 51*, 538–576. https://doi.org/10.1057/s41267-020-00318-w

Michie, S., & Williams, S. (2003). Reducing work related psychological ill health and sickness absence: A systematic literature review. *Occupational and Environmental Medicine, 60*(1), 3–9. https://doi.org/10.1136/oem.60.1.3

Moon, K. K., & Christensen, R. K. (2020). Realizing the performance benefits of workforce diversity in the U.S. Federal Government: The moderating role of diversity climate. *Public Personnel Management, 49*(1), 141–165. https://doi.org/10.1177/0091026019848845

Mor Barak, M. E. (2017). *Managing diversity: Toward a globally inclusive workplace* (4th ed.). SAGE Publications.

Mor Barak, M. E. (2019). Erecting walls versus tearing them down: Inclusion and the (false) paradox of diversity in times of economic upheaval. *European Management Review, 16*(4), 937–955. https://doi.org/10.1111/emre.12302

Mor Barak, M. E., & Levin, A. (2002). Outside of the corporate mainstream and excluded from the work community: A study of diversity, job satisfaction and well-being. *Community, Work and Family, 5*(2), 133–157. https://doi.org/10.1080/13668800220146346

Mor Barak, M. E., Cherin, D. A., & Berkman, S. (1998). Organizational and personal dimensions in diversity climate: Ethnic and gender differences in employee perceptions. *Journal of Applied Behavioral Science, 34*(1), 82–104. https://doi.org/10.1177/0021886398341006

Moztarzadeh, A., & O'Rourke, N. (2015). Psychological and sociocultural adaptation: Acculturation, depressive symptoms, and life satisfaction among older Iranian immigrants in Canada. *Clinical Gerontologist, 38*(2), 114–130. https://doi.org/10.1080/07317115.2014.990601

Muchiri, M. K. (2011). Leadership in context: A review and research agenda for sub-Saharan Africa. *Journal of Occupational and Organizational Psychology, 84*(3), 440–452. https://doi.org/10.1111/j.2044-8325.2011.02018.x

Nadeem, S. (2013). Manager-subordinate trust relationships in Pakistan. In P. Cardona & M. Morley (Eds.), *Manger-subordinate trust: A global perspective* (pp. 234–253). Routledge.

Newman, A., Herman, H. M., Schwarz, G., & Nielsen, I. (2018). The effects of employees' creative self-efficacy on innovative behavior: The role of entrepreneurial leadership. *Journal of Business Research, 89*, 1–9. https://doi.org/10.1016/j.jbusres.2018.04.001

Nishii, L. H. (2013). The benefits of climate for inclusion for gender-diverse groups. *Academy of Management Journal, 56*(6), 1754–1774. https://doi.org/10.5465/amj.2009.0823

OECD. (2020). *How's life? 2020: Measuring well-being*. OECD Publishing. https://doi.org/10.1787/9870c393-en

Ogbonna, E., & Harris, L. C. (2006). The dynamics of employee relationships in an ethnically diverse workforce. *Human Relations, 59*(3), 379–407. https://doi.org/10.1177/0018726706064181

OHCHR (2012). *Promoting and protecting minority rights: A guide for advocates*. Retrieved January 28, 2023, from https://www.ohchr.org/sites/default/files/Documents/Publications/HR-PUB-12-07_en.pdf

Ott, D. L., Russo, E., & Moeller, M. (2022). Neurodiversity, equity, and inclusion in MNCs. *AIB Insights, 22*(3), 1–5. https://doi.org/10.46697/001c.34627

Paolillo, A., Silva Silvia, A., & Pasini, M. (2016). Promoting safety participation through diversity and inclusion climates. *International Journal of Workplace Health Management, 9*(3), 308–327. https://doi.org/10.1108/IJWHM-01-2015-0002

Paolillo, A., Silva, S. A., Carvalho, H., & Pasini, M. (2020). Exploring patterns of multiple climates and their effects on safety performance at the department level. *Journal of Safety Research, 72*, 47–60. https://doi.org/10.1016/j.jsr.2019.12.009

Pitts, D. (2009). Diversity management, job satisfaction, and performance: Evidence from U.S. Federal Agencies. *Public Administration Review, 69*(2), 328–338. https://doi.org/10.1111/j.1540-6210.2008.01977.x

Platania, S., Morando, M., & Santisi, G. (2022). Organizational climate, diversity climate and job dissatisfaction: A multi-group analysis of high and low cynicism. *Sustainability, 14*(8), 1–19. https://doi.org/10.3390/su14084458

PwC. (2017). Time to close the gender gap. *PwC*. Retrieved October 25, 2022, from https://www.pwc.co.uk/women-in-technology/women-in-tech-report.pdf

Randall, D. M. (1993). Cross-cultural research on organizational commitment: A review and application of Hofstede's value survey module. *Journal of Business Research, 26*(1), 91–110. https://doi.org/10.1016/0148-2963(93)90045-Q

Raskovic, M. (2021). (Social) identity theory in an era of identity politics: Theory and practice. *AIB Insights, 21*(2), 1–7. https://doi.org/10.46697/001c.13616

Richard, O., Roh, H., & Pieper, J. R. (2013). The link between diversity and equality management practice bundles and racial diversity in the managerial ranks: Does firm size matter? *Human Resource Management, 52*(2), 215–242. https://doi.org/10.1002/hrm.21528

Roberson, Q. M. (2006). Disentangling the meanings of diversity and inclusion in organizations. *Group and Organization Management, 31*(2), 212–236. https://doi.org/10.1177/1059601104273064

Sabharwal, M. (2014). Is diversity management sufficient? Organizational inclusion to further performance. *Public Personnel Management, 43*(2), 197–217. https://doi.org/10.1177/0091026014522202

Sasikala, V., & Sankaranarayanan, V. (2022). Diversity in global mining: Where we are and what we need to do. *AIB Insights, 22*(3), 1–8. https://doi.org/10.46697/001c.33781

Sheldon, J. P., Oliver, D. G., & Balaghi, D. (2015). Arab American emerging adults' ethnic identity and its relation to psychological well-being. *Emerging Adulthood, 3*(5), 340–352. https://doi.org/10.1177/2167696815597601

Shen, J., Chanda, A., D'Netto, B., & Monga, M. (2009). Managing diversity through human resource management: An international perspective and conceptual framework. *International Journal of Human Resource Management, 20*(2), 235–251. https://doi.org/10.1080/09585190802670516

Shore, L. M., Randel, A. E., Chung, B. G., Dean, M. A., Holcombe Ehrhart, K., & Singh, G. (2011). Inclusion and diversity in work groups: A review and model for future research. *Journal of Management, 37*(4), 1262–1289. https://doi.org/10.1177/0149206310385943

Sliter, M., Boyd, E., Sinclair, R., Cheung, J., & McFadden, A. (2014). Inching toward inclusiveness: Diversity climate, interpersonal conflict and well-being in women nurses. *Sex Roles, 71*, 43–54. https://doi.org/10.1007/s11199-013-0337-5

Stahl, G. K., Tung, R. L., Kostova, T., & Zellmer-Bruhn, M. (2016). Widening the lens: Rethinking distance, diversity, and foreignness in international business research through positive organizational scholarship. *Journal of International Business Studies, 47*(6), 621–630. https://doi.org/10.1057/jibs.2016.28

Stryker S. (1980). Symbolic interactionism: A social structural version.

Szkudlarek, B. (2019). *Engaging business in refugee employment: The employer's perspective*. The University of Business School.

Szkudlarek, B., Roy, P., & Lee, E. S. (2022). How multinational corporations can support refugee workforce integration: Empathize globally, strategize locally. *AIB Insights, 22*(3), 1–5. https://doi.org/10.46697/001c.32998

Tajfel, H., & Turner, J. C. (1986). The social identity theory of intergroup behavior. In S. Worchel & W. G. Austin (Eds.), *Psychology of intergroup Relations* (pp. 7–24). Nelson-Hall.

Tekleab, A. G., Bartol, K. M., & Liu, W. (2005). Is it pay levels or pay raises that matter to fairness and turnover? *Journal of Organizational Behavior, 26*(8), 899–921. https://doi.org/10.1002/job.352

Tlaiss, H., & Kauser, S. (2011). The impact of gender, family, and work on the career advancement of Lebanese women managers. *Gender in Management: An International Journal, 26*(1), 8–36. https://doi.org/10.1108/17542411111109291

Tobias Neely, M. (2018). Fit to be king: How patrimonialism on wall street leads to inequality. *Socio-Economic Review, 16*(2), 365–385. https://doi.org/10.1093/ser/mwx058

Triandis, H. C. (2001). Individualism-collectivism and personality. *Journal of Personality, 69*(6), 907–924. https://doi.org/10.1111/1467-6494.696169

United Nations. (2015). Take action for the sustainable development goals. *Sustainable development goals*. Retrieved August 12, 2022, from http://www.un.org/sustainabledevelopment/sustainable-development-goals/

UNCTAD. (2020). Global investment trends and prospects. *World Investment Report 2020*. Retrieved October 25, 2022, from https://worldinvestmentreport.unctad.org/world-investment-report-2020/ch1-global-trends-and-prospects/

UNHCR. (2021). Refugee statistics. *Refugee data finder*. Retrieved October 25, 2022, from https://www.unhcr.org/refugee-statistics/

Uribes, M. (2021, October 25). *Five reasons why construction's gender deficit won't last*. Global Construction Review Retrieved October 24, 2022, https://www.global-constructionreview.com/five-reasons-constructions-gender-deficit-wont-last/

Utsey, S. O., Chae, M. H., Brown, C. F., & Kelly, D. (2002). Effect of ethnic group membership on ethnic identity, race-related stress, and quality of life. *Cultural Diversity and Ethnic Minority Psychology, 8*(4), 366–377. https://doi.org/10.1037/1099-9809.8.4.367

Vaara, E., Tienari, J., & Koveshnikov, A. (2021). From cultural differences to identity politics: A critical discursive approach to national identity in multinational corporations. *Journal of Management Studies, 58*(8), 2052–2081. https://doi.org/10.1111/joms.12517

Vertovec, S. (2007). Super-diversity and its implications. *Ethnic and Racial Studies, 30*(6), 1024–1054. https://doi.org/10.1080/01419870701599465

Volpone, S. D., Marquardt, D. J., Casper, W. J., & Avery, D. R. (2018). Minimizing cross-cultural maladaptation: How minority status facilitates change in international acculturation. *Journal of Applied Psychology, 103*(3), 249–269. https://doi.org/10.1037/apl0000273

Waddell, G., & Burton, A. K. (2006). *Is work good for your health and well-being?* The Stationery Office.

Wainwright, O. (2017). Why IKEA's flatpack refugee shelter won design of the year. *The Guardian*. Retrieved October 25, 2022, from https://www.theguardian.com/artanddesign/2017/jan/27/why-ikea-flatpack-refugee-shelter-won-design-of-the-year

Ward, C., Kim, I., Karl, J. A., Epstein, S., & Park, H. J. (2020). How normative multiculturalism relates to immigrant well-being. *Cultural Diversity and Ethnic Minority Psychology, 26*(4), 581–591. https://doi.org/10.1037/cdp0000317

Wilks, D. C., & Neto, F. (2013). Workplace well-being, gender and age: Examining the 'double jeopardy' effect. *Social Indicators Research, 114*(3), 875–890. https://doi.org/10.1007/s11205-012-0177-7

Williams, D. R., Yu, Y., Jackson, J. S., & Anderson, N. B. (1997). Racial differences in physical and mental health: Socio-economic status, stress, and discrimination. *Journal of Health Psychology, 2*(3), 335–351. https://doi.org/10.1177/135910539700200305

Williams, K. Y., & O'Reilly, C. A. (1998). Forty years of diversity research: A review. In B. M. Straw & L. L. Cummings (Eds.), *Research in organizational behavior* (pp. 77–140). JAI Press.

Wolfson, N., Kraiger, K., & Finkelstein, L. (2011). The relationship between diversity climate perceptions and workplace attitudes. *The Psychologist-Manager Journal, 14*(3), 161–176. https://doi.org/10.1080/10887156.2011.546170

Wong Espejo, A. (2021). *Government statistics and measures of wellbeing*. Institute of Development Studies. https://doi.org/10.19088/IDS.2021.029

Zander, L., Mockaitis, A. I., & Butler, C. L. (2012). Leading global teams. *Journal of World Business, 47*(4), 592–603. https://doi.org/10.1016/j.jwb.2012.01.012

Zea, M., Asner-Self, K., Birman, D., & Buki, L. (2003). The abbreviated Multidimentional acculturation scale: Empirical validation with two Latino/Latina samples. *Cultural Diversity and Ethnic Minority Psychology, 9*(2), 107–126. https://doi.org/10.1037/1099-9809.9.2.107

Zimmerman, C., Kiss, L., & Hossain, M. (2011). Migration and health: A framework for 21st century policy-making. *PLoS Medicine, 8*(5), 1–7. https://doi.org/10.1371/journal.pmed.1001034

Part IV

Migrants as an International Business Resource

16

Skilled Migrants: Stimulating Knowledge Creation and Flows in Firms

Pallavi Shukla and John Cantwell

Introduction

Skilled migrants have been shown to contribute to higher productivity, greater entrepreneurship, and increased cross-border trading in their host countries (OECD, 2011). Skilled migrants, according to the OECD (2011), are defined as foreign-born workers with a college degree (ISCED 5–6 education level) or more. Canada, Ireland, the United Kingdom, New Zealand, and the United States have the largest share of skilled migrants as a share of their foreign-born workforce, with numbers hovering around 46.9%, 43.5%, 38.9%, 31.5%, and 29.4%, respectively (OECD, 2011). To attract skilled workers from around the world to support their domestic employers' hiring needs, many countries have made changes to their migrant work authorization programs in recent years (e.g., Germany, France, and Poland), while others have launched pilot programs such as Canada's Atlantic Immigration Pilot to ease restrictive immigration policies (OECD, 2021).

It is important to acknowledge that while the definition of skilled migrants, as noted above, is an empirical convenience (as most national governments collect information on the education level of migrants), the definition of skilled migrants tends to be potentially broader in character. Conceptually

---

P. Shukla (✉) • J. Cantwell
Department of Management and Global Business, Rutgers University, Newark, NJ, USA
e-mail: pallavi.shukla@rutgers.edu; cantwell@business.rutgers.edu

speaking, skilled migrants are those ethnic individuals (primarily first-generation but also including second-generation migrants) who possess experiential or technical knowledge, vocational skills, or expertise in a specific domain; this broader definition of skilled migrants, therefore, includes college-educated individuals in engineering, medicine, or academia, as well as those in nursing, cooking, priesthood, tailoring, or carpentry, among others, who may not necessarily hold a traditional college degree. Similarly, many migrants may have valuable entrepreneurial skills that enable them to start and run businesses in ethnic niches and conduct cross-border trade through their social connections, but they may not necessarily have a college degree. For the purposes of this chapter, we use this broader definition of skilled migrants.

It is also important to acknowledge that first-generation skilled migrants may enter their CR using various visa routes, such as family, work, humanitarian, free movements, accompanying family of workers, or others. There might be a false presumption that skilled migrants enter their adopted CR because they are employed by a firm or university for their skills and that is the reason they come. But this may not always be the case as every visa category of migrants may have skilled workers. In other words, skilled migrants include both non-immigrant (or transient[1] as we call them) and immigrant categories of foreign-born workers. Non-immigrants comprise foreign students and business visa holders (or expatriates) sent by their firms on job assignments; immigrants include naturalized citizens and permanent residents, who may include refugees as well as asylees. In other words, refugees, asylees, or seasonal workers may be skilled workers as well. This distinction is quite relevant from a policy perspective and is often not understood.

Skilled migrants have long been considered valuable sources of knowledge for firms (Hornung, 2014). In addition to addressing the immediate labor shortage needs of employers in their receiving country, skilled migrants bring idiosyncratic knowledge to their receiving country. The unique knowledge about the culture, language, business system, and formal and informal institutions of their CO[2] is often gained through their interactions and experiences in their CO. This tacit knowledge is gained through their educational, business, and social experiences in their CO, in addition to the knowledge of their specific technological or functional domains and can be of interest to firms in their countries of residence.

---

[1] Transient migrants are defined as those who have lived in their CR for less than seven years, following Shukla and Cantwell (2018)

[2] An assumption made here is that these persons have lived in their CO for a considerable amount of time and are thus familiar with the cultural heritage and institutional environment in their CO.

Moreover, due to their transnational links to their compatriots in their CO, migrants in the information age are in a unique position to orchestrate cross-border social networks through their familial, business, or ethnic ties to facilitate knowledge flows. With the rise in teleworking opportunities facilitated by increasing digitalization in firms (Verhoef et al., 2021), especially since the start of the COVID-19 pandemic, several countries (like Estonia, Costa Rica, and Greece) have developed "digital nomad" visa schemes that allow foreign nationals to stay and work in these countries on a short-term visa (OECD, 2021). This is likely to facilitate greater flows of non-immigrant or transient migrants into these countries and create new migration corridors or pathways between countries. These new human flows can also boost local economies of these countries (Choudhury, 2022) through increased innovation and entrepreneurship (Azoulay et al., 2022; Hunt & Gauthier-Loiselle, 2010; Saxenian, 2006) and facilitate knowledge flows through long-distance social networks (Saxenian, 2002b) between migrants' CR and CO. In other words, increased digitalization and migration policy-related changes have further enabled migrants to serve as valuable cross-border conduits of knowledge flows between their CO and CR.

Migrants, Knowledge Creation, and the Cross-Border Activities of Firms: Taking Stock

Aharoni (1966) was one of the first scholars to examine the role of foreign-born workers in facilitating investments in their CO. He noted that "decision making in complex organizations is a very long social process, not solely an intellectual exercise" (Aharoni, 1966: 219). Some of the more recent and extensive case studies that examine the role of high-skilled Asian immigrants in affecting regional and international economic activities have been by Anna Lee Saxenian (1999, 2002c, 2006; Saxenian & Hsu, 2001). Saxenian (1999, 2006) found that highly skilled migrants of Indian, Chinese, and Taiwanese origin have contributed to the regional economy in California. Also, she argued that Asian scientists, engineers, and entrepreneurs have helped build long-distance social networks between Silicon Valley and Asia (Saxenian, 2002c). Following the seminal works by Aharoni (1966) and Saxenian (1999), a number of empirical studies have examined the role of skilled migrants in affecting the performance of firms in their emigrating and immigrating countries.

To take stock of the role of migrants in influencing the processes of knowledge creation, recombination and international knowledge connectivity that in turn facilitate the cross-border activities of firms, we conduct an extensive review of the literature using Thomson Reuters' Web of Science database to identify scholarly articles published in top-ranked journals between 1980 and 2022. We refine our results to focus on topics of the greatest interest to international business and management scholars at the firm level. So, we exclude articles that focus primarily on macro-level concepts such as labor market outcomes, remittances, and societal-level integration efforts and outcomes for the purposes of this study. Our final list comprises over 50 articles, as shown in Table 16.1. We divide this stream of literature into four domains based on the nature of research questions and outcomes being examined by researchers. The first domain focuses on skilled migrants affecting cross-border trade and foreign direct investment (FDI) flows, the second domain focuses on skilled migrants influencing technological innovation and knowledge flows in firms, the third domain focuses on migrant entrepreneurs and their characteristics in affecting cross-border activities of firms, and the fourth domain focuses on the expatriates and human resource management aspects of migrants in firms. We begin by elaborating on these streams of literature.

Foreign Market and Entry Strategy Selection

Several studies have examined how and to what extent skilled migrants affect the cross-border trade and FDI flows between countries. This stream of literature has argued that skilled migrants help reduce search costs for CR firms not only in the selection of foreign markets (Chung & Tung, 2013; Filatotchev et al., 2007) but also in the identification of partner firms in export–import relationships (Rauch & Trindade, 2002). For example, Ellis (2000) examined the foreign market entry decisions of toy manufacturers in Hong Kong (in 1997–1998), and found that information about foreign market entry opportunities is "commonly acquired via existing social ties" (Ellis, 2000: 462). Ellis (2000) argued that "knowledge of foreign market opportunities is contingent upon the idiosyncratic benefits of each individual's social network" (Ellis, 2000: 448). As a result, "information search activities would appear to be selectively influenced by those existing social ties linking the initiating decision-maker (i.e., seller, buyer, or third party) with others that are in some way connected to a particular foreign market" (Ellis, 2000: 448). In other words, social ties—business, family, or friendship ties—of migrants can help identify suppliers, distributors, bankers, merger or acquisition targets, and

Table 16.1 List of articles reviewed categorized by international business domains

Author/s	Year	Title	Journal
Foreign Market Selection and Entry Strategy			
Gillespie, K; Riddle, L; Sayre, E; Sturges, D	1999	Diaspora interest in homeland investment	Journal of International Business Studies
Ellis, P	2000	Social ties and foreign market entry	Journal of International Business Studies
Wong, PLK; Ellis, P	2002	Social ties and partner identification in Sino-Hong Kong international joint ventures	Journal of International Business Studies
Filatotchev, I; Strange, R; Piesse, J; Lien, YC	2007	FDI by firms from newly industrialized economies in emerging markets: corporate governance, entry mode and location	Journal of International Business Studies
Bhattacharya, U; Groznik, P	2008	Melting pot or salad bowl: Some evidence from US investments abroad	Journal of Financial Markets
Zaheer, S; Lamin, A; Subramani, M	2009	Cluster capabilities or ethnic ties? Location choice by foreign and domestic entrants in the services offshoring industry in India	Journal of International Business Studies
Madhavan, R; Iriyama, A	2009	Understanding global flows of venture capital: Human networks as the "carrier wave" of globalization	Journal of International Business Studies
Chung, HFL; Tung, RL	2013	Immigrant social networks and foreign entry: Australia and New Zealand firms in the European Union and Greater China.	International Business Review
Hernandez, E	2014	Finding a Home away from Home: Effects of Immigrants on Firms' Foreign Location Choice and Performance	Administrative Science Quarterly
Karreman, B; Burger, MJ; Oort, FGV	2017	Location Choices of Chinese Multinationals in Europe: The Role of Overseas Communities	Economic Geography
Shukla, P; Cantwell, J	2018	Migrants and multinational firms: The role of institutional affinity and connectedness in FDI	Journal of World Business
Li, Y; Hernandez, E; Gwon, S	2019	When Do Ethnic Communities Affect Foreign Location Choice? Dual Entry Strategies of Korean Banks in China	Academy of Management Journal
Gregoric, A; Rabbiosi, L; Santangelo, GD	2019	Diaspora ownership and international technology licensing by emerging market firms	Journal of International Business Studies

(continued)

Table 16.1 (continued)

Author/s	Year	Title	Journal
Useche, D; Miguelez, E; Lissoni, F	2020	Highly skilled and well connected: Migrant inventors in cross-border M&As	Journal of International Business Studies
Cai, H; Meng, Y; Chakraborty, S	2021	Migrants and exports: Decomposing the link	Journal of World Business
Moschieri, C.; Fernandez-Moya, M.	2022	A dynamic long-term approach to internationalization: Spanish publishing firms' expansion and emigrants in Mexico (1939–1977)	Journal of International Business Studies

Innovation and Knowledge Management

Author/s	Year	Title	Journal
Oettl, A; Agrawal, A	2008	International labor mobility and knowledge flow externalities	Journal of International Business Studies
Edler, J; Fier, H; Grimpe, C	2011	International scientist mobility and the locus of knowledge and technology transfer	Research Policy
Barnard, H; Pendock, C	2013	To share or not to share: The role of affect in knowledge sharing by individuals in a diaspora	Journal of International Management
Scellato, G; Franzoni, C; Stephan, P	2014	The mover's advantage: The superior performance of migrant scientists	Economics Letters
Wang, D	2015	Activating Cross-border Brokerage: Interorganizational Knowledge Transfer through Skilled Return Migration	Administrative Science Quarterly
Almeida, P; Phene, A; Li, S	2015	The Influence of Ethnic Community Knowledge on Indian Inventor Innovativeness	Organization Science
Breschi, Stefano, Lissoni, Francesco, & Miguelez, Ernest	2017	Foreign-origin inventors in the USA: testing for diaspora and brain gain effects	Journal of Economic Geography
Choudhury, P; Kim, DY	2019	The ethnic migrant inventor effect: Codification and recombination of knowledge across borders	Strategic Management Journal
Hernandez, E. & Kulchina, E.	2020	Immigrants and Foreign Firm Performance	Organization Science
Miguelez, E; Temgoua, CN	2020	Inventor migration and knowledge flows: A two-way communication channel?	Research Policy
Miguelez, E; Morrison, A	2022	Migrant inventors as agents of technological change	Research Policy

(continued)

Table 16.1 (continued)

Migrant Entrepreneurship			
Author/s	Year	Title	Journal
Bates, T	1997	Financing small business creation: The case of Chinese and Korean immigrant entrepreneurs	Journal of Business Venturing
Sequeira, JM; Carr, JC; Rasheed, AA	2009	Transnational Entrepreneurship: Determinants of Firm Type and Owner Attributions of Success	Entrepreneurship Theory and Practice
Prashantham, S; Dhanaraj, C	2010	The Dynamic Influence of Social Capital on the International Growth of New Ventures	Journal of Management Studies
Ellis, PD	2011	Social ties and international entrepreneurship: Opportunities and constraints affecting firm internationalization	Journal of International Business Studies
Ndofor, HA; Priem, RL	2011	Immigrant Entrepreneurs, the Ethnic Enclave Strategy, and Venture Performance	Journal of Management
Neville, F; Orser, B; Riding, A; Jung, O	2014	Do young firms owned by recent immigrants outperform other young firms?	Journal of Business Venturing
Sui, S; Morgan, HM; Baum, M	2015	Internationalization of immigrant-owned SMEs: The role of language	Journal of World Business
Dimitratos, P; Buck, T; Fletcher, M; Li, N	2016	The motivation of international entrepreneurship: The case of Chinese transnational entrepreneurs	International Business Review
Jiang, G; Kotabe, M; Hamilton III, RD; Smith, SW	2016	Early internationalization and the role of immigration in new venture survival	International Business Review
Kulchina E	2016	A path to value creation for foreign entrepreneurs	Strategic Management Journal
Morgan, HM; Sui, S; Baum, M	2018	Are SMEs with immigrant owners exceptional exporters?	Journal of Business Venturing
Kerr, SP; Kerr, W	2020	Immigrant entrepreneurship in America: Evidence from the survey of business owners 2007 & 2012	Research Policy
Fainshmidt, Stav; Smith, Adam W.; Aguilera, Ruth V.	2021	Where Do Born Globals Come from? A Neoconfigurational Institutional Theory	Organization Science
Czinkota, M; Khan, Z; Knight, G	2021	International business and the migrant-owned enterprise	Journal of Business Research
Azoulay, P., Jones, B. F., Kim, J. D., Miranda, J.	2022	Immigration and Entrepreneurship in the United States	American Economic Review-Insights

(continued)

Table 16.1 (continued)

Expatriate and Human Resource Management			
Author/s	Year	Title	Journal
Naumann, E.	1993	Organizational predictors of expatriate job-satisfaction	Journal of International Business Studies
Sergeant, A., & Frenkel, S.	1998	Managing people in China: Perceptions of expatriate managers.	Journal of World Business
Hung-Wen, L.	2007	Factors that Influence Expatriate Failure: An Interview Study	International Journal of Management
Tung, RL	2008	Brain circulation, diaspora, and international competitiveness.	European Management Journal
Farh, CIC; Bartol, KM; Shapiro, DL; Shin, J	2010	Networking Abroad: A Process Model of How Expatriates Form Support Ties to Facilitate Adjustment	Academy of Management Journal
Brannen, MY; Thomas, DC	2010	Bicultural Individuals in Organizations: Implications and Opportunity	International Journal of Cross-Cultural Management
Bruning, N. S., Sonpar, K., & Wang, X. Y.	2012	Host-country national networks and expatriate effectiveness: A mixed-methods study	Journal of International Business Studies
Fitzsimmons, SR	2013	Multicultural Employees: A Framework for Understanding How They Contribute to Organizations	Academy of Management Journal
Liu, X; Gao, L; Lu, J; Wei, Y	2015	The role of highly skilled migrants in the process of inter-firm knowledge transfer across borders	Journal of World Business
Furusawa, M; Brewster, C	2015	The bi-cultural option for global talent management: The Japanese/Brazilian Nikkeijin example	Journal of World Business
Kane, AA; Levina, N	2017	'Am I Still One of Them?': Bicultural Immigrant Managers Navigating Social Identity Threats When Spanning Global Boundaries	Journal of Management Studies
Vora, D; Kostova, T	2019	Antecedents of psychological attachment in multinational enterprises	Multinational Business Review
Hong, H. J., Minbaeva, D.	2022	Multiculturals as strategic human capital resources in multinational enterprises	Journal of International Business Studies

business partners in their CO markets (Useche et al., 2019; Wong & Ellis, 2002; Zaheer et al., 2009), as well as domestic markets (Bonacich & Modell, 1980). The knowledge shared by migrant inventors in cross-border mergers and acquisitions has been known to reduce the institutional distance between countries that are located geographically apart, especially in case of full acquisitions in high-tech sectors (Useche et al., 2019). Similarly, Foley and Kerr (2013) find that ethnic innovators in U.S. multinational firms help their firms in forming new affiliates abroad without the support of local joint venture partners in those foreign countries.

Moreover, highly educated skilled migrants who remain embedded in their CO, while establishing themselves in their adopted CR, often function as "opportunity-sensing, value-adding, and monitoring devices" (Madhavan & Iriyama, 2009: 1242); these professional and technical workers often work with venture capital partners in their CR to seek funding for new ventures in their developing CO (Madhavan & Iriyama, 2009). While Madhavan and Iriyama (2009) focused on investments from migrants' CR to CO, other more recent studies have examined the impact of ethnic migrant communities in attracting FDI from their CO (Hernandez, 2014; Karreman et al., 2017; Li et al., 2019; Shukla & Cantwell, 2018). For example, Hernandez (2014) examines the role of immigrants in the United States in influencing the location choice and survival of subsidiaries of firms from 27 countries (into the United States) between 1998 and 2003. He finds that the chances of locating operations and surviving in a state rise with increased concentration of same-nationality immigrants and that these effects are stronger for inexperienced firms. He also finds that the effects are stronger for locations where immigrants can help facilitate industry-specific knowledge spillovers and for knowledge-seeking subsidiaries.

Studies in this domain also find that skilled migrants help build valuable linkages between countries, especially between developed and developing economies. The lack of effective governance and a relatively weak institutional infrastructure in developing countries (Dunning, 2005) make it difficult for foreign investors to get information about the investment opportunities in those countries. Skilled migrants from developing countries in a (developed) CR can help fill this knowledge gap (Sonderegger & Taeube, 2010). Migrants' familiarity with regulatory procedures as well as their connections in local regions of their CO can give them an advantage over others who lack such connections. Anecdotal evidence suggests that migrants in top management teams are often involved in facilitating direct investments to their developing CO (Bhattacharya & Groznik, 2008; Filatotchev et al., 2007; Pandey et al., 2006; Schotter & Abdelzaher, 2013). More specifically, Zaheer et al. (2009)

argue that emerging markets, such as India, lack formal institutional structures to support entrepreneurial activity, therefore CEO's social ties with key stakeholders (such as, bankers, firm employees, bureaucrats, etc.) are important in the early stages of location decision-making. They examine the extent to which social ties as opposed to knowledge spillovers found in a cluster influence location choice for new entrants using 108 location decisions across 11 city clusters in the information technology-enabled service industry in India. They find that ethnic networks exert greater influence than cluster capabilities on location decisions of firms.

A few recent studies have taken a more nuanced look at firm heterogeneity (independent firms versus multinational firm subsidiaries, or privately owned/remotely located) when examining the role of migrants in affecting location and exporting decisions. Hernandez and Kulchina (2020) use data on foreign firms in Russia during 2006–2011 to find that independent firms have a greater need for resources from co-ethnic migrant community in a CR and depend on individual managers' social ties for accessing those resources. Similarly, Cai et al. (2021) analyze a dataset of 50,000 Chinese exporters with connections to migrants in 205 countries to find that "less-integrated migrants (in a CR) attract home exports, while privately-owned and remotely-located exporters (in a CO) with limited resources or external connections benefit more" from migrants in a foreign country.

Technological Innovation and Knowledge Flows

In this domain, studies have examined the role of highly educated skilled migrants, specifically inventors and scientists, in enhancing either new technological knowledge creation and recombination in CR firms, or on cross-border knowledge flows between CO and CR firms. For example, Choudhury and Kim (2019) use a dataset of Chinese and Indian herbal patents filed in the United States to find that an increase in the number of first-generation ethnic migrant inventors increases the herbal knowledge capability of CR firms by 4.5%. They note that ethnic migrant inventors due to their understanding of idiosyncratic cultural knowledge can help unlock knowledge "previously locked within the cultural context of their home regions," thereby facilitating the creation of novel technological solutions in their CR firms (Choudhury & Kim, 2019). They also find that knowledge recombination to develop new applications is more likely to be done by teams of inventors comprising different ethnic backgrounds in CR firms. Bahar et al. (2020) also analyze patent data to find that immigrant inventors enable new knowledge creation in same technologies their COs specialize in. Similarly, Miguelez and Morrison (2022) argue that migrants facilitate the process of regional technological diversification in their CR. They examine an original dataset of migrant inventors in European regions between 2003 and 2011 to find that migrants inventors not only contribute to the development of new technological specializations in their CR but also "trigger a process of unrelated diversification" providing further evidence of migrants acting as an international business resource.

While skilled migrants have been shown to contribute to increased technological innovation in their CR firms as noted above, international mobility of migrant inventors also plays a role in facilitating knowledge flows and technology transfer (Edler et al., 2011; Oettl & Agrawal, 2008b) across borders, thereby supporting the idea of brain circulation (Saxenian, 2002a; Tung, 2008; Wang, 2015) that can be crucial to new knowledge creation in various industries. For example, Foley and Kerr (2013) find that "increases in the share of a firm's innovation performed by inventors of a particular ethnicity are associated with increases in the share of that firm's affiliate activity in countries related to that ethnicity," suggesting that migrants provide invaluable cross-border knowledge linkages within multinational firms. Migrants who have lived in multiple countries or travel more regularly can be greater sources of knowledge in firms and can also provide greater connectivity between regions. Along these lines, research on return migrant inventors shows that they facilitate production of knowledge in their CO (Choudhury, 2016; Fry, 2023) and that this knowledge tends to be of higher quality (Perri et al., 2015). Acting as knowledge bridges between their CO and their CR, migrant inventors have been associated with greater integration of knowledge originating from their CO in the innovation process at their multinational firm (Marino et al., 2020). This is explained, in part, by a related finding that migrant inventors have been shown to have access to larger international research networks than native researchers who lack international background (Scellato et al., 2015).

Several studies find that migrants serve as valuable conduits of knowledge flows, especially between developed and developing countries. For example, Levin and Barnard (2013) using a sample of South African managers examine the value of interpersonal connections in facilitating knowledge flows across borders; they find that managers in less-developed countries benefit from their personal connectivity to compatriots living in more (technologically and economically) advanced countries, thus demonstrating that cross-national interpersonal ties provide a mechanism for knowledge flows and could be sources of useful knowledge, especially for firms in less-developed countries.

Evidence from the examination of patent citation data also suggests that migrants from developing countries living in developed countries facilitate the international diffusion of knowledge within the multinational network between their CO and CR (Miguelez & Temgoua, 2020).

Migrant Entrepreneurship

Several studies in the international entrepreneurship literature (Ellis, 2011; Neville et al., 2014; Sequeira et al., 2009) provide empirical and anecdotal evidence that migrant entrepreneurs leverage their unique knowledge and experience of their CO for their startup and born-global firms (Fainshmidt et al., 2021; Oviatt & McDougall, 2005; Oviatt et al., 1995). Due to their international orientation, access to capabilities (such as entrepreneurial skills, or unique technological knowledge), and knowledge of unique resources (such as availability of skilled and unskilled labor) in their CO, migrant entrepreneurs tend to be successful in foreign markets (Czinkota et al., 2021; Kulchina, 2016; Neville et al., 2014; Sui et al., 2015). For a systematic analysis of the migrant entrepreneurship literature, see Sinkovics and Reuber (2021).

Studies in this stream of literature find that socially embedded entrepreneurs capitalize on opportunities in their CO (Landolt et al., 1999; Sequeira et al., 2009) and benefit from "lower set-up, monitoring and enforcement costs" (Ellis, 2011). However, migrants' social network can also be constrained by linguistic and psychic distance and may limit internationalization horizons for the venture (Ellis, 2011). Therefore, it is essential to consider how different types of migrant entrepreneur's social networks, such as business advice networks, emotional support networks, or business resources networks, affect the growth prospects of entrepreneurial ventures (Arregle et al., 2015). Some evidence also suggests that while migrants with greater social capital or prior entrepreneurial experience tend to engage in ethnic markets (niche markets for cultural products or services), migrants with prior managerial experience (those who were employed as managers in CR firms) tend to engage in mainstream markets in their CR (Ndofor & Priem, 2011).

It is important to acknowledge here that there is a large literature in sociology on *ethnic entrepreneurship* that examines the various characteristics and motivations of immigrant entrepreneurs who start their small businesses in ethnic niches (Portes, 1997) to economically adapt in their new CR environment (Bonacich, 1973). While most small businesses in ethnic enclaves (Portes, 1995; Portes & Sensenbrenner, 1993) may not have the financial resources to engage in the internationalization of their firms (through acquisitions, joint ventures, or greenfields), it is important to note that they may still engage in international trade. Research suggests that small businesses often engage in different types of cross-border trading, resulting in the creation of a variety of firms, as noted in detail by Landolt et al. (1999) in the case of El Salvadoran migrants in the United States. Also, ethnic niches are crucial for the creation of institutional affinity in CR regions which, in turn, facilitate the development of a knowledge community for migrants from a CO (Shukla & Cantwell, 2018).

Expatriate and Human Resource Management

The initial focus by researchers in this domain was on examining the dimensions of successful expatriate acculturation (Oddou et al., 1985) and the individual and organizational attributes for success of employees sent on international assignments (Hung-Wen, 2007; Naumann, 1993) for increasing expatriate managerial effectiveness (Sergeant & Frenkel, 1998) in unfamiliar contexts. In the past two decades, however, researchers have delved deeper to understand the process of expatriate adjustment in foreign locations (Bruning et al., 2012; Farh et al., 2010) and have expanded their research questions to include bicultural (Brannen & Thomas, 2010) and multicultural managers (Fitzsimmons, 2013) due, in part, to the rise in the number of first- and second-generation immigrants in many countries (Baycan et al., 2012).

Several scholars (Brannen & Thomas, 2010; Fitzsimmons, 2013; Furusawa & Brewster, 2015) note that biculturals and multiculturals, "who are individuals with unique cultural knowledge, skills, abilities, and other characteristics," can be valuable resources for firms in the conduct of international business due to their ability to switch internalized cultural schemas. For example, evidence suggests that skilled migrants who are bilingual and possess bicultural competence can play a vital role at each step of the knowledge transfer process between firms from their CO and CR (Liu et al., 2015). More recent studies have examined the nuances under which these individuals are more likely to become strategic resources for international firms. Along these lines, Kane and Levina (2017) find that migrant managers with bicultural competencies who are able to "embrace their home country identity" can be more successful in their boundary-spanning activities, such as teaching new technical competencies, building new relationships in CO, and receiving inputs from CO employees in cross-border knowledge-intensive projects. Hong and Minbaeva (2022) conduct an ethnographic study over two years in two multinational firms to identify individual-, team-, and firm-level factors (which include a global mindset, language policy and practices, and team diversity, among others) that enable the transformation of a multicultural's cultural knowledge into human capital resources.

Our review of the literature that has examined the role of skilled migrants in influencing cross-border activities of export/import, born-global, and large multinational firms suggests that skilled migrants can help improve firm performance by stimulating new knowledge creation in their CR, reducing information and search costs for CR firms looking to internationalize, and in facilitating in intra-firm and inter-firm knowledge flows across borders. Their actions often result in enhanced innovation capabilities and improved firm performance through enrichment of firm-specific knowledge base, which could be market-specific knowledge, institutional knowledge, or technological knowledge, and identification of new resources and capabilities in CO location. In sum, migrants are viewed as valuable resources for places and firms.

Theoretical Perspectives on Skilled Migrants in Internationally Engaged Firms

Researchers have relied on three main theoretical lenses to study the effects of skilled migrants in firms: (1) the role of idiosyncratic knowledge held by skilled migrants drawing on the resource-based (Barney, 1991; Dierickx & Cool, 1989) and knowledge-based view (Nonaka, 1994; Nonaka & Takeuchi, 1995) of the firm; (2) the role of social ties and embeddedness, drawing on the relational governance perspective (Burt, 2000; Granovetter, 1985; Uzzi, 1997); and (3) the role of affinity, cohesion, and solidarity within a group drawing on the social identity theory (Lee, 1999; Moreland & Beach, 1992; Tajfel & Turner, 1979). The first perspective views skilled migrants as carriers of unique institutional, cultural, market-specific, and technological knowledge, in part due to their cultural heritage and CO experience but also, in many cases, due to their international experience of living in multiple countries (experiential knowledge). As the "experience and knowledge of a firm's personnel" (Penrose, 1959) determines "what it 'sees' in the external world" (Penrose, 1959: 79–80), migrants are viewed as valuable resources who have a comparative advantage, relative to natives, in markets for knowledge and intermediate products. Also, it is assumed that they are willing to share this knowledge due to a positive affect toward their CO (Barnard & Pendock, 2013).

The second approach draws on the relational governance perspective (Granovetter, 1985; Poppo & Zenger, 2002) to emphasize the importance of migrants as cross-border bridges who facilitate knowledge flows through their social networks. The underlying assumption is that international economic activities carry higher transaction costs (Coase, 1937; Williamson, 1981) due to increased liability of foreignness (Hymer, 1960; Zaheer, 1995), and skilled migrants help lower these costs through their cross-national interpersonal ties. The social proximity of migrants (in a CR) with their compatriots (in their CO), who often share a common understanding of the world (Naphiet & Ghoshal, 1998), makes the sharing, transfer, and absorption of knowledge about product ideas, technological, industry-specific, and entrepreneurial opportunities in mainstream and niche markets somewhat easier. While weak ties (as in acquaintance relationships) tend to be a source of new knowledge and ideas as they generally operate in different social circles (Granovetter, 1973; Levin & Cross, 2004), strong ties (such as those between migrants and their compatriots in their CO) have the benefit of increased "willingness to share" that plays a crucial role in cross-border knowledge transfer due to the inherent complexity of coordination arising from time zone differences, schedule conflicts, and long-distance communication (Levin & Barnard, 2013: 680). Ties also bring social benefits of trust, reciprocity, and commitment, and these translate into economic terms as lower search, transaction, and transformation costs in international transactions (Ellis, 2011).

The third theoretical perspective draws on the social identity theory (Tajfel & Turner, 1979), more specifically the psychological processes of social identification and social categorization to highlight the potential barriers and enablers for successful transformation of migrant's idiosyncratic knowledge and abilities into human capital resources that lead to improved financial outcomes for firms. While social categorization, on the one hand, can facilitate migrant employee's acculturation and adaptation to their CR environment, on the other hand, it could prevent migrants from sharing their knowledge in firms if migrants from a specific CO (migrants in general) face discrimination in that CR. Focusing on the individual level, this stream of literature argues that individual migrants may have access to more than one cultural profile and associated cultural schema (Brannen & Thomas, 2010) which can give them a comparative advantage relative to natives in boundary-spanning roles.

Skilled Migrants Stimulating Knowledge Creation and Flows: When, Why, and How

It follows from the above discussion that there are two main mechanisms/processes that explain how skilled migrants stimulate knowledge creation and cross-border knowledge flows in firms: (1) as *knowledge carriers*, and (2) as

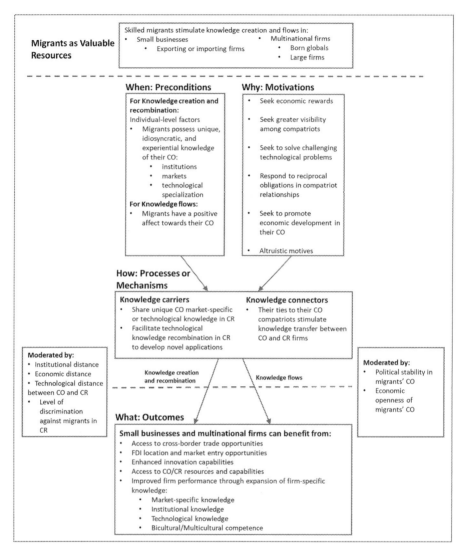

Fig. 16.1 Skilled migrants as international business resources: When, Why, and How

knowledge connectors. These are shown in the *How: Process or Mechanisms* component of our proposed conceptual model in Fig. 16.1. In their role as knowledge carriers, skilled migrants can be viewed as sources of distinctive knowledge and their unique contributions are visible through new knowledge creation efforts in their CR firms. A necessary precondition for this mechanism is that migrants possess idiosyncratic and experiential knowledge of their CO. In their role as knowledge connectors, on the other hand, skilled migrants can be viewed as valuable resources for their social capital and ability to use cross-national interpersonal ties to connect their CR firms to resources, capabilities, and markets across borders. A necessary precondition for this mechanism is that migrants' have a positive effect toward their CO else they may be unwilling to facilitate knowledge flows to their CO. The *When: Preconditions* component (see Fig. 16.1) shows the necessary conditions for knowledge creation and flows to come about. It is important to acknowledge the distinction between the knowledge carrier and knowledge connector process as it allows for a nuanced understanding of the phenomenon under examination (Shukla, 2016). In most situations, both processes are likely to interact positively to further enhance the effects of skilled migrants on the outcomes (shown as the *What: Outcomes* component in Fig. 16.1). But in some cases, this may not be true. In situations where skilled migrants' connectedness to their CO is absent, as in the case of refugees or asylees where political or economic instability in their CO (as observed in countries like Syria, Afghanistan, or Ukraine more recently) allows only limited connectedness, the knowledge carrier channel is still relevant and can contribute to knowledge development not only in CR firms but also in their CR community (Shukla & Cantwell, 2018).

Why: Motivations

Before elaborating on the knowledge carrier and knowledge connector processes, it is important to understand the motivations of skilled migrants for engaging in this behavior. Our examination of the literature suggests that there are four main reasons that motivate skilled migrants to share their knowledge or facilitate cross-border knowledge flows. First, migrants are often seeking economic rewards and career growth in their firms and by stimulating new knowledge creation or helping reduce information costs during their firm's internationalization efforts, they seek rewards for their efforts (Saxenian, 2006). Second, many migrants, specifically migrant inventors, are seeking to solve challenging technological problems, therefore, they engage in new knowledge creation through knowledge recombination efforts to develop novel applications to problems (Choudhury & Kim, 2019). Third, migrants may be responding to reciprocal obligations in their social, compatriot relationships (Agrawal et al., 2011). This is especially relevant in many collectivistic cultures (such as, China, India, Japan, and South Korea), where individuals are expected to return favors to other members of their community. Fourth, in some instances, skilled migrants may be engaging in altruistic behavior and, therefore, seeking to give back to their CO (Gillespie et al., 1999; Glennie & Chappell, 2010; Saxenian, 2006). For example, Saxenian (2006) notes that Hewlett-Packard (HP) senior manager, Radha Basu, was committed to contributing to India's economic development and took personal risks to establish HP's Indian operations in 1985. According to Saxenian, Basu used her credibility to gain confidence and trust of the HP management and Indian government officials to successfully establish the HP-India development center (Saxenian, 2006: 282). It is worth mentioning here that these four motivators are not mutually exclusive; it is quite likely that skilled migrants are motivated for one or more reasons.

How: Processes or Mechanisms

How do skilled migrants stimulate knowledge creation and cross-border knowledge flows in and across firms? To answer this question and improve our understanding of the two processes at work, we begin with the idea that each individual is a carrier of his own knowledge world—a world formed and continuously updated by one's life experiences, both sensory and internal, in a given societal context. As the societal context changes from one country to another, so do the life experiences of an individual. North (1994) has argued that the informal constraints that guide human interaction in a society vary from one country to another and are passed down from one generation to another as "customs, taboos, and myths that provided cultural continuity" (North, 1994: 363). This suggests that despite sub-national cultural and linguistic differences, a person of Indian origin is likely to have experiences that are common with other persons from India due to their exposure to similar economic, educational, legal, and political system across the Indian states. In other words, migrants from a CO are likely to have some shared experiences and a common understanding of the economic, political, social, legal, and educational systems of that country. These experiences are likely to provide migrants with some tacit knowledge (Polanyi, 1961) of their CO and this knowledge, as noted by several theorists of organizational culture, is unlikely to be gained by other persons new to that country, explicitly by reading a book. In sum, migrants by virtue of their experiences, interactions, and affiliations at school, and at their place of work in their CO, are likely to carry a variety of knowledge that may be relevant to their CR firms.

Migrants by virtue of their interactions with others, in the firms they work for, or the organizations in their social community (such as professional associations, cultural associations, etc.), are likely to engage in exchange and combination of knowledge through such "mechanisms as meetings and telephone conversations" (Nonaka, 1994: 19) in their CR. Combination of migrants' tacit knowledge and explicit knowledge through interactions with natives and other migrants leads to new knowledge creation in their CR (Almeida et al.,

2015; Oettl & Agrawal, 2008a). This knowledge, depending on the context and on the educational qualification and expertise of the migrant, could be of various types, such as industry-specific technological knowledge, product-specific knowledge, cultural knowledge, knowledge of business and social practices in their CO, knowledge of business contacts, and knowledge of investment opportunities, among others (Shukla, 2016). Through this process of converting tacit knowledge into explicit knowledge that can be shared with others, as well as assimilating explicit knowledge transmitted by other workers (natives and other migrants) in a firm (Nonaka, 1994), migrants are engaged in the process of sharing knowledge (or externalization) as well as learning (or internalization as Nonaka calls it) in their adopted CR. Migrants' experiential knowledge of their CO is likely to interact with firm-specific tangible and intangible assets in their CR leading to the creation of new capabilities (Barney, 1991; Teece et al., 1997) and ownership advantages (Dunning, 1980, 1988) in CR firms.

As a result of their prior connections and experience in their occupational industry as well as upstream and downstream industries in their CO, some migrants are likely to possess knowledge pertaining to technological specialization, product ideas, quality of labor, employees' attitude toward work, customer preferences, domestic competition, regulations, suppliers, and distributors; this knowledge can be a valuable resource for firms in the migrants' CR (Shukla, 2016). For example, migrant's tacit knowledge about customer preferences for differentiated ethnic products can be useful for product designers in firms in those industries (Gould, 1994) and can play a role in influencing foreign market entry decisions in their CO (Chung et al., 2010).

In sum, migrants' idiosyncratic knowledge and cross-national interpersonal ties can become a valuable and inimitable resource for firms (Barney, 1991; Zaheer et al., 2009) seeking to expand overseas, and could substitute for the experience gained by personnel in a foreign subsidiary, which is a critical factor in renewed commitment of resources in the internationalization process (Johanson & Vahlne, 1977).

Moderators

The usability of migrant's CO-specific (or CR-specific for return migrants) idiosyncratic knowledge depends on the level of information already available in the CR (or CO for return migrants). Broadly speaking, three distances—institutional distance (due to differing business systems and language, or lack of trade agreements and diplomatic relationships) (Liu et al., 2015; Moschieri & Fernandez-Moya, 2022), technological distance (technological specialization of countries in specific industries) (Useche et al., 2019), and economic distance (level of economic development) (Miguelez & Temgoua, 2020)—between CO and CR seem to affect meaningful and usable knowledge creation in a location and flows between CR and CO. The greater the distance between the CO and CR along these dimensions, the greater is gap in knowledge that migrants can fill in their firms. Knowledge flows are also moderated by political stability and economic openness of the countries being examined. For example, in the case of refugees or asylees from a CO that is facing political instability, cross-border knowledge flows may not be pronounced. But skilled migrants from these countries are still carriers of unique intangible knowledge that can be relevant to CR firms, hence, as noted earlier, there is a need to differentiate between migrants as knowledge carriers (and creators) and as knowledge connectors. Lastly, environmental-level factors such as biases or discrimination against migrants in general or specifically for migrants from a specific CO may raise barriers to knowledge sharing and severely constrain knowledge sharing by skilled migrants. On other hand, if social perception toward migrants is positive, the likelihood of knowledge sharing by individual skilled migrants would also increase. Figure 16.1 shows the key components and the relationships between the various components of our framework.

Conclusion and Avenues for Future Research

At a time when increasing political polarization is fueling and swaying public perception against immigrants in many countries in Europe, as well as the United Kingdom and the United States (Hainmueller & Hopkins, 2014), it is important for migration researchers to explore the nuances of this phenomenon at the country, industry, firm, and individual levels. In this chapter, we addressed the topic of skilled migrants as an international business resource in firms by examining the current state of literature in international business to explain when, why, and how skilled migrants influence the various outcomes in international, born-global, and multinational firms. This is relevant as one-third of all adult immigrants in OECD countries are skilled migrants; this share is even more for countries such as Canada (60%) and Australia (47%) which have selective migration policies, based on 2015/2016 data (d'Aiglepierre et al., 2020).

This chapter argues that skilled migrants who possess experiential knowledge of their CO business system and are also well integrated in their CR can offer useful and often novel knowledge to their firms in technological, institutional, and market entry domains that, in turn, leads to improved firm performance through enhanced innovation, new alliances, international expansion, or new product development. Due to their ability to access more than one cultural profile in their social and business interactions, many bicultural managers have a comparative advantage relative to natives in the boundary-spanning roles of firms (Brannen & Thomas, 2010). Consequently, an opportunity exists for organizational policymakers to proactively design talent search and human resource management practices to capitalize on the boundary-spanning competencies of these managers (Fitzsimmons, 2013; Furusawa & Brewster, 2015).

An opportunity also exists for organizational policymakers to create an inclusive firm environment where migrants feel motivated to share domain-specific, unique cultural knowledge of their CO that could be applied in the CR context to enable creation of novel applications in the CR. Such inclusion efforts would also send a strong positive signal to those migrant employees, who may be less willing to share their ideas on their own due to cultural or linguistic barriers, especially when the institutional, economic, or technological distance between migrants' CO and CR is high, as in the case of developing country migrants residing in developed country contexts.

While existing research in the domain of migration international business activities of firms has provided valuable insights for researchers, practitioners, and policymakers, several recent trends deserve more attention. Since the start of the COVID-19 pandemic, remote work has taken a life of its own. For many employees, this has translated to work-from-anywhere (Choudhury et al., 2021) and many countries are offering "digital nomad" visas to skilled workers who can provide proof of income and remote employment in addition to insurance and intent to depart the country (Choudhury, 2022). These trends can lead to the creation of new migration corridors between countries (quite distinct from colonial ties-related migration corridors) as policymakers change their migration policies to attract tourists and skilled transient workers to boost their local economies.

The changing patterns in the geography of global migration with greater immigration into Europe and increasing emigration from Latin America and Asia over the past few decades has implications for international business scholarship (Hajro et al., 2022). In terms of migrant-sending countries, India has the largest skilled diaspora in the OECD countries (over 3 million tertiary-educated migrants), followed by China (2 million) and Philippines (1.8

million), the United Kingdom (1.7 million), and Germany (1.4 million) based on 2015/2016 data (d'Aiglepierre et al., 2020), and several studies have examined the contributions of these migrants in the U.S., U.K., and German contexts. With emigration rates of more than 40% observed in countries such as Guyana, Trinidad and Tobago, Mauritius, Jamaica, and Fiji (d'Aiglepierre et al., 2020), there is an opportunity for learning more about the role of skilled migrants as an international business resource in these countries. Is the phenomenon of skilled emigration from these countries reflective primarily of the brain drain phenomenon or is brain circulation and technological upgrading (Agrawal et al., 2011; Docquier & Rapoport, 2012; Saxenian, 2002a) occurring in firms of these countries?

Lastly, a recent development that is creating or in many cases deepening migration pathways between countries is the Belt and Road Initiative (BRI), which is a massive, $838 billion infrastructure development initiative launched by China to connect over 160 countries. Especially relevant here is the increased migration observed between China and the countries on the African continent. China is Africa's largest trading partner, and an estimated 500,000 African migrants live in China (Cissé, 2021). It is important to note that African migrants to China tend to be highly educated people who are either business professionals, students, or English-language teachers (Politzer, 2008). In recent years, China has sought to attract more international students by offering scholarships, especially students from Africa and from the BRI countries (OECD, 2021). These trends present new and exciting avenues for research for scholars interested in examining the role of skilled migrants as an international business resource.

References

Agrawal, A., Kapur, D., McHale, J., & Oettl, A. (2011, January). Brain drain or brain bank? The impact of skilled emigration on poor-country innovation. *Journal of Urban Economics, 69*(1), 43–55. https://doi.org/10.1016/j.jue.2010.06.003

Aharoni, Y. (1966). *The foreign investment decision process* (Vol. 8, p. 13). Division of Research, Harvard University.

Almeida, P., Phene, A., & Li, S. (2015, January-February). The influence of ethnic community knowledge on Indian inventor innovativeness [Article]. *Organization Science, 26*(1), 198–217. https://doi.org/10.1287/orsc.2014.0931

Arregle, J. L., Batjargal, B., Hitt, M. A., Webb, J. W., Miller, T., & Tsui, A. S. (2015). Family ties in Entrepreneurs' social networks and new venture growth [Review]. *Entrepreneurship Theory and Practice, 39*(2), 313–344.

Azoulay, P., Jones, B. F., Kim, J. D., & Miranda, J. (2022, March). Immigration and entrepreneurship in the United States [Article]. *American Economic Review-Insights, 4*(1), 71–88. https://doi.org/10.1257/aeri.20200588

Bahar, D., Choudhury, P., & Rapoport, H. (2020). Migrant inventors and the technological advantage of nations. *Research Policy, 49*(9), 103947.

Barnard, H., & Pendock, C. (2013, March). To share or not to share: The role of affect in knowledge sharing by individuals in a diaspora. *Journal of International Management, 19*(1), 47–65. https://doi.org/10.1016/j.intman.2012.11.003

Barney, J. (1991). Firm resources and sustained competitive advantage. *Journal of Management, 17*(1), 99.

Baycan, T., Sahin, M., & Nijkamp, P. (2012, December). The urban growth potential of second-generation migrant entrepreneurs: A sectoral study on Amsterdam. *International Business Review, 21*(6), 971–986. https://doi.org/10.1016/j.ibusrev.2011.11.005

Bhattacharya, U., & Groznik, P. (2008, August). Melting pot or salad bowl: Some evidence from US investments abroad [Article]. *Journal of Financial Markets, 11*(3), 228–258. https://doi.org/10.1016/j.finmar.2008.01.004

Bonacich, E. (1973). A theory of middleman minorities. *American Sociological Review, 38*, 583–594.

Bonacich, E., & Modell, J. (1980). *The economic basis of ethnic solidarity: Small business in the Japanese American community*. University of California Press.

Brannen, M. Y., & Thomas, D. C. (2010). Bicultural individuals in organizations: Implications and opportunity. *International Journal of Cross Cultural Management, 10*(1), 5–16.

Bruning, N. S., Sonpar, K., & Wang, X. Y. (2012., May). Host-country national networks and expatriate effectiveness: A mixed-methods study. *Journal of International Business Studies, 43*(4), 444–450. https://doi.org/10.1057/jibs.2012.5

Burt, R. S. (2000). The network structure of social capital. *Research in Organizational Behavior, 22*, 345–423.

Cai, H., Meng, Y., & Chakraborty, S. (2021, 2021/02/01). Migrants and exports: Decomposing the link. *Journal of World Business, 56*(2), 101166.

Choudhury, P. (2016, May). Return migration and geography of innovation in MNEs: A natural experiment of knowledge production by local workers reporting to return migrants [Article]. *Journal of Economic Geography, 16*(3), 585–610. https://doi.org/10.1093/jeg/lbv025

Choudhury, P. (2022). How "digital nomad" visas can boost local economies. *Harvard Business Review*.

Choudhury, P., Foroughi, C., & Larson, B. (2021, 2021/04/01). Work-from-anywhere: The productivity effects of geographic flexibility. *Strategic Management Journal, 42*(4), 655–683. https://doi.org/10.1002/smj.3251

Choudhury, P., & Kim, D. Y. (2019, February). The ethnic migrant inventor effect: Codification and recombination of knowledge across borders [Article]. *Strategic Management Journal, 40*(2), 203–229.

Chung, H. F. L., Naruemitmongkonsuk, J., & Enderwick, P. (2010). Immigrant employee effects in international strategy: An exploratory study of international service firms. *International Marketing Review, 27*(6), 652–675. https://login.proxy.libraries.rutgers.edu/login?url=http://search.ebscohost.com/login.aspx?direct=true&db=edselc&AN=edselc.2-52.0-78349245875&site=eds-live

Chung, H. F. L., & Tung, R. L. (2013). Immigrant social networks and foreign entry: Australia and New Zealand firms in the European Union and greater China. *International Business Review, 22*(1), 18–31.

Cissé, D. (2021). As migration and trade increase between China and Africa, *Traders at Both Ends Often Face Precarity.*

Coase, R. H. (1937). The nature of the firm. *Economica, 4*(16), 386–405. http://www.jstor.org/stable/2626876 (New Series)

Czinkota, M., Khan, Z., & Knight, G. (2021). International business and the migrant-owned enterprise. *Journal of Business Research, 122*, 657–669.

d'Aiglepierre, R., David, A., Levionnois, C., Spielvogel, G., Tuccio, M., & Vickstrom, E. (2020). *A global profile of emigrants to OECD countries.* OECD iLibrary. https://doi.org/10.1787/0cb305d3-en

Dierickx, I., & Cool, K. (1989). Asset stock accumulation and sustainability of competitve advantage [Article]. *Management Science, 35*(12), 1504–1511.

Docquier, F., & Rapoport, H. (2012). Globalization. *Brain Drain, and Development., 50*, 681–731. http://search.ebscohost.com/login.aspx?direct=true&db=ofm&AN=79961450&site=ehost-live

Dunning, J. H. (1980). Toward an eclectic theory of international production: Some empirical tests. *Journal of International Business Studies, 11*(1), 9–31. https://doi.org/10.2307/154142

Dunning, J. H. (1988). The eclectic paradigm of international production: A restatement and some possible extensions. *Journal of International Business Studies, 19*(1), 1–31. https://doi.org/10.2307/154984

Dunning, J. H. (2005). Institutional reform, foreign direct investment and European transition economices. In R. Grosse (Ed.), *International business and government relations in the 21st century* (pp. 49–78). Cambridge University Press.

Edler, J., Fier, H., & Grimpe, C. (2011, July). International scientist mobility and the locus of knowledge and technology transfer [Article]. *Research Policy, 40*(6), 791–804.

Ellis, P. (2000). Social ties and foreign market entry [Article; Proceedings paper]. *Journal of International Business Studies, 31*(3), 443–469.

Ellis, P. D. (2011, January). Social ties and international entrepreneurship: Opportunities and constraints affecting firm internationalization. *Journal of International Business Studies, 42*(1), 99–127.

Fainshmidt, S., Smith, A. W., & Aguilera, R. V. (2021, 2022/07/01). Where do born Globals come from? A Neoconfigurational institutional theory. *Organization Science, 33*(4), 1251–1272. https://doi.org/10.1287/orsc.2021.1497

Farh, C. I. C., Bartol, K. M., Shapiro, D. L., & Shin, J. (2010, July). Networking abroad: A process model of how expatriates form support ties to facilitate adjustment. *Academy of Management Review, 35*(3), 434–454.

Filatotchev, I., Strange, R., Piesse, J., & Lien, Y. C. (2007, July). FDI by firms from newly industrialised economies in emerging markets: Corporate governance, entry mode and location [Article]. *Journal of International Business Studies, 38*(4), 556–572.

Fitzsimmons, S. R. (2013, October). Multicultural employees: A framework for understanding how they contribute to organizations. *Academy of Management Review, 38*(4), 525–549.

Foley, C. F., & Kerr, W. R. (2013). Ethnic innovation and U.S. multinational firm activity. *Management Science, 59*(7), 1529–1544. https://doi.org/10.1287/mnsc.1120.1684

Fry, C. V. (2023). Bridging the gap: Evidence from the return migration of African scientists. *Organization science (Providence, R.I.), 34*(1), 404–432. https://doi.org/10.1287/orsc.2022.1580

Furusawa, M., & Brewster, C. (2015, January). The bi-cultural option for global talent management: The Japanese/Brazilian Nikkeijin example [Article]. *Journal of World Business, 50*(1), 133–143.

Gillespie, K., Riddle, L., Sayre, E., & Sturges, D. (1999). Diaspora interest in homeland investment. *Journal of International Business Studies, 30*(3), 623–634. https://doi.org/10.1057/palgrave.jibs.8490087

Glennie, A., & Chappell, L. (2010). *Show me the money (and opportunity): Why skilled people leave home — And why they sometimes return.* Retrieved August 9, 2015, from.

Gould, D. M. (1994). Immigrant links to the home country: Empirical implications for U.S. bilateral trade flows. *Review of Economics & Statistics, 76*(2), 302. https://login.proxy.libraries.rutgers.edu/login?url=http://search.ebscohost.com/login.aspx?direct=true&db=buh&AN=5627792&site=ehost-live

Granovetter, M. (1985). Economic action and social structure: The problem of embeddedness. *American Journal of Sociology, 91*(3), 481–510.

Granovetter, M. S. (1973). The strength of weak ties. *American Journal of Sociology, 78*(6), 1360–1380. https://doi.org/10.2307/2776392

Hainmueller, J., & Hopkins, D. J. (2014, 2014/05/11). Public attitudes toward immigration. *Annual Review of Political Science, 17*(1), 225–249.

Hajro, A. A., Brewster, C. C., Haak-Saheem, W. W., & Morley, M. J. M. J. (2022). Global migration: Implications for international business scholarship. *Journal of International Business Studies, 1–17,* 1134. https://doi.org/10.1057/s41267-022-00565-z

Hernandez, E. (2014, March). Finding a home away from home: Effects of immigrants on Firms' foreign location choice and performance [Article]. *Administrative Science Quarterly, 59*(1), 73–108.

Hernandez, E., & Kulchina, E. (2020, July-August). Immigrants and foreign firm performance [Article]. *Organization Science, 31*(4), 797–820. https://doi.org/10.1287/orsc.2019.1331

Hong, H. J., & Minbaeva, D. (2022, February). Multiculturals as strategic human capital resources in multinational enterprises [Article]. *Journal of International Business Studies, 53*(1), 95–125. https://doi.org/10.1057/s41267-021-00463-w

Hornung, E. (2014, January). Immigration and the diffusion of technology: The Huguenot diaspora in Prussia. *American Economic Review, 104*(1), 84–122.

Hung-Wen, L. (2007). Factors that influence expatriate failure: An interview study [Article]. *International Journal of Management, 24*(3), 403–413.

Hunt, J., & Gauthier-Loiselle, M. (2010, April). How much does immigration boost innovation? [Article]. *American Economic Journal-Macroeconomics, 2*(2), 31–56.

Hymer, S. H. (1960). *The international operations of National Firms: A study of direct foreign investment*. MIT Press.

Johanson, J., & Vahlne, J.-E. (1977, Spring/Summer 77). The internationalization process of the firm: A model of knowledge development and increasing foreign market commitments [Article]. *Journal of International Business Studies, 8*(1), 25–34. http://search.ebscohost.com/login.aspx?direct=true&db=buh&AN=4668270&site=ehost-live

Kane, A. A., & Levina, N. (2017). 'Am I still one of them?': Bicultural immigrant managers navigating social identity threats when spanning global boundaries: Navigating identity threats in spanning boundaries. *Journal of Management Studies, 54*(4), 540–577.

Karreman, B., Burger, M. J., & van Oort, F. G. (2017). Location choices of Chinese multinationals in Europe: The role of overseas communities [Article]. *Economic Geography, 93*(2), 131–161. <Go to ISI>://WOS:000396851300003.

Kulchina, E. (2016, July). A path to value creation for foreign entrepreneurs [Article]. *Strategic Management Journal, 37*(7), 1240–1262.

Landolt, P., Autler, L., & Baires, S. (1999). From hermano lejano to hermano mayor: The dialectics of Salvadoran transnationalism. *Ethnic and Racial Studies, 22*, 290–315.

Lee, J. (1999). Retail niche domination among African American, Jewish and Korean entrepreneurs. Competition, coethnic advantage and disadvantage. *The American behavioral scientist (Beverly Hills), 42*(9), 1398–1416. https://doi.org/10.1177/0002764299042009014

Levin, D. Z., & Barnard, H. (2013). Connections to distant knowledge: Interpersonal ties between more- and less-developed countries. *Journal of International Business Studies, 44*(7), 676–698. https://doi.org/http://www.palgrave-journals.com/jibs/archive/index.html

Levin, D. Z., & Cross, R. (2004). The strength of weak ties you can trust: The mediating role of trust in effective knowledge transfer. *Management Science, 50*(11), 1477–1490.

Li, Y., Hernandez, E., & Gwon, S. (2019). When do ethnic communities affect foreign location choice? Dual entry strategies of Korean banks in China? *Academy of Management Journal, 62*(1), 172–195.

Liu, X., Gao, L., Lu, J., & Wei, Y. (2015, January). The role of highly skilled migrants in the process of inter-firm knowledge transfer across borders. *Journal of World Business, 50*(1), 56–68.

Madhavan, R., & Iriyama, A. (2009, October-November). Understanding global flows of venture capital: Human networks as the "carrier wave" of globalization [Article]. *Journal of International Business Studies, 40*(8), 1241–1259. https://doi.org/10.1057/jibs.2009.6

Marino, A., Mudambi, R., Perri, A., & Scalera, V. G. (2020). Ties that bind: Ethnic inventors in multinational enterprises' knowledge integration and exploitation. *Research Policy, 49*(9), 103956. https://doi.org/10.1016/j.respol.2020.103956

Miguelez, E., & Morrison, A. (2022). Migrant inventors as agents of technological change. *The Journal of technology transfer., 48,* 669. https://doi.org/10.1007/s10961-022-09927-z

Miguelez, E., & Temgoua, C. N. (2020). Inventor migration and knowledge flows: A two-way communication channel? *Research Policy, 49*(9), 103914.

Moreland, R. L., & Beach, S. R. (1992). Exposure effects in the classroom: The development of affinity among students. *Journal of Experimental Social Psychology, 28*(3), 255–276.

Moschieri, C., & Fernandez-Moya, M. (2022, July). A dynamic long-term approach to internationalization: Spanish publishing firms' expansion and emigrants in Mexico (1939-1977). *Journal of International Business Studies, 53*(5), 818–849. https://doi.org/10.1057/s41267-021-00489-0

Naumann, E. (1993). Organizational predictors of expatriate job-satisfaction [Article]. *Journal of International Business Studies, 24*(1), 61–80.

Ndofor, H. A., & Priem, R. L. (2011, May). Immigrant entrepreneurs, the ethnic enclave strategy, and venture performance [Article]. *Journal of Management, 37*(3), 790–818.

Neville, F., Orser, B., Riding, A., & Jung, O. (2014, January). Do young firms owned by recent immigrants outperform other young firms? [Article]. *Journal of Business Venturing, 29*(1), 55–71.

Nonaka, I. (1994). A dynamic theory of organizational knowledge creation [Article]. *Organization Science, 5*(1), 14–37. https://login.proxy.libraries.rutgers.edu/login?url=http://search.ebscohost.com/login.aspx?direct=true&db=buh&AN=7098440&site=ehost-live

Nonaka, I., & Takeuchi, H. (1995). *The knowledge-creating company: How Japanese companies create the dynamics of innovation.* Oxford University Press.

Oddou, G., Mendenhall, M., & Oddou, G. (1985). The dimensions of expatriate acculturation - a review. *The Academy of Management review., 10*(1), 39–47.

OECD. (2011). Skilled migration in OECD regions. In *OECD regions at a glance 2011.* OECD Publishing.

OECD. (2021). *International migration outlook 2021*. OECD. https://doi.org/10.1787/29f23e9d-en

Oettl, A., & Agrawal, A. (2008a, December). International labor mobility and knowledge flow externalities [Article]. *Journal of International Business Studies, 39*(8), 1242–1260.

Oettl, A., & Agrawal, A. (2008b). International labor mobility and knowledge flow externalities. *Journal of International Business Studies, 39*(8), 1242–1260.

Oviatt, B. M., & McDougall, P. P. (2005). Toward a theory of international new ventures. *Journal of International Business Studies, 36*(1), 29–41. https://doi.org/10.1057/palgrave.jibs.8400128

Oviatt, B. M., McDougall, P. P., & Marvin, L. (1995). Global start-ups: Entrepreneurs on a worldwide stage. *The Academy of Management executive (1993), 9*(2), 30–44.

Pandey, A., Aggarwal, A., Devane, R., & Kuznetsov, Y. (2006). The Indian diaspora: A unique case? In Y. Kuznetsov (Ed.), *Diaspora networks and the international migration of skills*. The World Bank Development Studies.

Penrose, E. T. (1959). *The theory of the growth of the firm*. Blackwell.

Perri, A., Scalera, V. G., & Mudambi, R. (2015). *An analysis of the co-inventor networks associated with the Chinese pharmaceutical industry*. DRUID15, June 15–17, 2015. LUISS.

Polanyi, M. (1961). *The tacit dimension*. University of Chicago Presss.

Politzer, M. (2008). China and Africa: Stronger economic ties mean more migration.

Poppo, L., & Zenger, T. (2002). Do formal contracts and relational governance function as substitutes or complements? [Article]. *Strategic Management Journal, 23*(8), 707.

Portes, A. (1995). Economic sociology and the sociology of immigration: A conceptual overview. In A. Portes (Ed.), *The economic sociology of immigration*. Russell Sage Foundation.

Portes, A. (1997). Immigration theory for a new century: Some problems and opportunities. *International Migration Review, 31*(4), 799–825. https://doi.org/10.2307/2547415

Portes, A., & Sensenbrenner, J. (1993). Embeddedness and immigration: Notes on the social determinants of economic action [Research article]. *American Journal of Sociology, 98*(6), 1320–1350.

Rauch, J. E., & Trindade, V. (2002). Ethnic Chinese networks in international trade. *Review of Economics & Statistics, 84*(1), 116.

Saxenian, A. (1999). *Silicon Valley's new immigrant entrepreneurs*. Public Policy Institute of California.

Saxenian, A. (2002a). Brain Circulation: How high-skill immigration makes everyone better off. *Brookings, 1*, 28.

Saxenian, A. (2002b). *Local and global networks of immigrant professionals in Silicon Valley*. Public Policy Institute of California.

Saxenian, A. (2002c). Transnational communities and the evolution of global production networks: The cases of Taiwan, China and India. *Industry and Innovation, 9*(3), 183–202.

Saxenian, A. (2006). *The new Argonauts*. Harvard University Press.

Saxenian, A., & Hsu, J. Y. (2001, December 1, 2001). The Silicon Valley–Hsinchu Connection: Technical Communities and Industrial Upgrading. *Industrial and Corporate Change, 10*(4), 893–920. https://doi.org/10.1093/icc/10.4.893

Scellato, G., Franzoni, C., & Stephan, P. (2015). Migrant scientists and international networks. *Research Policy, 44*(1), 108–120.

Schotter, A., & Abdelzaher, D. (2013, March). The boundary spanning effects of the Muslim diaspora on the internationalization processes of Firms from Organization of Islamic Conference Countries. *Journal of International Management, 19*(1), 82–98. https://doi.org/10.1016/j.intman.2012.09.002

Sequeira, J. M., Carr, J. C., & Rasheed, A. A. (2009, September). Transnational entrepreneurship: Determinants of firm type and owner attributions of success [Article]. *Entrepreneurship Theory and Practice, 33*(5), 1023–1044.

Sergeant, A., & Frenkel, S. (1998). Managing people in China: Perceptions of expatriate managers [Article]. *Journal of World Business, 33*(1), 17–34.

Shukla, P. (2016). *Migrants, institutional change and the geography of foreign direct investment*. Ph.D. Thesis, Rutgers University.

Shukla, P., & Cantwell, J. (2018). Migrants and multinational firms: The role of institutional affinity and connectedness in FDI. *Journal of World Business, 53*(6), 835–849.

Sinkovics, N., & Reuber, R. A. (2021, June). Beyond disciplinary silos: A systematic analysis of the migrant entrepreneurship literature [Article]. *Journal of World Business, 56*(4), 101223. https://doi.org/10.1016/j.jwb.2021.101223

Sonderegger, P., & Taeube, F. (2010, December). Cluster life cycle and diaspora effects: Evidence from the Indian IT cluster in Bangalore. *Journal of International Management, 16*(4), 383–397. https://doi.org/10.1016/j.intman.2010.09.008

Sui, S., Morgan, H. M., & Baum, M. (2015, October). Internationalization of immigrant-owned SMEs: The role of language [Article]. *Journal of World Business, 50*(4), 804–814.

Tajfel, H., & Turner, J. C. (1979). An integrative theory of intergroup conflict. In W. G. Austin & S. Worchel (Eds.), *The social psychology of intergroup relations* (pp. 33–47). Brooks/Cole.

Teece, D. J., Pisano, G., & Shuen, A. (1997). Dynamic capabilities and strategic management [Article]. *Strategic Management Journal, 18*(7), 509–533. https://login.proxy.libraries.rutgers.edu/login?url=http://search.ebscohost.com/login.aspx?direct=true&db=buh&AN=12493427&site=ehost-live

Tung, R. L. (2008). Brain circulation, diaspora, and international competitiveness. *European Management Journal, 26*(5), 298–304.

Useche, D., Miguelez, E., & Lissoni, F. (2019). Highly skilled and well connected: Migrant inventors in cross-border M&As. *Journal of International Business Studies, 51*(5), 737–763.

Uzzi, B. (1997, March). Social structure and competition in interfirm networks: The paradox of embeddedness [Article]. *Administrative Science Quarterly, 42*(1), 35–67. https://doi.org/10.2307/2393808

Verhoef, P. C., Broekhuizen, T., Bart, Y., Bhattacharya, A., Dong, J. Q., Fabian, N., & Haenlein, M. (2021, January). Digital transformation: A multidisciplinary reflection and research agenda [Article]. *Journal of Business Research, 122,* 889–901. https://doi.org/10.1016/j.jbusres.2019.09.022

Wang, D. (2015, March). Activating cross-border brokerage: Interorganizational knowledge transfer through skilled return migration [Article]. *Administrative Science Quarterly, 60*(1), 133–176. <Go to ISI>://WOS:000354860500008.

Williamson, O. E. (1981). The economics of organization: The transaction cost approach. *American Journal of Sociology, 87*(3), 548–577. https://doi.org/10.2307/2778934

Wong, P. L. K., & Ellis, P. (2002). Social ties and partner identification in Sino-Hong Kong international joint ventures [Article; Proceedings paper]. *Journal of International Business Studies, 33*(2), 267–289.

Zaheer, S. (1995). Overcoming the liability of foreignness. *Academy of Management Journal, 38,* 341–363. http://vnweb.hwwilsonweb.com/hww/jumpstart.jhtml?prod=OMNIFT&query=199509104830003+%3Cin%3E+an

Zaheer, S., Lamin, A., & Subramani, M. (2009). Cluster capabilities or ethnic ties? Location choice by foreign and domestic entrants in the services offshoring industry in India. *Journal of International Business Studies, 40*(6), 944–968. https://doi.org/10.2307/40262819

17

How Migration Enhanced a Mexican MNC's Socially Embedded Capability

Anabella Davila

Introduction

According to the International Labour Organization (ILO), in 2019, Latin America contained 3.5 percent of international migrant workers, including refugee flows. Although in the past, migrant workers followed the route to the developed North (United States or Canada), a recent trend is the mobility of individuals between neighboring countries, that is, the Venezuelan diaspora is migrating to Colombia and Peru.

The United Nations (UN) 2030 Sustainable Development Agenda acknowledges migration as an essential aspect of development policy, urging governments to facilitate orderly, safe, regular, and responsible migration and mobility, including implementing planned and well-managed migration policies. Unfortunately, however, much of the recent mass migration of low-skilled workers caught migration systems off guard and quickly overwhelmed them. In this vein, one can observe that private actors (e.g., businesses, non-governmental organizations [NGOs], or charity organizations) respond to the call to enhance factors that can make migration a pillar for regional development while building local migration governance.

Multinational corporations (MNCs) operating in emerging economies in primary sectors constantly receive demands from societies from hiring and

A. Davila (✉)
Tecnologico de Monterrey, Monterrey, Mexico
e-mail: anabella.davila@tec.mx

© The Author(s), under exclusive license to Springer Nature Switzerland AG 2023
A. I. Mockaitis (ed.), *The Palgrave Handbook of Global Migration in International Business*,
https://doi.org/10.1007/978-3-031-38886-6_17

training refugees as part of their corporate social responsibility (CSR) practices (Barnard et al., 2019; Reade et al., 2019). However, international institutions admit that some companies are unwilling to take the risks of hiring refugees because of the legal uncertainty surrounding them (OECD/UNHCR, 2018). This position could respond to several factors, including the lack of social embeddedness capability or specific political and economic circumstances that can harm the company's position within the community or with local governments. A socially embedded capability develops from the company's commitment to creating partnerships with various local organizations and institutions to build social infrastructure for community development (Gifford & Kestler, 2008; London & Hart, 2004). Thus, to understand how companies develop such socially embedded capability, there is a need to examine micro-level processes, interactions, and structures that explain the emergence, function, and effects of that capability (Elg et al., 2017).

The new migration flows of low-skilled migrants and refugees are becoming central to international business research (e.g., Barnard et al., 2019; Szkudlarek et al., 2022). However, we know minimal about how emerging markets MNCs (EMNCs) capitalize on their social embeddedness capabilities or face the contextual challenge of migration. Thus, drawing from a single case study, this chapter aims to understand how migration enhanced the global capability in the social embeddedness of a Mexican MNC. The case builds on today's Mexican contextual challenges of a massive migration flow of low-skilled migrants and refugees from northern Central and South America and the pressures of the United States to adopt the characteristics of a 'safe third country,' including granting refugees' jobs, housing, and health services.

The case discussed in this chapter is about FEMSA (A Mexican MNC in the beverage and diversified conglomerate, employing +320,000 employees), which operates in 13 countries. FEMSA enhanced its global capability in social embeddedness by hiring refugees as part of its diversity and inclusion policy. In addition, the company is under the mentorship of Tent Partnership for Refugees, a non-profit organization that helps the global business community include refugees in their workforce.

Through the migration lens, the case analysis uncovers how a diversity policy offered an alternative path to interact with the community, enhancing the company's social embeddedness by hiring refugees. A chronological examination of events published on the CSR and sustainability reports identified processes and structures that emerged toward building the company's diversity policy. Critical were the processes of internationalization that made the company adopt global standards on diversity issues and train employees to receive a diverse workforce. To manage the diversity policy, the company introduced structures for new human resources practices such as complaints systems, verification and audit mechanisms, and a diversity governance committee. The last event categorized added equality and inclusion to the structure of the policy as principles and actions. Thus, the diversity policy evolved through processes and structures within the firm serving the company to respond to the contextual challenges of migration and enhance its social embeddedness capability.

The remainder of this chapter consists of three parts. The first part outlines the concept of global capability in social embeddedness. The second part provides an overview of Latin America's political and economic migration context, focusing on factors that push the population out of their home countries and factors that make them stay as refugees in safe third countries. Finally, the chapter presents the case of FEMSA and discusses how hiring refugees enhanced the company's global capability in social embeddedness.

The Global Capability in Social Embeddedness

MNCs operate in multilocal social realities and encounter diverse demands and expectations linked to their economic activity (Macdonald, 2013). The literature on social embeddedness proposes that MNCs' economic activity depends on the social relationships in which they participate. MNCs become 'socially embedded' by an iterative process of external pressures and the corresponding responses aligned to the accepted local social processes and outcomes (Macdonald, 2013). Thus, to advance in understanding the MNCs' socially embeddedness capability, there is a need to analyze how the macro socioeconomic processes and global institutions evolved to the level of influencing corporate social behavior. At the same time, uncovering subjacent mechanisms by which local actors base their claims or demands on MNCs. However, external pressures can likely conflict with local claims or demands, influencing MNCs' social responses to privilege one over another (Macdonald, 2013). Thus, MNCs struggle between adhering to the international institutions' social agenda or responding to the needs of the local social actors. Moreover, corporate social behavior can receive coercive pressures or develop a voluntaristic approach when responding to external social pressures or local social demands (Macdonald, 2013).

The literature acknowledges that MNCs operating in emerging economies must understand the social contracts and institutions dominating the local economy. Thus, MNCs' socially embedded strategy in emerging economies requires a locally based community interaction model (London & Hart, 2004) to obtain local legitimacy (Gifford & Kestler, 2008). For example, in Latin America, local communities expect businesses to contribute to economic and social development. Such expectations might be because MNCs tend to invest in the extractive and raw materials sectors that provide low-value-added jobs and require little investment in industrial infrastructure. Therefore, local communities cannot perceive the benefit of letting MNCs operate and exploit their natural resources.

Moreover, local communities have a long history of receiving social investments in education, health, and living standards from local companies as part of their CSR practices (Davila, 2019). Therefore, MNCs seeking to fulfill the communities' social contract must develop a solid social orientation based on a reciprocal relationship with the community beyond providing jobs. The concept of socially embedded capability emerged to explain the MNCs' need to develop a competitive advantage in emerging economies through a different business model. This capability builds on the ability of MNCs subsidiaries to understand local markets based on information and knowledge of trusted individuals, communities, and NGOs, work together with indigenous groups to provide products and services according to their needs, and build social infrastructure for community development (Gifford & Kestler, 2008; London & Hart, 2004). However, scholars advise MNCs operating in emerging economies that seek a competitive advantage based on their social embeddedness capability might not be sustainable in the long run. There is a risk of substituting local institutions for community development or simply, and it could be challenging to create institutions for market governance. Therefore, there is a need to identify what social actions or practices competitors find difficult to imitate. Moreover, their implementation could be unique, making them non-transferable within the MNC (Lashitew & van Tulder, 2020).

The management of a social embeddedness capability requires the support of certain micro-foundations and routines within the company. The micro-foundation framework identifies individual capabilities, organizational processes, and routines of dynamic capabilities (Teece, 2007). Elg et al. (2017) adopted and extended the micro-foundation framework to study how MNCs in emerging economies cope with different institutional environments. They analyzed the micro-level components of individuals, processes and interactions, and structures. For them, the individual category includes behaviors and abilities. Process and interactions refer to the interplay between individuals and various organizational processes. And the structure category requires rules, norms, and systems. For this study, the micro-level analysis of the components only took the process and structures because of the unobtrusive research method.

Latin American MNCs' Social Actions and Practices

Some studies on the corporate social behavior of MNCs from advanced economies (e.g., European or North American) show how they respond more to the global social agenda and central corporate policies throughout their international operations than to the local societal needs (Huemer, 2010; Husted & Allen, 2006). In contrast, other studies show that MNCs from emerging economies (EMNCs) respond more to local social needs (Davila, 2021; Davila et al., 2018). Specifically, Davila et al. (2018) identified four mechanisms through which Latin American MNCs engage with their local stakeholders. One, Latin American MNCs report a partnership with local social organizations. Such organizations act as intermediaries between the company and the community groups. Local community organizations can reach out to silent (or nonvisible) stakeholders who can benefit from the company's social practices; otherwise, they may remain isolated or eventually generate conflict. Two, Latin American MNCs inform about a continuous dialogue with community members, although they tailor the dialogue mode according to specific stakeholder groups. For example, some stakeholder groups communicate better through group meetings with the company than individually. Three, Latin American MNCs show how they develop networks of volunteers (employees and community members) to help them implement the companies' social practices. And four, Latin American MNCs compensate for the social deficiencies in the community by creating social infrastructure in health, education, and living standards because of the lack of governmental capacity or resources to build such infrastructure. However, Latin American MNCs seek to respond to the global social agenda pressures, though they respond late and not constantly. With a few exceptions, Latin American MNCs publish corporate social responsibility or sustainability reports inconsistently with little content on the global social agenda (e.g., Global Reporting Initiative [GRI], UN Global Compact [UNGC], or UN Sustainable Development Goals) (Davila, 2022).

Although literature grants EMNCs, in general, valuable knowledge on the dynamics of local markets, Latin American MNCs also have a long tradition of compensating for social institutions' deficiencies impacting socioeconomic development (Davila, 2021; Schneider, 2013). Economic history shows how emblematic Mexican MNCs have offered education and health services to their employees, their families, and, by extension, the community since the late nineteenth century. These companies built primary and vocational schools, colleges and universities, health clinics, and hospitals. Moreover, some companies offered their employees credit for housing and other needs, aiming to improve their living standards (Davila, 2021; Saragoza, 1988).

Although Mexican MNCs have long understood the need to add to their CSR practices a community development approach as part of their business social responsibilities, a new challenge appears in the local social context. That is, the flow of thousands of migrants needing temporary jobs and housing in Mexican cities along the US northern border while waiting for a legal permit to migrate to the United States.

The next section of the chapter presents a brief overview of the political and economic contexts of Migration in Latin America before introducing the case of FEMSA.

Political and Economic Context of Migration in Latin America

An overview of Latin America's political and economic migration context focuses on factors that push the population out of their home countries and factors that make them stay as refugees in safe third countries. International institutions attribute forced human mobility to the social inequality, poverty, and violence migrants suffer in their home countries. In this case, migrants either ask for refugee status or a permit for free transit to the developed North—Canada and United States. However, any country that accepts refugees needs the appropriate infrastructure to offer shelter and assistance for health, educational, and legal services. Moreover, migrants need more attention to help adapt to the receiving country in their journey to the North. Finally, when appropriately processed, a positive view of the migration process is a form of socioeconomic investment.

The 2019 *Social Panorama of Latin America and the Caribbean*, published by the United Nations Economic Commission for Latin America and the Caribbean (ECLAC), urges nations to strengthen multilateral cooperation to protect migrants because the Latin American migration panorama is facing a humanitarian crisis (ECLAC, 2019). In other words, Latin American countries should closely follow recent migration flows from and between countries of northern Central America and Venezuela into South America to increase protection and ensure adherence to the neighboring countries to the regional development agreement plans. According to the ECLAC (2019), migrants constitute a complex and challenging group to categorize as part of the population in the region because they are diverse. For example, there are asylum seekers, economic migrants, unaccompanied children and adolescents, environmental migrants, irregular migrants, trafficked persons, victims of trafficking, and stranded migrants. This last and new category of migrants refers to those detained for lengthy periods, have had their asylum applications rejected, or are in an irregular migration status (ECLAC, 2019). Naturally, then, migrants with such a diverse profile require different needs.

Migratory Trends

Migratory trends indicate that intraregional migration in 2019 accounted for 63 percent of the total migration movement in Latin America and the Caribbean (ECLAC, 2019). Analysts also observed the increments of migrants according to the country of origin (e.g., Venezuela and some Caribbean countries) and the country's destination (e.g., Colombia, Chile, Ecuador, and Peru). In addition, UNs' population surveys indicate that in 2019, 40.5 million Latin American and Caribbean people lived outside the countries where they were born, accounting for 6 percent of the Latin American population (ECLAC, 2019).

Although the case of Venezuelan migrants is noteworthy, international institutions are not paying much attention or promoting funding to protect them (Van Praag, 2019). Analysts stress that Venezuela suffers from a humanitarian crisis in which the government cannot provide for the population's basic needs—food and health services (Van Praag, 2019). However, Venezuelan migrants are not leaving the country because of an armed conflict; therefore, their host countries do not consider them refugees, which would make them eligible for international aid. Moreover, Venezuelan migrants do not consider themselves refugees either. Van Praag (2019) informs that most Venezuelan migrants have a residency permit or other documents allowing them to stay or work in their destination country.

Migrants are a vulnerable group of the population, and they encounter violence, racism, and xenophobia during their transit to other countries or within the host countries. Mexico is a hospitable country for migrants. In various stages of the twentieth century, it received migrants escaping from dictatorship governments such as Argentina, Chile, and Spain or armed conflicts in Central America. However, since 2018, caravans, a form of a massive and organized collectivity of migrants from northern Central America, have entered Mexico in transit to the United States (Ortega Velázquez, 2020). Table 17.1 shows indicators of poverty, social inequality, and peace (because of the difficulties in measuring violence) in some of the migrants' home countries. The country profiles portray a significant deterioration in such indicators, a factor that can cause the expulsion of their population.

The Trump administration (2017–2021) intensified pressures on Mexico to stop such caravans of migrants to the United States. In 2019, Trump threatened Mexico that if the Mexican government did not stop the caravans in their northern borders, he would withdraw the United States from the North American Free Trade Agreement (NAFTA) under review at that time (El Norte, 2018). Later, Trump repeated his threat. Still, at that time, it was to impose a 5 percent tariff on all US imports from Mexico if the Mexican government would not stop undocumented migrants from El Salvador, Guatemala, Honduras, and Nicaragua. Moreover, Trump threatened countries that expelled citizens withdrawing financial support, such as Honduras.

The Mexican Foreign Affairs Minister informed the press that deploying more than 25,000 National Guard members to help with the migration flows

Table 17.1 Country profile indicators of poverty, social inequality, and peace (in contrast to violence)

Country	Poverty Rate[a]	Social Inequality[b]	Peace[c]
El Salvador	32.0% (2019)	38.8% (2019)	114
Guatemala	59.3% (2014)	48.3% (2014)	106
Honduras	48.0% (2019)	48.2% (2019)	117
Nicaragua	24.9% (2016)	46.2% (2016)	124

Source: Adapted by the author from World Bank (2023a, 2023b); Institute for Economics and Peace (IEP) (2022)
[a]The poverty rate is the number of people (expressed as a percentage) in each demographic group whose income falls below the poverty line. The numbers in this column indicate the percentage of people below the poverty line in each country and next to the year of the last data registered by the World Bank
[b]Social inequality refers to the different means people have to access and use resources for personal growth (e.g., health, education, and other societal goods) that result in unequal distribution across societal groups. Although analysts link social inequality to economic and wealth inequality, it is generally measured through the Gini Index, and expressed as a percentage. Next to the percentage of each country appears the year of the last data registered by the World Bank
[c]There are so many types of violence with a unique form of measurement that makes it difficult to compare the degree of violence among countries. Therefore, analysts propose to measure peace which is the absence of violence. Thus, in measuring peace, analysts measure violence. The Institute for Economics and Peace produces the Global Peace Index, a comprehensive assessment of a country's social, political, and economic factors that create peace. The numbers in this column indicate the country's ranking among 163 countries worldwide

on the southern border and not from the northern border succeeded. As a result, the flow of migrants reduced to 56 percent in three months, and the United States withdrew from the economic threats. Furthermore, although the official discourse was that Mexico did not accept to be a safe third country for migrants, it agreed on a series of measures to stop the flow of migrants. For instance, the United States will require asylum seekers to apply for asylum in Mexico before doing so in the United States, providing work opportunities and access to health and education services (Ortega Velázquez, 2020).

Although Mexico installed a policy of granting humanitarian visas for US asylum seekers to wait for their immigration and asylum resolutions, the migration systems were ineffective in responding to the high demand. Mexico failed to build safe zones to keep migrants under control and prevent their displacement within the country's borders, leaving them in lethal danger (Ortega Velázquez, 2020).

Migration Governance

Under the circumstances described above, other social actors emerged to help migrants in their social and economic integration and social adaptation while they continue their journey to the destination country. For example, the UNHCR is the UN agency for refugees in Mexico. There are also religious organizations such as the Jesuit Service for Migrants Mexico and other NGOs. However, it is essential to highlight that these organizations are not calling people to help them to emigrate to Mexico. Instead, their services are for migrants already in the country. Migrants seek to regularize their status. Such NGOs offer them legal assistance and new work skills to apply for local or temporary jobs or help them use government services such as health and education during their short-term stay. In addition, some NGOs offer liaison services with governmental agencies for migrants' human rights protection.

Most international and local organizations, NGOs, and governmental agencies focus on the individual and the migrant's needs or demands during transit. However, other organizations seek to help businesses develop their social capabilities and become part of the migration governance system. For example, the Tent Partnership for Refugees was founded in 2016 by Hamdi Ulukaya, a Turkish US migrant, to connect businesses with refugees to work and integrate them into their new community (Tent, 2023). For Tent, securing a job for a refugee is critical in building a new life. Thus, Tent focuses on training businesses on hiring, training, and mentoring refugees but does not provide direct programs for refugees. Though Tent is a foundation, it does not operate as such, instead, it partners with businesses and other organizations to meet its purpose through various initiatives. For instance, Tent's research shows that European consumers prefer to buy brands from companies that hire refugees because they pay taxes instead of depending on the government for assistance (Tent, 2023a). In another research, Tent partnered with New York University's Stern School of Business, revealing that North American consumers prefer to buy brands from companies that hire refugees expressing their support for various forms of corporate citizenship (Tent, 2022).

Moreover, Tent partnered with a US consulting company to map the status of the Venezuelan migrants in Colombia and Peru to provide advice on how businesses can help with such massive migration. The report informs about the limited access to the financial system and the high level of education of most Venezuelans who struggle to utilize their skills because of the lack of job opportunities. In addition, Colombian and Peruvian governments provide limited health and education assistance for Venezuelans, leaving them to rely upon their network for support. The report also highlights that most Venezuelans are unwilling to return to their country unless there is a significant political change and economic recovery. Therefore, the solutions host governments would require to implement should be permanent, focusing on the long-range stay of Venezuelans (Tent, 2019).

The Tent Partnership for Refugees reports a list of more than 300 MNC members committed to hiring and economically integrating refugees in various ways. MNCs come from a variety of industries around the world. The list includes, for example, large retail stores (e.g., H&M Group, GAP Inc.), global manufacturing consumer goods (e.g., Adidas, New Balance), global consulting companies (e.g., Accenture, Adecco, Deloitte), global banks (e.g., BBVA, Santander), online businesses and services (e.g., Amazon, Airbnb, Google), among many other industries. Next, the chapter analyzes the sustainability reports of one Mexican MNC member of the Tent Partnership for Refugees, aiming to understand how the company enhanced its social embeddedness capability by hiring refugees.

Method

This chapter aims to uncover how migration enhanced FEMSA's global capability in social embeddedness. FEMSA is an emblematic Latin American MNC characterized by its long tradition of commitment to the socioeconomic development of the local communities in which it operates (López-Morales & Ortega-Ridaura, 2018). Therefore, the analysis of FEMSA's social practices presents an opportunity to advance our knowledge of social embeddedness capability in the context of migration.

Corporate reports on sustainability issues are common primary data sources for research in Latin America (e.g., Gómez & García, 2020). Methodologists argue that corporate reports are primary data source because these documents offer multiple details on the actors' names, specific events or activities, statements by senior executives, and descriptions of operations and products, among other topics (Yin, 2015). Therefore, the analysis of the case followed a chronology of events regarding the social embeddedness of the company in the context of migration, as reported in the FEMSA's social responsibility and sustainability reports. Sixteen reports were analyzed for this case—from 2005 to 2021. The reports are available to the public on the company's website and easily downloaded in English. The analysis of consecutive corporate reports facilitated tracing the evolution of the initial practice of hiring individuals belonging to vulnerable groups as part of the company's social practices. Once the practice emerged, the analysis continued pursuing its trend until it reached hiring refugees as part of a corporate diversity policy. This analytical strategy also enabled the author to discern whether the reporting practice responded to pressures or demands according to what the company self-reported.

Data analysis followed the theoretical definitions of micro-level capabilities, processes, and structures (Elg et al., 2017). Thus, a continuous set of practices that allowed the interplay among individuals toward one end went into the process category. In this vein, data reported as practices with rules and norms entered the structural category. Grouping data into these two categories facilitated the analysis and, later, the case narrative.

Findings narrate supporting evidence for the emerging practice to explore what FEMSA reports as a diversity policy that supports its social embeddedness capability. Next, I present the case of FEMSA's social embeddedness capability.

FEMSA's Social Embeddedness Capability

FEMSA is an international conglomerate of businesses in the beverage, logistics, and convenience stores sectors, operating in 13 countries with more than 312,000 employees worldwide. FEMSA's origins can be traced back to 1890 in the desertic northeast city of Monterrey, Mexico. A group of Spaniards that migrated in the second half of the nineteenth century established a brewery as the parent company with subsidiaries along the brewery's supply chain. The brewery's steel and glass subsidiaries impressively impacted the North of

Mexico, becoming the region's industrial development engine (Beato & Sindico, 1983; Haber, 1995; Snodgrass, 1998).

The company also gained legitimacy within the local community for the welfare approach toward the employees. Since its foundation, the company and its subsidiaries encountered a precarious labor market and oriented the employee policies to compensate for the social deficit in which workers lived. First, the company offered employees basic education within its facilities and later opened a vocational school for their technical training. Later, the employees' children received basic education and opened the school doors to the community members. Second, the company offered the employees and their families health-related services such as clinical attention and subsidies on medicines. This benefit also included subsidies for hospital services extending the benefit to nearby communities. Third, in terms of living standards, the company began by granting housing subsidies, later offering housing construction loans, and then credits for housing and other needs. In this vein, FEMSA promoted workers' cooperatives to manage more employee benefits such as recreational centers, saving programs, and subsidized loans (Davila, 2021; Snodgrass, 1998). In the 1982 annual report, the company informed about providing technical training to the employees through the new company's educational centers, expanding recreational facilities to other parts of the country, and establishing a retirement program to prepare psychologically and physically employees close to retirement. Fourth, regarding health programs, the company introduced preventive healthcare programs for the employees' children (Valores Industriales [former corporate name], 1982). In sum, throughout the twentieth century, FEMSA built and sponsored primary and vocational schools, colleges and universities, hospitals, and health clinics and encouraged employees to own homes.

The literature attributes the social welfare approach of the company toward the employees to the familiar management style adopted by early entrepreneurs in the region (Davila, 2021; Snodgrass, 1998). Economic historians and political science scholars suggest that the management style observed the principles of the Social Doctrine of the Catholic Church that dictate how to manage companies and the obligations of businesses toward their employees and community (Salas-Porras, 2001a, 2001b; Saragoza, 1988). However, critical approaches argued that companies altered the labor market's conditions because not all companies could compensate workers similarly. Another critical view was that the welfare system prevented workers from migrating to the developed North; thus, companies needed to engage workers to stay in the region (Rojas Sandoval, 1997; Saragoza, 1988). Moreover, Snodgrass (1998) argued that the companies based the welfare system on an ideology that sought to generate workers' loyalty and commitment to the company. That is, to build an emotional barrier that would reject an external labor movement that attempted to unify the industry unions nationally under the authority of the federal government of the time. However, such labor initiatives were considered a managerial innovation to build good labor relations that prevail today (Davila, 2021).

The above summary describes FEMSA's underpinnings of an early CSR approach that focuses on practices centered on the employees' community. Framing CSR practices within the employees' socioeconomic context would offer a broader view of the social embeddedness capability as it emerged through such welfare practices. However, we need to know more about how the company transformed employee-centered CSR practices to respond to the social challenge of low-skill migration in the communities in which it operates today. The case now turns to tracing the company's modern CSR practices.

The company published its first social responsibility report in 2005. The report's cover letter highlights the simultaneous creation of economic and social value as the foundation of the company's business culture, highlighting principles and values that focus on developing and respecting human dignity. In addition to continuing the past social practices regarding education, health, and living standards of the employees, their families, and the community, the company reports an agreement with the Mexican Ministry of Economy to support the self-employment program of vulnerable groups. Furthermore, the company committed to opening 100 small convenience stores to integrate people with disabilities, senior citizens, single mothers, and people living in rural areas or extreme poverty. The commitment included training in in-store management subjects (FEMSA, 2005). This initiative could be the foundation of a diversity policy based on community development and social practices.

In 2005, the company reported operations in nine countries and export activities to the United States, Europe, and Asia. In addition, it lists a series of community-oriented social practices operating in Central America, Argentina, Brazil, Colombia, and Venezuela (FEMSA, 2005). Most of such social practices were donations in-kind to local foundations or additions to government social programs.

In 2007, the company informed of its adherence to the 10 principles of the United Nations Global Compact (UNGC), and the report used such a framework to inform about their social practices. Furthermore, regarding human rights and job protection, including the company's suppliers, FEMSA publishes its equal opportunity employer policy, offering work and development opportunities to all people without distinction of gender, age, religion, or condition, and including people with different abilities. Additionally, FEMSA reports about the community development programs in all the operating countries, emphasizing employees' children's education and community health prevention programs (FEMSA, 2007). Thus, in 2007, the company improved its diversity and inclusion policy through the principles of the UNGC.

In 2008, the company reported the adoption of the GRI indicators. Thus, following the GRI Labor Practices and Decent Work Performance Indicators, FEMSA expanded its diversity and inclusion policy. It added financial status, nationality, and race, assuring that the principle of equal employment opportunities guides hiring practices in all the countries of operations. As a result, the company presumed to have a blend of 15 different nationalities among the 120,000 employees in that year. The diversity and inclusion policy included specific training covering the fields of human rights, dignity at work, communication skills, and procedures for handling difficult situations. Additionally, the company reports the introduction of a communication system available to all employees and other stakeholders to make a complaint or claim regarding any behavior against the code of ethics, including discrimination acts or human rights violations (FEMSA, 2008).

Furthermore, in 2008, regarding social investment and in addition to the ongoing social practices, the company started the FEMSA Foundation, operating under a cooperation scheme with local organizations to improve the quality of life in the community (FEMSA, 2008). Thus, following the GRI framework, the company reports a more inclusive diversity employment policy with training and complaint systems. It also has partnerships with local organizations to support social investments in the community.

In 2009, the company re-established a hiring policy stating that an international company recruits directors, executives, and employees from the communities in which it operates. Furthermore, the company extends the training programs on human rights to the security and health center personnel across all business units. In this vein, the company assures its labor policies stipulate full respect for human rights and the fundamental rights established by ILO (FEMSA, 2009). Similarly, the 2010 and 2011 sustainability reports introduced the first-time gender equality issues regarding equal pay for men and women performing the same job. For this matter, the company informs the reviewing of the human resources practices to ensure hiring, promoting, and retaining women. Further, the report stresses a gender-blind job evaluation system based on performance, making no distinction between permanent and temporary workers (FEMSA, 2010, 2011). Hence, the introduction of gender equality issues strengthened the diversity policy.

The 2012 report announced the FEMSA Diversity Model considering six areas: gender, individuals with disabilities, ethnicity, age, sexual orientation, and sociocultural and economic levels. The company sought to build a more diverse and inclusive organization by implementing the model (FEMSA, 2012). In 2013, the company reported an audit process for all the hiring and retention policies in all the business units to confirm that all procedures are free of discriminatory practices. This auditing included economic compensation to ensure no distinction due to gender, age, nationality, or other individual traits (FEMSA, 2013). The structure supporting the diversity policy included a consciousness of inclusiveness in addition to human resources practices.

From 2013 to 2019, the sustainability reports maintained the same information about the company's diversity, equity, inclusion policy, training, and compliance mechanisms. However, the 2020 report announced the hiring of refugees. The company stressed the need to encourage an inclusive workforce by offering job opportunities to individuals of vulnerable groups such as refugees. For this matter, the company informed its partnership with the UNHCR and the Tent Partnership for Refugees (FEMSA, 2020). Moreover, the 2021 information included the creation of the corporate Sustainability, Inclusion, and Diversity Committee, emphasizing the strong commitment of the company from the governance standpoint to manage such issues effectively. In 2020, the company included 200 refugees in its workforce, and in 2021, more than 475 Latin American refugees. Therefore, the diversity policy strengthened the inclusiveness approach and made the company turn once more to the community to learn that refugees need a job. In addition, the company formed alliances with international organizations with experience with refugees and migrants (FEMSA, 2021).

Discussion

The literature on MNCs operating in emerging economies attributes their understanding and integration with the local environment to their socially embedded capability. This capability requires a locally based community interaction model (London & Hart, 2004). In other words, MNCs and communities that work together for community development build social infrastructure based on a network of trusted organizations and institutions. Also, companies work with indigenous groups to provide products and services according to their needs and build social infrastructure for community development (London & Hart, 2004). In turn, the community grants MNCs with local legitimacy (Gifford & Kestler, 2008).

The case of FEMSA stands out from the rest of Latin American MNCs because, since its origins, the company has built social infrastructure for its employees' community. Following the path of employees, employees' families, and relevant community members, FEMSA built and offered infrastructure and services in education, health, and living standards. The company provided all the means for individual and community development during precarious labor market conditions and poor economic performance in Mexico.

However, FEMSA emphasized strengthening its commitment to community development by adjusting its hiring policy to the new social reality of the countries in which it operates. The company introduced a diversity policy focusing on individuals belonging to vulnerable socioeconomic groups. Based on the company's CSR and sustainability reports analysis, the case presents how the policy evolved under specific influence parameters. First, as the company entered the process of internationalization, the company sought to comply with global guidelines on diversity issues. The UNGC and GRI standards played an essential role in how the company strengthened its diversity policy, modifying it according to international guidelines. Second, a specific training process accompanied the diversity policy to prepare the employees to treat individuals belonging to those vulnerable groups that the company hired. Third, new human resources practices, complaints systems, verification and audit mechanisms, and a governance committee supported the diversity policy. All these elements formed a new structure within the organization. Finally, the diversity policy made the company conscious of the need to add equality and inclusion as policy principles and actions.

The analysis of the diversity policy suggests another path to interact with the community. Although the company continues with its social contribution supporting local organizations and institutions that promote community development in the countries of operations, introducing a diversity policy seems to benefit the community differently than before. That is, by offering a job to individuals that belong to vulnerable groups, which usually are ignored by business organizations, seek to make a difference in the community because of the socioeconomic meaning of having a job. However, the company used its experience in building partnerships and alliances with local organizations and governmental agencies to implement the diversity policy. Moreover, the company followed the job-related guidelines of international organizations that helped to strengthen and enforce its diversity policy every year.

It is interesting to note that the evolution of the diversity policy incremented its scope every year until it reached the hiring of refugees. Mexico received a massive migration and the pressures of the United States to keep migrants in the country. However, the government lacks the infrastructure and procedures to receive migrants massively. Since 2019, migrants have entered the country in caravans, seeking help from the Mexican government and society to survive while waiting for the US approval of their migration applications. Many of these migrants in Mexico hold a refugee status but still need help to survive. As a company, FEMSA has experience in identifying the needs of community members and was quick to determine that this group of individuals needed a job. In alliance with the Tent Partnership for Refugees and the UNHCR, the company learned how to turn its diversity policy to tackle this phenomenon and include refugees in their workforce.

Conclusion

A social embeddedness capability might take alternative paths to compete in emerging markets or work with the community for development. Characteristics of such capability might change as the context changes. For example, competing in an emerging market requires a new business model for building products and services along the community needs and with the help of local organizations. In the context of migration, adopting a diversity policy with principles and actions of equality and inclusion built an alternative connection with the community. In this case, FEMSA's enhanced its social embeddedness capability through a diversity policy that included hiring refugees and preparing the company to work with them. Such critical processes and structures supported the company in continuing its social mission and connecting with the community. In this way, this chapter advances our knowledge of social embeddedness capability in the context of migration. Future studies can follow the impact of having refugees in the workforce and the difference that a job makes in the refugee community.

References

Barnard, H., Deeds, D., Mudambi, R., & Vaaler, P. M. (2019). Migrants, migration policies, and international business research: Current trends and new directions. *Journal of International Business Policy, 2*, 275–288. https://doi.org/10.1057/s42214-019-00045-6

Beato, G., & Sindico, D. (1983). The beginning of industrialization in Northeast Mexico. *The Americas, 39*(4), 499–518. https://doi.org/10.2307/981250

Davila, A. (2022). Global pressures and employee-centered reporting practices. In L. Casanova & A. Miroux (Eds.), *Emerging market multinationals report 2022: Reinventing global value chains* (pp. 120–127). S. C. Johnson School of Business, Cornell University/Emerging Markets Institute.

Davila, A. (2021). How Mexican companies contribute to human development. In J. Marques (Ed.), *Business with a conscience: A Routledge research companion* (pp. 211–224). Routledge.

Davila, A. (2019). Analysis of the MNEs' social practices in Latin America: Implications for development studies research. In P. Lund-Thomsen, M. W. Hansen, & A. Lindgreen (Eds.), *Business and development studies: Issues and perspectives* (pp. 310–328). Routledge.

Davila, A., Rodriguez-Lluesma, C., & Elvira, M. M. (2018). Engaging stakeholders in emerging economies: The case of Multilatinas. *Journal of Business Ethics, 152*(4), 949–964. https://doi.org/10.1007/s10551-018-3820-7

ECLAC. (2019). *Social Panorama of Latin America*. Economic Commission for Latin America and the Caribbean (ECLAC), LC/PUB.2019/22-P/Rev.1, Santiago: Chile. Retrieved on February 09, 2023, through https://www.cepal.org/en/publications/44989-social-panorama-latin-america-2019

Elg, U., Ghauri, P. N., Child, J., & Collinson, S. (2017). MNE micro-foundations and routines for building a legitimate and sustainable position in emerging markets. *Journal of Organizational Behavior, 38*(9), 1320–1337. https://doi.org/10.1002/job.2214

El Norte. (2018, April 2). Pide Trump a México frenar migración [Trump asks Mexico to stop migration]. *El Norte, Internacional*. Retrieved on February 6, 2023 through https://busquedas.gruporeforma.com/elnorte/Documento/Web.aspx?id=2841613|ArticulosCMS&url=https://img.gruporeforma.com/imagenes/ElementoRelacionado/7/840/6839162.jpg&text=caravanas+de+migrantes&tit=

FEMSA. (2021). *Sustainability report 2021*. Retrieved on April 29, 2022, through https://www.femsa.com/en/sustainability/resources/sustainability-reports/

FEMSA. (2020). *2020 Sustainability content*. Retrieved on December 29, 2020, through https://www.femsa.com/en/sustainability/resources/sustainability-reports/

FEMSA. (2013). *Sustainability report 2013*. Retrieved on February 19, 2016, through http://www.sustainabilityreport.femsa.com/2013/pdf/full.pdf

FEMSA. (2012). *Sustainability report 2012*. Retrieved on February 19, 2016, through https://www.unglobalcompact.org/system/attachments/21127/original/Sustainability_Report_2012.pdf?1364684836

FEMSA. (2011). *Sustainability report 2011*. Retrieved on February 19, 2016, through http://www.femsa.com/sites/default/files/SR_2011.pdf

FEMSA. (2010). *Sustainability report 2010*. Retrieved on February 19, 2016, through http://www.femsa.com/sites/default/files/SR_2010.pdf

FEMSA. (2009). *Sustainability report 2009*. Retrieved on February 16, 2016, through http://assets.coca-colacompany.com/c5/6f/99cdf032482dac2718bd19f5f3eb/2009_FEMSA.pdf

FEMSA. (2008). *Social responsibility report 2008*. Retrieved on February 19, 2016, through http://www.femsa.com/sites/default/files/SR_2008.pdf

FEMSA. (2007). *2nd social responsibility report*. Retrieved on August 31, 2016, through http://www.femsa.com/sites/default/files/SR_2007.pdf

FEMSA. (2005). *Primer Informe de Responsabilidad Social* [First Social Responsibility Report]. Retrieved on September 26, 2016, through http://www.femsa.com/sites/default/files/IS_2005.pdf

Gómez, N. A., & García, S. M. (2020). Governance and type of industry as determinants of corporate social responsibility disclosures in Latin America. *Latin American Business Review, 21*(1), 1–35. https://doi.org/10.1080/10978526.2019.1697185

Gifford, B., & Kestler, A. (2008). Toward a theory of local legitimacy by MNEs in developing nations: Newmont mining and health sustainable development in Peru. *Journal of International Management, 14*(4), 340–352. https://doi.org/10.1016/j.intman.2007.09.005

Haber, S. (1995). *Industry and underdevelopment: The industrialization of Mexico, 1890–1940*. Stanford University Press.

Huemer, L. (2010). Corporate social responsibility and multinational corporation identity: Norwegian strategies in the Chilean aquaculture industry. *Journal of Business Ethics, 91*, 265–277. https://doi.org/10.1007/s10551-010-0618-7

Husted, B. W., & Allen, D. B. (2006). Corporate social responsibility in the multinational enterprise: Strategic and institutional approaches. *Journal of International Business Studies, 37*(6), 838–849. https://doi.org/10.1057/palgrave.jibs.8400227

Institute for Economics & Peace (IEP). (2022). Global peace index 2022: Measuring peace in a complex world. Sydney, AU. Retrieved on February 15, 2023, through https://www.economicsandpeace.org/research/

Lashitew, A. A., & van Tulder, R. (2020). The limits and promises of embeddedness as a strategy for social value creation. *Critical Perspectives on International Business, 16*(1), 100–115. https://doi.org/10.1108/cpoib-02-2018-0021

London, T., & Hart, S. L. (2004). Reinventing strategies for emerging markets: Beyond the transnational model. *Journal of International Business Studies, 35*(5), 350–370. https://doi.org/10.1057/palgrave.jibs.8400099

López-Morales, J. S., & Ortega-Ridaura, I. (2018). Internationalization, corporate social responsibility, and poverty alleviation: The case of FEMSA in Latin America. In *Examining the private Sector's role in wealth creation and poverty reduction* (pp. 110–137). IGI Global.

Macdonald, K. (2013). The socially embedded corporation. In J. Mikler (Ed.), *The handbook of global companies* (pp. 371–387). Wiley-Blackwell.

OECD/UNHCR. (2018). *Engaging with employers in the hiring of refugees. A 10-point multi-stakeholder action plan for employers, refugees, governments, and civil society*. Retrieved on April 4, 2023, from https://www.unhcr.org/media/37169

Ortega Velázquez, E. (2020). Mexico as a "safe" third country? Instrumentalization of the right to asylum. *Frontera Norte, 32*, 1–28. https://doi.org/10.33679/rfn.v1i1.2019

Reade, C., McKenna, M., & Oetzel, J. (2019). Unmanaged migration and the role of MNEs in reducing push factors and promoting peace: A strategic HRM perspective. *Journal of International Business Policy, 2*, 377–396. https://doi.org/10.1057/s42214-019-00043-8

Rojas Sandoval, J. (1997). *Fábricas pioneras de la industria en Nuevo León [Pioneer industry factories in the state of Nuevo Leon]*. UANL Press.

Salas-Porras, A. (2001a). Corrientes de pensamiento empresarial en México (primera parte) (Streams of entreprenurial thought in Mexico, part one). *Revista Mexicana de Ciencias Políticas y Sociales, 44*(181), 181–210. https://nbn-resolving.org/urn:nbn:de:0168-ssoar-59504-6

Salas-Porras, A. (2001b). Corrientes de pensamiento empresarial en México (segunda parte) (Streams of entreprenurial thought in Mexico, part two). *Revista Mexicana de Ciencias Políticas y Sociales, 44*(183), 227–257. https://nbn-resolving.org/urn:nbn:de:0168-ssoar-59481-6

Saragoza, A. M. (1988). *The Monterrey elite and the Mexican state, 1880–1940*. The University of Texas Press.

Schneider, B. R. (2013). *Hierarchical capitalism in Latin America. Business, labor, and the challenges of equitable development*. Cambridge University Press.

Snodgrass, M. (1998). The birth and consequences of industrial paternalism in Monterrey, Mexico, 1890–1940. *International Labor and Working-Class History, 53*, 115–136. https://doi.org/10.1017/S0147547900013697

Szkudlarek, B., Roy, P., & Lee, E. S. (2022). How multinational corporations can support refugee workforce integration: Empathize globally, strategize locally. *AIB Insights, 22*(3), 1–5. https://doi.org/10.46697/001c.32998

Teece, D. J. (2007). Explicating dynamic capabilities: The nature and microfoundations of (sustainable) enterprise performance. *Strategic Management Journal, 28*(13), 1319–1350. https://doi.org/10.1002/smj.640

Tent. (2023). *About*. Retrieved on March 19, 2023, through https://www.tent.org/

Tent. (2023a). *How hiring refugees helps brands: Europe*. Retrieved on March 19, 2023, through https://www.tent.org/resources/how-hiring-refugees-helps-brands-europe-2023/

Tent. (2022). *How helping brands helps refugees: United States*. Retrieved on March 19, 2023, through https://www.tent.org/resources/helping-refugees-helps-brands-us-2022/

Tent. (2019). *The experience of Venezuelan refugees in Colombia and Peru and how the business community can help*. Retrieved on March 19, 2023, through https://www.tent.org/resources/venezuelan-refugees-colombia-and-peru/

Valores Industriales. (1982). *Informe Anual 1982 [Annual report 1982]*. Corporate Publication.

Van Praag, O. (2019). *Understanding the Venezuelan refugee crisis*. Wilson Center. Retrieved on February 10, 2023, through https://www.wilsoncenter.org/article/understanding-the-venezuelan-refugee-crisis

World Bank. (2023a). Poverty headcount ratio at national poverty lines (% of the population). *Data*. Retrieved on February 13, 2023, through https://data.worldbank.org/indicator/SI.POV.NAHC?locations=1W&start=1984&view=chart

World Bank. (2023b). Gini Index. *Data*. Retrieved on February 13, 2023, through https://data.worldbank.org/indicator/SI.POV.GINI?locations=1W&start=1984&view=chart

Yin, R. K. (2015). *Qualitative research from start to finish*. NY: The Guilford Press.

18

Female Diasporans and Diaspora Networks: A Neglected Resource for Business?

Maria Elo, Ilia Gugenishvili, and Maria Ivanova-Gongne

Introduction

Global migration discussions focus on flows, corridors, and "crises" and employ terms such as country, stock, flow, or direction to understand the phenomenon (e.g., Lee, 1966). In the business context, the role and history of migration as a resource are underexplored and partly misunderstood (Cohen, 2008; Heikkilä, 2017). Migration is perpetual and some diasporas span millennia, like the Jewish diaspora (Cohen, 2008). These social formations, that is, people on the move, have shaped the business per se, being more than a factor condition driving its competitiveness (cf. Porter, 1990; Tung, 2008). Contemporary diasporas that are aggregations of people who share ethnic connotations and heritage do not necessarily wish to return to their home country, partly due to digital participation and more accessible travel (Brinkerhoff, 2009; Elo & Minto-Coy, 2018, see also Cohen, 2008; Elo & Minto-Coy, 2018). In a similar vein, diasporas are becoming more individual and digital (Brinkerhoff, 2009), increasingly building on mobile labor force and talent (Tung, 2008; Habti & Elo, 2019) and less on distinct merchant or

---

M. Elo (✉)
University of Southern Denmark, Odense, Denmark
e-mail: melo@sam.sdu.dk

I. Gugenishvili • M. Ivanova-Gongne
Åbo Akademi University, Turku, Finland
e-mail: ilia.gugenishvili@abo.fi; maria.ivanova@abo.fi

trade diaspora logics as in the past (Cohen, 2008). Mass migrations today relate mainly to forced migration, for example, fleeing from danger, and less to voluntary migration, for example, moving for studies, marriage, or work (Heikkilä, 2009, 2017).

These contemporary trends of boundaryless career and global mobility (Tung, 2008; Habti & Elo, 2019) have created globally a more mobile version of diaspora, a diaspora where individual diasporans seize opportunities beyond one host country and where generations may not only be many but also increasingly mixed and superdiverse (Vertovec, 2007; Meyer, 2001). This development suggests that there exists a superdiverse, multiethnic, multilingual, and multicultural global landscape of diasporas which entails a range of different people, from those without any formal education to those with high skills and formal qualifications (e.g., Fludernik, 2003; Vertovec, 2007; Elo et al., 2022).

A common concern both in real-life and in multiple disciplines is postmigratory integration and economic participation, whether that is in the labor market or self-employment and entrepreneurship (Riaño, 2011; Aman et al., 2022). "Wrong" surname, accent, or skin color, for example, can be tremendous issues even for those diasporans who are local born "neo-locals" and have completed their education in the local context, a phenomenon also referred to as biopolitics (Fassin, 2001; Krivonos, 2020). In fact, many long-term migrants are diasporans who are naturalized and hence also citizens and locals but are not perceived through that lens due to their perceived otherness. Sociologists, among others, have investigated discrimination and barriers that migrants and diasporans face, but similar barriers exist also in entrepreneurship and other social contexts of everyday life, for instance, in interaction with public services and locals, as well as in relation to perceptions of migrants' as individuals/entrepreneurs and of their businesses (e.g., Mak & Nesdale, 2001; Ivanova-Gongne et al., 2021). Such non-inclusive practices, norms, and regulations waste the "brain" (Mattoo et al., 2008). As highly skilled and talented people are often perceived as male, not as women, women with dual careers (i.e., professional and family care careers) tend to be the most invisible and vulnerable "brain" in professional settings among the already invisible diasporans and migrants (Kofman, 2000; Habti, 2014; Eremenko et al., 2017; Elo et al., 2020a, b). Hence, migrant talent remains underemployed and gendered (Kofman, 2000; Christou & Kofman, 2022).

Another overlooked aspect, in addition to the female gender in the diaspora, is how the country of origin (COO) perceives their diasporas abroad. In many cultures, outmigration is associated with treason and egoism (e.g., Ahmed et al., 2018; Emmanuel et al., 2019). In diaspora engagement research, the focus is on positive diaspora engagement, being an act from the diaspora toward the old home country (Plaza & Ratha, 2011; Minto-Coy, 2016). However, these discourses take place largely in the setting of the Global South. More importantly, there is very little evidence of countries engaging with their diasporas and addressing their inherent talent on an individual level as a resource, that is, reverse engagement potential (Brinkerhoff, 2009; Elo & Ivanova-Gongne, 2020; Elo et al., 2022).

Despite the importance of diasporas and circular migration (Tung, 2008; Porter, 1990), COO businesses overlook the potential resource base of their diaspora diversity and skills abroad. Previous research has shown that diasporas generate diaspora pulls, internationalize products and services, act as markets or prosumers, bridge institutional divides, form connections with civil society, introduce and develop innovation, diffuse ethnic products, and possess particular diasporic marketing agility (Riddle & Brinkerhoff, 2011; Rana & Elo, 2017; Silva & Elo, 2017; Elo et al., 2020a, b). Diaspora research often centers on developing countries, leading to a one-sided view, as these findings and assumptions may not apply to developed countries (Plaza & Ratha, 2011; Nkongolo-Bakenda & Chrysostome, 2013). Therefore, it is interesting to consider if small and open economies (Luostarinen & Gabrielsson, 2006) actually employ the full resource base, including their diaspora, to enhance their global competitive advantage.

This study examines Finnish migrants and diasporans abroad, with a focus on Finnish-origin women located in various host countries. We ask: Do Finnish companies or state perceive them as a valuable diasporic resource abroad for business and the economy? This is assessed by examining: What kind of professional outreach have Finnish women abroad received from Finland, if any? Who have contacted them? What purpose or task can be identified in this reverse diaspora engagement? Is this outreach happening at an individual level or through associations and aggregate relations?

The purpose of the study is to introduce and examine the concept of reverse engagement as a talent-skill-resource strategy (cf. Tung, 2008; Gamlen, 2014) and shed light on this activity experienced by migrant-diasporic women. This is usually seen from the re-mobility perspective and country perspective representing a form of brain circulation, illuminating the talent flows and benefits. When addressing the "brain" flows and categories, the focus is on stock, direction, and circulation, but not on the "brain" *staying* in the host country (e.g., Güngör & Tansel, 2014; Subbotin & Aref, 2021). Hence, the migrant-diasporic women's impact and potential represents a conceptual gap. This study reflects experiences in multiple countries and shows if and how female talent and skill translate as resources when abroad.

This is a mixed-methods study combining perspectives and methods, for example, qualitative interviews, ethnographic and autoethnographic observations, and survey data (James, 2016). The lead author has 31 years of experience as a Finnish migrant and diasporan abroad in multiple countries, continents, and cultures, which provides a large network of women with diversity, autoethnographic material, and several insights into diverse organizations. The organization Finnish Women Worldwide and their Finnish professional women worldwide group form an overarching network, but also other networks, such as chambers of commerce, are addressed.

The study contributes to diaspora and migration research, female migrant resources, and resource-talent literature. It advances discussions on the Sustainable Development Goals (SDGs) about inclusion, gender, and work reflecting diasporic women.

Theories on Migration, Diaspora, and Brain Circulation

Migration and Diasporas

International migration refers to mobility across borders, migrating out of one's home country, and accounts for 3.6% of the world's population (IOM, 2022). Migration is becoming increasingly female as 47.9% of migrants are women of working age (ibid.). The economic impact of these women is crucial as they send home a higher percentage of their earnings than men while facing more restrictive labor policies and employment customs (United Nations, n.d.). According to IOM (2023), migrant women are less likely to participate in the labor markets when compared to migrant men, but they are more economically active than native women. This underlines the relevance of female migration, particularly for the Global South. On the individual level, gender is an important factor impacting mobility; it influences the migration decision in the pre-migration phase, the transit period, and the migration experience, as well as the aspirations to return. Gender affects access to services, labor markets, and opportunities (e.g., Aman et al., 2022). IOM calls for consideration of the gendered experiences and the needs and characteristics of different groups of people on the move (IOM Global Data Institute, 2023). As migration and diaspora are gendered, migrant women from the Global North are also not free from these impediments, even as highly skilled people or as entrepreneurs (Elo et al., 2020a).

Diasporas are social and cultural formations that evolve through human mobility; they are discussed in multiple ways but typically reflect some ethnonational glue as an entity (Brubaker, 2005). Diasporas are by no means limited to historical population movements and aggregations (Cohen, 2008); they also represent a variety of people in different types of contemporary groups (Brubaker, 2005; Elo & Minto-Coy, 2018). As Saxenian (2007) has noted, some contemporary diasporas do have the element of origin, but in addition also have a particular location and skill-related uniting factor, such as the Chinese and Indian IT-diaspora formation in Silicon Valley. Such talent diasporas are viewed as elite migrants (Leinonen, 2012; Elo & Leinonen, 2019). Diasporas form "spaces" in host countries that may enable and foster knowledge transfer and economic participation (Elo & Minto-Coy, 2018). However, despite the potential elite characteristics of high education, foreign languages, and developed country origin, female migrants from developed countries do not necessarily flourish professionally in the diaspora, whether in business or academia (Sang et al., 2013).

While general literature on diaspora talent and brain circulation tends to assume that there is a positive evolution and potential, also for women (e.g., Tung, 2008), gendered processes have an intersectional nature that leave an imprint on female diasporas (Elo et al., 2020a, b; Christou & Kofman, 2022). Prior studies point to a positive potential, such as trade facilitation by diaspora and internationalization via transnational entrepreneurial actors (Tung & Chung, 2010; Elo et al., 2020a, b). On the other hand, IOM's data suggest that these dynamics are potentially dissimilar for men and women, and women are perceived less as categories of "brain" or talent despite their contributions, which leads to brain waste (Elo et al., 2020a, b).

Methodology

The study explores how Finnish companies and institutions perceive Finnish women abroad as a diasporic resource for business and the economy. There is limited research on diasporic talent and resource identification, which also links to methodological scarcity in examining such themes.

We focus on the experiences and perceptions of women with a developed country origin, rather than perceptions of the state or business. The study observes and examines interpretations, views, and lived experiences of Finnish origin women, without attempting to generate factual data on the number or type of contacts. Finnishness, in this study, refers to origin, not citizenship.

The study combines qualitative thematic interviews, ethnographic and autoethnographic observations, and survey data (James, 2016). Method triangulation is used (Denzin, 1978). First, ethnographic observations took place between 2006 and 2019 on regular bases in the United States, 1993 and 2022 in Greece, and 1999 and 2022 in Germany. These took place in contexts of social and professional interaction in places of "passage" or "gathering", such as the Suomi-Talo (Finland House), Merimieskirkko (The Finnish Seamen's Mission), different business clubs, and Chambers of Commerce events. Manual field notes have been generated over time. Supplementing the observations, two surveys have been carried out in 2015–2016 and 2018–2019. First, small-scale research was carried out to understand the dynamics of Finnish women in terms of their mobility, family, and how that relates to their careers. This was largely a mixed-style survey building on open-ended questions with 16 respondents. The link to the survey was shared on social media (Facebook) and directly sent to targeted individuals. The second, more extensive survey followed especially the US context as this was found to represent one of the major "career" destinations of Finnish women abroad with more than 600,000 people of Finnish origin. The link to the survey was distributed through social media (Facebook, LinkedIn) and American-based networks and organizations associated with Finland. Fifty-eight women responded. The responses collected through the survey provide valuable descriptive information and help us understand the characteristics and experiences of our respondents. Specifically, among others, the survey provides information on their education, language skills, and past experiences as an immigrant. This information serves as a foundation for further investigation, analysis, and a deeper understanding of the participants' perspectives and insights. Thus, it sets a fruitful ground for the qualitative interviews and their analysis.

Finally, interviews with Finnish women were conducted in 2023. The targeted women share the following criteria: (a) They identify as women of Finnish origin; (b) they also use English and/or other foreign languages in their daily lives; (c) they reside primarily outside Finland; and (d) they are highly skilled/experienced professionals. These women have a personal migratory experience as professionals or have migrated as a spouse (Habti & Elo, 2019). These personal thematic, retrospective interviews represent different destination country contexts.

The majority of the participating women are highly skilled; they have bachelor's or master's degrees, and many of them also have a strong record of work experience. Their Finnish language skills are adequate or fluent for social engagement or work in Finnish. The respondents represent an adult age group, that is, working life age or senior, as many senior citizens continue to work in, for example, the United States or in family businesses. The lead author's experience as a Finnish migrant in multiple countries, cultures, and organizations provides access to diverse observations, autoethnographic material, and several insights into relevant organizations supporting the triangulation. The participant researcher status fostered understanding the phenomenon, creating trust, and accessing respondents. For relevance and validity, the organization Finnish Women Worldwide and their Finnish professional women worldwide group have been helpful in reflecting on the research process. The active approach by Finnish actors was questioned and validated. This was done first through one digital seminar where talent and brain waste were openly discussed among presenters (e.g., the lead author) and the participants, and second by validating those views through in-depth discussions.

The concept of reverse engagement as a talent-skill-resource strategy (cf. Tung, 2008; Gamlen, 2014) is often seen from the re-mobility perspective and country perspective, illuminating talent flows and benefits as a form of brain circulation. Yet, the activity and interest regarding their talent, experienced from the side of the migrant-diasporic women who stay in the host country, remain underexplored. To provide evidence on this discussion, a mixed method with multiple rounds can provide an understanding of the phenomenon and its contextualization, as well as its development over time (cf. era of globalization and digitalization). It is not just a question whether diasporic women are approached as talent, but also where, when, by whom, and how that happens, if it happens at all for the participants. Especially the digital dimension and the globalized context offer cheaper and better tools for accessing women and their talent abroad compared to the previous era where such identification of talent was highly complicated, expensive, and largely based on offline social capital.

Findings

Globalization and different paradigm changes have influenced the way people live and work (Heikkilä, 2017). The patterns of Finnish emigration have radically changed over time. The historical waves in the nineteenth century consisted of poverty and hunger-struck villages and peripheries pushing masses of people seeking livelihood abroad (see, e.g., Korkiasaari & Söderling, 2003); these were similar to the diaspora waves that we have today from developing countries labeled as "economic" and "climate" migrants. In the recent decades, globalization created more diverse, multiple entry-exit migrations and a range of transnational mobilities. These are often triggered by factors that attract and pull people to make such choices based on personal motivations and intentions as voluntary migration (e.g., Heikkilä & Koikkalainen, 2011; Heikkilä, 2009, 2017). These categories of emigration typically represent study, marriage, and work migrations.

Finland has been suffering from a leaking talent pipeline since it joined the European Union, as young and educated Finns leave and very few return (Elo, 2017). Finland has been aware of these concerns. Scholars have tried to actively build circular brain strategies since 2005 to create knowledge and concrete recommendations for policymakers to deliver effective brain circulation and talent policies that would benefit the Finnish economy and society as a whole (see e.g., Raunio, 2005). The new national strategy for 2022–2026 continues to emphasize strengthening the Finnish identity, language, culture, nationality, social participation, and attractiveness of return. The strategy aims to "*making use of expatriate Finns in support of trade and industry, export promotion, research and sustainable development*" (Sisäministeriö, 2021, p. 3).

The Finnish-origin people who have outmigrated from Finland and live abroad are called "ulkosuomalainen" which refers to "outside-Finns" being spatially out of the country. Translated as "expatriate Finns" in English. The term is misleading as they do not necessarily have any corporate expatriate agreements, theoretically, they may represent self-initiated expatriates (Habti & Elo, 2019). Other discussions suggest that living abroad means gradually becoming an outsider in line with the outsidership concept (see Johanson & Vahlne, 2009). Basically, this term addresses Finnish citizens living abroad and those Finnish citizens' descendants who identify themselves as Finns. They are not clearly defined, formally there are 300,000 Finns abroad, but other estimates suggest 1.6 to two million people (see e.g., Korkiasaari & Söderling, 2003). The most popular destination countries for Finns abroad are Sweden, the United Kingdom, Germany, the United States, and Spain (see more in Valtioneuvosto ja ministeriöt, n.d.). The overall trend in growing numbers of outmigration since 1995, interrupted by the Covid-19 pandemic, is visible in the formal statistics of emigration, see Fig. 18.1.

Contrary to popular assumptions on the economic development level, Finland has suffered from brain drain, outmigration, and even negative net migration since 2010. The Covid-19 pandemic and Brexit triggered some return migration. Migration per se is undergoing radical changes not only due to the pandemic but also due to digitalization. Already before the pandemic, Finland was among the leading countries in applying remote and online work practices which enables a vast human potential to work or venture in a location unbound manner (see more in Finnish Immigration Service, n.d.; Occupational Safety and Health Administration in Finland, 2021). It has

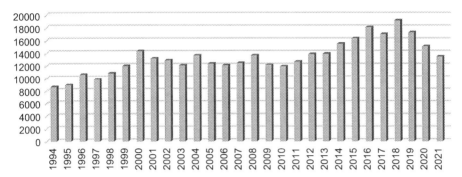

Fig. 18.1 Emigration from Finland. Source: Statistics Finland, compiled by the authors

become more usual for Finns to live and work in two or more countries or have temporary stays abroad. Young people and students benefit from mobility and exchange programs, such as ERASMUS. These foster international mobility of talent but build on brain circulation principle. Interestingly, the pandemic reduced international mobility in general (see more in The Finnish National Agency for Education, n.d.). Following global trends, Finnish study migration and student mobility are also becoming more female, further underlining the female potential.

Although the Ministry of Interior states that next to issues on citizenship services, Finnish schooling abroad, support for return, and political participation, the maintenance and support of Finnish language and culture abroad and the provision of expertise for the Finnish companies in the destination countries—by the Finns abroad—are important issues, the latter category is not perceived to be valued from the perspective of the Finnish women abroad (Valtioneuvosto ja ministeriöt, n.d.).

Findings from Finnish Women in the United States

Finnish women living in the United States are an interesting group due to the strict immigration policy and the opportunities for migrants in the United States. This context matters in multiple ways for their potential. The US immigration policy requires a work permit, entrepreneurial visa, green card, or naturalization. The United States represents a traditional, historical, and multi-category (i.e., study, marriage, work, and entrepreneurial migration) destination for Finns providing an excellent context to study women abroad without having a time or sample bias.

In our survey of Finnish women in the United States, we found that the 58 women had an average age of 22 years when they moved and were highly educated: 24% had a bachelor's degree, 48% had a master's degree, and 8.6% had a Ph.D. They showed multicultural and multilingual characteristics in terms of their families and citizenship as the majority had either acquired US citizenship or had multiple statuses-citizenships. Their spouses were largely non-Finnish, representing predominantly other Nordic country citizens or US Americans. The culturally mixed families represented the majority family pattern in this study. The data indicated linguistic-cultural superdiversity, 3.4% were Swedish speakers, 10.3% were mixed speakers, and the majority belonged to the Finnish-speaker group. The languages spoken in a professional context were Finnish, Swedish, English, Spanish, German, and French. Beyond the diverse areas of expertise, the STEM areas, such as biotechnology, medicine, information technology or engineering were dominating, followed by management, trade, and business while humanities, arts, social, and political sciences represented the smallest category of expertise. Interestingly, 73% of the women felt that they are well-integrated into the US American society, and 45% of women strongly agreed that career opportunities are better in the United States.

The respondents demonstrate valuable professional, linguistic, and cultural resources that are highly relevant for business and economy in general. They may be seen as a sample representing the mobility of Finnish women that are typically relatively young when outmigrating but well-educated (Elo, 2017). Based on this US study, we argue that there is a considerable female resource base in the diaspora that is competent, highly qualified, and able to contribute to business and the economy. This suggests that Finnish women abroad possess relevant and advanced skills, talents, and networks for their COO. This data advances the understanding of the respondents' characteristics and sets the ground for investigating a more comprehensive and nuanced explanation and understanding of the phenomenon.

Observations from Diaspora

During my 31-year work and residence in various countries and sectors, I (lead author), have observed different Finnish diasporas and the development of Finnish women abroad as they navigate their professional growth and career dynamics. The emergence of particular diasporas in these countries and cities have partly idiographic dynamics, but the continuation of professional activity and participation abroad is a common notion. Their development relates to institutions and framings that enable women to exercise their professions. Some locations do not allow working for spouses, have strict regulations on permits, or simply do not offer suitable opportunities. However, many Finnish women turn barriers into stimuli to entrepreneurial activities, creating an alternative path. Transnational activities form one option since digitalization and the internet opened the door to location unbound activity.

Deskilling and resignation are fought with multiple coping strategies. Finnish women seem to be keen to develop their language skills. There are even expectations to become fluent abroad. Finnish women often put very high standards in their professionalism and integration. Many women face difficulties in the early post-migratory stages, yet there is great resilience in developing solutions, skills, and additional languages into a professionally functioning level. Today, different events and female networking are supporting this process of re- and upskilling. For example, Finnish Worldwide Women organize theme evenings, the Finnish Seamen's Mission has already long been organizing specific events for women to provide information on local conditions, and many local groups are also active. There is an increase in developing bilateral chambers of commerce since we established the Finnish-Hellenic Chamber of Commerce in Athens in the mid-1990s. Such organizations are an important connecting element for business and professional networking. The observations suggest that the size of the host country and the intensity of the business matter, for example, the United States is too large to facilitate easy in-person professional networking for all women across the United States. Still, the country is of central importance as a trade and talent hub. For example, in the Finnish American Chamber of Commerce meeting in Washington DC in 2017, this networking concern was expressed as highly relevant. The case of Luxembourg is different, as a small host country with a central location, it gained importance as a female networking hub that is disproportionate to its size. Naturally, these diaspora engagement networks need primus motor individuals. Hence, it is highly important what kind of diaspora waves and flows exist in a location. Younger and working-aged women increase the interest in professional engagement and activity differently than elderly women in diaspora.

While women still tend to dominate in cultural organizations, festivities, and Finnish schooling affairs abroad, I have not encountered many female-focused movements or groups that focus specifically on professional and business development. My observations in more gender-conservative European countries suggest that the host country's gender disparity seems to influence such activities. Hence, there is no one template that Finnish women in the diaspora would use to enact opportunities for their professionalism, but there are certainly common directions and orientations, perhaps with different speeds.

My own experiences over the years echo those of the interviewees. Since 1991, only one Finnish company has proactively connected to help them in a notoriously difficult situation where they saw no other option, linguistically and practically. Acting as an entrepreneur in international business and consulting for decades, the majority of the activity I have encountered has been the other way around, that is, so-called passive internationalization where the request and impetus come from the foreign actors being interested in Finland or its products or services. I can confirm the pattern that Finnish diasporic women are rarely perceived as business resources by the Finnish actors, such as business, academia, or other institutions. The outreach of COO is rare and limited.

Findings from Interviews

In 2023, we interviewed seven highly skilled Finnish women with Ph.D. degrees or advanced skills in demand by industry and the economy. They have extensive experience living and working abroad which we examined. These women were followed retrospectively as internationally mobile Finns for approximately 30 years; hence, their life courses and experiences cover the period of globalization and the increasing internationalization of Finnish businesses. These purposefully and theoretically selected interviewees provide insights into their first-hand experiences on the outreach of Finnish companies or state regarding their professional resources, their experiences related to reverse diaspora engagement ("giving back"), and efforts in utilizing their resources. We explore the perceived interest in them and the actor types contacting them to understand the landscape of these activities and actors and their configurations. The findings are coded and organized into themes, see Table 18.1.

The Perceived Value of Finnish Female Diaspora

The qualitative inquiry based on the interviews shows that the Finnish highly skilled female diasporans, all of them with extensive migration and professional experience and expertise, are not seen by the Finnish institutional and organizational actors. These women have purposefully invested in their education, competences, re- and upskilling locally, and cultivating an extensive professional language skill portfolio. Many of them are competing with native

Table 18.1 Analysis of the interviews

Perceived value of Finnish Female Diaspora	
Perceived professionally driven outreach	
Perceptions on the situation	"However, I live in a country that the Finns don't have much interest in, which is a major mistake. Country X is seen as difficult, almost insolvent country that does not interest them, or it left to other cooperation partners, or it is handled through central European offices. Country X is perceived as a holiday place only, which is not correct. The gross national product has been top of the EU in recent years and there are big leaps in the digitalization of things, in other words, there are opportunities if you have the courage to exploit them". "I definitely feel that there are so many missed opportunities of building an interactive outreach network". "The Finnish government is not actively looking to interact with or enhance the network of the Finnish diaspora abroad. It seems that it is more geared towards the companies that want to go international from Finland instead of finding and creating networks abroad of the ones who are already there. They collect information about who moves abroad and where, but that information is not used". "Hard work to foster trade relations and develop understanding".
View on outreach	"I don't want to complain any more, mainly because Finnish firms are not interested in country X and therefore there exists no outreach". "I would be tempted to answer 'zero outreach'". "There is no information if there even exists any outreach for other companies besides these key areas of business. There is no gender-based outreach of any kind either. I've only heard that if you succeed well abroad, then the government and other agencies will contact you, but if you are an entrepreneur just starting or struggling to make a living abroad, there is no support whatsoever". "Little outreach and weaking over time". "there was no contact". "No, no, no, never. This [reaching out] has not happened to me and has not happened to any other women I know. It is a long way to go".
Outreach regarding professional capabilities	"Directly said, nobody has been contacting except the Finnish Olympic Committee who contacted before the XXXX Olympic games in order to have me organize their transportation and other daily local program. Which I did, but I was not with the sponsors here as I was working, I found another Finn to help them on the daily program locally. Even this contact was coming from an acquaintance from Finland who knew the people of the Finnish Olympic Committee". "10 years ago, I was contacted by a visiting Finnish delegation of parliament to host a tour around (A USA-based top) University. My Alma mater continues to invite me for guest lectures, a connection I am particularly happy to maintain", "organizing transportation and local program", "inexistent", "no outreach", "Yes, there has been some freelance work outreach from the Finnish companies I used to work with, but this has happened less and less the longer I have been abroad".

(*continued*)

Table 18.1 (continued)

Perceived value of Finnish Female Diaspora	
Contacting actors and reasons	
Content of outreach	"help in organizing visit", "the experiences of direct contact are connected to my scientific advisory roles", "inexistent", "my main source of income at the moment comes from a Finnish company, but the outreach in this case happened because of a friend contact, and surprisingly it is slightly different kind of work than my main working experience", "no such"
Type of actors contacting	"committee", "Finnish business agencies and Finnish universities", "no actors", "Finnish customer firm", "no one"
Level of contact and relationship to the actor	"professional acquaintance", "the majority of contact is based on institutional affiliation. Very recently I was invited by a Finnish organization to work with and support with responsibility themes and challenges, but this workshop was invited by a personal connection", "n/a", "Finnish customer/professional service", "no contact"
Task related to reverse diaspora involvement	"practical organizing", "scientific advisory task", "the purpose and criteria of contacting me have been exactly the same as if I had been in Finland, to get a professional service form a person that they were happy to work with earlier", "no task"
Task related particularities	"The purpose and criteria of contacting me have been exactly the same as if I had been in Finland, to get a professional service form a person that they were happy to work with earlier", "freelance work. My being abroad or having experience living/working abroad has not helped much in my case. Although with my main employer it has been beneficial that briefing and communication from their clients comes in English, and that is not a problem for me, while for some of my predecessors it was", "local daily program"
Views on reverse diaspora engagement	
Purpose and commitment on reverse diaspora involvement	"As I am now working in a firm concentrating on the Dutch market, the difference how the Dutch employ the Dutch abroad is really big. Whatever they are searching, they always first search some Dutch from that place, make contact and ask all kinds of things even if they were from a different field of business. Often these (contacts) lead to collaboration. Finnish companies are not able to (do not know how to) utilize this resource at all. Either they don't believe that local Finns would be useful or then they trust that they find somewhere else (e.g., from sales office in Germany or Italy) will provide that knowledge and help". "If I am completely open and honest, I always feel guilty for the feeling of not being able to contribute enough to my home country. Achieving the highest academic merit is demanding and takes its toll. Despite this, I don't ever recall saying 'no' when asked. I always make space and prioritize, sometimes even at the expense of my core responsibilities". "As there are a number of businesses and entrepreneurs abroad that have roots in Finland, it would make sense that someone would pay attention and use these resources to support further economic growth also in their home country because they have valuable information about their current residence and networks there".

(continued)

Table 18.1 (continued)

Perceived value of Finnish Female Diaspora	
Critical views on operations of the Finnish business or state	"Finland's embassy in Washington D.C. has a contact page for Team Finland. 'Team Finland is a network of public sector bodies, dedicated to helping Finnish companies grow and be successful abroad. It also promotes Finland's country image and attracts foreign investments and experts to Finland'. https://finlandabroad.fi/web/usa/contacts-and-networking. They also have a page for sales leads and business opportunities in various countries. However, the site and its opportunities are limited mostly to basic descriptions of the cities and countries, like Brussels is the capital of Belgium and offers multiple business opportunities in the middle of Europe. Stating basic facts that anyone learns at school is not supportive. In addition, most of the US partnerships and support are towards bioenergy, green energy, connectivity, maritime, and aerospace in chosen partner states". "The migrated people aboard feel belonging to the mother country and have some kind of ties (strong or not) to that place. They can be memories of places and people that used to be, but they also realize that going back is not a choice because they have rooted in their current country of residence, and have nothing to go back to, no network in their home country or means to live there. Thus, regardless of how they make their living and support their families, they feel stuck to their choices in life, and with no support from their old home country, they feel uprooted. This disconnection can also lead to hatred against the country of origin, its policies, and practices. For example, the Finnish government still wants you to pay taxes every year and television tax even if you have not lived there for years, and have not owned an apartment or television there. When you tell about this here in the new country of residence, the people laugh about it: why would you pay a television tax when you don't live there? The rules feel restricting and not supportive". "I do believe that if there was equivalent field of work in Finland as my main working experience here, I would be valued from a Finnish point of view as I have now worked in a large world-wide-known organization, but there isn't really, and thus no work in exactly that field in Finland". "They don't know how"

speakers in their work and operate multiple languages, have Ph.D. degrees in demanding areas, such as international business, chemistry, security, and sustainability, as well as extensive work experience. Counterintuitively, these knowledge and skills do not seem to be perceived by COO: They are not contacted for these reasons, we found no proactivity in shaping future resource pools or anything alike. Without their contact networks and self-organizing, there would be no linkage to Finland at all. Some of the interviewees complain about this ignorance directly, some have proactively contacted companies about their existence and potential, but without results. Great frustration exists among the interviewees about this situation as they are motivated to contribute to Finnish progress with their competencies and resources. They perceive this lack of outreach:

> As I am now working in a firm concentrating on the Dutch market, the difference how the Dutch employ the Dutch abroad is really big. Whatever they are searching, they always first search some Dutch from that place, make contact and ask all kinds of things even if they were from a different field of business. Often these (contacts) lead to collaboration. Finnish companies are not able to (do not know how to) utilize this resource at all. Either they don't believe that local Finns would be useful or then they trust that they find somewhere else (e.g., from sales office in Germany or Italy) will provide that knowledge and help. (Interview 1)

However, there are views supporting the assumptions present in diaspora studies on altruistic and patriotic behavior, supporting one's homeland when possible:

> If I am completely open and honest, I always feel guilty for the feeling of not being able to contribute enough to my home country. Achieving the highest academic merit is demanding and takes its toll. Despite this, I don't ever recall saying "no" when asked. I always make space and prioritize, sometimes even at the expense of my core responsibilities. (Interview 2)

The interviewees follow technological developments, networking possibilities, and available tools to update such processes and activate the outreach. There are clear expectations related to digitalization and instruments available:

> As there are a number of businesses and entrepreneurs abroad that have roots in Finland, it would make sense that someone would pay attention and use these resources to support further economic growth also in their home country because they have valuable information about their current residence and networks there. (Interview 3)

> At that time, it was difficult, there was no internet…, today we have different tools. (Interview 4).

These expectations indicate that they consider the unwillingness and uninterest of Finnish companies and public sector actors to perceive them as a mindset problem not as a problem of lacking ability to assess them or connect via technology. These Finnish women interviewed, thus, perceive lack of interest from companies and public sector actors as intentional. This is a strong interpretation that they voice, but it builds on their experiences over decades following the situation in different trade partner countries of Finland. While the survey data from the United States is limited, the overall positive perception from Finnish female diasporans on their life suggests them feeling professionally valued in US society. Similarly, women in other countries (e.g., Germany, the United Kingdom, Greece) see their resources valued by the local economy.

Assessing the Value of Finnish Female Diaspora

Interestingly, the respondents who are professionally active residents in different countries, without knowing each other, all agree that there is very little or no assessment of their value or interest shown by the COO. This is a shared view across multiple host countries. If they are perceived as useful for some occasion, their resources are valued in a very sporadic ad hoc manner by individual people who need some sort of help, not by formal organizational actors such as firms, groups of firms, or public sector institutions. These are members of the personal networks of these women that perceive them stimulated by an identified need. Surprisingly, their value as Finnish experts able to operate the language is appreciated mainly by local actors, for example, firms that need particular solutions. Hence, the outreach comes from the host country or other international context.

One Ph.D. holder explains the situation when considering returning or staying and further career after working abroad in a prestigious research institute:

> In research, positions are typically time-limited, which leads back to spending more time in politics, finding funding, and administration than in research. Additionally having a temporal contract many "normal" things like having a bank loan get challenging. I was offered a permanent position by the software company XXXX to be a software developer with not-so-bad conditions. XXXX was looking for someone who speaks Finnish to develop an XXXX payroll solution for the Finnish market. I was looking for a permanent position. The position was located only 50 km from my living place in country Y, which made it easy to accept due to having a social network here. Naturally, it is always rewarding to be able to use skills that you have collected on the way and collect new skills. This has been one of my motivations in my professional career together

with having a reasonable income and a healthy, interesting working atmosphere. When entering XXXX I could use my Finnish, after changing to a group where I could use my French and interest in law. Even if I'm more technical than a linguistic person. Again, changing position and applying my skills in statistics, and data science, which is coming back to my thesis. (Interview 6)

No attempt was made to pull her resources back to Finland after her Ph.D. even though her case is well-documented due to her academic prestige. These interviews illustrate that women, in their home country and abroad, wish to employ the capabilities and resources and develop their life. They possess professional agency and motivation. They are actively seeking opportunities in host contexts and transnational spaces to do so, but for some reason, they are not perceived or valued by Finnish actors. We identify a lack of assessment in all contexts. There is almost no professional-level contacting or networking that would document or assess these resources abroad in a systematic and active manner. At the same time, there is a strategy 2022–2026 for "ulkosuomalainen" that claims to be concerned and interested in these diaspora resources through workshops and hearings.[1] This is a step toward the wished direction but requires coordinated gender and intersectional approaches. In 2023, Finnish formal institutions collect data on Finnish firms and businesses abroad, not yet on the talent base. After an individual from Finland migrates to another country, especially within the EU border, they might not be traceable due to lack of institutional processes for doing that. An emerging discourse addresses Finns abroad "from below" but action reaching any groups of women in different countries to identify and assess their positions, competencies, or languages is due. The only notable institutions or networks identified that address women in diaspora are the Finnish Professional Women Worldwide network (LinkedIn) and International Working Women of Finland (Facebook), not formal institutions like ministries or chambers of commerce. The extant intelligence system potentially has a gender-related structural bias toward registered firms or even some assumptions about gender roles (Christou & Kofman, 2022). As one interviewee puts it "no, no, no, never. This [reaching out] has not happened to me and has not happened to any other women I know. It is a long way to go".

The resources for reverse diaspora involvement are there, like skills, motivation, and altruism. The women value their own experiences and would like to engage more; however, they see the current methods used for the

---

[1] See more in https://valtioneuvosto.fi/hanke?tunnus=SM001:00/2021. Retrieved 14.3.2023.

administration of diaspora resources in general critically. Activities of Business Finland and private businesses are seen as less effective or inclusive to women abroad.

We analyze the findings from the interviews regarding the Finnish women's perceptions of how Finnish companies and public sector actors value and keep in contact with them (see Table 18.1).

Taxonomy of Female Resources Abroad

Despite the indicated lack of perceived value from Finnish actors, we highlight that there exists significant resources that these diaspora women could bring to the Finnish economy. The identified resources can be organized into a taxonomy from the business value angle:

- Professional resources: Education, work experience, skillsets, business and market knowledge, capital, and entrepreneurial capabilities.
- Social resources: Local networks, business contacts, and ties, social capital, understanding of socio-behavioral patterns and practices, and market-specific knowledge.
- Cultural resources: Languages, interpretations, cultural practices, knowledge of cultural patterns and heritage, school and education systems, institutional styles, and -systems.
- Transnational resources: Ability to act as a connector and translator of systems, transnational communication and networking, transnational innovation and business development, and transnational entrepreneurial capabilities.

Finnish companies and public sector could draw more attention to diaspora resources and networks and utilize them to a larger extent and broader scope.

Discussion and Conclusion

Despite the emerging global talent and boundaryless career research, female diasporans remain in conceptual shadows (cf. Tung, 2008). International business and management theories rarely address female talent specifically (Latukha et al., 2021), even less so, when discussing individuals who have settled abroad or represent descendants of migrants. They are not perceived as talents, not theoretically or conceptually. Talent tends to refer to globally mobile expatriates who migrate because of their career. This negligence of a large global population as a business resource is closely linked to current debates on equality, inclusion, and diversity where gender is one focal element. The study found that women in diaspora have notable resource potential and willingness to contribute, but their potential is not utilized by COO actors.

Theoretically, there is an inherent bias as women tend to be represented as spouses, dependents, or marriage migrants, but not as dynamic networked professionals with valuable resources. The professional agency and dual careers remain theoretically interesting concerns in diaspora. The debates on the participation of women in labor markets due to aging societies suggest that the inherent and highly qualified resources in diaspora are not theorized as potential despite digitalization and boundaryless career concepts.

Against the conceptual challenges and framings, there are managerial implications that illustrate serious problem areas. When multilingual, highly competent, and professionally skilled women are not within the radar of the private and public sector, then the system is malfunctioning. These are resources that are capable, committed, and interested to contribute in and through diaspora. Moreover, they are easily identifiable and accessible via social media, and other networks like LinkedIn. As they are not contacted, employed, or assessed systematically, Finnish actors need to consider the research questions the women pose; are the Finnish actors (a) not aware of these resources in the era of internet and digitalization, (b) not convinced about these resources and their potential due to lack of data, or (c) simply not interested to develop their international relations, trade, and business? Many Finnish actors use considerable amounts of private and public funds employing foreign consultancies and experts for tasks that these Finnish women could do, perhaps even better and with higher aspirations, but surely more economically.

Resource bases addressing available resources of Finnish female diaspora abroad require strategic development and policies. Such resources should represent an element of national business intelligence and part of the national strategic governance of resources, for example, via chambers of commerce. Other countries, like the Philippines, operate their diaspora resources strategically and intentionally as a part of the national economy, development, and business strategy (Nicolas & Rodriguez, 2019). After the collapse of Nokia, we had resource assessment discussions in Germany regarding the information about these available diasporic STEM-resources and competencies that were available around the world. This useful experience was about to get "brain wasted". Then, we considered ways to introduce the idea of assessing and documenting our talents abroad to the Finnish side, but with little success. The Finnish actors did not perceive these people as useful talent, similarly as they do not perceive female diaspora value today. In 2023, the diminishing talent situation is increasingly discussed from the perspective of retaining international talent in Finland (Yle, 2023). Thereby, the problem of perceiving talent in diaspora prevails. It goes against the SDGs, which emphasize the importance of considering all types of talent and promoting the inclusion of minorities and migrants. We recommend Finland's public and private sector actors to develop diaspora strategies for international business and economic relations.

This study has numerous limitations. It is mainly a conceptual discussion on women's diaspora resources with qualitative notions. However, it contributes by presenting novelty; the women from the Global North who are overlooked as "brain" by their home countries and reverse engagement. It calls for future research on female resources and on developed countries that are perhaps latecomers to understand the value of their female diaspora networks. Moreover, these highly skilled women provide critical views on gaps and trigger discussions on deeper investigation on resource dynamics and their gender intersectionality.

References

Ahmed, J., Mughal, M., & Klasen, S. (2018). Great expectations? Remittances and asset accumulation in Pakistan. *Journal of International Development, 30*(3), 507–532.

Aman, R., Ahokangas, P., Elo, M., & Zhang, X. (2022). Migrant women entrepreneurship and the entrepreneurial ecosystem. In D. G. Pickernell, M. Battisti, Z. Dann, & C. Ekinsmyth (Eds.), *Disadvantaged entrepreneurship and the entrepreneurial ecosystem* (pp. 187–120). Emerald Publishing Limited.

Brinkerhoff, J. M. (2009). *Digital diasporas: Identity and transnational engagement*. Cambridge University Press.

Brubaker, R. (2005). The 'diaspora'diaspora. *Ethnic and Racial Studies, 28*(1), 1–19.

Christou, A., & Kofman, E. (2022). *Gender and migration: IMISCOE short reader* (p. 123). Springer Nature.

Cohen, R. (2008). *Global diasporas: An introduction*. Routledge.

Denzin, N. K. (1978). Sociological methods: A sourcebook. New York, NY: McGraw-Hill.

Elo, M. (2017). Against all odds–a diaspora entrepreneur developing Russian and Central Asian markets. In *The challenge of BRIC multinationals* (pp. 481–502). Emerald Group Publishing Limited.

Elo, M., & Ivanova-Gongne, M. (2020). Language resources and multiethnic central Asian economies. *Eurasian Journal of Economic & Business Studies, 3*(57), 5–23. https://doi.org/10.47703/ejebs.v3i57.17

Elo, M., & Leinonen, J. (2019). Dynamics of diasporic life – Entry and exit behavior of highly skilled migrants. In D. Habti & M. Elo (Eds.), *Global mobility of highly skilled people. International perspectives on migration* (Vol. 16, pp. 81–105). Springer. https://doi.org/10.1007/978-3-319-95056-3_4

Elo, M., & Minto-Coy, I. (2018). *Diaspora networks in international business.* Springer.

Elo, M., Aman, R., & Täube, F. (2020a). Female migrants and brain waste: A conceptual challenge with societal implications. *International Migration.* https://doi.org/10.1111/imig.12783

Elo, M., Minto-Coy, I., Silva, S. C. E., & Zhang, X. (2020b). Diaspora networks in international marketing: how do ethnic products diffuse to foreign markets? *European Journal of International Management, 14*(4), 693–729.

Elo, M., Kothari, T., & Ivanova-Gongne, M. (2022). Language diversity - Multiethnic migrant and diaspora resources for international business and entrepreneurship. In M. Latukha (Ed.), *Diversity in action: Managing diverse talent in global economies* (pp. 123–150). Emerald Publishing.

Emmanuel, N. D., Elo, M., & Piekkari, R. (2019). Human stickiness as a counterforce to brain drain: Purpose-driven behaviour among Tanzanian medical doctors and implications for policy. *Journal of International Business Policy, 2*, 314–332.

Eremenko, T., El Qadim, N., & Steichen, E. (2017). Southern Europeans in France: invisible migrants? In J. M. Lafleur & M. Stanek (Eds.), *South-North migration of EU citizens in times of crisis* (pp. 123–148). Springer.

Fassin, D. (2001). The biopolitics of otherness: Undocumented foreigners and racial discrimination in French public debate. *Anthropology Today, 17*(1), 3–7.

Finnish Immigration Service. (n.d.). *Frequently asked questions: Employment.* Migri.Fi. Accessed March 1, 2023, from https://migri.fi/en/faq-employment

Finnish National Agency for Education. (n.d.). *International mobility periods of students.* Oph.Fi. Accessed March 1, 2023, from https://www.oph.fi/en/statistics/international-mobility-finnish-higher-education

Fludernik, M. (2003). *Diaspora and multiculturalism: Common traditions and new developments* (Vol. 66). Rodopi.

Gamlen, A. (2014). Diaspora institutions and diaspora governance. *International Migration Review, 48*, 180–217.

Güngör, N. D., & Tansel, A. (2014). Brain drain from Turkey: Return intentions of skilled migrants. *International Migration, 52*(5), 208–226.

Habti, D. (2014). Spatialities of work and home in a dual-career context of highly skilled Arab women in Finland. *Journal of Finnish Studies, 17*(1–2), 92–125.

Habti, D., & Elo, M. (Eds.). (2019). *Global mobility of highly skilled people: Multidisciplinary perspectives on self-initiated expatriation* (Vol. 16). Springer.

Heikkilä, E. (Ed.). (2009). International migration of skilled persons from Finland. *Siirtolaisuus-Migration, 36*(1), 24–28.

Heikkilä, E. (Ed.). (2017). *Immigrants and the labour markets. Experiences from abroad and Finland*. Migration Institute of Finland.

Heikkilä, E., & Koikkalainen, S. (Eds.). (2011). *Finns abroad: New forms of mobility and migration*. Migration Institute of Finland.

IOM. (2022). IOM Issue Brief Building Capacity, 11.2.2022, IOM, Geneva.

IOM Global Data Institute. (2023). *Women & girls on the move: A snapshot of available evidence*. Migrationdataportal.com. Accessed March 1, 2023, from https://www.migrationdataportal.org/resource/women-girls-move-snapshot-available-evidence

Ivanova-Gongne, M., Lång, S., Brännback, M., & Carsrud, A. (2021). Sensemaking by minority entrepreneurs: Role identities and linguistic embeddedness. *Journal of Small Business & Entrepreneurship*, 1–24.

James, M. (2016). Diaspora as an ethnographic method: Decolonial reflections on researching urban multi-culture in outer East London. *Young, 24*(3), 222–237.

Johanson, J., & Vahlne, J. E. (2009). The Uppsala internationalization process model revisited: From liability of foreignness to liability of outsidership. *Journal of International Business Studies, 40*, 1411–1431.

Kofman, E. (2000). The invisibility of skilled female migrants and gender relations in studies of skilled migration in Europe. *International Journal of Population Geography, 6*(1), 45–59.

Korkiasaari, J., & Söderling, I. (2003). *Finnish emigration and immigration after World War II*. Turku: Siirtolaisuusinstituutti.

Krivonos, D. (2020). Swedish surnames, British accents: Passing among post-Soviet migrants in Helsinki. *Ethnic and Racial Studies, 43*(16), 388–406.

Latukha, M., Shagalkina, M., Kalinina, E., & Khasieva, D. (2021). Does gender matter? Gender talent migration and its implication for talent management. *Journal of Global Mobility: The Home of Expatriate Management Research, 9*(2), 191–216.

Lee, E. S. (1966). A theory of migration. *Demography, 3*(1), 47–57.

Leinonen, J. (2012). "Money is not everything and that's the bottom line": Family ties in transatlantic elite migrations. *Social Science History, 36*(2), 243–268.

Luostarinen, R., & Gabrielsson, M. (2006). Globalization and marketing strategies of born globals in SMOPECs. *Thunderbird International Business Review, 48*(6), 773–801.

Mak, A. S., & Nesdale, D. (2001). Migrant distress: The role of perceived racial discrimination and coping resources. *Journal of Applied Social Psychology, 31*(12), 2632–2647.

Mattoo, A., Neagu, I. C., & Özden, Ç. (2008). Brain waste? Educated immigrants in the US labor market. *Journal of Development Economics, 87*(2), 255–269.

Meyer, J. B. (2001). Network approach versus brain drain: lessons from the diaspora. *International Migration, 39*(5), 91–110.

Minto-Coy, I. D. (2016). Diaspora engagement for development in the Caribbean. In A. Chikanda, J. Crush, & M. Walton-Roberts (Eds.), *Diasporas, development and governance, global migration issues* (Vol. 5, pp. 121–139). Springer. https://doi.org/10.1007/978-3-319-22165-6_8

Nicolas, I. M., & Rodriguez, J. L. S. (2019). The Philippines experience in managing diaspora resources: Policies and initiatives in facilitating diaspora engagement. In *Diaspora networks in international business: Perspectives for understanding and managing diaspora business and resources* (pp. 513–528). Springer.

Nkongolo-Bakenda, J. M., & Chrysostome, E. V. (2013). Engaging diasporas as international entrepreneurs in developing countries: In search of determinants. *Journal of International Entrepreneurship, 11*, 30–64.

Occupational Safety and Health Administration in Finland. (2021). *Remote work*. Accessed March 1, 2023, from https://www.tyosuojelu.fi/web/en/working-conditions/work-environment/remote-work

Plaza, S., & Ratha, D. (2011). Harnessing diaspora resources for Africa. *Diaspora for Development in Africa*, 1–54.

Porter, M. E. (1990). The competitive advantage of nations. *Competitive Intelligence Review, 1*(1), 14–14.

Rana, M. B., & Elo, M. (2017). Transnational diaspora and civil society actors driving MNE internationalisation: the case of Grameenphone in Bangladesh. *Journal of International Management, 23*(1), 87–106.

Raunio, M. (2005). From brain drain to brain circulation – Top professionals as a key resource of Finnish economy. *EVA report, 2005*.

Riaño, Y. (2011). Drawing new boundaries of participation: Experiences and strategies of economic citizenship among skilled migrant women in Switzerland. *Environment and Planning A, 43*(7), 1530–1546.

Riddle, L., & Brinkerhoff, J. (2011). Diaspora entrepreneurs as institutional change agents: The case of Thamel.com. *International Business Review, 20*(6), 670–680.

Sang, K., Al-Dajani, H., & Özbilgin, M. (2013). Frayed careers of migrant female professors in British academia: An intersectional perspective. *Gender, Work and Organization, 20*(2), 158–171.

Saxenian, A. (2007). *The new argonauts: Regional advantage in a global economy*. Harvard University Press.

Silva, S. C., & Elo, M. (2017). How to internationalize a traditional Portuguese-style food–liability or asset of Portugueseness? In A. Verbeke, J. Puck, & R. V. Tulder (Eds.), *Distance in international business: Concept, cost and value* (pp. 425–442). Emerald Publishing Limited. https://doi.org/10.1108/S1745-886220170000012007

Sisäministeriö. (2021). *Ulkosuomalaisstrategia 2022-2026*. Accessed December 13, 2021, from http://urn.fi/URN:ISBN:978-952-324-544-0, Sisäministeriö/Valtioneuvosto

Subbotin, A., & Aref, S. (2021). Brain drain and brain gain in Russia: Analyzing international migration of researchers by discipline using Scopus bibliometric data 1996–2020. *Scientometrics, 126*(9), 7875–7900.

Tung, R. L. (2008). Brain circulation, diaspora, and international competitiveness. *European Management Journal, 26*(5), 298–304.

Tung, R. L., & Chung, H. F. (2010). Diaspora and trade facilitation: The case of ethnic Chinese in Australia. *Asia Pacific Journal of Management, 27*, 371–392.

United Nations. (n.d.). *Global compact for migration.* refugeesmigrants.un.org. Accessed March 1, 2023, from https://refugeesmigrants.un.org/migration-compact

Valtioneuvosto ja ministeriöt. (n.d.). *Ulkosuomalaisia yhdistää suomalainen identiteetti.* Intermin.Fi. Accessed March 1, 2023, from https://intermin.fi/maahanmuutto/ulkosuomalaiset

Vertovec, S. (2007). Introduction: New directions in the anthropology of migration and multiculturalism. *Ethnic and Racial Studies, 30*(6), 961–978.

Yle. (2023). *Yle News. APN's podcast: Finland's international talent brain drain.* Accessed March 23, 2023, from https://yle.fi/a/74-20022735

19

Non-Ethnic Inventor Sourcing of Immigrant Knowledge: The Role of Social Communities

Larissa Rabbiosi, Francesco Di Lorenzo, Anupama Phene, and Paul Almeida

Introduction

The international business literature suggests that global migration stimulates a process of knowledge circulation and includes several studies of the effects of knowledge flows related to immigrant inventors' innovative activities (e.g., Breschi et al., 2017; Choudhury, 2016; Oettl & Agrawal, 2008). This strand of work has focused so far largely on flows of knowledge enabled by ethnic ties between the immigrant inventor and his or her home country (Agrawal et al., 2008; Kerr & Lincoln, 2010; Saxenian, 2002). Work along these lines explores different types of ethnic community related knowledge flows—those that occur within broad ethnic communities (including flows from different locations worldwide), flows within the ethnic community in the immigrant inventors' host country, and flows within ethnic communities which include

---

L. Rabbiosi • F. Di Lorenzo (✉)
Copenhagen Business School, Copenhagen, Denmark
e-mail: lr.si@cbs.dk; fdl.si@cbs.dk

A. Phene
George Washington University, Washington, DC, USA
e-mail: anuphene@gwu.edu

P. Almeida
Georgetown University, Washington, DC, USA
e-mail: almeidap@georgetown.edu

home and host country members (Almeida et al., 2015; Breschi et al., 2017; Kapur, 2001; Marino et al., 2020).

Although in the U.S. immigrants from a range of ethnicities have contributed to positive economic gains, several studies highlight the particular influence of Indian and Chinese inventors—and especially in high-technology industries and regions (Kerr, 2007; Wadhwa et al., 2007). Based on their patenting and innovation activities, inventors from India comprise the second largest group (after Chinese inventors) of immigrant scientists and engineers (Saxenian et al., 2002). This significance of Indian inventors for innovativeness in high technology areas in the U.S. points to the importance of understanding the extent to which their innovativeness influences others. Previous studies show that immigrant communities, and Indian immigrant communities in particular, have important influences on entrepreneurship, trade and foreign direct investment (Kalnins & Chung, 2006; Rauch & Trindade, 2002; Shukla & Cantwell, 2018; Sonderegger & Täube, 2010), and that Indian inventors in high technology sectors exploit one another's knowledge and work intensively with fellow immigrants. We know also, that this tends to result in more valuable innovations (Almeida et al., 2015).

However, how ethnic Indian inventors' innovation activity affects their non-ethnic peers has attracted less research attention. It has been shown that inventor teams that include both ethnic and non-ethnic members enable flows of knowledge among team members from different cultures and that this leads to higher levels of knowledge recombination (Choudhury & Kim, 2019). Apart from this effect, we know little about other aspects that facilitate flows of immigrant knowledge held by ethnic inventor communities to inventors outside those communities. We suggest that Indian and other inventors belong to several social communities simultaneously. For instance, Indian inventors belong also to organizational, technological, and geographic communities by virtue of their employment, profession, and geographic location (Boschma, 2005). Drawing on insights from social identity and categorization theories (Tajfel, 1974; Tajfel & Turner, 1986), we suggest that common membership in a community allows non-Indian inventors to source knowledge from their Indian peers. In other words, in the same way that participation in an ethnic community facilitates intra-community flows of knowledge enabled by interaction and increased trust among community members (Almeida et al., 2015), the presence of Indians in other communities increases the chances of knowledge flows among the members of those communities including those belonging to other ethnic groups. Therefore, we suggest that the extent to which non-Indian inventors source knowledge from Indian inventors depends in part on the extent to which non-Indian inventors are exposed to Indians in the same organizational, technological, and geographic communities.

To explore flows of immigrant inventor knowledge outside the ethnic Indian community, we analyze data drawn from U.S. semiconductor industry patents to study the extent to which non-Indian inventors source knowledge from Indian inventors' patented inventions. Our data cover the period 1983 to 1998. Based on these data, we create matched samples of Indian and non-Indian inventors, and measure inventor knowledge sourcing based on backward citations. We use patent data to measure the percentage of Indian inventors in organizational and technological communities and employ U.S. Homeland Security data to measure the percentage of Indian immigrants in the geographic communities that include Indian and non-Indian inventors.

We find that both Indian and non-Indian inventors source knowledge from Indian immigrant inventors (immigrant knowledge), although as expected the extent of this activity is greater among Indian inventors. In line with our hypotheses, we find that for all three communities—organizational, technological, and geographic—a larger presence of Indians results in an increase in the immigrant knowledge sourced by non-Indian inventors. Overall, our results point to the positive role of ethnic Indians for enhancing innovativeness among both Indian and non-Indian inventors. We find that organizational, technological, and geographic communities facilitate knowledge flows both within communities and across the ethnic community boundaries.

We believe that our research makes several contributions. First, empirically, we add to previous research on immigrants and innovation by investigating the influence of Indian inventors' knowledge on other (non-Indian) inventors—an area of enquiry so far less addressed. Second, we highlight the facilitation mechanism provided by organizational, technological, and geographic communities. Third, we provide some implications for firms, managers, and policymakers. We suggest that it is important for managers and firms to be aware of the multiple communities to which their employees belong, and the knowledge flows and innovation activity they enable. Flows of knowledge within social communities that are beyond the firm's boundaries have potentially positive and negative implications for firm competitiveness, and firms should take account of this in their hiring and employee practices. The additional positive effects of immigrant inventors and even immigrant families highlighted by our findings should not be overlooked given the sensitivities of immigration in national policies. Our findings suggest that immigrant inventors contribute to the innovativeness of other inventors and that non-professional family members can also have an influence.

Theory and Hypotheses

Inventors and Social Communities

Innovation rarely happens in isolation (Diemer & Regan, 2022); it tends to be the result of multiple interactions among inventors that allow access to and exchanges of knowledge (Almeida & Kogut, 1999). Research has shown how social communities allow the sharing of norms and values and provide the means for knowledge to circulate (Boschma, 2005; Brown & Duguid, 1991; Cooke & Kemeny, 2017). Ethnic inventors tend to have affiliations with their relevant ethnic community which includes members with the same national, cultural and/or ethnic background (e.g., Almeida et al., 2015; Choudhury & Kim, 2019; Marino et al., 2020). However, inventors participate also in organizational communities (inventors share the same organizational context), technological communities (inventors working in the same technological/research domain) and geographic communities (inventors located in the same geographic space) (Crescenzi et al., 2016). Membership of these social communities allows Indian inventors and non-Indian inventors to meet and interact which makes them important sources of knowledge for both inventor groups.

Kogut and Zander (1992) proposed the idea of the firm as a social community which facilitates flows of knowledge among firm members in a particular location and internationally. For example, in a multinational firm context, organizational membership allows flows of knowledge among members of the multinational in different countries and with different national origins (e.g., Almeida & Phene, 2004; Foley & Kerr, 2013; Rabbiosi & Santangelo, 2013). From a learning and knowledge perspective, not only does the organization evolve and change based on its employees, but the firm's members evolve by learning from the organization. This results in a convergence of learning and knowledge in both the individual and the organization (March, 1991). The firm's structures, systems, and common norms and culture (the organizational community) can promote receptiveness to and absorption of knowledge from different domains.

In addition to organizational communities, technological communities are important for connecting members and facilitating knowledge flows. For example, in the case of inventors with a common culture, early work in this area conducted by Crane (1972) describes how the 'invisible college of scientists' helps to diffuse knowledge beyond the firm's boundaries. Similarly, Rappa and Debackere (1992) demonstrate that verbal exchanges (conversations) between experts in the same technological areas (within and across firms) result in the sharing of information and know-how of interest to all the members of the group. Technological communities allow development and use of a specialized vocabulary, and a common set of routines and cognitive bonds among members (Garud & Rappa, 1994). Inventors' participation in a technological community results in the creation and spread of a distinct epistemic community (Cetina, 1999; Powell & Giannella, 2010) which increases the likelihood of knowledge flows among inventors (e.g., Caragliu & Nijkamp, 2016; Crescenzi et al., 2016).

The third type of social community that affects knowledge flows is based on co-location within a geographic area (Almeida & Kogut, 1999; Boschma, 2005). By creating the conditions for the development of social ties and networks relevant for learning (Jacobs, 1969; Marshall, 1890; Saxenian, 1996), geographic proximity enables effective transmission of knowledge (e.g., Fleming et al., 2007; Lobo & Strumsky, 2008). Co-located invention networks favor access to and exchanges of knowledge (Breschi & Lissoni, 2009). Case studies on regional clusters of small and medium sized firms in Italy (Piore & Sabel, 1984) and Baden-Wuerttemberg in Germany (Herrigel, 1993) indicate the significance of geographic communities for knowledge flows across the firms in those regions. A seminal work by Saxenian (1996) provides an ethnography of engineers located in Silicon Valley, and attributes their success to robust exchanges of knowledge among the individuals and firms in that location.

Individual interaction and trust building based on organizational, technological, and geographical community membership provides opportunities that extend across ethnic community boundaries. The part played by the social communities within these groups in enabling knowledge flows suggests that they may affect the extent to which non-Indian inventors source knowledge from Indian inventors. In the next section, we explore in more depth the conditions rendering non-Indian inventors more likely to source immigrant knowledge in organizational, technological, and geographic communities which cross ethnic community boundaries.

Communities as Mechanisms for Knowledge Flows

The sourcing of knowledge from Indian inventors requires non-Indian inventors to recognize, understand and assimilate immigrant knowledge. Each of these fundamental aspects of knowledge flows benefits from participation of non-Indian inventors in social communities that include Indian inventors.

The opportunities for non-Indian and Indian inventors to interact increases within a social community. Increased presence of Indian inventors in non-Indian inventors' organizational, technological, and geographic communities allows proximity between Indian and non-Indian inventors which promotes direct social interaction. Social relationships among the members of a community facilitate access to information and resources (Owen-Smith & Powell, 2004). These effects are explained by the basic propositions of social identity and categorization theories (e.g., Tajfel, 1974; Tajfel & Turner, 1986). Within each community discernible similarities such as a shared interest in the same technological field promote social bonds and social cohesion within the community and separation from dissimilar others. The social identification of members belonging to the same community increases their ability to recognize and accept the value of others' knowledge and reduces the costs of collaboration and knowledge transfer among members (Brown & Duguid, 2001; Kane, 2010; Kane et al., 2005). Even in the absence of direct interactions, social identification with the community facilitates opportunities for interperson knowledge flows (Daft & Weick, 1984; Teece & Pisano, 1994). Overall, social proximity among non-Indian inventors and Indians enabled by membership of organizational, technological and/or geographic communities is likely to increase non-Indian inventors' familiarity with Indian inventors' attitudes, approaches, and knowledge, allow a better understanding of the ethnic community and promote greater appreciation of the value of the knowledge possessed by Indians. In turn, this can increase understanding of and receptivity to immigrant knowledge and may induce non-Indian inventors to search across ethnic community boundaries to acquire and use knowledge produced by Indian inventors.

Recognition, understanding and assimilation of immigrant knowledge is likely to depend on the inventor's reasons for participating in social communities. The literature suggests that this might depend on non-rational or instrumental motivations. Non-rational motivations are typical in ethnic communities where flows of knowledge build on social capital. Knowledge flows among members might be altruistic and rely on common values and norms which induce participants to share or transfer resources within the group on the basis of a shared ethnic identity (Almeida et al., 2015; Saxenian & Hsu, 2001), and not necessarily in expectation of a return or a reward (Nahapiet & Ghoshal, 1998). Instrumental motivations for joining a community in the expectation of gaining access to knowledge, are based on calculated and rational expectations and reciprocity. This means that membership of a social community is premised on mutual trust and compliance with the norms of reciprocity, that is, the expectation of some (not necessarily specific) kind of return at some point, for the resources shared (Kurzban & Neuberg, 2015) to avoid social sanctioning by the community (Portes, 1998).

Prior research suggests that participants use organizational, technological and geographic communities to enhance their economic well-being which includes access to innovation related knowledge (Dahl & Pedersen, 2004). For instance, Paruchuri and Awate (2017) demonstrate that inventors source organizational knowledge to support their creation of knowledge. Similarly, Owen-Smith and Powell (2004) describe how to increase their innovativeness individuals and groups working in biotechnology firms use informal collaborations to access knowledge from other institutions including firms, universities and government laboratories. The partner choices made by these individuals depend on the problem to be tackled and the complementary expertise they seek. Scientists collate lists of potential collaboration partners based on their knowledge and expertise and consult them about problems. Rogers (1983) describes the social exchanges among semiconductor engineers in Silicon Valley to share job and work related information useful for their careers and research. Knowledge is the currency allowing entry to these geographically, technologically, and organizationally mediated social groups whose members expect to receive and to provide knowledge. The motivation for this type of community participation appears to be instrumental and based on rational expectations of reciprocal exchanges of useful knowledge. Organizational, technological, and geographic social communities can include membership of multiple ethnicities not necessarily for altruistic reasons but for instrumental reasons related to effective sourcing of useful knowledge. If Indians are a useful source of knowledge in these communities, a larger Indian presence will provide non-Indian inventors with more opportunities to source knowledge.

Communities are also marked by dynamism and while social communities can vary in their degree of parochialism (Bowles & Gintis, 2004) they may enable participation in other communities. Membership in organizational, geographic and technological communities can and does change over time (Qin, 2015). Almeida and Kogut's (1999) work on semiconductor engineers shows that they move across geographic regions and between firms within the same region. As a result, the extent of Indian inventor participation in each of these communities is likely to vary, with consequences for their utility for non-Indian inventors' sourcing of immigrant knowledge.

Taken together, these arguments suggest:

Hypothesis 1: For non-Indian inventors, the sourcing of Indian immigrant inventor knowledge increases with the percentage of Indian immigrant inventors in the same organizational community.

Hypothesis 2: For non-Indian inventors, the sourcing of Indian immigrant inventor knowledge increases with the percentage of Indian immigrant inventors in the same technological community.

Hypothesis 3: For non-Indian inventors, the sourcing of Indian immigrant inventor knowledge increases with the percentage of Indian immigrants joining the same geographic community.

Method

Empirical Context and Data Sources

The Indian community in the U.S. is among the best educated national subgroups and includes many high-skilled science and technology workers, in particular. Since liberalization of its immigration law in 1965, the U.S. has experienced a steady inflow of skilled Indian professionals and students. This migrant inflow can be identified as: "The Early Movers" (1965–1979), Families (1980–1994), and "The IT Generation" (1995 to date) (Chakravorty et al., 2017, p. 29). The first group entered the U.S. based on their education and skills follow which family-related visas became an important entry category, with the families (spouses and children) and immediate relatives (parents, siblings, etc.) moving to join these highly skilled early movers. The third group, the IT workers, occurred due to the large involvement of Indians in computer systems and related services sectors. Their migration was pulled first by the "millennium bug" problem, and later by increased demand for computer and engineering-related labor in the U.S.

Whether early movers or later immigrants, Indians have emerged in the U.S. as a successful ethnic community with a high proportion of doctoral degree holders employed mostly in STEM (science, technology, engineering, mathematics) related jobs (Pew Research Center, 2013). Indian immigrants are contributing to overall U.S. innovative capacity and entrepreneurial activity, and the number of patents co-invented by Indians filed by U.S. firms in high-technology areas has increased (Almeida et al., 2015; Kerr, 2007; Saxenian, 1999). Given their education and work characteristics and their growing representation in patenting and innovation, we use Indian immigrant inventors in the U.S. as our empirical setting to study how and under what conditions immigrant knowledge flows to inventors outside the ethnic community. We focus on the semiconductor industry where ethnic Indian immigrant inventors play an important role.

Our dataset was constructed using the following sources of information. First, the National Bureau of Economic Research (NBER) database of the U.S. Patent and Trademark Office (USPTO) which allows us to identify patent applications by inventors with a U.S. location working in the semiconductor industry. These data are supplemented by information from the U.S. Department of Homeland Security (DHS) on the characteristics of Indian aliens who become permanent U.S. residents (immigrants).[1] We have ZIP (Zone Improvement Plan) codes for Indian immigrants' declared intended place of residence during this time period. We track this information for the period 1983–1997.[2] To compute the distribution of Asian Indians in each U.S. state and county we use U.S. Census data for 1980 and 1990.[3]

Sample

We constructed the sample using the data in Almeida et al. (2015). First, we identified 3228 Indian inventors during the longer period 1981–2002 and their 8984 semiconductor patents. Using NBER and USPTO patent data, we checked whether Indian inventors listed as first patent author were living in a U.S. inventor location during the period of observation. For the same sector and period, we identified 53,671 non-Indian inventors with a U.S. inventor

---

[1] These Indian permanent residents may be new arrivals or individuals already in the U.S. with temporary non-immigrant status (e.g., F-1, H-1, L-1).

[2] Since 1998, this information has been confidential.

[3] Census data differ from DHS data and refer to "Asian Indians" as individuals who were born in India (observed in the DHS data), American-born individuals with Indian ancestry, and individuals with Indian ancestry born-elsewhere. It is useful to examine the spatial distributions of Asian Indians in the Census data and Indian-born immigrants in the DHS data. Both show (very similar) spatial distribution of Asian Indians and India-born immigrants across U.S. states and counties. In 1990, 61% of Asian Indians were living in the states of California, New York, New Jersey, Illinois, and Texas and in 1983–1997, 62% of India-born migrants to the U.S. were living in the same five states. In 1990, the counties with Asian Indian presence amounting to 25% (and 25% of India-born immigrants) were Queens (New York State), Los Angeles (California), Cook (Illinois), Harris (Texas), Santa Clara (California) and Middlesex (New Jersey).

location listed as first patent author. Second, using NBER and USPTO data we extracted ZIP codes for inventor locations to identify county of residence in the U.S.[4] Then, for all inventors, we constructed yearly information on the community of Indian immigrants in the inventor's county of residence using DHS data. Since DHS data cover the period 1983–1997 and we use lagged values for our independent variables, the dataset resulted in 2184 Indian and 46,373 non-Indian inventors.

In order to control for unobserved factors that might affect patterns and rates of citations to immigrant knowledge by non-Indian inventors, and to achieve an identical number of inventors in both groups, we employed coarsened exact matching (CEM) with a "one-to-one" option. The idea behind this nonparametric matching method is to temporarily coarsen each variable into substantively meaningful groups (i.e., strata) to allow exact matching on the coarsened data, and then to retain only the original (uncoarsened) values of the matched data (Iacus et al., 2009, 2011). Several management and economics studies use CEM to deal with selection challenges (e.g., Azoulay et al., 2010; Campbell, 2012; Di Lorenzo & Van de Vrande, 2019). CEM reduces imbalances among the covariates between the groups of Indians and non-Indians which decreases statistical bias and improves causal interpretation of the effects. Our CEM procedure resulted in an exact matching between Indian and non-Indian inventors based on the following inventor covariates: total number of patents, patenting tenure, share of patents applied for and granted in semiconductor classes, county of residence, and year.[5] The CEM procedure significantly improved the imbalance between the Indian and non-Indian inventor groups; the overall imbalance provided by the L1 statistic moved from L1 = 0.826 to L1 = 0.501. From the initial 2184 Indian inventors, 35% are matched exactly. The resulting dataset at inventor-year level consists of 1528 inventors (764 Indian and 764 non-Indian) located in 116 different U.S. counties and observed between 1983 and 1998 for a total of 2230 observations. Although we test our hypotheses for the sample of matched non-Indian inventors, that is, 764 non-Indian inventors and 1116 observations, we conducted additional analysis and comparisons using the sample of Indian inventor observations.

---

[4] In order to map to DHS data and create a meaningful location match for Indian inventors we dropped inventors with missing ZIP code information and those with multiple ZIP codes in the same year.

[5] Following previous research using CEM (e.g., Di Lorenzo & Van de Vrande, 2019), we also exact-matched using the variable "matching year" which is the last year in each individual inventor time series and allows comparison and matching of Indian and non-Indian inventors along the selected covariates in the final years observed.

Variables

Our dependent variable is *immigrant knowledge sourced* which captures the knowledge sourced by the focal inventor from Indian inventors in each year. Following Almeida et al. (2015), we consider the inventor's patent portfolio in year t, and examine patents cited (backward citations) in this portfolio during the six years prior to year t. Our measure is the count of patents citing Indian inventors.[6]

Our independent variables consider the focal inventor's exposure to Indians in our three communities. First, we capture exposure to Indian inventors in the focal inventor's organizational community. The variable *ethnic organizational community* is the percentage of Indian inventors in all inventors granted semiconductor patents in the focal inventor's firm in year t – 1. Second, we capture exposure to Indians in the focal inventor's technological community by identifying the focal inventor's primary semiconductor technological class based on the three-digit semiconductor technology class in which the inventor patented the most in year t – 1. The variable *ethnic technological community* is the percentage of Indian inventors in all inventors with patents in the focal inventor's primary semiconductor technological class in year t – 1. Third, we measure the focal inventor's exposure to Indians in the geographic community by considering the focal inventor's county of residence. We include variables for two aspects of geographic community, namely professional and family milieux based on DHS data which classifies Indians transitioning to legal permanent resident status based on "class of admission" (i.e., status to immigrate to the U.S.). Classes of admission are mutually exclusive i.e., an immigrant can be classified in only one class. The U.S. immigration system includes a range of admission classes which fall into the following broad categories: (a) spouses and children of resident aliens or U.S. citizens, (b) other immediate relatives (e.g., siblings, parents) of resident aliens or U.S. citizens, (c) outstanding professionals and skilled workers, (d) other (e.g., refugees). We use categories (a) and (c) to capture the respective exposure to geographically situated Indian families and professionals. The variables *ethnic geographic professional community* and *ethnic geographic family community* are defined as the respective percentages in year t – 1 of outstanding professionals and skilled Indian immigrants in total Indian immigrants, and total Indian spouses and children in total Indian immigrants in the focal inventor's county.

---

[6] To obtain a more complete picture of immigrant knowledge flows, we also considered patents with at least one Indian inventor and classified these as knowledge sourced from an Indian inventor.

To rule out competing mechanisms we included the following control variables. An inventor's propensity to source knowledge from an ethnic community might be explained by overall knowledge sourcing behavior. Accordingly, we control for knowledge sourced by the focal inventor from the organizational, technological, and geographic communities. *Organizational knowledge sourced by the inventor* is the percentage of backward citations (filed between years t − 6 and t) in the inventor's patent portfolio (in year t) to patents assigned to the focal inventor's firm. Similarly, *technological knowledge sourced by the inventor* is the percentage of backward citations (filed between years t − 6 and t) in the inventor's patent portfolio (in year t) in the inventor's primary three-digit semiconductor technology class. *Geographic knowledge sourced by the inventor* is the percentage of backward citations (filed between years t − 6 and t) to the inventor's patent portfolio (in year t) to inventors living in the focal inventor's state.

At the focal inventor level, we control also for *inventor productivity* which is the total number of patents filed by the inventor between years t − 6 and year t, and *inventor technological breadth* which is the standard deviation of the technological classes in the focal inventor's portfolio of patents applied for in year t − 1. Both these characteristics might influence the inventor's ability to source immigrant knowledge. Since collaborations are important for knowledge sourcing, we control for *inventor collaboration propensity* as the average number of coinventors named on the focal inventor's patents in year t − 1, and *inventor ethnic collaboration propensity* is the average number of Indian inventors (collaborators) named the focal inventor's patents in year t − 1.

Finally, we control for other contextual factors. The sourcing of immigrant knowledge might be influenced by the quality of the knowledge created by Indian inventors and exposure to the Indian community in the county of residence. We include *immigrant knowledge quality* computed as the average number of forward citations received by Indian patents in year t − 1. Based on U.S. census data, for each county we compute the variable *Indian population in county* as the percentage of Asian Indians in the county's total population in year t − 1.

Results

Our variable of interest *immigrant knowledge sourced*, is a count variable characterized by a typical right-skewed citations data distribution which calls for a negative binomial regression model to test our hypotheses. We rule out possible non-independence of observations within groups and estimate robust

Table 19.1 Correlation matrix and summary statistics

Sample of Non-Indian Inventors (N = 1116)	(1)	(2)	(3)	(4)	(5)	(6)	(7)	(8)	(9)	(10)	(11)	(12)	(13)	(14)
(1) Immigrant knowledge sourced														
(2) Ethnic organizational community	0.068													
(3) Ethnic technological community	0.184	0.219												
(4) Ethnic geographic professional community	0.192	0.033	0.125											
(5) Ethnic geographic family community	0.079	−0.009	−0.050	0.178										
(6) Technological flows to inventor	0.064	0.076	0.173	0.040	−0.024									
(7) Organizational flows to inventor	0.093	0.014	−0.001	−0.011	−0.054	−0.046								
(8) Geographic flows to inventor	0.080	0.002	0.083	0.076	0.048	0.008	0.463							

(continued)

Table 19.1 (continued)

Sample of Non-Indian Inventors (N = 1116)	(1)	(2)	(3)	(4)	(5)	(6)	(7)	(8)	(9)	(10)	(11)	(12)	(13)	(14)
(9) Inventor productivity	0.378	0.111	0.174	0.158	0.041	0.122	0.097	0.102						
(10) Inventor collaboration propensity	0.148	0.043	0.109	0.056	-0.025	-0.007	0.104	0.059	0.240					
(11) Inventor ethnic collaboration propensity	0.134	0.304	0.120	0.026	-0.002	0.015	-0.006	0.047	0.169	0.354				
(12) Inventor technological breadth	0.381	0.060	0.175	0.113	-0.005	0.061	0.083	0.096	0.574	0.229	0.191			
(13) Immigrant knowledge quality	-0.106	-0.138	-0.445	-0.148	0.076	0.029	-0.016	-0.074	-0.104	-0.102	-0.112	-0.131		
(14) Indian population in county	0.024	0.145	0.312	0.186	0.052	-0.026	-0.015	0.265	0.079	0.068	0.024	0.107	-0.315	
Mean	7.839	0.058	0.054	0.161	0.395	0.503	0.106	0.207	0.896	1.411	0.094	-0.928	2.899	0.013
Std. Dev.	22.202	0.067	0.024	0.093	0.075	0.293	0.169	0.203	0.795	1.539	0.338	0.647	0.301	0.011

Sample of Indian Inventors (N = 1114)	(1)	(2)	(3)	(4)	(5)	(6)	(7)	(8)	(9)	(10)	(11)	(12)	(13)	(14)
(1) Immigrant knowledge sourced														
(2) Ethnic organizational community	−0.057													
(3) Ethnic technological community	0.147	−0.030												
(4) Ethnic geographic professional community	0.108	−0.005	0.153											
(5) Ethnic geographic family community	0.018	0.009	−0.008	0.176										
(6) Technological flows to inventor	0.055	0.002	0.180	0.019	0.009									
(7) Organizational flows to inventor	0.067	−0.171	0.033	0.022	−0.077	−0.040								
(8) Geographic flows to inventor	0.099	−0.005	0.097	0.111	0.000	0.025	0.481							
(9) Inventor productivity	0.341	−0.096	0.167	0.085	0.003	0.148	0.129	0.140						

(continued)

Table 19.1 (continued)

Sample of Indian Inventors (N = 1114)	(1)	(2)	(3)	(4)	(5)	(6)	(7)	(8)	(9)	(10)	(11)	(12)	(13)	(14)
(10) Inventor collaboration propensity	0.137	-0.151	0.054	0.015	-0.054	0.018	0.113	0.065	0.172					
(11) Inventor ethnic collaboration propensity	0.184	0.071	0.208	0.008	-0.008	0.069	0.076	0.032	0.149	0.421				
(12) Inventor technological breadth	0.360	-0.105	0.123	0.123	0.009	0.014	0.105	0.065	0.462	0.220	0.154			
(13) Immigrant knowledge quality	-0.093	0.026	-0.481	-0.126	0.083	0.004	-0.032	-0.061	-0.123	-0.072	-0.116	-0.125		
(14) Indian population in county	0.043	0.107	0.304	0.224	0.042	0.091	-0.051	0.274	0.118	0.095	0.159	0.106	-0.309	
Mean	14.008	0.169	0.06	0.157	0.396	0.551	0.091	0.200	0.965	1.392	0.282	-0.931	2.899	0.013
Std. dev.	45.585	0.214	0.022	0.091	0.078	0.279	0.152	0.203	0.784	1.396	0.582	0.645	0.299	0.011

Correlations greater than 0.050 are significant at least at $p < 0.10$

standard errors and the variance-covariance matrix by clustering at the individual inventor level.

Table 19.1 summarizes the descriptive statistics and correlations of the variables used in our analysis for the samples of non-Indian and Indian inventors.

On average, the extent of immigrant knowledge sourcing is around 7.8 citations for a non-Indian inventor (6.5% of the inventor's total backward citations) and 14 citations (10.6% of the inventor's total backward citations) for an Indian inventor. This suggests that Indian inventors' use of immigrant knowledge is approximately twice that of non-Indian inventors ($p < 0.01$). In terms of potential exposure to Indians in different communities we also find differences between Indian and non-Indian inventors. On average, the possibility of interactions with Indians in the workplace (*ethnic organizational community*) is twice as high for Indian compared to non-Indian inventors (0.169 vs 0.058; $p < 0.01$). The results for the variable *ethnic technological community* and the t-test of mean values (0.054 vs 0.060; $p < 0.01$) suggest that the difference in the exposure to potential interactions with Indians within their technological community between the two groups of inventors is significant but relatively small (0.006).[7]

In relation to the control variables, the results for knowledge sourced from their technological, organizational, and geographic communities, and average number of collaborators are similar for Indian and non-Indian inventors. However, for collaboration with Indian inventors the results differ significantly with Indians more likely to collaborate with other Indians.

Table 19.2 reports the results of our models.

Before discussing our hypotheses, we consider model 1 which includes the full sample, that is, the combined sample of non-Indian and Indian inventors. The coefficient of the dummy variable *Indian inventors* is positive and statistically significant ($p < 0.05$) suggesting that Indian inventors draw more on knowledge patented by Indian inventors than do non-Indian inventors. This result is in line with prior findings which suggest ethnicity facilitates access to and flows of knowledge among co-ethnic group members (Agrawal et al., 2008).

Next, we consider the implications of immigrant knowledge for the sample of non-Indian inventors (models 2–7). Model 2 is the baseline model which includes the control variables. We find that the greater the exposure of non-Indian inventors to Indians in different communities, the greater the amount

---

[7] There is no difference between Indian and non-Indian inventors in terms of *ethnic geographic professional community* and *ethnic geographic family community* which is as expected due to the exact matching on *county of residence* between Indian and non-Indian inventors which smooths differences at the county level between the two groups.

Table 19.2 Negative binomial regression for ethnic community knowledge sourced by non-Indian inventors

	Full Sample	Sample of Non-Indian Inventors						Sample of Indian Inventors	Full Sample
	Model 1	Model 2	Model 3	Model 4	Model 5	Model 6	Model 7	Model 8	Model 9
Indian inventor	0.388** (0.157)								0.438*** (0.150)
Ethnic organizational community			4.486*** (1.464)				3.973** (1.545)	−0.516** (0.253)	−0.0614 (0.260)
Ethnic technological community				28.16*** (4.814)			30.22*** (4.808)	17.44*** (4.284)	23.81*** (3.747)
Ethnic geographic professional community					2.886* (1.542)		3.576*** (1.229)	1.401 (0.954)	2.390*** (0.890)
Ethnic geographic family community						5.021*** (1.154)	3.588*** (1.085)	0.864 (1.488)	2.638** (1.060)
Technological flows to inventor	(0.157)	0.572 (0.384)	0.437 (0.381)	−0.104 (0.346)	0.697** (0.352)	0.677** (0.341)	−0.0591 (0.282)	0.304 (0.286)	0.176 (0.208)
Organizational flows to inventor	0.490* (0.257)	1.965* (1.193)	1.886 (1.192)	1.778 (1.082)	2.088* (1.207)	1.753* (1.013)	1.564* (0.851)	−1.192** (0.492)	0.603 (0.587)
Geographic flows to inventor	0.515 (0.676)	0.502 (0.537)	0.636 (0.534)	0.776* (0.467)	0.211 (0.510)	0.553 (0.529)	0.678 (0.431)	1.324*** (0.392)	0.823*** (0.310)
Inventor productivity	0.955*** (0.345)	0.736*** (0.116)	0.706*** (0.117)	0.865*** (0.100)	0.664*** (0.107)	0.722*** (0.102)	0.739*** (0.0936)	0.823*** (0.0865)	0.790*** (0.0652)
Inventor collaboration propensity	0.766*** (0.0714)	0.0640	0.0907**	0.0793*	0.0615	0.0751*	0.102**	0.0463	0.0694**

19 Non-Ethnic Inventor Sourcing of Immigrant Knowledge: The Role...

	(1)	(2)	(3)	(4)	(5)	(6)	(7)	(8)	(9)
Inventor ethnic collaboration propensity	0.0531 (0.0384)	0.172 (0.0438)	−0.0689 (0.0453)	0.0193 (0.0469)	0.249 (0.0392)	0.169 (0.0417)	−0.113 (0.0418)	0.328*** (0.0516)	0.182* (0.0344)
Inventor technological breadth	0.287*** (0.0977)	0.347*** (0.169)	0.373*** (0.181)	0.221** (0.152)	0.308*** (0.190)	0.351*** (0.153)	0.219** (0.182)	0.435*** (0.119)	0.329*** (0.0990)
Immigrant knowledge quality	0.426*** (0.0890)	−0.112 (0.0951)	−0.106 (0.0947)	0.875*** (0.100)	−0.188 (0.0927)	−0.377 (0.0879)	0.652** (0.104)	0.414 (0.105)	0.477** (0.0803)
Indian population in county	−0.124 (0.215)	7.785 (0.261)	1.800 (0.254)	1.339 (0.296)	10.99 (0.266)	10.90 (0.266)	−2.333 (0.291)	−8.540 (0.293)	−4.268 (0.224)
Constant	0.755 (7.241) 1.035	0.736 (10.57)	0.600 (10.51)	−3.630*** (10.91)	0.420 (9.511)	−0.627 (9.627)	−5.280*** (9.964)	−1.490 (7.389)	−3.510*** (7.031)
									(0.759)
Observations	2230	1116	1116	1116	1116	1116	1116	1114	2230
Clustered Errors	YES	YES	YES	YES	YES	YES	YES	YES	YES
Wald Chi2	290.3	204.1	216.1	346.4	235.4	258.1	521.9	256.7	608.9
Prob > chi2	0.000	0.000	0.000	0.000	0.000	0.000	0.000	0.000	0.000

Robust standard errors in parentheses. *** $p < 0.01$, ** $p < 0.05$, * $p < 0.1$

of immigrant knowledge sourced by non-Indian inventors. Model 3 supports hypothesis 1. The coefficient of *ethnic organizational community* is positive and significant at $p < 0.01$ suggesting that knowledge sourced from Indian inventors by non-Indian inventors increases with the number of Indian inventor patenting in the organizational context of the focal inventor. In model 4, the coefficient of *ethnic technological community* is positive and significant at $p < 0.01$ suggesting that exposure to Indian inventors is important also in the relevant technological context of the non-Indian inventor; this supports hypothesis 2. Our results also support hypothesis 3 that exposure to Indians through membership of the same geographic community promotes knowledge sourcing by non-Indian inventors from Indian inventors. The coefficients of *ethnic geographic professional community* and *ethnic geographic family community* are positive and significant ($p < 0.1$ and $p < 0.01$, respectively). That is, the greater the exposure to Indian professionals and (interestingly) Indian families in the U.S. county of residence the greater the amount of immigrant knowledge sourced by non-Indian inventors. These results are confirmed by model 7 which includes all the independent variables.

Model 8 provides the results for exposure to the organizational, technological, and geographic communities for our matched samples of Indian inventors. Since each focal Indian inventor is a member of the ethnic Indian community, we find different patterns for Indian inventors' exposure to interactions with other Indians for knowledge sourcing from the other communities. For an Indian inventor sourcing immigrant knowledge, what matters is exposure to other Indian inventors in the technological community, and co-inventing with other Indian inventors both of which are positive and statistically significant ($p < 0.01$). However, increased exposure to Indian inventors patenting in the organization seems detrimental to immigrant knowledge sourcing which might be explained in part by competition. As the number of Indian inventors in the organizational community increases, Indian inventors may reduce their sourcing of immigrant knowledge to differentiate themselves in terms of their knowledge creation compared to other Indian organizational peers. For Indian inventors, colocation with immigrant professionals and immigrant families for promoting potential interactions and facilitating knowledge sourcing is less important—shown by the lack of significance of the variables *ethnic geographic professional community* and *ethnic geographic family community*. The existing embeddedness of Indian inventors in their ethnic community might remove the need for participation in geographic communities to source immigrant knowledge.

Robustness Checks

We conducted some robustness checks (results available upon request). First, since our sample was constructed using CEM which allows a one-to-one exact matching procedure we matched one non-Indian inventor to one Indian inventor. However, our results are robust to different matching alternatives such as a many-to-one matching which allows more than one non-Indian inventor to be matched to an Indian inventor and matching of inventor locations based on the same state rather than the same county. Second, we conducted an ordinary least squares (OLS) estimation and obtained results largely consistent with our main results.

Although full investigation of the relationship between our dependent variable *immigrant knowledge sourced* and the innovation quality of non-Indian inventors is beyond the scope of the present study, preliminary testing using our data suggests a positive correlation between knowledge sourced from Indian inventors and innovation quality for non-Indian inventors which is similar to the effects found by Almeida et al. (2015) in their study of Indian inventors. This initial evidence is reassuring and corroborates the importance of studying how and to what extent immigrant knowledge spills over outside the ethnic community.

Discussion and Conclusions

Research at the intersection of the international business and innovation literatures has for long emphasized the importance of ethnicity as a mechanism for the transfer of knowledge between inventors. Shared language and sense of identity and similar norms promote trust and reciprocity and reduce information costs, allowing easier knowledge flows among inventors in the same ethnic community (Agrawal et al., 2008; Breschi et al., 2017; Kerr, 2008; Oettl & Agrawal, 2008; Saxenian, 1999). It has been shown also that the sourcing of knowledge from ethnic communities enhances the quality of the innovations produced by immigrant inventors (Almeida et al., 2015). However, if it remains within the ethnic community the significance of immigrant knowledge will be limited. Our research goes beyond a "community-centered perspective" (Lissoni, 2018) and proposes and explores a new perspective on immigrant inventors by considering the influence of their knowledge outside the ethnic community (e.g., Choudhury & Kim, 2019). We draw on insights in the sociology literature to explore how ethnic inventors' knowledge is disseminated. Since knowledge flows are socially situated (Brown & Duguid, 1991), we posit that socialization processes which allow inventors outside the ethnic community to interact with the members of that community serve to straddle ethnic community boundaries and enable knowledge sourcing. In line with previous work, we focus on three communities—the organizational, technological, and geographic communities—in which inventors are embedded simultaneously and where socialization takes place (Boschma, 2005).

The overall finding that the knowledge created by the Indian inventors contributes as prior knowledge to non-Indian inventors' innovations constitutes an important contribution to scholarship. This area tends to be overlooked—the dominant focus being on immigrant knowledge influencing other members of the ethnic community. In other words, our study complements and extends work on innovation and entrepreneurship (Almeida et al., 2015; Choudhury, 2016; Elo et al., 2019; Kenney et al., 2013), and foreign investment (Foley & Kerr, 2013; Hernandez, 2014; Miguelez, 2017) which focuses on ethnic community interactions and the benefits that accrue to ethnic community members as a result of community membership. For instance, Rauch and Trindade (2002) show how ethnic Chinese communities support trade across borders through the sharing of knowledge related to markets and supply and by sanctioning which discourages opportunistic behavior by the community. Similarly, Shukla and Cantwell (2018) show that the presence of immigrants in the host country influences its patterns of foreign investment; and in the area of entrepreneurship, the success of the "motel industry" has been shown to be shaped by the sharing of knowledge and preferred access to capital among ethnic Indians (Kalnins & Chung, 2006). In a high technology and innovation context, Saxenian (2002) discusses the existence of a variety of Chinese and Indian professional associations in Silicon Valley, aimed at sharing scientific and technical information and enabling co-operation between engineers and scientists within the ethnic community. She documents the role of associations for facilitating cross-generation mentoring and resources to facilitate entrepreneurial activity. In the patent and knowledge creation space, Agrawal et al. (2008), provide evidence of co-ethnicity in increased flows of knowledge represented by citations. They show also that co-location seems to serve a similar purpose by supporting the development of social capital.

Our research builds on these studies and suggests that different communities—organizational, technological, and geographic—play a part in disseminating inventor knowledge from the ethnic community to inventors outside that community. Specifically, we suggest that organizational, technological, and geographic communities can bridge ethnic community boundaries and enable social interactions. We contribute to research on social communities by investigating the implications of simultaneous embeddedness in different communities for flows of knowledge across ethnic community boundaries. Crescenzi et al. (2016) show that inventors within the same organization are more likely to collaborate. We complement this finding by showing that organizational communities can bridge ethnic community boundaries. Specifically, our results suggest that the presence of Indian inventors in the organizational community is more likely to increase the probability of socialization with non-Indians and lead in turn to knowledge flows. We support the view that geographically situated social communities facilitate flows of immigrant knowledge to members outside the ethnic community. We argue that embeddedness in co-located professional and family communities triggers interactions with Indians and enables a better understanding of the ethnic community and a greater appreciation of the knowledge available within it. This evidence echoes previous findings on the importance of family communities for the geographic distribution of skilled labor (Dahl & Sorenson, 2010).

From a policy perspective, the issue of immigrant inventors and their contribution to host economies has been the subject of controversial debate on immigration. Despite evidence of the benefits reaped by the host economy from the presence of high skilled immigrants, questions remain about the negative effects such as the crowding out from science and engineering of native born scientists and inventors (Stephan & Levin, 2001). In the current climate, policy decisions appear to be driven by concerns about the negative effects of immigration which are resulting in greater scrutiny of the H1B visa program that allows immigrant inventors to work in the U.S., and recent increased suspension of premium fast track processing of these visas (Da Silva, 2018). Our study provides evidence which should be informative for policy makers. Our findings build on work which challenges the idea of the displacement (of natives) effects of immigration (Kerr & Lincoln, 2010; Moser et al., 2014) and suggests the positive benefits for the non-Indian community based on the knowledge created by Indian inventors—effects which are enhanced by the increased presence of immigrant inventors and their families in organizational, technological and geographic communities. In particular, our findings about the role of ethnic geographically situated professional communities echo empirical evidence on the reduced flows of knowledge due to policies that limit the international mobility of skilled workers and students (Orazbayev, 2017). Thus states, professional associations and organizations should exploit the presence of immigrant inventors and their family members in order to obtain the benefits for the wider community.

Our research has some limitations. Our findings for the flow of immigrant knowledge beyond community members might not be generalizable directly to other ethnic groups than the Indian community. An interesting extension to our work would be to study other ethnic immigrant communities (Chinese, Russian) which show predominantly skilled migration. It would be interesting also, to explore whether our results could be replicated for other destination countries for example, by studying the sourcing of immigrant knowledge in the UK—another important destination country for Indian immigrants. Theoretically, we posit that the presence of Indians in the organizational, technological, and geographic communities of non-Indian inventors promotes knowledge sourcing from the ethnic community through interactions and social processes. Our results point to the importance of a greater presence of Indians in the communities of non-Indian inventors. However, we do not observe the nature of their interactions. While availability of data to investigate these types of interactions is scarce, the need to understand the specific interaction channels that support flows of immigrant knowledge should be an important topic for future research. Also, with some exceptions (Choudhury & Kim, 2019) the influence of immigrant knowledge on individuals outside the ethnic community remains an under-researched phenomenon and should be prioritized on future research agendas. For example, our results show that the sourcing of immigrant knowledge could have important implications for the quantity and quality of the innovation output of non-members of the ethnic community. A deeper exploration of the implications of the intersection between ethnic community knowledge sourcing and the social realm would add to our understanding of innovation by providing practical insights for inventors and firm managers, and prescriptions for policy makers to maximize the benefits of this knowledge.

Acknowledgments This work was supported by the Independent Research Fund Denmark | Social Sciences.

Grant: "The role of diaspora investors in developing countries: A study of firm internationalization and inter-firm collaborations" (DFF—4182-00053).

References

Agrawal, A., Kapur, D., & McHale, J. (2008). How do spatial and social proximity influence knowledge flows? Evidence from patent data. *Journal of Urban Economics, 64*(2), 258–269. https://doi.org/10.1016/j.jue.2008.01.003

Almeida, P., & Kogut, B. (1999). Localization of knowledge and the mobility of engineers in regional networks. *Management Science, 45*(7), 905–917. https://doi.org/10.1287/mnsc.45.7.905

Almeida, P., & Phene, A. (2004). Subsidiaries and knowledge creation: The influence of the MNC and host country on innovation. *Strategic Management Journal, 25*(8–9), 847–864. https://doi.org/10.1002/smj.388

Almeida, P., Phene, A., & Li, S. (2015). The influence of ethnic community knowledge on Indian inventor innovativeness. *Organization Science, 26*(1), 198–217. https://doi.org/10.1287/orsc.2014.0931

Azoulay, P., Zivin, J. S. G., & Wang, J. (2010). Superstar extinction. *The Quarterly Journal of Economics, 125*(2), 549–589.

Boschma, R. (2005). Proximity and innovation: A critical assessment. *Regional Studies, 39*(1), 61–74. https://doi.org/10.1080/0034340052000320887

Bowles, S., & Gintis, H. (2004). Persistent parochialism: Trust and exclusion in ethnic networks. *Journal of Economic Behavior & Organization, 55*(1), 1–23. https://doi.org/10.1016/j.jebo.2003.06.005

Breschi, S., & Lissoni, F. (2009). Mobility of skilled workers and co-invention networks: An anatomy of localized knowledge flows. *Journal of Economic Geography, 9*(4), 439–468. https://doi.org/10.1093/jeg/lbp008

Breschi, S., Lissoni, F., & Miguelez, E. (2017). Foreign-origin inventors in the USA: Testing for diaspora and brain gain effects. *Journal of Economic Geography, 17*(5), 1009–1038. https://doi.org/10.1093/jeg/lbw044

Brown, J. S., & Duguid, P. (1991). Organizational learning and communities-of-practice: Toward a unified view of working, learning, and innovation. *Organization Science, 2*(1), 40–57.

Brown, J. S., & Duguid, P. (2001). Knowledge and organization: A social-practice perspective. *Organization Science, 12*(2), 198–213. https://doi.org/10.1287/orsc.12.2.198.10116

Campbell, B. A. (2012). Earnings effects of entrepreneurial experience: Evidence from the semiconductor industry. *Management Science, 59*(2), 286–304. https://doi.org/10.1287/mnsc.1120.1593

Caragliu, A., & Nijkamp, P. (2016). Space and knowledge spillovers in European regions: The impact of different forms of proximity on spatial knowledge diffusion. *Journal of Economic Geography, 16*(3), 749–774. https://doi.org/10.1093/jeg/lbv042

Cetina, K. K. (1999). *Epistemic cultures: How the sciences make knowledge*. Harvard University Press: Cambridge, MA.

Chakravorty, S., Kapur, D., & Singh, N. (2017). *The other one percent: Indians in America*. Oxford University Press.

Choudhury, P. (2016). Return migration and geography of innovation in MNEs: A natural experiment of knowledge production by local workers reporting to return migrants. *Journal of Economic Geography, 16*(3), 585–610. https://doi.org/10.1093/jeg/lbv025

Choudhury, P., & Kim, D. Y. (2019). The ethnic migrant inventor effect: Codification and recombination of knowledge across borders. *Strategic Management Journal, 40*(2), 203–229. https://doi.org/10.1002/smj.2977

Cooke, A., & Kemeny, T. (2017). Cities, immigrant diversity, and complex problem solving. *Research Policy, 46*(6), 1175–1185. https://doi.org/10.1016/j.respol.2017.05.003

Crane, D. (1972). *Invisible colleges; diffusion of knowledge in scientific communities.* Chicago, University of Chicago Press.

Crescenzi, R., Nathan, M., & Rodríguez-Pose, A. (2016). Do inventors talk to strangers? On proximity and collaborative knowledge creation. *Research Policy, 45*(1), 177–194. https://doi.org/10.1016/j.respol.2015.07.003

Da Silva, C. (2018). *H-1B visa premium processing fast-track program on hold until 2019.* Newsweek. Accessed from https://www.newsweek.com/h-1b-visa-premium-processing-fast-track-program-hold-until-2019-1094370.

Daft, R. L., & Weick, K. E. (1984). Toward a model of organizations as interpretation systems. *Academy of Management Review, 9*(2), 284–295. https://doi.org/10.5465/amr.1984.4277657

Dahl, M. S., & Pedersen, C. Ø. R. (2004). Knowledge flows through informal contacts in industrial clusters: Myth or reality? *Research Policy, 33*(10), 1673–1686. https://doi.org/10.1016/j.respol.2004.10.004

Dahl, M. S., & Sorenson, O. (2010). The migration of technical workers. *Journal of Urban Economics, 67*(1), 33–45. https://doi.org/10.1016/j.jue.2009.09.009

Di Lorenzo, F., & Van de Vrande, V. (2019). Tapping into the knowledge of incumbents: The role of corporate venture capital investments and inventor mobility. *Strategic Entrepreneurship Journal, 13*(1), 24–46.

Diemer, A., & Regan, T. (2022). No inventor is an Island: Social connectedness and the geography of knowledge flows in the US. *Research Policy, 51*(2), 104416. https://doi.org/10.1016/j.respol.2021.104416

Elo, M., Täube, F., & Volovelsky, E. K. (2019). Migration 'against the tide': Location and Jewish diaspora entrepreneurs. *Regional Studies, 53*(1), 95–106.

Fleming, L., King, C., & Juda, A. I. (2007). Small worlds and regional innovation. *Organization Science, 18*(6), 938–954. https://doi.org/10.1287/orsc.1070.0289

Foley, C. F., & Kerr, W. R. (2013). Ethnic innovation and U.S. multinational firm activity. *Management Science, 59*(7), 1529–1544. https://doi.org/10.1287/mnsc.1120.1684

Garud, R., & Rappa, M. A. (1994). A socio-cognitive model of technology evolution: The case of Cochlear implants. *Organization Science, 5*(3), 344–362. https://doi.org/10.1287/orsc.5.3.344

Hernandez, E. (2014). Finding a home away from home: Effects of immigrants on firms' foreign location choice and performance. *Administrative Science Quarterly, 59*(1), 73–108. https://doi.org/10.1177/0001839214523428

Herrigel, G. (1993). Large firms, small firms, and the governance of flexible specialization: The case of Baden Wuerttemberg and socialized risk. In *Country competitiveness.* Oxford University Press.

Iacus, S. M., King, G., & Porro, G. (2009). CEM: Software for coarsened exact matching. *Journal of Statistical Software, 30*(9).

Iacus, S. M., King, G., & Porro, G. (2011). Causal inference without balance checking: Coarsened exact matching. *Political Analysis, 20*(1), 1–24.

Jacobs, J. (1969). *The life of cities*. Random House.

Kalnins, A., & Chung, W. (2006). Social capital, geography, and survival: Gujarati immigrant entrepreneurs in the U.S. lodging industry. *Management Science, 52*(2), 233–247. https://doi.org/10.1287/mnsc.1050.0481

Kane, A. A. (2010). Unlocking knowledge transfer potential: Knowledge demonstrability and superordinate social identity. *Organization Science, 21*(3), 643–660. https://doi.org/10.1287/orsc.1090.0469

Kane, A. A., Argote, L., & Levine, J. M. (2005). Knowledge transfer between groups via personnel rotation: Effects of social identity and knowledge quality. *Organizational Behavior and Human Decision Processes, 96*(1), 56–71. https://doi.org/10.1016/j.obhdp.2004.09.002

Kapur, D. (2001). Diasporas and technology transfer. *Journal of Human Development, 2*(2), 265–286. https://doi.org/10.1080/14649880120067284

Kenney, M., Breznitz, D., & Murphree, M. (2013). Coming back home after the sun rises: Returnee entrepreneurs and growth of high tech industries. *Research Policy, 42*(2), 391–407. https://doi.org/10.1016/j.respol.2012.08.001

Kerr, W. R. (2007). *The ethnic composition of U.S. inventors*. Harvard Business School Press.

Kerr, W. R. (2008). Ethnic scientific communities and international technology diffusion. *The Review of Economics and Statistics, 90*(3), 518–537. https://doi.org/10.1162/rest.90.3.518

Kerr, W. R., & Lincoln, W. F. (2010). The supply side of innovation: H-1B visa reforms and U.S. ethnic invention. *Journal of Labor Economics, 28*(3), 473–508. https://doi.org/10.1086/651934

Kogut, B., & Zander, U. (1992). Knowledge of the firm, combinative capabilities, and the replication of technology. *Organization Science, 3*(3), 383–397. https://doi.org/10.1287/orsc.3.3.383

Kurzban, R., & Neuberg, S. (2015). Managing Ingroup and outgroup relationships. In *The handbook of evolutionary psychology* (pp. 653–675). Wiley. https://doi.org/10.1002/9780470939376.ch22

Lissoni, F. (2018). International migration and innovation diffusion: An eclectic survey. *Regional Studies, 52*(5), 702–714. https://doi.org/10.1080/00343404.2017.1346370

Lobo, J., & Strumsky, D. (2008). Metropolitan patenting, inventor agglomeration and social networks: A tale of two effects. *Journal of Urban Economics, 63*(3), 871–884. https://doi.org/10.1016/j.jue.2007.07.005

March, J. G. (1991). Exploration and exploitation in organizational learning. *Organization Science, 2*(1), 71–87. https://doi.org/10.1287/orsc.2.1.71

Marino, A., Mudambi, R., Perri, A., & Scalera, V. G. (2020). Ties that bind: Ethnic inventors in multinational enterprises' knowledge integration and exploitation. *Research Policy, 49*(9), 103956. https://doi.org/10.1016/j.respol.2020.103956

Marshall, A. (1890). *Principles of economics*. Macmillan.

Miguelez, E. (2017). Inventor diasporas and the internationalization of technology. *World Bank Economic Review*. https://doi.org/10.1093/wber/lhw013

Moser, P., Voena, A., & Waldinger, F. (2014). German Jewish Émigrés and US invention. *American Economic Review, 104*(10), 3222–3255. https://doi.org/10.1257/aer.104.10.3222

Nahapiet, J., & Ghoshal, S. (1998). Social capital, intellectual capital, and the organizational advantage. *Academy of Management Review, 23*(2), 242–266.

Oettl, A., & Agrawal, A. (2008). International labor mobility and knowledge flow externalities. *Journal of International Business Studies, 39*(8), 1242–1260. https://doi.org/10.1057/palgrave.jibs.8400358

Orazbayev, S. (2017). International knowledge flows and the administrative barriers to mobility. *Research Policy, 46*(9), 1655–1665. https://doi.org/10.1016/j.respol.2017.08.001

Owen-Smith, J., & Powell, W. W. (2004). Knowledge networks as channels and conduits: The effects of spillovers in the Boston biotechnology community. *Organization Science, 15*(1), 5–21. https://doi.org/10.1287/orsc.1030.0054

Paruchuri, S., & Awate, S. (2017). Organizational knowledge networks and local search: The role of intra-organizational inventor networks. *Strategic Management Journal, 38*(3), 657–675. https://doi.org/10.1002/smj.2516

Pew Research Center. (2013). *The rise of Asian Americans*. Accessed from http://www.pewsocialtrends.org/2012/06/19/the-rise-of-asian-americans/.

Piore, M. J., & Sabel, C. (1984). *The second industrial divide: Possibilities for prosperity*. Basic Books.

Portes, A. (1998). Social capital: Its origins and applications in modern sociology. *Annual Review of Sociology, 24*(1), 1–24. https://doi.org/10.1146/annurev.soc.24.1.1

Powell, W. W., & Giannella, E. (2010). Collective Invention and Inventor Networks. In B. H. Hall, N. Rosenberg (Eds.), *Handbook of the Economics of Innovation*, Vol. 1 (pp. 575–605). North-Holland.

Qin, F. (2015). Global talent, local careers: Circular migration of top Indian engineers and professionals. *Research Policy, 44*(2), 405–420. https://doi.org/10.1016/j.respol.2014.08.007

Rabbiosi, L., & Santangelo, G. D. (2013). Parent company benefits from reverse knowledge transfer: The role of the liability of newness in MNEs. *Journal of World Business, 48*(1), 160–170.

Rappa, M. A., & Debackere, K. (1992). Technological communities and the diffusion of knowledge. *R&D Management, 22*(3), 209–220. https://doi.org/10.1111/j.1467-9310.1992.tb00811.x

Rauch, J. E., & Trindade, V. (2002). Ethnic Chinese networks in international trade. *The Review of Economics and Statistics, 84*(1), 116–130. https://doi.org/10.1162/003465302317331955

Rogers, E.M. (1983). *Diffusion of innovations*. The Free Press. Accessed from http://repository.experience-capitalization.net/handle/123456789/83

Saxenian, A. (1996). Inside-out: Regional networks and industrial adaptation in Silicon Valley and Route 128. *Cityscape, 2*(2), 41–60.

Saxenian, A. (1999). *Silicon Valley's new immigrant entrepreneurs*. Public Policy Institute of California.

Saxenian, A. (2002). Silicon Valley's new immigrant high-growth entrepreneurs. *Economic Development Quarterly, 16*(1), 20–31. https://doi.org/10.1177/0891242402016001003

Saxenian, A., & Hsu, J.-Y. (2001). The Silicon Valley–Hsinchu connection: Technical communities and industrial upgrading. *Industrial and Corporate Change, 10*(4), 893–920. https://doi.org/10.1093/icc/10.4.893

Saxenian, A., Motoyama, Y., & Quan, X. (2002). *Local and global networks of immigrant professionals in Silicon Valley*. Public Policy Institute of California.

Shukla, P., & Cantwell, J. (2018). Migrants and multinational firms: The role of institutional affinity and connectedness in FDI. *Journal of World Business, 53*(6), 835–849. https://doi.org/10.1016/j.jwb.2018.07.003

Sonderegger, P., & Täube, F. (2010). Cluster life cycle and diaspora effects: Evidence from the Indian IT cluster in Bangalore. *Journal of International Management, 16*(4), 383–397. https://doi.org/10.1016/j.intman.2010.09.008

Stephan, P. E., & Levin, S. G. (2001). Exceptional contributions to US science by the foreign-born and foreign-educated. *Population Research and Policy Review, 20*(1), 59–79. https://doi.org/10.1023/A:1010682017950

Tajfel, H. (1974). Social identity and intergroup behaviour. *Social Science Information, 13*, 65–93.

Tajfel, H., & Turner, J. C. (1986). The social identity theory of intergroup behavior. In *Psychology of intergroup relations* (pp. 7–24). Nelson-Hall.

Teece, D., & Pisano, G. (1994). The dynamic capabilities of firms: An introduction. *Industrial and Corporate Change, 3*(3), 537–556. https://doi.org/10.1093/icc/3.3.537-a

Wadhwa, V., Saxenian, A., Rissing, B. A., & Gereffi, G. (2007). *America's new immigrant entrepreneurs: Part I (SSRN scholarly paper ID 990152)*. Social Science Research Network. Accessed from https://papers.ssrn.com/abstract=990152

Part V

The Migrant's Journey

20

Unfolding the Dynamics of Refugees' Entrepreneurial Journey in the Aftermath of Forced Displacement

Solomon Akele Abebe and Ziad El-Awad

Introduction

Refugee entrepreneurship (RE) entails the process of founding and developing ventures by refugees, who are individuals that have fled war, conflict, and persecution across international borders, in their new host country (Abebe, 2023). Having been forcibly displaced from their original contexts and relocated to completely foreign contexts, refugees often need to rebuild their lives from scratch, resulting in significant challenges when they undertake entrepreneurship (Harima, 2022). Scholars reveal that refugee entrepreneurs face complex and much harder obstacles to overcome compared to their immigrant counterparts (Alrawadieh et al., 2019; Ram et al., 2022; Wauters & Lambrecht, 2008). Nonetheless, the global number of refugee business start-ups is on the rise (Desai et al., 2021). For instance, *The Economist* (2018)

S. A. Abebe (✉)
Sten K. Johnson Centre for Entrepreneurship, School of Economics & Management, Lund University, Lund, Sweden
e-mail: solomon_akele.abebe@fek.lu.se

Z. El-Awad
Sten K. Johnson Centre for Entrepreneurship, School of Economics & Management, Lund University, Lund, Sweden

School of Business, Innovation and Sustainability, Halmstad University, Halmstad, Sweden
e-mail: ziad.el-awad@fek.lu.se

reported that even in resource-deficient settings like the Zaatari camp in Jordan, refugees have established over 3000 startups, generating a revenue of $13 million per month. This paradox that refugees thrive in entrepreneurship despite their detrimental challenges is labeled the "paradox of refugee entrepreneurship" (Collins et al., 2017). As such, the question remains as to how refugees, after undergoing disruptive life circumstances in their most extreme form, can start and grow their ventures and generate societal wealth through their businesses (Jiang et al., 2021). Nonetheless, current RE literature provides limited insight to address this question.

While RE research dates back to the 1980s (Fass, 1986), it has been gradually expanding but rapidly within the last few years with a growing body of literature (Desai et al., 2021). However, much of the existing knowledge has primarily tended to focus on refugee entrepreneurial entry as driven by ethnocultural characteristics linked to the home country (Bizri, 2017; Gold, 1988, 1992; Halter, 1995) and their experience of disadvantages in the host country structure (Barak-Bianco & Raijman, 2015; Garnham, 2006; Johnson, 2000). As such, many studies primarily focus on the antecedents of RE while also considering it a group-level phenomenon determined by cultural and structural factors rather than individual journeys. At the same time, the paradigm featured in the bulk of extant RE literature views refugees as submissive to their surroundings or external factors and does not show how they act independently to manage their circumstances (Abebe, 2023). However, the last few years have seen emerging streams of literature focusing on the contextual responsiveness of refugees (Harima, 2022; Obschonka et al., 2018; Ram et al., 2022; Refai et al., 2018). These studies show the relevance of individual entrepreneurial agency in the specific case of refugees, who need to manage their disruptive circumstances and orchestrate their career paths.

Our study draws on and extends the current scholarly conversation on RE by investigating how recently arrived refugees proactively pursue entrepreneurship in their host country after forced displacement. We build on the notion of "embedded agency" (Garud et al., 2007) as an underlying concept to complement the overwhelming situational and circumstantial focus of RE research. The embedded agency approach provides the conceptual foundation to theorize on refugees as individual entrepreneurial agents who consciously reflect, decide, and actively orchestrate their entrepreneurial path under "substantial adversity" (Shepherd et al., 2020), and within the frame set by their home and host country contexts. To capture this empirically, we applied a process research design and inductively studied 21 refugees from Syria who fled the violent "Syrian Conflict" to Sweden during the period coinciding with the "European refugee crisis" of the mid-2010s and engaged in

RE. Relying on rich qualitative data drawn from 40 interviews, which were collected over two years, and a theory-building inductive analysis (Gioia et al., 2013), we provide a conceptual framework unfolding the dynamics of refugees' entrepreneurial journeys.

We make four contributions to the literature on (refugee) entrepreneurship. Firstly, we focus on the process of RE and develop a theoretical model that outlines the dynamics of this process, including the different phases, underlying mechanisms, and enabling factors of this process. Our processual approach updates the current static or snapshot approach, which mainly considers cultural and structural-level factors that influence refugees' entrepreneurial entry. Secondly, we expand the realm of entrepreneurship literature by providing an inductive comprehension of the phenomenon in the context of individuals experiencing extreme life disruption as opposed to those who benefit from a continuous life flow and accumulated resources. Thirdly, we achieve a balanced application of the agency/structure dialectic to RE, departing from the concept of embedded agency (Garud et al., 2007). We highlight how refugees' ability to proactively orchestrate their entrepreneurial journey, reflecting their entrepreneurial agency, is intertwined with detrimental circumstances and structural barriers arising from forced migration. Our approach chimes with recent studies (Ram et al., 2022; Villares-Varela et al., 2022) in providing a balanced role to refugee entrepreneurial agency, a factor less accounted for by the prevailing perspectives on RE (Abebe, 2023) but vital in the case of refugees who need to rebuild their lives after relocation.

The study has three implications for policy and practice. Firstly, by highlighting the pre-organizational intricacies of RE, the study provides insights for policymakers on appropriate intervention strategies to improve its preconditions and outcomes. Secondly, the study demonstrates that refugees pursue viable business opportunities in the later stages of their journey, but their initial businesses are necessity-based and informal, with small profit margins and long working hours. This increases the risk of perpetuating segregation and inequality rather than promoting integration. However, specific policies and entrepreneurial support systems for refugees can help alleviate this issue by enhancing their entrepreneurial skills and knowledge of business rules and regulations in the host country through early training. This way, they can pursue more viable business opportunities from the outset. Finally, for aspiring refugee entrepreneurs, our study clearly shows the mechanisms by which they can rework their disadvantages and expedite their entrepreneurial journey.

Conceptual Background

Refugee Entrepreneurship

RE is an emerging field of research that has gained increasing attention in recent years, particularly in the aftermath of the "refugee crisis" of the mid-2010s (Desai et al., 2021). At its core, RE provides a conceptual framework for investigating the complex interplay between refugeehood and entrepreneurship, which is further influenced by issues such as gender, ethnicity, and social class (Adeeko & Treanor, 2021). Refugeehood pertains to the situation of being a refugee, which is typified by extreme life disruption triggered by involuntary and abrupt displacement from one's home country and resettlement in often completely foreign contexts (UNHCR, 2022). Entrepreneurship refers to the process of establishing and growing a business (Gartner, 1985). RE, therefore, can be defined as the process of founding and developing a venture carried out in a new host country by individuals who have fled their countries of origin due to war, conflict, or persecution across international borders (Abebe, 2023; Fuller-Love et al., 2006). Refugee entrepreneurs are forced migrants who undertake entrepreneurial activities during their early resettlement in the host country, where they have been granted refugee status according to international law (Heilbrunn et al., 2018). RE is a form of entrepreneurship distinguished by the additional challenges that refugees face as a result of their liabilities linked with their refugeeness and foreignness while attempting to establish and expand businesses in their host countries.

RE is not an entirely new phenomenon, as forced migration has existed throughout human history (Bernard, 1977). However, as an area of research, it is still in its infancy. For many years, the topic did not receive much attention within the broader field of scholarship on refugees' economic behavior, which primarily focused on their wage labor outcomes (Abebe, 2023). Research on migration and entrepreneurship mainly concentrated on voluntary migrant entrepreneurs, and analysis of refugee entrepreneurs was often subsumed under the established research stream on immigrant entrepreneurs by conflating the two, despite ontological differences arising from their departure motives, migration patterns, and legal circumstances (Heilbrunn & Iannone, 2020). Although Gold (1988, 1992) acknowledged the distinctiveness of RE and called for separate analysis, his ideas were not widely recognized for many years until the recent "refugee crisis." However, RE has now become globally significant for both political and academic reasons due to its potential benefits for refugees' socioeconomic integration and host societies (Harima et al., 2021). The current scholarly urgency and increased research interest in the topic indicate that RE is becoming a vibrant area of research with a rapidly accumulating body of knowledge, in contrast to its modest origins in the 1980s and sporadic development over the years (Desai et al., 2021). Given the growing number of refugees, RE is likely to gain more prominence in the future.

The body of literature emerging in the RE research stream is primarily rooted in the social sciences and humanities fields, with limited theory development within the entrepreneurship scholarly conversation. For the most part, RE research has been dominated by scholars from fields such as cultural anthropology, sociology, economic geography, and psychology, while entrepreneurship and management scholars have only recently begun to investigate the topic (Heilbrunn & Iannone, 2020). The predominance of social sciences and humanities scholars has significantly influenced the current understanding of RE. Although there is a wealth of knowledge on group ethnocultural characteristics, resources, and macro-level structural factors that affect refugees' entry into and outcomes in entrepreneurship, the literature lacks a deeper understanding of individual refugee actors and their agency in the entrepreneurial process (see reviews by Abebe, 2023; Lazarczyk-Bilal, 2019). In other words, the current literature primarily explains the determinants of RE but does not provide accounts of the dynamics of entrepreneurship as actively organized by individual refugees. Therefore, the conceptualization of RE as an entrepreneurial undertaking and occurrence requires further development by emphasizing the perspectives of individual refugee actors, their agency, and the processuality of entrepreneurial activity. This study seizes this opportunity to address and deepen our understanding of RE.

Understanding the Dynamics of Refugee Entrepreneurship: The Embedded Agency Approach

Many RE studies are conceptually grounded in cultural, structural, and mixed embeddedness (ME) perspectives derived from sociological research on immigrant entrepreneurship. Studies informed by cultural theories focus on refugees' entrepreneurial predisposition, enabled by their home cultural values, beliefs, group characteristics, and possession of ethnocultural resources (Campbell, 2007; Gold, 1988; Halter, 1995; Kaplan, 1997). Those with structural theories, on the other hand, focus on how disadvantages in the economy's structure, labor market policies, and regulatory-institutional conditions in the host country influence refugees' entry into entrepreneurship (Garnham, 2006; Kupferberg, 2008). Other studies departing from the ME framework fuse aspects of cultural and structural perspectives (Price & Chacko, 2009; Wauters & Lambrecht, 2008). However, these perspectives often emphasize the weight of external factors in the analysis of RE and lack conceptual foundations to account for the dynamics of RE by explaining how refugees voluntarily decide to start a business and proactively orchestrate their journey toward it. As a result, in the literature, refugee entrepreneurs are frequently understood as being submissive to external factors and their circumstances, rather than how they act as entrepreneurial agents and overcome their constraints.

Nevertheless, in recent years, a number of scholars have begun to theorize on the active involvement of refugees in entrepreneurship as they rebuild their lives and career paths (Obschonka et al., 2018; Ram et al., 2022; Shepherd et al., 2020). These studies provide different accounts of refugees' contextual responsiveness as they engage in entrepreneurship to rebuild their lives and career paths. While scholars acknowledge the exercise of entrepreneurial agency by refugees, they often do not clearly define its interplay with external factors or the structural context, instead emphasizing refugees' individual traits such as identity (Adeeko & Treanor, 2021; Refai et al., 2018), resilience (Shepherd et al., 2020), and motivations (Mawson & Kasem, 2019). There are a few exceptions that provide an understanding of the interplay of contextual factors and the personal agency of refugee entrepreneurs (Ram et al., 2022; Villares-Varela et al., 2022). These studies argue that external factors and conditions facing refugees shape their entrepreneurial actions while also constraining them. Therefore, as entrepreneurial agency in the context of RE must be seen as having relative autonomy, it is necessary to have a balanced theoretical exploration of RE that captures the interplay between agency and structure.

The embedded agency approach (Garud et al., 2007) provides the conceptual backdrop to complement the current focus on situational and circumstantial factors in research on entrepreneurship by refugees. This concept addresses the longstanding debate between structure and agency in the literature on institutions and entrepreneurship. It contends that an overemphasis on structure or context in early institutional literature and RE research can result in causally deterministic understandings that exclude individuals' volitional choices and purposeful behavior. At the same time, an excessive emphasis on agency in entrepreneurship research can lead to a lack of understanding of the context in which it takes place. The embedded agency approach brings together the tenets of institutional and entrepreneurial theories under one concept and highlights the mutuality between structure and agency (c.f. Gartner, 1985; Jack & Anderson, 2002). It suggests that external circumstances and structures do not necessarily limit agency but rather provide the platform and resources for the unfolding of (refugee) entrepreneurship (McMullen et al., 2021). Informed by this approach, this study strives to capture the true dynamics of the phenomenon by investigating how refugees proactively orchestrate their entrepreneurial journeys despite facing various disadvantages and adverse circumstances and within the framework of their home and host country contexts.

Methodology

Research Design and Participant Selection

Our research question involves developing a process-oriented theory that explores the dynamics of refugees' entrepreneurial journeys after they are forced to migrate to a new host country. Due to the limited number of existing studies that theorize on the refugee entrepreneurship process, our study focuses primarily on building a theory rather than testing one. To accomplish this objective, we are using a qualitative, inductive research approach with a longitudinal orientation. This approach enables us to start with the research question in mind and detect new theoretical ideas and insights on RE emerging from the data. It also allows us to capture the specificities of the refugee entrepreneurial journey and foster a better understanding of its processual nature (Gioia et al., 2013). Additionally, this research design enables us to stay close to our refugee participants and capture the dynamics of events that occur before, during, and after their flight, as well as their entrepreneurial journey after relocation. These dynamics could have otherwise been overlooked in survey-based designs (e.g., Obschonka et al., 2018). By capturing these details, we aim to deepen our understanding of the refugee entrepreneurial journey and its distinct nature.

The study focuses specifically on Syrian refugees who were relocated to Sweden as a result of the violent conflict in Syria since 2011. The choice to focus on this group is supported by their high proportion during the study period, with more than 6.8 million Syrians being forced to flee due to the civil war (UNHCR, 2022). The study exclusively focuses on Sweden to ensure that differences in institutional contexts do not impact refugees' entrepreneurial journeys (Harima, 2022). During the period known as the "European refugee crisis," Sweden was one of the European countries that accepted the highest number of refugees per capita (Konle-Seidl, 2018). In Sweden, refugees typically stay at camps until a decision is made on their asylum application, which can take 6 to 18 months. Successful applicants receive a residence permit based on their refugee status, with Syrian refugees arriving before Fall 2015 receiving permanent residence permits and those arriving after receiving temporary ones. All refugees participate in the "establishment program" for immigrants (Etableringsprogrammet) to prepare for the labor market, including language and cultural training and skill validation (Konle-Seidl, 2018). The political and institutional context in Sweden during the study period was relatively favorable toward refugees and RE. However, our model may be context-specific and require further testing to explain RE in other contexts.

We employed a purposive sampling approach to select participants for our study based on theoretical relevance criteria (Eisenhardt & Graebner, 2007). Participants had to be (1) Syrians who fled the civil war, (2) with legally recognized refugee status in Sweden, and (3) either self-employed or operating their businesses in Sweden as recent arrivals. To ensure that the participants' experiences were unique to refugees, we excluded those who had obtained Swedish citizenship, which would have given them access to international markets and made them act like transnational entrepreneurs (Halilovich & Efendić, 2021). Besides, we selected participants who were "acute refugees" according to Kunz's Kinetic Model of Refugee Theory (1973), meaning they were forced to leave Syria suddenly and without preparation, unlike "anticipatory refugees," who could sense danger early and depart in an orderly fashion. Moreover, we confirmed that the participants had started their businesses during the early stages of their resettlement in Sweden, when they were still acutely experiencing the challenges of being a refugee and facing uncertainty about their future. These measures allowed us to capture the unique circumstances and behaviors associated with RE that stem from the challenges of being a refugee and adjusting to a foreign environment and different institutional frameworks, setting them apart from immigrant entrepreneurs (Harima et al., 2021).

Due to the specificity of our selection criteria and the "hard-to-reach" nature of refugee populations (Bloch, 2004), we employed a snowballing strategy (Sulaiman-Hill & Thompson, 2011) to identify study participants. We utilized the contacts of a research assistant of Syrian origin who was employed at Lund University and had previous experience working on government-sponsored refugee integration projects to recruit 17 participants. Additionally, the first author utilized an established contact (Atkinson & Flint, 2001) from his participation in entrepreneurship training for refugees during the crisis to recruit four participants. Table 20.1 provides brief

Table 20.1 Participant's characteristics

Participants	Sex	Age	Education	Pre-adversity experience	Arrival date	Location	Type of business	Company date
Participant 1	M	49	Accounting degree	Accountant; credit manager	2014	Landskrona	Small kiosk	2017
Participant 2	M	42	Engineering degree	Property developer; owner of a real estate	2014	Landskrona	Water scooters, kayaks, and beach gear renting shop	2017
Participant 3	M	40	Engineering degree	Engineer in a company selling generator sets; worked in family business in the same branch; work experience in emirates	2014	Malmö	A small watch shop	2016
Participant 4	M	43	Elementary	Grew up in a family that owned roastery	2015	Malmö	Syrian specialty nut store	2017
Participant 5	M	22	High school	No formal work experience, but grew up in a family business.	2012	Lund	A combined food retail store and hairdressing store	2018
Participant 6	M	30	No university education	He had been developing own business	2011	Stockholm	Online store for oriental treats	2019
Participant 7	M	35	Uncompleted university education	Owned a business in Syria	2014	Stockholm	Importing and selling Syrian dessert online	2019
Participant 8	F	40	No university education	Owned her business in Lebanon	2018	Uppsala	Informal apparel trading	2019
Participant 9	F	45	University education	Co-owned a business with husband	2017	Umeå	Work-integrated cooperative	2019
Participant 10	M	40	Primary school	Owned different types of businesses	2015	Ronneby	Syrian bakery	2018

(continued)

Table 20.1 (continued)

Participants	Sex	Age	Education	Pre-adversity experience	Arrival date	Location	Type of business	Company date
Participant 11	M	42	Degrees in auto mechanics and business administration	Accountant in an oil company; owned manufacturing workshop on the side	2015	Ronneby	Supermarket	2019
Participant 12	M	29	Interrupted environmental engineering degree	No formal work experience	2017	Stockholm	Online platform for Arabic clothes	2019
Participant 13	F	50	Degree in advertising, design and printing	Co-owned a printing press with husband	2015	Malmö	Women's beauty center	2018
Participant 14	M	52	No formal education	Owned dairy product trading	2014	Karlskrona	Small shop for Syrian dairy products	2019
Participant 15	M	54	Highschool education	Owned an apparel store	2015	Ronneby	Arabic clothing store	2018
Participant 16	F	35	Degree in media and journalism; diploma in teaching	Teaching math and informatics; owned an educational channel	2015	Karlskrona	E-platform for children	2018
Participant 17	M	40	Highschool	Owned an apparel business	2015	Kallinge	Arabic clothing line for women and children	2017
Participant 18	F	45	No formal education	Grew up in an entrepreneurial family; sales person in her husband's wedding shop	2017	Lund	Informal décor service for weddings and birthdays	2019

Participant 19	M	54	Chartered accounting license, and diplomas in business	Accountant in different countries	2015	Lund	Small restaurant	2017
Participant 20	M	35	Low formal education	Owned a bakery for 20 years	2014	Lund	Syrian bakery	2018
Participant 21	F	37	Informatics engineering degree	IT support for tech company	2014	Örebro	E-platform for programming kids	2019

descriptions of each of the 21 refugee entrepreneurs. They are listed in the order of their first interview.

Data Collection

Data for this study was collected between 2018 and 2020 with the aim of gaining an in-depth understanding of the dynamics in the personal lives of refugees, both before, during, and after flight, and their overall entrepreneurial journey. Multiple rounds of in-depth individual interviews were conducted, with all participants except two interviewed over two rounds. During the first round, participants were asked open-ended questions to explain their previous lives and backgrounds, forced migration experiences and their impact on their lives, sources of entrepreneurial motivation and types of businesses, challenges in resettling and starting their businesses, and overall entrepreneurial activity in Sweden. The average length of these interviews was around 50–60 minutes per participant. The author and a researcher colleague examined the transcriptions in order to develop early insights for the following round.

The second round focused more on gaining an in-depth understanding of the RE process, although some follow-up questions were also included to triangulate previous responses. The interview guide was designed to encourage informants to provide a chronological account of the preconditions for their venture founding activity, as well as pre-entry and startup stages. Participants were asked for detailed accounts of their venture development activity and plans, with exit strategies excluded from the study as it was too early for participants to discuss them. A timeline-based interview approach was used to verify and explain how events related to the entrepreneurial journey unfolded chronologically, which helped guard against memory failure associated with retrospective accounts (Miller et al., 1997). Table 20.2 shows that the average length of the second-round interviews was about 1 hour and 25 minutes.

All rounds of interviews except for four were conducted in the informants' mother tongue of Arabic to capture the nuances and ensure data quality (Chidlow et al., 2014) by a well-trained Syrian research assistant employed at Lund University, under the supervision of the author and a researcher colleague. Face-to-face meetings or Skype calls were used to collect data, and all interviews were recorded; those in Arabic were immediately translated into

Table 20.2 Data sources

Participants	Interview 1 date	Length in hours	Interview 2 date	Length in hours	Interview formats
Participant 1	17/08/2018	2:00	03/06/2019	1:34	In person
Participant 2	10/09/2018	1.37	15/08/2019	1:57	In person
Participant 3	17/09/2018	2:27	N/A	N/A	In person
Participant 4	24/10/2018	2:40	N/A	N/A	In person
Participant 5	19/11/2019	2:00	10/08/2020	1.30	In person, Skype
Participant 6	09/01/2020	2:30	22/08/2020	1:45	Skype
Participant 7	22/01/2020	1:45	23/08/2020	1:20	Skype
Participant 8	23/01/2020	2:00	25/08/2020	1:30	Messenger
Participant 9	28/01/2020	2:00	27/08/2020	1:30	Skype
Participant 10	04/03/2020	2:30	29/08/2020	1:15	Skype
Participant 11	21/03/2020	2:00	31/08/2020	1:45	Skype
Participant 12	30/01/2020	1:30	13/10/2020	1:00	Skype
Participant 13	05/05/2020	1:45	17/10/2020	1:20	Skype
Participant 14	09/03/2020	1:45	21/09/2020	1:30	Skype
Participant 15	28/03/2020	2:00	19/09/2020	1:45	Skype
Participant 16	27/04/2020	1:45	09/09/2020	1:15	Skype
Participant 17	25/02/2020	2:00	21/09/2020	1:00	In person
Participant 18	19/06/2020	1:30	15/10/2020	1:35	In person
Participant 19	06/07/2020	3:30	21/10/2020	1:15	In person
Participant 20	07/07/2020	1:30	13/10/2020	1:10	Skype
Participant 21	07/07/2020	2:00	09/10/2020	1:25	Skype

English, and all of them were transcribed word-for-word, creating more than 500 pages of text for the final analysis.

Data Analysis

Although our data analysis began during the interviewing process (Charmaz, 2006), it evolved in three iterative stages, involving sorting, reducing, and theorizing (Gioia et al., 2013), with the goal being to uncover theoretical constructs unfolding the dynamics of RE.

First-Order Codes: Creating a Time-Sensitive Representation of Critical Events Unfolding in the Lives of Refugee Entrepreneurs

We began by sorting the empirical material to bring order and structure to our data. We spent a significant amount of time analyzing the details and identifying initial categories. Our analysis of the interview material focused on identifying critical events during refugees' life transitions, such as preflight, flight, asylum seeking, reestablishment, and entrepreneurial carrier periods, as well as their interpretations of these events. Using the informants' own terms and phrases, we created initial labels reflecting key instances and events in each period, which were later converted into summaries, resulting in over 200 first-order codes. We highlighted sections in the data that revealed refugees' experiences of loss, trauma, resilience, motivations for entrepreneurship, and resource mobilization. We then sorted the first-order codes chronologically (Rennstam & Wästerfors, 2018) and developed an order of events reflecting the basic steps in the life transition process of refugees, with a focus on their entrepreneurial journey.

Second-Order Categories: Linking Empirical Observations to Abstract Concepts

In the next stage, we reduced the data into a more manageable set by focusing on the most relevant first-order themes. Drawing on the basic stages of the entrepreneurial process (Gartner et al., 2004), we tentatively categorized informants' entrepreneurial journey into three phases: pre-conditions for business startup, pre-entry, and startup and development, for analytical purposes. We reorganized the first-order codes based on these phases and then categorically reduced them by studying and evaluating them, selecting 34 initial codes that revealed patterns. To make sense of our empirical findings, we engaged with a diverse body of literature on migrant, refugee, and mainstream entrepreneurship, following established practices of qualitative data analysis (Gioia et al., 2013). Some literature (e.g., Bayon et al., 2015; Townsend et al., 2010) was not part of our a priori conceptual framework but was closely related to the emerging themes from the coding and used to label the second-order codes. For example, we used the existing literature (Townsend et al., 2010) to term the two first-order concepts that showed refugees' positive beliefs and feelings about understanding the host country to start and manage a business as *perceived entrepreneurial self-efficacy*. Finally, we grouped all selected first-order codes with common themes and linked them to higher-level conceptual categories (i.e., second-order codes) that captured the embedded meanings.

Developing a Process Model

After coding our data and abstracting it into conceptual themes, we moved on to the last step of our processual analysis, which was to find out how the concepts we had found interact with each other. We went back and forth between the first-order themes and the literature until we settled on 12 second-order concepts, which we then put into four overarching aggregate themes. The first three dimensions represented the stages in refugees' entrepreneurial journey, which we coded as *detrimental entrepreneurial resource circumstances, re-acquisition of entrepreneurial resources*, and *entrepreneurial action and exploration*. The final aggregate theme represented the factors explaining the transition from one stage to the next, which we coded as *enabling factors*. Finally, we uncovered the dynamic interrelationships between the identified second-order concepts themselves as well as with the four aggregate themes to form the building blocks of the process model that unfolds the dynamics of RE, as presented in Fig. 20.3, after multiple iterative versions (Gioia et al., 2013). The data structure that illustrates the link between these concepts and first-order observations is presented in Figs. 20.1 and 20.2, and the model is discussed in the discussion and conclusion section.

Findings

This section presents our findings on how the entrepreneurial journey of refugees unfolds after their forced displacement to a new host country, based on empirical observations of Syrian refugee entrepreneurs in Sweden. Our data analysis identifies three phases, and we explain the dynamics of entrepreneurial behaviors inherent in each phase along with the enabling factors that trigger the transition from one phase to the next.

Phase 1. War, violence, and conflict, and subsequent forced displacement, leading to detrimental entrepreneurial resource circumstances.

Refugees face detrimental entrepreneurial resource circumstances as a result of their experience of war, violence, and conflict, as well as their subsequent forced displacement to completely foreign contexts. The emerging data structure emphasizes that three factors—*homeland resource loss, restrained cognitive framing*, and *hindered interaction in the host country*—interact recursively to cause this.

Homeland resource loss entails the permanent destruction or deactivation of refugees' pre-disaster physical, social, financial, and human capital resources critical for venture founding and development activity (Harima, 2022). Our

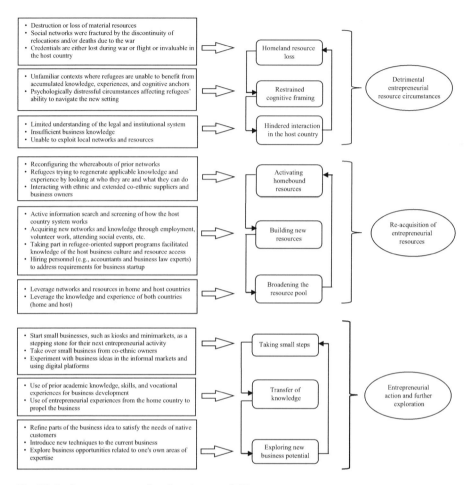

Fig. 20.1 Data structure for the phases of RE

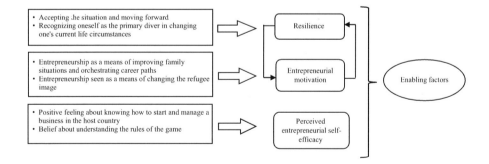

Fig. 20.2 Data structure for the enabling factors

informants stated that their physical capital resources, such as real estate, properties, and shops, as well as their credentials, were destroyed due to extensive barrages and shelling during the Syrian war. Participant 2 stated, *"I had a real estate business in Aleppo, and it was burned to the ground."* Additionally, participants mentioned that they were left with nothing, having used their years of savings to pay for ransoms and smugglers or not being able to access them after relocation. Participant 13 illustrated this by saying, *"My husband was kidnapped by ISIS, and we had to pay [our savings] to get him back."* Furthermore, refugees' social networks became fractured due to the loss of pre-existing contacts and relationships in Syria, caused by death (Participant 14: *"Two of my best suppliers for my business were killed by airstrikes"*) or separation from friends, family, and acquaintances because of the discontinuity of relocations (Participant 19: *"…after these years, I still don't know where most of my friends and relatives are."*)

According to our analysis, when refugees experience the loss of homeland resources, it creates new context and psychologically distressing circumstances. This causes them to lose their cognitive anchors, or what is familiar to them. We describe this as **restrained cognitive framing.** In cognitive psychology, "cognitive framing" refers to how individuals interpret and respond to information based on their prior knowledge (Huhn et al., 2016). Refugees facing retrained cognitive framing are unable to use their accumulated knowledge, skills, and cognitive anchors, resulting in psychological distress that affects their ability to react, navigate, and adapt to their new environment (Jiang et al., 2021). Participant 1 reflects on this situation as follows: *"When I realized that I had lost everything, I was so affected psychologically that I wasn't able to function normally, perform tasks, or plan for my future for some time."* Similarly, Participant 19 states, *"With everything being new, I don't feel that I belong here… I also realized that I couldn't use any of my previous knowledge or skills, […] this affected me as I did not know how to react."* Our data reveals that the loss of cognitive anchors, coupled with additional stressors and challenges in the host country, such as language, further hinders refugees' interaction in the host country.

Hindered interaction in the host country entails refugees' limited capacity to navigate and exploit externally complex networks and resources in the host country's social, economic, and institutional environments (Schnell & Sofer, 2002). Participant 11 states, *"[…] being in a new country and the nature of different people and the language […] limit my capabilities and do not give me the opportunity to put all my energy into it."* Our results suggest that refugees' hindered interaction further exacerbates the loss of home country resources. Participant 21 stated, *"As my knowledge of how things work here is limited, my* *home country experiences and knowledge continue to be irrelevant."* Hence, the iterative mechanism by which refugees lose resources means that they continue to encounter detrimental resource constraints before engaging in business startup activity.

Despite their adverse situations, refugees are driven forward to rebuild their lives by manifesting strong dimensions of **resilience** (see also Obschonka et al., 2018; Shepherd et al., 2020). Resilience serves as a positive driving force for RE by allowing refugees to function positively and overcome previous and current adversities. Participant 11 states, *"[…] With everything that happened to me, the most important thing is to accept the situation and move forward […] This is normal when you leave your country."* Strong resilience, in turn, drives refugees' **entrepreneurial motivation**, as stated by Participant 6: *"I am not a son of this country […] I have to be the main driver to change my life situation […] That is why I was motivated to start a business."*

Our data demonstrates that refugees were motivated toward entrepreneurship by a combination of intrinsic and extrinsic factors. For example, some were motivated to change the refugee image, as stated by Participant 11: *"[…] I can't accept the status I am looked at as a refugee. I was determined to start this business […] I kept going until I made it happen."* Others were motivated by extrinsic factors, such as improving their family's economic situation, as stated by Participant 9: *"I [was motivated] to start this business because my husband became disabled due to the war, and after we moved [to Sweden], I had to support him and the family […] that is why I was persistent despite the challenges."* As reflected in these excerpts, our data overall indicates that refugees' resilience enhances their entrepreneurial motivation, and vice versa, and the interplay between the two helps refugees rebound from adverse circumstances and drive them forward in the entrepreneurial journey.

Our overall analysis shows that refugees face a greater risk of harm and danger compared to migrants because they are forced to move suddenly and unexpectedly, resulting in experiences of destruction and dangerous journeys that lead to the loss of essential resources such as finances and relevant credentials needed for entrepreneurial activities (Harima, 2022). In contrast, migrants who plan ahead have more time to choose a resettlement country and leave with their resources intact, making them better equipped to utilize their resources back home and in third countries to pursue opportunities. Additionally, migrants tend to have better psychological readiness to adapt to new environments (Leong, 2014). Trauma and sudden displacement cause severe cognitive disruptions for refugees, affecting their interaction and knowledge base and making it challenging for them to access critical entrepreneurial resources (Jiang et al., 2021). Therefore, unlike immigrant entrepreneurs, refugees need to engage in additional steps to (re)acquire entrepreneurial resources.

Phase 2. Re-bouncing from the adversity of forced displacement triggering re-acquisition of entrepreneurial resources.

While refugees recover from the adversity of forced displacement and are motivated to start businesses, being aware of their precarious resource situation prompts them to engage in resource-seeking behaviors. As shown in Fig. 20.1, the interplay of three second-order themes underlies refugees' resource re-acquisition process relevant for undertaking entrepreneurial action: *activating homebound resources, building new resources,* and *broadening the resource pool*.

After deciding to start their businesses, refugees proactively engage in resource-seeking behaviors by **activating homebound resources**. This entails revitalizing accessible or available resources related to their home country by reconfiguring them and reinterpreting their value and function for business startup in the new host environment (Harima, 2022). In contrast to voluntary immigrants, whose resources from home are often automatically transposed into their new environment (Christensen et al., 2020), our data shows that refugees must reconfigure their prior networks and resources with the help of both their remaining and new connections to reactivate entrepreneurial resources. For example, Participant 7 stated: *"After deciding to have my business, I thought about how to get the necessary resources. […] Then, I started to look for the whereabouts of my previous business networks. […] you know some of them are dead; others are dispersed. After several efforts, I found two of them, who lent me money and also found ways to supply me with products."* Other participants leveraged their relevant knowledge and experience from their home country by looking at the knowledge at their disposal (Participant 10: *"I have knowledge of the behavior of Syrian customers and products. That was my major resource when I thought of starting a business in Sweden."*). Additionally, some participants (e.g., participant 20) actively socialize with co-ethnic and extended co-ethnic business owners and suppliers to obtain information and financing.

Developing an initial resource repertoire through activation enables refugees to build up new resources in the host country. Participant 10 explains, *"[...] being aware of the value of my previous knowledge is relevant because it gives me the base to further build new connections and understand how things work [in Sweden]."* **Building new resources** refers to various activities that refugees undertake to assemble relevant entrepreneurial resources in the host country (Harima, 2022). Some refugees actively seek and screen information in order to understand how the Swedish system works. Participant 1 shares, *"After my* decision [to start a business], I started to actively look for information about the Swedish system."* In some cases, refugees hire accountants and lawyers to gain a good understanding of the business environment and its different requirements and procedures. Participant 8 says, *"[...] I paid a Swedish accountant on an hourly basis. He provided me with all of the information I required."* Other refugees start to build new networks through different activities such as internships, employment, voluntary work, attending social events, and more. Participant 9 explains, *"I started working at Umeå municipality, and this helped me meet different people and expand my network."* Many participants actively participate in refugee support programs provided by the Swedish state, where they acquire relevant knowledge of the Swedish administrative and legal structure for doing business and accessing finance.

Building new resources helps refugees with **broadening the resource pool** as they can leverage knowledge, experience, networks, and resources in both their home and host countries. Participant 2 explains, *"This helps me expand my possibilities. I reached out to all my previous business networks and connections, who are dispersed in different places after the war, to provide me with any help they can. At the same time, I explored all my options in this country."* Participant 11 concurs with this statement, saying, *"When you start a business as a refugee in a new country after losing everything, you always start with your previous knowledge and experience and help from your close networks. Then, you understand the country in which you start a business. In that way, you have more resources."* Broadening the refugee's resource pool further triggers the activation of homebound resources, reflecting the iterative nature of resource mobilization in RE. Participant 1 explains, *"The more knowledge and information I get here, the more I clearly see how all my skills and experiences from my home country are relevant."*

Engaging in resource-seeking behavior enhances refugees **perceived entrepreneurial self-efficacy**. Actively searching for the necessary resources to establish themselves in a new country can boost refugees' self-efficacy, or their confidence in their ability to accomplish goals, increasing their motivation and determination to succeed as entrepreneurs (Townsend et al., 2010). This stands in contrast to immigrants who had the opportunity to prepare for their move and may have already established networks, connections, and financial resources in their destination country, providing them with a strong sense of belief and advantages in starting their business (Christensen et al., 2020). Participant 19 stated: *"No one came with information to tell me how to do this. I found everything by myself through trial and error, but this has created positive feelings that I can manage this [starting a business]."* Similarly, Participant 2 remarked, *"I know the game now [...] I know how to run things. I think I can *handle [the next steps]."* Our findings overall suggest that refugees' entrepreneurial mobilization process develops their belief in their capacity to perform tasks and roles associated with venture founding and development.

Phase 3. Perceived entrepreneurial self-efficacy triggering entrepreneurial actions and further exploration.

Our data indicates that the development of perceived entrepreneurial self-efficacy drives the transition to the phase where refugees undertake entrepreneurial action and further exploration. During this phase, refugees utilize their available resources to establish a venture and engage in the gradual development of new business possibilities. As shown in Fig. 20.1, this phase can be explained by three iterative second-order codes: ***taking small steps, transfer of knowledge,*** and ***exploring new business potential***.

Taking small steps refers to a strategy in which refugees become self-employed in the host country by starting or taking over small businesses with manageable risks. This approach allows them to test out different business possibilities and gain a better understanding of the host country's business environment (Zhang & Chun, 2018). Taking small steps can thus manifest as taking over small businesses or starting new ones with minimal risk. Excerpts from Participant 1 illustrate this point: *"When I started thinking about my own business, [I asked myself]: what kind of business can I manage in this country? Can I have a construction company? Or do I start small and learn the business step by step? So, I said to myself, the easiest thing is to have a small business, which doesn't need a lot of qualifications, and try my luck with it."* Some refugees started small businesses, such as kiosks and minimarkets, as stepping stones for their next entrepreneurial activity. Participant 3 explains, *"I started this small shop for the sole purpose of collecting information for the next step."* Participant 5 took over a small supermarket from a co-ethnic owner where he worked for two years and says, *"I knew this business well and the customers, and when I sorted out the finances, I bought the store."* For some refugees, the internet provides a medium for experimenting with business ideas without a significant investment of resources.

Even after mobilizing resources, refugee businesses at this early stage are typically necessity-oriented and operate in informal or low-value sectors with small profit margins and long working hours (e.g., Participants 8 and 18). While these businesses may be challenging to operate, this approach allows refugees to mitigate the risks associated with starting a business in a new and unfamiliar environment. This approach enables them to test the viability of their ideas and potentially scale up or pivot their business as they gain more knowledge and resources.

Taking small steps helps refugees understand the context of the host country and facilitates the transfer of their knowledge to the country. **Transfer of knowledge** refers to the cognitive process by which refugees recognize that their vocational and entrepreneurial experiences and qualifications from their home country can be applied and used for business development in the host country. Participant 19 describes, *"The experience I got from [the initial activities], like the registration, knowing the procurement, and all the details and steps that I went through in opening the business, allowed me to understand the Swedish bureaucracy much more. [...] this has made me realize that I can now apply my previous knowledge and experiences in the business and tap into better business opportunities."* Participant 14 also states, *"I have learned a lot through this business. I've grown into a more mature person. I have grown in all aspects. [...] now, I can even use my previous [entrepreneurial] experiences to further develop my business."*

Overall, the data suggests that refugees can benefit from taking small steps in their business procedures, as this can help them better understand the context of the host country and facilitate the transfer of their knowledge from their home country. Through this transfer of knowledge, refugees can leverage their previous entrepreneurial experiences and knowledge to navigate the host country's institutional context, leading to better business opportunities. As they gain experience and confidence, they can scale up their businesses toward a more stable and prosperous entrepreneurial career. By starting with small-scale business activities that facilitate the transfer of knowledge, refugees can enhance their entrepreneurial abilities and explore new business potential in their new environment. However, compared to voluntary immigrants, who plan their move in advance, are more explorative from the beginning, and are more willing to take bigger risks and pivot (Christensen et al., 2020; Cortes, 2004), refugees often start small and gradually build their businesses due to the challenges of forced displacement and resettlement. This approach allows them to mitigate risks and gradually gain experience and resources to grow their businesses.

Exploring new business potential for refugees involves actively seeking out fresh opportunities to develop their current ventures or embark on new entrepreneurial ventures, drawing on their past experiences and qualifications. This may entail refining certain aspects of their current business or modifying existing practices using knowledge from their previous entrepreneurial endeavors. Some of the participants in the study considered this stage an opportunity to improve and grow their business by utilizing their previous experience and knowledge (*"I want to re-shuffle the larger part of this business and make it more profitable and efficient through new techniques. [...] my* *previous business experience in this area will be relevant"* - Participant 19). The data also indicates that some refugee entrepreneurs explore business opportunities related to their areas of academic knowledge and vocational experience (*"I now want to tap into a new business [...] related to my previous expertise [in auto mechanics] [...] some kind of manufacturing involving heavy machinery. [...] What I learnt from here is that it doesn't need to be big from the beginning but I can start by taking small steps and gradually develop it"* - Participant 11).

Participants expressed their intention to gradually develop their businesses with small steps, learning as they go and applying their skills to explore new business potential. This highlights the iterative nature of the process. The data also shows that several participants planned to pursue international business opportunities after obtaining Swedish citizenship, indicating their ambition and willingness to expand their business beyond the host country (*"When I get my Swedish citizenship sooner [hopefully], I plan to pursue the possibility of business trading between Syria, the United Arab Emirates, and Sweden"* - Participant 3). This highlights that RE is a temporal phenomenon, and the acquisition of citizenship marks a significant step in the process by opening up new opportunities for refugees and potentially changing the trajectory of their businesses.

Discussion and Conclusion

A Dynamic Process Model of Refugee Entrepreneurship

In this section, we present an integrated processual model (Fig. 20.3) that synthesizes our findings and unfolds the dynamics of RE. The model is based on the premise that entrepreneurship is shaped by extreme life disruption in the refugee context, which has been referred to as "substantial adversity" (Shepherd et al., 2020). Although there are theoretical explanations of entrepreneurs responding to unfavorable events (Shepherd & Williams, 2020), the circumstances faced by refugee entrepreneurs are particularly extreme. These circumstances include the complete destruction of their original context that had been favorable to them, exposure to trauma related to violent conflicts and perilous flight, resettlement in unfamiliar settings, and complex legal issues (Harima et al., 2021). As a result, our model demonstrates that entrepreneurship in such circumstances is a dynamic process encompassing three iterative phases: adverse entrepreneurial resource circumstances caused by forced displacement; bouncing back from adversity, triggering re-acquisition of entrepreneurial resources; and developing perceived entrepreneurial

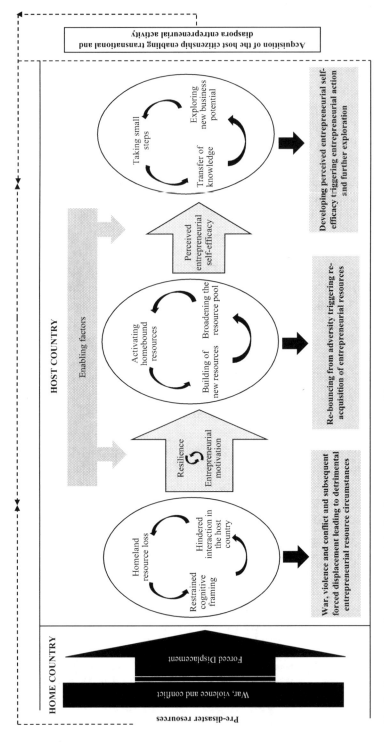

Fig. 20.3 A dynamic process model of refugee entrepreneurship

self-efficacy, triggering entrepreneurial action and further exploration of opportunities. The transition from one phase to another is driven by enabling conditions that demonstrate refugees' personal capabilities to proactively rebuild their personal and professional lives. By emphasizing how refugees actively influence the prerequisites of venture founding and development, our model highlights the individual agency of refugees, which generates the energy necessary to move from a disadvantaged position toward being entrepreneurial agents in the host society and generating societal wealth through their ventures. Below, we provide a more detailed explanation of our dynamic model in light of the empirical data and relevant literature.

The RE process differs from entrepreneuring in non-disruptive contexts, such as in the case of voluntary immigrants, where individuals continuously benefit from accumulated resources (Vinogradov & Elam, 2010). However, compared to immigrants, refugees face a greater risk of harm and danger as they are forced to move suddenly and unexpectedly, resulting in the loss of essential resources such as finances and relevant credentials needed for entrepreneurial activities (Harima, 2022). Hence, refugees often experience detrimental entrepreneurial resource circumstances due to the loss of home country resources caused by forced disembedding from their original context, which is either completely destroyed by war or no longer exists as it did (Giddens, 1990; Harima, 2022). The loss of home country resources has catastrophic impact, creating unfamiliar and distressful circumstances for refugees, which can restrain refugees' cognitive framing, leading to further underembeddedness due to their hindered interaction in the host country and limiting their capacity to navigate and exploit external complex networks and resources (Jiang et al., 2021; Schnell & Sofer, 2002). Our results suggest that refugees' underembeddedness further leads to the loss of home country resources, creating an iterative and cyclical process. In contrast, immigrants and ethnic minorities tend to have better psychological readiness to adapt to new environments and can form ethnocultural networks and intra-ethnic and enclave resources that support their entrepreneurial activities (Gold, 1992; Wauters & Lambrecht, 2008).

One model illustrates that the mechanism by which refugees suffer from detrimental entrepreneurial resource circumstances is iterative/cyclical rather than stemming solely from the dual processes of disembedding and underembedding, as explained by Harima (2022). The iterative and cyclical nature of the process of refugees losing entrepreneurial resources highlights the unique challenges they face when pursuing entrepreneurship compared to voluntary migrants. Therefore, our model reveals that, unlike immigrant entrepreneurs, refugees need to engage in additional steps to (re)acquire entrepreneurial resources. The differences between refugees and immigrants demonstrate how the context of migration can influence the ability to (re)acquire entrepreneurial resources and the importance of understanding the unique challenges that refugees face during the entrepreneurial process.

Despite the adverse circumstances perpetuating resource constraints, refugees are driven forward in their entrepreneurial journeys by the interplay of resilience and entrepreneurial motivation. Resilience refers to refugees' positive functioning in rebuilding their lives (Obschonka et al., 2018). Passive responses are not likely to be effective in this context, and refugees must take entrepreneurial action to succeed (Shepherd et al., 2020). Refugees' intrinsic and extrinsic entrepreneurial motivation further strengthens their resilience and vice versa, enabling them to recover from the hardship of forced displacement and spark the reacquisition of resources. As Harima (2022) argues, forced displacement evokes refugees' cognitive processes, making them aware of their resource loss and constraints and leading them to engage in resource-seeking behaviors. Our model reveals that refugees first seek to activate any remaining or deactivated resources in their home country. Reactivating these resources serves as a foundation for building resources in the host country, expanding the refugees' resource base, triggering further reactivation of homebound resources, and so on. In contrast, migrants who plan their migration to a specific country may not go through a similar process, as they have time to research and prepare for their move (Christensen et al., 2020). However, refugees must adapt their deactivated resources to the new context, whereas immigrants have the foresight to plan for this in advance.

Our model presents a more dynamic perspective on the resource mobilization process in RE. Harima (2022) has suggested that refugees undergo a disembedding process that leads to re-embedding in their home country, while their underembedding results in re-embedding in the host country. The outcomes of these two separate processes help refugees mobilize resources through resource activation and building, respectively. However, our framework reveals that this is a cyclical/iterative process rather than a direct and dual one. We found that refugees develop an initial resource repertoire through the activation of accessible resources, which provides the base to build new resources in the host country. Building resources, in turn, broadens refugees' resource pool, allowing them to leverage knowledge, experience, networks, and resources in both their home and host countries, further triggering the activation of additional homebound resources, and so on. This finding expands the insights put forth by Jiang et al. (2021) that only highlight the value of resources after disruption (i.e., those built in the host country) as more beneficial to the RE process than prior resources (i.e., those reactivated from the home country). Overall, our model considers resource mobilization in RE as a recurrent process that links both home and host countries, in contrast to other approaches that highlight the duality of refugee resources (Harima, 2022; Jiang et al., 2021; Sandberg et al., 2019).

Re-acquiring resources enhances refugees' perceived entrepreneurial ability, which leads to a positive perception of their capacity to undertake entrepreneurship, prompting them to take entrepreneurial action and explore opportunities (Townsend et al., 2010). Our model shows that, at this stage, refugees' entrepreneurial action involves setting up ventures on a small scale by taking small steps to test out business possibilities and gain a better understanding of the host business environment. In this regard, our study supports previous arguments that refugee ventures are often survival-oriented or necessity-driven, easy-to-implement, and located in the informal and low-value sectors (Luseno & Kolade, 2023). But we show that taking small steps enables the transfer of refugees' pre-disaster human capital and enhances their self-confidence in their actual entrepreneurial ability (Bayon et al., 2015), enabling them to actively explore new opportunities for either developing their existing ventures or taking further steps based on their skills and qualifications, thereby repeating the cycle. In contrast, voluntary migrants who plan their move in advance are more exploitative from the outset and are more willing to take bigger risks and pivot (Cortes, 2004). Immigrants who have the opportunity to prepare for their move may have already established networks, connections, and financial resources in their destination, home, and other countries, giving them a strong sense of belief and advantages in creating better business opportunities (Christensen et al., 2020). Refugees attain this stage with the acquisition of a new nationality, which reinstates their homeland access and enables them to explore opportunities in the international market, making their entrepreneurial behavior more similar to that of transnational and diaspora entrepreneurs (Halilovich & Efendić, 2021). In our model, this marks the boundary of RE.

Research Contributions

While much of the existing literature on RE has examined the reasons behind refugees' engagement in entrepreneurial activities in their host countries, less attention has been paid to the actual processes involved in starting and developing their ventures and how their entrepreneurial journeys are structured. For example, previous studies have explored how refugees' ethnocultural characteristics and resources (Campbell, 2007; Gold, 1988, 1992; Halter, 1995), as well as the economic and institutional environment in the host country, or a combination of both (Price & Chacko, 2009; Tömöry, 2008; Wauters & Lambrecht, 2008), influence their entrepreneurial motivations following resettlement. However, our study focuses on the process of RE and develops a theoretical model that outlines the dynamics of this process, including the various phases and underlying mechanisms, as well as the enabling factors that facilitate the transition from one phase to another. Our findings demonstrate how refugees are able to bounce back from adversity and become successful entrepreneurs by building their personal capabilities and proactively influencing the prerequisites for starting and developing their businesses.

Second, this study expands the realm of entrepreneurship research by providing an inductive comprehension of the phenomenon in the context of refugees, who face severe life disruption. Prior research has highlighted the significance of recognizing opportunities (Bhave, 1994) and the role of human and social capital (Jack & Anderson, 2002; Mamabolo & Myres, 2020; Vinogradov & Elam, 2010) in establishing and developing ventures, but has not explored how individuals facing war, conflict, and forced displacement can manage this process. Our study reveals that entrepreneurship in the refugee context is characterized by unfavorable resource loss and constraints, necessitating the cultivation of entrepreneurial abilities and behaviors like resilience, resource reactivation, and resource building. Unlike in non-disrupted scenarios where capital resource accumulation propels the process's continuity, the refugee context necessitates a focus on personal agency and adaptability. By broadening the purview of entrepreneurship research to include extreme life disruption, our study demonstrates how individuals can still create wealth and successful ventures despite confronting significant challenges.

Our final contribution departs from the concept of embedded agency (Garud et al., 2007) to offer a balanced application of the agency/structure dialectic to RE. Prior research has portrayed refugee entrepreneurs as facing insurmountable obstacles and taking a passive role in addressing them or has attributed their entrepreneurial behavior to cultural and structural factors, both of which overlook the interplay between individuals and their context (Abebe, 2023). However, we highlight how refugees' ability to proactively orchestrate their entrepreneurial journey, which reflects their entrepreneurial agency, is intertwined with detrimental circumstances and structural barriers arising from forced migration. We use the embedded agency approach as a sensitizing concept to explore the interplay between refugee entrepreneurs (as agents) and their contexts (as structures). This approach recognizes how forced migration shapes refugees' pursuit of entrepreneurship in two directions. On the one hand, the extreme life disruption associated with it drives refugees to become small business owners in order to circumvent their life situation. On the other hand, it created detrimental circumstances that constrained their business entry and further progression in the entrepreneurial process but also enabled them to build their capabilities to move forward. Hence, our approach chimes with recent studies (Ram et al., 2022; Villares-Varela et al., 2022) in providing a balanced role to refugee entrepreneurial agency, a factor less accounted for by the prevailing cultural, structural, and mixed embeddedness perspectives (Abebe, 2023) but vital in the case of refugees who need to rebuild their lives after forced displacement.

Implication for Policy and Practice

Beyond its research contributions, our study offers implications for RE policy and practice. Our study has revealed a cyclical process of resource loss and mobilization that refugees experience during their journey toward founding and developing their ventures. The loss of resources from their home country creates unfamiliar and distressful circumstances in the host country, hindering their ability to navigate and understand the new context. As a result, they require additional support to mobilize resources before starting a business. To expedite the process of RE, we recommend two policy actions. Firstly, policymakers should create initiatives that enable refugees to use their previous human capital by developing appropriate tools for skill assessment and qualification recognition. This will allow refugees to benefit from their accumulated cognitive abilities (Jiang et al., 2021) and facilitate the building of new resources in the host country, which is crucial for venture founding and development, and also enable the reactivation of additional home country resources. Secondly, policymakers could organize trainings related to language, cultural knowledge, and business rules and regulations for refugees as early as the asylum-seeking phase. This will support refugees' efforts to build up host country resources and better equip them to navigate the new context. These policy actions can facilitate the resource mobilization process for refugees, leading to a more successful journey toward entrepreneurship and economic self-sufficiency.

Our findings also show that refugees often take small steps and establish ventures on a limited scale, even after mobilizing entrepreneurial resources. This is because they want to test the waters and explore business opportunities before fully committing themselves. It is only after gaining self-confidence in their entrepreneurial abilities that they engage in opportunity-driven entrepreneurship, which involves pursuing business opportunities with a higher level of ambition and risk-taking. As such, our findings highlight that, due to their limited entrepreneurial skills and unfamiliarity with the host country's business environment, most of the businesses established by refugees are necessity-based, informal, and of low value. This underscores the importance of providing tailored entrepreneurial support infrastructures for refugees, such as startup incubators and training programs (Meister & Mauer, 2019). These initiatives can offer practical support to aspiring refugee entrepreneurs by empowering them and developing their skills, ultimately helping them to overcome the challenges they face in the host country's business environment and achieve success. Such support structures should offer business training, advisory, and coaching services, as well as knowledge of local market mechanics, as these help refugees leverage their personal capabilities and enhance their entrepreneurial knowledge, skills, and competence. Such practical support schemes boost refugees' actual entrepreneurial self-efficacy (Bayon et al., 2015) during pre-startup, allowing them to pursue more viable business opportunities from the start.

Limitations and Research Outlook

While our study provides valuable insights into the dynamics of RE, it has certain limitations. Firstly, we relied on retrospective interviews, which could have been subject to recollection bias. To mitigate this, we structured our questions around event sequences and asked informants to verify their accounts (Miller et al., 1997). However, future research could use longitudinal designs and prospective data collection methods to capture the real-time nature of refugees' entrepreneurial behaviors (Langley, 2009). Secondly, our participants are all from Syria, where entrepreneurship is highly valued (Mawson & Kasem, 2019), and this may raise questions about the homogeneity of our sample. To address this, future research should test our conceptual model on refugees from different ethnic backgrounds. Thirdly, our sample size of 21 may be considered small, but we believe it is sufficient for our initial efforts in theorizing the entrepreneurial journey of refugees. However, we acknowledge the value of including data from field observations and other data sources from different stakeholders in future studies (Überbacher, 2014). Fourthly, our model shows a linear process of RE, but it may not apply to failed refugee entrepreneurs, which could be an interesting aspect to consider in future studies. Finally, the institutional environment in which refugees undertake entrepreneurship plays a crucial role in shaping their experiences and outcomes (Harima et al., 2021). Studying the topic in other contexts may yield different findings, and we encourage cross-national and cross-continental research designs. This will further enrich our understanding of the nature, dynamics, and specificity of RE.

References

Abebe, S. A. (2023). Refugee entrepreneurship: Systematic and thematic analyses and a research agenda. *Small Business Economics, 60*(1), 315–350.

Adeeko, N., & Treanor, L. (2021). Negotiating stigmatised identities: Enterprising refugee women in the United Kingdom. *International Small Business Journal, 40*(1), 23–46.

Alrawadieh, Z., Karayilan, E., & Cetin, G. (2019). Understanding the challenges of refugee entrepreneurship in tourism and hospitality. *The Service Industries Journal, 39*(9–10), 717–740.

Atkinson, R., & Flint, J. (2001). Accessing hidden and hard-to-reach populations: Snowball research strategies. *Social Research Update, 33*(1), 1–4.

Barak-Bianco, A., & Raijman, R. (2015). Asylum seeker entrepreneurs in Israel. *Economic Sociology: The European Electronic Newsletter, 16*(2), 4–13.

Bayon, M. C., Vaillant, Y., & Lafuente, E. (2015). Initiating nascent entrepreneurial activities: The relative role of perceived and actual entrepreneurial ability. *International Journal of Entrepreneurial Behavior & Research, 21*(1), 27–49.

Bernard, W. S. (1977). Immigrants and refugees: Their similarities, differences and needs. *International Migration, 14*(4), 267–281.

Bhave, M. P. (1994). A process model of entrepreneurial venture creation. *Journal of Business Venturing, 9*(3), 223–242.

Bizri, R. M. (2017). Refugee-entrepreneurship: A social capital perspective. *Entrepreneurship & Regional Development, 29*(9–10), 847–868.

Bloch, A. (2004). Survey research with refugees: A methodological perspective. *Policy Studies, 25*(2), 139–151.

Campbell, E. H. (2007). Economic globalization from below: Transnational refugee trade networks in Nairobi. In M. J. Murray & G. A. Myers (Eds.), *Cities in contemporary Africa* (pp. 125–148). Palgrave Macmillan.

Charmaz, K. (2006). *Constructing grounded theory: A practical guide through qualitative analysis*. Sage.

Chidlow, A., Plakoyiannaki, E., & Welch, C. (2014). Translation in cross-language international business research: Beyond equivalence. *Journal of International Business Studies, 45*(5), 562–582.

Christensen, L. J., Newman, A. B., Herrick, H., & Godfrey, P. (2020). Separate but not equal: Toward a nomological net for migrants and migrant entrepreneurship. *Journal of International Business Policy, 3*(1), 1–22.

Collins, J., Watson, K., & Krivokapic-Skoko, B. (2017). *From boats to businesses: The remarkable journey of Hazara refugee entrepreneurs in Adelaide*. University of Technology Sydney. Accessed from https://researchoutput.csu.edu.au/ws/portalfiles/portal/21074866/From_Boats_to_Businesses_Full_Report_Web.pdf

Cortes, K. E. (2004). Are refugees different from economic immigrants? Some empirical evidence on the heterogeneity of immigrant groups in the United States. *Review of Economics & Statistics, 86*(2), 465–480.

Desai, S., Naudé, W., & Stel, N. (2021). Refugee entrepreneurship: Context and directions for future research. *Small Business Economics, 56*, 933–945.

Eisenhardt, K. M., & Graebner, M. E. (2007). Theory building from cases: Opportunities and challenges. *Academy of Management Journal, 50*(1), 25–32.

Fass, S. (1986). Innovations in the struggle for self-reliance: The Hmong experience in the United States. *International Migration Review, 20*(2), 351–380.

Fuller-Love, N., Lim, L., & Akehurst, G. (2006). Guest editorial: Female and ethnic minority entrepreneurship. *The International Entrepreneurship & Management Journal, 2*(4), 429–439.

Garnham, A. (2006). Refugees and the entrepreneurial process. *Labour, Employment and Work in New Zealand, 9*(1), 156–165.

Gartner, W. B. (1985). A conceptual framework for describing the phenomenon of new venture creation. *Academy of Management Review, 10*(4), 696–706.

Gartner, W. B., Gartner, W. C., Shaver, K. G., Carter, N. M., & Reynolds, P. D. (Eds.). (2004). *Handbook of entrepreneurial dynamics: The process of business creation*. Sage.

Garud, R., Hardy, C., & Maguire, S. (2007). Institutional entrepreneurship as embedded agency: An introduction to the special issue. *Organization Studies, 28*(7), 957–969.

Giddens, A. (1990). *The consequences of modernity* (Vol. 53). Stanford University Press.

Gioia, D. A., Corley, K. G., & Hamilton, A. L. (2013). Seeking qualitative rigor in inductive research: Notes on the Gioia methodology. *Organizational Research Methods, 16*(1), 15–31.

Gold, S. J. (1988). Refugees and small business: The case of Soviet Jews and Vietnamese. *Ethnic and Racial Studies, 11*(4), 411–438.

Gold, S. J. (1992). The employment potential of refugee entrepreneurship: Soviet Jews and Vietnamese in California. *Review of Policy Research, 11*(2), 176–186.

Halilovich, H., & Efendić, N. (2021). From refugees to trans-local entrepreneurs: Crossing the borders between formal institutions and informal practices in Bosnia and Herzegovina. *Journal of Refugee Studies, 34*(1), 663–680.

Halter, M. (1995). Ethnicity and the entrepreneur: Self-employment among former Soviet Jewish refugees. In M. Halter (Ed.), *New migrants in the marketplace: Boston's ethnic entrepreneurs* (pp. 43–58). University of Massachusetts Press.

Harima, A. (2022). Theorizing disembedding and re-embedding: Resource mobilization in refugee entrepreneurship. *Entrepreneurship & Regional Development, 34*(3–4), 269–293.

Harima, A., Periac, F., Murphy, T., & Picard, S. (2021). Entrepreneurial opportunities of refugees in Germany, France, and Ireland: Multiple embeddedness framework. *International Entrepreneurship and Management Journal, 17*(2), 625–663.

Heilbrunn, S., & Iannone, R. L. (2020). From center to periphery and back again: A systematic literature review of refugee entrepreneurship. *Sustainability, 12*(18), 1–37.

Heilbrunn, S., Freiling, J., & Harima, A. (2018). *Refugee entrepreneurship: A case-based topography*. Palgrave Macmillan, Cham.

Huhn, J. M., Potts, C. A., & Rosenbaum, D. A. (2016). Cognitive framing in action. *Cognition, 151*, 42–51.

Jack, S. L., & Anderson, A. R. (2002). The effects of embeddedness on the entrepreneurial process. *Journal of Business Venturing, 17*(5), 467–487.

Jiang, Y. D., Straub, C., Klyver, K., & Mauer, R. (2021). Unfolding refugee entrepreneurs' opportunity-production process—Patterns and embeddedness. *Journal of Business Venturing, 36*(5), 106138.

Johnson, P. J. (2000). Ethnic differences in self-employment among southeast Asian refugees in Canada. *Journal of Small Business Management, 38*(4), 78.

Kaplan, D. H. (1997). The creation of an ethnic economy: Indo-Chinese business expansion in Saint Paul. *Economic Geography, 73*(2), 214–233.

Konle-Seidl, R. (2018). *Integration of refugees in Austria, Germany and Sweden: Comparative analysis*. European Parliament, Policy Department A: Economic and Scientific Policy. Accessed from http://www.europarl.europa.eu/supporting-analyses

Kunz, E. F. (1973). The refugee in flight: Kinetic models and forms of displacement. *International Migration Review, 7*(2), 125–146.

Kupferberg, F. (2008). Migrant men and the challenge of entrepreneurial creativity. In U. Apitzsch & M. Kontos (Eds.), *Self-employment activities of women and minorities* (pp. 145–157). VS Verlag für Sozialwissenschaften.

Langley, A. (2009). Studying processes in and around organizations. In D. A. Buchanan & A. Bryman (Eds.), *The SAGE handbook of organizational research methods* (pp. 409–429). Sage.

Lazarczyk-Bilal, N. (2019). Refugees or immigrants—How does it matter for entrepreneurship? Systematic review of refugee entrepreneurship literature inspired by the immigrant entrepreneurship research. In A. Kuzminska (Ed.), *Management challenges in the era of globalization* (pp. 153–162). Wydawnictwo Naukowe Wydziału Zarządzania Uniwersytetu Warszawskiego.

Leong, C. H. (2014). Social markers of acculturation: A new research framework on intercultural adaptation. *International Journal of Intercultural Relations, 38*, 120–132.

Luseno, T., & Kolade, O. (2023). Displaced, excluded and making do: A study of refugee entrepreneurship in Kenya. *Journal of Entrepreneurship in Emerging Economies, 15*, 808. https://doi.org/10.1108/JEEE-04-2021-0163

Mamabolo, A., & Myres, K. (2020). A systematic literature review of skills required in the different phases of the entrepreneurial process. *Small Enterprise Research, 27*(1), 39–63.

Mawson, S., & Kasem, L. (2019). Exploring the entrepreneurial intentions of Syrian refugees in the UK. *International Journal of Entrepreneurial Behaviour & Research, 25*(5), 1128–1146.

McMullen, J. S., Brownell, K. M., & Adams, J. (2021). What makes an entrepreneurship study entrepreneurial? Toward a unified theory of entrepreneurial agency. *Entrepreneurship Theory and Practice, 45*(5), 1197–1238.

Meister, A. D., & Mauer, R. (2019). Understanding refugee entrepreneurship incubation: An embeddedness perspective. *International Journal of Entrepreneurial Behavior & Research, 25*(5), 1065–1092.

Miller, C. C., Cardinal, L. B., & Glick, W. H. (1997). Retrospective reports in organizational research: A reexamination of recent evidence. *Academy of Management Journal, 40*(1), 189–204.

Obschonka, M., Hahn, E., & Bajwa, N. U. H. (2018). Personal agency in newly arrived refugees: The role of personality, entrepreneurial cognitions and intentions, and career adaptability. *Journal of Vocational Behavior, 105*, 173–184.

Price, M., & Chacko, E. (2009). The mixed embeddedness of ethnic entrepreneurs in a new immigrant gateway. *Journal of Immigrant & Refugee Studies, 7*(3), 328–346.

Ram, M., Jones, T., Doldor, S., Villares-Varela, M., & Li, H. (2022). What happens to refugee-origin entrepreneurs? Combining mixed embeddedness and strategy perspectives in a longitudinal study. *Ethnic and Racial Studies, 45*(16), 1–27.

Refai, D., Haloub, R., & Lever, J. (2018). Contextualizing entrepreneurial identity among Syrian refugees in Jordan: The emergence of a destabilized habitus? *The International Journal of Entrepreneurship and Innovation, 19*(4), 250–260.

Rennstam, J., & Wästerfors, D. (2018). *Analyze! Crafting your data in qualitative research*. Studentlitteratur AB.

Sandberg, S., Immonen, R., & Kok, S. (2019). Refugee entrepreneurship: Taking a social network view on immigrants with refugee backgrounds starting transnational businesses in Sweden. *International Journal of Entrepreneurship and Small Business, 36*(1–2), 216–241.

Schnell, I., & Sofer, M. (2002). Unbalanced embeddedness of ethnic entrepreneurship: The Israeli Arab case. *International Journal of Entrepreneurial Behavior & Research, 8*(1–2), 54–68.

Shepherd, D., & Williams, T. (2020). Entrepreneurship responding to adversity: Equilibrating adverse events and disequilibrating persistent adversity. *Organization Theory, 1*(4), 1–25.

Shepherd, D. A., Saade, F. P., & Wincent, J. (2020). How to circumvent adversity? Refugee-entrepreneurs' resilience in the face of substantial and persistent adversity. *Journal of Business Venturing, 35*(4), 105940. https://doi.org/10.1016/j.jbusvent.2019.06.001

Sulaiman-Hill, C. M., & Thompson, S. C. (2011). Sampling challenges in a study examining refugee resettlement. *BMC International Health and Human Rights, 11*(1), 1–10.

The Economist. (2018, April 3). *The rise of the refugee startup*. Accessed January 7, 2023, from https://www.dailymotion.com/video/x6h9pyg

Tömöry, E. (2008). Immigrant entrepreneurship: How the '56-ers helped to build Canada's economy. *Hungarian Studies Review, 35*(1–2), 125–142.

Townsend, D. M., Busenitz, L. W., & Arthurs, J. D. (2010). To start or not to start: Outcome and ability expectations in the decision to start a new venture. *Journal of Business Venturing, 25*(2), 192–202.

Überbacher, F. (2014). Legitimation of new ventures: A review and research programme. *Journal of Management Studies, 51*(4), 667–698.

UNHCR. (2022). *Global trends: Forced displacement in 2021*. Accessed October 25, 2022, from https://www.unhcr.org/62a9d1494/global-trends-report-2021

Villares-Varela, M., Ram, M., & Jones, T. (2022). Thwarted or facilitated? The entrepreneurial aspirations and capabilities of new migrants in the UK. *Sociology, 56*(6), 1140–1158.

Vinogradov, E., & Elam, A. (2010). A process model of venture creation by immigrant entrepreneurs. In C. G. Brush, L. Kolvereid, L. O. Widding, & R. Sorheim (Eds.), *The life cycle of new ventures: Emergence, newness and growth* (pp. 109–126). Edward Elgar Publishing.

Wauters, B., & Lambrecht, J. (2008). Barriers to refugee entrepreneurship in Belgium: Towards an explanatory model. *Journal of Ethnic and Migration Studies, 34*(6), 895–915.

Zhang, Z., & Chun, D. (2018). Becoming entrepreneurs: How immigrants developed entrepreneurial identities. *International Journal of Entrepreneurial Behavior & Research, 24*(5), 947–970.

21

Supporting Skilled Migrants' International Career Success Across the Micro, Meso, and Macro Levels

Marian Crowley-Henry, Shamika Almeida, Santina Bertone, and Asanka Gunasekara

Introduction

The global phenomenon of migration is cross-disciplinary, multi-level and complex. Public policy academics question if migration is a step too far for the contemporary global order (Goodman & Schimmelfennig, 2020), where globalization and the liberalization of global mobility on the one hand is met with fragmented and disintegrated migration policy and supports by independent states on the other. Skilled migrants journey largely into the unknown when they seek to pursue their careers internationally. Increasingly, research on skilled migrants in business, management and policy academic

M. Crowley-Henry (✉)
Maynooth University, Maynooth, Ireland
e-mail: marian.crowleyhenry@mu.ie

S. Almeida
University of Wollongong, Wollongong, NSW, Australia
e-mail: shamika@uow.edu.au

S. Bertone
Central Queensland University, Melbourne, VIC, Australia
e-mail: s.bertone@cqu.edu.au

A. Gunasekara
Swinburne University of Technology, Melbourne, VIC, Australia
e-mail: agunasekara@swin.edu.au

publications detail the precarity (Al Ariss et al., 2012) of their employment, their discrimination and under-employment (Almeida & Fernando, 2017; Bertone, 2009; Hawthorne, 2011; Kostenko et al., 2012), and the invisibility of their talents to the powerful influencers (in organizations, at national policy level) in the host countries (Almeida & Fernando, 2017; Crowley-Henry & Al Ariss, 2019). However, skilled migrants possess cross-cultural competencies which should facilitate them taking up boundary-spanning roles within international businesses to help improve the organizations' international performance. To more fully utilize skilled migrants' cross-cultural competencies, better integration and support policies are required at the individual (micro), organizational (meso), and country (macro) levels. Our focus in this chapter responds to calls to share career *success* stories of skilled migrants and policy recommendations that are supportive of skilled migrants' careers (Crowley-Henry et al., 2018).

We define skilled migrants as being educated to third level with "at least a bachelor's degree or equivalent" (Hajro et al., 2019, p. 329), and legally living/working in a host country (Zikic, 2015). In the academic literature on career theory and career studies, the complexity of influences that direct career orientations is underscored (Zikic et al., 2010; Crowley-Henry et al., 2019). Moreover, for skilled migrants' careers, the variation across host and home country supporting institutions is noted (Wall & São José, 2004; Wiß, 2017). Career success has been described as "positive psychological or work-related outcomes or achievements one has accumulated as a result of one's work experience" (Judge et al., 1995, p. 486), and comprises objective and subjective elements. Objectively, career success can be seen as progression in a given career path: a hierarchical or financial advancement. Stumpf and Tymon Jr (2012) include mobility, promotions and salary change as measures of objective career success, with Hughes (1937, p. 413) defining it as including a "series of statuses and clearly defined offices". Subjectively, career success focuses on the subjective "meaning" of success (Hughes, 1937, p. 413), and "enjoyment of work and positive work values" (Crowley-Henry & Al Ariss, 2019, p. 11). Embracing both the subjective and objective elements of career success accords with research into aspects that many skilled migrants value in their working lives in host countries (Rajendran et al., 2017).

This chapter considers factors across different levels that lead to skilled migrants' career success stories and focuses on policy recommendations to support skilled migrants within organizations internationally. In sharing positive initiatives and supporting factors, we do not seek to mitigate the challenges faced by skilled migrants, but rather to celebrate and emphasize the facilitating factors leading toward successful career outcomes for skilled migrants. This strengths-based approach potentially offers a richer understanding of the multi-level forces at play in skilled migrants' careers, forces that we argue may be harnessed through meso- and macro-policy interventions and individual, agentic strategies adopted by the skilled migrants themselves.

We develop a multi-level framework of skilled migrant career success by drawing on secondary data (policy reports, academic literature, practitioner reports and existing published empirical studies) and the inductive coding of in-depth qualitative interviews with 63 skilled migrants. We categorize this secondary and primary data across the dimensions of intelligent career theory (Arthur et al., 1995). Several researchers have previously adopted similar integrative pluralistic approaches that bridge the macro-micro divide (Rousseau, 2011, p. 429). For example, Hajro et al. (2019) used a multi-level framework of individual, organizational, and societal levels to assess how migrants acculturate and cope in host countries (Gunasekara et al., 2019). Similarly, Zikic (2015) considered the relational interplay at the individual and organizational levels, by using intelligent career theory at the individual level and the resource-based view at the organizational level, to identify ways that employers may leverage skilled migrants' career capital.

To showcase the practical significance of our framework, we detail rich qualitative interview data from six participants in our sample, two each in the host countries of the USA, Australia, and Ireland, respectively. By drawing on the cases from three immigrant-receiving countries, we are able to more broadly contemplate how appropriately our multi-level framework represents global factors influencing skilled migrants' career success rather than those based only on one country. This leads us to proposing policy recommendations for actors at the micro, meso, and macro levels that would help promote skilled migrants' career success.

Intelligent career theory (Arthur, et al., 1995; Zikic, 2015) or career capital (DeFillippi & Arthur, 1994) refers to the three types of knowing that are accepted as contributing to the career attributes an individual possesses. The first, 'knowing why', focuses on the motivations and ambitions an individual has which spurs them forward in their careers. The second, 'knowing how', equates closest to human capital theory in that it represents the knowledge, skills and abilities an individual possesses in order to complete their work tasks. For skilled migrants, this may be reflected in their educational qualifications and skills accreditations. Finally, the third, 'knowing whom', considers the social capital an individual possesses, with both strong and weak ties (Granovetter, 1973).

While intelligent career theory was developed and has been used at the individual level in career research projects, our chapter extends the theory to the meso and macro domains, in exploring knowing why (e.g. the attraction mechanisms engaged at the meso and macro levels to encourage skilled migrants to move to and remain in the organization/host country); knowing how (e.g. skills required/sought after at the meso and macro levels respectively); and knowing whom (e.g. social networks and support groups at the meso and macro levels which enable positive career outcomes). Zikic (2015) previously conceptualized the relationship between the micro-level intelligent career capital of skilled migrants and the resource-based view theory applied to the competitive advantages of diversity at the organizational level. We extend this further in line with the focus of this book on international business, by including the national/country level and including policy literature, thereby providing a cross-disciplinary (migration policy/international management/human resource management/career theory) overview of facilitating factors. Consequently, we consolidate the characteristics/strategies at the individual level, human resource management (HRM) practices and policies at the organizational level, and strategies at the national/state/provincial level, which promote skilled migrants' career advancement in the host country in our multi-level career success framework.

The next section provides an overview of the literature which informed the development of our multi-level conceptual framework. Here we consider micro-, meso- and macro-level intelligent career theory factors. Then, we outline our empirical research approach and present empirical validation of our framework. Subsequently, we make recommendations for policy-makers at the national and organizational levels.

Micro-Level Influences on Skilled Migrants' Career Success

This section considers intelligent career theory at the individual level of analysis. It is at the micro level of analysis that intelligent career theory (with the three types of knowing that constitute an individual's career capital) is theorized. One's attitude to work ("knowing why") is significant for subsequent employment opportunities (Brown et al., 2016). Hard-working traits are indications of an individual's character and moral fiber, an important part of their self-legitimation (Sennett, 2003). Rajendran et al. (2017) illustrate how skilled migrants' "can do" attitude, work ethic, and willingness to learn about the host culture facilitates their career advancement internationally.

Motivations and attitudes vary across individuals (Hajro et al., 2019). Mary Yoko Brannen cautions against stereotyping on cultural generalizations (Horak et al., 2019, p. 475). Some individuals may strive for objective career success such as financial rewards or positions with prestigious status to impress significant others in the home and/or host country, while others may wish to satisfy subjective career success such as the attainment of work-life balance and a high quality of life. Understanding the heterogeneity of motivations skilled migrants possess is important as perceptions of career success, at the individual level, may vary widely depending on the respective motivations and expectations.

With regard to "knowing how", as per the principles of human capital theory (Schultz, 1961), skilled migrants should be able to access employment that aligns with their experience and qualifications (Zikic, 2015). However, in practice, soft skills such as communication skills and cultural intelligence (Presbitero, 2017) facilitate their career progression more than academic qualifications. Skilled migrants' technical, soft, and relational skills can promote their career advancement in the host country. Linguistic skills are particularly beneficial (Ellis, 2013; Gunasekara et al., 2019), especially in the initial work-seeking phase after moving to a host country. Using language skills was seen to bridge the social, economic and cultural aspects of capital (Al Ariss & Syed, 2011) since skilled migrants, working as linguists, are able to build social capital in the host community while maintaining their cultural links and earning money.

The personality traits from the Big Five of extraversion, openness, emotional stability, agreeableness, and conscientiousness combined are the best predictors of expatriate success and superior job-role performance (Caligiuri & Bonache, 2016). Caligiuri and Bonache (2016, p. 134) suggest that "successful and adjusted expatriates are higher in openness" as a personality trait. They continue that expatriates who thrive when presented with opportunity at work and easily make cross-cultural adjustment are able to achieve career success, which benefits them personally and their employers.

Finally, pertaining to "knowing whom", the social ties that skilled migrants have and build in the host country impacts positively on their career capital. Caligiuri and Bonache (2016) apply Amir's (1969) contact hypothesis, that "the more peer-level interaction expatriates have with others from a given cultural group, the more positive their attitudes will be toward the people from that cultural group" (Caligiuri & Bonache, 2016, p. 136). Their analysis suggests that the longer a migrant is amongst another cultural group (e.g. host country nationals), the better their social network and capital with that cultural group will develop and become. This suggests that skilled migrants in a host country have the potential to develop strong local networks over time, thereby developing their social capital in the host country.

At the individual level, the combination of one's knowing why, how and whom creates individualized career capital which dictates their career success and the spill-over effects for employing organizations and international business.

Meso-Level Influences on Skilled Migrants' Career Success

In this section, we move to the meso/organizational level, and consider meso-level policies from the literature which can be mapped to each of the three intelligent career dimensions respectively. Organizations, through their policies and activities, may inspire and motivate skilled migrants to develop their careers, or create disincentives, leading either to separation or skilled migrants establishing their own businesses in response to blocked career paths (Miller & Le Breton-Miller, 2017). In this chapter, we focus on examples of positive approaches by organizations—the meso-level "knowing why"—which support skilled migrants' careers. Communication is most important here: those organizations which have clear policies with regard to the competencies required for particular positions, for which skilled migrants have the technical abilities, will be more successful in attracting skilled migrants with the requisite skills (Almeida & Fernando, 2017).

At the organizational level, "as the demand for culturally agile business professionals increases, there is a greater need for a wider array of international experiences to help these professionals gain cross-cultural competencies" (Caligiuri & Bonache, 2016, p. 136). Where organizations are willing to provide tailored support for their international workers, the results are positive in terms of performance. Stoermer et al.'s (2018) study of 175 expatriates in South Korea found that perceived organizational support positively affects job satisfaction.

Concerning the meso-level "knowing how" dimension, when organizations hire employees who possess skills, expertise as well as social resources embedded in social relationships, organizations can gain access to resources critical to a firm's success (Ortlieb & Sieben, 2014; Hillman & Dalziel, 2003). For instance, the skilled migrants' language skills and cultural intelligence (Thomas

& Inkson, 2017) in relation to their originating countries can create benefit to the host country organizations that operate in the international markets (Zikic, 2015). Skilled migrants' international cultural competencies may create a competitive advantage for these organizations, encouraging them to recruit skilled migrants to avail of their "knowing how" at the organizational level (Zikic, 2015).

Finally, pertaining to the "knowing whom" dimension, involvement in voluntary work and/or participate in community-organized activities (Almeida & Bertone, 2016) enables local employers to establish links with skilled migrants and for them to evaluate the skilled migrants' ability to apply their skills in the local organizational and community context. Similarly, a study conducted in China on expatriates (Wang & Kanungo, 2004) indicates that building networks with both peer expatriates and local partners comprising people from different backgrounds facilitates faster learning and adaptation to the local environment. Many multinational organizations have formalized mentoring programs where they assign a "buddy" for new recruits to ensure a greater level of acculturation to the organization and social environment within an organization (Almeida & Fernando, 2017), thereby encouraging further "knowing whom" by skilled migrants to support their career progression.

In summary, at the meso level, organizational support in attracting skilled international workers/migrants (knowing why), addressing skills gaps and training (knowing how), and the thoughtful induction (knowing whom) of skilled migrants results in positive business outcomes.

Macro-Level Influences on Skilled Migrants' Career Success

In this section, we focus on unpacking the macro/national level supports of skilled migrants' careers in a host country. With regard to "knowing why" factors at the macro level, we focus here on the attraction policies that countries put forward to encourage skilled migrants to enter and remain in the host country. In other words, these are the strategies employed by countries which motivate skilled migrants, at the individual level, to migrate to specific countries. Froese (2012) introduces three categories explaining the initial motivation to move internationally. These are the job market, family, and regional interest. When the job market in the country is buoyant, or if living standards and quality of life are better than the home country, this may promote the motivation to relocate to another country. Transnational marriage migration is another reason for mobility across borders (Nehring & Sealey, 2020). The ease of entry to the host country and the supports provided encourage skilled migrants to consider that country as a destination of choice, offering a positive future to the skilled migrant and their family. Global indicators of, for instance, cost of living standards, educational standards, and happiness indices, will enable skilled migrants to make a more informed decision with regard to expectations in the host country (Organization for Economic Co-operation and Development, 2011), as does word of mouth through transnational professional or family/friendship networks. Similarly, when countries such as Australia and New Zealand publish lists of skills shortages and occupations in demand, along with clear guidelines on the process of migrating, these countries facilitate inward skilled migration (Department of Home Affairs, 2023a).

Theoretically, we view these macro-level factors as drawing from academic sub-disciplines such as immigration, integration, multiculturalism, and labor market economics. How potential and actual immigrants become aware of push and pull factors and the various immigration policies operating in host countries has been a topic of research for some decades (for example, Borjas, 1989; Birrell, 2003; Berry, 2011; Miller & Castles, 2014; Boucher, 2016, cited in Opare-Addo, 2018). Approaches to integration and settlement have focused initially on human capital theory, but more recently have incorporated elements of Bourdieu's social and cultural capitals, cultural competence, cultural pluralism, and the role of labor market institutions in host countries which seek to fill skilled labor vacancies (Opare-Addo, 2018). Labor market segmentation theory has been a longstanding critical approach by scholars to explain how employers in host countries seek out ethnic and racialized groups to fill undesirable niches in the host country (see Colic-Peisker & Tilbury, 2007). In combination, the theoretical literature around skilled migrants in developed countries suggests powerful economic and social forces both promoting and inhibiting the successful attraction and integration of skilled migrants in employment. From the "global race for talent" (Boucher, 2016) to exclusionary policies of some employers and professional associations toward skilled migrants, the picture is complex and fragmented. It suggests that pro-immigration policies of national governments and employment institutions may be undermined, facilitated, or mediated by other social and economic practices at the macro level.

We consider the "knowing how" factors at the macro level to include policies pertaining to acquiring and developing skilled migrants with the skills required in the respective country. Immigration policy that enables skilled immigrants to both study and work at a high skill level in the host country before settling permanently is an important factor (Chiou, 2017; Green & Hogarth, 2017); it allows them to acculturate, as students, prior to more permanent settlement. Recent Office for National Statistics (ONS) migration statistics in the UK highlights the valuable role migrants play in minimizing skills shortages in countries (Chartered Institute of Personnel and Development, 2018). For example, European countries have implemented policies to attract skilled and high-skilled migrants such as academics, medical personnel, and engineers (Cerna & Czaika, 2016), encouraging those with scarce "know-how" to migrate easily.

However, the attraction of skilled immigrants alone is not always sufficient. Once onshore, these immigrants may require assistance to navigate an unfamiliar labor market. Nationally funded agencies such as Adult Multicultural Education Services in Australia provide bridging programs and mentorship opportunities for newly arrived skilled immigrants. For example, the Skilled Professional Migrants Program offers skilled migrants a combination of job preparation training (resume writing, interview skills, the Australian job market and culture) and professional mentoring for up to six months, to assist them to enter or re-enter skilled employment in their new country (Thomson et al., 2016). In addition, industry and professional associations (such as Engineers Australia, Diversity Council of Australia (DCA)) have been known to provide valuable research and skilled immigrant development programs (Engineers Australia, 2020; DCA, 2018). In this way, skilled migrants' host country specific knowing how skills are developed. These are just some examples of macro-level policies and practices related to acquiring and developing skilled migrant relevant "knowing-how" in host countries, while also supporting skilled migrants' transition to the host workplace.

Granovetter's (1973) hypothesis of "the strength of weak ties" is relevant when the bonding and bridging capital of skilled migrants is considered. Bonding capital refers to the links between like-minded people, or the networks for homogeneous groups who build strong ties, while bridging capital builds connections between people from different walks of life and therefore includes heterogeneous groups (Putnam, 2007) and weaker ties. Typically, skilled migrants tend to have more bonding capital via networks with other migrants from their own country, but tend to lack bridging capital with host country employers (Briggs, 2003), thus hindering their integration into mainstream society. However, there are national and regional policies which may help to address this problem. For instance, in Canada, TRIEC (Toronto Regional Immigrant Employment Council, 2017) runs the CanPrep program to facilitate talent acquisition from overseas by Canadian employers. The Connector program, which helps migrants build their professional networks

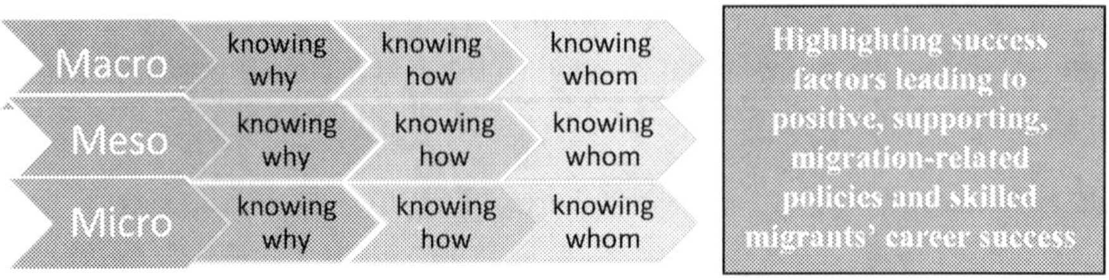

Fig. 21.1 Intelligent career theory through a multi-level lens—supporting skilled migration and skilled migrants' career success. *Knowledge and understanding of intelligent career theory through micro, meso, and macro levels highlights positive policies and practices that support skilled migration and skilled migrants' careers across levels and stakeholders*

connects them with an occupation-specific mentor located in Canada and matches them to employers who are looking to hire, is a combined macro/meso-level initiative developed by a tripartite collaboration between education bodies, employers, and local government. This program focuses on knowing whom, by linking people together in mutually beneficial professional networks they would otherwise have not been able to develop.

Therefore, supports at the macro level pertaining to knowing why, how, and whom aid skilled migrants' transition to the host country and provide positive results in terms of their workplace integration, work readiness and productivity.

We summarize our conceptualization of intelligent career theory across the micro, meso and macro levels in Fig. 21.1.

Empirical Research and Exemplar Cases

Supplementing the literature presented so far in this chapter which informed our theoretical multi-level application of intelligent career theory, we draw on the work and career experiences of a diverse sample of 63 skilled migrants in western host countries (Ireland, USA, and Australia) to further unpack the institutional and structural influences on their careers which they faced after migration. Qualitative studies are appropriate for the study of poorly understood phenomena (Maguire & Phillips, 2008). We used purposeful sampling (Creswell, 2014), personal contacts and snowball sampling (Saunders et al., 2009) to source interviewees. In total, 63 skilled migrants employed in organizations in Australia, Ireland and the USA participated in this study (23 in the USA, 20 in Ireland and Australia respectively). The participants stemmed from 26 different home countries: Germany, Ireland, South Africa, UK,

Switzerland, Spain, Italy, Poland, USA, Bulgaria, Jordan, Brazil, Lebanon, Colombia, Argentina, Peru, Singapore, Taiwan, China, South Korea, Vietnam, Malaysia, Sri Lanka, India, and Pakistan. Each interview was approximately an hour long, audio recorded and transcribed. The same semi-structured interview guide was used for all participants. This included questions on topics such as background (family, motivation to migrate etc.), adjustment (adjustment to host country, likes and dislikes, regrets etc.) and career (current position, how they progressed, career aims, factors that influence their career progression etc.). We coded the interviews under micro, meso, and macro levels of "knowing why", "knowing how" and "knowing whom" factors that had impacted on their careers. This approach enabled us to build a descriptive, multi-level perspective and interpretive analysis of factors that influence skilled migrants to succeed in their careers.

For the purposes of this chapter, we draw on the lived experiences from six exemplar cases from the full sample to present our framework's explanatory potential. These cases are Sen (Sri Lankan, male, Business Operations manager, IT, 42, married, one child) and Liz (Indian Fijian, female, Director of Finance and Administration, married, two children) who moved to Australia; Sam (Indian, male, Director IT architecture, 45, married, one child) and Carmel (Irish, female, registered nurse, 56, married, four children) who moved to the USA; Luke (Italian, male, Banker, 44, long term relationship, no children) and Celina (Argentinian, female, clinical psychologist, 42, married, two children) who moved to Ireland. These are outlined next.

Considering Intelligent Career Theory Across Multi-Levels in Practice

Beginning with the micro level, all of the six skilled migrant cases we elaborate on here could be characterized as curious, motivated to learn, flexible, stoic, and resilient in their approach to new experiences and career challenges. As Sen (Sri Lankan, Business Operations manager, IT, 42, married, one child) who moved to Australia explained:

> Both of us [he and his wife] didn't find it hard at all because we are very flexible. … I was ready for the worst. I came with the anticipation that I would be without a job for the first twelve months. So there were no disappointments….

Sen explained that his chief motivations for migrating to Australia were quality of life, gaining a second passport, and retiring at age 50. He and his wife had left good professional employment in Sri Lanka in search of a safer and more satisfying life in Australia. His interview showed a highly focused, strategic approach to his career in Australia, overcoming early difficulties with determination, exemplifying a strong sense of knowing why:

> I have two objectives: First, I want financial independence and two, I believe we need to give back to society. That's … my major driving factors.

Sam, an Indian-born IT director in the USA, had his own knowing why factors that drove his career ambitions:

> I was always ambitious, because I'd seen my Dad, he grew from being a chemist to a manager… So someday I'd like to be in a managerial or leadership role… So I would like to get up to chief architect level. (Sam, Indian in the USA, Director IT architecture, 45, male, married, one child).

With regard to knowing how, Luke, an Italian skilled migrant working in Ireland summarized this well when he said:

> I think it probably helped that in my high school we had foreign teachers as well. Like English and French. So you would study…economics and business and then language as well… and that helped me learn the language before I left the country. (Luke, Italian in Ireland, Banker, 44, male, long term relationship, no children).

Having extended family members in Australia, knowing whom, supported Sen's move to Australia:

> One of (wife's) cousins was here so that made us become more biased towards Australia. (Sri Lankan, Business Operations Manager, IT, 42, male, married).

Moving to the meso level, knowing why was shown to be relevant in skilled migrant career success as it is linked to the skills' requirements that organizations had. The skilled migrants we interviewed were all employed and so their motivation to move to the respective host country for work was attained. Organizations supported skilled migrants' language competency and knowing how through peer networks (knowing whom), as Sam explains. Sam, the Indian in the US IT industry spoke about the cultural training he was involved in at work, where paradoxically, because he spoke English so well, his employer utilized him to mentor others from India in how to use American idiom:

> I studied in a convent school so my English has been a little better than average Indian's English. … So instead of me getting cultural training, it was sometimes trying to help others … what the words mean and how one's pronunciation actually changes the meaning of what somebody hears.

Luke, the Italian skilled migrant working in the banking industry in Ireland, mentioned the mentoring support he received from his managers:

> I think had a couple of managers that were really good managers. They were kind of passionate, they gave feedback that really helped me. (Luke, Italian, Banker, 44, male, long term relationship, no children).

And the direct encouragement he had been given in his career by his managers:

> Sometimes what happened was management approached me saying: 'you would be good for this position' and then of course I would be receptive to that. And I would also apply for the job as well. We had mutual interest.

Luke's case shows not only the support he attained from the organization at the meso level in terms of his personal development, but also the knowing whom element, where managers he had impressed acted as mentors in his ongoing career progression. Similarly, Celina, an Argentinian skilled migrant in Ireland, who was working as a psychologist, spoke highly of the mentoring she received from a local health organization:

> Through the different placements, I made good connections with the XYZ principal psychologist from the area, and I went to meet them and they are actually mentoring me. (Celina, Argentinian in Ireland, clinical psychologist, charitable family support organization, female, 42, married, two children).

The opportunity for development within a profession or organization at the meso level is also pronounced in the exemplars' interviews. For example, Carmel, an Irish skilled migrant in the USA working as a registered nurse stated:

> I'm a nurse clinician there right now… It's great, I love it. I love working within the team I work with… I go to every single floor and I problem-solve… (Carmel, Irish in the USA, registered nurse, health facility, female, 56, married, four children).

These organization-led supports for skilled migrants aided their career outlook and perceptions of career success.

At the macro level, the knowing why motivation to move to a particular host country was definitely related to host country migration policies in attracting skilled migrants. One of our exemplar participants, Sen, explained why he and his wife chose Australia as their destination of choice. According to the macro-level "knowing why" and "knowing how" rationale, the Australian migration policies were clear and transparent and skilled migrants had a feasible avenue to apply for permanent residency under the skill migration points system (Department of Home Affairs, 2023b).

> We thought it was very easy to get migration status, because we were qualified accountants In 2006, the(se) skills were in great demand, so you got 25 marks (points)…Why didn't we consider anything like US? Because it was difficult, more difficult. We only thought Australia is good. Canada didn't even cross our minds…. (Sri Lankan, Business Operations Manager, IT, 42, male, married).

Liz, a Fijian Indian accountant working in Australian real estate, spoke frequently in her interview about the value of networking with a range of other professionals and members of the community and her professional association:

> And then I also … do a lot of volunteer work with XYZ Australia. So I set up a women's committee, I used to chair the women's committee and I also mentored people… I also helped them out in IT, their business competitions and checking of CVs… I have also helped Indian executives, they have business competition, I was one of the judges for that. I have also helped, have been on with CPA on … committees as a chair and helped them with the task.

Our conceptual framework (see Fig. 21.1) of multi-level factors influencing skilled migrants' host country integration and career success is confirmed among the exemplar cases and broader sample of participants. However, in practice, a more complex relational/hybrid scaffolding of factors at and across different levels of analysis was apparent. For instance, Sam, the Indian skilled migrant in the USA explained the knowing why and knowing how factor at the labor market (macro level), which had motivated his choice of profession:

> IT was booming, so I got into the IT space. (Director IT architecture. IT, 45, male, married).

Subsequently, Sam chose to migrate to the USA when he was attracted by job offers from that country.

Apart from the macro-level policies attracting certain skills to a host country, as alluded to above under knowing why, we also found evidence of the importance of knowing how at the macro level in supporting skilled migrants in the host country. One of our exemplar cases, Liz (Indian Fijian, Director of Finance and Administration, Real Estate, female, married, two children), referred several times to the beneficial influence of the Certified Practicing Accountants Association (CPA), a national professional association, which she credited with equipping her with skills to practice as an accountant and also with the networks (the knowing whom at the micro, meso, macro levels) to find her first and subsequent professional jobs after graduating in Australia. Here again, the blurred boundaries between micro, meso and macro career capital elements is pronounced.

Overall, our multi-level intelligent career theory framework appropriately conceptualizes the empirical data and secondary data, confirming the importance and relevance of the micro-, meso-, and macro-level career capital elements. Moreover, the complexity and overlap between elements in the framework in practice is pronounced.

Policy Recommendations to Support Skilled Migrants' Career Success

Our conceptual framework (see Fig. 21.1) which incorporates a micro, meso, and macro dimension to intelligent career theory is confirmed in our empirical research. Career knowing why, how and whom factors were found to be relevant at and across levels of analysis when proactively advocating skilled migrants' career success. To better enable skilled migrants' skills usage and employment, we recommend that decision-makers at the meso and macro (country/region) levels consider where gaps or shortcomings may be in the different elements of the framework, and then focus on improving policies in those particular areas. Our aim is for the framework to be used, as far as practicable, to ensure that all skilled migrants may realize their full career potential. In so doing, we aim to avoid the economic waste, social disruption, and personal malaise inherent in the under-utilization of skilled immigrants' talents associated with stunted career paths (Bertone, 2008).

Our framework and analysis suggest that there are many ways that governments, industry and professional bodies, community organizations and organizations have contributed to facilitating and promoting the careers of skilled migrants. There are also personal and social factors at the individual level which have been demonstrated to assist skilled migrants to take advantage of opportunities and 'cut through' barriers identified in previous literature. The fact that such barriers continue to be documented and unequal career outcomes in employment evidenced, however, indicates the need to disseminate and proliferate these success factors more broadly across individuals and institutions at the three levels of our analysis and apply them in a more integrated, holistic way. Based on our analyses of the literature and our empirics, there are a number of practical policy recommendations that we believe will better support skilled migrants' careers in the host country across different levels. These policy recommendations would reduce the career obstacles faced by skilled migrants and avoid the costly skills wastage and social drawbacks associated with the blocked careers of skilled migrants. We present these multi-level policy recommendations together in Table 21.1.

Limitations and Future Research Opportunities

This chapter focuses on the research-informed success factors pertaining to skilled migrants' career success in "western", developed host countries. With this as the particular focus in this chapter, we do not provide a balanced representation of the challenges and obstacles to career success, which skilled migrants face across the levels. It is not our intention to belittle or ignore the discrimination, racism, and inequality skilled migrants experience in navigating their host country careers. These are real and efforts must be made to address these concerns. Further studies could mirror our approach, but focus on the alternative angle of obstacles and challenges at each level. Both these approaches, combined, would give more rounded guidance to the parties at various levels with regard to skilled migrant careers in different host countries, as experienced by the skilled migrants with varying intersectional characteristics.

However, we argue that the framework provides an important starting point for future studies focusing on strengths rather than failures in skilled immigration policies, leading toward skilled migrants' career success in the host country. We found a very good fit between the framework and the lived experiences reported by our six skilled migrant cases, enabling a sophisticated and reasonably comprehensive analysis of the success factors and strategies

Table 21.1 Policy recommendations across levels, supporting skilled migration and skilled migrants' career success

Level	Policy recommendations
Macro	• Open advertisement of skills requirements in the host country, including host country related information (such as quality of living indices, cost of living indices, etc.) (knowing why and how) • Recognition of skills; further education & development opportunities for skilled migrants to encourage them to remain in the host country (knowing why & how) • Expansion of socialization opportunities for skilled migrants in the host country, fostering community and broad professional links (knowing whom) • Involvement of employer organizations and professional associations in national and local initiatives to provide mentoring and work experience programs for new skilled migrants • Provision of online professional and industry induction programs for new skilled migrants seeking employment
Meso	• Acknowledgment of value of multicultural mindset and language skills for competitiveness in the international marketplace (knowing why and how) • Tailored support and career development policies and practices for skilled migrants, including access to social skills' training, buddy systems to aid socialization at work, and customized mentoring opportunities (knowing why, how, and whom) • Addressing unconscious bias around ethnic and racial stereotypes in the workplace through behavioral change programs particularly for organizational leaders • Creation of policies specifically focusing on socialization and skill needs of skilled immigrants in the workplace • Establishment of skilled migrant diversity committees in organizations to advise and advocate on behalf of migrants
Micro	• Research on skills requirements and talent gaps in the host country (knowing why & how) • Active engagement in language, cultural training, and socialization opportunities in the host country (knowing how and whom). • Provision of work experience and buddying programs customized to individual migrants' career backgrounds and needs

which had contributed to their career success. We suggest that our multi-relational framework and analysis makes a contribution to literature and policy recommendations pertaining to skilled migrant career success and likely strategies for success. The framework could be applied to and quantitatively tested in larger scale studies of skilled migrants in different host country and organizational contexts, with skilled migrants from different originating countries, and across genders, ages and races.

Conclusions

Intelligent career theory has traditionally centered on the micro level in career studies in the management discipline. In this chapter, we extend its reach by also applying it to the meso (organizational supports) and macro (national migration policies) levels with regard to the respective "knowing why", "knowing how", and "knowing whom" dimensions which facilitate and support skilled migrants' career success in the host country. By adopting a multi-level analysis of career supporting initiatives through the intelligent career theory lens, enabling supports (at/across the different levels) can be emphasized.

The six exemplar cases qualitatively show how the framework, in practice, adequately consolidates the global factors influencing skilled migrants' career success across three host countries. The complex overlap of micro-, meso-, and macro-level factors is evidenced in the lived experiences of the migrants: the hybrid nature of career influences at the micro, meso, and macro levels is pronounced.

In synthesizing literature across levels through intelligent career theory, we propose policy recommendations aimed at individuals, organizations and national or provincial/state agencies which seek to ensure greater integration and utilization of skilled migrants' human capital. With claims that much of the human capital of skilled migrants is being under-utilized or wasted, we argue that it is imperative to critically examine and build on the success factors within national and international contexts if nations, organizations, and skilled migrants are to attain mutual, reciprocal benefits from skilled migration.

Acknowledgments We would like to thank the anonymous reviewer for their suggestions on the earlier draft(s) of this chapter. We would like to acknowledge the funding from the Irish Fulbright Commission which enabled the data collection in the USA and Ireland. We would also like to acknowledge the internal research grant received from the University of Wollongong which facilitated research visits to Australia to collaborate on this project.

References

Al Ariss, A., & Syed, J. (2011). Capital mobilization of skilled migrants: A relational perspective. *British Journal of Management, 22*(2), 286–304.

Al Ariss, A., Koall, I., Özbilgin, M., & Suutari, V. (2012). Careers of skilled migrants: Towards a theoretical and methodological expansion. *Journal of Management Development, 31*(2), 92–101.

Almeida, S., & Bertone, S. (2016). The influence of regional community characteristics on employer recruitment decision making. *New Zealand Journal of Employment Relations, 41*, 22–40.

Almeida, S., & Fernando, M. (2017). Making the cut: Occupation-specific factors influencing employers in their recruitment and selection of immigrant professionals in the information technology and accounting occupations in regional Australia. *The International Journal of Human Resource Management, 28*(6), 880–912.

Amir, Y. (1969). Contact hypothesis in ethnic relations. *Psychological Bulletin, 71*(5), 319–342.

Arthur, M., Claman, P., & DeFillippi, R. (1995). Intelligent enterprise, intelligent careers. *Academy of Management Executive, 9*(4), 7–19.

Berry, J. W. (2011). Integration and multiculturalism: Ways towards social solidarity. *Papers on Social Representations, 20*(1), 2.1–2.2.1.

Bertone, S. (2008). *From factory fodder to multicultural mediators: A new typology of immigrant work experiences in Australia*. VDM Verlag.

Bertone, S. (2009). Immigration and the labour market in Australia. In J. Higley, J. Nieuwenhuysen, & S. Neerup (Eds.), *Nations of immigrants: Australia and the USA compared*. Elgar.

Birrell, B. (2003). Immigration policy and the Australian labour market. *Economic Papers: A Journal of Applied Economics and Policy, 22*(1), 36–45.

Borjas, G. J. (1989). Economic theory and international migration. *International Migration Review, 23*(3), 457–485.

Boucher, A. (2016). The global race for talent: Global context, skill and gender: Navigating the theoretical terrain. In A. Boucher (Ed.), *Gender, migration and the global race for talent* (pp. 13–52). Manchester University Press.

Briggs, X. (2003). *Bridging networks, social capital, and racial segregation in America*. Harvard University, John F. Kennedy School of Government, Faculty Research Working Papers Series (rwp02-011). Accessed from https://www.researchgate.net/profile/Xavier_Briggs/publication/4892608_Bridging_Networks_Social_Capital_and_Racial_Segregation_in_America/links/54c5605b0cf219bbe4f4c7c6/Bridging-Networks-Social-Capital-and-Racial-Segregation-in-America.pdf

Brown, P., Power, S., Tholen, G., & Allouch, A. (2016). Credentials, talent and cultural capital: A comparative study of educational elites in England and France. *British Journal of Sociology of Education, 37*(2), 191–211.

Caligiuri, P., & Bonache, J. (2016). Evolving and enduring challenges in global mobility. *Journal of World Business, 51*, 127–141.

Cerna, L., & Czaika, M. (2016). European policies to attract talent: The crisis and highly skilled migration policy changes. In A. Triandafyllidou & I. Isaakyan (Eds.), *High-skill migration and recession*. Palgrave Macmillan.

Chartered Institute of Personnel and Development. (2018). *Latest ONS migration stats highlight valuable role of migrants in minimising skills shortages: CIPD Press Release*. Accessed from https://www.cipd.co.uk/about/media/press/261115-ons-response

Chiou, B. (2017). Two-step migration: A comparison of Australia's and New Zealand's policy development between 1998 and 2010. *Asian and Pacific Migration Journal, 26*(1), 84–107. https://doi.org/10.1177/0117196817695272

Colic-Peisker, V., & Tilbury, F. (2007). *Refugees and employment: The effect of visible difference on discrimination* (pp. 1–50). Centre for Social and Community Research, Murdoch University.

Creswell, J. (2014). *Research design: Qualitative, quantitative, and mixed methods*. Sage.

Crowley-Henry, M., & Al Ariss, A. (2019). Talent management of skilled migrants: Propositions and an agenda for future research. *International Journal of Human Resource Management, 29*(13), 2054–2079.

Crowley-Henry, M., O'Connor, E., & Al Ariss, A. (2018). Portrayal of skilled migrants' careers in business and management studies: A review of the literature and future research agenda. *European Management Review, 15*(3), 375–394. https://doi.org/10.1111/emre.12072

Crowley-Henry, M., Benson, E., & Al Ariss, A. (2019). Linking talent management to traditional and boundaryless career orientations: Research propositions and future directions. *European Management Review, 16*(1), 5–19. https://doi.org/10.1111/emre.12304

DeFillippi, R., & Arthur, M. (1994). The boundaryless career: A competency-based perspective. *Journal of Organisational Behavior, 15*, 307–324.

Department of Home Affairs. (2023a). *Skilled Migration – Skilled Occupation list*. Accessed from https://immi.homeaffairs.gov.au/visas/working-in-australia/skill-occupation-list

Department of Home Affairs. (2023b). *Skilled Migration*. Accessed from https://immi.homeaffairs.gov.au/what-we-do/skilled-migration-program

Diversity Council of Australia. (2018). *Leading practice case studies – Culture and religion*. Accessed from https://www.dca.org.au/topics/culture-religion/leading-practice-case-studies-culture-religion

Ellis, B. (2013). Freelancing eagles: Interpretation as a transient career strategy for skilled migrants. *Journal of Management Development, 32*(2), 152–165.

Engineers Australia. (2020). *About overseas qualified engineers*. Accessed from https://www.engineersaustralia.org.au/About-Us/Divisions/Overseas-Qualified-Engineers/OQE-Victoria/

Froese, F. (2012). Motivation and adjustment of self-initiated expatriates: The case of expatriate academics in South Korea. *The International Journal of Human Resource Management, 23*(6), 1095–1112.

Goodman, S. W., & Schimmelfennig, F. (2020). Migration: a step too far for the contemporary global order? *Journal of European Public Policy, 27*, 1103–1113.

Granovetter, M. (1973). The strength of weak ties. *American Journal of Sociology, 78*(6), 1360–1380.

Green, A., & Hogarth, T. (2017). Attracting the best talent in the context of migration policy changes: The case of the UK. *Journal of Ethnic and Migration Studies, 43*(16), 2806–2824.

Gunasekara, A., Grant, S., & Rajendran, D. (2019). Years since migration and well-being among Indian and Sri Lankan skilled migrants in Australia: Mediating effects of acculturation. *International Journal of Intercultural Relations, 70*, 42–52.

Hajro, A., Stahl, G., Clegg, C., & Lazarova, M. (2019). Acculturation, coping, and integration success of international skilled migrants: An integrative review and multilevel framework. *Human Resource Management Journal, 29*, 328–252.

Hawthorne, L. (2011). *Competing for skills: Migration policies and trends in New Zealand and Australia*. Department of Immigration and Citizenship and Department of Labour, Wellington, International Migration Settlement and Employment Dynamics.

Hillman, A., & Dalziel, T. (2003). Boards of directors and firm performance: Integrating agency and resource dependence theories. *Academy of Management Review, 28*(3), 383–396.

Horak, S., Farndale, E., Brannen, M., & Collings, D. (2019). International human resource management in an era of political nationalism. *Thunderbird International Business Review, 61*, 471–480.

Hughes, E. (1937). Institutional office and the person. *American Journal of Sociology, 43*, 404–413.

Judge, T., Cable, D., Boudreau, J., & Bretz, R. (1995). An empirical investigation of the predictors of executive career success. *Personnel Psychology, 48*(3), 485–519.

Kostenko, W., Harris, M., & Zhao, X. (2012). Occupational transition and country of origin effects in the early stage occupational assimilation of immigrants: Some evidence from Australia. *Applied Economics, 44*, 4019–4035.

Maguire, S., & Phillips, N. (2008). 'Citibankers' at Citigroup: A study of the loss of institutional trust after a merger. *Journal of Management Studies., 45*, 372–401.

Miller, M. J., & Castles, S. (2014). *The age of migration: International population movements in the modern world* (5th ed.). Palgrave Macmillan.

Miller, D., & Le Breton-Miller, I. (2017). Underdog entrepreneurs: A model of challenge-based entrepreneurship. *Entrepreneurship Theory and Practice, 41*, 7–17.

Nehring, D., & Sealey, C. (2020). Intimate citizenship and the tightening of migration controls in the United Kingdom. *Social Policy & Administration, 54*, 427–440.

Opare-Addo, J. (2018). *Public policies and the labour market integration of skilled immigrants in Canada and Australia*. Doctor of Philosophy, Swinburne University of Technology, Melbourne, Australia, pp. 1–397.

Organisation for Economic Co-operation and Development. (2011). *How's life?: Measuring wellbeing*. OECD Publishing. Accessed from https://read.oecd-ilibrary.org/economics/how-s-life_9789264121164-en#page4

Ortlieb, R., & Sieben, B. (2014). The making of inclusion as structuration: Empirical evidence of a multinational company. *Equality, Diversity and Inclusion: An International Journal, 33*(3), 235–248.

Presbitero, A. (2017). It's not all about language ability: Motivational cultural intelligence matters in call center performance. *The International Journal of Human Resource Management, 28*(11), 1547–1562. https://doi.org/10.1080/09585192.2015.1128464

Putnam, R. (2007). E Pluribus unum: Diversity and community in the twenty-first century. *Scandinavian Political Studies, 30*, 137–174.

Rajendran, D., Farquharson, K., & Hewege, C. (2017). Workplace integration: The lived experiences of highly skilled migrants in Australia. *Equality, Diversity and Inclusion: An International Journal, 36*(5), 437–456.

Rousseau, D. (2011). Reinforcing the micro/macro bridge: Organisational thinking and pluralistic vehicles. *Journal of Management, 37*, 429–442.

Saunders, M., Lewis, P., & Thornhill, A. (2009). *Research methods for business students* (5th ed.). Pearson Education Limited.

Schultz, T. (1961). Investment in human capital. *American Economic Review, 51*(1), 1–17.

Sennett, R. (2003). *Respect: The formation of character in an age of inequality*. Penguin.

Stoermer, S., Haslberger, A., Froese, F., & Kraeh, A. (2018). Person–environment fit and expatriate job satisfaction. *Thunderbird International Business Review, 60*(6), 851–860.

Stumpf, S., & Tymon, W., Jr. (2012). The effects of objective career success on subsequent subjective career success. *Journal of Vocational Behavior, 81*(3), 345–353.

Thomas, D. C., & Inkson, K. (2017). *Cultural intelligence. Surviving and thriving in the global village* (3rd ed.). Berrett-Koehler Publishers.

Thomson, L., O'Dwyer, M., & Chan, A. (2016). *Hidden assets: Partner-migration, skilled women and the Australian workforce*. AMES Australia Research and Policy Unit and the Office for Women, Department of Prime Minister and Cabinet.

Toronto Region Immigrant Employment Council (TRIEC). (2017). *TRIEC initiatives*. TRIEC. Accessed from http://triec.ca/triec-initiatives/

Wall, K., & São José, J. (2004). Managing work and care: A difficult challenge for immigrant families. *Social Policy & Administration, 38*(6), 591–621.

Wang, X., & Kanungo, R. N. (2004). Nationality, social network and psychological well-being: Expatriates in China. *International Journal of Human Resource Management, 15*(4–5), 775–793.

Wiß, T. (2017). Paths towards family-friendly working time arrangements: Comparing workplaces in different countries and industries. *Social Policy & Administration, 51*(7), 1406–1430.

Zikic, J. (2015). Skilled migrants' career capital as a source of competitive advantage: Implications for strategic HRM. *International Journal of Human Resource Management, 26*, 1360–1381.

Zikic, J., Bonache, J., & Cerdin, J. (2010). Crossing national boundaries: A typology of qualified immigrants' career orientations. *Journal of Organisational Behavior, 31*, 667–686.

22

Career Capital Development of Highly Skilled Self-Initiated Expatriates

Rodrigo Mello and Vesa Suutari

Introduction

Self-initiated expatriates (SIEs) usually expatriate themselves to a country of their preference to seek career development and personal interests (Jokinen et al., 2008), often with no definite duration in mind (Tharenou, 2013). Such international mobility shapes the life paths of individuals and impacts their careers both during expatriation and after they have returned home, moved on to another destination, or put their stay on a more permanent footing.

Although the immigration literature typically excludes a requirement to work from the definition of migrant (see Andresen et al., 2013), it does commonly use the terms skilled migrants (e.g., O'Connor, 2018) and SIEs (e.g., Suutari et al., 2018) when individuals decide to live and work abroad (Mello et al., 2020; Andresen et al., 2013). Whether referred to as high-skilled immigrants or SIEs, the literature discusses the global mobility of highly skilled people living and working overseas (Fitzsimmons et al., 2020). This chapter explores the developmental experiences of highly skilled business and engineering professionals at the university level who have moved abroad to work on their own initiative.

R. Mello (✉)
University of Vaasa, Vaasa, Finland
e-mail: rodrigo.mello@uwasa.fi

V. Suutari
School of Management, University of Vaasa, Vaasa, Finland
e-mail: vesa.suutari@uwasa.fi

© The Author(s), under exclusive license to Springer Nature Switzerland AG 2023
A. I. Mockaitis (ed.), *The Palgrave Handbook of Global Migration in International Business*,
https://doi.org/10.1007/978-3-031-38886-6_22

Previous empirical studies have found work requirements are higher in global than domestic jobs (e.g., Shin et al., 2007). Consequently, international career scholars have defined global work as a *high-density* work experience that substantially affects individuals' career trajectories, motivation, and competencies (Tesluk & Jacobs, 1998; Shaffer et al., 2012). Scholars have also argued that the learning and developments experience abroad is so meaningful to expatriates that they often consider such development as one aspect of career success (Mello et al., 2021; Shen et al., 2015; Brisco et al., 2021). Such an outcome may be assessed through their career capital (CC) developed abroad (Shaffer et al., 2012).

The conceptualization of CC assumes that people invest in their careers through three *ways of knowing*, broadly reflecting an individual's physiological capital (knowing-why), intellectual capital (knowing-how), and social capital (knowing-whom) (Parker et al., 2009). This concept seems particularly suited to exploring the career of SIEs as it incorporates their motivation and identity, skills and expertise, and also their social networks (Mäkelä et al., 2009; Parker et al., 2009). All of the above add meaning to their experience abroad and are consequently perceived as an important aspect of career success. Accordingly, the CC concept is increasingly used in global careers research (Dickmann et al., 2018; Shaffer et al., 2012). Understanding the CC of SIEs is important for employers because international mobile professionals offer an ever-expanding recruitment pool for international companies seeking internationally experienced talent. In addition, recruiting such people can reduce the costs typically associated with traditional expatriation (Dickmann et al., 2018).

In light of this background, this chapter aims to assess the CC development of SIEs during expatriation. We asked the Finnish Association of Business School Graduates and the Academic Engineers and Architects in Finland to contact members who were SIEs working abroad or had done so recently. We received replies from 114 SIEs whose developmental experiences we analyze below. We support that analysis with illustrative quotations from interviews of SIEs representing those same associations.

Theory

The Developmental Nature of Global Work

Many studies on expatriates' career development are theoretically grounded in the boundaryless career paradigm (Arthur & Rousseau, 1996; Sullivan & Arthur, 2006). That stresses developmental opportunities arising from moving across organizational and national borders. Such transitions offer SIEs opportunities to engage in various forms of learning to develop new career competencies (Arthur et al., 1995). However, such changes in job duties, social relations, and work environments also incur various costs and risks that might adversely impact career development (Guan et al., 2019; Morgeson et al., 2015). Given this context, global work is described as high-density work involving international relocation and a need to *adjust thought patterns and scripts to effectively interact with people and adapt to situational demands across cultures* (Shaffer et al., 2012, p. 1300). The work role requirements also disrupt or interfere with employees' usual activities and routines outside work and affect the whole family. Expatriates are also often reported to be responsible for a wider variety of tasks than in their previous jobs and to have more autonomy (Mello et al., 2023). However, this may be more typical among assigned expatriates (AEs) than among SIEs. The SIE population includes groups such as young people heading abroad, while companies typically only send highly skilled professionals and managers abroad. In any case, expatriate work is highly developmental, and the experience can have major career implications for expatriates (Shaffer et al., 2012). In turn, expatriates might face problems finding what they perceive to be sufficiently challenging and interesting jobs after the expatriation (Suutari & Brewster, 2003).

Existing Research on Characteristics of SIEs

The experiences of AEs have received the most attention in the literature on international human resource management. However, the body of research on SIEs is gradually increasing (Brewster et al., 2021). Consequently, we are starting to understand how SIEs differ from traditional AEs and the characteristics of those SIEs. It is well-known that SIEs are motivated by different factors than AEs (Doherty et al., 2011), that their career paths (Peltokorpi & Froese, 2009) and psychological contracts are different (Casado & Caspersz, 2021), and their commitment to their current employer also seems to differ (Casado & Caspersz, 2021; Lapointe et al., 2020; Linder, 2019). Furthermore, AEs usually have managerial or senior technical roles that make them more likely to work than the SIE group as a whole. The AE is also, by definition, more likely to work for a sizable multinational enterprise than an SIE (Meuer et al., 2019; Andresen et al., 2015). In turn, they get more organizational and financial support from their employer, while SIEs rely more on their own resources (Hussain & Deery, 2018).

An AE must learn to work in a new country, in a new division of their employer, and an SIE must adjust to working in a new organization. While

AEs are often enthusiastic about the opportunity to move abroad, most will follow their employer's suggestion. The assignment process often means they have little time to prepare for the move (Doherty et al., 2011). In contrast, SIEs decide independently to go to a certain country. The limitations in the choice of host country and restricted preparation time mean AEs may experience greater adjustment gaps and have a more significant cognitive difference from people in the host country (Haslberger & Brewster, 2009).

Finally, SIEs tend to be abroad longer than AEs (Farcas & Goncalves, 2017), have more interest in considering more permanent international careers (Doherty et al., 2011), and have a higher degree of on-the-job embeddedness in the host country than AEs (Meuer et al., 2019). As SIEs have also, by definition, looked for a new job abroad when expatriating, they have no repatriation agreement like SIEs and typically no organization to return to back at home, which may cause them to face greater repatriation challenges than AEs (Begley et al., 2008). Nevertheless, it has recently been reported that SIEs' repatriation adjustment may not always be as difficult as commonly thought (Ellis et al., 2020).

The brief discussion above indicates SIEs have various work and career-related characteristics that differentiate them from AEs. Consequently, their developmental experiences may differ somewhat from those of AEs, who have been studied more than SIEs (Dickmann et al., 2018). We will next discuss the limited evidence we have on the development of SIEs during their expatriation.

CC and Its Development During Self-Initiated Expatriation

Expatriates' high-density work abroad means they are in a constant state of learning. Researchers have recently used the CC framework to analyze such developments (Shaffer et al., 2012). The conceptualization and operationalization of CC are built on the concept of the intelligent career rooted in this literature (Dickmann et al., 2018; Haslberger & Brewster, 2009). Intelligent career theory was first developed by DeFillippi and Arthur (1994) and revised by Arthur et al. (1995). The theory suggests that people invest in their careers through three *ways of knowing* that broadly reflect an individual's values, motivation, and identity (knowing-why), skills and expertise (knowing-how) and relationships and reputation (knowing-whom) (Mäkelä et al., 2009; Parker et al., 2009). This theory has been used in different studies, including those focusing on the CC of knowledge workers in the global economy (Lamb & Sutherland, 2010) on CC needed by business leaders to facilitate their organizational role transition (Brown et al., 2020), and on senior women managers' CC development during the transition to entrepreneurship (Terjesen, 2005).

In the context of expatriation, scholars have used the intelligent career framework to understand the development of expatriates' CC (Dickmann & Cerdin, 2018; Dickmann & Doherty, 2010; Stahl et al., 2002; Suutari et al., 2018; Suutari & Mäkelä, 2007) and also on CC development among expatriate partners (Kanstrén & Suutari, 2021; McNulty et al., 2019). Nevertheless, the few studies to address CC development among SIEs offer apparently contradictory results.

Knowing-Why CC

Knowing-why CC supplies SIEs with energy, self-assurance, and a sense of purpose and identification with work (Cappellen & Janssens, 2005; Dickmann et al., 2018; Inkson & Arthur, 2001). It relates to a person's self-concept, personal dispositions, values, and interests (Inkson & Arthur, 2001; Parker et al., 2009). The existing research indicates that during their global careers, expatriates develop their knowing-why CC as they encounter new issues and constantly have to put their career development at risk due to the uncertainty of international careers (Jokinen et al., 2008). This is even more relevant for SIEs as they need to look for a job abroad in a new environment and start working in a new organization. Simultaneously, a lack of organizational support and training increases the probability of their facing unexpected challenges. Coping with such experiences involves constant self-analysis, learning, paying attention to personal growth, and bolstering self-confidence. Accordingly, identity shifts can be linked to knowing-why CC (Defillippi & Arthur, 1994; Kohonen, 2005).

There is some evidence that SIEs appear to develop their knowing-why CC quite extensively during expatriation. Dickmann et al. (2018) and Jokinen et al. (2008) reported a very high level of development (a mean of 4.94 on a 7-point scale in the first study and a mean of 5.03 in the second). Expatriation also helps SIEs to develop an openness to change and new experiences (Andresen, 2021). Interestingly, Jokinen et al. (2008) found that overall knowing-why CC increased equally among both AEs and SIEs, while Dickmann et al. (2018) reported AEs acquire even more knowing-why CC than SIEs. So, the findings are inconclusive regarding whether the extent of development differs between expatriate types.

Knowing-How CC

Knowing-how CC relates to the competencies, knowledge and insights that global careerists develop to undertake international work (Harvey et al., 2000). Accordingly, scholars have addressed the value of international assignments as a developmental tool in competency training with future Multinational Corporation (MNC) leaders (Kohonen, 2005; Stahl et al., 2002). Owing to SIEs operating in a high-density work environment with no organizational support (Mello et al., 2023), they accumulate skills such as general social skills, change management skills, and global leadership skills (Jokinen et al., 2008). However, as they are individuals who need to find jobs alone, some SIEs may work in lower hierarchical positions than AEs. That situation naturally limits the learning of knowing-whom CC among such SIEs.

A few quantitative studies report that, on average, SIEs developed considerable knowing-how CC during their expatriation experiences (Dickmann et al., 2018 reported a mean of 4.77 and Jokinen et al., 2008 a mean of 4.76 on a 7-point scale knowing-how scale). In addition, it has been reported that expatriation helps SIEs develop general and job-specific knowledge, skills, and abilities (Andresen, 2021; Rodriguez & Scurry, 2014). Furthermore, Rodriguez and Scurry (2014) found that SIEs tend to develop their international competencies as a consequence of acquiring awareness of the dualities between globalization and localization. In their study of Irish repatriates, Begley et al. (2008) included some SIE accounts of how expatriation had developed skills, business knowledge, and cross-cultural awareness when working in high-level positions abroad. Unfortunately for those SIEs, the same study reported that the Irish job market did not value such issues following repatriation.

Makkonen (2015) reported on the perceived employability of SIEs in China. Some SIEs felt that the experience did not develop their expertise that much. Instead, they felt they were exploited to benefit local co-workers or superiors; thus, their perceived employability declined. Similarly, scholars reported SIEs' temporary de-skilling process due to career breaks when there was a mismatch between their educational background and local labor market demand (Mendoza, 2022; Begley et al., 2008). These perceived career outcomes were connected with limited organizational support and development opportunities offered to SIEs in host country. Similarly, Felker (2011) reported that the experiences of well-educated Eastern European SIEs indicated the situation was not very positive as they experienced down-skilling, meaning the SIEs worked in positions below their levels of education and capability.

Consequently, fewer development opportunities were available to those SIEs, and they feared losing their competencies and struggled to maintain them. Such findings indicate that the expatriation context may have important impacts on the extent of the development of knowing-how CC when abroad.

Regarding expatriate types, it is interesting to observe that, on a general level, the accumulation of knowing-how CC does not differ significantly between SIEs and AEs (Jokinen et al., 2008; Dickmann et al., 2018), there are a few observable distinctions. For example, AEs experience more learning in terms of organizational knowledge (Jokinen et al., 2008; Dickmann et al., 2018). That may relate to the type of jobs AEs have and also to their role as representatives of the whole organization in the host unit (e.g., integration and coordination responsibilities across borders).

Knowing-Whom CC

Knowing-whom CC concerns the social networks SIEs develop during expatriation and their abilities to build and utilize such networks in their work and career. Mäkelä and Suutari (2009) argue that the real challenge lies in knowing whether such networks can be utilized after repatriation or when moving to other countries. The networks of expatriates in their home country typically weaken during expatriation, which adversely affects employability. Those SIEs who do not have good networks in their home country can thus find securing suitable employment problematic (Begley et al., 2008). Owing to a lack of long-term organizational attachment, SIEs have less internal social capital than AEs, who leverage stronger internal ties within MNCs due to their work roles (Mäkelä & Suutari, 2009; Suutari et al., 2018). Before being sent abroad, AEs typically also have considerable experience working in the same company and have thus created good internal connections in the home country. For their part, SIEs move to a new organization abroad and lack broader networks. They typically develop closer contacts with locals through working in local organizations and are more interested in integrating into a local community than AEs. The latter rely more on their internal connections with the idea of repatriation back to their home country in a few years (Mäkelä & Suutari, 2013). Rodriguez and Scurry (2014) observed that SIEs still tend to perceive weak social and professional integration with locals owing to encountering cultural and gender differences. Furthermore, SIEs tend to stay abroad longer than AEs and often even consider more permanent stays. That attitude facilitates the integration with locals in the longer term.

The evidence on SIEs is quite limited, but it has been reported that SIEs develop their knowing-whom CC during expatriation (Dickmann et al., 2018 reported a mean of 4.57 and Jokinen et al., 2008 a mean of 4.62 in a 7-point knowing-whom scale). It is noteworthy that the available SIE studies tend to focus on SIEs developing the ability to build networks rather than on the extent of the networks ultimately acquired. In addition, it has been reported that SIEs perceive a certain degree of social recognition after their expatriate experiences, as peers in new jobs seem to value such experiences (Andresen, 2021). Nevertheless, as SIEs can face periods of unemployment after repatriation, that perception was not as common among SIEs as among AEs (Andresen, 2021). Jokinen et al. (2008) and Dickmann et al. (2018) reported significant differences between SIEs and AEs in terms of their overall knowing-whom capital acquisition, as AEs reported acquiring more social capital than SIEs. That may have important effects as a high stock of knowing-whom CC offers expatriates access to future career opportunities and the critical job-related information required to succeed internationally (Burt, 2005; Mäkelä & Suutari, 2009).

In summary, the number of studies on the development of CC among SIEs remains limited, and some present quite a negative view of the topic (Rodriguez & Scurry, 2014; Makkonen, 2015), while a few others offer a more positive view (Jokinen et al., 2008; Dickmann et al., 2018). Accordingly, it can be concluded that more research is needed. We will next describe the methods of our study before presenting our findings.

Methods

We used an internet survey to collect data from expatriate members of two Finnish trade associations to investigate the CC development of Finnish SIEs. Because trade association membership figures in Nordic countries are high, the sample provided by the Business School Graduates association and the association of Academic Engineers and Architects in Finland (TEK) is likely to represent almost all Finnish university level graduates working abroad in these fields (Suutari et al., 2018). The two associations identified individuals working abroad in 2015 and 2016, and they received our questionnaire in 2020. The present study is informed by the questionnaire responses of 114 SIEs, which were analyzed using SPSS to describe the development experiences of the respondents. Table 22.1 below presents the sample. The sample of highly skilled SIEs includes men and women of various ages, most of whom worked in Europe. Reflecting their high level of education, they also worked

Table 22.1 Sample characteristics (survey)

Sample characteristics	
Gender	*n*
Men	68
Women	46
Age	
From 27 to 40	45
From 41 to 60	56
Over 60	13
Country	
Europe	83
Asia	19
America	10
Oceania	2
Repatriates vs. expatriates	
Repatriates	31
Re-expatriates	83
Organizational position[a]	
Mean	6.7
Standard deviation	1.4
Educational background	
M.Sc. (Econ.)	53
M.Sc. (Techn.)	61
Total	114

[a]Scale from 1 (lowest level) to 10 (highest level)

typically in higher organizational levels. A surprisingly large proportion of the SIEs in our sample had decided to continue their international career after their initial SIE experience.

We used the CC scale devised by Dickmann et al. (2018) to measure CC development. Participants were asked: "To what extent did your international work experience (2015/16) develop the following abilities in you?" All items were measured on a 7-point Likert scale anchored with *did not improve/increase at all* (1) and *improved/increased very much* (7). The scale consists of 28 items measuring expatriates' development on three dimensions of CC: knowing-how CC (18 items), knowing-why CC (4 items), and knowing-whom CC (6 items) while working abroad (see Dickmann et al., 2018 for the items). Cronbach's alphas were 0.930 for knowing-how CC, 0.864 for knowing-why CC, and 0.905 for knowing-whom CC.

In addition to the quantitative analysis and reporting of CC development, we used data from semi-structured interviews of expatriates to illustrate their developmental experiences in key areas. That input was elicited via a qualitative extension of the survey in the form of interviews addressing the overall developmental and career experiences of expatriate members. In the survey,

Table 22.2 Sample characteristics (interviews)

Sample characteristics				
Gender	Age	Education	Location	Profession
1. Male	48	M.Sc (Econ.)	Netherlands	Controller
2. Male	55	M.Sc (Econ.)	USA	General manager
3. Male	38	M.Sc (Econ.)	Austria	Entrepreneur
4. Male	52	M.Sc (Econ.)	Switzerland	General manager
5. Female	34	M.Sc (Econ.)	China	Project manager
6. Female	62	M.Sc (Econ.)	Germany	Sales manager
7. Male	42	M.Sc (Econ.)	Germany	International sales repr.
8. Male	50	M.Sc (Econ.)	China	Unit manager

the respondents were asked if they are willing to participate to further interviews. Invitations to such interviews were send by e-mails. As an outcome overall 20 interviewees were reached for further interviews. In the present chapter, we use only the qualitative data from the interviews with SIEs ($n = 8$). The sample size is very small and thus there are clear limitations with regard to generalizability of these findings. In turn, we have above reported quantitative evidence with broader sample and this qualitative evidence is used just to illustrate the key developments that SIEs have reported in the survey. Thus, instead of doing systematic analysis of few qualitative interviews, we looked for interview quotations to illustrate how development in the three areas of CC were verbally described during interviews. The sample characteristics of these SIEs are described in Table 22.2.

Results

Overall, the survey data ($n = 114$) suggested that SIEs develop CC quite extensively when working abroad. As can be seen from Table 22.3, the development of CC was seen to be high across all three dimensions of CC. In turn, the data also indicated that SIEs accumulated, to some extent, higher "stock" of knowing-how and knowing-why CC than knowing-whom CC. Table 22.3 shows SIEs' perceptions of how much they believe they accumulated knowing-how CC.

A similar view on the extensive development opportunities that living and working abroad offered also appeared during the interviews of SIEs as it was commented like this:

> *I think that starting to live and work abroad on your own is probably the most extensive learning opportunity that one can face… The first half of years are always*

Table 22.3 Self-initiated expatriates' development abroad across three aspects of career capital

Aspect of CC	Mean	Std. dev.
Knowing-how	4.9137	1.14966
Knowing-why	4.8990	1.29054
Knowing-whom	4.6301	1.60647

Table 22.4 Self-initiated expatriates' development abroad across subdimensions of knowing-why career capital

	Mean	Std. dev.
Knowing self	**4.88**	**297**
I am able to recognize my own strengths and weaknesses, needs and motives	5.21	1.347
I understand what other people think about me	4.51	1.483
I acknowledge my personal values and beliefs	4.92	1.559
Personal development	**4.91**	**1.539**
I set goals for personal development	4.96	1.644
I undertake activities to enhance my skills and competencies	4.92	1.621
I want to know more than is required for task accomplishment	5.35	1.644

the most difficult ones when you have to learn everything from the beginning… You will for sure face some conflicts and challenges. Those offer the best situations for personal growth… Finally, you experience that you can win the challenges and always 'land on your feet'… When such positive experiences emerge, it develops you and gives you self-confidence (Interviewee 1)

Development of Knowing-Why CC

With regard to knowing-why CC, both knowing self and personal development orientation are perceived as equally important areas of development in the eyes of SIEs. Table 22.4 shows SIEs' perceptions of how much they believe they accumulated knowing-how CC.

Knowing-why-related developments were also raised in interviews. It was argued that challenging experiences were perceived as transitional experiences, which increased the self-understanding:

Definitely, I am now more aware of my strengths and weaknesses. I have sometimes been in personal profile analyses, and I am now really good now in describing what kind of person I am… I would say that international experiences have developed my strengths further. With regard to my weaknesses, I have done my best to develop myself in those areas as well. (Interviewee 2)

Through your international experiences, one is almost forced to think about their own values… Through such situations, one also starts to better understand oneself. As an outcome, I also aim to behave more consciously on the basis of my values. (Interviewee 3)

These transitional experiences have also increased their understanding of constant learning and also their interest in future development and personal growth:

I have become more open-minded, and the experiences have increased my willingness to grow as a person and learn new issues. I see that no one is ever 'ready' as a person. (Interviewee 4)

When there have been career options to choose from after my international experiences, I have typically chosen the options that involve the best changes to try new issues and to develop something new and also to develop myself. I am always in favor of new adventures and development opportunities (Interviewee 3)

At the same time, such experiences have typically given confidence that one is able to handle challenging experiences also in the future and thus able to take on even more responsibilities in the future career:

This experience has given me self-confidence; I don't get so easily scared if all doesn't go as expected… It gives you perseverance when all doesn't happen as quickly as you expect. (Interviewee 5)

You learn to tolerate uncertainty as the international work environment is more uncertain when you can never know what to expect, how people react in different situations and so on. (Interviewee 1).

Development of Knowing-How CC

The data presented in Table 22.5 on knowing-how CC shows that the most extensive development concerns the development of social skills and social judgment skills. In addition, more general cognitive ability development increased when working in more complex and uncertain international work environments. A new job in a new cultural context also offered a very good starting point for learning new job-related and cross-cultural skills.

Table 22.5 Self-initiated expatriates' development abroad across subdimensions of knowing-how career capital

	Mean	Std. Deviation
Social skills	**5.94**	**1.273**
Ability to interact socially with people from diverse cultural backgrounds	6.06	1.241
Ability to make yourself understood in multicultural environments	5.87	1.334
Cognitive ability	**5.20**	**1.364**
Ability to separate relevant knowledge from irrelevant	5.18	1.436
Ability to switch the target of concentration quickly	5.27	1.518
Social judgment skills	**5.14**	**1.295**
Recognizing the principles of social functioning/interaction	5.13	1.360
Understanding your own role in social organization	5.18	1.364
Task knowledge	**5.06**	**1.302**
Knowledge of norms central to your own tasks	4.97	1.379
Professional/functional knowledge/expertise central to your own tasks	5.33	1.455
Knowledge of the trends and latest achievements of professional development in your area of responsibility	4.86	1.558
People knowledge	**5.03**	**1.453**
Understanding factors causing variety in the needs of different people	4.96	1649
Understanding how behavior may reflect different values	5.14	1.580
Understanding different factors differentiating cultures	5.25	1.632
Knowledge of general factors guiding human behavior	4.84	1.596
Organization knowledge	**4.67**	**1.711**
Understanding the strategic roles of different units of the international organization	5.11	1.797
Understanding the components of the organization's international competitive advantage	4.58	1.824
Knowledge of international management systems of the organization	4.33	2.011
Business knowledge	**3.27**	**1.914**
Understanding financial options typical for the business area	3.25	1.976
Understanding shareholders' interests	3.30	2.137

Among the seven dimensions measured, the development of organizational knowledge regarding how international organizations operate and business knowledge scored the lowest. The lower level of learning in these areas may reflect the type of jobs that SIEs have, as some work in lower-level positions in local, less-international companies. Accordingly, in terms of such tasks, there is less to learn about how international companies operate. However, all SIEs share a general level of learning on cross-cultural issues when working abroad.

Our quantitative findings indicate that the social aspects of learning were the most emphasized. This aspect encompasses general social skills and also cross-cultural skills:

The competence that I developed the most abroad relates to how to interact with people… I overall learned how important relationships are. You also need to find out who are the important persons in the organization. (Interviewee 6).

This experience has expanded my thinking. If someone behaves in a different way, it is easier to accept that some people have very different values and culture-based behavioral styles… You can still succeed when interacting with them. (Interviewee 7)

As SIEs learned different ways of working abroad and saw how international organizations operate, they acquired learning on task-related knowledge and skills and organizational knowledge:

When you work abroad, you see different working cultures, and through that, you start questioning your ways of working, and thus you learn task-related skills… You also learn to watch issues from different and broader angles. (Interviewee 7)

Important learning aspects also relate to technical issues; those have progressed so quickly over the last ten years… Working abroad also helped to understand the different views and relationships between national units and HQ (Interviewee 4)

Development of Knowing-Whom CC

Table 22.6 illustrates that SIEs report developing their knowing-whom competencies quite considerably during expatriation. The most extensive development occurs in the area of being competent in building inter-organizational networks and teams across borders. The information clearly reflects the experiences of SIEs working in international work environments as expatriates. The slightly lower scores on the extent to which SIEs had learned to know the important people in the organization or their ability to develop external networks may again reflect the work roles of SIEs. That is because many SIEs do not work in the most senior roles, and those roles involve less external representation than those typically held by AEs. Furthermore, as organizational newcomers and also as foreigners in a new country, they may not have easy access to people at the highest levels of the organization. Because SIEs tend not to have international roles and are more likely to work in local organizations that are not particularly internally oriented, their international abilities concerning knowing-whom CC may not be developed extensively.

Table 22.6 Self-initiated expatriates' development abroad in terms of knowing-whom career capital

	Mean	Std. Deviation
Knowing- whom CC, in total	4.63	1.606
Ability to build inter-organizational networks and teams across boundaries	4.96	1.867
Knowledge of people with influential power within organizations	4.65	1.875
Ability to build and maintain the external network	4.46	1.810
Ability to link resources and activities internationally	4.45	1.885

During the interviews, SIEs stressed how important networks are in international work environments, how they have developed their skills in networking, and how they use such networks to succeed in their work.

> *I have developed strong networks internationally when I have been moving around. I can find connections to almost any work situation that I face and need to find out how to handle the situation. Both in Finland and abroad. It has huge benefits for my work and also for any personal challenges I face abroad. (Interviewee 8)*

In turn, it was also recognized that networks are, to some extent, national; thus, it is sometimes difficult to maintain or use them in future careers.

> *I have learned to use my networks. Which ones depend on the situation as networks are, to some extent, country-specific, but I have managed to utilize those. Those have given me concrete help in my work and career. (Interviewee 1)*

Conclusions

The present study's findings support the view that SIEs generally develop their CC fairly extensively when working abroad. These findings thus confirm those described in a few earlier quantitative studies (Dickmann et al., 2018; Jokinen et al., 2008). This view contrasts with findings from other studies that emphasize more negative views on the development of SIEs, who are described as facing challenges in finding suitable jobs abroad that fit their level of education and CC (Begley et al., 2008; Rodriguez & Scurry, 2014; Makkonen, 2015). Therefore, the context in which the SIEs work may impact their learning opportunities and perception of the value of such international work experience. For example, Makkonen (2015) studied the experiences of SIEs in China and found that the development and career opportunities for SIEs were limited in that context. In contrast, the average SIE contributing to the present study and previous larger surveys (Dickmann et al., 2018; Jokinen et al., 2008) may have more commonly chosen to move to developed European countries. Accordingly, there may be better development opportunities for them. Therefore, studies addressing SIEs should consider the context in which SIEs work when reporting and interpreting the findings (Andresen et al., 2021). It is also important to note that there are different kinds of SIEs, from top managers in MNCs to young graduates heading abroad to gain international experience (e.g., Selmer et al., 2022). Consequently, findings reported from a particular group of SIEs may differ extensively from those derived from other groups and from more general samples of quite different types of SIEs.

Examining our findings across three distinct aspects of CC first revealed the extensive accumulation of knowing-why CC. Such development has been reported among all expatriates, but it may be even higher among SIEs due to the highly boundaryless nature of the careers of SIEs (Biemann & Andresen, 2010). Those SIEs find themselves in a more vulnerable position and exposed to different risks, such as being able to adjust to a new country, organization, and role during international career transitions. At the same time, they lack organizational support. However, in line with modern career theories, SIEs may grasp the opportunity to learn from such a challenging context (2023 Mello et al., 2023). Experienced global careerists also view the opportunities for constant development in an international career context as among the best sides of an international career while acknowledging that the working environment is challenging (Suutari & Mäkelä, 2007). In addition, SIEs face a similar transition stage after expatriation when they typically need to find a new job and employer upon repatriation (Andresen et al., 2013) or re-expatriation (Mello et al., 2022).

In such transitions, SIEs may need to act proactively and take the initiative to acquire the resources necessary to adapt their career to the challenges of international career transitions (Smale et al., 2019; Andresen et al., 2020). Due to such career uncertainties and transitions, SIEs might face periods of unemployment (an employment gap) or underemployment (where they have to take a job that does not match their skills or abilities). Nevertheless, SIEs may still develop their knowing-why CC while experiencing different career transitions.

Regarding the development of knowing-how CC, the findings show that the foreign sojourns of SIEs substantially increase it. In most of the subdimensions of knowing-how, the means were very high (i.e., over five on a 7-point scale). The exceptions were organizational and business knowledge. This finding is similar to those of Jokinen et al. (2008) and Dickmann et al. (2018). Those studies reported that the real gain from international career transitions relates to intellectual capital aspects that transcend the limits of one single organization, such as social skills and cognitive abilities. An SIE's career is characterized by being less dependent on organizations, which justifies a lower accumulation of knowledge connected with a specific organization or specific business. Hence, SIEs tend to accumulate more knowing-how CC that allows them to use it in multiple contexts, as SIEs tend to be exposed to various contexts during their career.

Finally, our findings on knowing-whom CC indicate that even though SIEs do improve their stock of it during international career transitions, less development is reported in that area than in the two other aspects of CC. As discussed earlier, this may partly relate to the type of jobs some SIEs have and the type of organizations in which they work. An SIE may also find themselves in a context where the development of abilities to build social networks across counties suffers from the lack of organizational support for building and maintaining ties across countries. As an AE, one may already have internal connections before moving to the host country, or at least they have their established company network to draw on, whereas SIEs do know no one in the organization when starting. It may also be challenging for SIEs to maintain and leverage these connections during international career transitions as they move across organizational and national borders and also to bridge individuals from different social groups across countries (Kwon & Adler, 2014). During expatriation, international social ties expand while home-country connections typically weaken (Mäkelä & Suutari, 2009).

Overall, our findings across all aspects of CC reinforce the idea that SIEs may acquire less knowing-whom CC than other expatriates because they are on their own (Suutari et al., 2018). As an SIE's career is more boundaryless than that of an AE, the concept of the boundaryless career can help understand the dynamics of the SIE career. The boundaryless nature of international careers refers to the freedom to earn work experience in global environments across national and often also across organizations. (Guan et al., 2019). Unlike the accumulation of knowing-why and knowing-how CC, knowing-whom CC depends exclusively on a single individual's learning process. Knowing-whom CC is limited to relationships with other social actors, where individuals leverage resources through such relationships (Dickmann et al., 2018). Hence, SIEs' greater boundarylessness (more freedom and less dependence on organizational support) can challenge the accumulation of knowing-whom CC because they do not have the internal professional network of an organization during transitions across countries.

While providing some new evidence on the development of SIEs, the present study also has some limitations. First, like most expatriation research (e.g., Ren et al., 2013; Breitenmoser et al., 2018), the study relies on cross-sectional data. Accordingly, longitudinal studies on the development process for SIEs abroad would help improve our understanding of CC development among that group. Because SIEs work in quite different jobs and societal contexts, it would be good to investigate the antecedents of CC development in the future. That line of research could provide a more comprehensive view of why some experiences are more developmental than others.

Furthermore, all SIEs contributing to the present study were university-educated engineers and business professionals. The career benefits of an international assignment could manifest differently among less educated people with different career expectations and realities. All expatriates were also Finnish and different cultures might value IA experiences differently (Andresen et al., 2020).

In terms of practical implications, our findings show that organizations would benefit from recognizing that the SIE group represents an important pool of talent that could aid organizations' globalization efforts. The SIE cohort offers an interesting recruitment pool for MNCs and could also offer cheaper recruitment solutions than using AEs. As SIEs are usually recruited from the local labor market and invariably managed as part of the local labor force, they add knowledge gained from living in other countries, including language skills and internationalization experience that would be difficult to match among local employees. So, SIEs not only accumulate CC but also add value to the local learning environment. In turn, an increasing number of businesses are starting to view SIEs as boundary-spanners: People able to speak the local language, understand the local culture and have good local connections (Furusawa & Brewster, 2018; Brewster et al., 2021). There is clearly scope for far more research focused on the employers of SIEs.

References

Andresen, M. (2021). When at home, do as they do at home? Valuation of self-initiated repatriates' competences in French and German management career structures. *The International Journal of Human Resource Management, 32*(4), 789–821.

Andresen, M., Bergdolt, F., & Margenfeld, J. (2013). What distinguishes self-initiated expatriates from assigned expatriates and migrants. In *Self-initiated expatriation: Individual, organizational, and national perspectives*, pp. 11–41.

Andresen, M., Biemann, T., & Pattie, M. W. (2015). What makes them move abroad? Reviewing and exploring differences between self-initiated and assigned expatriation. *International Journal of Human Resource Management, 26*(7), 1–16. https://doi.org/10.1080/09585192.2012.669780

Andresen, M., Pattie, M. W., & Hippler, T. (2020). What does it mean to be a 'self-initiated' expatriate in different contexts? A conceptual analysis and suggestions for future research. *The International Journal of Human Resource Management, 31*(1), 174–201.

Andresen, M., Brewster, C., & Suutari, V. (2021). *Conclusions: Self-initiated expatriates in context: recognizing space, time and institutions* (pp. 214–227). Routledge.

Arthur, M. B., & Rousseau, D. M. (1996). Introduction: The boundaryless career as a new employment principle. In M. B. Arthur & D. M. Rousseau (Eds.), *The Boundaryless career: A new employment principle for a new Organisational era* (pp. 3–20). Oxford University Press.

Arthur, M., Claman, P., & DeFillippi, R. (1995). Intelligent enterprise, intelligent career. *Academy of Management Executive, 9*, 7–20.

Begley, A., Collings, D. G., & Scullion, H. (2008). The cross-cultural adjustment experiences of self-initiated repatriates to the Republic of Ireland labour market. *Employee Relations, 30*(3), 264–282. https://doi.org/10.1108/01425450810866532

Biemann, T., & Andresen, M. (2010). Self-initiated foreign expatriates versus assigned expatriates: Two distinct types of international careers?. *Journal of Managerial Psychology, 25*(4), 430–448.

Breitenmoser, A., Bader, B., & Berg, N. (2018). Why does repatriate career success vary? An empirical investigation from both traditional and protean career perspectives. *Human Resource Management, 57*(5), 1049–1063. https://doi.org/10.1002/hrm.21888

Brewster, C., Suutari, V., & Waxin, M. F. (2021). Two decades of research into SIEs and what do we know? A systematic review of the most influential literature and a proposed research agenda. *Journal of Global Mobility: The Home of Expatriate Management Research.* https://doi.org/10.1108/JGM-05-2021-0054

Briscoe, J. P., Kaše, R., Dries, N., Dysvik, A., Unite, J. A., Adeleye, I., et al. (2021). Here, there, & everywhere: Development and validation of a cross-culturally representative measure of subjective career success. *Journal of Vocational Behavior, 130*, 103612. https://doi.org/10.1016/j.jvb.2021.103612

Brown, C., Hooley, T., & Wond, T. (2020). Building career capital: Developing business leaders' career mobility. *Career Development International, 25*(5), 445–459.

Burt, R. S. (2005). *Brokerage and closure: An introduction to social capital.* Oxford University Press.

Cappellen, T., & Janssens, T. (2005). Career paths of global managers: Towards future research. *Journal of World Business, 40*, 348–360.

Casado, R., & Caspersz, D. (2021). Changing psychological contracts and organisational commitment: A longitudinal comparison of assigned and self-initiated expatriates in Australia. *International Journal of Human Resource Management, 32*(18), 3950–3972. https://doi.org/10.1080/09585192.2019.1660701

Defillippi, R., & Arthur, M. (1994). The boundaryless career: A competency-based perspective. *Journal of Organizational Behavior, 15*, 307–324.

Dickmann, M., & Cerdin, J.-L. (2018). Exploring the development and transfer of career capital in an international governmental organization. *The International Journal of Human Resource Management, 29*(15), 2253–2283.

Dickmann, M., & Doherty, N. (2010). Exploring organizational and individual career goals, interactions, and outcomes of developmental international assignments. *Thunderbird International Business Review, 52*(4), 313–324.

Dickmann, M., Suutari, V., Brewster, C., Mäkelä, L., Tanskanen, J., & Tornikoski, C. (2018). The career competencies of self-initiated and assigned expatriates: Assessing the development of career capital over time. *International Journal of Human Resource Management, 29*(16), 2353–2371. https://doi.org/10.1080/09585192.2016.1172657

Doherty, N., Dickmann, M., & Mills, T. (2011). Exploring the motives of company-backed and self-initiated expatriates. *International Journal of Human Resource Management, 22*(33), 595–611.

Ellis, D., Thorn, K., & Yao, C. (2020). Repatriation of self-initiated expatriates: Expectations vs experiences. *Career Development International, 25*(5), 539–562. https://doi.org/10.1108/CDI-09-2019-0228

Farcas, D., & Goncalves, M. (2017). Motivations and cross-cultural adaptation of self-initiated expatriates, assigned expatriates, and immigrant workers: The case of Portuguese migrant workers in the United Kingdom. *Journal of Cross-Cultural Psychology, 48*(7), 1028–1051. https://doi.org/10.1177/0022022117717031

Felker, J. A. (2011). Professional development through self-directed expatriation: Intentions and outcomes for young, educated Eastern Europeans. *International Journal of Training and Development, 15*(1), 76–86.

Fitzsimmons, S. R., Baggs, J., & Brannen, M. Y. (2020). The Immigrant Income Gap. *Harvard Business Review Digital Articles,* 2–8. https://hbr.org/2020/05/research-the-immigrant-income-gap

Furusawa, M., & Brewster, C. (2018). Japanese self-initiated expatriates as boundary spanners in Chinese subsidiaries of Japanese MNEs: Antecedents, social capital, and HRM practices. *Thunderbird International Business Review, 60*(6), 911–919.

Guan, Y., Arthur, M. B., Khapova, S. N., Hall, R. J., & Lord, R. G. (2019). Career boundarylessness and career success: A review, integration and guide to future research. *Journal of Vocational Behavior, 110*(May 2018), 390–402. https://doi.org/10.1016/j.jvb.2018.05.013

Harvey, M., Novicevic, M., & Speier, C. (2000). An innovative global management staffing system: A competency-based perspective. *Human Resource Management, 39,* 381–394.

Haslberger, A., & Brewster, C. (2009). Capital gains: Expatriate adjustment and the psychological contract in international careers. *Human Resource Management, 48*(3), 379–397. https://doi.org/10.1002/hrm.20286

Hussain, T., & Deery, S. (2018). Why do self-initiated expatriates quit their jobs: The role of job embeddedness and shocks in explaining turnover intentions. *International Business Review, 27*(1), 281–288. https://doi.org/10.1016/j.ibusrev.2017.08.002

Inkson, K., & Arthur, M. B. (2001). How to be a successful career capitalist. *Organizational Dynamics, 30*(1), 48–61. https://doi.org/10.1016/S0090-2616(01)00040-7

Jokinen, T., Brewster, C., & Suutari, V. (2008). Career capital during international work experiences: Contrasting self-initiated expatriate experiences and assigned expatriation. *International Journal of HRM, 19*(6), 979–998.

Kanstrén, K., & Suutari, V. (2021). Development of career capital during expatriation: partners' perspectives. *Career Development International, 26*(6), 824–849.

Kohonen, E. (2005). Developing global leaders through international assignments: An identity construction perspective. *Personnel Review, 34*(1), 22–36.

Kwon, S. W., & Adler, P. S. (2014). Social capital: Maturation of a field of research. *The Academy of Management Review, 39*(4), 412–422. https://doi.org/10.5465/amr.2014.0210

Lamb, M., & Sutherland, M. (2010). The components of career capital for knowledge workers in the global economy. *The International Journal of Human Resource Management, 21*, 295–312.

Lapointe, E., Vandenberghe, C., & Fan, S. X. (2020). Psychological contract breach and organizational cynicism and commitment among self-initiated expatriates vs host country nationals in the Chinese and Malaysian transnational education sector. *Asia Pacific Journal of Management, 39*, 319–342. https://doi.org/10.1007/s10490-020-09729-7

Linder, C. (2019). Expatriates' motivations for going abroad: The role of organizational embeddedness for career satisfaction and job effort. *Employee Relations, 41*(3), 552–570.

Mäkelä, K., & Suutari, V. (2009). Global careers: A social capital paradox. *International Journal of Human Resource Management, 20*(5), 992–1008. https://doi.org/10.1080/09585190902850216

Mäkelä, K., & Suutari, V. (2013). The social capital of traditional and self-initiated expatriates. In *Talent management of self-initiated expatriates* (pp. 256–277). Palgrave Macmillan.

Mäkelä, K., Björkman, I., & Ehrnrooth, M. (2009). MNC subsidiary staffing architecture: Building human and social capital within the organisation. *The International Journal of Human Resource Management, 20*(6), 1273–1290.

Makkonen, P. (2015). Perceived employability development of Western self-initiated expatriates in local organisations in China. *Journal of Global Mobility, 3*(4), 350–377. https://doi.org/10.1108/JGM-05-2015-0015

McNulty, Y., Lauring, J., & Selmer, J. (2019). Highway to hell? Managing expatriates in crisis. *Journal of Global Mobility, 7*(2), 157–180.

Mello, R., Dickmann, M., Brewster, C., & Suutari, V. (2020). The Long-Term Effects of Self- Initiated Expatriation on the Future Careers of Assignees 1. In Self-Initiated Expatriates in Context (pp. 91–109). Routledge.

Mello, R., Dickmann, M., Brewster, C., & Suutari, V. (2021). The long-term effects of self-initiated international assignments on future careers of assignees. In

M. Andresen, C. Brewster, & V. Suutari (Eds.), *Self-initiated careers: Recognizing space, time, and institutions*. Routledge. https://doi.org/10.4324/9780429352690

Mello, R., Suutari, V., & Dickmann, M. (2022). How career adaptability, job fit, and job characteristics impact expatriates' career success. In *Academy of management proceedings* (Vol. 2022, p. 13308). Academy of Management.

Mello, R., Suutari, V., & Dickmann, M. (2023). Taking stock of expatriates' career success after international assignments: A review and future research agenda. *Human Resource Management Review, 33*(1), 100913.

Mendoza, C. (2022). Illuminating the shadows of skilled migration: Highly qualified immigrants from Latin America in Spain. *International Migration, 60*(5), 60–73.

Meuer, J., Tröster, C., Angstmann, M., Backes-Gellner, M., & Pull, K. (2019). Embeddedness and the repatriation intention of assigned and self-initiated expatriates. *European Management Journal, 37*(6), 784–793. https://doi.org/10.1016/j.emj.2019.03.002

Morgeson, F. P., Mitchell, T. R., & Liu, D. (2015). Event system theory: An event-oriented approach to the organizational sciences. *Academy of Management Review, 40*, 515–537.

O'Connor, E. (2018). Skilled Migrants and International Careers: A Qualitative Study and Interpretation of the Careers and Perceived Career Success of Skilled Migrant Workers in Ireland (Doctoral dissertation, National University of Ireland, Maynooth (Ireland)).

Parker, P., Khapova, S. N., & Arthur, M. B. (2009). The intelligent career framework as a basis for interdisciplinary inquiry. *Journal of Vocational Behavior, 75*(3), 291–302.

Peltokorpi, V., & Froese, F. J. (2009). Organizational expatriates and self-initiated expatriates: Who adjusts better to work and life in Japan? *International Journal of Human Resource Management, 20*(5), 1096–1112. https://doi.org/10.1080/09585190902850299

Ren, H., Bolino, M. C., Shaffer, M. A., & Kraimer, M. L. (2013). The influence of job demands and resources on repatriate career satisfaction: A relative deprivation perspective. *Journal of World Business, 48*(1), 149–159. https://doi.org/10.1016/j.jwb.2012.06.015

Rodriguez, J. K., & Scurry, T. (2014). Career capital development of self-initiated expatriates in Qatar: Cosmopolitan globetrotters, experts and outsiders. *The International Journal of Human Resource Management, 25*(7), 1046–1067.

Selmer, J., Suutari, V., & Brewster, C. (2022). Self-initiated expatriates. In *Expatriates and Managing Global Mobility* (pp. 114–136). Routledge.

Shaffer, M. A., Kraimer, M. L., Chen, Y. P., & Bolino, M. C. (2012). Choices, challenges, and career consequences of global work experiences: A review and future agenda. *Journal of Management, 38*(4), 1282–1327.

Shen, Y., Demel, B., Unite, J., Briscoe, J. P., Hall, D. T., Chudzikowski, K., et al. (2015). Career success across 11 countries: Implications for international human resource management. *International Journal of Human Resource Management, 26*(13), 1753–1778. https://doi.org/10.1080/09585192.2014.962562

Shin, S. J., Morgeson, F. P., & Campion, M. A. (2007). What you do depends on where you are: Understanding how domestic and expatriate work requirements depend upon the cultural context. *Journal of International Business Studies, 38*(1), 64–83.

Smale, A., Bagdadli, S., Cotton, R., Dello Russo, S., Dickmann, M., Dysvik, A., et al. (2019). Proactive career behaviors and subjective career success: The moderating role of national culture. *Journal of Organizational Behavior, 40*(1), 105–122.

Sullivan, S. E., & Arthur, M. B. (2006). The evolution of the boundaryless career concept: Examining physical and psychological mobility. *Journal of vocational behavior, 69*(1), 19–29.

Suutari, V., & Brewster, C. (2003). Repatriation: Empirical evidence from a longitudinal study of careers and expectations among Finnish expatriates. *International Journal of Human Resource Management, 14*(7), 1132–1151. https://doi.org/10.1080/0958519032000114200

Suutari, V., & Mäkelä, K. (2007). The career capital of managers with global careers. *Journal of Managerial Psychology, 22*(7), 628–648.

Suutari, V., Brewster, C., Mäkelä, L., Dickmann, M., & Tornikoski, C. (2018). The effect of international work experience on the career success of expatriates: A comparison of assigned and self-initiated expatriates. *Human Resource Management, 57*(1), 37–54. https://doi.org/10.1002/hrm.21827

Terjesen, S. (2005). Senior women managers' transition to entrepreneurship: Leveraging embedded career capital. *Career Development International, 10*(3), 246–259.

Tesluk, P. E., & Jacobs, R. R. (1998). Toward an integrated model of work experience. *Personnel Psychology, 51*(2), 321–355.

Tharenou, P. (2013). Self-initiated expatriates: An alternative to company-assigned expatriates? *Journal of Global Mobility, 1*(3), 336–356. https://doi.org/10.1108/JGM-02-2013-0008

23

Expatriates' Quality of Life During the Pandemic: Two Sides of the Same Coin

Anh Nguyen and Maike Andresen

Introduction

Only when the tide goes out do you discover who's been swimming naked.—Warren Buffett

The COVID-19 pandemic marked its outbreak worldwide in March 2020. It changed the lives of workers significantly through lockdowns, health hazards, and economic crises. The conditions led to stressful experiences for individuals, especially expatriates, that is, those who relocate and execute their employment abroad (Andresen et al., 2014). During turbulent times, individuals require substantial resources, ranging from physical and economic to sociopsychological, to cope with stressors and sustain the quality of life (Hobfoll, 1989; Shelef et al., 2022). As expatriates tend to possess fewer resources than natives, they are more vulnerable during a crisis. For example, border restrictions during the pandemic hindered their ability to travel internationally, which prevented expatriates from securing desired employment (ILO, 2021b). They were also overrepresented in sectors and occupations where telework was not possible, increasing the risk of infection in the workplace (European Commission, 2020). Furthermore, they suffered from stress and negative affectivity (Rosa González et al., 2022), deterioration of mental health

---

A. Nguyen (✉) • M. Andresen
University of Bamberg, Bamberg, Germany
e-mail: Anh.Nguyen@uni-bamberg.de; maike.andresen@uni-bamberg.de

(Solà-Sales et al., 2021; Spiritus-Beerden et al., 2021), loss of income, and job instability (ILO, 2021b), which were more severe than in the native population (Global Migration Data Portal, 2022; Shelef et al., 2022). At the same time, a more nuanced view suggests that the availability of and access to resources is likely to vary widely among expatriates, suggesting heterogeneous experiences during the pandemic. This means, for instance, that if resources were sufficient or increased, some expatriates may have been little constrained by the pandemic or even benefited, for instance, due to improved work–life balance, affluent monetary assets, or job security (Mello & Tomei, 2021).

In order to design effective support for expatriates during the pandemic, it is crucial to obtain a comprehensive view of how various aspects of their lives changed during this period of turbulence. However, existing studies on this topic suffer from three major shortcomings. First, they primarily employed a *variable-centered* approach (cf. Gama et al., 2022; Hall et al., 2021; Solà-Sales et al., 2021), which assumes that the influences of the pandemic on expatriates' quality of life can be estimated uniformly and generalized to all expatriates (cf. Meyer & Morin, 2016). This excludes the diverse experiences of expatriates during the pandemic, which can range from negative to positive. For example, some expatriate groups reported improvements in work–life harmony (Mello & Tomei, 2021), transnational networks (Rosa González et al., 2022), and work engagement (Sahoo et al., 2022), suggesting facilitation in quality of life. Second, by assuming that the pandemic affected expatriates equally, the variable-centered approach provides insufficient knowledge for practitioners to build support and coping strategies suited to expatriates' individual experiences. Third, as the literature has focused primarily on the consequences of the pandemic, there is little understanding of the factors that contribute to these outcomes. The lack of insight into protective and risk factors also results in inapt measures to aid expatriates with different levels of vulnerability.

In this light, we adopted a *person-centered* approach to investigate how expatriates perceived the impact of the pandemic on their quality of life. This method allowed us to identify subgroups within the expatriate population, the impact of the pandemic on whose life demonstrated similar and statistically identifiable patterns (cf. Meyer & Morin, 2016). We further investigated the resources (or lack thereof) associated with the emergence of patterns, including gender, marital status, expatriate mode, community embeddedness, and personal initiative, thereby identifying the most vulnerable, as well as resilient groups. The links between perceived changes in quality of life and expatriates' work outcomes were also examined, including job embeddedness, intention to stay, career resources, and international relocation mobility readiness.

The findings of this study are important for several reasons. First, by illustrating the diverse expatriate experiences during turbulent times, we emphasize the importance of customizing policies and procedures for this population based on individual factors. Second, the identification of harmful and helpful elements serves to further illuminate the most vulnerable and resilient groups, thereby enhancing the reliability and delivery of organizational support. Therefore, the results are instrumental in developing practical recommendations for policymakers to manage expatriates during crises such as the pandemic and prepare them for the challenges of the aftermath.

In the following section, we elaborate on our research questions using the Conservation of Resource (COR) theory (Hobfoll, 1989; Hobfoll et al., 2018), followed by a literature review of related concepts and an illustration of the methods and data analysis. We then present the results of our study and implications for research and practice. The chapter ends with a report of limitations and suggestions for future research, along with the conclusions of the study.

Expatriates' Quality of Life Amid the COVID-19 Pandemic, Resources, and Work Consequences

According to COR theory, individuals strive to obtain, maintain, and enrich resources (Hobfoll, 1989; Hobfoll et al., 2018). The threat of or actual resource losses, which are typically prevalent during turbulent times, triggers stress response (Shelef et al., 2022). Evidence generally showed that expatriates were more vulnerable than the natives to stress and damage during crises (Global Migration Data Portal, 2022; Shelef et al., 2022), because they tend to possess limited *resources* to cope with such situations (Shelef et al., 2022). Their lack of resources is manifested in various aspects, such as language deficiencies, which obstructed their access to government information, and dampened their adherence to control measures (Kumar et al., 2021). The *consequences* of resource losses were also more severe among expatriates than the national population: risk of infection, mortality rates, and several mental health problems were more pronounced among the former than the latter groups (Hayward et al., 2021; Kumar et al., 2021). Expatriates are more likely than natives to suffer from mass unemployment, and stressful and hazardous working conditions (ILO, 2021b). In terms of *quality of life*, most studies indicated physical and material damages that expatriates perceive in the epidemic (cf. Bailey, 2021; Haist & Kurth, 2022; ILO, 2021b; Koveshnikov et al., 2022), while overlooking other facets such as relationships, fulfillment, work and career, recreation, socialization, social, community, and civic activities and self-understanding (Flanagan, 1982).

In this light, the COR theory posits that during crises, individuals with more resources at the beginning are less prone to stress and dampened their quality of life (Hobfoll, 1989; Shelef et al., 2022). This means that even among the expatriate population, individuals may have different views on how the pandemic has affected their quality of life, depending on their personal resource pool. They can differ in terms of (1) the perceived overall connotation of the impact, that is, whether the pandemic had a positive, negative, or negligible influence on their quality of life; and (2) the way the pandemic changed the different facets of their quality of life, for example, some aspects of quality of life changed during the crisis but the others did not. Both dimensions constitute distinct and statistically identifiable patterns that describe expatriates' personal experiences of the *quality of life* during the pandemic.

Assuming that expatriates' perceptions of quality of life in the pandemic are manifold, the potential *consequences* of this diversity are an intriguing topic. Specifically, we are interested in their retention intentions, international relocation mobility readiness, and career resources, which the literature indicated to transform during the pandemic (Haist & Kurth, 2022; ILO, 2021b; Schmidt, 2021; Végh et al., 2022), without considering the diversity of expatriates' experiences. Another aspect is the *factors* under which these different patterns emerge. Aside from demographic features (i.e., gender, marital status), which appear to be associated with how individuals cope with the pandemic (Kowal et al., 2020; Shelef et al., 2022), social and personal resources, such as community embeddedness, expatriation mode, and personal initiative, are crucial for expatriates to sustain the quality of life in turbulent times. The factors contributing to perceived quality of life and the consequences resulting from the perceived quality of life are summarized in Fig. 23.1.

Consequences of Expatriates' Quality of Life in the Pandemic on Their Work Outcomes

Intention to Stay in the Host Country and Organization

The intention to stay in the host country and organization appears to be the most common consequence identified in relation to the pandemic among

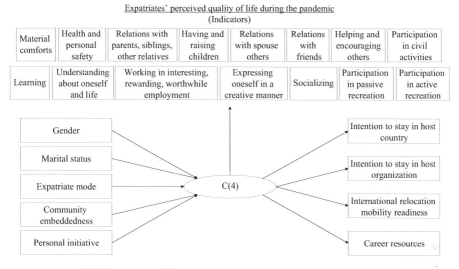

Fig. 23.1 Model illustration of 4-class LCA with covariates and distal outcomes

expatriates. Various sources indicate that the pandemic has triggered a desire among workers originating from abroad to return home (ILO, 2021b; Koveshnikov et al., 2022; Rosa González et al., 2022). The reasons varied widely, ranging from a lack of a secure job (ILO, 2021b) to concerns about family health in the host country (Chan et al., 2022) and in the home country (Rosa González et al., 2022). Nonetheless, it appears that the majority of expatriates opted to stay in their destination country during the crisis, claiming that it was safer and preferable for the continuity of their work and personal lives (Rosa González et al., 2022; Végh et al., 2022). Likewise, the intention to stay with the host organization was negatively related to expatriates' perceived non-work constraints during the pandemic (Chan et al., 2022). However, many expatriates indicated a desire to continue their employment during the pandemic, especially those living in less severely affected countries (Végh et al., 2022).

International Relocation Mobility Readiness

Another notable consequence is the readiness for international relocation mobility. An ILO survey (ILO, 2021b) shows that the number of migration plans among internationally relocated workers dropped from 60% to 23% in the first year of the pandemic. Ubiquitous and emerging forms of work, such as virtual and remote work, may lead to a decrease in the number of long- and short-term assignments, especially in the form of assigned expatriation (Mello & Tomei, 2021; Végh et al., 2022). The crisis has also changed the motivation of expatriates to move abroad (Végh et al., 2022). Health, safety, and security, which were considered relatively trivial before the outbreak of the pandemic, became more important among the motivations for global mobility (Végh et al., 2022). In contrast, motives such as new experiences and career development decreased in importance among the factors influencing mobility (Végh et al., 2022). The readiness to relocate during and after the pandemic seemed ambivalent for many expatriates, who feared uncertainty or preferred to work online (Mello & Tomei, 2021; Végh et al., 2022). For others, however, relocation and mobility were an indispensable part of their lives, so the COVID-19 pandemic acted as an accelerating factor in their relocation plans, especially after vaccines became widely available (Végh et al., 2022).

Career Resources

Expatriate careers in the midst of the pandemic are an overlooked area. Specifically, career resources, which include human capital, career management behaviors, and environmental and motivational resources, are essential for predicting the career success of expatriates in turbulent times (Hirschi et al., 2018). The pandemic was undoubtedly a peculiar circumstance for obtaining career resources. Due to the lockdown, expatriates reportedly lacked opportunities to enrich their human capital and effectively manage their career behaviors, such as attending language classes (Haist & Kurth, 2022), developing soft skills (e.g., communication), and networking (Schmidt, 2021). The uncertainty associated with the pandemic affected expatriates' confidence in developing and achieving career goals (i.e., motivational resources) (Végh et al., 2022) and deprived them of organizational support (i.e., environmental resources) (Bailey, 2021). However, the exacerbation only applied to a certain group of expatriates; various other cases showed improvement or invariance in the acquisition of career resources. For instance, the lockdown allowed these expatriates to focus on developing their career agency, as demonstrated by their participation in online self-development courses (Haist & Kurth, 2022). The strenuous situation during the pandemic challenged them to develop new skills, such as time management, multitasking, and technical skills (Schmidt, 2021).

In summary, the evidence on how the pandemic has influenced expatriates' core work outcomes is generally inconsistent, with some suggesting facilitation and others suggesting stability or deterioration. Thus, it is unlikely that the pandemic was consistently dampening expatriates' work outcomes, but rather that individual perceptions of quality of life during the pandemic, which vary across the population, are the influencing factors of such consequences. Therefore, it is necessary to obtain a classification of expatriates' individual experiences of their quality of life during the pandemic and, from there, determine the extent to which these personal perceptions differentiated work outcomes.

Factors Associated with Expatriates' Quality of Life During the Pandemic

Gender

Female expatriates were among the most vulnerable groups during the pandemic (Shelef et al., 2022; UN Women, 2020). The literature illustrates that they are inherently disadvantaged in terms of possessing resources to cope with different types of crises, which is even more notable when they belong to minority groups such as expatriates (Shelef et al., 2022). During the crisis, they were at five times greater risk of job loss than male expatriates (ILO, 2021a). Their physical and mental health was also more at risk than men's during the crisis (Gama et al., 2022; Spiritus-Beerden et al., 2021). Intimate partner violence and sexual abuse against women increased during the epidemic (UN Women, 2020). Isolation and lockdown led to a surge in domestic violence, while physical and verbal attacks threatened female expatriates working in women-dominated occupations (e.g., health care and domestic care) (UN Women, 2020). Given these impediments to women, we expect *gender* to be a factor contributing to perceived quality of life in the pandemic.

Marital Status

Akin to that, marriage generally acts as a resource for coping with stressors (Williams et al., 2009). However, it is unclear whether and how it affected expatriates' quality of life during the pandemic. Recent literature suggests that family ties may have become stronger and facilitated their work life (Mello & Tomei, 2021). Staying with family also reduced feelings of loneliness during the lockdown and anxiety about ambivalence (Rosa González et al., 2022). However, for expatriates who stayed with family, the pandemic situation could have placed greater demands and depleted resources, for instance, in terms of work and household responsibilities (Végh et al., 2022). Isolation and lockdown similarly proved stressful for those who were separated or divorced, due to the distance from their children and concerns about their children's safety (Finell et al., 2021; Végh et al., 2022).

Expatriation Mode

Another factor that seemed to determine expatriates' experiences with the pandemic is their expatriation mode, that is, whether they were assigned expatriates (AEs) or self-initiated expatriates (SIEs). AEs tended to possess more resources, including job stability and organizational support, than SIEs during the crisis, which relieved them of financial and social threats. Research indicates that virtual assignments in lieu of travel may be attractive to many AEs who often endure work–life conflicts due to frequent business travel (Mello & Tomei, 2021; Végh et al., 2022). Flexible work has paved the way for AEs to strengthen ties with their family members (Mello & Tomei, 2021) and to manage their work more efficiently (Mello & Tomei, 2021; Schmidt, 2021). In contrast, SIEs are more likely than AEs to work in low-status occupations and were, therefore, faced with a higher likelihood of layoffs and precarious working conditions during the pandemic (Haist & Kurth, 2022). Border closures and lockdowns were overwhelming for them, as they prevented them from visiting their families (Haist & Kurth, 2022; Végh et al., 2022). The contrast in the resource pool thus implies a role of the expatriate mode in shaping the quality of life of expatriates during the pandemic.

Community Embeddedness

Further, the pandemic highlighted the crucial role of expatriates' community embeddedness in turbulent times, their enmeshment in the local community encompasses links (i.e., connections with people, figures, associations, etc.), fit (i.e., perceived compatibility with the local community), and sacrifice (i.e., anticipated losses from leaving their place of residence) (Mitchell et al., 2001). In the wake of the pandemic, connectedness to the local community, for example, in terms of access to government information and supportive authorities, was vital to avoid higher rates of contagion, actual infection, and excessive stress (Finell et al., 2021; Haist & Kurth, 2022; Kumar et al., 2021). Relationships with community members were fundamental to overcoming infectious diseases (e.g., checking in and buying food during quarantine)

(Finell et al., 2021). Trust in local authorities also eased their worries about health and safety, not only for themselves but also for their families back home (Rosa González et al., 2022). In contrast, expatriates with loose enmeshment in the host community tended to suffer more from loneliness and anxiety (Haist & Kurth, 2022), as well as greater risks of illness, violence, and exploitation due to their inability to obtain necessary social support (Kumar et al., 2021; UN Women, 2020). Hence, the extent to which expatriates are connected to the host community can shape their quality of life in critical times.

Personal Initiative

While community embeddedness provides essential social resources, personal initiative represents expatriates' agency to overcome a crisis. Personal initiative refers to the behavioral tendency to take the initiative, be proactive, and overcome difficulties to achieve goals (Frese et al., 1997). Expatriates who possess this trait were likely to tackle problems despite the constraints of their circumstances, such as taking online self-development courses and finding new activities during the lockdown (Haist & Kurth, 2022). In other cases, proactivity was useful for forming collective action, such as helping others navigate bureaucracy and sharing preventative information (Finell et al., 2021). This helped to diminish unpleasant emotions such as hopelessness, reduce loneliness in isolation (Haist & Kurth, 2022), and strengthen ties to the local community (Finell et al., 2021). In the work context, the personal initiative was beneficial in overcoming technical challenges (e.g., the time lag in remote work) and creating ways to communicate more effectively in the virtual environment (Schmidt, 2021).

Overall, evidence suggests that gender, marital status, expatriate mode, community embeddedness, and personal initiative tended to be associated with expatriates' quality of life during the pandemic. It is unclear whether these factors diversified expatriates' perception of their quality of life during the crisis from a person-centered perspective.

Methods

An Overview of Latent Class Analysis

We employed the latent class analysis (LCA) using the maximum likelihood (ML) three-step procedure (Asparouhov & Muthén, 2014; Vermunt, 2010). This method relaxes the linear assumption in relationships between the pandemic's impacts on quality of life with predictors and outcomes, which typically requires a mediation model and regression analysis in a variable-centered approach (Meyer & Morin, 2016). This person-centered method, by contrast, focuses on identifying personalized experiences of expatriates (i.e., latent classes), which allows further exploration of factors explaining the emergence of classes (i.e., covariates or predictors), as well as the difference between classes in terms of consequences (i.e., distal outcomes) (Nylund-Gibson et al., 2019; Vermunt, 2010). In our research model (Fig. 23.1), the latent classes emerged from expatriates' perceived quality of life in the pandemic, which was associated with gender, marital status, expatriate mode, community embeddedness, and personal initiative. At the same time, expatriates in different classes demonstrated different levels of intention to stay, international mobility relocation readiness, and career resources.

The analysis procedure entailed the following steps. First, we identified a latent class model using class indicators (i.e., perceived changes in quality-of-life facets during the pandemic). Then, in Step 2, we computed a pseudo-class with a latent class posterior distribution to fix misclassification errors. In Step 3, by applying multinomial regression and Chi-square tests, we investigated the association between error-controlled classes, as well as covariates (i.e., predictors of classes). We also examined the mean differences between classes as to the work outcome variables using the Wald test (Nylund-Gibson et al., 2019).

Data Collection and Sample

Our quantitative cross-sectional data consists of employed expatriates living and working in the United Kingdom, France, and Germany during the first wave of the pandemic (July to November 2020). We disseminated a recruitment call in a Consumer Panel, Prolific, and Facebook groups for expatriates. A total of 2860 individuals from these sources accessed our invitation link, of whom 921 were eligible and completed the online survey. We examined the quality of the responses by employing indicators such as consistency between answers, response time, and outliers, to remove 214 careless answers (Meade & Craig, 2012), resulting in a response rate of 24.7%.

Our sample (41.3% men, 58.7% women) encompassed 707 employed expatriates originating from 98 countries who resided in France (11.9%), Germany (25.6%), and the United Kingdom (62.5%). The majority were highly qualified, with 38% having a bachelor's degree, 36.4% a master's degree, and 6.8% a doctorate. The remainder completed secondary education or lower (8.2%) or post-secondary non-tertiary or short-cycle tertiary degrees (10.6%). As to marital status, 43.4% of the respondents were married, 33.1% were living in a partnership, 21.4% were single, and 2.1% were separated or divorced. Our sample consisted of 9.1% AEs (i.e., those who were relocated abroad by their employer) and 91.1% SIEs (i.e., those who relocated abroad on their own initiative).

Measures

Quality of Life Scale

We adapted the *Quality of Life* Scale (Flanagan, 1982) to measure expatriates' perceived impact of the pandemic on their life quality. At the time of data collection, a scale ranging from 1 ("highly negative") to 7 ("highly positive"), with a midpoint of 4 denoting no perceived influence ("neither negative nor positive"), was used to ask the participants to rate the impact of the COVID-19 pandemic on several aspects of their quality of life. The scale encompassed 15 items, each describing an aspect of quality of life (Flanagan, 1982). Sample items were "A. Material comfort—things like a desirable home, good food, possessions, convenience, an increasing income, and security for the future" and "E. Close relationship with a husband/wife/a life partner". The instrument obtained desirable reliability ($\omega = 0.91$) (Hayes & Coutts, 2020).

Scales to Measure Expatriates' Work Outcomes

Intention to stay: We measured intention to stay *in the employer organization* using the 5-item scale developed by Price and Mueller (1986) ($\omega = 0.89$). Sample items included "I plan to stay in this company as long as possible" and "I plan to leave this company as soon as possible" (reverse code). To measure the intention to stay *in the host country*, we applied the mobility scale from the Employment Opportunity Index developed and validated by Griffeth et al.

(2005). The instrument encompasses three items, for instance, "I am unable to move to another country now even if a job came along". All the items were rated from 1 ("strongly disagree") to 5 ("strongly agree"). The reliability test of the scale yielded a satisfactory result (ω = 0.73).

International relocation mobility readiness: We employed a translated version of the German scale for measuring international relocation mobility readiness (Dalbert, 1999; Otto, 2004). The questionnaire contained 13 items, which were ranked from 1 ("strongly disagree") to 5 ("strongly agree"). A sample item reads, "There are many places in the world where I could imagine living and working". Testing of internal consistency yielded a desirable result (ω = 0.85).

Career resources: To measure career resources, we used the Career Resources Questionnaire developed by Hirschi et al. (2018). Specifically, we included occupational expertise, soft skills, job challenges, and career confidence subscales. The instrument consists of 13 items rated on a scale from 1 ("not true at all") to 5 ("completely true") and obtained good internal consistency (ω = 0.91).

Scales to Measure Factors Associated with Expatriates' Quality of Life

Gender: Codes for the gender of participants were 1 ("male") and 2 ("female").

Marital status: Participants had the following options to describe their marital status: 1 ("married"), 2 ("in partnership"), 3 ("single"), 4 ("separated"), 5 ("divorced"), and 6 ("widowed"). In the survey, no participant chose option 6 ("widowed"), so it was removed from further analysis.

Expatriation mode: We asked participants whether they were sent to work abroad by their employer, in order to determine their expatriate mode as AE (1 - "yes") or SIE (2 - "no").

Community embeddedness: To measure community embeddedness, we employed the original scale and revised two items about links to fit the internationally relocating population (Mitchell et al., 2001; Tharenou & Caulfield, 2010). An example of a revised item is "Do you have any relatives living in the country where you now live?" and "How many children are currently living with you?" Most items measuring links have dichotomous options ("yes" or "no") or require manual entry of numbers (i.e., number of friends and children). Sample items for the "fit" and "sacrifice" dimensions read "I really love the place where I live" and "Leaving this community would be very hard". These items are rated on a Likert scale from 1 ("strongly disagree") to 5 ("strongly agree"). The instruments demonstrated an acceptable internal consistency ($\omega = 0.75$).

Personal initiative: We employed the scale developed by Frese et al. (1997) ($\omega = 0.84$) to measure the personal initiative of expatriates. The scale consists of seven items, which are rated on a scale from 1 ("hardly ever or never") to 5 ("very often or always"). An example of an item included is "I actively attack problems".

Results

Latent Class Analysis

Table 23.1 illustrates the results of the LCA. We scrutinized the following fit indices to determine the best-fit model: Akaike's information criterion (AIC) (Akaike, 1987), Bayesian information criterion (BIC) (Schwarz, 1978), sample size adjusted BIC (ABIC) (Sclove, 1987), entropy values (Celeux & Soromenho, 1996), and the Lo-Mendell-Rubin likelihood ratio test (LMR LRT) (Lo et al., 2001). LMR LRT yielded a significant result for the 2-class model, proving that the impact of the pandemic on expatriates' quality of life was likely to be diverse. The four-class model was, thus, confirmed by a comparison of the fit criteria. Therefore, we can statistically classify the impact of the pandemic on expatriates' quality of life into four distinguishable patterns.

Figure 23.2 demonstrates differences between the classes explained by the means of the pandemic's impact on expatriates' quality of life facets. The first class (12.4%) indicated significant "negative" impacts, especially on health and personal safety; relationships with parents, siblings, and other relatives; relationships with close friends; helping and encouraging others; participating in civil activities; learning; and participation in active recreation. Moreover, this class showed a strong deterioration in socializing and a slightly negative impact on other facets, such as material comfort, having and raising children,

Table 23.1 Latent class analysis results

Fit indices	1-class model	2-class model	3-class model	4-class model
AIC	38248.892	35610.769	34829.125	**34496.26**
BIC	38385.723	35820.576	35111.909	**34852.027**
Adjusted BIC	38290.466	35674.516	34915.045	**34604.359**
Entropy		**0.920**	0.877	0.884
LMR LRT		$p < 0.001$	**$p < 0.05$**	$p = 0.07$

Note: The most preferable model for each of the fit indices was marked as bold

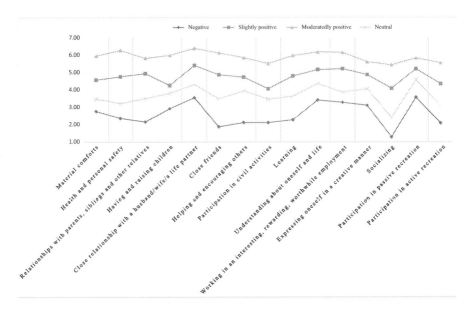

Fig. 23.2 Illustration of latent classes based on the experienced quality of life. *Note:* Scale ranging from 1 ("highly negative") to 7 ("highly positive") and a midpoint of 4 indicating no perceived impact ("neither negative nor positive")

close relationship with life partner, an understanding of self and life, working in interesting, rewarding, and worthwhile employment, creativity, and participation in passive recreation. In contrast, the second class (26.3%) showed a "slightly positive" effect of the pandemic on all variables affecting the quality of life, excluding socializing. A notable improvement in the quality of life emerged in class three (9.1%), in which expatriates experienced "moderately positive" impacts on all quality-of-life facets, especially health and personal safety, close relationships with a life partner, close friends, understanding about oneself and life, and working in interesting, rewarding, and worthwhile employment. The last class accounted for the majority of the population (52.2%) and represented relatively "neutral" influences of the pandemic on expatriates' quality of life. Individuals in this class perceived slightly negative impacts on health and personal safety, as well as on socializing. Other facets of their quality of life, however, held steady during the pandemic.

In summary, the pandemic generally did not significantly affect the quality of life of the majority of expatriates. A quarter of our sample even perceived the pandemic as slightly positive for their life quality and, most interestingly, a minority reported notably ameliorated living during the pandemic. Nevertheless, one-fifth of the expatriate population experienced a deterioration in the quality of their lives.

Relationships Between Classes of Expatriates' Quality of Life and Distant Work Outcomes

Given the evidence of the variety of impacts of the pandemic on expatriates' quality of life, we proceeded further to examine whether their experiences affected work outcomes. Figure 23.3 illustrates a summary of these findings.

Pairwise Wald test revealed that intention to stay in the organization was significantly different within each pair of all classes ($p < .001$). Specifically, intention to stay in the organization was lowest among those who experienced "*negative*" impacts of the pandemic ($M = 2.27$, $SD = 3.94$), followed by those in "*slightly positive*" ($M = 2.98$, $SD = 3.00$) and "*neutral*" ($M = 3.50$, $SD = 2.15$) classes, and comparably highest in the "*moderately positive*" classes ($M = 4.04$, $SD = 3.62$).

The test on intention to stay in the host country showed striking differences between expatriates who experienced "*moderately positive*" impacts ($M =$

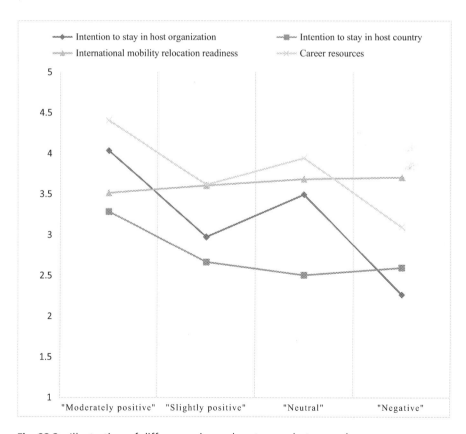

Fig. 23.3 Illustration of differences in work outcomes between classes

3.29, $SD = 4.12$) and all other classes, including those perceived "*slightly positive*" ($M = 2.67$, $SD = 2.52$) ($p < 0.01$), "*neutral*" ($M = 2.51$, $SD = 1.89$) ($p < 0.001$), and "*negative*" influences of the crisis ($M = 2.60$, $SD = 3.56$) ($p < 0.01$). However, the intention to remain in the host country did not differ significantly between the latter three classes.

In terms of international relocation mobility readiness, results revealed that expatriates with "*moderately positive*" experiences during the pandemic showed the least preparedness to relocate ($M = 3.52$, $SD = 1.94$). This result distinguished them from those who perceived "*negative*" ($M = 3.71$, $SD = 1.89$) ($p < 0.10$) and "*neutral*" ($M = 3.69$, $SD = 1.22$) ($p < 0.10$) impacts, but not those with "*slightly positive*" perception ($M = 3.61$, $SD = 1.49$). These latter three classes—encompassing expatriates whose impact of the pandemic was "*negative*", "*neutral*", and "*slightly positive*"—demonstrated no significant differences in international relocation mobility readiness.

Finally, the mean values of career resources were strikingly different within each pair of classes ($p < 0.001$). Expatriates who perceived the "*moderately positive*" effects of the pandemic scored highest on career resources ($M = 4.41$, $SD = 1.86$), far above those who perceived "*neutral*" ($M = 3.95$, $SD = 1.12$), "*slightly positive*" ($M = 3.62$, $SD = 1.57$), and "*negative*" influences ($M = 3.10$, $SD = 3.40$) of the crisis.

Relationships Between Factors and Classes of Expatriates' Quality of Life

In the last step, we explored the role of protective and harmful factors on expatriates' quality of life in the midst of the pandemic (see Table 23.2).

Table 23.2 Summary of the relationship between classes and covariates (predictors)

	Covariates								
		Marital status					Expatriate	Community	Personal
Class	Gender	(1)	(2)	(3)	(4)	(5)	mode	embeddedness	initiative
"Moderately positive"	n.s.	+	–	–	–	–	–	+++	+++
"Slightly positive"	n.s.	–	–	+	+	–	–	+	+
"Neutral"	–		–	+	+	+	+	++	++
"Negative"	+		–	–	–	–	+	n.s	–	–

Notes: Gender: 1 ("male") and 2 ("female"); *Marital status*: 1 ("married"), 2 ("in partnership"), 3 ("single"), 4 ("separated"), 5 ("divorced"); *Expatriation mode*: AE (1 - "yes") or SIE (2 - "no")

The Chi-square test revealed that females were more likely than males to experience "*negative*" influences of the pandemic on quality of life, $\chi^2(3, N = 707) = 6.93$, $p = 0.07$, $p < 0.10$. Only 9% of the men perceived negative effects of the pandemic, compared to 14.7% of women. In contrast, males' quality of life after the pandemic was more likely to remain "*neutral*" (57.2%) compared with that before the outbreak, a perception that was less prevalent among females (48.7%).

Pertaining to other parameters, the data demonstrated a strong correlation between marital status and the standard of living among the expatriates during the pandemic, $\chi2(12, N = 707) = 32.74$, $p < 0.01$. Specifically, 14.5% of married expatriates reported "*moderately positive*" impacts of the pandemic, whereas this number was only 7.3% among those living in a partnership, 1.3% of single, and 0% of separated and divorced expatriates. Being married was also associated with a lower probability of perceiving the impacts of this crisis as "*neutral*". Only 46.3% of them perceived no change as a result of the pandemic, whereas the numbers were much higher among those who were single (55%), living with their partner (57.7%), separated (66.7%), and divorced (55.6%). Divorced participants had the highest risk of exacerbation, with 22.2% of them claiming "*negative*" impacts of the pandemic on their quality of life, compared with 14.3%, 10.7%, 11.3%, and 0% for those who were married, partnered, single, and separated, respectively. The "*slightly positive*" impact of the pandemic on life quality was strongest among single (32.5%) and separated (33.3%) expatriates. Only 24.8% of married participants, 24.4% of those living in a partnership, and 22.2% of divorced people reported the same experiences.

The results further provide evidence on the role of expatriation mode on expatriates' quality of life during the pandemic, $\chi2(3, N = 707) = 10.07$, $p < 0.05$. AEs were more likely than SIEs to view their quality of life as either "*moderately positive*" (15.2% versus 8.4%) or "*slightly positive*" (36.4% versus 25.3%). In contrast, the pandemic changed the lives of SIEs less than AEs, with 54% of SIEs reporting a "*neutral*" impact on quality of life, while only 34.8% of AEs had the same perception.

Community embeddedness appeared to be a significant resource for expatriates' quality of life during the epidemic. One increase in the unit in community embeddedness resulted in 6.08 more odds of experiencing "*moderately positive*" than "*negative*" influences of the pandemic (Odds Ratio [OR] = 6.08, 95% Confidence Interval [CI] (2.79, 13.26), $p < 0.001$), 3.58 more odds to perceive "*moderately positive*" than "*slightly positive*" experiences (OR = 3.58, 95% CI (1.90, 6.76), $p < 0.001$), and 6.89 times more chances to perceive "*moderately positive*" than "*neutral*" impacts (OR = 6.89, 95% CI

(3.77, 12.5), $p < 0.001$) of the pandemic. Akin to that, as community immersion was raised by one unit, the probability of experiencing "*neutral*" impact increased by 1.91 times compared to perceiving a "*slightly positive*" experience (OR = 1.91, 95% CI (1.32, 2.79), $p < 0.01$).

Lastly, personal initiative appeared to be a strong resource for expatriates to cope with the pandemic. As personal initiative increased by one unit, the odds of being in a "*moderately positive*" class increased by 41.14 times compared to enduring "*negative*" influences (OR = 41.14, 95% CI (14.23, 118.92), $p < 0.001$), by 12.05 times compared to obtain "*neutral*" perception (OR = 12.05, 95% CI (5.23, 27.78), $p < 0.001$), and by 18.96 times compared to perceiving "*slightly positive*" impacts (OR = 18.96, 95% CI (8.38, 42.89), $p < 0.001$). Higher levels of proactivity and persistence similarly resulted in a higher probability of being "*neutral*" in the pandemic compared to experiencing "*negative*" influences (OR = 3.41, 95% CI (1.68, 6.94), $p < 0.01$) and a "*slightly positive*" perception (OR = 1.57, 95% CI (1.01, 2.45), $p < 0.05$). Likewise, those with higher levels of initiative possessed a greater chance of perceiving "*slightly positive*" than "*negative*" changes in quality of life (OR = 2.17, 95% CI (1.12, 4.20), $p < 0.05$).

The results shed light on how the pandemic shaped expatriates' quality of life, as well as their relationships with work outcomes and explanatory factors. In the following section, we elaborate on the implications of the study results and provide recommendations for practices to support expatriates during and after the pandemic.

Discussion

Contrary to previous studies that used a variable-centered approach, we clearly illustrated that the pandemic did not affect expatriates uniformly. This finding is reflected in our opening quote, "Only when the tide goes out do you discover who's been swimming naked", in that some were equipped with significantly more resources than others ("with a bathing suit or without", so to speak). The results of the data analysis revealed that the pandemic influenced expatriates' quality of life in four ways: "*negative*", "*slightly positive*", "*moderately positive*", and "*neutral*". Each class differed from the others in terms of their work outcomes, and most interestingly, the group that perceived a positive impact on their quality of life did not consistently show positive work consequences.

The expatriates who perceived "*moderately positive*" experiences notably reported additional positive outcomes, such as a greater willingness to stay and enrichment of their career resources. At the same time, this amelioration reduced their readiness to be internationally mobile. The analysis shows that being married, being an AE, having fewer previous mobility experiences, being tightly connected with the host community, and having high levels of initiative and persistence increased the chances of perceiving "*moderately positive*" benefits during the pandemic. Expatriates' embeddedness with the host-country environment serves as a personal resource that can facilitate coping with country-related challenges and motivate them to stay on the assignment (Andresen, 2015). Thus, these conditions were reliable resources for expatriates to tackle challenges in such turbulent times.

In contrast, expatriates who experienced "*negative*" influences of the pandemic significantly reduced their intention to stay and reported a decline in career resources. The pandemic represented a high-demand situation for them that occasioned physiological or psychological costs and, thus, resource loss (cf. Hobfoll et al., 2018). Consequently, this aggravation increased their international relocation mobility readiness; leaving the current employer and country of residence would allow expatriates to withdraw entirely from the stressful situation in the host country to halt the resource loss spiral and regain resources elsewhere (cf. Hobfoll et al., 2018). This experience was more prevalent among females, divorced expatriates, those with low community embeddedness, and those with low personal initiative. Thus, it is likely that these expatriates had insufficient resources to cope with the crisis, which called for further support from organizations and societies.

We found that the majority of expatriates perceived the impact of the pandemic on their quality of life as "*neutral*", except for their health and personal safety. Their work outcomes, including their intention to stay and their career resources, were generally less favorable than those who perceived "*moderately positive*" changes, but better than those who had a "*negative*" experience and even those with a "*slightly positive*" perception. The crisis encouraged their tendency to pursue international relocation mobility, in contrast to expatriates who enjoyed "*moderately positive*" benefits. Further analysis pointed out that men, unmarried individuals, SIEs, and those with average connections to the host society and average personal initiative were representative of this group.

Lastly, it is interesting to note that expatriates who had "*slightly positive*" experiences during the pandemic did not benefit at work as much as those who perceived "*moderately positive*" impacts, and their work outcomes were far inferior to those whose lifestyles remained "*neutral*". We presume that the explanatory factors in this class are responsible for this result. We found that such an experience is associated with being single, living independently, having relatively low levels of community embeddedness, and having low levels of personal initiative. It has long been known that families play a crucial role in expatriate success (Schütter & Boerner, 2013) by transferring resources to the expatriate. If individuals lack these additional family resources, the expatriate might be less willing to stay abroad (Zimmerman & Darnold, 2009). Thus, although expatriates in this group believed that their quality of life improved during the pandemic, their propensity and ability to use these resources for work outcomes were limited.

Given this, it is positive in terms of work consequences if expatriates can achieve an improvement or at least stabilization of their quality of life during a crisis. Mello and Tomei (2021) showed that the use of flexible work arrangements has a significant effect on the quality of life by making expatriates' work and private lives much easier. It is worth noting that some factors of quality of life actually improved under pandemic conditions, such as health and personal safety or understanding of oneself and life, which may have previously received little attention from many expatriates and organizations (Rosa González et al., 2022; Végh et al., 2022). This could be a call for organizations to exert further efforts to promote these quality-of-life factors, also under non-pandemic conditions, for example, through the provision of medical services, psychological counseling, sports activities, or meditation practices.

There is a need to provide aid to vulnerable expatriates such as women, divorcees, people with less community embeddedness (e.g., newcomers), and those with less initiative and persistence. Key impairments in their lives include insecurity and health impairments, a lack of close friendships, and limited opportunities to learn, socialize, participate in civil activities, and actively recreate (e.g., travel). During the pandemic, meeting these needs presented challenges for both individuals and organizations. Therefore, in similar crises, organizations can alternatively offer their expatriates interactive events and online communication to reduce uncertainty and mitigate loneliness (Schmidt, 2021). They can also equip expatriates with skills to manage virtual and remote work more efficiently, such as technical expertise, time management, and online communication (Schmidt, 2021). Virtual environments can also be used for learning activities, which proved beneficial for several expatriates during the pandemic (Rosa González et al., 2022). For those whose host country language is deficient, it may be beneficial to disseminate preventive information and provide them with an interpreter when needed (e.g., when communicating with health authorities) (cf. Kumar et al., 2021). Lastly, employers should maintain close contact with female expatriates during a crisis, such as the pandemic, and provide them with information and access to sources of protection (e.g., women's associations, family offices, police, etc.).

On the one hand, the pandemic posed a challenge for many organizations and expatriates. On the other hand, it stimulated some reflections on future Human Resource Management practices for expatriates. For instance, for AEs and married expatriates, transitioning back to the pre-pandemic state may be challenging since they had a positive experience with the altered working arrangements implemented during the pandemic. Many would prefer to introduce more virtual assignments instead of physical ones (Mello & Tomei, 2021; Schmidt, 2021; Végh et al., 2022). In line with that, they may exhibit less motivation to take on long-term assignments (Mello & Tomei, 2021) and require further guarantees of health care and the safety of their families (Végh et al., 2022). Organizations, thus, may need to reposition their global mobility activities by shifting to more virtual work and assignments and advancing their digitalization even after the pandemic. Likewise, the pandemic has shed light on expatriates' needs for personal growth, self-awareness, and self-actualization, which may require the attention of organizations during the post-crisis phase.

Limitations and Directions for Future Research

Our study has some limitations that may impede the interpretation of the research results. First, the small proportion of AEs in our sample may alter the percentage of latent classes. To confirm our findings, further quantitative research with a larger proportion of AEs is necessary. Second, we conducted this study by employing a sample located across three European countries. The results of the study, therefore, can differ depending on the region. For instance, empirical evidence suggests that expatriates consider their quality of life to be more stable in countries with less stringent regulations (Végh et al., 2022). Similarly, how the host country's government managed the crisis (pandemic), as well as the host country nationals' sentiments, can significantly affect expatriates' perceptions of their lives (Finell et al., 2021; Végh et al., 2022). Lastly, we employed cross-sectional data for the analysis, hence limiting the causality interference of the results. Future research should, therefore, replicate our model with longitudinal data. Furthermore, it is insightful to explore the long-term effects of the pandemic, such as whether the experience of the pandemic influences expatriates' career changes.

Conclusion

In terms of the impact of the pandemic on quality of life, expatriates could be categorized into four main groups: "negative", "slightly positive", "moderately positive", and "neutral" experience. The categorization was also associated with various conditions such as gender, marital status, relocation experiences, community embeddedness, and personal initiative. The respective quality of life experience is a crucial factor that determines expatriates' intention to stay in the host country and with the employing organization, their international relocation mobility readiness, and their career resources.

Acknowledgments This research has received funding from the European Union's H2020 research and innovation program under the Marie Skłodowska-Curie grant agreement no. 765355.

References

Akaike, H. (1987). Factor analysis and AIC. *Psychometrika, 52*(3), 317–332. https://doi.org/10.1007/BF02294359

Andresen, M. (2015). What determines expatriates' performance while abroad? The role of job embeddedness. *Journal of Global Mobility: The Home of Expatriate Management Research, 3*(1), 62–82. https://doi.org/10.1108/JGM-06-2014-0015

Andresen, M., Bergdolt, F., Margenfeld, J., & Dickmann, M. (2014). Addressing international mobility confusion – Developing definitions and differentiations for self-initiated and assigned expatriates as well as migrants. *The International Journal of Human Resource Management, 25*(16), 2295–2318. https://doi.org/10.1080/09585192.2013.877058

Asparouhov, T., & Muthén, B. (2014). Auxiliary variables in mixture modeling: Three-step approaches using M plus. *Structural Equation Modeling: A Multidisciplinary Journal, 21*(3), 329–341. https://doi.org/10.1080/10705511.2014.915181

Bailey, L. (2021). International school teachers: Precarity during the COVID-19 pandemic. *Journal of Global Mobility: The Home of Expatriate Management Research, 9*(1), 31–43. https://doi.org/10.1108/JGM-06-2020-0039

Celeux, G., & Soromenho, G. (1996). An entropy criterion for assessing the number of clusters in a mixture model. *Journal of Classification, 13*(2), 195–212. https://doi.org/10.1007/BF01246098

Chan, H. L., Zawawi, D., Toh, P. S., & Emily Gunn, S. M. (2022). Exploring perceived organisational support and resilience as antecedents of expatriates' work and non-work spheres amid the Covid-19 pandemic. *International Journal of Business & Society, 23*(2), 967–986. https://doi.org/10.33736/ijbs.4853.2022

Dalbert, C. (1999). *Mobilitätsbereitschaften (MOB-BG)* [Unpublished data]. Martin-Luther-Universität Halle-Wittenberg, Halle-Wittenberg.

European Commission. (2020). *A vulnerable workforce: Migrant workers in the COVID 19 pandemic*. Publications Office. https://doi.org/10.2760/316665

Finell, E., Tiilikainen, M., Jasinskaja-Lahti, I., Hasan, N., & Muthana, F. (2021). Lived experience related to the COVID-19 pandemic among Arabic-, Russian- and Somali-speaking migrants in Finland. *International Journal of Environmental Research and Public Health, 18*(5). https://doi.org/10.3390/ijerph18052601

Flanagan, J. C. (1982). Measurement of quality of life: Current state of the art. *Archives of Physical Medicine and Rehabilitation, 63*(2), 56–59.

Frese, M., Fay, D., Hilburger, T., Leng, K., & Tag, A. (1997). The concept of personal initiative: Operationalization, reliability and validity in two German samples. *Journal of Occupational and Organizational Psychology, 70*(2), 139–161. https://doi.org/10.1111/j.2044-8325.1997.tb00639.x

Gama, A., Rocha, J. V., Marques, M. J., Azeredo-Lopes, S., Pedro, A. R., & Dias, S. (2022). How did the COVID-19 pandemic affect migrant populations in Lisbon, Portugal? A study on perceived effects on health and economic condition. *International Journal of Environmental Research and Public Health, 19*(3). https://doi.org/10.3390/ijerph19031786

Global Migration Data Portal. (2022). *Migration data relevant for the COVID-19 pandemic*. Accessed from https://www.migrationdataportal.org/themes/migration-data-relevant-covid-19-pandemic

Griffeth, R. W., Steel, R. P., Allen, D. G., & Bryan, N. (2005). The development of a multidimensional measure of job market cognitions: The employment opportunity index (EOI). *The Journal of Applied Psychology, 90*(2), 335–349. https://doi.org/10.1037/0021-9010.90.2.335

Haist, J., & Kurth, P. (2022). How do low-status expatriates deal with crises? Stress, external support and personal coping strategies during the COVID-19 pandemic. *Journal of Global Mobility, 10*(2), 209–225. https://doi.org/10.1108/JGM-03-2021-0039

Hall, B. J., Zhao, P., Xiong, M. Z., Latkin, C., Yang, B., & Wang, C. (2021). Exploring correlates of depression, quality of life and alcohol misuse: A nationwide cross-sectional study of international migrants during the COVID-19 epidemic in China. *BMJ Open, 11*(3), e048012. https://doi.org/10.1136/bmjopen-2020-048012

Hayes, A. F., & Coutts, J. J. (2020). Use omega rather than Cronbach's alpha for estimating reliability. But…. *Communication Methods and Measures, 14*(1), 1–24. https://doi.org/10.1080/19312458.2020.1718629

Hayward, S. E., Deal, A., Cheng, C., Crawshaw, A., Orcutt, M., Vandrevala, T. F., Norredam, M., Carballo, M., Ciftci, Y., Requena-Méndez, A., Greenaway, C., Carter, J., Knights, F., Mehrotra, A., Seedat, F., Bozorgmehr, K., Veizis, A., Campos-Matos, I., Wurie, F., et al. (2021). Clinical outcomes and risk factors for COVID-19 among migrant populations in high-income countries: A systematic review. *Journal of Migration and Health, 3*, 100041. https://doi.org/10.1016/j.jmh.2021.100041

Hirschi, A., Nagy, N., Baumeler, F., Johnston, C. S., & Spurk, D. (2018). Assessing key predictors of career success. *Journal of Career Assessment, 26*(2), 338–358. https://doi.org/10.1177/1069072717695584

Hobfoll, S. E. (1989). Conservation of resources: A new attempt at conceptualizing stress. *American Psychologist, 44*(3), 513–524. https://doi.org/10.1037/0003-066X.44.3.513

Hobfoll, S. E., Halbesleben, J., Neveu, J.-P., & Westman, M. (2018). Conservation of resources in the organizational context: The reality of resources and their consequences. *Annual Review of Organizational Psychology and Organizational Behavior, 5*(1), 103–128. https://doi.org/10.1146/annurev-orgpsych-032117-104640

ILO. (2021a). *ILO monitor: COVID-19 and the world of work* (7th edn). International Labour Organisation (ILO). Accessed from https://www.ilo.org/global/topics/coronavirus/impacts-and-responses/WCMS_767028/lang%2D%2Den/index.htm

ILO. (2021b). *Locked down and in Limbo: The global impact of COVID-19 on migrant worker rights and recruitment*. International Labour Organisation (ILO).

Koveshnikov, A., Lehtonen, M. J., & Wechtler, H. (2022). Expatriates on the run: The psychological effects of the COVID-19 pandemic on expatriates' host country withdrawal intentions. *International Business Review (Oxford, England), 31*(6), 102009. https://doi.org/10.1016/j.ibusrev.2022.102009

Kowal, M., Coll-Martín, T., Ikizer, G., Rasmussen, J., Eichel, K., Studzińska, A., Koszałkowska, K., Karwowski, M., Najmussaqib, A., Pankowski, D., Lieberoth, A., & Ahmed, O. (2020). Who is the most stressed during the COVID-19 pandemic? Data from 26 countries and areas. *Applied Psychology: Health and Well-Being, 12*(4), 946–966. https://doi.org/10.1111/aphw.12234

Kumar, B. N., Hargreaves, S., Agyemang, C., James, R. A., Blanchet, K., & Gruer, L. (2021). Reducing the impact of the coronavirus on disadvantaged migrants and ethnic minorities. *European Journal of Public Health, 31*(Suppl 4), iv9–iv13. https://doi.org/10.1093/eurpub/ckab151

Lo, Y., Mendell, N., & Rubin, D. (2001). Testing the number of components in a normal mixture. *Biometrika, 88*(3), 767–778. https://doi.org/10.1093/biomet/88.3.767

Meade, A. W., & Craig, S. B. (2012). Identifying careless responses in survey data. *Psychological Methods, 17*(3), 437–455. https://doi.org/10.1037/a0028085

Mello, S. F., & Tomei, P. A. (2021). The impact of the COVID-19 pandemic on expatriates: A pathway to work-life harmony? *Global Business & Organizational Excellence, 40*(5), 6–22. https://doi.org/10.1002/joe.22088

Meyer, J. P., & Morin, A. J. (2016). A person-centered approach to commitment research: Theory, research, and methodology. *Journal of Organizational Behavior, 37*(4), 584–612. https://doi.org/10.1002/job.2085

Mitchell, T. R., Holtom, B. C., Lee, T. W., Sablynski, C. J., & Erez, M. (2001). Why people stay: Using job embeddedness to predict voluntary turnover. *Academy of Management Journal, 44*(6), 1102–1121. https://doi.org/10.2307/3069391

Nylund-Gibson, K., Grimm, R. P., & Masyn, K. E. (2019). Prediction from latent classes: A demonstration of different approaches to include distal outcomes in mixture models. *Structural Equation Modeling: A Multidisciplinary Journal, 26*(6), 967–985. https://doi.org/10.1080/10705511.2019.1590146

Otto, K. (2004). *Geografische und berufliche Mobilitätsbereitschaft im Berufsverlauf: Der Einfluss von Persönlichkeit, sozialem Umfeld und Arbeitssituation* [Dissertation]. Martin-Luther-Universität Halle-Wittenberg, Halle-Wittenberg.

Price, J. L., & Mueller, C. W. (1986). *Handbook of organizational measurement*. Pitman.

Rosa González, J. M., Barker, M., & Shah, D. (2022). COVID-19 and self-initiated expatriate health workers: Spanish nurses in Germany. *Journal of Global Mobility, 10*(2), 242–264. https://doi.org/10.1108/JGM-03-2021-0028

Sahoo, A., Xechung, N. L., Mostafiz, M. I., & Krishnaswamy, J. (2022). Perceived risk and sensitivity and their influence on expatriate performance during the COVID-19 pandemic. *Global Business & Organizational Excellence, 41*(4), 68–84. https://doi.org/10.1002/joe.22152

Schmidt, S. L. (2021). *The development of career capital through international consulting work: A German case study during the COVID-19 pandemic* [Vaasa, Finland]. osuva.uwasa.fi. Accessed from https://osuva.uwasa.fi/handle/10024/12773

Schütter, H., & Boerner, S. (2013). Illuminating the work-family interface on international assignments. *Journal of Global Mobility: The Home of Expatriate Management Research, 1*(1), 46–71. https://doi.org/10.1108/JGM-09-2012-0012

Schwarz, G. (1978). Estimating the dimension of a model. *The Annals of Statistics, 6*(2), 461–464. https://doi.org/10.1214/aos/1176344136

Sclove, S. L. (1987). Application of model-selection criteria to some problems in multivariate analysis. *Psychometrika, 52*(3), 333–343. https://doi.org/10.1007/BF02294360

Shelef, L., Schiff, M., Pat-Horenczyk, R., & Dekel, R. (2022). Covid-19 vs. terrorism: Contribution of the COR theory to the process of coping with invisible threats. *Journal of Psychiatric Research, 147*, 176–182. https://doi.org/10.1016/j.jpsychires.2022.01.023

Solà-Sales, S., Pérez-González, N., van Hoey, J., Iborra-Marmolejo, I., Beneyto-Arrojo, M. J., & Moret-Tatay, C. (2021). The role of resilience for migrants and refugees' mental health in times of COVID-19. *Healthcare (Basel), 9*(9). https://doi.org/10.3390/healthcare9091131

Spiritus-Beerden, E., Verelst, A., Devlieger, I., Langer Primdahl, N., Botelho Guedes, F., Chiarenza, A., de Maesschalck, S., Durbeej, N., Garrido, R., Gaspar de Matos, M., Ioannidi, E., Murphy, R., Oulahal, R., Osman, F., Padilla, B., Paloma, V., Shehadeh, A., Sturm, G., van den Muijsenbergh, M., et al. (2021). Mental health of refugees and migrants during the COVID-19 pandemic: The role of experienced discrimination and daily stressors. *International Journal of Environmental Research and Public Health, 18*(12). https://doi.org/10.3390/ijerph18126354

Tharenou, P., & Caulfield, N. (2010). Will I stay or will I go? Explaining repatriation by self-initiated expatriates. *Academy of Management Journal, 53*(5), 1009–1028. https://doi.org/10.5465/amj.2010.54533183

UN Women. (2020). *Addressing the impacts of the COVID-19 pandemic on women migrant workers.* UN Women. Accessed from https://www.unwomen.org/en/digital-library/publications/2020/04/guidance-note-addressing-the-impacts-of-the-covid-19-pandemic-on-women-migrant-workers

Végh, J., Jenkins, J., & Claes, M.-T. (2022). "Should I stay or should I go?"—Why the future of global work may be less binary: Lessons on approaches to global crises from the experiences of expatriates during the COVID-19 pandemic. *Thunderbird International Business Review, 1,* 21. https://doi.org/10.1002/tie.22309

Vermunt, J. K. (2010). Latent class modeling with covariates: Two improved three-step approaches. *Political Analysis, 18*(4), 450–469. Accessed from http://www.jstor.org/stable/25792024

Williams, K., Frech, A., & Carlson, D. L. (2009). Marital status and mental health. In *A handbook for the study of mental health* (2nd ed., pp. 306–320). Cambridge University Press. https://doi.org/10.1017/cbo9780511984945.020

Zimmerman, R. D., & Darnold, T. C. (2009). The impact of job performance on employee turnover intentions and the voluntary turnover process. *Personnel Review, 38*(2), 142–158. https://doi.org/10.1108/00483480910931316

24

"Bringing It All Back Home": Capital Utilization of Irish Repatriates in the Irish SME Animation Industry

Adele Smith-Auchmuty and Edward O'Connor

Introduction

Situated within the context of the Irish animation industry, our study holistically unpacks the international transfer and utilization of various forms of capital by repatriated Irish self-initiated expatriates (SIEs). The context of our study features the highly globalized Irish animation industry, where small to medium enterprises (SMEs) dominate. The success of the Irish animation industry is built on having a strong network of connections, international and domestic, a 'membership of a group' (Bourdieu, 1986). Therefore, the Irish animation companies and their founders represent an under-researched example of Irish SIEs, as a 'novel' sector in Ireland, seen as a small growing successful industry operating in a limited domestic market with many push and pull factors.

This multi-level qualitative study applies Pierre Bourdieu's forms of capital (economic, cultural, and social) to unpack the capital utilization of repatriated SIEs. Bourdieu's forms of capital offer a relational explanation (Al Ariss & Syed, 2011) of how the repatriated SIEs utilize their capital in pursuit of a career and business in the Irish animation industry (Inkson & Myers, 2003; Inkson et al., 2015). While there is a growing literature on SIEs, this has tended to focus on the act and experience of expatriation, with little emphasis

---

A. Smith-Auchmuty (✉) • E. O'Connor
Maynooth University, Maynooth, Ireland
e-mail: Adele.SmithAuchmuty@mu.ie; Edward.OConnor@mu.ie

on repatriation (Ellis et al., 2020; Kraimer et al., 2016). Likewise, though international mobility studies emphasize the role of economic, social, and cultural capital in shaping SIEs' decisions and outcomes (Crowley-Henry et al., 2016; Zikic, 2015), the extant literature is not prolific on the capital utilization of repatriated SIEs (Inkson, 1997; Israel et al., 2019).

The following section details the theories utilized to unpack the interviewees' narratives, beginning with international mobility and SIEs, followed by an understanding of the different forms of capital utilized by SIEs.

Theoretical Background

International Mobility

The extant literature on international mobility contains a variety of terms for the different types of internationally mobile workers. However, despite the diversity of names, the literature tends to focus on three main forms of mobile worker when referring to the international mobilization of workers. These are Organization Assigned Expatriates (AEs), SIEs and (Skilled) Migrants. This study focuses on SIEs as its research population, with a concentration on their repatriation to their home country. This variety of terms has meant the difference between the different internationally mobile worker concepts is not always clear and several studies, such as Crowley-Henry et al. (2016), Andresen et al. (2014), and Cerdin and Selmer (2014), have drawn attention to several conceptual concerns.

Organization AEs (Alshahrani & Morley, 2015; Brewster & Scullion, 1997) are generally defined as employees who are sent by their home country organization on assignment to a foreign subsidiary, with the intention of repatriating to the home country base once the assignment is finished. AEs are provided with organizational support for the full duration of their expatriation and repatriation (Cerdin & Selmer, 2014). The fact that AEs have organizational support is a strong differentiating factor between AEs and the other two forms of mobile worker, SIEs and skilled migrants (Brewster et al., 2021). However, we do not have such a strong differentiating factor in the extant literature's treatment of SIEs and skilled migrants, with a blurring of the boundaries between SIEs (Al Ariss & Crowley-Henry, 2013) and skilled migrants (Brewster et al., 2021; Crowley-Henry et al., 2016).

Skilled migrants tend to be seen to be moving to developed countries from developing ones (Baruch et al., 2007), and tend to be portrayed in the extant literature as a lacking agency to advance their careers (Al Ariss et al., 2012), sometimes vulnerable (O'Connor & Crowley-Henry, 2020), disadvantaged and discriminated against (Cook et al., 2011). Migrants move to another country or region to better their material or social conditions and improve prospects for themselves and/or their families. They are generally deemed to settle in the host country for long periods or permanently, one aspect that supposedly differentiates them from SIEs. (Cerdin & Selmer, 2014).

SIEs (Jokinen et al., 2008; Suutari & Brewster, 2000) are individuals who choose, independent of any employer or organization, to go abroad for career, professional experience, travel or lifestyle reasons (Brewster et al., 2021; Doherty, 2013). The existing literature tends to present SIEs, when compared to the studies on skilled migration, as being more career agentic (Andresen et al., 2014; Suutari et al., 2017), and "endowed with agency" (Al Ariss et al., 2012, p. 94), possessing the ability to travel freely across national boundaries, and are assumed to have, and be in control of, an international career (Carr et al., 2005). However, not all SIE literature reflects this positive view, with several studies, such as Scurry et al. (2013) and O'Connor and Crowley-Henry (2020), finding evidence in SIE narratives of both positive and negative career opportunities and development, which were of an intricate and sometimes contradictory nature.

The SIE concept evolved from the Overseas Experience (OE) concept, which, in its original incarnation, was not a career-orientated concept. The concept originally was concerned with travel, exploration, and personal development, where the individual would "shuttle between jobs and between different areas or countries and… spend leisure and vacation time visiting new places" (Inkson et al., 1997, p. 352). In later work, Cerdin and Selmer (2014) identified four criteria (which must all be fulfilled at the same time) to define SIEs. The four criteria are: (1) Self-initiated international relocation, (2) intention to seek regular employment, (3) intentions of a temporary stay and (4) possess a skill and/or professional qualifications. The research population for this study simultaneously meets all four criteria: They have professional or skilled qualifications, their relocation was self-organized, as their move was for career reasons, they sought and obtained employment and they always intended to repatriate back to Ireland. The act of expatriation was used to build up various forms of capital, which were then utilized after the interviewees' repatriation to re-establish their careers back in Ireland. In the following section, we discuss Bourdieu's forms of capital (economic, cultural, and social), which we apply to unpack the capital utilization of repatriated SIEs in the Irish animation industry.

Forms of Capital

Extant research on capital mobilization by internationally mobile workers (migrants, AEs & SIEs) tends to adopt a human capital view on the capital mobilization of the studied population (Phan et al., 2015). While social capital and knowledge transfer of AEs have been studied from the meso perspective (Amir et al., 2020). However, several studies on international careers see human capital studies as too narrow (Al Ariss & Syed, 2011) and lacking the depth and holistic approach needed to obtain a full multifaceted understanding of international careers (Syed, 2008). In human capital theory, "there is no place for institutional factors, such as firm-specific employment policies, the strategies of professional associations, or the effects of government vocational training and welfare bodies" (Ho & Alcorso, 2004, p. 239). To holistically unpack the repatriated SIEs' capital utilization, it was decided that this study needed to move beyond the traditional human capital viewpoint. To achieve this, we utilize Bourdieu's forms of capital to explore how repatriated Irish SIEs mobilize their different forms of capital. Bourdieu's forms of capital are a "multi-layered framework conceptualizing individuals as producers of social practices in social space" where they "utilize their respective capitals, economic, social or cultural, that are recognized as symbolic capital in their respective fields" (Chudzikowski & Mayrhofer, 2011, p. 22). This study draws on this holistic view of capital to unpack the interviewees' accounts of their career transitions, actions, and outcomes.

There are four main capital constructs in Bourdieu's theory of practice: These are cultural capital, social capital, economic capital, and symbolic capital. See Fig. 24.1 for an illustration of Bourdieu's Forms of Capital.

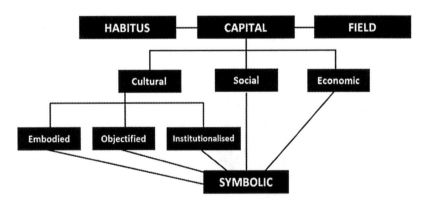

Fig. 24.1 Bourdieu's Forms of Capital. Created by authors from Bourdieu (1986)

Loury (1977) originally introduced the concept of social capital, which he defined as "intangible resources in families and communities that help to promote social development" (Palloni et al., 2001, p. 1263). However, Bourdieu (1986) realized the wider implications of the concept for the study of human society. Bourdieu and Wacquant (1992) describe the conceptualization of social capital as "the sum of the resources, actual or virtual, that accrue to an individual or a group by virtue of possessing a durable network of more or less institutionalized relationships of mutual acquaintance and recognition" (Bourdieu & Wacquant, 1992, p. 119). Social capital consists of resources or power, based on connections in society, membership of a group, class, and so on (Bourdieu, 1986; Mayerhofer et al., 2004; Fernando & Cohen, 2016). The act of expatriation can result in the SIE needing to establish new host country-based social capital or a dependency on previous connections already established in the host country, such as friends, family, or alumni (White & Ryan, 2008; Phan et al., 2015).

Bourdieu (1986) defines cultural capital as forms of knowledge, education, and advantages that a person has and that support the individual's social mobility within society. Creese and Wiebe (2012) found the operation of cultural capital plays a large role in the deskilling of migrants, concurring with Bourdieu's argument that cultural capital is instrumental in the transmission of power, privilege, and inequality. Bourdieu divides cultural capital into three forms: Embodied Capital is defined as "long-lasting dispositions of the mind and body" (Bourdieu, 1986, p. 17), such as language, dialect and mannerisms, amassing over time and can be both intentionally acquired and passively inherited. Objectified cultural capital is more tangible than embodied capital, as in material objects that one can possess such as paintings, books, and so on. Finally, institutionalized capital refers to academic credentials or professional qualifications, for example, such as a degree in classical animation, that symbolize cultural proficiency and influence.

Economic capital is capital that "is immediately and directly convertible into money and may be institutionalized in the form of property rights" (Bourdieu, 1986, p. 16), and it is "more easily converted into cultural, social or symbolic capital than vice versa" (Chudzikowski & Mayrhofer, 2011, p. 23). An example of converted economic capital is how individuals can pay for entry to specialized educational institutions, such as the specialized qualifications offered at Ballyfermot College of Further Education which converts this financial output into a form of institutionalized cultural capital in the qualifications they achieve, such as a degree in animation. This also creates a form of social capital in the alumni networks they develop among their peers while studying in the educational institution.

Additionally, symbolic capital is the "degree of accumulated prestige, celebrity, consecration, or honor" (Bourdieu, 1993, p. 7) that a person possesses within a social space. It is the power gained through the accrual and mobilization of any form or combination of capital (Al Ariss & Syed, 2011). When the other forms of capital, that is cultural, social, or economic capital, are recognized as legitimate, they become symbolic capital, which in turn helps the individual gain access to and accumulate further resources (Chudzikowski & Mayrhofer, 2011). For example, a degree in classical animation is a form of institutionalized cultural capital, which becomes symbolic capital when the holder uses it to gain employment in successful and famous animation studios, such as Warner Brothers. However, as can happen with SIEs' qualifications, if the degree in classical animation is not accredited in the host country it will then lose its power and value and no longer be symbolic capital. This highlights the importance of the international recognition of the degrees held by the majority of the research population of this study.

In conclusion, while many terms can be used to understand internationally mobile workers, our study focuses on SIEs and their ability to utilize the four forms of capital from Bourdieu's (1986) theory. For qualitative researchers, their findings are the products of varied contextual influences (Roller & Lavrakas, 2015), and the following section sets the context for the research setting.

Research Context

The Introduction and Development of Animation in Ireland[1]

The context of the study helps explain the push and pull factors influencing the interviewees' expatriation and repatriation decisions (Krings et al., 2009). The study is situated within the context of the indigenous Irish Digital, Film and TV production industry and, focuses on its largest division—the animation sector. Due to its context, company founders within the Irish animation industry represent an under-researched example of Irish SIEs. Understanding this high-end technology-based industry from a historical context is necessary to fully contextualize this research.

Animation developed as a result of experimentation by J. Stuart Blackton, given his fascination with light and motion (Solomon, 1989). Throughout

---

[1] Elements of this section have been published in Smith et al., (2012).

the years, animation has been seen to be similar to drawing cartoons (Solomon, 1989). Animation has been described as a 'young art' which evolved in the USA in the 1920s (Clancy, 2005). At this time, New York was known as the hub for animation centers, according to Solomon (1989). Later, European countries such as those under communist rule, for example, Hungary and Czechoslovakia began to develop a political type of animation. This brought about a division in animation works. The productions from the USA were heavily Disney-dominated, while the Europeans focused on work for "art-house viewing" unlike "mainstream" work in the case of Disney productions (Clancy, 2005).

Experimentation on animation began in Ireland in the early 1920s. However, it wasn't until the 1970s that the industry began to develop when numerous individuals sought full-time employment within the sector, marking many industry successes (Clancy, 2005). In the early 1980s, the Industrial Development Authority (IDA) introduced sizeable tax incentives to entice international animation studios to invest in Ireland (Monster, 2002; Clancy, 2005). As a consequence, three American animation companies were set up in Ireland. By 1990, an animation industry had developed in Ireland, which comprises three significant studios, employing 530 employees (Clancy, 2005). As a result of the formation of a new industry, there was a need for a skilled labor force, after which Ballyfermot College of Further Education offered an animation course, to educate amateur animators, followed by Dun Laoghaire College of Art and Design, allowing students to solely focus on animation.

Even though the industry was beginning to grow as a result of American influence, the early 1990s witnessed a turbulent time for the 'bigger players' in the Irish market. For example, Sullivan Bluth Studios experienced financial difficulty and as a result ceased trading, as did Emerald City. This resulted in employees from these studios taking up employment at Fox Animation in the USA (Clancy, 2005). Murakami Wolf Swenson changed ownership and traded in a much smaller studio. These closures almost marked the end for the Irish animation industry, as the industry experienced a complete "lull" (Clancy, 2005). However, many small indigenous studios were established during this difficult time, having gained the necessary technical and business experience as a result of previous employment at Sullivan Bluth (Clancy, 2005). As Clancy (2005) stated, the introduction of these businesses into the industry was the real beginning of the success of the animation industry in Ireland. During this time the independent Irish animators had established their credentials in the industry, picking up their first awards at international festivals.

The Irish Digital, Film and TV Production industry heavily depends on a 'tax shelter,' known as Section 481, which commenced in 1997, as an industry aid to promote and encourage companies to invest in Irish-produced films. Enterprise Ireland has also been very supportive in terms of promoting the Indigenous industry at home and in the international arena. Up until 2009, Ireland's film industry had achieved 45 international awards (Audiovisual Federation Review, 2009). During the next 20-plus years, the "ink hasn't run dry" for the Irish animators, as the flourishing industry employs over 2000 professionals (Abbatescianni, 2020) across 69 companies Olsberg (2023) having accumulated a plethora of Academy Awards, British Academy Film Awards (BAFTAs) and international recognition as Olsberg (2023) notes, the industry is composed of quality animators, producing superior work.

The Industry's Push and Pull Factors

Ireland's animation sector has a "small domestic [animation] market, insufficient home country audience base and consequent negligible local market potential" (Ryan et al., 2019, p. 8). This limited domestic market, acting as a 'push' factor, meant many of the new animation graduates and entrants to the animation job market became SIEs, generally seeking work in countries with centers of production excellence (pull factors), such as Hollywood USA. Push or negative factors motivate people to leave a country; these can include a lack of economic (Al Ariss & Özbilgin, 2010) or professional opportunities (O'Connor & Crowley-Henry, 2020) in the home country. Pull or positive factors, on the other hand, motivate people to move to a certain host country, which in this study tended to be the UK or USA. These pull factors may be better economic conditions (Cook et al., 2011), better lifestyle (Doherty, 2013), professional experience (Ryan et al., 2019) or career opportunities (O'Connor & Crowley-Henry, 2020). It is important to note that while push factors can cause people to leave one country, they must be accompanied by pull factors to attract people to the new host country (Dobson & Sennikova, 2007). Ryan et al. (2019) found that Irish animators were 'pushed' to relocate because of the limited opportunities available in the then moribund Irish animation market, and 'pulled' toward countries like the USA by the career and development opportunities offered by its renowned animation studios.

SIEs found placements, internships, and employment opportunities among the big-name studios such as Warner Brothers, Walt Disney Feature Animation, twentieth Century Fox, MTV New York, and Universal Studios. It was through these opportunities that many of our interviewees started to build up the international experience and network necessary (cultural and social capital) for working in the industry. This host country developed capital was then later utilized, or mobilized (Al Ariss & Syed, 2011), by the SIEs to repatriate and establish a career/business in Ireland's small but growing, highly globalized, high-intensity animation industry, which in turn acted as a pull factor for the now experienced SIEs to repatriate. The next section of this study focuses on the research methods employed to generate the data to understand this process further.

Methodology

This section describes the research methodology employed in this study, involving a fundamentally qualitative approach with in-depth interviews.

Research Design

This study adopted an inductive/qualitative research approach. This paradigm enables the researcher to draw an understanding of the human experience and the arrangements in which we understand the world (Lee & Lings, 2008). The research methodology employed considers a single case study exploration of SMEs in an indigenous Irish Industry consisting of practicing SIEs. Yin (2003) believes a case study approach is most suitable for unpacking contemporary issues set within specific contexts. As part of a multi-phase research design, this multi-firm embedded case study considers the career narratives of 12 repatriated SIEs drawn from eight companies.

Utilizing an explanatory case study design (Eisenhardt, 1989; Yin, 2003), this study aims to understand how the various forms of capital (economic, cultural, and social), developed in both home and host countries, affect the repatriated SIEs careers, business motivations, actions, and outcomes in firms operating in the Irish animation sector. In concentrating on a single industry grouping, with multiple SMEs all operating internationally, the study examines the repatriated Irish SIEs' narratives concerning their international transfer and utilization of various forms of capital by.

Firstly, the participating firms were carefully selected. The screening used in the selection method necessitated that a firm included in the study met three criteria:

1. The firm had to be indigenous to Ireland.

2. Involved in principal animated content and created in Ireland, with a core business module of designing and producing animated films and /or TV content.
3. The firm must have achieved at least 25 per cent of sales in at least two countries within three years from inception.

However, all firms exceeded the minimum criteria of 25 per cent and became involved in international activity within a shorter period, than the minimum of three years.

Secondly, the practicing SIEs was uncovered using the following criteria, an individual of Irish origin, expatriated from Ireland and repatriated back to Ireland. Initially, we developed a database of all Irish-based animation companies using Animation Ireland's website (www.animationIreland.com), followed by creating a 'company and founder information profile' for each company and founding members using secondary sources.

Company Profile

Throughout the screening process, we identified 8 SMEs and 12 repatriated SIEs that met the criteria. All respondents were Irish. These are represented in our study population table, (see Table 24.1). All identified SIEs agreed to take part and contribute to the study. To ensure the interviewees' anonymity, the names used in this work are pseudonyms.

Employee numbers are one measure that can be used to gage the size of a firm. Most of the firms in this study could be classified as small, typically employing less than 20 employees. While two companies employ between 20 and 50, the additional three companies employ just over 100 employees. Moreover, these employee figures can fluctuate and are determined by the project at hand at any given time. As a result, numerous freelance animators are 'floating' and always seeking work. The second measure used to evaluate the size of the company is its turnover, this ranged from some of the 'younger' operators with a turnover of almost €1 million, while some of the more established companies had a turnover of €5–€13 million. In general, it was suggested that turnover was a 'variable' factor and given the industry's success, it has increased year on year. The third measure used to estimate a company's size relates to the number of offices a company operates in. All of the firms in this study operate in one office, all mainly headquartered in the Irish animation hub, Dublin.

Table 24.1 SIE profile

Pseudonym	Education	Year company Est.	Expatriation host country	Years expatriated
James	Degree	2003	Czech Rep.	2 years
Lucy	Degree	2003	Germany UK	2 years and 4 months
Brian	Specialized certificate and degree	2002	USA	3 years
Richie	Specialized certificate and degree	2000	USA	1 year and 6 months
David	Degree (incomplete)	1997	USA	3 years
Peter	Degree and degree	1999	UK	1 year and 4 months
Timmy	Degree	1999	UK	2 years
Tony	Design & Masters	2008	UK	1 year
Martin	Degree	2002	USA	2 years
Adam	Degree	2002	France	2 years
Joseph	Degree and Masters	2002	USA	4 years
George	Diploma	2004	UK Australia	2 years

Source: Created by Authors, 2023

Data Collection

The primary data collection technique used in this investigation was in-depth interviews. Interviewing has been identified as the most used technique for gathering qualitative research, given its flexibility, in terms of time and content, which can be tailored to suit any research topic (Lee & Lings, 2008). The interviews were conducted in English with native English speakers. To source the initial interviewees for the study, the researchers, utilizing purposeful sampling (Creswell, 2007), used personal contacts they had developed in the Irish animation industry.

With purposeful sampling, the researcher selected the respondents and location for the research from those that can purposely provide information and knowledge about the phenomenon under critique (Creswell, 2007). The researchers then combined 'Cold-Calling' and Snowball sampling (Browne, 2005) to continue the process. For Snowball sampling, the initial interviewees, using their work and social networks, were encouraged to recommend appropriate interviewees for the next round of research interviews (Bryman, 2008). With the 'Cold Calling' approach, the researchers utilized a directory from Animation Ireland, cross-referenced with Enterprise Ireland and the Irish Film Board.

Semi-structured interviews, utilizing topic guides, were deemed most suitable for this study (Lee & Lings, 2008). This approach allowed the researchers to structure a topic, guide the questions and ensure all interviews were performed comparably. Narrative inquiry was preferred as one of its stated aims is to construct an in-depth understanding of the individuals' perspectives of their contextual experiences (Miller, 2000), creating knowledge of the participants' everyday life and experiences, as well as the meanings they attach to these experiences.

Triangulation was also conducted by gathering secondary material from many industries-related websites, press releases, industry and company reports, online podcasts, published media content, and founder and company social media platforms. This information provided a richer context for our research.

Data Coding and Analysis

All interviewees were carried out by the researchers. On average each interview was 1 hour and 15 minutes. All interviews were recorded and transcribed straight after the interview precisely. The data gathered was analyzed by NVivo which allowed the researcher to conduct cross-case comparisons (Myers, 2009). Many quotes were then selected to demonstrate the SIEs' mobilization of various forms of capital, which the final analysis is based on, such as the impact of context on career actions. The following section provides a detailed account of the findings obtained.

Findings and Discussions

This section sets out the research findings of data gathered from semi-structured, in-depth interviews in a small 'friendly' industry sector (Smith, 2014) of practicing SIEs. All interviewees have returned to live and advance their careers and/or business in the animation industry in Ireland. It was through this experience that entrepreneurs gained experienced and built a network which practices the concept of capital mobilization (Al Ariss & Syed, 2011).

Push and Pull Factors

Cementing the animation industry in Ireland in the early days was incubated by the animation education providers, Ballyfermot College of Further Education and Dun Laoghaire College of Art and Design. Therefore, the studied SIEs story in this investigation began with their time in education. The majority of graduates attended Ballyfermot College of Further Education. This training and education experience acted as a form of institutionalized cultural capital, which transferred internationally when the graduates were expatriated. These courses not only produced skilled individuals but also were loci wherein early connections were established between digital animators and later bolstered between digital animation firm's founders, thus the beginning of their social capital building, within a small, closely knit industry, O'Gorman and Evers (2011).

> *Several of us went to Ballyfermot college… Many of the main players in the industry went or taught there. It is a very close 'community'. (James).*

The participants' education was also responsible for developing additional forms of capital, such as increased cultural capital from work experience within the Irish animation sector. However, the animators knew Ireland's animation sector was small, offering limited opportunities for development and career, in what was then also a declining and struggling animation industry. This combination of factors acted as push factors in the recently graduated animators' decisions to leave Ireland.

> *I knew it was time to exit Ireland, opportunities were declining, so I got work in the USA for a few years… that was a difficult move and a steep learning curve.....but so valuable* (George)

Supplementing the lack of opportunities in the domestic market (push factors) was the career attractions in the international animation arena (pull factors). For example, Hollywood in the USA was the center of excellence for animation involvement. Therefore, some animators used their existing social capital to access host countries.

> *Many of my friends had left Ireland already… Many of my graduating class had moved to the states…. AN Other at XY Ltd. Helped us a lot by helping us connect in Ireland and abroad. After all, we were all colleagues at college (Lucy).*

This networking opportunity allowed many graduates to gain employment in big-name studios, such as Warner Brothers, and Disney, which was a result of the mobilization of their symbolic capital, that is, their degrees and training specialisms in animation. In all cases this was the SIEs first experience of the global animation industry, thus translating into many forms of capital, for example social (international network), cultural (work experience) and economic (an insight into funding opportunities) and later mobilized as symbolic capital in the act of repatriation as captured in the work of Al Ariss and Özbilgin (2010).

> *The international experience was what shaped me….I knew there was no area that I wasn't comfortable in, I wasn't necessarily an expert in the area, but I had a greater awareness of what was going on and even working with the others on projects was a great experience. It was my baptism of how animation works* (Brian).

The majority of our studied SIEs (10 out of 12) left Ireland with the intention to return home. While the time frame varied from one to four years, depending on the placement/contract opportunity and experience, James notes,

> *I went abroad to get work experience in the field, it gives us that edge. To establish how the world of animation works. We then returned home, set up in Ireland, that was always the plan* (James).

While this introduces the reasons for the interviewees accessing the host country, the next section reveals the repatriation process.

Repatriation

The act of repatriation (Cerdin & Selmer, 2014) occurred when the interviewees felt that they had gained the necessary experience, that is, capital in the host country to then repatriate to Ireland. During the time of their experience abroad, the domestic animation industry was recovering with many new openings arising which strongly influenced their desire to return home and establish a new venture that is acting as a strong pull factor.

> *Irish animation getting… winning awards…well, that helps internationally* (Timmy).

A meso-level pull factor, and one that played a major role in the resurgence of the Irish animation industry, was a government-funded representative body—Animation Ireland. Animation Ireland, sponsored by Enterprise Ireland, is an 'umbrella brand' beneath which Ireland's leading animation enterprises organize and wherein the member firms work together to promote the animation industry. Its key personnel have an intimate knowledge of each animation company and became an additional form of capital for the repatriated animators now operating from Ireland. For example, Animation Ireland's personnel also recommend international tradeshows or festivals to entrepreneurs, as well as highlighting individuals with whom contact could prove fruitful. Key personnel have critical contacts within the industry. One founder stated that "they will set up meetings which kick start new connections" (Lucy). She also stated that they are supportive,

> …. in terms of encouragement, for example you should talk to this person, meet that person etc., they have been excellent (Lucy).

The re-establishing process involved the repatriated SIEs mobilizing various forms of capital which they have acquired during their experience in the host country. The following sections uncover the mobilization of social, cultural, economic, and symbolic capital.

Social Capital

The mobilization of social capital proved to be one important form of capital in the repatriation process shadowed by the respondents as identified by Bourdieu and Wacquant (1992). Social capital involved engagement with colleagues, friends and family, in both the home and host country as well as professional and alumni networks. The combination of the interviewee's education, gained in the home country and work experience, obtained in the host country resulted in network connections which were leading sources of social capital.

> *People want to work with people they know, they know what they are capable of, this experience was not only critical but also we were building our networking while building on our career. (James)*

While the respondents had gained much experience and shared many credentials in the international animation industry, re-establishing themselves in their home country and setting up their new enterprise was a challenge. The smallness of the domestic market which was originally the push factor for their expatriation was still a legacy issue that remained. However, interviewees continued to maximize their broader international capital.

> *Our international experience was key, it helped us understand the business, the industry culture, what the industry wants and how to tap into those niche opportunities… we had a lot of connections built in LA and I knew I could use these at any stage to tap into the market and use them as a support while I started my own business… when I returned home to Ireland, within 3 months, I was up and running, all because I had the groundwork done while I was in LA (Brian).*

Given the highlighted successes of the social capital gained by these successful entrepreneurs, the following section outlines the importance of cultural capital in a small, unique, and novel industry setting.

Cultural Capital

As Bourdieu (1986) captures, cultural capital includes cultural, educational, professional skills and languages as forms of capital which can endorse social mobility in society. For example, the repatriates knew about Ireland and had a cultural adverse understanding of the current business environment.

> *We are all friends here, we built our network from our first days in Ballyfermot. But we are in our own league in terms of our offerings (George).*

One of the main reasons for the respondents moving to the host country was to gain industry know-how and as George noted, to *"learn the ropes."* Adam also remarks,

> *I had probably 10 years of experience or more in animation. Primarily in feature film… I worked with Sullivan Bluth… Disney Paris… Disney LA and I had been in LA with Rich Animation a couple of years prior to that… This combination of knowledge, gave [a] great footing and a great understanding of the industry when we set up [in Ireland]… (Adam).*

In other words, the acquired skills and experience are other forms of social capital mobilized by the interviewees as they repatriated to Ireland. Additionally, the cultural capital acquired from the respondents was mobilized as symbolic capital which greatly benefited the entrepreneurs in the early set-up stages.

We [now] had the experience in the industry after being abroad. Regardless of everything else, nobody is going to work with you if you can't do the work… you have to prove yourself when it comes to being successful (James).

After a very slow uncertain start for the Irish animation industry in the early days, the industry is now thriving as Joseph highlights, the Irish animators are "punching well above their weight" in the international arena, bringing home many high-status awards, which proves the success of the industry as well as each animation studio. This success internationally has raised the profile of Irish firms collectively as well as individually and it has helped Irish firms win new sales and commissions. This converts to cultural capital, building on symbolic capital. As Peter notes, "winning awards…. that's the tool we use to open the next door." Overall the Irish animation sector has benefited greatly from the successful moves of all of its players.

Economic Capital

Market knowledge of funding opportunities has played a large role in the re-establishment of the interviewees in the Irish animation sector. The Irish tax incentive—Section 481, acts as a strong aid for the industry, which not only kick-started the industry in the early days but also has continued to encourage international partnering, through investment and engagement with overseas firms. This initiative has not only offered many new opportunities but also acted as a strong pull factor for the SIE returning home. Lucy highlights the importance of the Section 481 tax incentive and source of economic capital as captured by Chudzikowski and Mayrhofer (2011) playing a crucial role for SIEs developing new Irish firms,

Section 481 (tax incentives) encouraged us to come back home and set up in Ireland. We also had the experience in the industry after being abroad (Lucy).

The smallness of the Irish animation sector means that the Irish animation sector is unable to support all the animation that it produces, therefore some firms needed to mobilize their international capital to source international funding, exercising the government incentive of co-producing. This funding doesn't come without snags, for example, to qualify for EU funding, the production must be co-produced by producers from a minimum of three EU countries.

> *Well we have always known that Ireland is such a small country, that it can't support all of the animation that is produces… the thing about the funding schemes means that you have to co-produce most of your projects. You have to co-produce with other countries to qualify for the European funding… There are certain countries that have very strong animation industries and the smaller countries would depend on them to come in on their projects (Peter).*

Therefore, playing to their advantage the SIEs use their international social capital to source economic capital in the form of funding opportunities and partner experiences to develop and grow their highly innovative product and service offerings.

In conclusion, the findings and discussions highlight that these Irish SIEs have successfully maximized each opportunity to exploit the various forms of capital throughout their careers to help them during each stage of their business. The following section concludes the chapter.

Conclusion

In this chapter, we have highlighted the impacts of capital (economic, cultural, and social) utilization of repatriated SIEs. By adopting Bourdieu's (1986) perspective of capital, we have captured the impacts on career/business motivations, actions, and outcomes of the various forms of capital mobilized and transferred by a unique set of repatriated Irish SIEs. Despite the number of studies that have examined SIEs, there is limited focus on how international capital is transferred and utilized or regarded as a 'tool' for shaping the successful careers and firms established, particularly those in the Irish animation industry. We note that social capital is accumulated and deployed collectively for tangible or symbolic gains, thus monopolizing the firms' resources. This is because animation firms individually pitch for commissions or are sought out for their product by commissioners rather than competitively tendering for projects (Ryan et al., 2019). Thus, the founders of these SMEs, practicing Irish animation firms, have carefully planned their accumulation and transfer of international and domestic capital to build successful firms with the support of solid network connections.

Futureproofing the success of these SMEs involves maximizing each opportunity to capture, transfer, and utilize various forms of capital during these repatriated and re-established stages of business initiation, growth, and success.

References

Abbatescianni, D. (2020) *The Animation sector generates half of Ireland's production spend*. Accessed February 12, 2023, from https://cineuropa.org/en/newsdetail/388238/

Al Ariss, A., & Crowley-Henry, M. (2013). Self-initiated expatriation and migration in the management literature. Present theorizations and future research directions. *Career Development International, 18*(1), 78–96. https://doi.org/10.1108/13620431311305962

Al Ariss, A., & Özbilgin, M. (2010). Understanding self-initiated expatriates: Career experiences of Lebanese self-initiated expatriates in France. *Thunderbird International Business Review, 52*(4), 275–285. https://doi.org/10.1002/tie.20355

Al Ariss, A., & Syed, J. (2011). Capital mobilization of skilled migrants: A relational perspective. *British Journal of Management, 22*(2), 286–304. https://doi.org/10.1111/j.1467-8551.2010.00734.x

Al Ariss, A., Koall, I., Ozbilgin, M., & Suutari, V. (2012). Careers of skilled migrants: Towards a theoretical and methodological expansion. *Journal of Management Development, 31*(2), 92–101. https://doi.org/10.1108/02621711211199511

Alshahrani, S. T., & Morley, M. J. (2015). Accounting for variations in the patterns of mobility among conventional and self-initiated expatriates. *International Journal of Human Resource Management, 26*(15), 1936–1954. https://doi.org/10.1080/09585192.2015.1041757

Amir, S., Okimoto, T. G., & Moeller, M. (2020). Informal repatriate knowledge transfer: A qualitative analysis of Malaysian corporate executives. *Journal of Global Mobility: The Home of Expatriate Management Research, 8*(1), 107–140. https://doi.org/10.1108/JGM-09-2019-0043

Andresen, M., Bergdolt, F., Margenfeld, J., & Dickmann, M. (2014). Addressing international mobility confusion – Developing definitions and differentiations for self-initiated and assigned expatriates as well as migrants. *The International Journal of Human Resource Management, 25*(16), 2295–2318. https://doi.org/10.1080/09585192.2013.877058

Audiovisual Federation Review. (2009). *Film and television production in Ireland*. Audiovisual Federation of IBEC, Affiliated to ICT Ireland.

Baruch, Y., Budhwar, P. S., & Khatri, N. (2007). Brain drain: Inclination to stay abroad after studies. *Journal of World Business, 42*(1), 99–112. https://doi.org/10.1016/j.jwb.2006.11.004

Bourdieu, P. (1986). The forms of capital. In J. G. Richardson (Ed.), *Handbook of theory and research for the sociology of education* (pp. 241–258). Greenwood.

Bourdieu, P. (1993). The Field of Cultural Production: Essays on Art and Literature. Columbia University Press, New York.

Bourdieu, P., & Wacquant, L. (1992). *An invitation to reflexive sociology*. University of Chicago Press.

Brewster, C., & Scullion, H. (1997). A review and agenda for expatriate HRM. *Human Resource Management Journal, 7*(3), 32–41. https://doi.org/10.1111/j.1748-8583.1997.tb00424.x

Brewster, C., Suutari, V., & Waxin, M. (2021). Two decades of research into SIEs and what do we know? A systematic review of the most influential literature and a proposed research agenda. *Journal of Global Mobility: The Home of Expatriate Management Research, 9*(3), 311–337. https://doi.org/10.1108/JGM-05-2021-0054

Browne, K. (2005). Snowball sampling: Using social networks to research non-heterosexual women. *International Journal of Social Research Methodology, 8*(1), 47–60. https://doi.org/10.1080/1364557032000081663

Bryman, A. (2008). *Social research methods.* Oxford University Press.

Carr, S. C., Inkson, K., & Thorn, K. (2005). From global careers to talent flow: Reinterpreting 'brain drain'. *Journal of World Business, 40*(4), 386–398. https://doi.org/10.1016/j.jwb.2005.08.006

Cerdin, J. L., & Selmer, J. (2014). Who is a self-initiated expatriate? Towards conceptual clarity of a common notion. *International Journal of Human Resource Management, 25*(9), 1281–1301. https://doi.org/10.1080/09585192.2013.863793

Chudzikowski, K., & Mayrhofer, W. (2011). In search of the blue flower? Grand social theories and career research: The case of Bourdieu's theory of practice. *Human Relations, 64*(1), 19–36. https://doi.org/10.1177/0018726710384291

Clancy, M. (2005). *Possible worlds: Animation in Ireland.* Accessed October 10, 2022, from http://www.ncad.ie/faculties/visualculture/research/thoughtlines/mclancy.shtml/

Cook, J., Dwyer, P., & Waite, L. (2011). The experiences of accession 8 migrants in England: Motivations, work and agency. *International Migration, 49*(2), 54–79. https://doi.org/10.1111/j.1468-2435.2009.00595.x

Creese, G., & Wiebe, B. (2012). Survival employment': Gender and deskilling among African immigrants in Canada. *International Migration, 50*(5), 56–76. https://doi.org/10.1111/j.1468-2435.2009.00531.x

Creswell, J. W. (2007). *Qualitative inquiry & research design.* Sage.

Crowley-Henry, M., O'Connor, E., & Al Ariss, A. (2016). Portrayal of skilled migrants' careers in business and management studies: A review of the literature and future research agenda. *European Management Review.* https://doi.org/10.1111/emre.12072

Dobson, J. R., & Sennikova, I. (2007). From fundamental freedom to political and economic 'hot potato' in 50 years: Labour mobility and migration within the EU. *Journal of Business Economics and Management, 8*(2), 123–136. https://doi.org/10.3846/16111699.2007.9636160

Doherty, N. (2013). Understanding the self-initiated expatriate: A review and directions for future research. *International Journal of Management Reviews, 15*(4), 447–469. https://doi.org/10.1111/ijmr.12005

Eisenhardt, K. (1989). Building theories from case study research. *Academy of Management Review, 14*(4), 532–550. https://doi.org/10.2307/258557

Ellis, D. R., Thorn, K., & Yao, C. (2020). Repatriation of self-initiated expatriates: Expectations vs. experiences. *Career Development International, 25*(5), 539–562. https://doi.org/10.1108/cdi-09-2019-0228

Fernando, W. D. A., & Cohen, L. (2016). Exploring career advantages of highly skilled migrants: A study of Indian academics in the UK. *The International Journal of Human Resource Management, 27*(12), 1277–1298. https://doi.org/10.1080/09585192.2015.1072101

Ho, C., & Alcorso, C. (2004). Migrants and employment: Challenging the success story. *Journal of Sociology, 40*(3), 237–259. https://doi.org/10.1177/1440783304045721

Inkson, K. (1997). Expatriate assignment versus overseas experience: Contrasting models of international human resource development. *Journal of World Business, 32*(4), 351–368. https://doi.org/10.1016/S1090-9516(97)90017-1

Inkson, K., & Myers, B. (2003). "The big OE": Self-directed travel and career development. *Career Development International, 8*(4), 170–181. https://doi.org/10.1108/13620430310482553

Inkson, K., Arthur, M. B., Pringle, J., & Barry, S. (1997). Expatriate assignment versus overseas experience: Contrasting models of international human resource development. *Journal of World Business, 32*(4), 351–368. https://doi.org/10.1016/S1090-9516(97)90017-1

Inkson, K., Dries, N., & Arnold, J. (2015). *Understanding careers* (2nd ed.). Sage.

Israel, E., Cohen, N., & Czamanski, D. (2019). Return on capital? Determinants of counter-migration among early career Israeli STEM researchers. *PLoS One, 14*(8), e0220609. https://doi.org/10.1371/journal.pone.0220609

Jokinen, T., Brewster, C., & Suutari, V. (2008). Career capital during international work experiences: Contrasting self-initiated expatriate experiences and assigned expatriation. *The International Journal of Human Resource Management, 19*(6), 979–998. https://doi.org/10.1080/09585190802051279

Kraimer, M., Bolino, M., & Mead, B. (2016). Themes in expatriate and repatriate research over four decades: What do we know and what do we still need to learn? *Annual Review of Organizational Psychology and Organizational Behavior, 3*(1), 83–109. https://doi.org/10.1146/annurev-orgpsych-041015-062437

Krings, T., Bobek, A., Moriarty, E., Salamonska, J., & Wickham, J. (2009). Migration and recession: Polish migrants in post-Celtic Tiger Ireland. *Sociological Research Online, 14*(2), 1–6. https://doi.org/10.5153/sro.1927

Lee, N., & Lings, I. (2008). *Doing business research: A guide to theory and practice*. Sage.

Loury, G. C. (1977). A dynamic theory of racial income differences. In P. A. Wallace & A. LaMond (Eds.), *Women, minorities, and employment discrimination* (pp. 153–186). Heath.

Mayerhofer, H., Hartmann, L. C., & Herbert, A. (2004). Career management issues for flexpatriate international staff. *Thunderbird International Business Review, 46*(6), 647–666. https://doi.org/10.1002/tie.20029

Miller, R. L. (2000). *Researching life stories and family histories*. Sage Publications.

Monster, A. (2002). *Articles: The budding Irish animation industry.* Accessed November 3, 2022, from https://arts.monster.ie/articles/budding/

Myers, M. (2009). *Qualitative research in business management*. Sage.

O'Connor, E., & Crowley-Henry, M. (2020). From home to host: The instrumental kaleidoscopic careers of skilled migrants. *Human Relations, 73*(2), 262–287. https://doi.org/10.1177/0018726719828452

O'Gorman, C., & Evers, N. (2011). Network intermediaries in the internationalization of new firms in peripheral regions. *International Marketing Review, 28*(4), 340–364. https://doi.org/10.1108/02651331111149930

Olsberg. (2023) The cultural dividend generated by Ireland's Section 481 film and television incentive. Accessed February 14, 2023, from https://www.screenireland.ie/industry-insights/industry-reports/olsberg-report

Palloni, A., Massey, D. S., Ceballos, M., Espinosa, K., & Spittel, M. (2001). Social capital and international migration: A test using information on family networks. *American Journal of Sociology, 106*(5), 1262–1298. https://doi.org/10.1086/320817

Phan, M. B., Banerjee, R., Deacon, L., & Taraky, H. (2015). Family dynamics and the integration of professional immigrants in Canada. *Journal of Ethnic & Migration Studies, 41*(13), 2061–2080. https://doi.org/10.1080/1369183X.2015.1045461

Roller, M. R., & Lavrakas, P. J. (2015). *Applied qualitative research design: A total quality framework approach*. The Guilford Press.

Ryan, P., Evers, N., Smith, A., & Andersson, S. (2019). Local horizontal network membership for accelerated global market research. *International Marketing Review, 36*(1), 6–30. https://doi.org/10.1108/IMR-03-2017-0061

Scurry, T., Rodriguez, J., & Bailouni, S. (2013). Narratives of identity of self-initiated expatriates in Qatar. *Career Development International, 18*(1), 12–33. https://doi.org/10.1108/13620431311305926

Smith, A. (2014) *Inside the 'Black Box' of the Born Global Network, National University of Ireland, Galway, PhD*. Accessed November 3, 2022, from https://aran.library.nuigalway.ie/bitstream/handle/10379/4177/PhD_Adele_Smith_2014_PDF.pdf?sequence=2

Smith, A., Ryan, P. A. and Collings, D. (2012) Born global networks: The role of connectors. *European Journal of International Management, 6*(5). ISSN 1751–6757. https://doi.org/10.1504/EJIM.2012.049642.

Solomon, C. (1989). *The history of animation – Enchanted drawings*. Alfred A. Knopf.

Suutari, V. and Brewster, C. (2000) Making their own way: international experience through self-initiated foreign assignments. *Journal of World Business, 35*(4), 417–436. https://doi.org/10.1016/S1090-9516(00)00046-8

Suutari, V., Brewster, C., Mäkelä, L., Dickmann, M., & Tornikoski, C. (2017). The effect of international work experience on the career success of expatriates: A comparison of assigned and self-initiated expatriates. *Human Resource Management, 57*(1), 37–54. https://doi.org/10.1002/hrm.21827

Syed, J. (2008). Employment prospects for skilled migrants: A relational perspective. *Human Resource Management Review, 18*(1), 28–45. https://doi.org/10.1016/j.hrmr.2007.12.001

White, A., & Ryan, L. (2008). Polish 'temporary' migration: The formation and significance of social networks. *Europe-Asia Studies, 60*(9), 1467–1502. https://doi.org/10.1080/09668130802362227

Yin, R. (2003). *Case study research: Design and methods* (3rd ed.). Sage.

Zikic, J. (2015). Skilled migrants' career capital as a source of competitive advantage: Implications for strategic HRM. *The International Journal of Human Resource Management, 26*(10), 1360–1381. https://doi.org/10.1080/09585192.2014.981199

Index[1]

A

Absenteeism, 333
Academic Engineers and Architects, 524
Accelerated processing, 59
Accessibleness, 284
Acculturation, 123, 125, 169, 177, 328, 334, 369
Achievement, 169
Acquisition of a new nationality, 491
Acquisitions, 367
Adaptation, 185, 196, 507
   cultural adaptation, 183
   socio-cultural adaptation, 183
Adjustment, 209, 214, 367, 526
Administration of diaspora resources, 425
Adult Third Culture Kids (ATCKs), 206
Adversity, 492
Afrikaans migrants, 86
Age, 267
   age effect, 130
   aging of the population, 60
Agency/structure dialectic, 492
Agentic strategies, 503
Agents of change, 255
AI technology, 242
Alliance partners, 259
Alliances, 253, 399
Altruistic behavior, 371
Ambivalence, 69
Animation, 579, 582
Annual profit, 262
Anti-discrimination laws, 239
Arabic, 476
Assigned expatriates (AEs), 554
   See also Expatriates
Assimilation, 121, 438
   policies, 125
Associate physicians, 57
Asylees, 374
Asylum, 393
Australia, 49
Austria, 252, 261

B

Backlog, 50
Barriers, 102
   cultural and linguistic barriers, 292
   (*see also* Language, barrier)

---

[1] Note: Page numbers followed by 'n' refer to notes.

Barriers (*cont.*)
   to internationalization, 102 (*see also* Internationalization)
   regulatory barriers, 60
Belongingness, 283, 284, 287
Belt and Road Initiative (BRI), 376
Benevolence, 170
Biculturals, 328, 367
   bicultural managers, 375
Birth country, 123
Body language, 286
Border closures, 554
Boundaryless career, 408, 425
   boundaryless career paradigm, 524
Boundary-spanning, 502
Bourdieu's Forms of Capital, 576
Brain circulation, 409, 411, 413
Bridging programs, 509
Broadening the resource pool, 484
Building new resources, 483
Burnout, 333
Business professionals, 540

C

Canada, 49
Canvas ceiling, 336
Capabilities, 99, 368
Capital, 585
   bonding capital, 509
   bridging capital, 509
   capital mobilization, 584
   cultural capital, 198, 577
   forms of capital, 575
   human capital, 576
Capital-intensive, 239
Capitalist logic, 235
Caravans, 391
Career, 61, 216, 339, 503
   advancement, 308, 309, 312
   development, 214, 314–317, 525
   growth, 371
   influences, 518
   international career, 538, 575, 576
   paths, 470
   progression, 319, 513
   success, 502, 514, 516
Career capital, 503–505
   framework, 526
   scale, 531
   theory, 217
Career resources, 550, 552, 562
   Career Resources Questionnaire, 558
Career supporting initiatives, 518
Caribbean, 391
Categorization theories, 438
Central government, 241
Change agents, 239, 240
Childhood, 217
China, 157, 228
   Chinese economy, 229
   Chinese government, 240
   Chinese workplace, 234–235
   mainland China, 229
Circular brain strategies, 414
City governments, 241
Climate for inclusion, 327
   See also Inclusion
Cluster capabilities, 364
Coarsened exact matching (CEM), 442
Cognitive dissonance, 158
Collaboration, 253
Collective identity, 121
Collectivism, 130, 149, 159, 170, 171
Collectivistic cultures, 154, 157, 334
Colonial, 337
Commitment, 334
Common membership, 434
Communication, 215
   barriers, 107
   formal communication, 286
Communities, 435
   development, 398
   embeddedness, 554
   family communities, 455

geographic communities, 436
immigrant communities, 434
interactions, 454
local communities, 394
membership, 454
migrant communities, 363
organizational communities, 436
research on social communities, 454
social communities, 435, 436
technological communities, 436
Compatriot, 371
Competencies, 506, 524
  cross-cultural competencies, 502
  cultural competence, 508
Conflict, 145
Conformity, 170, 171
Connectivity, 365
Consensual decision-making, 152
Conservation, 170, 171
Conservation of Resources (COR) theory, 549
Constant learning, 534
Contact, 258
Context, 538
Cooperation, 217
Coping strategies, 417
Corporate social responsibility, 389
Country of origin, 108, 166, 178, 252
COVID-19, 47, 144
  pandemic, 25, 547
  response to COVID-19, 155
Credential recognition, 55, 57
Crime, 75
Crisis, 80
Cross-cultural training, 36
Cultural
  background, 331
  biases, 280
  capital, 194, 588–589
  conflict, 254
  differences, 105, 145, 147, 158, 251–254, 332
  distance, 101, 187

group, 211
homelessness, 212
hybrids, 217
intelligence, 505, 506
knowledge, 94, 108, 267
and linguistic boundaries, 281
map, 152
match, 197
norms, 145
orientations, 127
remembering, 193
schemas, 367
sensitivity, 255
shifts, 340
stability, 134
Culture, 119, 146, 191, 252, 282
  cultural traits, 195
  culture change, 125
  first culture, 206
  heritage culture, 123
  national culture, 120
  third culture, 206

D

Debate on immigration, 455
  See also Immigration
Decent Work, 398
Decision-making, 149
De-contextualization, 243
De-qualification, 305
De-skilling, 305, 309, 417
Destination countries, 168
Developing countries, 230, 363
Development of abilities, 539
Development opportunities, 538
Diaspora, 121, 185, 198, 256, 375
  contemporary diasporas, 407
  diasporans, 408
  ethnic diaspora, 119
  resources, 426
  strategies, 427
  talent, 411

Digital age, 242
Digital divide, 30, 306
Digitalization, 242, 313, 417, 422
Digital nomad, 357, 375
Disagreement, 149
Discrimination, 71, 236, 291, 292, 327, 369, 398
   discriminatory behavior, 291
   discriminatory regulations, 237
   employment discrimination, 305
   non-discrimination practices, 338
Displacement, 393, 455
Dissimilarities, 282
Diversity, 280, 326, 399
   climate, 327, 339
   Diversity Committee, 399
   management practices, 336
   policy, 395, 400, 401
"Diversity climates," 330
Doctors, 54
Domestic migration
   domestic migrants, 241 (*see also* Migration)
Duality of refugee resources, 491

E

Early movers, 440
Economic barriers, 241
Economic capital, 577
Economic development, 371
Economic distance, 374
Education, 209
   education systems, 215
The efficiency-driven logic, 241
Efficiency wage, 235
Egalitarian leadership, 152, 156
Embedded agency, 470
Emerging economies, 243, 336
Emerging markets, 336
Emigrants, 167
Emigration waves, 121, 134
Employment, 333
   contract, 235

Employment Opportunity Index, 557
   meaningful employment, 318
   opportunities, 336
Enculturation, 187
Entrepreneurial motivation, 482
Entrepreneurs, 96, 410
   migrant entrepreneurs, 358
Entrepreneurship, 185, 454, 466, 494, 527
   dynamics of entrepreneurship, 469
   entrepreneurial action, 491
   entrepreneurial activity, 184, 364, 441, 469
   entrepreneurial journey, 467, 476
   entrepreneurial process, 469
   entrepreneurial self-efficacy, 487–489
   entrepreneurial skills, 356
   entrepreneurial ventures, 366
   migrant entrepreneurship, 366–367
Entry barriers, 316
Entry strategy, 358–364
Epidemic, 75
Equal opportunity, 331, 397
Equity, 399
'Essential' work, 35
Ethical consumer and investor movements, 244
Ethnic, 334
   communities, 438
   generations, 119, 134
   innovators, 363
   products, 373
   ties, 433
Ethnicity, 120
Ethnocentric, 328
Europe, 530
   European Union (EU), 168
European, 567
European refugee crisis, 466
European Union (EU), 123
Expatriates, 205, 356, 525, 547
   children, 209
   success, 505

Expatriation, 528, 578
  expatriation cycle, 207
Experience, 490
  challenging experiences, 533
  transitional experiences, 533
Experiential knowledge, 373
Explanatory factors, 564
Exploring new business potential, 486

F

Fairness, 331
Families, 218
Family-related training and
    support, 214
Family reunification, 75
Female expatriates, 553
Female migrants, 261, 269
FEMSA, 395
Finland, 192, 524
  Finnish actors, 424
  Finnish emigration, 413
  Finnish settlers, 191
  Finnish-speaker, 416
  Finnish women, 411
  Finns, 189
Finnish emigration
  expatriate Finns, 414
Finnish women
  Finnish women abroad, 416
Firm competitiveness, 435
Firm internationalization, 101
Flexible work, 566
Forced displacement, 466, 479,
    487, 490
Foreign-born, 356
Foreign direct investment (FDI),
    234, 358
  inflows, 229, 233
Foreigners, 329
Foreign language, 104, 107
Foreignness, 468
Foreign-owned enterprises, 239
Formal and informal institutions, 238

Fourth Industrial Revolution, 242
Future development, 534
Futureproofing, 340

G

Gender, 256, 260, 337, 408
  differences, 267
  disparity, 417
Generations, 120, 197
  cohorts, 134
  effects, 134
  first-generation, 356
  subculture theory, 123
Ghoshal, S., 369
Global capability, 386, 387
Global indicators, 508
Global job opportunities, 81
Global labor shortage, 71
Global migration, 375
  See also Migration
Global Reporting Initiative (GRI), 389
Global talent, 53, 280
  global war for talent, 60, 67
Global virtual team, 339
Global work, 240, 242, 524
Going digital, 319
Government, 567
Government regulations, 237
Green cards, 50
Greenfields, 367
Grounded theory, 312

H

Hard currency, 79
Hard work, 191
Health, 565
Healthcare sector, 49
  healthcare and nursing, 319
  healthcare managers, 60
  healthcare workers, 54
Healthcare systems, 29
Hedonism, 169

Heritage culture, 187
Hierarchies, 237
High-density work, 525
  experience, 524
Highly skilled, 412
  jobs, 308
Hoffman, J., 337
Home country resources, 489
Home/host cultures, 212
Homeland, 121
  attachment, 123
  resource loss, 479
Honesty, 195
Host country, 121, 145, 197, 516, 526, 551
  developed host countries, 516
  migration policies, 514
  nationals, 145
Host culture, 125
Host organization, 551
Household registration system, 232
Hukou, 229
  hukou-based discrimination, 237, 240 (*see also* Discrimination)
  hukou-based HRM discrimination, 237
  hukou-based human resource management, 235–237
  rural-hukou, 232
  status, 237
  system, 232
  urban-hukou, 232
  urban-hukou holders, 232
Human beings, 340
Humanistic mission, 336
Humanitarian crisis, 390, 391
Human resource initiatives, 332
  See also Human Resource Management (HRM)
Human Resource Management (HRM), 242, 367–368
  HR practices, 239
  socially embedded HRM, 244
Human rights, 398

Identification, 286
Identity/identities, 119, 120, 137, 159, 166, 169, 185, 188, 212, 453, 524
  cultural identity, 119, 125
  ethnic identity, 334
  formation, 197, 252
  group, 329
  hybrid identity, 120, 188
  migrant identities, 124
  national identity, 196
Image, 192, 196
Immigrant inventors, 364, 433
Immigrant knowledge sourcing, 449
Immigrants, 125, 143, 147, 191, 357, 374, 465
  annual immigrants, 51
  effect, 107
  employees, 158
  families, 435
  groups, 122
  hidden immigrants, 215
  prioritizing, 54
Immigration, 47, 166, 306, 334, 435, 508, 523
  annual immigration target, 53
  effects of immigration, 455
  integration, 59
  policies, 516
Incisive event, 144
Inclusion, 283, 290, 319, 326, 339, 399
  migrant inclusion, 304, 327
  migrants' inclusion at work, 312
  policy, 399
  task-related inclusion, 284
  at work, 312
  workplace inclusion, 280
Inclusionary activities, 283
Inclusive firm, 375
Inclusiveness, 280, 289
  dimensions of inclusiveness, 289
  research, 283

Inclusive societies, 336
In-depth interviews, 581
India, 375
   Indian community, 440
   Indian inventors, 434
Indigenous, 581
Individual agency of refugees, 489
Individualism, 149, 152, 154, 156, 157, 170, 171
Industry bodies, 338
Inequality, 68, 332, 467
Informal collaborations, 439
Informal constraints, 372
Informal relationships, 292
Information, 258
Information and communication technology, 285
Ingroup, 251, 283, 328
   in-group favoritism, 258
Innovation, 435, 441, 454
Innovativeness, 434
Insider position, 101
Institutional adaptation, 238
Institutional changes, 228
Institutional distance, 363
   See also Dissimilarities
Institutional entrepreneurship, 239
Institutional environment, 232, 238, 494
Institutionalism, 238
Institutional isomorphism, 238
Institutional tension, 238
Instrumental motivations, 439
Integration, 317, 408, 508, 529
   challenges, 282
   migrant integration, 34, 339
   policies, 269
   programs, 55
   promoting integration, 467
Intelligent career theory, 503, 504, 515, 518, 526
   multi-level intelligent career theory framework, 515
Intention to migrate, 166
Intention to quit, 333
Intention to stay, 550, 557, 561
Interaction, 97, 258, 288
Interactivity, 184
Intercultural competence, 101
Interfirm relationships, 97
Intermediaries, 102
International aid, 391
International alliances, 251
International assignment, 540
International business, 67, 93, 136, 184, 185, 198, 207, 227, 240, 244, 281, 326, 358, 433, 487
   activities, 266
   international firms, 502
   resources, 365
   theories, 243
International capabilities, 218
International diffusion of knowledge, 366
International experience, 101, 106, 213, 266, 538
International exposure, 217
International human resource management, 205
International industry, 337
Internationalization, 94, 98, 99, 108, 109, 242, 256, 366, 400
   firm internationalization, 94
International joint ventures, 253
   performance, 261
International knowledge connectivity, 358
Internationally mobile workers, 574, 578
International markets, 99
International migrant flows, 339
International migration, 240
International minorities, 287, 288
International mobility program (IMP), 52
International opportunities, 102

604 Index

International Organization on Migration (IOM), 326
International orientation, 100
International regulations, 238
International relocation, 550
International relocation mobility readiness, 558, 562
International roles, 213
International travel, 144
International work environments, 536
International workers, 506
Interorganizational networks, 536
Interpersonal connections, 259, 365
Interpersonal ties, 255, 373
Intersectional disadvantages, 31
Intersectionality, 338
    gender intersectionality, 427
Interviews, 304
Investments, 254
Invisible diasporans, 408
Iron-rice bowl, 234
Isolated crises, 81
Isolation, 554
Italy's Equitable and Sustainable Wellbeing Framework, 326

J

Job satisfaction, 330
Job security, 236
Joint ventures, 367
Judgment skills, 534

K

Knowing how, 503
Knowing who, 503, 529–530
Knowing why, 503
Knowledge, 97, 252, 255, 356, 435, 436, 490, 528
    business knowledge, 535
    carriers, 369
    community, 367
    connectors, 370
    creation, 365, 370
    cross-border knowledge linkages, 365
    cultural knowledge, 367
    experiential knowledge, 370
    flows, 357, 365, 433, 438
    idiosyncratic knowledge, 373
    immigrant knowledge, 435, 440
    organizational knowledge, 535
    recombination, 364
    spillovers, 255, 364
    tacit knowledge, 372 (*see also* Experiential knowledge)
    task-related knowledge and skills, 536 (*see also* Skills)
    technological knowledge, 364
    transfer, 369, 438, 576
    world, 372
Knowledge-based view, 368
Knowledge sharing, 259
    barriers to knowledge sharing, 374

L

Labor-intensive industries, 230
Labor-intensive manufacturing, 238
Labor market, 235
    institutions, 508
Labor shortages, 316
Lack of perceived value, 425
Language, 30, 93, 100, 136, 168, 215, 282
    barrier, 97, 109
    borders, 99
    bridges, 106
    choice, 103
    competency, 512 (*see also* Language, skills)
    differences, 282
    foreign language, 98, 100
    native language, 94, 98, 196
    paths, 99
    shared language, 105, 453
    skill portfolio, 418
    skills, 94, 103, 108, 317, 505, 506

Index   605

Latent Class Analysis (LCA), 556
Latin America, 391
Leadership, 149
Leaking talent pipeline, 414
Learning opportunities, 537
Legitimacy, 396
Liability of outsidership, 94, 101, 106
Licensing requirements, 55–56
Life course interviews, 190
Life stages, 123
Lifetime employment, 235
Lingua franca, 97, 103, 104
Linguistic blind, 100
Linguistic inclusiveness, 281
Lithuania, 120, 166
    Lithuanians, 177
Location advantage, 243
Location unbound, 414
Lockdown, 552
Long-term assignments, 567
Long-term effects, 567
Long-term orientation, 134
Loss of informal face-to-face interaction, 286
Low cost labor, 336

M

Mackenzie, W., 337
Macro level, 335
    macro-level policies, 509
    macro/national level, 507
Majority settled populations, 334
Malpractice insurance, 56
Managerial interventions, 291
Managerial practices, 239
Market mechanisms, 234–235
Masculinity, 130
Meaningful employment, 312, 313
Mechanical skill, 97
Mental health, 333
Mental illnesses, 326
Mentoring, 331, 513
Mentorship, 509

Mergers and acquisitions, 363
Meso level, 337, 506
Mexico, 393, 400
    Mexican government, 401
Micro level, 338, 504–506
Micro-foundation, 388
Middle-income countries, 68
Migrants, 98, 143, 188, 252, 282, 325, 357, 523
    characteristics, 256
    elite migrants, 411
    employment hierarchy, 320
    groups, 197
    high-skilled migrants, 509
    inventors, 363
    older migrants, 261 (*see also* Age)
    populations, 326
    precarious migrants, 26
    skilled migrants, 355, 501, 574
    vulnerable migrants, 26, 32
    wellbeing, 240–241
Migrant workers, 34, 228
    migrants working in MNCs, 279
    temporary legal migrants, 50
Migration, 167, 185, 186, 227, 255, 325, 376, 395, 401, 407, 551
    background, 252
    circular migration, 409
    corridors, 375
    determinants of migration, 80, 81
    drivers of migration, 68, 79, 167
    female migration, 410
    flows, 392
    forced migration, 476
    intentions, 167
    internal migration, 233
    international migration, 143, 410
    motivations for migrating, 512
    pathways, 376 (*see also* Migration, corridors)
    patterns, 468
    research, 267
    studies, 145
    waves of migration, 74, 86

Migratory birds, 229
Minorities, 329, 330
Minority employees, 338
Mismatched employment, 305
Mobility, 26, 184, 410, 412, 552
   global mobility, 567
   international mobility, 455, 523
Monolinguals, 100
Motivation, 567
Multicultural, 328, 367, 416
Multiculturalism, 508
Multi-level factors, 514
Multilingual, 416, 426
Multinational corporation, 281
Multinational enterprises, 96, 97, 227, 244, 335, 336
   MNE subsidiaries, 244
   multinational firm subsidiaries, 364
   multinational organizations, 507
Multinational firm, 367, 436
Multinational network, 366
Multiple levels of analysis, 28
Multi-relational framework, 517

N

Nahapiet, J., 369
National business intelligence, 426
Nationality-based subgroups, 257
Native language, 107
   See also Language
Naturalized citizens, 356
Networking, 514, 537
   possibilities, 422
Networks, 101, 107, 366, 399, 416, 484, 490, 529, 577
   peer networks, 512
New capabilities, 373
New normal, 37
Non-governmental organizations (NGOs), 393
Non-rational, 85
Non-rational motivations, 438

Norms, 122, 453
   accepted norms, 146
North, 372
North American Free Trade Agreement (NAFTA), 392
Number of migrants, 262
Nurses, 54

O

Occupational health and safety (OHS), 36
Occupational position, 256
Online environment, 290
Online inclusion, 280, 287–289
Online or virtual work environments, 280
Online virtual means, 289
Online work, 285
Open confrontation, 154, 157
Open management style, 292
Openness to change, 170, 171
Opportunistic behavior, 239
Opportunities, 196
Organizational and national borders, 539
Organizational demography, 331
Organizational field, 337
Organizational level, 330
Organizational performance, 338
Organizational policymakers, 375
Organizations, 565
Outgroup, 251, 283, 328
Outmigration, 414
Outreach, 418, 422
Overseas Experience (OE), 575

P

Pandemic, 149, 319, 357, 548, 564
   management, 149, 151, 153
Parenthood, 218
Patent citation, 366

Paternalism, 239
Patriarchal, 337
Perceived entrepreneurial self-efficacy, 484
Perceived social distance, 286
Perceptions, 70, 152, 195, 198, 411
Performance, 254, 368
Performance of IJVs, 259
    See also International joint ventures (IJVs)
Personal development, 513
Personal differences, 331
Personal growth, 534
Personal initiative, 555
Personal level, 330
Personal networks, 423
Personal resources, 328, 565
Personal safety, 565
The planned economy, 233
Points-based migration system, 233
Policies, 237
Policy changes, 61
Policymakers, 375
Policy recommendations, 518
Political polarization, 374
Political stability, 374
Politicization of migration, 335
Pollock, D. C., 206
Population diversification, 335
Positivity, 198
Post-Soviet, 123
Potential, 333
Poverty, 390
Power, 170
Power distance, 130, 149, 152, 154, 156
Pre-departure, 214
    training, 208
    views, 207
Prioritized urgent worker, 51
Privilege, 328
Pro-active approach, 337
Proactivity, 421
Processing times, 53

Processual analysis, 479
Professional activity, 416
Professional agency, 424
Professional context, 416
Psychic distance, 97, 99, 102
Psychological contracts, 525
Pull factors, 580
Push factors, 580, 585
Push-pull models, 167

Q

Qualification recognition, 493
Qualifications, 318
Qualitative, 190, 581
Quality of life, 512, 548
Quality of living, 71

R

Race, 337
Refugee entrepreneurs, 468, 494
    paradox of refugee entrepreneurship, 466
    refugee entrepreneurial agency, 493
    (see also Refugees)
Refugeehood, 468
Refugeeness, 468
Refugees, 26, 136, 307, 326, 356, 390, 394, 443, 494
    acute refugees, 472
    crisis, 468
    life transitions, 478
Regional development, 390–391
Relational governance perspective, 368
Relocation, 183, 208, 552
Repatriates, 528
Repatriation, 207, 208, 210, 578, 586
    programs, 211
    repatriation adjustment, 215, 526
    (see also Adjustment)
Reputation risk, 244
Research on alliance success, 267

Resettlement, 468
Resilience, 482
  resilient, 549
Reskill, 242
Resource-based, 368
Resources, 99, 366, 439, 484, 538, 548
  accumulation, 492
  constraints, 490
  loss, 565
  mobilization, 491
Responsible investors, 241
Restlessness, 212, 215
Restrained cognitive framing, 481
Retention, 550
Return migrant inventors, 365
Reverse engagement, 409, 413
  reverse diaspora engagement, 418
Rokeach Values Survey (RVS), 169
Rootlessness, 215
Rumor transmission, 86
Rumor transmission model, 73
Rural-hukou holders, 232
Rural migrants, 236
Rural migrant workers, 241
Rural-urban migration, 229, 235

S

Safe third countries, 390
Schwartz Values Survey (SVS), 166, 169
Secondary labor market, 240
Security, 170, 171
Segregation, 467
Self-direction, 169
Self-enhancement, 170, 172
Self-expression, 171
Self-initiated expatriates (SIEs), 554, 573
  highly skilled SIEs, 530
  See also Expatriates
Self-transcendence, 170, 172
Semi-structured interviews, 531
Senior care, 57

Sensemaking, 144–147, 155, 156
  perspective, 144
Settlement culture, 187
Shared national identity, 105
Shock, 144
Shortage of healthcare professionals, 55
Shortages, 308, 315
Skilled migrants, 136, 502, 516
  skilled immigrants, 48
  skilled migrants' career success, 503–506 (*see also* Career, success)
Skilled workers, 443
Skills, 74, 509, 524, 528
  cross-cultural skills, 213
  requirements, 512
  shortages, 508
  wastage, 516
Small-and medium-sized enterprises (SMEs), 93, 573
Social bonds, 282
Social capital, 366, 454, 506, 524, 529, 577, 587–588
Social categories, 257
Social categorization, 257, 291, 369
  dynamics, 282
Social change, 340
Social communities, 439
Social comparison, 257
Social contagion, 67
  model of social contagion, 71
Social distance, 258
Social embeddedness, 395
Social fragmentation, 286
Social groups across countries, 539
Social identities, 251, 268, 434, 438
  building, 252, 253
  theory, 369
Social indifference and neutrality, 286
Social inequality, 390
Social integration, 241
Social interaction, 255, 438
The socialist logic, 235
Socialization, 124, 454
Socialization hypothesis, 124
  See also Socialization

Social legitimacy, 238
Socially constructed, 146
Socially embedded entrepreneurs, 366
Socially responsible MNEs, 244
Social networks, 357, 481, 506, 524, 539
Social perception, 374
Social recognition, 530
Social resources, 555
Social segregation, 241
Social skills, 534
Social status, 334
   low-status migrants, 29
Social ties, 260, 267, 334, 358
Social welfare systems, 234
Societies, 565
Socioeconomic development, 394
Socio-emotional orientations, 284
South Africans, 77
Soviet era, 122
Soviet Union, 124
Spillover effects, 243
Stability, 171
Stakeholders, 389
State governments, 57
State-owned enterprises, 232
Stereotypes, 189
Stereotyping, 257
Stigmatization, 30
Stimulation, 169
Strategic response, 239
Stress, 209, 333
Structural bias, 424
Subgroups, 256
Subsidiaries, 254
   See also Multinational enterprises
Superdiversity, 335, 339
Superior job-role performance, 505
Support, 214, 565
   network, 212
   organizational and financial
      support, 525
   organizational support, 527, 549
   systems for refugees, 467
Sweden, 479
Symbolic capital, 578
Syria, 481
Syrian refugees, 471, 472

Tacit knowledge, 260
Tailored entrepreneurial support, 494
Taking small steps, 485
Talent, 524
   international mobility of talent, 415
   migrant talent, 408
Targeted drawing, 59
Targeted draws, 56
Task-related orientations, 284
Taxonomy, 425
Tax shelter, 580
Technological distance, 374
Technological diversification, 365
Technological innovation, 365
Temporary Foreign Work Program
     (TFWP), 52
Temporary licensing, 60
Temporary low-skilled work, 308
Temporary Residents to Become
     Permanent Residents
     (TR2PR), 52
The Tent Partnership for Refugees,
     336, 393
Thematic analysis, 148
The theory of institution
     co-evolution, 238
Third culture, 206
   TCK background, 216
Three-D jobs, 236
   dangerous, 236
   difficult, 236
   dirty, 236
Top management teams, 363
Tradition, 170, 171
Training, 331, 398, 527
   possibilities, 314
   programs, 218
   and support, 208

Transient migrants, 356n1
Transit, 392
Transnational, 189
　links, 357
　mobilities, 413
Trauma, 478
Traumatic emigration, 122
Travel, 75
Travel restrictions, 144
Trust, 195, 369, 453
Turnover intentions, 334

U

Uncertainties, 538, 566
Uncertainty avoidance, 130, 149, 152, 154, 156
Underemployment, 33, 538
Underserved regions, 56
Undocumented migrants, 35
Unemployed, 33
Unemployment, 538
UN Global Compact (UNGC), 389
Uniqueness, 284
United States (US), 49, 393
Universalism, 170
University-educated engineers, 540
UN Sustainable Development Goals, 389
Upskill, 242
Urban ills, 236
Urbanization, 228, 241
Urban labor, 237
Urban migrants, 241
Urban-rural segregation, 229
Usefulness, 284
U.S. immigration system, 443

V

Vaccine hesitancy, 30
Values, 119, 191
　differences, 165
　dimensions, 126
　individual-level values, 120
　migrant values, 177
　personal values, 120, 169
　sub-dimensions, 169
　systems, 165
Venezuela, 391
　Venezuelan migrants, 394
Violence, 390
Virtual environments, 566
Virtual inclusiveness, 290
Virtual work, 280
Voluntary migration, 229
Vulnerable groups, 400
Vulnerable migrants, 549

W

Wage discrimination, 237
War for talent, 48
Ways of knowing, 524
Weak ties, 369
Well-being, 217, 335
　migrant well-being, 326
　workforce well-being, 325
Willingness to emigrate, 177
Willingness to move, 207
Worker shortages, 53
Work experience, 75
Workforce, 355
　diversity, 327
　well-being, 327
Working abroad, 532
Working conditions, 333
The World Bank, 233
World factory, 231
Worldviews, 119
Worldwide diaspora, 120

X

Xenophobic, 269

Y

Yin, R. K., 395

Printed in the United States
by Baker & Taylor Publisher Services